GERMANY, EUROPE AND THE POLITICS OF CONSTRAINT

PROCEEDINGS OF THE BRITISH ACADEMY • 119

GERMANY, EUROPE AND THE POLITICS OF CONSTRAINT

Edited by
KENNETH DYSON & KLAUS H. GOETZ

Published for THE BRITISH ACADEMY
by OXFORD UNIVERSITY PRESS

Oxford University Press, Great Clarendon Street, Oxford OX2 6DP

Oxford New York

Auckland Bangkok Buenos Aires Cape Town Chennai
Dar es Salaam Delhi Hong Kong Istanbul Karachi Kolkata
Kuala Lumpur Madrid Melbourne Mexico City Mumbai Nairobi
São Paulo Shanghai Singapore Taipei Tokyo Toronto

Oxford is a registered trade mark of Oxford University Press
in the UK and certain other countries

Published in the United States
by Oxford University Press Inc., New York

© The British Academy 2003

Database right the British Academy (maker)

British Library Cataloguing in Publication Data
Data available

ISBN 0–19–726295–3

Typeset by J&L Composition, Filey, North Yorkshire
Printed in Great Britain
on acid-free paper by
Antony Rowe Limited
Chippenham, Wiltshire

Contents

PART IV: Europeanization of Public Policies

PART V: Europeanization Compared

List of Figures

List of Tables

Notes on Contributors

Jeffrey J. Anderson is Graf Goltz Professor and Director of the Center for German and European Studies at the Edmund A. Walsh School of Foreign Service, Georgetown University. He specializes in comparative political economy, with special emphasis on Germany and European integration. His most recent book is *German Unification and the Union of Europe* (Cambridge University Press, 1999).

Simon Bulmer is Jean Monnet Professor of European Politics and Head of the Department of Government at the University of Manchester. He has written extensively on the interaction of Germany with the European Union. His most recent book is *Germany's European Diplomacy: Shaping the Regional Milieu* (Manchester University Press, 2000) (with C. Jeffery and W. E. Paterson).

David Dolowitz is Senior Lecturer in Politics at the University of Liverpool He is author of *Learning From America* (Sussex Academic Press, 1998) and co-author of *Policy Transfer and British Social Policy* (Open University Press, 1999). He has also published in a wide range of academic journals.

Kenneth Dyson is Research Professor in the School of European Studies, Cardiff University. He is a Fellow of the British Academy and an Academician of the Learned Society of the Social Sciences. In 1996 and 2001 he chaired the Higher Education Funding Council research assessment panel for European Studies. His most recent books include *The Road to Maastricht: Negotiating Economic and Monetary Union* (Oxford University Press, 1999) (with Kevin Featherstone), chosen as an academic book of the year by the American library journal *Choice*; *The Politics of the Euro-Zone: Stability or Breakdown?* (Oxford University Press, 2000); and *European States and the Euro: Europeanization, Variation and Convergence* (Oxford University Press, 2002). He is co-editor of the journal *German Politics*.

Christiane Eilders is Senior Researcher at the Hans-Bredow-Institut in Hamburg, where she is mainly concerned with studies on political communication. She was a researcher at the Social Science Centre in Berlin and at the Ludwig-Maximilians-Universität Munich and also taught communications at the Free University Berlin. Her research focuses on the interrelations of media and politics, a broad range of issues regarding the public sphere as well as on news values and information processing. She is author of *Nachrichtenfaktoren* *und Rezeption* (Westdeutscher Verlag, 1997) and several articles on political communication issues.

Rainer Eising is Assistant Professor of Political Science at the FernUniversität Hagen. His main research interests are European integration, policy analysis, and interest intermediation. He is author of *Liberalization and Europeanization: The Regulatory Reform of the Electricity Supply Industry in Great Britain, the European Community and Germany* (Leske und Budrich, in German). He is co-editor with Beate Kohler-Koch of *The Transformation of Governance in the European Union* (Routledge, 1999), and he has published in a range of international journals.

Klaus H. Goetz is Senior Lecturer in Government at the London School of Economics. He specializes in the comparative study of European executives. His most recent publications include *Europeanised Politics? European Integration and National Political Systems* (Frank Cass, 2000) (with Simon Hix) and a special issue of the *Journal of European Public Policy* (December 2001) on executive governance in Central and Eastern Europe. He is co-editor of *West European Politics*.

Markus Haverland is Lecturer in the Department of Political Science, Nijmegen School of Management, The Netherlands. He is interested in the effects of European integration on national social and environmental policy and in comparative welfare state research. Recent publications include *National Autonomy, European Integration and the Politics of Packaging Waste* (Thela Thesis, 1999) and several articles on comparative social policy.

Peter Humphreys is Professor of Politics at the University of Manchester. He has published extensively on comparative communications policy, including *Mass Media and Media Policy in Western Europe* (Manchester University Press, 1996) and *Media and Media Policy in Germany: The Press and Broadcasting since 1945* (Berg, 1994).

Charlie Jeffery is Director of the ESRC's Devolution and Constitutional Change Programme and Deputy Director of the Institute for German Studies at the University of Birmingham. His most recent publications include *Germany's European Diplomacy: Shaping the Regional Milieu* (Manchester University Press, 2000) (with S. Bulmer and W. E. Paterson). He is co-editor of *German Politics*.

Martin Lodge is Lecturer in Political Science and Public Policy at the Department of Government and the ESRC Centre for Analysis of Risk and

Regulation at the London School of Economics. His main research interests lie in the areas of comparative public administration and public policy, with particular emphasis on regulation and regulatory reform.

Alister Miskimmon is Lecturer in European Politics/International Relations at Royal Holloway, University of London. His Ph.D. deals with the development of Germany's CFSP policy in the 1990s. Recent publications include: 'Recasting the Security Bargains: Germany, European Security Policy and the Transatlantic Relationship', in D. Webber (ed.), *New Europe, New Germany, Old Foreign Policy? German Foreign Policy since Unification* (Frank Cass, 2001).

Jörg Monar is Professor of Contemporary European Studies at the University of Sussex and Associate Director of the Sussex European Institute. He is also a Professor and member of the Academic Council of the College of Europe (Bruges) and joint editor of the *European Foreign Affairs Review*. He has published widely on EU matters, notably on EU justice and home affairs and on institutional reforms. His most recent book is *The European Union after the Treaty of Amsterdam* (Continuum, 2001) (co-editor).

Oskar Niedermayer is Professor for Political Science at the Free University of Berlin. His research interests are in the fields of party research as well as political attitudes and behaviour. Recent publications include *Bürger und Politik* (Opladen, 2001), *Die Parteien nach der Bundestagswahl 1998* (Opladen, 1999) (editor); *Demokratie und Partizipation* (Opladen, 2000) (co-editor); *Parteiendemokratie in Deutschland*, 2nd revised edn (Opladen, 2002) (co-editor).

Stephen Padgett is Professor of Politics at the University of Strathclyde. He has written extensively on German and European politics and policy. His recent publications include *Organizing Democracy in Eastern Germany; Interest Groups in Post-Communist Society* (Cambridge University Press, 2000) and *Continuity and Change in German Politics: Beyond the Politics of Centrality* (Frank Cass, 2002) (co-edited). He is co-editor of *German Politics*.

William E. Paterson is Professor of German Politics and Director of the Institute for German Studies at the University of Birmingham. He has published widely on various aspects of German politics. The theme of Germany and European integration has been an abiding preoccupation. His current interests include the management of bilateral relations and policy transfer in the communist successor parties of East Central Europe. He was awarded an OBE in 1999 for 'Scholarship in German Studies'. His most recent book publication is *Developments in German Politics 3* (Palgrave, 2003) (co-editor).

Thomas Saalfeld is a Senior Lecturer in Politics at the University of Kent at Canterbury. His publications include *Bundestagswahl '98: End of an Era*? (Frank Cass, 2000) (co-editor) and *Members of Parliament in Western Europe: Roles and Behaviour* (Frank Cass, 1997) (co-editor). He is associate editor of *The Journal of Legislative Studies* and co-editor of *German Politics*.

Gunnar Folke Schuppert is Professor of State and Administrative Sciences at the Humboldt-Universität zu Berlin, Visiting Professor at the Social Science Centre Berlin, and Fellow at the Max-Weber-Kolleg in Erfurt. He has published widely on public law and, in particular, administrative law. His most recent books include *Verwaltungswissenschaft—Verwaltung, Verwaltungsrecht, Verwaltungslehre* (2000); *Bundesverfassungsgericht und gesellschaftlicher Grundkonsens* (2000) (editor); and *Die Konstitutionalisierung der Rechtsordnung* (2000) (with C. Bumke), all published by Nomos Verlagsgesellschaft.

Katrin Voltmer is Senior Lecturer in Political Communications at Leeds University. Before coming to Britain, she taught at the Free University Berlin and worked as a researcher at the Social Science Centre in Berlin. She is author of *Medienqualität und Demokratie* (Nomos Verlagsgesellschaft, 1999) and numerous articles and chapters on the media in post-communist countries, political news and their impact on audiences. Her current research interests include the role of the media in transitions to democracy, the quality of media reporting, and campaign communications.

Rüdiger K. W. Wurzel is Lecturer in the Department of Politics and International Studies at the University of Hull. His main research interests are European and EU environmental policy, on which he has published widely. He is currently the principal investigator for an ESRC-funded research project on environmental governance. His most recent book is *Environmental Policy-Making in Britain, Germany and the European Union. The Europeanisation of Air and Water Pollution Control* (Manchester University Press, 2002). He co-edited a special issue for *Environmental Politics* on 'New Instruments in Environmental Governance' (2003).

Acknowledgements

The project documented in this volume arose out of a convergence of interests in the research of the two editors, both of whom have paid increasing attention to Europeanization as a variable in understanding domestic politics. The chapters explore the importance of Europeanization in relation to Germany and examine how it has affected polity, politics, and public policies. The present volume seeks to make a contribution both to Europeanization studies and to German studies. The contribution to the former goes beyond adding greater depth by detailed country study to seeing how Germany has fitted into the wider experience of Europeanization. The contribution to German studies involves a systematic examination of Germany and Europe from the perspective of Europeanization.

The book has been made possible by generous financial support from the British Academy, the Economic and Social Research Council (ESRC) and STICERD–LSE. We would like to offer particular thanks to Professor Edward C. Page, director of the ESRC Future Governance Programme, for his faith in this project. A special debt of gratitude is owed to Angela Pusey, who is responsible for lectures and symposia at the British Academy, for the patient, courteous, and efficient way in which she organized the research workshop and the conference that helped prepare this book.

The research workshop in November 2001 and the conference in May 2002 were important in enabling the contributors to exchange ideas with each other and with other experts in Europeanization studies. The final revision of chapters benefited greatly from the comments of those who served as discussants at both events, and we are most grateful to them for making available their expertise. They included: Professor Tanja Börzel (Heidelberg), Professor David Farrell (Manchester), Professor Christopher Flockton (Surrey), Professor Colin Hay (Birmingham), Professor Jack Hayward (Hull), Professor Robert Hazell (University College London), Professor Christopher Hill (LSE), Professor Christoph Knill (Jena), Professor Michael Moran (Manchester), Professor Edward C. Page (LSE), Professor Philip Schlesinger (Stirling), Professor Gordon Smith (LSE), Dr Ulf Sverdrup (ARENA, Oslo), Dr Eiko Thielemann (LSE), Professor Lord Wallace (LSE), Professor Stephen Wilks (Exeter), and Professor Robert Worcester (MORI/LSE).

The book was prepared under the umbrella of the Association for the Study of German Politics (ASPG), and many of the contributors have been drawn from its membership. We would like to express our gratitude to the ASGP for its support. Thanks are also due to James Rivington and the publications team at the British Academy for their support at every stage in preparing the book. Above all, we have been fortunate to have contributors who have displayed good humour in conducting business and seriousness of purpose and efficiency in producing draft chapters on time. Any shortcomings in the final product remain the responsibility of the editors.

KENNETH DYSON
DysonKH@cardiff.ac.uk

KLAUS H. GOETZ
k.h.goetz@lse.ac.uk

Part I
Understanding Europeanization

1

Living with Europe: Power, Constraint, and Contestation

KENNETH DYSON & KLAUS H. GOETZ

Introduction

AT THE BEGINNING OF THE TWENTY-FIRST CENTURY Europe is a continent of contrasts: more and more states wish to join Europe, in the sense of seeking membership of the European Union (EU), and yet some long-standing member states appear to find it increasingly difficult to live with the implications of progressive integration. While the borders of the EU move eastwards and southwards, the traditional North-Western core states face growing problems in balancing the 'enabling' and the 'constraining' aspects of their engagement in Europe and in achieving congruence between domestic and European priorities and preferences. In much of Europe, governments have to contend with vocal anti-integrationist sentiments, which have provided a springboard for the rise of populist parties (Taggart 1998).

Against the background of a European integration process that is marked by continued deepening and widening, on the one hand, and growing evidence of domestic disquiet and dissent, on the other, this volume explores three key themes. The first revolves around the challenge to the power of member states—as subjects of European integration—to determine the course of the integrationist project and to shape European public policies. The second concerns the increasing constraints in the domestic political arena experienced by member states as objects of European integration. The third and final theme relates to domestic contestation over both the 'constitutive politics of the EU'—i.e. the 'rules, norms, and framework of integration' (Bulmer 1997: 50)—and specific policy choices or, in a broad understanding of the term, the 'regulative politics' of the EU (Anderson 1997: 82ff.). These three themes—power, constraint and contestation—and their interdependence are explored with specific reference to contemporary Germany.

Germany and the EU: A Relationship Under Scrutiny

No single relationship has been more critical to the success of European integration than that between Germany and the EU (and its predecessors). For five decades, this relationship has been the yardstick for what is achievable in European integration and for the timing and tempo of major advancements in the 'European project'. Germany is the most populous member, Europe's biggest economy and exporter, and by far the largest contributor to the EU budget. In contrast to Britain and France, Germany's engagement in Europe has not been distracted by other international role conceptions, whether of a post-colonial global player or a sovereign nation-state. German national interests have, first and foremost, been defined as European. The EU has, moreover, been the most attractive institutional arena for putting into practice a historically conditioned German commitment to multilateralism, 'good neighbourliness', the primacy of international law, and the purposive 'taming' of state power (Katzenstein 1997a). Through integration, Germany has been able to take a leading part in shaping an institutional arena that embodies its own post-war role conception as a 'civilian power' (Maull 1992); to dissociate itself from a 'failed' past; and to regain credibility and respect as an international actor.

Germany's oft-noted emphasis on the importance of economic, social and political reconstruction as the basis for international security and peace reflects, in essence, its own early post-war experience of overcoming the handicap of being a 'failed' state. Within the EU, Germany has been able to exercise 'soft' or 'institutionalized' power (Anderson 1997; Katzenstein 1997a) through 'exporting' its domestic institutional models, policy preferences, and 'ways of doing things'. As a consequence of German success in shaping its regional milieu (Bulmer, Jeffery and Paterson 2000), the EU feels familiar. Germany has immense political capital invested in the EU and considerable resources of power at its disposal to shape the integration process on terms that are favourable to its interests.

Given the centrality of Germany in the integration process, it is not surprising that German–EU relations have attracted a great deal of scholarly attention, especially in the wake of the end of the Cold War, German unification, the termination of remaining Allied rights over Germany, and Germany's re-emergence as a 'normal' state (see, e.g., Anderson 1999a; Baring 1996; Bulmer, Jeffery and Paterson 2000; Haftendorn 2001; Harnisch and Maull 2001; Katzenstein 1997a; Kohler-Koch and Knodt 2000; Rittberger 2001; Schneider, Jopp and Schmalz 2002; Webber 2001). This debate has—with some exceptions—been conducted with reference to variants of 'sociological' and 'historical' institutionalism, stressing the ideational aspects of Germany's relationship to the EU and 'path-dependent' patterns of continuity and change. Despite new pressures and strains from the international, European, and domestic arenas, the emphasis has been on the continuity of a pro-European élite consensus, a 'permissive' public consensus and a basic accommodation between EU and German institutions and policies. The dominant image is of peaceful co-existence and co-evolution between the two levels (or three, if one includes the Länder); and of pragmatic and incremental change in the definition and projection of national interests in a context of continuity in macro-political strategy towards European integration. The basic congruence between German and EU interests, institutions, and policies does not appear in doubt.

To the extent that the consequences of integration for Germany have featured in these debates, the emphasis has been on the theme of 'enabling constraints', in particular in the processes and substance of public policies. At the risk of oversimplification, one might say that the theme of 'congruence' deals with the domestic facilitating factors of Germany's success in shaping integration, while 'enabling constraints' has served as shorthand for the domestic effects. Of course, the interconnection, if not co-incidence, between facilitating factors and effects has not escaped previous analysts. In fact, the distinction between the two is analytical rather than empirical. Thus, 'institutional similarities' between Germany and the EU are considered key to 'the softness of German power in Europe' (Katzenstein 1997a: 4), but 'institutionalized power can also be seen to mould the identity of the states themselves' as is evidenced by 'the remarkably internationalized state identity' of Germany' (Katzenstein 1997a: 5). But it is only recently, as part of the growth of comparative Europeanization studies, that more systematic scholarly attention has begun to be paid to how integration shapes the German political system across the polity, politics and public policy dimensions and that first comprehensive assessments are being attempted (Sturm and Pehle 2001).

Structural or Contingent Congruence?

The prevalent understanding of congruence stresses its structural bases in Germany's post-war political culture, in the maturation of the Federal Republic's institutions within the framework of the EU, and in a 'goodness of fit' between domestic and EU institutions. These factors help to explain why Germany's relationship with the EU has been defined by a combination of co-existence and co-evolution. 'Co-existence' refers to a situation in which German and EU institutions, politics, and public policies operate alongside each other, with few, if any, mutual effects. 'Co-evolution' occurs when the different levels are engaged in intensive mutual interaction. As a result of co-existence and, in particular, co-evolution, Germany's relationship with the EU has taken on a 'path-dependent' character, confined within a fairly narrow and predictable range of responses to events and developments and, above all, manifesting continuity.

The historical circumstances giving rise to congruence are well known. Post-war German political identity and macro-political strategy were formed in the crucible of the horrors of the Third Reich and of total defeat in the Second World War. For Germany, this was a 'critical juncture' of the first order. It resulted in a recasting of political institutions and a reordering of policy paradigms, including the entrenchment of the democratic *Rechtsstaat* anchored in institutional guarantees of basic rights; a 'negotiation' democracy based on a complex division and sharing of powers through coalition government, federalism, and neo-corporatism; a new economic policy paradigm constructed around the ideas of a 'social market economy'; and a new foreign and security policy paradigm centred on unambiguous support for Western integration in its political, economic, and military dimensions. At a deeper cultural level, the problematizing of German identity by these historical experiences created space for a 'comprehensive transformation of post-World War II nation-state identity', facilitating the rise of 'German Europatriotism' (Risse 2001: 209). As Risse (2001: 209) points out, the 'European integration process did not create this identity', but 'reinforced and stabilized it by demonstrating that Germany can prosper economically and regain political clout in Europe through a policy of "self-binding" in European institutions'. This pro-European and cosmopolitan bias was linked to the development of a 'privileged partnership' (Simonian 1985) with France in building Europe and its institutionalization on a bilateral basis (Cole 2001; Webber 1999).

Proximity in time between the foundation of the Federal Republic in 1949 and the creation of the European Coal and Steel Community (ECSC) in 1950–1 fostered congruence; but the latter was by no means a political 'given'. Chancellor Konrad Adenauer had to fight hard for political acceptance of the ECSC and later the European Economic Community (EEC), and, in 1963, the Elysée Treaty that institutionalized Franco-German co-operation. There was opposition within his own Christian Democratic Union (CDU), in particular from Ludwig Erhard over the ECSC, and from a number of leading figures to the 'Gaullist' dimension of Adenauer's policy. However, the main resistance came from the opposition Social Democratic Party (SPD). It was not until the early 1960s that one can speak of the emergence of a strong pro-integrationist, cross-party, élite consensus, as the SPD accommodated to the electoral approval of Adenauer's policy. Germany's post-war political order grew to maturity in the framework of European institution-building, whether co-evolving or just co-existing. But it is worth remembering—not least for the sake of a proper historical contextualization of current developments—that, in the 1950s, European integration was associated with fierce domestic political contest and party polarization.

Since the early 1960s, the pro-integrationist consensus has proved broad, deep, and stable. As Niedermayer (Chapter 7 in this volume) shows, it has, on occasions, been challenged, notably in the 1990s over Economic and Monetary Union (EMU) and popular fears about losing the cherished D-Mark, a potent symbol of post-war economic success. There have been other sources of irritation and tension, notably Germany's EU budget contribution at a time of relative economic decline and fears over the implications of EU enlargement for both internal security and the labour market. But these issues have not created a new political cleavage, ignited Euro-sceptic politics or had a lasting influence on electoral behaviour (Lees 2002). The pro-integrationist élite consensus has had a symbiotic relationship with a 'permissive' popular consensus. For decades, Germany's political élite was, accordingly, able to pursue its integrationist objectives without having to spend much time on explaining or defending them before a sceptical or even hostile public. Equally, its members had little electoral incentive to focus on European issues and careers (Saalfeld, Chapter 4 in this volume).

A further key structural prop of congruence was institutional. There was a basic 'goodness of fit' between Germany and the EU in constitutional order, norms and conventions, patterns of meso-level governance, and policy goals (Bulmer 1997). As Katzenstein (1997a: 33) noted: 'The system of governance in the European polity is based on what one might call "associative sovereignty," pooled competencies in overlapping domains of power and interest, which is characteristic also of Germany's "semi-sovereign" state.' A norm of consensus-seeking behaviour within the European Council fitted closely with that of Germany's 'negotiation democracy' in which ways had to be found of accommodating different interests within and across the different sub-systems of coalition government, federal politics, and neo-corporatist politics. 'Network governance' at the EU level had much in common with the complex sharing of power between public and private actors in Germany (Kohler-Koch and Eising 1999). As Eising (Chapter 8 in this volume) shows, German business associations were disproportionately successful in playing the game of 'multi-level' players by extending their domestically learned and acquired competence to the EU level. This sense of 'goodness of fit' was strengthened by Germany's success in exporting its domestic policy goals to the EU, for instance those of 'sound' money and 'sound' finance within EMU (Dyson, Chapter 10 in this volume).

There is much to be said for congruence as a domestic factor facilitating integration; but it is possible to see Germany's relationship with the EU as more finely and precariously balanced and congruence as more contingent and fortuitous than is suggested by the preceding arguments. In such a perspective, domestic actors have more discretion in exercising their—institutionally circumscribed—power, domestic structures offer actors opportunities to pursue change in European policy, European integration has unintended and unanticipated consequences, public opinion on Europe is dynamic rather than locked into a 'permissive consensus' and, most importantly, institutional change at both European and domestic levels challenges congruence. As Anderson (1999b: 188) has suggested, a shift may be occurring 'away from mutually reinforcing dynamics—the national-supranational equilibrium established in the postwar period—to a much more differentiated pattern', with growing signs of integration effects, in particular in the societal sphere, 'that can only be described as system transforming or even system debilitating'.

Certainly, the contingent character of congruence has become increasingly evident in recent years. Generational change—represented by Chancellor Gerhard Schröder's discourse of 'normalization'—has been linked to a new willingness to redefine Germany's relationship to Europe by a more assertive pursuit of German interests and even willingness to talk about a 'German way' (Miskimmon and Paterson, Chapter 16 in this volume). Domestic structures have been shown to have their own interests and institutional philosophies to protect. Thus, the Bundesbank was reluctant to embrace EMU because it threatened to undermine domestic price stability (Dyson and Featherstone 1999). The Federal Constitutional Court has displayed ambivalence about the primacy of EU law to the extent that this primacy should not threaten the protection of the basic rights contained in the Basic Law and its role in guaranteeing those rights (Ress 1994; Schuppert, Chapter 16 in this volume). Länder governments—led by Bavaria— have used the platform of their new rights in European policy secured through the revised Article 23 of the Basic Law to stake out positions on a new constitutional agenda, central to which has been a catalogue of competences that would delimit the EU's powers and protect Länder autonomy (Jeffery, Chapter 5 in this volume). Both Schröder and Länder politicians have displayed increasing frustration at the way in which EU competition policy threatens their domestic capacity to pursue industrial and regional policies (Lodge, Chapter 11 in this volume) and undervalues the importance of 'services of general economic interest'. In consequence, direct political pressure has been put on the EU Commission to pay closer attention to German industrial interests.

Congruence can also be seen as reflecting a particular historical stage in the European integration process defined by membership based on a dominant North-Western core. Its members were founders of the EU, fully engaged in all the EU pillars and fully committed to 'closer political union'. Germany and France shared in occupying the 'motor' role within this core group, a position that was long relatively uncontested. As long as this core could continue to dominate agenda-setting and decision-making, Germany could shape European policies and, if necessary, block initiatives that were inimical to its interests. The dominance of the principle of unanimity within the European Council ensured that proposals that conflicted with domestic preferences could ultimately be stopped by Germany; the attempted reform of the European Monetary System (EMS) into an EMS II in the early 1980s provides a case in point (Dyson and Featherstone 1999). Finally, there was a restricted policy core to EU integration before the mid-1980s. In short, controlling agenda-setting and decision-making was a relatively easy process to manage in a smaller EU organized around the Franco-German alliance, with a limited policy core, and under conditions of unanimity.

These important underpinnings of congruence are being progressively eroded, as will be argued at greater length below. Thus, enlargement has been a catalyst for change in the character of the EU, as, successively, Nordic, Mediterranean, and Eastern Central European 'worlds' of integration and Europeanization have been grouped around the North-West core. The breadth and depth of the policy content of European integration have grown enormously, notably with the internal market programme, EMU, justice and home affairs (JHA), and environmental policies. Unanimity has given way to qualified majority voting (QMV) across a widening range of issues. The Nice Treaty can be seen as an attempt to fix Council voting in a way that better protects German interests in an enlarged EU, for instance by giving a new weighting to the demographic factor. But it does not solve the prospective problems of greater uncertainty and indeterminacy in EU policy. Germany's ability to 'upload' its institutional models, policy preferences, and 'ways of doing things' to the EU level can be expected to decline. This decline is set to accelerate further with a continuing erosion of 'soft' power consequent on the relative economic weakening of Germany and a greater reluctance of other EU states to emulate Germany. The inability of Germany to maintain its traditional 'paymaster' role in Europe has, in any case, already led to a loss of both centrality in key EU decision processes and 'leverage' over policy outcomes.

Increasingly, Germany has been confronted with unintended and unanticipated consequences of EU policy commitments, whether in competition policy (Lodge, Chapter 11 in this volume), EMU (Dyson, Chapter 10 in this volume), environmental policy (Wurzel, Chapter 14 in this volume) or justice and home affairs (Monar, Chapter 15 in this volume). The result is a heightened sense of the domestic costs associated with integration, for instance from a European Central Bank (ECB) monetary policy that is pro-cyclical for Germany and fiscal policy rules that threaten to be deflationary. The structural changes consequent on EU enlargement to embrace a range of smaller and poorer member states promise further consequences that could disadvantage German interests. Particular anxiety has focused on increased labour-market competition from newly mobile workers from the east, downward pressure on wages at a time when Germany is experiencing high unemployment, and worries over the internal security implications of open borders. Hence, despite its principled support for EU enlargement, the German government has taken the lead in seeking time-scales for the introduction of freedom of movement of workers and—in the case of its removal of its border controls—conditionality on the quality of the border-control capacity of new members like Poland.

Against this background, German political élites have displayed a heightened awareness of the brittleness of the mass 'permissive consensus' and of latent anti-EU sentiments (Korte and Mauer 2002). The effect has been greater hesitation about pursuing a strongly pro-integrationist agenda and willingness to explore how Germany's approach might be redefined. Responses have ranged from increased caution for fear of awakening latent anti-EU sentiments, attempts to stop right-wing populists from exploiting these sentiments by a more robust statement of German interests, to occasional willingness to tap into these sentiments for political advantage, for instance over the German budget contribution or excessive interference by the European Commission. In itself, this does not suggest that congruence no longer matters; but it serves as reminder that congruence has been based on a complex blend of structural factors and contingency. As will be argued below, developments at both the EU and the domestic levels threaten to undermine the particular configuration of structural and contingent conditions that have supported a relationship between Germany and the EU characterized by mutually reinforcing co-evolution and co-existence.

Beyond 'Enabling Constraints'?

When it comes to the effects of integration on Germany, perhaps the single most important theme in both political and academic discourse has been the interdependence between the enabling and the constraining dimensions of Germany's participation in integration. 'Enabling constraints' have been noted in terms of both Germany's international position and its domestic constitution, and the external and internal dimensions are seen as intimately connected. The basic pattern of the argument was already established by the 1960s, in work that stressed the link between European integration and domestic democratic consolidation (Hanrieder 1967). In the language of current Europeanization research, there was a 'feedback loop' between patterns of participation in European integration and patterns of domestic effect. One may speak of Europeanization research *avant la lettre*. Integration, the argument ran, constrained domestic political and institutional choices, and, in so doing, enabled (or at least assisted) democratization and stabilization. The same logic applied to Germany's international role. European integration allowed the Federal Republic to regain a degree of manoeuvre (sovereignty) in international affairs—the enabling effect. At the same time, it imposed systemic restrictions on Germany, if judged by the standards of traditional notions of sovereignty—the constraining effect. The idea of 'Europeanization' as a strategy of self-assertion (*Selbstbehauptung*) can, thus, be traced back to the earliest stages of the European integration process (Kohler-Koch and Knodt 2000).

The notion of a co-incidence or indivisibility between enabling and constraining effects also informed much of the domestic political debate at the time of German unification. Deeper European integration was said to be vital to the eventual success of the unification project. In Chancellor Helmut Kohl's words, borrowed from Adenauer, German unification and European unification were two sides of one and the same coin. Enabling and constraining effects were seen as intimately related in terms of a larger German interest in European security and putting in place the conditions in which future war was ruled out as an option in European politics (Dyson and Featherstone 1999).

While the notion of 'enabling constraints' discourages thinking in terms of trade-offs, enabling and constraining effects may also be seen as a matter of strategic calculation about the appropriate balance to be struck between the two. In such a reading, it is a matter for rational political determination of what costs in external and domestic constraints are worth paying for presumed external and domestic benefits of further integration. One of the key issues to be explored in this book is whether this oft-assumed harmony and balance between, or even coincidence of, constraining and enabling effects is coming increasingly under pressure. The very success of the EU in assuring European security opens up the possibility that the Kohl vision will give way to a more calculative approach to European integration, one that is more selective and conditional.

One of the arguments to emerge from this book is that the enabling effects of further integration—both domestic and international—are becoming more ambiguous and attenuated. There are two dynamics at play here. First, the returns of further integration are slowly diminishing for Germany, at least in the external dimension. Integration and unification have 'enabled' the Federal Republic to an extent where its power in Europe is safely established. It is difficult to see how further integration could enhance this gain; in fact, the changing nature of the integration process poses a risk of power losses rather than promising further gains. At the same time, the domestic constraining effects are more direct and experienced as intrusive. The prospect is, then, that European integration will be seen as less obviously enabling and more overtly constraining for Germany. The intimations are already apparent in EU competition policy, which is viewed increasingly as negative for German industrial policy, and in EU environmental policy, which is regarded as threatening the German belief in the value of a detailed regulatory approach based on best technology. There is also the potential to contest ECB monetary policy and EU fiscal policy rules as pro-cyclical and deflationary for Germany, with negative effects on growth and unemployment. In addition, EU enlargement holds out the prospect of a heightened focus on problematic consequences, not least as the position of the North-West core—and Germany as the lead player in that core—is challenged.

Reopening the Debate

Against this background, the volume seeks to re-examine the conventional wisdom about the domestic conditioning and the effects of integration, paying particular attention to 'soft power' grounded in harmonious co-existence and co-evolution, constraints, and emerging patterns of contestation. There are at least three major grounds that motivate this exercise: the new perspectives afforded by developments within the field of comparative European politics and integration studies; the changing nature of European integration; and the changing character of the German political system.

- The period since the mid-1990s has witnessed the emergence of a more focused debate on 'Europeanization', which—differences of emphasis notwithstanding—is at heart about the consequences of European integration for domestic political systems. As noted above, there was discussion of such effects before. But systematic empirical research was thin on the ground and individual contributions were not oriented towards a common empirical and intellectual agenda and remained at the margins of both integration studies and comparative politics. The rise of 'Europeanization' as a core theme in contemporary European political science has provided a shared agenda that brings together students of European integration and comparativists. Reflecting the different 'faces' of the EU as a political, economic, legal and, perhaps, cultural union, it has attracted students of political science (including international relations), political economy, law, and sociology. More importantly, the Europeanization literature is shedding new light on the complexity of processes and outcomes associated with the domestic conditioning and effects of European integration. What is emerging is a more differentiated picture—in both empirical and conceptual terms—of how the EU affects domestic polities, politics, and public policies.
- Since the mid-1980s, momentous shifts have taken place in the European integration process, including, in particular, the Single Market, the single currency, second- and third-pillar developments, Mediterranean, Nordic, and Eastern enlargement, institutional reform (including the European Convention), and the spread of the 'open' method of co-ordination. These changes are altering the character of Europeanization through their effects on both Germany's participation in integration and the domestic political system.
- The manner in which Germany participates in European integration and how it deals with its effects has also been affected by shifts within the German political system since unification. These have been summarized as the transition from the 'Bonn Republic' to the 'Berlin Republic'.

The next section examines in greater depth the concept of Europeanization and the main strands of research, with an emphasis on key differences in understanding and approach. The following two sections survey changes in the European integration process and in the political system of unified Germany. In each case, their implications for patterns of Europeanization, and for the themes of power, constraint, and contestation are considered.

Particular attention is paid to the way in which Europeanization manifests itself in different types of interaction between domestic and EU levels. Three key dynamics can be identified in the relationship between domestic (national and sub-national) and EU levels—co-existence, co-evolution, and contest. As noted earlier, co-existence refers to a situation in which the two levels display a high degree of autonomy and self-containment in policy and political terms. Europeanization is absorbed because it does not have direct effects on core policy beliefs or key policy instruments and does not affect in essentials how institutions work. Indeed, it seems reasonable to argue that in this case Europeanization is so marginal that it is scarcely relevant to understanding domestic politics.

More relevant are the dynamics of co-evolution and contestation. 'Co-evolution' stresses the supportive mutual interaction between domestic and EU levels in terms of policy beliefs and instruments and of timing and tempo of changes. It is seen, for instance, in telecommunications regulation (see Bulmer *et al.*, Chapter 12 in this volume). German negotiators focused on accommodating the timing and tempo of regulatory changes across the two levels. 'Contestation' involves a clash of policy beliefs and preferences. Its Europeanization effects are seen either in domestic transformation or domestic retrenchment.

Europeanization: Between 'Attention-Directing Device' and 'Theory'

Scholarly reflection on Europeanization is coming of age, as is evidenced by the rapid expansion of academic studies of the impact of European integration on the political life of current and future EU member states that explicitly engage with the notion of Europeanization (see, e.g., Dyson 2002*a*; Featherstone and Kazamias 2001; Featherstone and Radaelli 2003; Hix and Goetz 2000*b*; Green Cowles, Caporaso and Risse 2001; Héritier *et al.* 2001; Kassim, Peters and Wright 2001; Knill 2001; Schmidt 2002). The maturation of the field is also apparent in growing empirical, conceptual, and theoretical ambitions. Building on Olson (2002) and Buller and Gamble (2002), one may identify six main uses of the notion of Europeanization: as the development of institutions of governance at the European level; as the export or transfer of European models outside Europe's borders; as the achievement of the political unification of Europe; as a process whereby domestic politics becomes increasingly subjected to European policy-making, focusing on 'top-down' effects; as an element in domestic polit-ical manoeuvres and in legitimating domestic reforms, focusing on 'bottom-up' effects; and as a situation where distinct modes of European governance have transformed aspects of domestic politics.

The risk of 'concept stretching' has encouraged attempts to examine critically the notion itself and to give it greater conceptual clarity and precision (e.g., Buller and Gamble 2002; Radaelli 2001). The key challenge here is to distinguish it from established concepts such as 'integration', 'political unification', 'convergence', and 'policy transfer' and to identify its added value. As regards the first three of the above uses of Europeanization, it is difficult to see where their added value lies, and they will not, therefore, be pursued in this book. Europeanization as employed here is more than an 'attention-directing device' (Olson 2002), but less than a theory. It is best understood as a heuristic concept that has evolved in a variable and open-ended way, as scholars have responded to, and tried to capture, the complex, interactive changes underway on different levels and the variable, contingent nature of the phenomenon. Its differing uses also reflect disagreement about the scope and nature of empirically observable effects. One issue is whether 'Europeanization' is present only in situations where it has 'transformed' domestic politics (Buller and Gamble 2002; Radaelli 2001); another, whether it includes the 'bottom-up', discursive construction of European effects, even where no European policy model exists to 'down-load' (Kallestrup 2002). Accordingly, definitions or, more typically, implicit understandings range from the narrow—seeking parsimony—to the broad—seeking inclusiveness. They also stretch from a focus on Europeanization as a process that is associated with a broad range of effects (including inertia, accommodation, retrenchment and transformation) to Europeanization as a situation in which a particular effect—transformation—can be demonstrated to have occurred.

No less problematic than the risk of 'concept stretching' is that of confusing levels of analysis. The study of Europeanization is bound up with dynamics of change at, and across, different levels, stretching from the global to the supranational, national, sub-national, and local. Hence there is a challenge of distinguishing it from 'globalization' (see Anderson, Chapter 2 in this volume) as well as from other sources of change at the domestic level (Hix and Goetz 2001). Inevitably, Europeanization research soon becomes entangled in analysis of a complex field of forces. In our view, this problem can be managed only if its 'added value' is recognized as bestowing analytical primacy to the impact of European integration on the domestic level, as compared to 'integration', which draws attention to the impact of domestic actors on the European level. The key research questions are about how domestic actors are responding to European integration. Part of the answer may be that Europeanization is a catalyst for recasting integration by seeking to 'upload' domestic institutional models, policy preferences and 'ways of doing things' to the EU level (Jeffery, Chapter 5 in this volume). In this way, we are reminded that concepts are interdependent and that there is an interactive relationship in which Europeanization can be refashioned. But the challenge is to stay on the firm ground of what European integration is doing to domestic political systems.

Diversity in Europeanization studies reflects such differences of conceptual understanding and of empirical emphasis. These differences must not be overdrawn and should not be understood as evidence for the emergence of rival schools of thought. But is useful to keep them in mind in seeking to map the field. A first difference revolves, as already indicated, around the relative emphasis placed on a 'downloading' perspective that sees Europeanization as a vertical and hierarchical process versus a perspective that understands Europeanization as part of a dynamic and interactive process that includes 'downloading' as well as 'uploading' processes. The narrower approach is to examine the impact of European integration from a 'downloading' perspective that stresses the hierarchical relationship between the EU and its member states. Empirically, the focus is, first and foremost, on EU laws and policies and the manner in which they are dealt with at the domestic level. Europeanization here is often linked to coercive pressures. The broader approach is to see Europeanization as a distinct part of a dynamic interaction across levels. For example, institutional adjustment within national core executives to EU membership, especially demands for improved co-ordination of national responses, are at least as much bound up with the 'projection' of domestic preferences onto the EU level as with the 'reception' of EU laws and policies (Bulmer and Burch 2001; Kassim, Peters and Wright 2001). Success in 'uploading' domestic preferences to the EU level reduces adaptive pressures from above. Hence constraining effects do not just appear 'from above', but may be purposely 'uploaded' by domestic actors so that Europeanization serves as an external (and perhaps internalized) discipline and catalyst for domestic reforms (Dyson and Featherstone 1996). Europeanization is then bound up in a circular process. Yet, in order to safeguard the internal coherence of the concept and to differentiate it from others, notably integration, it seems sensible to distinguish between Europeanization's 'defining' properties — 'downloading' — and its 'accompanying' properties — 'uploading'.

It is important also to bear in mind that the nature of the vertical relationship itself is changing, as new forms of policy-making and governance emerge in the EU context. 'Softer' forms of integration — such as the 'open' method of co-ordination or benchmarking best practice among the member states — are supplementing the traditional reliance on the 'hard' instrument of commonly applicable EU law. 'Integration through law' may still be the chief integrationist method, but other methods — involving transnational exchange among policy professionals and mimetic effects — are gaining in relative importance. As a result, the EU's relationship to the member states is becoming less that of a superior legislator and increasingly resembles that of a catalyst, moderator, facilitator and, at times, of exhorter. To the extent that the EU is best understood as an arena rather than an actor, the horizontal dimension of Europeanization deserves increased attention, as there is a great deal of bilateral and multi-lateral interaction within the overall EU framework that reshapes national institutions and policies. This theme is prominent in the rapidly growing literature on cross-national policy transfer and policy learning both among current EU member states and between the latter and the applicant states (Bulmer *et al.*, Chapter 12 in this volume).

With a focus on patterns of 'downloading', two outlooks may be distinguished (Figure 1.1): a 'top-down' perspective, which examines a range of mechanisms, from coercive (requirements to comply) through mimetic effects (such as benchmarking) to transnational exchange of ideas and practices among policy professionals; and a 'bottom-up' perspective, which stresses the use that domestic actors make of the EU in order to legitimate policy reforms, to develop new policy solutions, and to alter policy beliefs (Knill and Lehmkuhl 2002; Kallestrup 2002). In the latter case, the emphasis is on the discursive construction of policy change, and Europeanization is understood as part of the narratives of domestic governance. The resultant conception of Europeanization adopts a more voluntarist viewpoint, seeing 'top-down', coercive adjustment as a limiting case rather than the norm.

This difference has direct implications for the question of whether a 'misfit' between the European and the domestic levels—especially in terms of institutional arrangements, policy content and instruments—is regarded as a necessary precondition for national reactions to take place, as some notable contributions to the debate assume (see, in particular, Risse, Green Cowles and Caporaso 2001; Börzel and Risse 2003). In accordance with this assumption, the empirical research focus is on how domestic actors and institutions 'cope with', 'accommodate', 'evade', or 'resist' the resulting adaptational pressures. Without 'misfit', European integration cannot be expected to provoke change at the national level.

Others have challenged this 'misfit' assumption head-on (for a recent review and rebuttal see Börzel, forthcoming). At least three principal objections tend to be advanced. First, EU and domestic legal frameworks, institutions, and public policies have no 'absolute' existence. They are open to interpretation. There is nothing fixed or given about 'fits' or 'misfits'. Unless one side or the other perceives a conflict, and is willing to give it salience, any potential 'misfit' remains dormant. Moreover, misfits are open to renegotiation. They can be dealt with by changing the terms of European integration in the form of seeking to 'upload' new policy preferences. This behaviour has been seen on the part of the German Länder (Jeffery, Chapter 5 in this volume) and has surfaced—albeit in a much more cautious manner—in relation to the EU's fiscal rules (Dyson, Chapter 10

Figure 1.1. Europeanization.

in this volume). Second, one needs to take account of institutional and policy 'voids' (Goetz 2001). Not all current member states joined the EU with a fully developed set of public institutions and domestic public policies, an observation that applies, in particular, to the Southern member states of Spain, Portugal, and Greece. Here, EU membership has often been associated with institutionalization *ab ovo* rather than institutional change. This argument is also of relevance in the case of the accession states in Central and Eastern Europe. Finally, as the discussion about the 'uploading' of member state preferences underlines, domestic actors routinely seek to 'export' their preferences. They have, accordingly, a key influence over any resulting 'fit' or 'misfit'. There are many examples of domestic policy-makers using EU-level initiatives to create pressures for domestic reform—in this case, 'misfits' have been more or less purposefully 'engineered' (see, e.g., Bulmer *et al.*, Chapter 12 in this volume). Equally, there are many examples where states have successfully managed to minimize national adaptive requirements. For example, in 2001, Germany successfully prevented a proposal that would have required the creation of an independent national regulatory authority for electricity.

Consequently, it has been suggested that, instead of focusing on 'misfit' as a key explanatory variable, Europeanization studies should examine domestic opportunity structures, policy beliefs and ideas, and discourse (see, e.g., Hix and Goetz 2000), as the key explanations for diverging trajectories of Europeanization within domestic politics. In rational choice inspired accounts, EU models—whether as 'requirements', 'recommendations', or 'suggestions'—are used by domestic actors to pursue their strategic interests, for instance in institutional aggrandisement. Dyson's discussion of the German Finance Ministry and EMU (Chapter 10 in this volume) provides an illustration. In constructivist accounts, EU models are 'internalized' in the belief systems of key domestic actors and crafted into a domestic discourse about the 'logic' of domestic policy change. Whether the accounts are strategic or cognitive, both stress the challenging of domestic 'veto points' (Haverland 2000).

The difference between explanatory accounts that focus on 'misfit' and those that advocate the explanatory power of domestic opportunity structures can be easily overstated. Advocates of the 'misfit' approach have argued that it is a precondition for domestic adaptation but, in itself, does not explain outcomes (Green Cowles, Caporaso and Risse 2001; Börzel and Risse 2003). The careful tracing of whether and how 'misfit' triggers domestic adaptation has to pay attention to domestic institutional and cultural variables, ranging from veto points, through capacity for political leadership, to depth of support for the European idea in conceptions of national identity. Nevertheless, 'misfit' may be more applicable to mechanisms of Europeanization based on clear prescriptive EU institutional models to be 'downloaded' than to other mechanisms of Europeanization in which domestic politics figures more prominently (Knill and Lehmkuhl 2002).

Devices such as 'benchmarking' best practice are used less to import new ideas than to legitimate existing domestic policy arguments.

Early studies of the impact of integration on domestic political systems, in particular, often associated Europeanization with transformation of domestic politics towards cross-national convergence over time, as part of the emergence of a European polity. States were seen as responding to the standardizing pressures 'from above', most evident in the extension and intensification of the common *acquis* and manifested in the rapid expansion of EU law. While not obsolete, national institutional and policy traditions could be expected to lose some of their distinctness. Wolfgang Wessels' writings on 'institutional fusion' serve as a well-argued and instructive example of this line of thinking (see, e.g., Wessels and Rometsch 1996). By contrast, most recent analyses highlight the way in which domestic arrangements 'refract' the effects of European integration. The result is a 'differential' impact of Europe, a persistent theme in Héritier *et al.* (2001) and Knill (2001), who focus on administrative and policy effects, but also in recent writings by Hall and Soskice (2001) and Schmidt (2002), who stress the variety of domestic institutional arrangements within European capitalism and how these refract Europe in different ways. To the extent that there is convergence, it appears clustered around particular types of capitalism. Thus 'co-ordinated' capitalisms of the Dutch and German type have responded to the adaptational pressures of EMU by trying to develop national social pacts in which employers and trade unions negotiate package deals to contain unit labour costs and improve labour-market efficiency (Dyson, Chapter 10 in this volume).

Finally, Europeanization studies have come to be interested in an increasingly broad range of effects. For example, an interest in material effects, such as is manifested in the structures of incentives and constraints at the EU level to which domestic policy-makers respond, is complemented by growing empirical attention being paid to cognitive effects, as demonstrated by policy learning and mimetic processes consequent on increased interaction at the EU level, notably in professional policy communities (Dyson 2002a). Policy-makers internalize a particular 'logic of appropriateness' in terms of which they legitimate proposals. Similarly, direct effects, which involve the presence of a clear EU model that is 'downloaded', are examined alongside indirect effects that take the form of 'spillover', as EU-level action in one area affects related areas and generates adaptational pressures there (see, e.g., Haverland, Chapter 13 in this volume). 'Process-oriented' accounts of Europeanization also see transformation of institutional arrangements and policy beliefs and instruments as only one of a range of possible impacts. Thus, Europeanization may be associated with 'system maintenance', as it serves to rule out certain kinds of domestic transformation, such as an extension of industrial subsidy policies or certain types of budget deficit and debt policies, thereby underpinning continuity in domestic politics. Again, subject to the constraints on macro-political strategy represented by degree of attachment to the European idea and identity, impacts may go beyond absorption to inertia—unwillingness to adapt to European requirements—and even retrenchment.

Before turning to the question of how Europeanization may be best conceptualized for the purposes of the present project, two additional features of recent work deserve highlighting. First, early work focused on the policy and polity dimensions of Europeanization (Hix and Goetz 2000). The domestic impact was primarily examined in selected fields of public policy—notably agricultural policy, regional policy, and industrial policy—that were at the heart of the Community *acquis*. Effects on the domestic polity in the form of national institutional adjustments provided a second focus of interest, in particular the implications of integration for national executives (government and central administrations), national legislatures and the intergovernmental systems of member states. More recently, however, there has been a broadening of discussion to the Europeanization of domestic politics, in other words processes of opinion formation and conflict resolution. This involves effects of European integration on political cleavages, partisan identification, electoral behaviour, and parties and party systems. Any conceptualization of Europeanization should be able to capture effects across all three dimensions.

Second, although the majority of empirical studies focus on the North-West core of founding member states, there is an increasing interest in states that joined later—the Southern periphery and the Nordic states; those that are actively seeking membership, such as the countries of Central and Eastern Europe, Malta, Cyprus, and Turkey; or are not yet seeking membership, but, are, nonetheless, affected by integration (notably Norway and Switzerland). This widening is welcome for several reasons, which we will take up again Chapter 17. First, it highlights the different stages in the historical development of European integration and the potential implications of time of accession and state of integration for patterns of Europeanization. Second, it draws our attention to the specificity of the Europeanization experience of the North-Western core. Third, emerging themes and arguments about EU-periphery members and non-members may be instructive for understanding the German experience. Their experience of 'downloading' and limited capacity to 'upload' might be especially instructive as Germany's capacity to exercise 'soft' power in the EU declines, constraining effects become more acutely felt, and domestic contestation increases.

The growing aspirations emerging from recent writing on Europeanization are to be welcomed, but there is a danger of a gap between an increasingly ambitious and demanding conceptualization and theoretical approaches to Europeanization and what empirical work can reasonably be expected to deliver. Conceptual and theoretical discussion can, at times, seem in danger of running away with itself. The working definition of Europeanization suggested here and the empirical questions that contributors were asked to address (see below) seek to avoid this pitfall. The definition is framed in a way that encourages careful empirical work on tracing the effects European integration. It attempts to be simple and concise and—by distinguishing 'defining' properties from 'accompanying' properties—to differentiate Europeanization from related concepts, notably integration. It focuses on processes rather than the characterization of an end-state and allows for variability in effects. Thus,

> Europeanization denotes a complex interactive 'top-down' and 'bottom-up' process in which domestic polities, politics and public policies are shaped by European integration and in which domestic actors use European integration to shape the domestic arena. It may produce either continuity or change and potentially variable and contingent outcomes.

It is important to distinguish these 'defining' properties of Europeanization from 'accompanying' properties (like 'uploading') that will vary in particular instances. In particular:

- The definition does not arbitrate between the 'fit/misfit' requirement and an emphasis on domestic political triggers and opportunity structures. Their explanatory value is to be tested by empirical observation.
- It leaves open for empirical investigation the respective importance of direct and indirect effects and of material and cognitive effects.
- It adopts an open specification of European integration. Depending on the case to be investigated, European integration may be specified as being synonymous with the EU; narrowed even further to the Community method and supranational integration; or—to take account of other institutional forums and processes—be understood as 'distinct modes of European governance' (Buller and Gamble 2002). In this volume, the focus is firmly on EU integration and its effects, but, as Helen Wallace (2001*a*: 5) has stressed, the EU is only part of 'a variegated pattern' that reveals 'several different transnational Europes, serving a mixture of functional, territorial and affiliational purposes'.
- Possibly most important of all, our definition does not incorporate the 'uploading' or export of domestic institutional models, policy preferences, and 'ways of doing things' to the European level. In this way, Europeanization is not confused with European integration. But, of course, Europeanization is frequently accompanied by the efforts of domestic actors to shape the terms of European integration, and consequent adaptational requirements, through 'uploading'. One effect of European integration may be intensified efforts of domestic actors to 'upload'. This interrelation cannot be ignored in empirical research on Europeanization, but is not strictly a defining property of Europeanization.

The Changing Nature of European Integration

The evolving conceptual understanding of Europeanization and the emergence of new foci for empirical investigation are, in part, a reflection of changes in the nature of the European integration process itself (for a succinct survey see Wallace 2001*b*). They include:

- the progressive extension and deepening of the *acquis communautaire*, in particular through the single market, EMU, justice and home affairs, and foreign and security policy;
- novel forms of co-operation and co-ordination that are gaining in importance in EU governance and indicate a partial move away from the Community method;
- Eastern and Mediterranean enlargement, leading to growing diversity among the member states; pressures for major policy reforms (especially to the EU budget and the Common Agricultural Policy (CAP)); differentiated policy regimes; and a further impetus to the formation of regional sub-groupings in the EU;
- institutional reform, as crystallized in the work of the European Convention in 2002–3.

This agenda is too well known to require extensive review; but, in the present context, it is important to draw out its implications for patterns of Europeanization in general, and for power, constraint, and contestation in the German case, in particular.

Extension and Deepening of the Acquis

The Single Market and EMU have far-reaching implications for national political economies. EMU's effects on domestic monetary, fiscal, and economic policies go to the core of the national political economies of the member states. 'Though a narrow, closed and privileged policy domain, EMU's effects on states are pervasive. Their scope stretches over fiscal, labour-market, and welfare policy . . . while technocratic in origin and ethos, EMU's effects as a macro-level cultural form stretch to the level of the polity' (Dyson 2000*b*: 657). Germany has played a key role in shaping the institutional framework, policy principles, and operating procedures of EMU (notably the European Central Bank and the Stability and Growth Pact). But although this success in uploading may have made abandonment of the D-Mark more acceptable to the German electorate, it has not avoided domestic adaptational pressures and conflicts. Germany faced serious problems in meeting the Maastricht convergence criteria, with a rather desperate last-minute action by then Finance Minister, Theo Waigel, to draw on the Bundesbank's gold reserves, which led him to open conflict with the

Bundesbank. In February 2002, Germany fought hard to avoid a formal warning from the European Commission over potential breach of the Stability Pact, only to have to bow to the inevitable less than a year later, as German budget deficits escalated. By December 2002 the European Commissioner for economic and financial affairs, Pedro Solbes, was referring to Germany as the problem of the Euro-Zone. Similarly, the German Länder became increasingly irritated at what they saw as excessive intervention of the European Commission in their industrial policies under the internal market programme, and they were joined in this defence, if not led, by Chancellor Schröder. With the backing of the Länder, in particular, which most resented EU interference, German interests were redefined in terms of either seeking a clear catalogue of competences for the EU, the federation, and Länder or at least a clear statement of mutual responsibilities.

The effects of deepening and widening in the second and third pillars have become more apparent in the wake of the new security agenda after the terror attacks of 11 September 2001 and the divisions revealed in 2002 over the planned military strike against Iraq. In relation to both common foreign and security policy and justice and home affairs Germany was a major 'uploader' with the end of the Cold War in Europe, not least because of its vulnerable borders (Miskimmon and Paterson and Monar, Chapters 16 and 15 in this volume). But justice and home affairs have raised political sensitivities for Germany because of the Länder's competences for criminal law and for police. In 2002, the common foreign and security policy had to cope with the fallout from Schröder's assertion of a distinctive 'German way' in response to the planned US attack on Iraq.

Novel Forms of Co-operation and Co-ordination

The 'open' method of co-ordination was pioneered in economic policy, and then quickly extended to other domains. Practices such as benchmarking best practice, target-setting and peer review take the place of standardized common legal regulation. According to Hodson and Maher (2001: 731) 'the open method provides real flexibility and marks a further maturation of the integration process. The desire of the EC to control outcomes, as manifested in the directive as the rule of choice in the single market, is overcome by recognition of the importance of diversity at the national level in relation to policy formation, legal frameworks, ideational references and popular perceptions and reactions to either the European project more generally or the specific policy being co-ordinated.' The open method also characterizes policy-making under the second and third EU pillars. It is at the core of what Helen Wallace (2000: 34) calls 'intensive transgovernmentalism', i.e. 'the active involvement of the European Council in setting the overall direction of policy; the predominance of the Council of Ministers (or an equivalent forum of national ministers) in consolidating cooperation; the limited or marginal role of the Commission; the exclusion of the EP and the ECJ from the circle of involvement; the involvement of a distinct circle of key national policy-makers; the adoption of special arrangements for managing co-operation; the opaqueness of the process, to national parliaments and publics; but the capacity on occasions to deliver substantive joint policy'.

The extension of the open method may be regarded as an indication of the steady broadening of the 'soft' *acquis* so that it is now difficult to think of domestic or foreign policies that are not subject to institutionalized co-operation and co-ordination. In this sense, it is suggestive of progressive Europeanization. But the open method may also be indicative of changes in the character of Europeanization, indicating a shift from coercive, 'top-down' imposition to negotiated co-ordination and imitation in which certain domestic actors seek legitimation for their policy proposals from benchmarking (a dynamic that is detailed in Dyson, Chapter 10 in this volume). The spread of this 'intensive transgovernmentalism' calls into question the association of Europeanization with a 'top-down', hierarchical process.

Germany actively sponsored the 'open' method of co-ordination as a means of developing EMU, not least because of its consistency with the principle of subsidiarity as enshrined in the Maastricht Treaty, and has been supportive of its extension. Germany's support would appear consistent with its traditional and effective reliance on 'soft' power. However, the spread of the open method is occurring at a time when a combination of faltering economic growth and high unemployment casts doubts on Germany's continuing credibility as a 'benchmark' from which others may wish to learn and copy and when increasing domestic budgetary problems reduce Germany's capability to be at the centre of EU problem-solving. The 'open' method is, therefore, unlikely to enhance German 'soft' power and may, in fact, produce the opposite effect.

Enlargement

The enlargement of the EU, with the accession of ten new member states as agreed at the Copenhagen summit in December 2002, marks a fundamental change in the scope and nature of European integration. The character of the enlarged Union remains a subject of controversy, as both the effects of integration on the accession states and the repercussions of enlargement for the EU and its current member states are uncertain. But the enlarged EU will in key respects be a much more heterogeneous union than the EU-15:

- The balance between 'large' and 'small' member states is changing. With the exception of Poland, all new members belong to the latter category, and some micro-states are added. In the Nice Treaty, Germany sought to offset this effect defensively by a re-weighting of votes in the Council to better reflect the demographic factor. Yet, it is clear that a traditionally dominant, but now relatively shrinking North-Western core faces a much enlarged 'periphery'. In many respects, the 'periphery' experience of integration becomes the norm in the EU.

- With the accession of the new member states, economic and social disparities within the EU increase decisively, and problems arise about how nominal and real economic convergence can be combined. There is an incentive for the new members that are subject to Treaty requirements of exchange-rate discipline to externalize the domestic costs of adjustment by seeking enlarged EU fiscal transfers. These costs would fall heavily on Germany and could lead German leaders into conflict with new members. This conflict could be more serious if new members are successful in building coalitions on this issue with some existing members.
- There will be a considerable advance in asymmetrical membership, as a result of derogations and transitional arrangements. In particular, new members will enter stage two of EMU as states with a derogation, and transitional arrangements exist on freedom of movement of labour, on the full implementation of Schengen, and on many aspects of the CAP.
- 'Bilateralization' will play a greater role within the EU, as some restrictions imposed on the new entrants are applied by some existing member states, but not others, such as restrictions on the freedom of the movement of labour which are to be applied by Germany, but not the UK.

Of course, enlargement to East-Central Europe can be seen as a major boost for German interests (Katzenstein 1997c). It allows Germany to build on the economic and political advantages of its central geographical location within an expanded EU. Germany stands to benefit both from its traditional economic dominance of this region and from enhanced geo-strategic security by stabilizing its eastern borders. Eastern enlargement has also been perceived as a counterweight to Southern enlargement, and the potential 'Mediterraneanization' of the EU.

The ambivalent effects of enlargement come to the fore over the labour market—where Germany has sought transitional arrangements on freedom of movement of labour—and over budgetary policy. With the 'periphery becoming the norm', the interests and policy concerns of peripheral states assume a much higher profile in the EU. Germany faces in consequence much greater assertiveness, notably from Spain on behalf of the South, and Poland on behalf of the Eastern accession states. Increased disparities within the enlarged EU add further pressure for more extensive EU-level fiscal transfers in the interest of economic and social cohesion. The question arises of whether the North-Western core can continue to manage this agenda as its shaping role declines.

The complexity of German interests is also evident over the issue of whether enlargement should be linked to the promotion and defence of regulatory harmonization or to regulatory competition. Traditional German ordo-liberal ideas favour common, authoritative rules to ensure competitive markets, while German economic interests could be threatened by lower regulatory standards in East-Central Europe. At the same time, some of the most prosperous German Länder have been increasingly critical of excessive Commission interference in their industrial policies. Insistence on new entrants meeting demanding standards loses credibility when these standards are seen not to be respected by those who promote them for others. The challenge of trying to foster relatively higher economic growth in new member states is likely to lead to new pressures for the relaxation of regulatory harmonization, which could trigger thorny domestic debates about German interests. A similar dynamic can be expected in the case of the central issue of exchange-rate policy for new member states as they attempt to meet the Maastricht convergence criteria for stage three of EMU. The internal adjustment problems and lost output and jobs associated with the external discipline of being tied to the euro in ERM2 will lead to powerful political pressures for EU-level compensation. These pressures will put Germany in a potentially very difficult position, caught between its interest in the new entrants' position in the EU and its interest in reducing its financial burdens within the EU. Finally, as will be discussed in Chapter 17, the issue of Turkish membership of the EU constitutes an important potential catalyst for increased domestic contestation and even polarization about the course of integration.

Institutional Reform

Enlargement is one of the main driving forces behind the discussion about a fundamental reform of the EU institutional framework and new forms of co-operation among the member states and between the latter and EU institutions. There is a basic political consensus in Germany on the need for major institutional reforms as a prerequisite of enlargement. Accordingly, Germany has played an agenda-setting role in stimulating the 'post-Nice' process, notably with Foreign Minister Joschka Fischer's speech of May 2000 on the 'finality' of European integration and Schröder's role in the SPD's resolution on 'responsibility for Europe' of November 2000. After the 2002 federal elections, Fischer took on one of the German seats in the European Convention, underlining the serious political commitment of Germany to the convention process. The debates in and around the European Convention clarified a consensus about German objectives, including:

- the incorporation of basic rights in an EU treaty, with the European Court of Justice (ECJ) empowered to enforce these rights;

- a clearer division of competences between the EU and the member states, recognizing, however, that scope for flexibility in developing integration was necessary especially in external and internal security;
- a strengthening of the powers of the European Parliament (EP);
- a president of the European Commission elected by the European Parliament, alongside a new president of the European Council;
- greater use of qualified majority voting, notably in foreign policy, in particular to reduce the number of veto points and the potential for blockage.

These positions were designed to improve both efficiency and democratic legitimacy of the EU institutions. At the same time, they were likely to be associated with greater contestation between the German and EU levels. Member states would still be able to seek to 'upload' their preferences. But such an institutional structure would reduce the capacity of a member state like Germany to obstruct or block the initiatives of others. The gain for German macro-political interests in promoting the integration process would be accompanied by more complex domestic adjustment problems to the effects of this process.

In sum, the developments in European integration that we have briefly sketched here have potentially far-reaching implications for German patterns of Europeanization. 'Uploading' might become more difficult for Germany, as the centrality of the Franco-German alliance is threatened in an enlarged and more diverse EU; as other member states, such as Spain and Poland, flex their muscles; and as the number of member states increases and, therefore, the options for effective coalition-building that exclude Germany. The concerns of the 'periphery' will become more central, and here the drivers of policy will be the peripheral states themselves. To this must be added the internal factors undermining the projection of German 'soft' power consequent on relative economic decline and budgetary restrictions after unification. Germany can no longer play the 'paymaster role' for Europe. In consequence, it is less obviously at the centre of EU problem-solving and is losing 'leverage' over policy outcomes. It is also less capable of convincing others by its policy arguments when its own performance is well below average. Benchmarking on Germany—i.e. exporting the German model—has given way to benchmarking by Germany (Dyson, Chapter 10 in this volume).

Europeanization in the Berlin Republic

The second chief source of change that affects patterns of Europeanization is domestic. It has become common to refer to unified Germany as the 'Berlin Republic', a term suggestive of a major domestic transformation consequent on unification. It coincides with generational change, a more complex and indeterminate party system, relative economic decline, a more visible and assertive international role by Germany, and sharper polarization on economic, social, and cultural policies since the coming into office of the first centre-left government. These variables influence how Germany interacts with Europe.

The transition from the Bonn to the Berlin Republic has been gradual and to some extent concealed until the end of the Kohl era, which stood for stability and continuity (or, in a critical reading, increasing immobility and inertia). More than a decade after unification, the quality, magnitude, and durability of change in the German political system are becoming more evident, as is the need to re-examine key analytical concepts developed in the context of the pre-unified Federal Republic. Thus, Padgett and Poguntke (2002) and their collaborators have revisited the 'politics of centrality' with the aim of exploring whether it is still of relevance in unified Germany; Kitschelt and Streeck (2003) have led a collective effort to re-examine *Modell Deutschland* and to re-evaluate the 'perspectives on a stable state' first developed by Paterson and Smith (1982) some twenty years ago; and a team of scholars led by Simon Green and William E. Paterson are re-examining Katzenstein's (1987) influential characterization of the Federal Republic as a 'semi-sovereign' state.

Many of the chapters in this volume engage with this debate on the changing face of the German political system. Our purpose here is not to provide a comprehensive survey of these changes, but to highlight—by reference to the politics-polity-policy distinction—those that may be expected to have a major impact on patterns of Europeanization.

The Political Realm

- The formation of the first Red–Green government under Schröder in 1998 represented a historical landmark in at least three senses: the first complete change of the federal government since the foundation of the Federal Republic; the instalment of the first centre-left government in its history; and a generational change in government as politicians whose formative personal and political experiences were in the Federal Republic (or, in a few cases, the German Democratic Republic) assumed office. Its re-election in 2002 confirmed a cultural change away from the Kohl generation and placed in question the traditional assumption that Germany was defined by a structural majority for conservatism.

The *Europeanization implications* included a new set of actors, who maintained continuity in macro-political strategy for Europe, but who were more pragmatic and robust (or, in an alternative reading, less dexterous and more short-sighted) in pursuing German interests within this context. Their success in doing so was qualified by an early lack of international experience, by the implications of

Germany's relative economic decline and absorption in domestic problems, and by a failure to build effective coalitions, whether with the French or with others. Schröder proved a less influential and committed European player than Kohl, more interested in short-term tactics and managing public opinion than in macropolitical strategy. The result was a sense of incoherence and confusion about European policy. Fischer sought to play a strong European role and develop a profile on macro-political strategy but, at least until 2002, lacked the domestic power base within the coalition to make up for Schröder's lack of engagement. The Blair–Schröder Paper of 1999 had limited positive domestic resonance; attempts to reanimate the Franco-German partnership proved problematic; while initial high hopes that Germany might co-operate with other Social Democrat-led governments to build a 'social' Europe, focused on growth, employment, and closer social and economic cohesion, were largely disappointed and withered as the centre-right regained power in key European states. The second Red–Green government of 2002 offered a new opportunity for Fischer to profile himself on macro-political strategy for Europe, which he tried to exploit. But the dramatic deterioration of relations with the Bush administration over Iraq during the election of 2002 meant that Germany found herself increasingly isolated on foreign and security issues, with a dramatic reduction in her capacity to shape policy European choices in this crucial policy domain.

- An increasing polarization of the party systems at federal and Länder levels was evident with the stabilization of the Party of Democratic Socialism (PDS) as the third party in the new Länder and a clear West–East divide in electoral behaviour and party system characteristics (Niedermayer, Chapter 7 in this volume). This development was halted, if not reversed, by the 2002 federal elections, in which the SPD strengthened its performance in the East at the cost of the PDS and the electoral landscape reverted to its traditional North–South divide as the CDU/CSU's key gains were confined to the South. Nevertheless, the East displayed much greater electoral volatility than the West, with little party loyalty, and a strong disposition to measure politicians and parties by their solidarity with the East (hence the impact of Schröder's crisis management of the floods in the East in August 2002). This disposition advantaged the PDS and after 2002 strengthened the position of Eastern representatives inside the SPD. The Eastern electorate showed less trust in EU institutions and was more critical of the EU than the Western electorate.

The *Europeanization implications* were limited by the fact that, with the exception of the PDS, all the main parties shared a consensus on the main elements of integration policy. However, there were notable indirect effects, primarily in terms of the patterns of coalition formation and policy co-ordination in the intergovernmental system. Competition for resources between Länder, especially between East and West, was heightened by progressive budget consolidation in the framework of the Stability and Growth Pact and by the recognition that the East had been crucial for the federal election result in 2002 and needed to be rewarded. Increased Länder competition introduced new stresses and strains into both party behaviour and EU–domestic relations (Jeffery, Chapter 5 in this volume), and the pluralization of coalition formulas in both West and East reduced the co-ordinating capacity of political parties in the intergovernmental system.

- There are signs of increasing stresses and strains within and among the key economic associations in Germany and in their relations with the federal government. The Alliance for Jobs reflected the political will of the new Red–Green government in 1998 to undertake economic reforms by consensus between the federal government, the employer organizations, and the trade unions. However, its work was blocked by their reluctance to co-operate. This reluctance reflected, in part, a lack of an underlying consensus about the causes of unemployment and, therefore, an inability to agree on solutions (even major reforms to job placement required a crisis in 2002). It also reflected fears of association leaderships about the exit of firms from employer organizations (especially because of the lack of flexibility in area wage agreements) and of trade unions about declining membership. Both reacted by strengthening their mobilizing role on behalf of their clientèles, in the process taking up uncompromising positions that made negotiated reforms very difficult. The main proposals on labour-market reform followed a different route: a crisis followed by Schröder's intervention to establish an independent commission under Peter Hartz from Volkswagen. Against this background, the Alliance for Jobs achieved little and—to appease employers who might exit from negotiations— trade unions shifted to greater flexibility in collective bargaining and accepted, however reluctantly, a stronger role for works councils in managing industrial relations.

The *Europeanization implications* are far-reaching. They included, in the first instance, difficulties in making effective use of benchmarking best practice as a catalyst for domestic reforms. The analyses and recommendations of the Benchmarking Group attached to the Alliance for Jobs were rejected by the trade unions as 'not discussable'. In part, this reflected an ideological rejection of proposals that were identified as grounded in the American model of labour markets and neo-liberal in inspiration. The Hartz Commission on labour-market reform was, in contrast, more effective by focusing on the benchmark of reducing the length of unemployment in Germany to the EU average. In part, the problem lay in the climate of confrontation and distrust between employer organizations and trade unions. The former welcomed the internal market and EMU as disciplining agents for domestic liberalization in product, financial, and labour markets and in wages policy. Seeing the German model as threatened, German trade unions sought a stronger influence at the EU level in promoting a 'social' Europe, a relaxation of the Stability and Growth Pact in the interests of higher public investment, and a more growth-oriented monetary policy. The unwillingness of the Schröder government to pursue this agenda actively at the European level damaged relations with the trade unions. Europeanization put the German trade unions on the defensive, particularly as it drew attention to wages as the only macro-economic variable left at the domestic level and increased domestic political pressures for a clear, long-term formula for wage bargaining. Hence, employers and trade unions were increasingly pursuing different agendas of European policy.

The Institutional Realm

- The increased scope and depth of European integration acted as a catalyst for a debate about the appropriate form of European policy coordination within the federal executive (Goetz, Chapter 3 in this volume). Before the 2002 elections, Schröder toyed with the idea of a European minister within the Federal Chancellery, in effect of taking responsibility away from the Foreign Minister. This option was ruled out by Fischer's strengthened position after the elections, but a division focusing solely on European policy was created in the Chancellery for the first time. Also before the elections, Werner Müller, the Federal Economics Minister, let it be known that he would seek to regain responsibility for macro-economic policy from the Finance Ministry, which had been lost to the Finance Ministry, then headed by Oskar Lafontaine, in 1998. After the 2002 elections, the new 'super-minister' for Economics and Labour, Wolfgang Clement, succeeded in repatriating economic policy and started to call for a more relaxed ECB monetary policy.

The *Europeanization implications* have included, in particular, a strengthening of the domestic role of the Finance Ministry and the centrality of budget consolidation within the first Schröder government. Hans Eichel used the requirements of the Stability and Growth Pact to bolster his standing within the government. From 2002 there was a greater potential for divided German views about macro-economic policy.

- Integration of the Bundesbank into the European System of Central Banks (ESCB) meant that it was no longer the 'bank that rules Europe' (Marsh 1992), but just one among many equals in setting ECB monetary policy. It had to look for other roles to strengthen its domestic presence and to undergo a major structural reform to adapt to its changed responsibilities.

The *Europeanization implications* included a domestic debate about the appropriate roles of the Bundesbank and a major structural reform in 2002 to accommodate its changed responsibilities (Dyson, Chapter 10 in this volume). Central to this debate were, first, the implications for the federal character of the Bundesbank of a proposed centralization of authority and, second, the question of whether it should have prime responsibility for banking supervision. Beyond this, the traditional 'signalling power' of the Bundesbank in disciplining domestic wage bargaining by the powerful employer and trade union organizations has gone, leaving a potential vacuum in which the outcomes of wage bargaining could have negative effects on ECB monetary policy. The result was a debate about the appropriate form of wage-policy co-ordination to replace the lost 'signalling power' of the Bundesbank. This included greater self-discipline through a productivity-oriented wage formula and 'negative', 'implicit' co-ordination in the form of the EU-level Macro-Economic Dialogue.

- The combination of the primacy of EU law over national law and the increasing scope and depth of European integration caused problems for the German Federal Constitutional Court. These problems centred on the safeguarding of the basic rights enshrined in the German Basic Law and the democratic legitimacy of European institutions compared to their national counterparts. They led the Court to take a critical approach in some key rulings, notably on the Maastricht Treaty in 1993, stressing an element of conditionality. The primacy of EU law had its limits in the role of the Court in protecting constitutionally enshrined basic rights. In consequence, domestic debate focused on the paramount need to finalize a European constitution that would enshrine a statement of basic rights and give the European Court of Justice an explicit role in protecting them. In its absence, there were grounds for potential frictions between the European Court of Justice and the Federal Constitutional Court. This issue was pressed strongly by German representatives in the European Convention in 2002. Earlier, a former president of the Federal Constitutional Court, Roman Herzog, had chaired the convention that produced the EU charter of basic rights.

The *Europeanization implications* included greater activism by the European Court of Justice in its rulings on basic rights, with important effects in Germany (see Schuppert, Chapter 6 in this volume).

The Policy Realm

- Perhaps the single most important domestic development was relative economic decline from 1993 onwards, represented by an economic growth rate below both the EU and the OECD averages and an employment and job creation record that compared unfavourably with other states. The 'German model' lost credibility as the basis for Germany to argue convincingly for the 'export' of its domestic institutional arrangements, policies, and 'ways of doing things' to the EU level. The 'paymaster of Europe' role was no longer sustainable, with the result that German leverage over policy outcomes declined. The result was a decline of 'soft' power at a critical moment when the EU was both completing EMU and enlarging.

The *Europeanization implications* included potentially greater 'misfit' between EU and domestic arrangements (see, e.g., Lodge, Chapter 11 in this volume), more conflicts as domestic reformers sought to use EU requirements to force the scope and pace of change (notably, structural reforms in fiscal policy, market liberalization, and labour-market flexibility), and a growing recognition of the need to 'benchmark' others.

- German unification was a key factor in this relative economic decline and led to the emergence of two distinct political economies, East and West. They were characterized by cultural differences rooted in the very different experiences of the Federal Republic and the German Democratic Republic. They could be contrasted as individualistic and solidaristic cultures or as cultures based on self-responsibility and state-orientation. A combination of poor productivity, high costs, and lost markets led to rapid de-industrialization and very high unemployment in the East and massive fiscal transfers from the West to support basic social services. Most seriously of all, the East German economy failed to achieve the rate of economic growth that would allow reasonably rapid 'catch-up' with the West and enable the reduction of these transfers. The result was a massive rise in public debt, restricting the room for manoeuvre in fiscal policy and, hence, the opportunities for the federal and Länder governments to pursue active employment policies, whether by public investment programmes or tax cuts.

The *Europeanization implications* included serious problems in meeting the requirements of the Stability and Growth Pact, especially with low tax revenues and high public spending pressures and accumulated debt. Budget consolidation emerged as the top priority of economic policy for the Schröder governments, the precondition for regaining a measure of macro-economic capacity to tackle problems of growth and employment. Similarly, Länder governments in the East hovered between welcoming EU Structural Fund measures and resenting the interventions of the Commission in enforcing competition policy rules and a liberalizing agenda that was hard to reconcile with the economic and social realities of the East.

- The domestic economy was remodelled by privatization and new types of regulatory regimes, particularly in telecommunications and energy policies (see Lodge and Bulmer *et al.*, Chapters 11 and 12 in this volume). Similar pressures were also underway in transport, notably the airlines and railways.

The *Europeanization implications* included an ongoing debate about whether the regulatory regimes that had evolved in Germany were compatible with EU templates, at least as defined by the European Commission and by new entrants to these sectors. Thus, there was criticism of the weak powers of the *Eisenbahn Bundesamt* in regulating railways, of the slowness of the regulatory office for telecommunications and postal services in liberalization, and of the absence of a regulatory authority for electricity and for gas and a reliance on negotiated sectoral regulation.

- In the face of a series of international crises, security policy under the Kohl and Schröder governments shifted from an exclusive focus on territorial defence to more flexible forms of 'out-of-area' operation. This began in Bosnia under the Kohl government, took on a new form of engaging in military action in the Kosovo war, reached a further stage with the intervention in Afghanistan, and culminated in a statement by the Minister of Defence that territorial defence was no longer the task of the Bundeswehr. The Kosovo war underlined the need for Germany to engage in a more effective European defence and security policy, and the terrorist attacks of 11 September 2001 gave a new priority to both EU internal and external security. At the same time as pressures for a permanent reorientation of foreign and security policy mounted, the distinctive German position of opposing the use of troops to effect regime change in Iraq showed up the limits to such a repositioning. Thus, the Iraq crisis was crucial in drawing out a new clarity about the purposes for which German troops could be deployed and emphasized the depth of commitment to UN mandates and the preference for peace-related and humanitarian roles.

The *Europeanization implications* included, in particular, the need to reform the Bundeswehr to prepare its for its fundamentally changed role (Miskimmon and Paterson, Chapter 16 in this volume). This issue was difficult because it went to the heart of post-war understandings about German political identity as a civilian power in which the armed forces were intimately linked to the rest of society.

Questions and Themes

The preceding sections have made the case for re-examining the impact of European integration on the German political system. Against this background, the contributors were invited to examine patterns of Europeanization with reference to the conceptual definition offered in this chapter, taking into consideration, where relevant, shifts in the European integration process and in the German political system. The contributions range across polity, politics, and public policies. The book, thus, covers areas where there is a 'received wisdom' that can be 'revisited'—for example, the Europeanization of the federal executive, the intergovernmental system, and some traditional public policy areas; public policies that have only recently begun to attract more systematic attention, like justice and home affairs; and aspects of politics that have suffered from relative neglect in the Europeanization debate, at least as regards Germany, such as the party system and political communications.

In their substantive coverage, the contributions are guided by a common set of empirical questions (these are virtually identical to those proposed by Featherstone and Radaelli 2003, although both sets were formulated independently). They include:

- *The 'what' or substantive question.* What has been affected by Europeanization? What form has Europeanization taken—accommodation, transformation, reaffirmation or retrenchment? What have been the level and the magnitude of change (core or marginal; change to goals, instruments or just their use)?
- *The 'why' or causal question*, dealing with the preconditions for change and the causal triggers. Has there been a 'misfit' between EU and domestic institutions, practices, and beliefs that has served as a trigger? What have been the effects of European integration on domestic political opportunity structures and how have actors used European integration?
- *The 'how' or modal question.* How do domestic institutional arrangements shape the way in which European integration affects polity, politics, and policy? To what extent are mechanisms of Europeanization related to clear EU institutional templates, where the relationship is more hierarchical, or to the EU as an arena for policy transfer and learning?
- *The 'who' or actor question.* Who are the key domestic actors affected by, and shaping, European integration? What are their motives? Are they to be seen as instrumentalizing Europe, or as normatively engaged?

- *The 'when' or temporal question.* Is it possible to identify major phases of Europeanization and changes in the timing and tempo of Europeanization?

Beyond a common working definition of Europeanization and a shared set of empirical questions, there has not been an attempt to impose a particular theoretical position on contributors, but, in common with most recent work on Europeanization, the majority of the analyses assembled here adopt variants of the neo-institutionalist approach.

2

Europeanization in Context: Concept and Theory

JEFFREY J. ANDERSON

Introduction

THE PURPOSE OF THIS VOLUME IS TO EXPLORE the extent of Europeanization in key spheres of the Germany political system, and to draw out the implications both for Germany and for the future trajectory of integration. This raises several thorny conceptual and methodological challenges. Empirical investigations of Europeanization should proceed from a common understanding of the phenomenon, especially if one hopes to gain insights into the cumulative impact of Europeanization on the national political system, as well as to generate useful comparisons with other states in Europe. Moreover, one should be able to differentiate the outcomes and processes associated with Europeanization from other large-scale causal forces that act on and within the nation-states.

The objective of this chapter is to explore the theoretical and empirical challenges associated with the use of Europeanization as an explanatory variable in accounting for domestic institutional and policy developments. It covers a broad range of issues, but focuses primarily on the relationship between Europeanization and globalization. In the course of this discussion, I elaborate on the challenges involved in distinguishing globalization and Europeanization as cause and effect of domestic dynamics and processes. In fact, in many respects, this chapter is an extended exercise in conceptual differentiation. This is an important and in key ways analytically prior objective, for no other reason than that we cannot hope to assess accurately the extent of Europeanization and its implications if we are unable to distinguish it from other large-scale processes at work in contemporary Europe. Globalization is just one of many such phenomena —others include micro-level forces of technological change in the economy and temporally circumscribed 'events' such as German unification and the end of the Cold War. Domestic systems are subject to a vast range of causal forces both endogenous and exogenous, and selecting one—in this case, Europeanization— for close, careful examination presupposes an ability to differentiate it conceptually and empirically.

Proceedings of the British Academy, **119**, 37–53. © The British Academy 2003.

Globalization

As a concept, globalization predates Europeanization, and, therefore, deserves first treatment. Ubiquitous yet amorphous,[1] it typically refers to the growth in economic transactions between and among countries since the late 1970s—specifically, international trade in goods and services, currency trading, and foreign direct investment (FDI) (Milner and Keohane 1996). Sociopolitically, globalization can also refer to a broader range of interdependent trends and developments: the increased volume and speed of information flows among nations, whether through traditional channels such as the print and broadcast media or through new technologies such as the internet; the emergence of transnational advocacy groups like Greenpeace and Amnesty International; the growing influence of international agencies such as the World Bank, the International Monetary Fund (IMF), and the United Nations; and even the international diffusion of common values and norms, such as human rights. At its most encompassing level, globalization implies the diminishing importance of national boundaries in circumscribing the way people act and think.

Defining globalization, as opposed to describing it impressionistically, has proved to be an elusive objective. Some scholars have sought to incorporate an anticipated or even desired final state of affairs into a process-oriented characterization of globalization. For example, many definitions begin with a vision of a truly global economy in which transnational markets operate free of locational constraints or national institutional impediments; working backward, globalization becomes the process by which this end-state is brought into being (Ohmae 1990). A major problem with such approaches is that the presumed empirical consequences of globalization—for example, the eclipse of the state and the narrowing of national policy choices—are built into the definition.

Other scholars, wary of these pitfalls, opt for conceptualizations that lend themselves more easily to empirical measurement and validation. An example is Milner and Keohane's definition of internationalization (1996: 4; emphasis in original), which '*refers to the processes generated by underlying shifts in transaction costs that produce observable flows of goods, services, and capital. . . .* [I]nternational trade, investment, and currency trading have grown dramatically during the last two decades, especially relative to the size of national economies; hence, internationalization, as we define it, has grown.' The problem with such an approach is the narrowness of the frame of reference. It is difficult to see how the more explicitly political and social elements of globalization, as we commonly perceive and understand them, can be extracted from such a restricted focus on flows and volumes of goods, services, and capital.

---

[1] For sceptical perspectives on the globalization phenomenon, see Berger and Dore (1996) and Hollingsworth and Boyer (1997).

In light of these various considerations, Philip Cerny's definition (1995: 596–7) offers a useful starting point for thinking about globalization and its relationship to other large-scale phenomena, like Europeanization:

> Globalization is defined . . . as a set of economic and political structures and processes deriving from the changing character of the goods and assets that comprise the base of the international political economy—in particular, the increasing structural differentiation of those goods and assets. 'Structures' are more or less embedded sets—patterns—of constraints and opportunities confronting decision-making agents . . . ; 'processes' are dynamic patterns of interaction and change that take place on or across structured fields of action.

This way of thinking about globalization carries several advantages. First, it directs attention to structures and processes, which—admittedly with prior effort—can be cast in terms of empirical referents that are observable and measurable. Second, the empirical manifestations of globalization are linked to underlying dynamics that appear to be largely economic in nature, which suggests that there is nothing inevitable or inexorable about globalization (i.e. it could conceivably wane as well as wax). Third, there is nothing intrinsically desirable or undesirable about globalization; rather, its effects and implications must be identified empirically and assessed on their own terms. And finally, again relating to impact and implications, the definition casts globalization in terms that are intimately related to behavioural patterns. In short, there is a healthy dose of rationalist institutionalism in Cerny's approach to the concept. Historically conditioned structures and processes to which human behavioural patterns have conformed are now in the process of being reordered and reshaped by deep-seated changes in the character of the goods and assets that comprise the base of the international political economy.

The multi-faceted nature of globalization leads inexorably to a search for cause and effect. The economic manifestations of globalization result from an inherently unco-ordinated process involving countless actors such as firms, governments, non-governmental organizations (NGOs), and even individuals. Increases in the volume of trade in goods and services, and the expansion of international capital markets, are linked intimately to technological innovations such as the microchip and internet revolutions. Economic globalization has also been spurred by the conscious efforts of firms, particularly large multinational enterprises, to achieve a global reach, as well as by the adoption of neo-liberal economic policy programmes by governments around the world. Political globalization carries more evidence of human design or at least intentionality, yet, even here, the processes have unfolded in a manner beyond the control of any single political authority. The European integration process itself, premised on completion of the internal market and a general orientation toward free trade with third countries, has provided a major impetus to globalization (Fligstein and Merand 2001; Milner and Keohane 1996: 24).

As globalization unfolds, the implications for nation-states grow more significant. National borders, whether by design or accident, become more permeable both economically and politically, and this in turn carries potentially weighty implications for domestic politics and even for elemental regime characteristics. Scholars have argued convincingly that the meaning and implications of national sovereignty have been transformed in significant and permanent ways (Biersteker 1999). With the progress of globalization, countries grow more interdependent and consequently become more vulnerable to impulses transmitted by the international system. Even a modest decline or rise in prices on international markets can mean the difference between prosperity and penury for individuals, firms, sectors, regions, and even nations. Granted, this is nothing new, but in today's world the speed and scope of exogenous economic shocks are vastly greater than in previous decades. And as nations' vulnerability to exogenous economic shocks has grown, so, too, has the likelihood of externally induced political crises.[2]

Nation-states are also unable to shield the domestic arena from political scrutiny, counsel, and even demands originating in the international community, which are often backed by the implicit or explicit threat of co-ordinated sanctions. Within the past decade, the fact, and occasional significance, of 'world opinion' has been demonstrated numerous times, whether in the Balkans or, more recently, in the aftermath of the terrorist attacks in the USA on 11 September.

Globalization also creates a situation in which the preferences and capabilities of domestic actors—from individuals to government agencies—become bound up, sometimes intimately and inextricably, with extranational factors. Contemporary research in the fields of comparative and international political economy focuses a great deal of attention on two such areas. First, the autonomy of national governments has diminished in the face of globalization, insofar as their standard policy repertoires have lost efficacy because of the undermining influences of international forces (Milner and Keohane 1996: 16–18). Attention here has focused primarily but not exclusively on the political left, which has been forced to abandon or at least substantially modify long-standing commitments and objectives to working-class constituencies and the like.

Second, global economic forces have the capacity to rearrange issue cleavages in society and thereby to shape the nature of domestic political conflict. For example, the interplay of international price changes and the relative scarcity or abundance of production factors at the national level have produced shifts in domestic political coalitions with important consequences for government policy choices and outcomes (Rogowski 1989). As economic globalization has progressed, issue conflicts at the national level have fallen increasingly along sec-

---

[2] Again, this is a matter of degree. Two studies that chart the impact of the international economy on national politics over the centuries are Gourevitch (1986) and Rogowski (1989).

toral lines, dividing mobile international capital and its labour forces from capital and labour relatively more rooted to particular production locations (Frieden 1991). Sectoral politics is expected to become more salient than the traditional politics of class. To the extent that globalization reshapes large swaths of national politics along sectoral lines, it is likely to create unresolved tensions in democracies that are universally based on the principle of territorial representation and that, in the vast majority of cases, have political parties and party systems organized around the clash of class-based interests. Finally, to the extent that nation-states attempt to manage the effects of globalization collectively, a causal link emerges between globalization and various modes of inter-state co-operation, up to and including regional integration, of which the EU is a prime example.

Europeanization

For well over a decade, students of European integration have pointed to the gradual emergence of incontrovertible empirical facts: domestic political behaviour, processes, institutions, and outcomes are increasingly shaped by, and even bound up with, European integration. Anecdotal evidence abounds that elected and appointed officials, as well as interest group representatives, see things differently and do things differently owing to the presence of the EU. Findings generated by systematic research reveal extensive effects in the realm of domestic institutions and, in particular, public policies (Ladrech 1994). Moreover, there are instances of domestic continuity—i.e. an absence of change—that can be traced back to European integration.[3] Alan Milward (1992), for example, presents a classic version of this thesis in his study of the rescue of the European nation-state. In sum, domestic political, economic, and social systems exhibit clear signs of what we wish to describe as 'Europeanization'. However true empirically, we must acknowledge the vast scope of the concept. Researchers will have to narrow the frame of reference to render the concept serviceable.

A few observations about the strengths of the definition of Europeanization offered by Dyson and Goetz (Chapter 1 in this volume) are in order before moving on to outline the relationship between globalization and Europeanization as well as the associated research challenges. By proceeding in this manner, Dyson and Goetz eschew two definitional approaches that are not at all well suited to the analytical agenda set out in this volume. The first and in some ways obvious approach is to define Europeanization as the regional manifestation of globalization. The concept then refers principally to the dramatic growth in intra-regional transactions—trade in goods and services, currency flows, and foreign direct investment—that has been especially pronounced in Europe since the late 1970s,

---

[3] Hix and Goetz characterize Europeanization as 'continuity and change in domestic political systems' (2000*b*: 2).

and perhaps even to the myriad social, political, and economic consequences that have accompanied these transactions. Paraphrasing Cerny (1995: 596–7), Europeanization would be defined as a set of economic and political structures and processes deriving from the increasing structural differentiation of the goods and assets that comprise the base of the European political economy.

Scholars who have taken this path (implicitly, for the most part) have argued that, when viewed in historical perspective, a good case can be made that Europeanization is causally prior to globalization. Fligstein and Merand (2001: 15) outline 'the important role that European market integration played in changes in trade in the world over the past 20 years', and conclude for all intents and purposes that globalization is Europeanization on a grand scale. Especially since the mid-1980s, which marked the launch of the Single Market initiative, European countries increasingly trade more with each other and less with the rest of the world. European multinational firms are 'much more Eurocentric than multinationals in general. They tend to invest more in Europe, export more of what they produce in general than large multinationals, and export most of their products to the rest of Europe. Over time, they have increased their investments and sales to the rest of Europe and have shifted away from the home market. It is no exaggeration to say that EU multinationals are predominantly "Europeanized"' (Fligstein and Merand 2001: 19).

There is at least one advantage to conceptualizing Europeanization as a regional microcosm of a global process: the metric by which these processes are identified and measured is identical, which naturally makes the tasks of comparing as well as modelling causal interactions much more transparent. The problem, or course, is that by essentially equating globalization and Europeanization, we have not advanced the discussion very far. Pursuing this line of reasoning also risks obscuring the distinctive *political* forces at work on the European continent in the post-war period. In other words, although there is a robust economic foundation to the regional integration process, at critical junctures the impetus for deepening and widening the European project has originated in geopolitical and even ideological factors that were at best only remotely connected with the structural differentiation of goods and assets in the region. As we shall see below, valuable insights can be gained by viewing Europeanization as a 'nested' phenomenon, in that it is taking place within a broader process of globalization, and may even be contributing to it. Europeanization interacts with, but is not subsumed by, globalization.

A second definitional approach equates Europeanization with the European integration process itself. Green Cowles, Caporaso and Risse (2001: 3) define Europeanization as 'the emergence and development at the European level of distinct structures of governance'. As such, Europeanization is nothing more and nothing less than the accretion of institutional arrangements produced by integration. Its origins extend back before the Second World War, but its decisive milestones are found in the post-1945 period. Together, they represent the incremental and sometimes halting forward march of integration in Western Europe: the Treaty of Paris, which established the European Coal and Steel Community (ECSC) in 1951; the Treaty of Rome, which launched the European Economic Community (EEC) in 1957; the Single European Act of 1987; the Treaty on European Union (1993); the Amsterdam Treaty (1998); and the still unratified Treaty of Nice. These, of course, represent the major, quasi-constitutional bargains over the years. In between, significant steps along the path of Europeanization were taken as well, such as the creation of the CAP, the elaboration of the EC/EU's external trade policy, and the establishment of social and regional policy frameworks operating at the European level. In short, the institutional manifestations of the integration process—decision-making processes and structures; an administrative apparatus designed to formulate, implement, and monitor policy; or legal frameworks—are the result of a process of Europeanization.

The sole advantage of employing this particular definition is that it places the researcher on familiar ground—thanks to decades of intensive study and reflection, we possess a firm empirical and intuitive grasp of the integration process and how it has progressed over the past half-century or so. Although serious disagreements over the causes of integration and its implications have arisen and will continue to do so, there is something approaching a solid consensus over the basic empirical referents of the process.

The drawbacks associated with this approach, however, are significant. In the first place, we already have a term for the empirical object of this definition. Admittedly, 'integration' often requires modifiers—political, economic, positive, negative—but the same would apply with equal force to any perfect substitute. More problematic, we are still left with the same task that confronted us at the start of this project: how to conceptualize, catalogue, and explain the domestic effects of 'Europeanization' (formerly 'integration')? In fact, there is the danger of embedding, however implicitly, an assumed transformation of the domestic level in the definition itself, which begins to resemble a transitive identity:

Integration = Europeanization = Domestic transformation

Since at best this definitional exercise would put us no closer to the target of this scholarly investigation, it makes sense to reserve the term 'Europeanization' for phenomena that are no doubt intimately bound up with, but nonetheless conceptually, empirically, and causally distinct from, the integration process itself.

Dyson and Goetz opt for a process-oriented approach that unpacks the 'bottom' node of Europeanization—the domestic context—and its links to the integration process as well as the larger globalization dynamic. This is accomplished by recasting the domestic arena in terms of complex configurations of interests, institutions, and ideas. Interests are causally important because they directly shape policy responses by establishing a distribution of societal preferences that national officials take into account as they seek to build electoral coalitions capable of winning and then holding political power. Institutions influence what actors do (or do not do) by allocating power to some actors but not others, structuring the content and sequence of policy-making, and providing opportunities for, and constraints on, the state as its officials seek societal support for their policy choices. Ideas matter because they enable actors to manage uncertainty about the expected consequences of alternative choices, and they provide actors with a symbolic and conceptual language to advance their causes. In the context of strategic interaction among numerous actors, shared ideas can bring about the convergence of expectations and strategies, facilitating agreement and co-operative outcomes.

Domestic interests, institutions, and ideas are not independent of one another. Interests are typically formulated in material terms—that is, they arise from the position of actors in the domestic and international economies. However, interests are shaped not only by the material world, but also by the realm of the possible, which is itself a function of the institutional context in which actors operate. Similarly, ideas are bound up with both interests and institutions. Ideas that achieve political ascendance are almost always intimately tied to the interests they serve. Over time, though, the belief system may begin to serve as an independent rationale for choice, and even to reshape the very interests that originally propelled it into prominence. Moreover, once an ascendant idea emerges through political competition, it is very likely to become institutionalized, as adherents of the belief system enact laws and create agencies to secure the policy outputs consistent with the idea. Ideational effects, mediated by institutions, will often persist long past the point where the idea ceases to command broader support and legitimacy. In fact, the institutionalized idea continues to influence politics because it serves interests—specifically, those of the individuals charged with carrying out government activities based on its principles. Interests still matter, although they are not necessarily the same ones that gave rise to the idea in the first place.

National configurations of interests, ideas, and institutions are not hermetically sealed off from the external environment, least of all in Europe. Indeed, member states are literally 'in' Europe; that is, they belong to an ongoing and in many ways unique supranational venture (Katzenstein 1997*b*). Political, economic, and social interactions are shaped by a national context that is itself embedded in a larger system of political and economic governance. This system embraces actors who operate within institutions that are independent of the member states, who hold and pursue interests that are in no way purely derivative of the member states, and who are infused with ideas situated at the supranational level. And so membership in the EC/EU 'matters', in that it automatically entails multi-layered interactions of interests, institutions, and ideas at and across the national and supranational levels (Sandholtz 1996). By casting Europeanization in these terms, Dyson and Goetz enable us to think more deeply about the phenomenon.

Their definition also allows for not just the 'top-down' effects of European integration on the domestic level, which tend to be the principal focus of the existing literature, but also subsequent 'bottom-up' effects at the supranational level. In other words, the definition embraces the possibility of recursive processes. Clearly, not all empirical instances of Europeanization contain a recursive component. In subsequent chapters, we find many examples of 'top-down' integration effects on the member states that to date have had no meaningful implications for the integration process itself (but have been significant domestically nonetheless). Frequently, however—perhaps more often than expected—domestic changes in institutional or ideational frameworks, for example, have significant return effects at the supranational level. Charlie Jeffery's Chapter 5 on the Germany Länder and Kenneth Dyson's Chapter 10 on economic policy in this volume are just two of several examples of the recursive dimension of Europeanization.

Studying Europeanization: The Empirical and Analytical Agenda

Conceptualizing Europeanization in these terms permits a more systematic search for empirical manifestations. Given the intricate configurations of interests, ideas, and institutions that have emerged within the countries of Europe since the end of the Second World War, and the political, economic, and social dynamics that have been sustained by these configurations, it is clear that even modest, externally induced changes in one or more of the domestic triad could have potentially far-reaching effects for the country in question and perhaps even for the EU, in whole or in part. What are the most effective research strategies for identifying and explaining Europeanization?

Clearly, the most direct approach is essentially inductive, and should centre, at least initially, on what one might describe as 'most likely' instances of Europeanization.[4] Many studies of EU policy implementation conform, often implicitly, to this template. More binding forms of EU-level decisions, particularly regulations and, to a lesser extent, Directives, require of the member states varying degrees of administrative adaptation to meet new EU-level requirements and objectives. The effects of integration—'Europeanization'—are empirically obvious, and are confined at least initially to structural innovations, additions, and adaptations. However, its subsequent impact on, and implications for, the domes-

---

[4] As this research area matures, it would make sense to move to 'least likely' case studies, which are more theoretically powerful; see Eckstein (1975).

tic system, as well as its recursive impact on the supranational integration process, are anything but obvious, and are often not pursued systematically. New laws, administrative procedures, and policy instruments and objectives can set in motion complex causal sequences that can and often do lead to a reformulation of interests on the part of government agencies, interest groups, and individual citizens. Insofar as the new structures embrace policy doctrines and value sets imported from the European level, these integration effects can lead to changes in the constellation of ideas and even identities at the domestic level.[5]

A 'supranational action–national reaction' approach to Europeanization also lends itself to the study of the periodic big bangs of integration: the Treaty of Rome; the Single European Act; the Treaty on European Union; and most recently the Amsterdam and Nice treaties. In these instances, the act of process tracing from supranational outputs (treaty amendments) to national and sub-national manifestations of Europeanization is likely to be more circumspect, as the causal linkages are often submerged and indirect. Often, however, this is not the case. For the countries that signed up for EMU in 1991, the structural impli-cations of membership—central bank independence, for example—were clear and unavoidable. In other cases, though, the domestic responses have been less predictable, and slower in coming. The proliferation of EC/EU oversight committees formed within national parliaments as integration intensified after 1986 would be a good example.

Far more challenging is the detection of Europeanization in response to 'busi-ness as usual' at the supranational level—that is, the day-to-day operations of the EU. 'Business as usual' is centred around discrete policy areas administered by the Commission, the push and pull of politics in the European Parliament and the Council of Ministers, the functioning of the European judicial system, and the horizontal diffusion of 'best practices' among the member states. Long-range studies that are capable of tracking the interactions between the emergence and operation of a separate EU policy or political system, on the one hand, and the domestic actors, structures, and processes connected to it, on the other, are best suited to capture any top-down effects stemming from the integration process. Much of the literature on the Structural Funds, with its emphasis on regionalism and sub-national empowerment, fits this description well. The growing body of literature that seeks to assess the impact of European integration on the democratic constitutions, broadly conceived, of the member governments is another case in point (Anderson 2002).

For all its advantages, proceeding with this particular conceptualization of

---

[5] In the mid-1990s, a European model of regional development was imported *wider Willen* into the new eastern territories of the Federal Republic of Germany, with significant consequences for the structure of intergovernmental relations, the specific economic regeneration priorities of the eastern state governments and the Federal Republic's general policy toward the Structural Funds in Brussels. See Anderson (1999a: Ch. 6).

Europeanization still poses at least two major empirical challenges to researchers. The first has to do with ascertaining whether the observed changes or continuities attributed to European integration would have occurred anyway—that is, even in the absence of a supranational impulse. The second revolves around determining whether the observed changes or continuities attributed to European integration in fact originated somewhere else: for example, globalization.

Challenge I: The Implicit Counterfactual

Counterfactuals are causal arguments about events that did not occur, and are useful in small N research designs, with $N = 1$ as the limiting case.[6] The technique enables a researcher to introduce, via a mental experiment, variation in an independent variable that otherwise cannot vary in the case study. In effect, one constructs an imaginary case in which the variable in question takes on a different value and, by means of a mental comparison, tests its impact not by gauging frequencies of association, as in statistical studies and $N > 1$ comparisons, but by argumentation about what would have happened. Credible counterfactuals invoke 'general principles, theories, laws, or regularities distinct from the hypothesis being tested ... and [draw] on knowledge of historical facts relevant to a counterfactual scenario' (Fearon 1991: 176). Until recently, counterfactual analysis has drawn little explicit attention in the field of Community studies.[7]

Philippe Schmitter (1999: 296–7) insists that to assess the impact of European integration on the member states, researchers at some point must explore a counterfactual: namely, 'what national democracies might have looked like today if they had not benefited and suffered from several decades of European integration'. He concludes on a sceptical note, arguing that 'it is difficult to separate out a distinctive, much less a definitive, contribution since *the net effect of the EU seems to complement (and, probably, to enhance) trends that were already affecting domestic democracies*' (emphasis in the original). Hix and Goetz (2000b: 21) reply that '[c]ounterfactuals might be desirable, but, in this case at least, they can be no more than interesting, though ultimately inconclusive, thought experiments'. This is a fair description of a counterfactual, but it leaves Schmitter's larger point unaddressed and, therefore, uncontested. It pays to look into this issue more deeply. In the first place, it is not at all clear that 'the net effect of the EU' is something that can be perceived, let alone measured accurately. Integration is an extraordinarily complex phenomenon, and the structures

---

[6] For a balanced discussion of the strengths and weaknesses of this approach, as well as concrete methodological guidelines for constructing a valid (or 'cotenable') counterfactual claim, see Fearon (1991).

[7] For a critique of the methodological underpinnings of conventional EC/EU analysis, see Anderson (1995).

of supranational governance it has bequeathed to Europe are similarly manifold, opaque, and complex. As such, aggregate and net effects of integration are in all likelihood phantom concepts.

If one chooses to unpack integration, and disassemble the EU into its component institutions or spheres of collective activity, the tangible supranational effects become more visible on the ground, and by extension the task of counterfactualizing grows more manageable. Of course, one could imagine all manner of counterfactual exercises in which European integration is taken out of the equation, and the anticipated 'effect' on the member states is clear but rather trivial in consequence. For example, without the pressures and in some cases legal dictates imposed by the EU, domestic institutional frameworks designed to monitor and where possible influence EU decisions—e.g. those attached to national and subnational legislatures, bureaucracies, and even interest groups—would never have been created in the first place, and undoubtedly would hardly be missed.

Take away the EU and imagine other facets of domestic politics or political economy, however, and the anticipated impact is much more salient and the implications more far-reaching. The absence of the EU Structural Funds, which not only attempt to direct and divert resources to disadvantaged regions but also, in conjunction with EU competition policy, place an overall cap on the competition for mobile investment among regions and even states, would have a tangible effect on economic development trajectories and central–regional political relations across Europe. Working out the effects of the absence of a CAP would lead to similar conclusions for national farming sectors throughout Europe. All of which is to say that if one retreats from the quixotic goal of assessing net integration effects, counterfactual analysis not only becomes feasible, but profitable too as a way to assess the significance of specific instances of Europeanization.

Challenge II: Europeanization versus Globalization

Implicit in Schmitter's assessment of counterfactual analysis and the EU is a second thorny problem—that of separating out the impact of European integration from another force pushing in a similar direction, namely globalization. Apart from measurement, this is perhaps the greatest methodological challenge associated with the study of Europeanization. This is so for several reasons. First, globalization and European integration are largely contemporaneous phenomena, emerging in the post-war period, and their respective pace and intensity have picked up over the course of the last twenty years or so. In fact, according to a recent index of globalization, EU members occupied eleven of the top twenty slots (Anonymous 2002: 39). The concurrent nature of these phenomena complicates research strategies based on temporal or sequential approaches to establishing causality.

Second, globalization and European integration cannot be conceptualized as purely independent variables; on the contrary, each has fed and shaped the other, in complex and often reinforcing ways. As alluded to above, the free trade orientation of the EU, and in particular the Single Market project—the core objective behind the launching of the European project in the late 1950s and its relaunching in the mid-1980s—have provided a major, ongoing push for globalization, at least as defined narrowly in terms of increasing cross-border economic flows and transactions. Fligstein and Merand (2001: 15) maintain that Europeanization is, in fact, causally prior to globalization.

There is also a great deal of evidence that globalization, or rather the perception of globalization, has had an impact on the European integration process itself. For example, persuasive analyses of the origins of the Single European Act look to, among other causal factors, the contextual effects of shifts in the international economy—specifically, the rise of Japan and the newly industrializing countries (NICs), combined with the decline of American military and economic hegemony—on the decision by the European Community to rejuvenate European economic prospects through deepening. Specifically, the change in the international distribution of economic power 'triggered' the deadline of 1992, insofar as it presented European élites with challenges and ultimately elicited policy choices that, filtered through major transformations of domestic politics within key Community members during the early 1980s, resulted in the Single European Act (Sandholtz and Zysman 1989). Thus, the Single European Act can be viewed as an anticipated reaction by the EC to cope with one of the manifestations of globalization. In as much as EMU represented the next logical step in the completion of the internal market, much the same can be said for this far-reaching monetary initiative. And, of course, there are additional examples of the EU resorting to integration as an anticipatory measure intended to contain the undesirable effects of internationalization; supranational programmes designed to ease economic adjustment in the steel and shipbuilding sectors come to mind as one example.

European integration and globalization are capable of reshaping the domestic landscape independently and in combination. In fact, Europeanization and globalization can interact in three broadly distinctive ways: (1) independent; (2) reinforcing; and (3) countervailing. The task, of course, is to devise research strategies for exploring these three categories, particularly the latter two, which are of greatest interest to social scientists. As outlined earlier, the Single Market and single currency initiatives—milestones in European integration that have been shown to have led to complex patterns of 'Europeanization' at the domestic level—appear to be examples of EU initiatives that are responses to, but ultimately work in tandem with, globalization. Just to show how important it is to parse empirical reality when examining this issue, however, the strengthening of the Structural Funds, an important component of both the Single Market and single currency initiatives, can be seen as an attempt to put in place regional structures and capabilities that can act in a countervailing manner to global/ European market forces.

What seems clear is that, given the comprehensiveness of the EU, particularly in the realm of economic activity, the effects of globalization are universally subject to the mediating influences of supranational governance in Europe. In other words, the relationship between Europeanization and globalization is quite likely to be 'nested'. Insightful examples of how 'nesting' plays out empirically in Germany can be found in Markus Haverland's Chapter 13 on social policy and Kenneth Dyson's examination of German economic policy-making in Chapter 10 in this volume.

The technique of process tracing, most commonly associated with the historical institutionalist tradition in comparative politics, offers a reliable, if not particularly efficient, means of teasing out the effects of European integration from the universe of potential causal factors, including globalization, that impinge on the nation-state in Europe. Such an approach could be applied fruitfully to Europeanization puzzles that are either inductively or deductively formulated. In the case of inductively inspired puzzles, a researcher would begin with what looks to be on the surface an apparent case of Europeanization—for example, a change in domestic interests, ideas, identities, and/or institutions that appears to be linked to the European integration process. The change could well be limited to a single country, or it could be a larger pattern among the EU membership, or sub-sets thereof. Through process tracing, the researcher would work back along the temporal causal chain, identifying the factors that brought about the observed changes. For example, through the analysis of investment data, company reports, as well as open-ended interviews with relevant actors, the researcher can discover what prompted changes in the investment strategies of export-oriented firms, as well as associated changes in their internal organization. Confirmation that they came about as the result of a new understanding of the exigencies of global economic competition, and not of developments in the Single Market or specific policies propagated by the European Commission, would suggest that globalization provided the principal impetus, even if a plausible preliminary hypothesis might have pointed to Europe as the source of the changes.

More powerful theoretically, yet more difficult to design, are deductive hypotheses about change and continuity in the inner workings of the European nation-state that are expected to flow from the process of European integration. Here, the researcher would start with the fact of integration or some aspect thereof, and attempt to work out deductively the expected impact on the domestic configuration of interests, ideas, and/or institutions of the member states. Sorting out the interaction (or non-interaction) of integration and globalization would be an essential task *a priori*, i.e. completed before the actual empirical investigation commences.

None of this, it should be underscored, necessitates the invention of new methodological techniques or new field research strategies. The tried-and-true methods of comparative politics and comparative sociology should stand the researcher in good stead. The voluminous literature on voting behaviour, for example, reveals many insightful ways of dealing with contending hypotheses about the determinants of voting. Rather, what is needed is, for lack of a better term, 'peripheral vision' when doing empirical research on Europeanization. In other words, one must always hold out the possibility, and take steps to honour that possibility in the conducting of the research, that the observed effects (or non-effects) may well result from an alternative source, in this instance processes and outcomes associated with globalization, not European integration.

Whatever the basic approach taken—inductive or deductive—both entail the selection of cases from among the set of countries that are subject simultaneously to the parallel and sometimes combined or synergistic effects of integration and globalization. No matter how careful the empirical process tracing or airtight the logic of deduction, there is always the risk of analytical oversight—of failing to see how integration's effects are overshadowed by, or a straightforward function of, broader forces of globalization. To avoid this situation, cross-regional comparisons may offer more convincing insights than can be garnered from an exclusive reliance on counterfactuals. Specifically, employing other advanced industrial democracies such as Japan, the United States, or Canada as control cases could enable the researcher to get a better handle on overall causal significance of integration. For example, if an instance of domestic change (or continuity) is common to both the European and non-European cases, then—to the extent a plausible chain of causality can be established—the link is unlikely to be related to European integration, and is more likely the result of larger contextual forces like globalization. The difficulty, of course, is that finding cases of globalized, yet unintegrated, polities comparable to those in Europe may be possible, but it is another matter entirely to locate integrated, yet unglobalized, polities that are strictly comparable to Europe's. What this means is that although researchers conceivably can control for integration, they cannot easily control for globalization, which limits the range of empirical questions that can be addressed via the comparative method.

Conclusion

Instead of casting Europeanization as the reincarnation of integration or as a macroscopic pattern of convergence around European templates, Dyson and Goetz present a working definition based on a looser conceptualization—namely, continuities and changes in domestic configurations of interests, ideas, and institutions that follow from the process of European integration. Potentially, this approach embraces a dizzying array of phenomena—some isolated, others more systematic and ubiquitous; some trifling, others consequential; some self-contained at the domestic level, others leading to significant recursive effects on supranational processes and outcomes.

As suggested above, the only feasible research strategy is to abandon a macro or aggregate perspective on Europeanization in favour of the approach adopted in this volume, which is premised on the wisdom and logic of parsing—that is, taking articulated components of the domestic system and devising rigorous searches for the presence or absence of Europeanization. What, if any, Europeanization has occurred in circumscribed policy areas such as social policy, competition policy, or environmental regulation? What is the impact of integration on the classic functions performed by national legislatures, or on the balance of institutional power between national legislatures, political executives, and judiciaries? To what extent is Europeanization mediating or simply conducting the effects of globalization in a particular policy area or locus of institutional activity?

Some puzzles are obviously more challenging than others but, if properly framed, interesting and illuminating answers can be gleaned from the empirical record. A significant problem, of course, is how to make sense of the assembled findings. Put another way, how can one aggregate the myriad conclusions of this potentially sprawling research programme, and thereby contribute to an accumulation of knowledge? The discipline of political science is replete with instances of similar conceptual hurdles that have yet to be cleared, and we appear to be adding another item to the list. There does not, however, appear to be a ready alternative and, as the ensuing chapters demonstrate, there is reason for hope.

The empirical studies in this volume, taken as a whole, suggest that the reformulation of domestic interests and identities in response to integration pressures remains more hypothetical than real. Jörg Monar's study of justice and home affairs in Chapter 15 as well as Rüdiger Wurzel's analysis of environmental policy in Chapter 14 in this volume, for example, argue that Germany had had considerable impact on EU policy initiatives in these areas over the past decade or so—an 'uploading' dynamic. But the recursive effects on the respective domestic policy-making communities have been modest, although signs of change are evident in both instances. Typically, domestic interests and identities have proved to be quite resilient. Instances of mutually reinforcing dynamics of 'uploading' from Germany to Europe and 'downloading' from Europe to Germany occur principally when these chains are consistent with the requirements of domestic actors (see here Simon Bulmer *et al.*'s Chapter 12 on sectoral governance and Charlie Jeffery's Chapter 5 on the Länder and Europe in this volume).

Recursive processes that result in domestic institutional changes are, perhaps, more commonplace. National engagement in a particular policy area, resulting in the 'uploading' of national preferences and frameworks, is followed by institutional adaptation as domestic élites respond to 'downloading' initiatives from the strengthened European policy regime. These institutional transformations, however, rarely rise to the systemic level, as Rainer Eising's Chapter 8 on interest organizations and Kenneth Dyson's Chapter 10 on economic policy-making in this volume point out. Klaus Goetz's examination of the German national executive in Chapter 3 points up an intriguing pattern of bifurcation, in which administrative structures exhibit evidence of Europeanization but political ones prove highly resistant to the conditioning effects of integration. These cumulative findings are robust in their own right, and raise a host of important questions that will bear careful examination in the future.

Note. I would like to thank Kenneth Dyson, Klaus Goetz, Colin Hay, Ed Page, and members of the conference group on 'Germany and Europe: A "Europeanized" Germany?' for their helpful comments, advice, and assistance in the researching and writing of this chapter.

Part II
Europeanization of the German Polity

3

The Federal Executive: Bureaucratic Fusion versus Governmental Bifurcation

KLAUS H. GOETZ

European Integration and the Federal Executive: A Long Story in Brief

THE STUDY OF THE IMPACT OF EUROPEAN INTEGRATION on the Federal executive in Germany has a surprisingly long pedigree, which goes back to the early 1970s (see Hesse and Goetz 1992 for a review of the early literature). In the rapidly expanding field of Europeanization studies, polity impacts were among the first to be explored systematically (Hix and Goetz 2000*a*), and the German case has long featured prominently in this type of inquiry. There was an early focus on linkage (Goetz 2000*a*), i.e., the institutional arrangements that connect national executives and EU authorities and the institutional practices that have evolved at the national level to support domestic–EU connections. This concentration on executive capacities for 'reception' and 'projection', to use the terminology employed by Bulmer and Burch (2001), has since remained at the heart of much writing on the executive impact. The key question has been how the German ministerial executive goes about the business of EU-related policy-making, i.e., the structures, processes and personnel involved (the 'projection' aspect) and how the downloading of the *acquis communautaire* affects the operation of the executive (the 'reception' side).

Early studies of the executive machinery for integration policy have been followed by a steady flow of empirical analyses of the executive consequences of 'opening up the state' (Wessels 2000); some contributions have been based on cross-country comparative designs (see, e.g., Bulmer and Burch 2001). At the centre of attention have been specialist linkage bodies, such as special EC/EU units—notably in the Chancellery, the Ministry of Foreign Affairs, and the Ministry of Economics—or the Permanent Representation of Germany in Brussels, with its specific remit to act as a conduit between the Federal executive and the European institutions (for a detailed analysis of the latter see recently Maurer and Wessels 2000, 2001, with comprehensive references to earlier work).

Proceedings of the British Academy, **119**, 57–72. © The British Academy 2003.

With progressive integration and the steady extension and intensification of the *acquis*, academic interest has widened beyond a concern with direct, highly visible, but discrete effects, such as the establishment of specialized EU units, to examine the more diffuse, but also, perhaps, more profound, consequences of integration. For example, in their comparative analysis of the Europeanization of central government in Germany and the UK, Bulmer and Burch (2001) differentiate between systemic, organizational, regulative, procedural, and cultural dimensions of change in an attempt to grasp what might be called the 'subterranean effects' of integration (see also Derlien and Murswieck 1999; Wessels 1999).

As far as the dominant pattern of the institutionalization of 'projection' capacities is concerned, there has been long a broad academic consensus on its defining features; but there is disagreement on the issue of efficacy. Thus, when it comes to how the Federal executive makes EU policy, there is a common emphasis on what Bulmer, Jeffery and Paterson (2000: 28) have called the 'syndrome of sectoral conflict, weak coordination and the arrival at a German position only at a late stage in negotiation'. EU-related powers and responsibilities are dispersed among a range of ministries and the Chancellery; policy-making is strongly sectorized; and capacities for hierarchical, impositional interministerial co-ordination are generally weak. There is a 'twin-track' approach to EU policy (Derlien 2000), with a 'diplomatic track', which is built around the Foreign Ministry and the Chancellery and focuses on constitutional and polity issues; and a 'sectorized expert track', which deals with the specifics of public policies.

On the whole, scholars of the executive have tended to be reticent about the policy effects of variations in executive arrangements. Thus, Wright and Hayward's summary of the key findings of their comparative study of executive co-ordination (2000) provides many insights into types and styles of co-ordination, but offers little in the way of concrete guidance for 'institutional engineering', since '"optimal" co-ordination will depend on a host of variables, such as the nature of co-ordination ambitions and constitutional, institutional, political and administrative opportunity structures' (2000: 45). Similarly, Wright's comparative analysis of the national co-ordination of EU policy-making (Wright 1996: 165, quoted in Kassim 2000) is extremely cautious about linking institutions and effects, noting that 'the effectiveness of a country's domestic EU co-ordination capacity must be judged according to the issue, the policy types, the policy requirements and the policy objectives. Merely to examine the machinery of co-ordination is to confuse the means and the outcomes.' The conclusions of a more recent comparative effort on the same subject are equally modest as regards the effectiveness of different national co-ordination systems: 'The question of effectiveness—what it means in an EU context and whether there is a recipe for success in the form of a particular national strategy—though undoubtedly an important concern, is extremely problematic' (Kassim 2000: 254).

In marked contrast to such hesitant comparative assessments, the literature on the Europeanization of the German executive has been very upfront about seeking to establish causal links between the domestic institutional bases of EU policy-making and patterns of EU-related policy co-ordination, in particular, on the one hand, and the substantive profile of German integration policy and Germany's role in European integration, on the other. Thus, the constraints associated with sectorization and the weakness of 'positive' co-ordination have long been controversially debated. For much of the time, these constraints were seen to contribute to Germany 'punching' below her weight in EU policy. Reflecting long-running and unresolved rivalries between the Chancellery, the Ministry of Foreign Affairs and the Ministry of Economics, German EU policy-making is marked by the absence of a 'single and unambiguously authoritative "ringmaster" to oversee coherence' (Bulmer, Jeffery and Paterson 2000: 25): 'Overall, the mind-set and institutional arrangements of the European policy-makers in the Federal Government are simply not attuned to the most effective representation of governmental policy' (2000: 28). This 'received wisdom' has recently been challenged by accounts that apply the familiar figure of 'enabling constraints' (see Dyson and Goetz, Chapter 1 in this volume) to the specific setting of intra-executive relations (Derlien 2000; Wessels 1999). Thus, Derlien (2000: 56) suggests that 'the German pattern of *ex post* co-ordination, a policy style resembling management by exception, is ultimately superior to a practice of *ex ante* co-ordination of all policy matters regardless of their salience. Such a strategy is counter-productive, for it leaves little room for the recurrent, multi-issue bargaining process at the European level and the informal norm of reciprocity'. At any rate, some of the traditional constraints arising from the combination of departmental autonomy and coalition politics, which both limit the scope for positive hierarchical co-ordination, may be weakening, not least because of the oft-noted progressive centralization of powers in the Chancellery, which is well documented for the Kohl chancellorship (Froelich 2001) and would appear to have continued under Chancellor Schröder (Goetz 2003*b*).

The Federal 'European policy-making machinery' (Bulmer, Maurer and Paterson 2001) has not, of course, been static. Governments and key personnel change; and, as many chapters in this volume attest, policy domains previously more or less untouched by Europeanization become drawn into the integration process, so that the role of responsible national ministries is partly transformed. For example, EMU has pushed the Ministry of Finance from an observer of EU policy into a central player, with far-reaching implications for the domestic inter-ministerial balance of powers (Dyson, Chapter 10 in this volume); and intensified co-operation in justice and home affairs has been associated with increased Europeanization pressures for the Ministry of the Interior (Monar, Chapter 15 in this volume). But although it is not always easy to keep track of the changes in institutions, processes and personnel, there is a broad empirical bases on which assessments about the 'projection' capacities of German EU policy can draw.

By comparison, rather less is known about the adaptive requirements arising from the 'downloading' of the *acquis* into the domestic context. Of course, implementation has scarcely been neglected in the study of the effects of integration; on the contrary, it has long been a mainstay of Europeanization research. However, in the German case, the primary responsibility for the administrative implementation of EU and domestic law lies with the Länder administrations and local government, whereas the Federal ministerial administration is principally geared to policy formulation and the monitoring of implementation. Accordingly, the vertical dispersal of implementation powers and responsibilities in Germany—or, in other words, the proliferation of veto points—regularly features prominently in accounts that seek to explain patterns of policy Europeanization in Germany (e.g., Knill 2001). In particular, difficulties in transposing European legislation into national law can often be traced directly to reluctance on the part of the Länder to approve legal measures in the Bundesrat for which they have prime administrative responsibilities (Haverland 2000).

Against this background of empirically well-informed and analytically increasingly sophisticated studies of the Europeanization of the German executive, the following discussion focuses on a central attribute of the Federal executive, the full ramifications of which are sometimes overlooked: its dual nature, combining the attributes of a political government and an administration. The chapter sets out to investigate how integration has affected this dual nature. Briefly, the argument developed below suggests that these two qualities of the executive have been affected in a differential way. On the administrative side, progressive integration has, indeed, been associated with growing 'multi-level fusion' (Wessels 1999), through which the ministerial administration becomes part of a closely interconnected multi-level system. By contrast, the governmental dimension of the executive is characterized by growing bifurcation. Government takes place at two levels—the European and the domestic—but institutional linkage between the two levels is limited and some of the defining features of German government, notably the defining tenets of party government, coalition government, and how parliamentary government, show few signs of Europeanization. This contrasting pattern of effects can be explained with reference to the differing opportunity structures within which officials and executive politicians operate. For officials, progressive integration provides opportunities for 'bottom-up' Europeanization, in that powers and responsibilities at the EU can be used for bureau-shaping at the national level. Executive politicians, too, have to operate at both levels, but European opportunities and constraints generally translate only loosely into power gains and losses at domestic level. The chief reason for this lies in the continued non-Europeanization of key actors and processes of domestic politics and democratic decision-making.

The remainder of this chapter seeks to substantiate this argument. After briefly commenting on the dual nature of the executive in general terms, the discussion characterizes the German executive system more specifically. It then reconsiders the differential European effect and puts forward an explanatory account that focuses on institutional opportunity structures and individual incentives. In the conclusion, the discussion turns to the question of whether the Europeanization pattern found—administrative fusion versus governmental bifurcation—supports the oft-advanced thesis of a progressive bureaucratization of public policy-making consequent upon European integration.

The Dual Nature of the Executive[1]

The institutionalization of executives has tended to be analysed from two distinct perspectives. The first, which is situated firmly in Comparative Government, is essentially concerned with the location of the executive in the political system. As such, it draws on, and engages with, the major comparative classifications of political systems. The location of the executive is central to the distinction between presidential, semi-presidential, and parliamentary systems, and it also marks a key difference between majoritarian and consensus democracies. As regards the Europeanization debate, this 'external' dimension of executive institutionalization has been addressed, in particular, with a view to the impact of European integration on executive–legislative relations; domestic intergovernmental relations; and changing patterns of executive relations with the associations of organized civil society.

The second major perspective is principally interested in the inner workings of the executive; it is this perspective that is central to the following discussion. The comparative study of European executives from this perspective is placed at the interface of Comparative Government and Comparative Public Administration. The first—Comparative Government—focuses on the political and governmental aspects of the executive, the executive as *Regierung*. It deals, for example, with the role of prime ministers and ministers in government; cabinets and cabinet committees; coalition governments, including how they are formed and terminated, how portfolios are allocated among coalition parties, and how political decisions are made; or the relationships between governments and governing parties. One may characterize this approach as executive studies 'from above', in that the executive territory is typically surveyed from the vantage point of political and governmental leadership.

By contrast, Comparative Public Administration is interested, first and foremost, in the bureaucratic parts of the executive that extend beneath its thin political veneer. Such studies concentrate on the executive as *Verwaltung*, in particular, the ministerial administration and other types of central agencies; the status, organization, and role of non-elected executive personnel, notably the civil

---

[1] This section draws heavily on Goetz (2003a).

service, and its relations to elected officials; and, increasingly, the importance of administrative law in governing executive action. With an emphasis on the bureaucratic foundations of executive power, Comparative Public Administration studies the executive 'from below'.

This, admittedly, rather simplified divergence in empirical focus reflects the duality of executives as political and administrative entities. As political institutions, executives are oriented towards acquiring, securing, and exercising political power. This function often predominates at the centre of government, where the requirements of political management drive the organization (Peters, Rhodes and Wright 2000). At the same time, however, executives are administrative institutions, which typically form the apex of a hierarchically structured administrative organization. Thus, in Germany, the Federal ministries are classed as supreme Federal authorities (*oberste Bundesbehörden*) and the minister is the head of the authority.

The tension between politics and administration is central to understanding the institutionalization of executives. This tension is not only about the tasks executives are expected to perform, but, perhaps more importantly, about the most appropriate organization of the executive, including its personnel.

The second key dimension of executive institutionalization concerns the relation between the formal office (including elected offices) and office holders. It has been argued that political institutions, in general, and the political parts of the executive, in particular, are distinguished by the exceptionally close connection between office and office holder (Göhler 1994). Certainly, mainstream executive studies, especially of chief executives (i.e. heads of government) and ministers, regularly note the importance of the personal qualities, dispositions, and motives of incumbents and the extent to which individuals shape the office they occupy. In fact, much of the literature concerned with political leadership in Western democracies revolves around this theme. There are, of course, great differences in the degree to which individuals can remould or reinterpret the formal position that they occupy. But at the top levels of the executive, consisting of heads of government and core ministers, it would appear that the 'man maketh the office' as much as the 'office maketh the man'. This is particularly the case where, as in Germany after 1945, new or fundamentally revised constitutions needed to be brought to life and discredited institutional legacies had to be overcome. Under such conditions, enterprising elected executives may be able to define their office in a way that sets the path for decades to come. The impact of Chancellor Adenauer on the long-term development of the German chancellorship is a case in point (Padgett 1994).

Whether executive politicians 'make a difference' to the offices they hold has long been subject to a lively debate, which, more recently, has spilled over to the administrative realm. Thus, from a rational choice perspective, attempts have been made to model the behaviour of officials with reference to individual utility calculations; in this connection, the debate between those who understand officials as either 'budget maximisers' or 'bureau shapers' has been particularly fruitful (Dunleavy 1991; Marsh, Smith and Richards 2000). The degree to which office and office holder are separated or merged, i.e. the extent to which it is possible to analyse, and to generalize about, the former without reference to specific office holders, constitutes the second key dimension of executive institutionalization. European countries differ significantly in the emphasis they place on clear role differentiations within the executive; the intensity with which they seek to regulate political and administrative offices and the behaviour of office holders; and the changeability of organizational arrangements over time.

Attention to these two dimensions of institutionalization allows us to draw out the diverging impact of integration on the governmental and the administrative dimensions of the executive and, as will be argued below, can help to understand the interaction between institutional opportunity structures and individual incentives in shaping differential trajectories of Europeanization.

The Internal Life of the Federal Executive

Before turning to more detailed consideration of patterns of executive Europeanization, it is useful to sketch briefly the salient features of the German variant of executive institutionalization. These provide the reference point against which Europeanization effects can be assessed. As regards the politics–administration nexus, perhaps its most notable feature is the traditionally close linkage between the political–governmental and the administrative spheres of the executive. In Germany, unlike in the UK, for example, there is little concern about the demarcation between politics and administration in the executive, and the boundaries between the two are fuzzy. Executive politicians and officials cooperate closely in the policy-making process, and there are no conventions that would bar officials from engaging in what might elsewhere be considered as work with a party-political aspect. Officials do not just advise and propose, and there are no formal dividing lines between policy and political work. In personnel policy, ministers have long taken a keen interest in appointments to top administrative positions and promotions, and they enjoy wide-ranging discretion, including the recruitment of outsiders with a party-political background. The political nature of the top civil service is formally recognized in the institution of the *politische Beamte* ('political civil servants'), and it is not unknown for top civil servants to have had a previous career as party politicians, although such cases are still fairly rare. The proximity of government and administration—in functional, organizational and personnel terms—is most evident in the key co-ordination units within the Federal executive, including the Chancellery and the *Leitungsstäbe* in the ministries. The latter, although overwhelmingly staffed by officials, are principally engaged in political co-ordination between the executive, the governing parties, parliament, and the Länder.

A second point worth emphasizing is the high degree of continuity in executive arrangements. The Federal Republic has at times been described as a 'Chancellor democracy', a notion associated with the centralization of powers in the office and the person of the chief executive. However, this characterization has always been contentious, and most standard accounts of successive chancellorships have stressed the manifold restraints—constitutional, institutional, political—on the capacity of the Chancellor to set the government agenda and to impose his will on the Cabinet and the governing parties. There is evidence of a progressive increase of the involvement of the Chancellor in certain policy domains, and EU-related policy tends to feature prominently among the examples given. Moreover, unification has shown that the routine limitations on chancellorial authority can be effectively suspended, at least for a certain period. But, despite a strong media focus on the Chancellor, the political executive cannot be described as a prime ministerial system.

The constraints on the personalized exercise of power are largely explained by the specific institutional underpinnings of the political executive. These institutions reflect the character of the executive as a cabinet government, coalition government, party government, parliamentary government, and a government that operates in a federalized political system. The interlocking of these principles is most evident in the elaborate machinery for policy co-ordination that has developed over the decades. It is notable that accounts of executive co-ordination in Germany tend to emphasize institutions—be they coalition rounds, interdepartmental working groups, joint executive-parliamentary working groups, or other such devices—at the expense of personalized administrative networks. While it used to be argued that the 'bottom-up' nature of the Federal policy process provided the head of the highly specialized policy sections (*Referate*) with a great deal of influence over the shape of public policy (Mayntz and Scharpf 1975), there is evidence to suggest that the strengthening of political co-ordination units noted above has increasingly reduced the mainline units to a more reactive role (Goetz 1999).

Despite an inevitable degree of tension between the political and administrative rationalities and between office and office holder, the German executive system has shown a remarkable degree of continuity over time. Such continuity is particularly evident in the internal ministerial organization, which is regulated in great detail in the Common Standing Orders of the Federal Ministries and has not altered fundamentally since the 1970s. Perhaps surprisingly, the division of the Federal ministerial administration between Bonn and Berlin has not been accompanied by a more far-reaching reorganization addressing long-standing points of critique, such as the proliferation of small sections. Even in the Chancellery, the basic organizational building blocs have remained largely intact since the time of Chancellor Schmidt, a degree of continuity that is all the more remarkable given the eminently political nature of the Chancellery's work. Unlike in many other

European states, there has also been no major change in the status of senior ministerial personnel.

The European Effect Reconsidered

Let us now turn to consider in more detail and depth the effects of progressive integration on the two key dimensions of executive institutionalization. The most influential account of the Europeanization of the German Federal executive has been put forward by Wolfgang Wessels, in collaboration with Dietrich Rometsch (Rometsch 1996; Wessels 1999, 2000, the latter with a comprehensive bibliography). Their chief argument is that progressive integration is accompanied by a process of horizontal and vertical 'fusion' in which the governments and administrations of several levels—EU, national, regional—share in the process of political–administrative decision-making. Politics and administration in Germany have reacted to this increasing fusion of statehood with a political–administrative Europeanization pattern that shows '*comprehensive mobilization and a co-existence of decentralization and co-ordination*' (Wessels 1999: 26, emphasis in the original). There has been an 'administrative–political multi-level fusion' (1999: 26).

What is the evidence for such an assessment? As far as the administrative component is concerned, there is a great deal of quantitative and qualititative data that can be adduced to support the fusion thesis. Clearly, there has been both a steady intensification of multi-level interaction and a continuous expansion of national administrative resources devoted to supporting effective German participation in this multi-level system. At the EU level, one finds evidence of a continuous growth in the number, frequency of meetings, and workload of the decision-making and implementing committees in which national officials participate. Not only has this necessitated a correspondent expansion in the staffing of the German Permanent Representation in Brussels, which acts as key link between the Brussels and the Bonn–Berlin bureaucracies (Maurer and Wessels 2000, 2001); perhaps more importantly, more and more officials from Bonn and Berlin participate directly in the Brussels committee system, so that as many German officials appear to take the shuttle between Brussels and Bonn or Berlin than between the latter two. New Councils of Ministers; the broadening of agendas as the *acquis* widens and deepens; resource-intensive forms of co-operation and co-ordination, such as the open method of co-ordination, which go beyond legislation and the monitoring of its implementation and rely on the administrations of the member states rather than the European Commission; and the close involvement of existing members in accession negotiations and applicant vetting have all meant that many national ministerial officials spend a growing amount of their time in Brussels.

This intensified participation in all stages of the EU policy-making process has required a qualitative and quantitative expansion of domestic administrative resources devoted to EU business. While the Federal ministerial administration as a whole has been shrinking since the mid-1990s, resources devoted to EU matters have continued to increase. The most visible sign is the increase in the number of divisions and sections with an explicit EU remit, which, by 2001, reached nine and ninety-nine, respectively (Sturm and Pehle 2001: 45). Growth over the years has been particularly marked in the case of the Ministry of Finance, which witnessed a massive expansion of its EU-related activities as a consequence of EMU. After the change of government in 1998, Oskar Lafontaine cemented the centrality of the Finance Ministry in the domestic EU process by insisting on the transfer of the Economics Ministry's key European division to his own department.

Of course, such specialized EU units are merely the tip of the iceberg. Already in 1987–9, some 20 per cent of all ministerial units were involved in European business (Wessels 2000: 313) and it would not seem unreasonable to assume that this percentage has at least doubled since. Evidently, this trend has not affected all ministries uniformly. As the policy-oriented studies in this volume highlight, patterns of Europeanization continue to differ markedly across policy areas and there remain central domains of domestic public policy, perhaps most notably social policy, where Europeanization is, at best, incipient (Haverland, Chapter 13 in this volume). Yet, in the field of justice and home affairs, long considered a hard 'core' of state sovereignty, Europeanization is progressing rapidly, requiring adjustments on the part of the relevant ministries—notably the Ministries of Justice and the Interior—which have not always been able to keep pace with the dynamics of policy developments (see the comments by Monar, Chapter 15 in this volume, on the Ministry of the Interior).

To this picture of administrative engagement must be added the many officials occupied with the management of bilateral and multi-lateral communication, co-operation and co-ordination involving current and prospective EU member states. The intensity of these relationships is best documented for the Franco-German alliance. While not all aspects of such relationships are directly connected to the EU integration project, there can be no doubt that it has decisively contributed to their growing intensity.

Effective participation at European level of a large number of German administrative actors requires a well-functioning co-ordination machinery within the Federal executive. As noted earlier, there is broad agreement in academic comment on the main features of the German co-ordination culture (among more recent accounts see Bulmer and Burch 2001; Bulmer, Jeffery and Paterson 2000; Bulmer, Maurer and Paterson 2001; Derlien 2000); disagreements centre on the effects of co-ordination on Germany's capacity to shape European policy, with some authors stressing the restrictive effects of dispersed powers, whereas others highlight their—potential—enabling effects. The main features of the co-ordination machinery were established in the 1950s (Hesse and Goetz 1992), and it was only in the 1990s that major changes were effected (Bulmer and Burch

2001) with the decisive extension of the range of core ministries involved in routine co-ordination, and the transfer of key co-ordinating responsibilities from the Economics Ministry to the Finance Ministry. Before the 2002 Federal elections, Chancellor Schröder had mooted the creation of a specialized Ministry of European Affairs, with the Minister located in the Chancellery ('Schröder macht Fischer die Europapolitik streitig', *FAZ*, 19 March 2002; Eckart Lohse, 'Die Europapolitik als Streitobjekt', *FAZ*, 20 March 2002). This plan was dropped after the elections in the face of strong opposition from Foreign Minister Joschka Fischer, but, for the first time, a dedicated unit devoted exclusively to EU matters was established in the Chancellery, asserting Schröder's claims in this policy domain.

Wessels's assessment of a comprehensive mobilization of the ministerial administration in Germany is also supported by the fact that the German ministerial bureaucracy is principally oriented towards policy formulation and the preparation of political decision-taking, rather than implementation, which is largely left to specialized non-ministerial authorities, and, in particular, Länder administrations and local authorities.

A central point to note about the Europeanization pattern on the administrative side is the functional, institutional, and personnel linkage between the EU and Federal levels (and also the Länder). Federal officials do not just operate at two or three levels but their activities at one level have direct implications for what they can and cannot do at another. In other words, the multi-level system is closely integrated. Both 'top-down' and 'bottom-up' Europeanization are clearly in evidence here, as Federal officials need to respond to legislative and policy initiatives emanating from the EU level and are able to use 'Brussels' to gain policy leverage in the domestic contest. This point is explored in the next section.

The present account departs from the fusion thesis when it comes to the political–governmental aspects of the executive. Here, the pattern of Europeanization cannot be described as fusion, but rather as 'bifurcation'. To be sure, Federal executive politicians do, of course, operate at both levels, European and domestic. Federal executive politicians certainly need to spend a growing share of their time on European business, in EU councils and meetings and on the bilateral and multilateral preparation of EU decision-making. But key arenas of domestic executive governance—party government, coalition government, and parliamentary government—show few signs of Europeanization.

Analyses of 'government at the centre' in Germany regularly point to the intricate patterns of political management in Germany's 'negotiation' and 'co-ordination' democracy (Goetz 2003*b*; Holtmann 2001; Padgett 1994). The Federal government is a *parliamentary government* and parliamentary account-ability is not secured only through formal means, such as the right of parliament to elect the Chancellor; regular reporting requirements imposed on the government; parliamentary questions and interpellations; the exhaustive scrutiny of bills introduced by the government; or the detailed parliamentary monitoring of the implementation of the Federal budget. There are also many informal mechanisms by which parliament reaches into the executive process (Saalfeld 1999), such as regular meetings between ministers and MPs from the governing parties to consider forthcoming legislative initiatives. The majority parliamentary parties and the government are, accordingly, said to constitute a 'composite actor' (*Handlungsverbund*) (von Beyme 1997: 358). The Federal government is also a *party government*. It is constituted after the Federal elections on the basis of coalition negotiations between the main representatives of the national parties and their parliamentary groups; majority party leaders typically join the government as ministers or, in the case of the largest party, Chancellor; major political initiatives are usually approved by the governing parties' national decision-making bodies prior to their submission to Cabinet; and the withdrawal of support by one of the political parties that make up the governing coalition inevitably spells the end of the government. Political parties do not just decide on the formation and termination of the government; given the intermeshing between government and majority parties, the latter can themselves be regarded as governing institutions. Finally, the Federal government is a *coalition government*, and coalition management is an abiding preoccupation of both the Chancellor and other key figures in the government.

Whereas there is, as noted, ample evidence to support the notion of administrative fusion, evidence of Europeanization of parliamentary, party and coalition government is scant. Neither the Federal parliament (Saalfeld, Chapter 4 in this volume) nor political parties (Niedermeyer, Chapter 7 in this volume) are part of an effective multi-level system extending to the EU. More importantly for the present argument, the institutional arrangements underpinning parliamentary, party and coalition government—especially the elaborate network of formal and informal mechanisms for synchronization between government, parliament, and governing parties—show no signs of effective functional or institutional linkage with the EU level. Of course, there is overlap in key personnel—the Chancellor or the Minister of Finance are central figures both in domestic management and at the European stage—but otherwise linkage is weak and, as will be argued below, even the identity of actors should not be overestimated in terms of linkage effects. It is certainly true that much less is known about the Europeanization of executive government than administration; for example, I am not aware of studies that would have investigated how the time budgets of German executive politicians and the relative share accorded to EU business have changed over the years; what share of cabinet time is taken up by the discussion of EU matters; or how frequently the latter are part of the agenda of coalition committees. The apparent non-Europeanization of central arenas of government may, therefore, at least in part be attributable to the fact that relevant systematic evidence has not been collected. But it is noticeable that analyses of structures and procedures of German government regularly highlight domestic rather than external sources of change (Helms 2001; Holtmann 2001; Manow 1996; Niclauß 2001; Saalfeld 1999).

Fusion versus Bifurcation: Towards an Explanation

How can one account for the differential pattern of executive Europeanization? Why should there be administrative fusion but governmental bifurcation? The pattern described here certainly cannot be reduced to one explanation, but, in line with the general approach outlined in Chapter 1 in this volume, the combination of institutional opportunity structures and individual incentives is of critical importance. Briefly, the opportunity structures within which officials operate provide them with strong incentives for 'bureau-shaping', in the sense of translating EU-level powers and responsibilities into their domestic settings. They operate both under pressures of 'top-down' Europeanization and it is in their interest to explore opportunities for 'bottom-up' Europeanization. By contrast, national political institutions—and notably the logics of parliamentary, party and coalition government—act as shields for executive politicians from Europeanization pressures from above. At the same time, domestic payoffs for 'bottom-up' Europeanization are, on the whole, fairly restricted, so that executive politicians only exceptionally act as strong Europeanizers.

This argument requires some further elaboration. As noted earlier, Federal officials are closely involved in the political policy process and they are used to operating in an environment in which officials have a proactive role in the policy process rather than being seen as agents for carrying out ministers' wishes. The extension and intensification of the *acquis* and new forms of European co-operation and co-ordination mean that they are inevitably drawn into the administrative multi-level game, for, in the German case, ministers do not act as gatekeepers to the European process. In other words, officials expect to act with considerable discretion and can be assumed to seek to protect, if not increase, such discretion when it comes to EU matters. Officials are at least as likely to seeks opportunities for 'bottom-up' Europeanization than to respond to 'top-down' pressures. The strength of national bureaucracies in EU policy-making implies that Europeanization provides a means of escaping some of the constraints associated with a domestic decision-making process in which parliament and political parties reach deeply into the executive; at the same time, Europeanization provides effective justification for seeking additional competences and resources (notably personnel) in the domestic departmental context. There are then not only functional and institutional ties binding administrative actors in a linked multi-level system; but officials also have a personal incentive to strengthen such linkage.

However, German officials are also unlikely to be tempted 'to go native', in the sense of distancing themselves from the political core concerns and objectives of their departments, as, in the German executive, close involvement of officials in the political policy process comes at the price of close involvement of executive politicians in personnel policy (Goetz 1997, 1999). Although a career system, the higher Federal ministerial civil service allows a great deal of scope for politicians' involvement in ministerial personnel policy—notably decisions on promotions—and this discretion is used at least from the level of head of section upwards, i.e. it is not limited to the ranks of administrative state secretaries and heads of division, which are officially classed as 'political civil servants', but reaches at least two ranks below. Being visible to ministers and parliamentary state secretaries (in effect, deputy ministers who must be members of the Bundestag) is, thus, an important facilitator, if not, in fact, a precondition, for individual advancement. This helps to explain why ambitious German officials are often reluctant to be seconded to the European authorities.

Turning to the institutional opportunity structures and individual incentives of executive politicians, it is clear that they differ decisively from those of officials and rarely favour active Europeanization or effective multi-level linkage. The opportunity structures are most congruent when executive politicians are considered purely in their capacity as heads or deputy heads of department. In this role, they can, indeed, be assumed to seek to protect their departmental turf in the process of 'top-down' Europeanization and to exploit opportunities for bottom-up Europeanization in an effort to enhance departmental powers and resources. Oskar Lafontaine's determination to transfer decisive EU competences of the Economics Ministry to the Ministry of Finance, justified with reference to the need to match the superior co-ordination capacity of the French and the British in the EMU project, provides an instructive illustration (Dyson, Chapter 10 in this volume). This motivation is likely to be most pronounced in the case of technocratic ministers, who have been appointed for their specialist policy expertise and identify closely with the particular mission of their department. However, the experience of the Kohl and the Schröder governments shows that such ministers quickly come to be seen as dispensable, unless they invest time and effort in building a solid basis of support in one of the governing parties. Put differently, ministerial effectiveness depends decisively on political capabilities and standing within the party. Nurturing such a basis is, therefore, an abiding preoccupation of successful ministers. Yet, in this respect, EU-level powers and responsibilities are of little help—Oskar Lafontaine was able to raid the Economics Ministry because he was leader of the SPD at the time, not because of his EU-level competences, and Hans Eichel, his successor as Finance Minister, has no effective veto position in the government, since his position in the party is not unassailable. In short, the linkage between EU-level and domestic power and influence is much looser in the case of executive politicians than in the case of officials. What matters just as much, if not more, are party-political standing, support in the parliamentary party, close links to relevant interest groups, and, more and more, skilful media management and presence.

The incentives for executive politicians to act as Europeanizers are, therefore, much less powerful and more ambiguous than in the case of officials. With the exception of technocratic ministers, their departmental role is but one they have to fulfil (as noted, they have a strong incentive to seek to become members of the Bundestag and to assume leadership positions in the party); and effectiveness in leading the department and exercising power in cabinet depends at least as much on political capital than on formal powers and resources. The politicians' decisive battles are won in the interlinked arenas of cabinet, party, parliament, and coalition, giving a strong external orientation to their work; by contrast, although officials certainly require political craft (Goetz 1997), their scope of action is much more narrow and inward-looking. Moreover, the generally low salience of European policy among the electorate (Niedermeyer, Chapter 7 in this volume) and the low visibility of EU-level successes and failures compared to political battles won and lost in the domestic arena mean that executive politicians face few electoral incentives to devote scarce time to EU issues. Only if these are subject to controversial domestic debate will politicians be encouraged to take an active lead.

Is Bureaucratization Inevitable?

The above analysis would appear to suggest that there is, indeed, a strong link between Europeanization and the bureaucratization of public policy-making. Whereas officials operate in an integrated multi-level system, executive politicians do not, and key arenas of national politics with which the political executive is inextricably intertwined—party, parliament, coalition—seem virtually immune to Europeanization. Germany would, thus, appear to provide support for the oft-voiced thesis that the EU is not only a 'Europe of executives', but, more specifically, a 'Europe of administrations'.

However, before subscribing to such a characterization, at least two points need to be considered. First, as noted, politics and administration are closely intertwined in the executive in functional, organizational, and personnel terms. True, few ministers and even fewer parliamentary state secretaries have a background as senior Federal officials, and it is still fairly uncommon for administrative secretaries or heads of divisions to be recruited from among the ranks of former party politicians, although such cases certainly exist. But while their career patterns are clearly distinct (Goetz 1999) and there is no tightly integrated politico-administrative élite, executive politicians and officials certainly do not constitute rigidly separate caste. The institution of the 'political civil servant' provides for a flexible passage between administration and politics and, in functional terms, policy and political work are closely intertwined, especially in political co-ordination units, which have gained in strength over the years (Goetz 1997). In short, while it makes sense to distinguish politics and administration analytically, in reality the distinction is fluid rather than dichotomous.

A second consideration concerns the capacity of political actors to direct and control the activities of officials. Are there reasons to assume that officials' discretion is greater when they participate in decision-taking at EU level and in the domestic handling of EU politics than in a purely domestic setting? In the domestic setting, the close linkage between government, governing parties, and parliament makes for a policy process in which politics is ever-present and the scope for bureaucratic drift is small. The weak Europeanization of these arenas certainly provides increased opportunities for administrative discretion. Moreover, as argued above, executive politicians will have weaker incentives to track officials' activities at EU level than in a domestic context. The conditions for bureaucratization are, therefore, favourable, but close political involvement in promotions for senior administrative posts means that officials have an incentive to second-guess politicians' intentions rather than to circumvent or undermine them.

Note.   Early drafts of this chapter were presented at two workshops held at the British Academy in London. I wish to thank Jack Hayward and Tanja Börzel, who acted as discussants for my paper, for their insightful and constructive comments and suggestions.

4

The Bundestag:
Institutional Incrementalism and
Behavioural Reticence

THOMAS SAALFELD

Introduction

IN A JOINT RESOLUTION, members of the *Délégation pour l'Union Européenne* of
the French National Assembly and of the European Union Affairs Committee of
the German Bundestag agreed in 2001 that successful enlargement of the EU
'will require far-reaching reform of the Treaties, aimed at providing an enlarged
Union with an architecture that has more legitimacy and greater transparency for
its citizens' (French National Assembly 2001). This reflects a consensus among
the German (and, of course, French) political élites across party lines that enlargement will require, apart from more efficient decision-making procedures at EU
level, enhanced legitimacy and transparency at EU and national levels in order to
connect the EU more effectively to its citizens. This is not to say that there was
agreement about solutions. Reform proposals aiming at 'connecting' European
citizens more effectively to the EU policy process range from a 'maximalist' to a
'minimalist' position. The former advocates the direct election of the President of
the Commission by the citizens of the member states, the 'parliamentarization' of
the Commission by strengthening its relationship with the European Parliament,
and the preservation of the status quo with respect to the powers of the national
parliaments as well as the Council. The 'minimalist' approach seeks to strengthen
national parliaments in the EU policy process and to maintain the status quo with
respect to the dominance of the Council, the appointment of the Commission
essentially through intergovernmental negotiations, and the powers of the
European Parliament (*Economist* 2002).

There is, however, a striking discrepancy between, on the one hand, an
emphatic consensus among the vast majority of members of the German political
élite about the crucial importance of European integration for Germany and, on the
other, the slow pace of institutional adaptation to the consequences of European
integration. This is accompanied by a certain behavioural reticence of members of
the Bundestag (MdBs) about making use of parliament as the classical device in

Proceedings of the British Academy, **119**, 73–96. © The British Academy 2003.

representative democracies to connect citizens with the EU policy process. Voting behaviour is a good example. Voters' opportunities to participate in the electoral process were improved by the introduction of direct elections to the European Parliament in 1979. But they are far less willing to participate in these elections than in elections to national, regional, or local assemblies. The élites in political parties reflect and reinforce this lack of enthusiasm by, at least generally, not politicizing EU-related issues in election campaigns—even in campaigns for the elections to the European Parliament.

This discrepancy may be partly due to the peculiar nature of the EU where '[c]ountry-defined policy demands and policy capabilities are set in a shared European framework to generate collective regimes, most of which are then implemented back in the countries concerned' (Wallace 2000: 7). Yet, as this chapter argues, a significant part of this discrepancy is due to choices made by the political élites, especially the political parties in campaign headquarters and parliament. Despite slowly, but significantly, improving institutional capabilities to subject EU policies to parliamentary scrutiny at the national level, MdBs have been reluctant to devote their scarcest resource—time—to the public and controversial debate of EU policies—a precondition of meaningful voter choice. Admittedly, EU policies now profoundly influence a large number of policy areas implicitly and in ways that are often difficult to understand and articulate in parliamentary debates. But debate about European integration and its reverbera-tions is strikingly low given the importance of issues such as enlargement, the deepening of European integration, and the 'democratic deficit' and potential remedies. This is all the more regrettable if one considers the frequency with which the EU is 'blamed' for unpopular policy outcomes by national politicians, and the problems associated with EU policies in such areas as agriculture and trade.

This chapter explores the evidence of a mismatch between the perceived importance of democratic, representative EU politics at the German élite level and institutional design as well as political behaviour. It investigates the extent to which there has been a gradual process of Europeanization of representation at the institutional and behavioural levels. It examines how this adaptation has been mediated by institutional structures and traditions and why institutional adapta-tion to the growing quantity and qualitative importance of EU law has been so slow. It asks why German political behaviour in the process of democratic repre-sentation has been affected so little by European integration. The emphasis is less on the peculiarities of the EU as a political body than on the way elected politicians respond strategically to these structural constraints.

Representation as Process of Delegation and Accountability

Despite its ambiguity and contestation, the notion of political 'representation' is a key concept in democratic theory. It describes political decisions that 'are made by elected representatives and implemented by appointed officials to whom the representatives delegate some of the tasks of governing. The representatives decide what citizens must and cannot do, and they coerce citizens to comply with their decisions' (Manin, Przeworski and Stokes 1999: 1). Representation can lead to a 'drastic reduction of the universe of those represented to a small group of representatives' (Sartori 1987: 223) and permits a simultaneous reduction of the transaction costs and external risks of collective decision-making (197: 216–23; Buchanan and Tullock 1962).

From a normative perspective, democratic conceptions of representation are problematic at the EU level, because 'individual citizens voting in free, equal, fair and competitive Euro-elections cannot influence the composition of Euro-authorities, much less bring about a rotation of those in office. . . . In general, the EU is not a political system in which rulers are held accountable for their policies and actions in the public realm by citizens, and where competing élites offer alternative programmes and vie for popular support at the European level' (Andersen and Burns 1996: 227). Given the lack of any collective accountability of the Council as the main decision-making body of the EU (for example, *vis-à-vis* the European Parliament), the relationship between national parliaments and governments is still crucial for a democratic process of representation. 'It is only through accountability to their national parliament, of ministers attending the Council, that democratic influence can be brought to bear on the Council's deliberations' (Cygan 2001: 6).

In the ideal-typical model of 'responsible party government' (underlying much of the normative debate on modern representative democracy at the national level), electoral competition between the government and opposition parties provides the main incentive for opposition MdBs to bear some of the costs of monitoring the executive (supported by the majority parties) and of using parliamentary debates as well as the mass media as devices to transmit information critical of the government's record to the electorate, thus forcing the government defend its policies in public. MdBs of the government parties also have incentives to monitor the making and implementation of government policies and to keep a watchful eye on 'their' leaders. Their electoral chances are tied to their leaders' performance in office, although their monitoring and influence will be more discreet. With regard to committees of the US Congress, Krehbiel (1991) has established that heterogeneity of preferences and competition in a committee or any other parliamentary body will make that body collectively more informative *vis-à-vis* the parent chamber and/or voters.

Whether MdBs have opportunities and incentives to effectively engage in EU-related oversight activities—thus ensuring a degree of accountability and responsiveness—is conditional on a number of factors. First, they need the institutional capacity to do so. The EU policy process poses specific problems for parliamentary oversight through national parliaments (Bulmer 1986), some of which were tackled through the reforms of 1992–4 (see below). Secondly, there needs to be a political will on the part of MdBs to make use of their institutional oversight capabilities or, if necessary, extend their capabilities through institutional reform. The representatives of the German people in the Bundestag seem to have lacked this political will, if compared to the scrutiny of purely domestic legislation and government activity.

The hypothesis advanced to explain this discrepancy between institutional capability and perceived importance, on the one hand, and lack of political will, on the other, is based on the incentive structure illustrated in the simple heuristic model sketched in Figure 4.1. This model is based on the assumption that parties and their candidates are rational actors with bounded rationality who primarily seek to advance their re-election chances. Their decision to engage in (or to avoid) legislative oversight activities depends on an analysis of electoral (opportunity) costs and benefits.[1] Whether or not MdBs are willing to bear the cost of parliamentary oversight depends on the institutional environment and the nature of the political issue. However, constitutional and organizational improvements (for example, through an improved committee structure) are necessary but insufficient conditions of improvements in political accountability and responsiveness, two key ingredients of democratic representation.[2] The resources available to MdBs—time in particular—are scarce (Döring 1995). Thus, the extent to which MdBs will utilize available monitoring arrangements in order to hold the federal government accountable for its EU policies depends on a cost-benefit analysis involving:

- The (differential) electoral benefit that MdBs expect from the outcomes of their oversight activities. This benefit largely depends on the salience of the respective policy (here: EU policy) in the domestic political arena. The domestic salience of EU issues is assumed to be high, if it affects clearly defined groups at the domestic level and the issue allows 'credit-claiming' or 'blame-avoiding' strategies. The salience is assumed to be low, if the matter is highly technical, does not affect a clearly defined constituency, and public awareness is low.

---

[1] It is not assumed that they are 'policy-blind' or disinterested in parliamentary or governmental office and career advancement, but it is argued that policy and office benefits follow from successful re-election (for a discussion of the trade-offs involved see Strøm and Müller 1999).

[2] Accountability is, as outlined above, an important element in the process of democratic representation, because it generates the information required for citizens to make meaningful electoral choices and for governments to remain responsive to citizens' preferences. It should be added that institutions are not set in stone. Despite historical path dependency they can be changed by actors and often do not completely determine actors' behaviour. They usually allow actors to make choices (within limits) concerning the extent to which they wish to use the opportunities and powers provided to them within given institutional constraints.

Variable 1: Institutional Context and Capacity

Variable 3: Uncertainty about the link between policy, oversight activity and outcome

		High	Low
	Low	Low oversight effort	
	High	Low oversight effort	High oversight effort

Variable 2: Domestic salience of EU issue

Figure 4.1. Conditional heuristic model of Bundestag scrutiny of EU policies.

- The probability MdBs assign to their chance of making a difference by investing time and other scarce resources into parliamentary oversight. This depends on the uncertainty of the link between policies and outcomes in a particular area (the more complicated the policy and the more uncertain MdBs are about the possible outcomes, the more likely they are assumed to be to grant the executive maximum leeway, especially MdBs of the government parties whose political views are generally close to the government's; see Bianco 1994); and the uncertainty about the efficacy of parliamentary oversight activities in a particular area (the higher the probability that oversight is efficacious, the higher the probability that MdBs will engage in such activities).
- The costs of oversight in terms of time and opportunity costs.[3]

MdBs will engage in oversight activities in EU affairs (as in any other policy area) if the expected utility, discounted by the probabilities mentioned under the second point, exceed the costs, that is, if the expected utility is greater than zero. This can be formalized in the following equation:

$$(4.1a) \quad EU(O_n) = 0;$$
$$(4.1b) \quad EU(O_1) = (1\text{-}P_{L[O1]})(1\text{-}P_{E[O1]}) \, U(O_{[O1]}) \, - \, C_{(O1)}.$$

$EU(O_n)$ is the expected utility of not engaging in any oversight activities in a particular policy issue; $EU(O_1)$ represents the expected utility of engaging in

---

[3] Figure 4.1 does not specify these costs, because there is no reason to assume that legislative oversight of EU-related policies is more 'costly' for MdBs than would be the case with regard to national issues. The main differences, here, are assumed to be in the benefits and levels of uncertainty.

oversight activities, $P_{L(OI)}$ (varying between 0 and 1) is the uncertainty about the link between a particular policy and a policy outcome, $P_{E(OI)}$ (varying between 0 and 1) represents the uncertainty about the efficacy of parliamentary oversight in the particular policy area; $U(O_{[OI]})$ is the political value or benefit that MdBs associate with a successful oversight activity in the particular policy area (mainly in terms of his or her re-election chances) and $C_{(OI)}$ represents the costs of the oversight activity (Table 4.1).

Everything else being equal, the rational MdB is likely to engage in oversight activities in a particular policy area, if $EU(O_1)$ is larger than $EU(O_n)$ which equals zero. If the electoral salience of the issue is low, MdBs will not invest a great deal of their resources in monitoring activities. If it is high, it depends on the uncertainty associated with the policy and its expected outcome as well as on the oversight mechanisms available. High uncertainty reduces the terms $(1-P_{L[OI]})$ and $(1-P_{E[OI]})$ and, hence, the incentives for MdBs to engage in oversight activities, even if the expected benefit $EU(O_1)$ is high. Low uncertainty may increase the incentives, if the salience is high (Figure 4.1). A number of examples of the expected utilities, given certain hypothetical values (ranging from zero to one), for the terms in equation (4.1b) shows that the utility reaches an upper bound of 1 under ideal (but unrealistic) circumstances with maximum salience of an issue (and therefore a maximum electoral benefit from oversight activities), zero costs, and zero uncertainty both about the link between policy and outcome and between oversight activity and its effect. As the values for the components of the equation are changed to more realistic levels, the expected utilities quickly

Table 4.1. Examples of expected utilities for different hypothetical values in (1b).

Example no.	$P_{L(OI)}$	$P_{E(OI)}$	$U_{[OI]}$	$C_{(OI)}$	$EU(O_1)$
1	0	0	1	0	1
2	0.5	0	1	0	0.500
3	0.5	0.5	1	0	0.250
4	0.5	0.25	0.25	0.25	−0.156
5	0.5	0.5	1	0.5	−0.250
6	0.5	0.5	0.5	0.5	−0.375
7	0.5	0.5	0.2	0.5	−0.450
8	0.9	0.9	0.1	0.5	−0.499
9	0.9	0.9	0.1	0.9	−0.899

Note: $P_{L(OI)}$: uncertainty (varying between 0 and 1) about the link between a particular policy and a policy outcome; $P_{E(OI)}$: uncertainty (varying between 0 and 1) about the efficacy of parliamentary oversight in the particular policy area; $U(O_{[OI]})$: political benefit the parliamentarian associates with a successful oversight activity; $C_{(OI)}$: costs of the oversight activity; $EU(O_1)$: expected utility of engaging in oversight activities.

become negative. Therefore, rational MdBs have few incentives to engage in such oversight activities (Figure 4.2).

Figure 4.2 shows the expected utility of engaging in EU-related oversight activities as the value of the variables in equation (4.1b) increases from a lower boundary of 0 to a maximum of 100 (or, 1) holding all the other variables constant at a level of 50 (or 0.5). If all the other variables are held constant, but the uncertainty about the link between policy and outcome increases, the expected utility will decline gradually. The same is true for the uncertainty about the efficacy of oversight activities. The expected utility increases gradually with increasing electoral benefits (owing to issue salience). But even if all other variables are held constant at 0.5, a maximum benefit will not push the expected utility above zero. The strongest leverage in this equation can be observed for the (opportunity) costs of oversight. Increases in the cost of oversight lead to a fairly steep decline of the utility, if all other variables are held constant.

While the predictions sketched above are of a generic nature, the incentive structure for parliamentarians is particularly unfavourable in EU-related matters. The uncertainty about the link between policy and outcome is often greater than in national politics, as is the uncertainty about the efficacy of parliamentary intervention. While we can present only circumstantial evidence for these two assertions, there is a considerable body of evidence in support of the claim that the electoral benefit (owing to issue salience) is generally lower than for national policy issues.

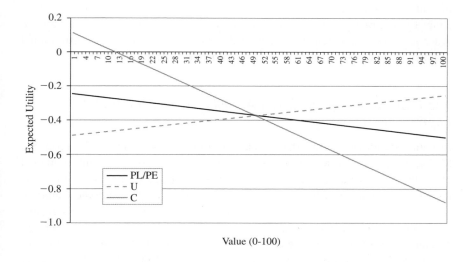

Figure 4.2. Expected utility for values of $P_{L(01)}$, $P_{E(01)}$, $U_{[01]}$, and $C_{(01)}$ between 0 and 100 (all other values constant at 50).

Parliamentary Oversight of EU Affairs: Institutional Constraints and Behavioural Patterns

In comparison to other West European parliaments, the Bundestag has relatively strong oversight capabilities, mainly owing to the federal government's lack of control of the plenary agenda and the high degree of professionalization of specialized parliamentary committee work (Döring 1995; Saalfeld 1998). Yet there is agreement that the Bundestag's efforts to scrutinize and influence the federal government in EU affairs through parliamentary channels have been more sporadic and less intense than in some important areas of domestic policy, at least until the reforms of 1994 (e.g., Bulmer 1986; Cygan 2001; Hölscheidt 2000; Ismayr 2001; Saalfeld 1995; Töller 1995; Weber-Panariello 1995). According to one interpretation, which could be termed the 'deparliamentarization' thesis (Börzel 2000), this is largely due to structural characteristics of the EU decision-making system, which is said to have led to a further shift of power from parliaments to the executive. 'Traditional mechanisms of parliamentary accountability have been weakened. National legislatures have seen their position weaken both formally—through erosion of sovereignty—and politically, as the executives and the civil servants dominate decision-making on EU issues to a greater extent than on domestic matters' (Raunio and Hix 2000: 144). An alternative position claims 'that notwithstanding the transfer of constitutional, executive and legislative powers to the European level, the overall impact of European integration on parliamentary government in the domestic arena has actually been rather modest' (Raunio and Hix 2000: 143). This section will seek to identify some important institutional constraints imposed on the Bundestag, examine attempts to overcome these structural constraints, and look at some behavioural indicators in order to assess the extent to which MdBs have actually used the institutional channels available to them in the context of EU-related affairs.

The Problem of Informational Asymmetry: Constitutional Improvements

In their attempt to monitor the federal government's activities at EU level, the MdBs, especially on the opposition side, have faced formidable informational obstacles that are largely of a technical–procedural nature and stem from the intergovernmental character of much of the EU's policy process. The confidentiality of interministerial negotiations is largely incompatible with parliament's need for transparency of government activity. In addition, even the reduced amount of information has often been available too late for the Bundestag to scrutinize and influence the government's position. The Bundestag has frequently received relevant information only after the national governments had reached an agreement in the Council. At this point, the scope for parliamentary influence (for example, through the parliamentary majority party or policy experts from a committee) is minimal, because any changes would require the unpacking of the entire result of complicated intergovernmental negotiations (Ismayr 2001: 292).

Clause 2 of the Act of Ratification of the Treaty of Rome (passed by the Bundestag in 1957) stipulated that the Federal government 'shall keep the Bundestag and the Bundesrat continually informed of developments in the Council of the European Economic Community and in the Council of the European Atomic Energy Community. Insofar as a decision of a Council requires the making of a German law or has immediate force of law in the Federal Republic of Germany, notification should be made prior to the Council making its decision' (quoted from Bulmer 1986: 225, 250). Despite Clause 2, the extent and timeliness of information accessible to the Bundestag was a serious problem. For example, about two-thirds of the small minority of EU regulations and Directives that were debated on the Bundestag's floor between 1980 and 1986 were already in force at the time of the debate (Ismayr 2001: 293; see also Bulmer 1986: 227–9).

The initial impetus for reform came from developments at the EC/EU level. Committed MdBs had fought for decades for the strengthening of parliamentary rights that eventually followed the Maastricht Treaty. But it was the ratification of the Maastricht Treaty that forced the federal government to clarify and improve the rights of the representation of the Länder governments—the Bundesrat—to information and participation. Most of these rights were then extended to the Bundestag. The decisive factor in breaking the federal government's resistance against more and earlier information was the credible threat of a refusal of the Bundesrat majority to ratify the Maastricht Treaty. As a result, the Bundesrat's and Bundestag's right to information in EU affairs were codified in an amendment to the Basic Law in December 1992. Article 23 of the Basic Law, which had become obsolete owing to German unification, was rewritten and became the 'Article on European Union' (Möller and Limpert 1993; Ress 1994).

According to Article 23, any further transfers of sovereign rights to the EU require ratification by a two-thirds majority in Bundestag and Bundesrat, thus safeguarding the rights of both chambers. Of more immediate relevance, the Federal government now has the constitutional duty to inform the Bundestag and Bundesrat 'comprehensively' and 'as early as possible' about all plans at the EU level that 'could be of interest to the Federal Republic'. Before a proposal is decided in the Council of Ministers, the Federal government must give the Bundestag an opportunity to express a view and has the duty to 'take this view into account' ('berücksichtigen') in the negotiations. Clause 4 of the 'Act on Co-operation between the Federal Government and the Bundestag in European Union Matters' (Co-operation Act [Bundestag])[4] lays down specific statutory

---

[4] The German title of the Act is 'Gesetz über die Zusammenarbeit von Bundesregierung und Deutschem Bundestag in Angelegenheiten der Europäischen Union'.

rules for the implementation of Article 23. According to this clause, the Federal government must send even first drafts of EU directives and guidelines to the Bundestag's EU Affairs Committee, along with an explanation of the draft measure and the government's own position on the matter. In addition, the Federal government must provide the Bundestag with a more detailed written report and any further oral explanations within five sessional days.

The Amsterdam Protocol (European Parliament 1999) annexed to the Treaty on European Union reinforced these legal provisions. Paragraph 1 of this Protocol requires that all Commission documents be forwarded promptly to the national parliaments of the member states. One of the most significant developments, as Cygan (2001: 9) points out, is that 'all Commission documents' now have to be forwarded, including green and white papers as well as communications which are preliminary discussion documents that were not necessarily made available to national parliaments as a matter of course. In addition, Paragraph 2 of the Protocol requires that Commission proposals for legislation be made available in good time 'so that the government of each Member State may ensure that the "national parliament receives them as appropriate"' (Cygan 2001: 10). The governments agreed in the Amsterdam Treaty that the Council would not decide until six weeks after the publication of the Commission's proposal in order to give national parliaments time to deliberate and, if necessary, influence their national government.

The Co-operation Act (Bundestag) places even more constraints on the Federal government. Clause 5 stipulates that the Federal government has to give the Bundestag 'sufficient' opportunity to express a view before it can agree to any EU measure. If sufficient time is not available, the Federal government may only give conditional agreement to a measure in the Council. Only after the Bundestag has expressed a view can the Federal government either convert its conditional into a final agreement or restart negotiations in the light of the arguments presented by the Bundestag.

The Conference of European Union Affairs Committees (COSAC— *Conférence des Organes spécialisés en Affaires communautaires*), introduced in 1989, has gained in status through its codification in the Amsterdam Treaty. It has proved to be a useful means of information exchange and source of institutional learning, although its resolutions are not binding for national parliaments. So far, the Bundestag has not supported a stronger institutionalization of COSAC in order to avoid a re-nationalization of EU policy-making (Ismayr 2001: 297). Nevertheless, the gradual institutionalization of transnational parliamentary co-operation is remarkable.

First assessments of the effectiveness of these changes are ambivalent. Ismayr (2001: 291) believes that the institutional changes since 1992 have clearly strengthened the Bundestag *vis-à-vis* the federal government in the EU's policy process. In particular, the Bundestag's opportunities to get involved in the process at an early stage have improved significantly. Such early involvement is crucial for the Bundestag to have any chance of exerting some influence (Deutscher Bundestag: EU-Ausschuss 1998: 21). The device of the federal government's 'conditional agreement' in the Council has worked well (Ismayr 2001: 293). The secretariat of the EU Affairs Committee concludes in a first self-assessment of the effectiveness of this new parliamentary body (see below) that the views expressed by the parliamentary parties' (especially the government parties') policy experts have had 'considerable weight' (Deutscher Bundestag: EU-Ausschuss 1998: 48, 29). Although the federal government is not formally bound by the views expressed by the Bundestag (Möller and Limpert 1993: 28–9), it may be forced to justify publicly why it has chosen not to follow the views of the Bundestag. These changes have contributed to a reduction of MdBs' uncertainty about the efficacy of their scrutiny. How significant this reduction has been needs to be assessed on a broader empirical basis, although the EU Affairs Committee's first evaluation after one parliamentary session (Deutscher Bundestag: EU-Ausschuss 1998) has been positive.

In addition, the EU Commission itself has increasingly become an important source of government-independent, up-to-date and—crucially for our theoretical argument—low-cost background information about the Federal government's performance in a large number of policy areas. Benchmarking and cross-national comparisons carried out by the EU increase the opportunities for national legislators to hold their governments accountable at the domestic level. This constitutes one example for the interaction between 'top-down' and 'bottom-up' processes in political representation and accountability in the EU's complex system of multi-level governance.

Bundestag Committees and the Union: Formal Convergence, Low Profile

Specialization and division of labour in parliamentary committees are among the chief ways for legislators to reduce the uncertainty between legislative measures and their outcomes (Krehbiel 1991). In the case of EU-related policies, committees need to cooperate beyond the boundaries of specific departmental committees with a high level of policy-specific expertise, because policy-specific expertise needs to be combined with specialist knowledge about the policy process at the EU level and the complicated processes of intergovernmental bargaining. In combination with the improved right to information according to the new Article 23 of the Basic Law, the powers granted to the committee (see below) also have a potential to reduce MdBs' uncertainty about the efficacy of their oversight in EU-related matters. According to our model, this should have had a modest, but positive, impact on the incentives for MdBs to engage in the oversight of the Federal government's activities at EU level.

Until the constitutional amendments of December 1992, the Bundestag had failed to appoint a permanent Committee comparable to the one regularly appointed by the Bundesrat or other parliaments in EU member states (Saalfeld 1995; Sturm and Pehle 2001). Following the insertion of the new Article 45 into the Basic Law, the Bundestag is now required to appoint a Standing Committee on European Union Affairs. The appointment of the first European Affairs Committee in 1994 marked a clear—albeit delayed—convergence with the practice in other EU member states—not a 'top-down' process, but rather an instance of horizontal institutional learning. Partly, the delay is the result of the Bundestag's attempt to integrate EU-level policy- making into its traditional organizational framework for scrutinizing and influencing the federal government, which was jealously guarded by the existing departmental standing committees.

After the first direct elections to the European Parliament in 1979 and the phasing out of 'dual mandates', it was felt that a scrutiny body was required that would not only co-ordinate the activities of the departmental standing committees, but also maintain links with the European Parliament through the inclusion of EP members. This caused some technical problems. The organizational form of an ordinary standing committee on European affairs could not be used, because — according to the Bundestag's rules of procedure—standing committees can be composed only of MdBs. Thus, members of the European Parliament could not be included in a regular standing committee, at least not with voting rights. In 1983, the Bundestag, therefore, established a Commission for European Affairs (*Europakommission*) that largely took the form of a Commission of Enquiry (*Enquête-Kommission*) (Pöhle 1984: 352–9). Such a Commission may be composed of MdBs and non-parliamentarians who enjoy the same rights as parliamentarians.

The Commission on European Community Affairs met only thirty-five times between 1983 and 1986 and was not considered to have been successful (Mehl 1987: 66–7, 92). It was not, therefore, reappointed, but replaced by a sub-committee of the Committee on Foreign Affairs consisting of thirteen MdB and thirteen German members of the European Parliament, the latter without voting rights (Schindler 1999: 3615). This solution, too, turned out to be less than successful, as the sub-committee's activities were confined to matters explicitly delegated to it by the Foreign Affairs Committee. Since the sub-committee did not have the power to make recommendations to the plenum, all proposed recommendations had to be agreed by the Foreign Affairs Committee. But this Committee was reluctant to grant too much of its scarce time to the discussion of matters raised by the Sub-Committee on European Affairs, especially questions that transcended the Foreign Affairs Committee's own jurisdiction (Brück 1988: 221–4; Hänsch 1986: 197). In 1991, therefore, the Bundestag appointed its first, short-lived EU Affairs Committee, whose successor was given constitutional rank in 1992 and appointed for the first time in 1994.

The Bundesrat, by contrast, had had a special EEC/EC/EU Affairs Committee since 1957. The difference between the two chambers can be explained by a number of factors. The lower level of partisan control of the federal government in the Bundesrat may have played a certain role. But there are also technical reasons. A large percentage of EU draft legislation is of a complicated, technical nature. Being largely responsible for the implementation and administrative detail of EU legislation, the Länder governments represented in the Bundesrat have had a stronger interest in influencing the detail of the implementation of EU policies, even if they are not politically salient. Backed by the administrations of the Länder, the Bundesrat has also had larger resources at its disposal than the Bundestag to scrutinize draft EU legislation.

After the amendments to the Basic Law in December 1992, the Bundestag Standing Committee on European Union Affairs was appointed for the first time in 1994. Given its constitutional rank, it is no longer at the discretion of a simple parliamentary majority to decide whether or not such a committee is to be established. Hence, the committee has the institutional continuity that it needs to build up the necessary expertise and provide a longer-term career perspective for EU specialists in the parliamentary parties. The committee serves as 'integration committee', specializing in fundamental issues of European integration, and as a 'linking' committee, co-ordinating the activities of other departmental standing committees in policies emanating from the EU, if and when such policies cut across departmental boundaries. It receives all EU draft legislation and acts as a parliamentary 'clearing house'. Its chair makes a formal proposal to the speaker of the Bundestag about which departmental standing committees should be involved in scrutinizing a particular matter. The chair is aided by the Europe Office (*Europa-Büro*), which is part of an extended committee secretariat (Ismayr 2001: 295–7). The federal government regularly informs the committee about imminent decisions in the Council and explains its own bargaining strategy, including its intended voting behaviour in the Council and its working groups (Deutscher Bundestag: EU-Ausschuss 1998: 32). Ministers and members of the Commission are heard as witnesses on a regular basis (Ismayr 2001: 297). One of the most important constitutional innovations is the fact that the Bundestag may empower the European Affairs Committee to express a view on EU draft legislation on behalf of the whole House.

The Committee consists of thirty-six MdBs and eleven German members of the European Parliament (the latter without voting rights). The MdBs are generally also members of other departmental standing committees in order to facilitate inter-committee co-ordination through cross-membership. The presence of members of the European Parliament is designed to establish regular links with the parliamentary representatives at the EU level and to add EU-specific expertise to the committee deliberations. Most assessments of the committee's impact so far have been sceptical (Sturm and Pehle 2001a: 68–70). The committee's right to express a view on behalf of the Bundestag, a real constitutional innovation at first glance, has in practice not had the anticipated effect of accelerated scrutiny and influence, because the European Affairs Committee still has the duty to consult all relevant departmental committees before it articulates the Bundestag's view. By 2000, therefore, this possibility of accelerated scrutiny and influence had not been used in a single case (Hölscheidt 2000: 34–5). The attendance of members of the European Parliament has suffered from the fact that the two legislatures' sessional timetables are not always compatible (Ismayr 2001: 295). Sturm and Pehle (2001: 70) concluded, therefore, that the European Affairs Committee has, in practice, not gained a dominant status in EU matters *vis-à-vis* the departmental standing committees that have defended their jurisdictions jealously.

The committee reforms have improved the Bundestag's monitoring capabilities in a structural sense and assisted coordination, but have not led to a significant intensification of parliamentary scrutiny in EU affairs, at least not beyond the small circle of EU experts in the committee. Committee recommendations (either from the EU Affairs Committee or any other departmental standing committee) about EU matters to the plenary are rare. In the 1994–8 Bundestag, for example, the relevant 'committees-in-charge' (*federführende Auschüsse*)—which co-ordinate the co-operation between several committees and report to the plenary if a matter is referred to more than one committee—made recommendations with regard to 158 out of a total of 2,070 EU documents (i.e. approximately 8 per cent). Only if a committee makes a recommendation will the issue be put on the Bundestag's agenda for debate. Yet, in the 1994–8 Bundestag, the chamber simply took note of such recommendations without any debate in four out of five cases. In other words, only about 1.5 per cent of all EU documents referred to the Bundestag get discussed in the plenary at all. In only two cases did the plenary amend a committee recommendation (Ismayr 2001: 297).

Hence the committee reforms have contributed to a reduction of uncertainty about the efficacy of parliamentary scrutiny and influence and, in conjunction with improved rights to information, reduced the Bundestag's cost of obtaining information. The reforms also stabilized and enhanced parliamentary career perspectives in EU affairs. However, the transmission of information from committee to the plenary and the general public has been modest.

Reducing Information and Oversight Costs Through 'Arena-Coupling' within Political Parties

One informal, but highly efficient, mechanism of information exchange and of keeping information costs down are political parties and their ability to link different levels of the political system from the local to the supranational. Intra-party channels of communication may be more efficient than official parliamentary channels, but are understudied in the empirical literature. More research is needed to understand the extent to which such channels of information supplement formal parliamentary channels and reduce the information costs in systems of multi-level governance. In the case of the SPD, for example, the Bundestag parliamentary party organizes regular conferences of the chairs of the parliamentary parties on the Länder, national, and European Parliament levels. These conferences are prepared by working groups within the parliaments (Leonardy 2002: 191). Regular conferences of policy experts within the parties at all levels of Germany's system of multi-level governance can play an equally important role. Similarly, the Bundestag's communication with firms, interest groups and NGOs—bodies with considerable resources operating at the EU level that may have incentives to inform MdBs about EU policies—needs to be studied more carefully to gain a realistic picture of the quality and cost of information that MdBs encounter.

Parliamentary Questions and Debates

Collecting information and generating parliamentary expertise through specialized standing committees is one aspect of parliamentary scrutiny of the executive. Transmission of the information extracted by experts to the chamber and to the general public is another dimension. For the US Congress, Krehbiel (1991) has demonstrated theoretically and empirically that information transmission between committees and chamber is generally problematic (Table 4.2).

Formally, the Bundestag receives a large number of EU documents for scrutiny, and this number has increased dramatically, especially between the early 1970s and the late 1980s (Table 4.2). As we have seen, the number of EU proposals

Table 4.2. Number of EEC/EC/EU documents, German Bundestag, 1957–98.

Bundestag period	No.
1957–61	13
1961–5	224
1965–9	745
1969–72	946
1972–6	1,759
1976–80	1,706
1980–3	1,355
1983–7	1,828
1987–90	2,413
1990–4	1,860
1994–8	2,070

Source: Sturm and Pehle (2001a: 58).

referred from committees back to the floor of the Bundestag has remained relatively small. The interaction between committees and floor is minimal. Nevertheless, the Bundestag, especially the opposition parties, may use various means of parliamentary interpellation in order to extract information and generate debate about European integration or EU policy, independent of a particular measure.

The Bundestag parties have rarely made use of these instruments to initiate debates on fundamental questions of European integration, but the content of interpellations such as *Aktuelle Stunden* and *Große Anfragen* has increasingly had a 'European dimension'. *Aktuelle Stunden* are one-hour adjournment debates on topics of current interest, frequently (but not necessarily) tabled as a follow-up to issues raised in question time. *Große Anfragen* are often relatively comprehensive written questions to the government, followed by a debate on the government's answer. Both forms of interpellation can only be tabled at the request of a parliamentary party or at least 5 per cent of the MdBs (Table 4.3).

Table 4.3 shows that interpellations about the EU as an organization and fundamental issues of European integration have not figured prominently, at least in quantitative terms, among the topics selected for *Aktuelle Stunden* and *Große Anfragen* in the legislative sessions between 1976 and 2002. If the Bundestag databases are searched more generally for references to a 'European dimension' in interpellations about policy (using the keyword index of the Bundestag's electronic data base), a clear increase of *Große Anfragen* with a 'European dimension' can be observed for the period since the early 1980s. There is only a slight

Table 4.3. Information transmission to the Bundestag plenum, 1983–2002: *Große Anfragen* and *Aktuelle Stunden*.

Bundestag	Große Anfragen			Aktuelle Stunden		
	Total no.	Explicitly on EC/EU as institution	Explicitly mentioning a European dimension	Total no.	Explicitly on EC/EU as institution	Explicitly mentioning a European dimension
1976–80	47	0	0	9	0	0
1980–3	32	0	5	12	1	2
1983–7	175	0	40	117	3	3
1987–90	145	12	37	126	4	6
1991–4	98	3	32	103	3	14
1994–8	156	8	54	103	4	6
1998–2002[a]	103	1	53	137	5	13

Note: [a] Until August 2002.

Source: Compiled from Deutscher Bundestag: DIP, http://dip.bundestag.de.

increase of *Aktuelle Stunden* with a European content since the beginning of the 1990s. In the 1998–2002 Bundestag, over one-half of all *Große Anfragen* and just under one-tenth of all *Aktuelle Stunden* had such a 'European dimension'. *Aktuelle Stunden* are predominantly short, controversial debates used by the opposition to challenge the government at short notice on current issues, whereas *Große Anfragen* are comprehensive written questions followed by more substantial debates about policy. Hence it is plausible to conclude that the 'European dimension' of policy seems to be strongly and increasingly present in debates between the policy experts of the parliamentary parties (*Große Anfragen*), but less relevant in controversial, topical exchanges which have a stronger potential to attract public interest (*Aktuelle Stunden*).

Explaining the Discrepancy between Structural Improvements and Behavioural Conservatism: The Electoral Connection

The above discussion has shown that Bundestag's institutional capacity to scrutinize and influence the Federal government's activities at the EU level has improved, especially since the constitutional amendments of 1992. The behavioural indicators presented suggest, however, that MdBs have not made full use of these improved opportunities, especially with regard to the transmission of the information generated in committees to the wider public. The chief reasons are the low electoral salience of the EU as an organization (to which MdBs respond) and the highly complex nature of EU policy, including a high degree of uncertainty about political responsibility. These factors make informed political choices highly problematic from a voter's perspective and reduce the incentives for MdBs to invest scarce resources in legislative oversight.

These factors may at least partly explain why many MdBs consider the scrutiny of the federal government's activities at EU level to be predominantly an issue for the European Parliament. In a survey of members of national parliaments and the European parliament, Katz and Wessels (1999) confronted parliamentarians at both levels—the national and the European—with the statement: 'Some people regard the European Parliament as the democratic heart of the Union, because democratic legitimacy of the Union can only be based on a supranational parliament. Others say that this is a wrong ambition because the legitimacy of the Union is already based on the national parliaments' (Katz 1999: 27). Respondents were then asked to locate their personal opinions on a seven-point scale, ranging between democratic legitimization based on the European Parliament (1) and on the national parliaments (7). On average, MdBs had a score of 3.16, whereas German MEPs were more clearly in favour of the European Parliament as the preferred locus of legitimization, with an average score of 1.84. Yet even the MdBs remained, on average, below the scale's mid-point of four, which clearly distinguishes them from their colleagues in the national parliaments of Greece,

Ireland, Luxembourg, Portugal, and Sweden who, on average, preferred the national parliament as the preferred locus of legitimization (Katz 1999: 29).

Low Political Salience of EU Matters on the 'Demand Side'

For analytical purposes, voters can be seen to constitute the 'demand side' of a political market, whereas political parties can be treated as the 'supply side'. On the demand side, German voters consider elections to the European Parliament to be clearly less important than elections to the national, *Länder* and even local assemblies (Table 4.4). Table 4.4 demonstrates that German voter turnout at elections to the European Parliament has remained consistently and significantly below the levels recorded for elections to the Bundestag. One of the reasons for these differences between national-level and European elections is revealed in Table 4.5. Asked in 1991 whether they felt that elections at the local, regional, national and European levels were 'very important', 'important', 'less important', and 'unimportant', barely more than one-half of the West Germans and just over one-third of the East Germans responded that elections to the European Parliament were very important or important. In both West and East Germany, elections to the European Parliament are clearly seen to be less important than national, regional, and even local elections.

The data above refer to the 'importance' of elections to the European Parliament in relation to elections at other levels of the German political system. This relatively utilitarian conceptualization could be replaced by survey questions

Table 4.4. Turnout in elections to the Bundestag and the European Parliament, 1976–99 (per cent).

Year	Elections to Bundestag	Elections to European Parliament (turnout in Germany only)	Difference between elections to European Parliament and proximate Bundestag election	Elections to European Parliament (turnout in all member states)
1976	90.7			
1979		65.7	−22.9	63.0
1980	88.6			
1983	89.1			
1984		56.8	−32.2	61.0
1987	84.3			
1989		62.4	−15.4	58.5
1990	77.8			
1994	79.0	60.0	−19.0	56.6
1998	82.2			
1999		45.2	−37.0	49.5

Source: Karl-Rudolf Korte, *Wahlen in der Bundesrepublik Deutschland*, 3rd edn (Bonn: Bundeszentrale für politische Bildung, 2000: 71, 99).

Table 4.5. Perceived importance of elections at different levels of the political system in Germany, 1991 (per cent).

Level	Very important or important		Less important or unimportant	
	West	East	West	East
Local elections (*Kommunalwahlen*)	85	81	14	15
Regional elections (*Landtagswahlen*)	91	75	8	21
National elections (*Bundestagswahlen*)	96	78	3	19
European elections (*Europawahlen*)	51	35	47	60

Source: Karl-Rudolf Korte, *Wahlen in der Bundesrepublik Deutschland*, 3rd edn (Bonn: Bundeszentrale für politische Bildung, 2000: 83).

asking respondents about the extent to which they define their political identities primarily as 'European' compared to local, regional, and national identities — without improving the result. The available survey material suggests that, if anything, the German population has become less 'European' since the 1980s in terms of the focus of their political identities, which has remained the town, followed by the region, and then Germany as a whole, while 'Europe' has declined in importance (Duchesne and Frognier 1995; European Commission 2001*a*).

Among voters, on the demand side of political competition where electoral accountability in representative democracies is based, the EU and related issues are of secondary importance. This reduces the political salience of European integration and EU-related policy issues. In addition, uncertainty about the link between policies promised and carried out by politicians and policy outcomes is high, not only for MdBs but also for voters. In the EU's multi-level political system, citizens are even more uncertain about 'exogenous conditions' and about the effect of policies on outcomes than on the local, regional, or national level. If such uncertainty exists, citizens 'cannot be sure which policies are in their best interest or how much they can expect from the government' (Manin, Przeworksi and Stokes 1999: 11–12). Hence, the incentives for citizens to go to vote and use the vote to hold elected representatives accountable for their EU-related policies or oversight activities are greatly reduced. The same uncertainty creates incentives for elected representatives to focus on regional and national issues with clearer and more promising opportunities to 'claim credit'. In other words, the decision-making process in the EU tends to combine low levels of issue salience with high levels of uncertainty about outcomes and responsibilities. In terms of our explanatory framework, this provides the worst possible incentive structure for actors—voters and MdBs alike—to invest scarce resources such as time into activities aimed at holding the executive accountable for EU-level activities.

So far, the EU's attempts to contribute to the creation of a European political community through strengthening European citizenship in the Maastricht Treaty and the role of national parliaments in the Amsterdam Treaty (signed in 1992 and 1997, respectively) have not led to a significantly stronger sense of a European political identity in Germany. The Maastricht Treaty set out the basic components of European citizenship, stating that all EU citizens who reside in a member state which is not their country of origin are entitled to vote, or stand, at elections to the European Parliament and at local elections. According to the Council Directive 94/80/EC, this provision was intended 'to enable citizens of the Union to integrate better in their host country', and, therefore, to complement the freedom of movement and residence of citizens within the EU (Wiener 1998). Yet, the number of persons benefiting from these provisions is small, and it remains to be seen whether they will contribute to the development of a stronger European sense of political community and citizenship beyond national allegiance as mobility increases. Owing to the small number of German and EU citizens involved, and the fact that such rights (at least in Germany) are restricted to local elections and elections to the European Parliament, the effect is still minor. It is unlikely to influence the voters' perceptions of the relatively low political importance of elections to the European Parliaments and the parties' overall incentive structure.

The fact that many voters consider elections to the European Parliament as second-order elections may, however, have indirect beneficial effects for democratic representation and accountability, demonstrating once again the complex interaction of 'top-down' and 'bottom-up' processes involved in European integration. Hix and Goetz (2000: 11) point out that 'direct elections to the European Parliament have indirect implications for domestic electoral processes, parties and party systems. The creation of a new and nation-wide (rather than regional) "second-order" contest gives opposition and protest parties the opportunity to undermine support for governing parties, and gives voters the chance to punish the parties they support or signal their genuine policy preferences.' This demonstrates the extent to which the EU has become a system of multi-level governance where democratic accountability may cut across different levels in more complicated ways than simplistic analyses of the consequences of European integration suggest.

Low Political Salience of EU Matters on the 'Supply Side'

Although interest in EU matters is low among voters on the 'demand side' of political competition, politicians and political parties could choose to act as political entrepreneurs and politicize EU-related issues (or any other issue), as in such member states as Austria, Denmark, and the UK. But the high degree of con-

sensus in the German political élite about the fundamental necessity and normative desirability of European integration has largely prevented this issue from
becoming contentious and, therefore, electorally salient in inter-party competition (Sturm and Pehle 2001: 150–2). Nevertheless, we can observe a gradually
growing impact of EU-related issues on the supply side of the national policy
agenda, especially since the 1990s. Whether this will amount to a significant
Europeanization of political competition will have to be evaluated on the basis of
longer time-series data. A secondary analysis of the data that is provided by the
Manifesto Research Group (Budge *et al.* 2001) allows us to gauge the extent to
which parties have made commitments with regard to European integration in
national election manifestoes. These commitments would enable voters to make
EU-related choices at the national level. Figure 4.3 is a scattergram of the percentage of favourable sentences in the election manifestos of each of the main parties
of the 1990s (y-axis) and the year of the election (x-axis) between 1949 and 1998.
The trend line indicates that the percentage of favourable sentences has gradually
increased over time, that is, the EC/EU has increasingly become a topic that parties
have highlighted in their national election manifestos in a positive way. The fact
that, in the 1998 elections, all Bundestag parties have percentages clearly above the
longer-term general trend line indicates an acceleration of this trend.

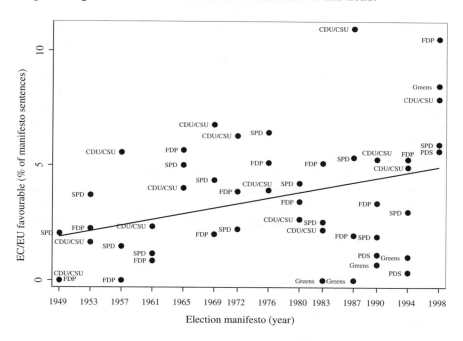

Figure 4.3. Number of sentences with favourable statements about the EC/EU in German
election manifestos, 1949–98 (trend).

The party labels permit us to trace the 'trajectories' of individual parties over time. Since the 1980s, the two major parties, and especially the CDU/CSU, have generally been more positive in their election manifestoes as far as European integration is concerned. Fluctuations at individual elections notwithstanding, the PDS and the Greens (with the exception of 1998) have generally been the least positive parties. This largely concurs with Niedermayer's findings in Chapter 7 of this volume. But the question of whether there is a longer-term supply-side-driven trend towards politicizing European integration needs to be evaluated in the light of longer time series than are currently available.

Reform Proposals and 'Uploading' of the German 'Model'?

The problems of efficiency, transparency, and representative democracy in the EU have fuelled a permanent discussion about institutional reform, not only in the EU but also in Germany. The pressure for reform expressed itself in the announcement of a constitutional convention at the Laeken Summit in December 2001. The Convention started its work in February 2002 and considered—among others— proposals for the roles of the European Parliament and the national parliaments in a future EU, including ways to connect the EU more effectively to its citizens. The Convention's deliberations had been preceded and accompanied by statements of leading German politicians, mainly from the ruling SPD–Green government, setting out models for the future of the EU. The proposals presented by Chancellor Gerhard Schröder, Foreign Minister Joschka Fischer, and Federal President Johannes Rau are close to the 'maximalist' scenario outlined in Chapter 1 in this volume. They address the incentive problems described in the previous sections by advocating the 'parliamentarization' of the EU and establishing a system of representative governance at the EU level that is close to the model of responsible party government.

In its 2002 election manifesto, for example, the SPD (2002) supported the idea of 'parliamentarizing' the EU by allowing the European Parliament to elect the next President of the Commission from among its own ranks. In other words, the party proposes to strengthen the democratic accountability relationship between the Commission and the European Parliament. Leading politicians of the Social Democrats and Greens agree that the Council of Ministers should be converted into a 'Chamber of the Member States'. Foreign Minister Fischer (2000) identified two models for a second chamber and argued that '[f]or the second chamber a decision will have to be made between the Senate model, with directly-elected senators from the member states, and a chamber of states along the lines of Germany's Bundesrat'. Chancellor Gerhard Schröder (*Süddeutsche Zeitung* 29 April 2001) argued unequivocally for an 'uploading' of the German Bundesrat model to the EU level, where the Council of Ministers would become an institution resembling the German representation of the Länder governments.

The Christian Democrats have been slightly more circumspect about detailed models. Nevertheless, party leader Angela Merkel called Schröder's reform plans for the EU, including an 'uploading' of the Bundesrat model, 'interesting' (*Süddeutsche Zeitung* 29 April 2001). In their election manifesto, the Christian Democrats, too, showed signs of 'uploading', in this case of elements of the Federal Republic's federalism, especially the principle of subsidiarity to the EU level. The Christian Democrats advocated more democratic legitimacy for the EU, more qualified majority voting in the Council, a move towards one-citizen-one-vote in elections to the European Parliament (with continued overrepresentation of the 'smallest member states'), and shared budgetary powers for Council and European Parliament. This was coupled with a clear indication that the EU should have responsibility only for policies that could not be devised more efficiently at a lower level of governance (CDU/CSU 2002).

Conclusions

The impact of European integration on political representation in Germany has been incremental in institutional and hesitant in behavioural terms, especially in relation to the Bundestag. At the beginning of the 1990s and following decades of experimentation, the German Bundestag improved significantly the institutional and organizational conditions for holding the federal government accountable. Yet, despite the strengthening of the Bundestag's information rights through the 1992 amendment to the Basic Law and the Amsterdam Treaty, which came into force in 1999, evaluations of the Bundestag's legislative oversight *vis-à-vis* the federal government and its policies in Brussels have remained ambivalent. This applies especially to the transmission of expert knowledge about EU policy to the floor of the Bundestag and the wider public.

In part, these problems can be ascribed to the technical problems involved in the establishment of a new and unique system of multi-level governance with complex chains of representation and accountability. Also, the Bundestag's institutional performance in the area of EU policies does not differ strongly from its performance in other areas: a strong emphasis on committee work coupled with deficits as a debating chamber. However, explanatory factors are also to be sought in the electoral incentive structure faced by MdBs. The evidence produced in this chapter is not a rigorous test of the expected-utility model presented in the second section, but corroborates many of its assumptions with a high level of plausibility. The context is provided by the generally low electoral salience of EU policies; by the unusually high levels of uncertainty (a) about the link between policies and outcomes at EU level and (b) about the potential efficacy of attempts by national parliamentarians to hold the Federal government to account for its actions at the EU level; and, finally, by the high opportunity costs of legislative oversight. In consequence, MdBs have—given their scarce resources—only limited incentives to prioritize legislative oversight in EU affairs. Despite institutional reforms, a significant element of mismatch remains.

However, there is some evidence that the behaviour of parties and their élites is gradually changing. The increased role of European integration in recent election manifestos at the national level and the increased EU content in parliamentary debates are early indications, although the fundamental 'permissive' consensus in the German élite is likely to limit the extent to which such debates can engage a wider public.

Note. I owe thanks to the editors of this volume as well as Tanja Börzel, Gisela Hendriks, Christoph Knill, Martin Lodge, Mehmet Ümit Necef, Eiko Thielemann, and Rüdiger Wurzel for their helpful comments on an earlier draft of this chapter. Needless to say, all remaining opacities are the author's responsibility alone.

5

The German Länder:
From Milieu-Shaping to Territorial Politics

CHARLIE JEFFERY

Introduction

Understandings of Europeanization

MUCH OF THE LITERATURE ON EUROPEANIZATION has the concept of 'goodness of fit' as its starting point, and so does this chapter. The notion of 'goodness of fit' has to do with how European integration impacts domestically on the polities, policies, and politics of member states. It is commonly held in the recent rash of Europeanization studies that a poor 'fit' of domestic institutional structures, policy portfolios and identitive norms creates adaptational pressures on the member states to conform with 'Europe'. The worse the fit, the stronger the adaptational pressure exerted by 'Europe' (Börzel and Risse 2000; Knill 2001; Knill and Lehmkuhl 1999; Risse, Green Cowles and Caporaso 2000).

This linkage of goodness of fit and an adaptational pressure in the member states caused by 'Europe' is problematic in two ways, as Dyson and Goetz confirm in Chapter 1 in this volume. First, it seems highly static. It implies that there is some fixed point 'out there' (Bulmer and Burch 2001) in 'Europe' to which the member states are ineluctably drawn. But 'Europe'—the whole gamut of policy portfolios, institutional forms, and political projects that make up the European Union—is hardly a static entity. Nor, of course, are the member states, in which institutions, policies, and norms change for all sorts of reasons, not many of which have any obvious connection to Europe. So while the dynamics of change in Europe and the member states may move in some kind of linkage with one another, there is no necessary connection between their trajectories. The goalposts of goodness of fit are, in other words, always changing, never static.

Second, there seems in the notions of fit and adaptation to be a unidirectional assumption of 'top-down' causality. The assumption is that 'Europe' causes change in the member states. This is clearly unsatisfactory when it is the member states that constitute and, therefore, help 'cause', the European Union. It is not enough to acknowledge the existence of 'feedback loops' (Börzel and Risse 2000: 1). Europeanization has to be conceived as a two-way process in which

Proceedings of the British Academy, **119**, 97–108. © The British Academy 2003.

member states and EU interact to cause change in one another. Bomberg and Peterson (2000: 2) hit the nail on the head:

> Europeanization is a shorthand term for a complex process whereby national and sub-national institutions, structures and populations adapt to and seek to shape the trajectory of European integration in general and EU policies in particular.

Europeanization and Germany

Germany provides a clear example of this interactive, two-way process. The German case has been discussed most comprehensively in these terms by Simon Bulmer in an influential paper in 1997, in which he identified a 'strikingly good fit', even a 'congruence' of constitutional order, norms and conventions, patterns of meso-level governance, and policy goals between Germany and the EU (Bulmer 1997). This 'congruence' had not emerged (just) because Germany had had to adapt to pressures for compliance and convergence emanating from the EU. It resulted much more from a complex of three factors:

- *A Europeanized identity*: multilateral co-operation in the EU had been internalized over the post-war period as a normative value by German policy-makers.
- *Institutional power*: value-driven multilateralism meant that Germany became an instinctive *demandeur* for multilateral solutions. In doing so it frequently proposed, or in a stronger interpretation, 'exported' (Bulmer, Jeffery and Paterson 2000) structures, norms, and policy principles for the EU which were drawn from domestic German practice.
- *Systemic empowerment*: institutional export mobilized 'a bias in the character of EU governance' (Bulmer 1997: 74), creating an 'institutional setting [which] is remarkably familiar and natural for Germany', 'a milieu in which Germany actors can feel at home' (Katzenstein 1997*b*: 40–1).

'Europeanization' understood from this perspective is about Germany 'shaping the regional milieu' (Bulmer, Jeffery and Paterson 2000) in Europe, about a member state actively shaping the character of EU governance with the result that it 'fitted' well with the character of German governance. The adaptational pressure evident here is clearly not just a 'top-down' process, but also one in which causality flows from the 'bottom up'.

This chapter looks at Europeanization through the lens of how the German Länder have responded to challenges posed by European integration since the mid-1980s. It focuses primarily on their 'horizontal' relations with one another rather than on their 'vertical' relations with the federal authorities in EU matters. It does this by understanding 'Europeanization' as a two-way process in which the EU imposes adaptational pressures on the Länder, but is also subject to adaptational pressures from the Länder. It also uses the timescale of fifteen years to explore the dynamics of Europeanization. In doing so it suggests that the goodness of fit Bulmer, Jeffery, Paterson, Katzenstein *et al.* identified was, in some respects at least, a temporary and contingent situation, which is now beginning to break down. The causes of breakdown have been new adaptational pressures rooted in wider dynamics of change in both domestic and EU politics, and the result has been new adaptational pressures largely emanating from within the domestic arena, not just from 'Europe'.

The chapter, therefore, provides a test case for the assumption outlined by Dyson and Goetz in Chapter 1 in this volume that Europeanization is a dynamic and interactive process between EU and domestic actors. The discussion, first, explores the interaction of the Länder and the EU through to the early 1990s, before addressing developments since then. It then explores how the dynamic of Europeanization has changed over time. Finally, some concluding reflections review the findings in the light of the empirical questions that link the contributions to this volume.

The German Länder and Europe I: Bringing about Goodness of Fit

For at least thirty years there was a poor fit between European integration and German federalism. The German Basic Law was, on the one hand, '*europaoffen*', open to Europe and more specifically to the transfer of German sovereign powers to international institutions. On the other hand, and seen from the Länder perspective, it was '*europablind*', blind to the implications that transfers of sovereignty had for the division of powers in the federal system. European integration was a federal responsibility, which meant *inter alia* that the federal authorities had—and used—the right to transfer sovereign competences of the Länder to the European level. At the European level, the Federal government then acted for the German member state in the collaborative exercise of former Länder competences together with the other member states and the other European institutions.

This was a manifestly unsatisfactory situation, in which the essence of Länder statehood—a significant scope for 'self-rule'—and with it the broader federal system had a vulnerable 'open flank'. This unsatisfactoriness was, though, for a long time a matter more for debate in the common rooms of German law schools than one of political importance for two reasons: first, the Länder were, on the whole, unequivocally integrationist, wholly in line with the élite consensus that European integration was a guiding value for German politics; second, the scale of transfers of Länder competences to Europe was rather modest as the integration process inched forward past de Gaulle, Eurosclerosis, and Mrs Thatcher's handbag.

This situation changed with the debates leading to the Single European Act. Consistent with their integrationist tradition, the Act was greeted in principle with outright enthusiasm by the Länder. The problem lay in the scale and scope of transfers of (Länder) competences envisaged for the Single Market process. This had an energizing effect—or, to use the Europeanization terminology, imposed an adaptational pressure—on the Länder. There followed a concerted campaign to gain adequate access to Europeanizing/-ized decision-making processes concerning those matters for which the Basic Law said the Länder had some kind of responsibility. That campaign ended only several years later in the context of the Maastricht Treaty on European Union (Jeffery 1993).

In this campaign, causality was clearly two-way. The aim throughout was as much to adapt 'Europe' to fit better with the domestic constitutional order in Germany as it was to adapt the Basic Law to the demands of accelerating European integration. The arguments of the Länder revolved around the concept of 'European domestic policy'. They argued that post-SEA European integration policy could no longer be considered as 'foreign policy' (and, therefore, a federal competence), given the direct effect of European legislation in member states, and given the growth of supranational (as opposed to intergovernmental) decision-making processes. The Länder were, therefore, entitled to a quality of input into decision-making for this 'European domestic policy' equivalent to that they would have in 'traditional' domestic policy.

This argument had and has no recognition in constitutional law, and is probably incompatible with the Constitutional Court's notion of the EU as a *Staatenverbund*, an 'association of states'. It was, nonetheless, pursued vigorously and won, not least because the Länder had a constitutional right to veto both the Single European Act and the Maastricht Treaty. On each occasion, the threat of veto was wielded to extract concessions from the Federal government. The process of upgrading Länder rights of input into European decision-making was not, in other words, the consensual working through of a co-operative 'culture' of politics as Börzel (1999) argues, but a fractious test of wills, which also spilled over into other areas of Länder Euro-engagement (and occasionally still does as periodically vexed Foreign Office officials confirm). The process was not so much co-operative as a concerted expression of a collective determination to which the federal level by and large and unwillingly had to submit. This robust approach of the Länder produced two forms of adaptation to the challenges of post-SEA Europeanization:

- The Basic Law was amended to close the 'open flank' by giving the Länder[1] a veto over transfers of sovereignty and to give expression to

---

[1] 'The Länder' here is a shorthand for the Länder acting collectively through their federal-level body and the federal second chamber, the Bundesrat.

the notion of European domestic policy. The result—Article 23 of the Basic Law—effectively 'Europeanized' the domestic practices of 'co-operative federalism'. It sets out a series of procedures, graded according to the scope of the competence the Länder have for particular issues in the Basic Law, which create an interdependence of the federal authorities and the Länder essentially the same as would apply to a purely domestic treatment of those issues.[2] This was 'top-down' Europeanization, the result of key domestic actors reacting to the adaptational pressures caused by a misfit of European integration with German federalism.

- But there was also 'bottom-up' adaptation. Using the same veto threat the Länder also forced the Federal government to represent a set of key demands to the Intergovernmental Conference (IGC) on Political Union. These demands were designed to make the European integration process more sensitive to the domestic context of member states that had a constitutionally entrenched regional tier of government. They won most of these demands: the incorporation of the principle of subsidiarity into the Maastricht Treaty (albeit in a weak form not in principle focused on the regional tier); the establishment of a new principle of regional representation in the EU in the form of the Committee of the Regions (CoR); and, most significantly, the right of regional ministers to speak for their member state's delegation in the Council of Ministers (in circumstances defined in domestic law, and in the German context in Article 23 of the Basic Law).[3] This was 'bottom-up' Europeanization, a form of institutional export (Bulmer, Jeffery and Paterson 2000: 40–3), designed to adapt the institutional framework of the EU to the domestic needs of the Länder.

The outcome of these domestic and European processes of adaptation pushed on by the Länder was to bring about some of the congruence Bulmer referred to. The combination of treaty change and the new Article 23 made the EU a more 'familiar' place where the Länder could, indeed, feel a little more 'at home'.

The German Länder and Europe II : The New Territorialism

That they would continue to feel 'at home' was, of course, not guaranteed by their achievements. The term 'congruence' refers to a condition of agreement or

---

[2] Though there is a partial 'get-out' clause for the federation, whose 'greatest possible respect' for Bundesrat positions can be overridden by its 'responsibility for the nation as a whole' (Article 23/5 and 23/6).

[3] This demand was introduced by the Belgian government at Maastricht, pushed on by the Belgian regions, and endorsed by the German Federal government.

conformity between two (or more) things. That condition may be broken if either, or both, of those two things change over time. The Maastricht Treaty was finally ratified in Germany in 1993, around eight years after the (West) German Länder were mobilized to act by the debates on the Single European Act. Neither the EU nor German federalism stayed still over that period. Domestic and European dynamics pulled in different directions to create a new incongruence which has, in turn, generated new (two-way) adaptational pressures.

Dynamic I: Competitive Federalism

The first dynamic is that which has become known as 'competitive federalism'. The old co-operative federalism, which was so successfully Europeanized by the new Article 23, is proving much more difficult to operate amid the territorial politics of united Germany. It was geared to the definition and implementation of common, nationwide standards in most fields of public policy and rested on a strong sense of solidarity among the Länder whose clearest expression was in the fiscal equalization process (Jeffery 2002*a*).

Financial solidarity is, in the context of a bigger federation with bigger gaps between the financially stronger and the financially weaker Länder, clearly under pressure. Despite the conclusion of the Solidarity Pact II in 2001, which is supposed to set in stone fiscal equalization processes until 2019, it is highly likely that contributor Länder will continue to take steps to limit their contributions to recipient Länder. The underlying sense of disquiet about the scale of financial transfers has been mildly assuaged, but clearly not resolved (Jeffery 2002*a*). At the same time, economic and financial disparity, meshed with sharper territorial differences in political culture and social identity, are leading to the emergence of a new quality of federalism that is focused on giving expression to territorially diverse preferences rather than delivering co-ordinated policy standards. This new quality of federalism has not found a formal institutional form. It has emerged alongside a set of institutional structures designed to embed co-operation and solidarity. There is, however, a growing disjunction between co-operative structure and competitive practice that is frequently overlooked by a German tradition of federal studies overinformed by a dry legalism (Jeffery 2002*a*). As Arthur Benz (1999: 56) has put it, 'federalism in Germany is much more flexible and open to institutional adaptation and policy change than is often assumed . . . the German federal state has to be acknowledged as a dynamic system'.

The new dynamics of territorialism naturally enough also impact on Länder European policy (Jeffery 1999: 57–8). The Länder now display a much more overt 'what's-in-it-for-me? mentality' focused (depending on the material situation 'at home') on bringing back structural funding or (at times: and/or!) limiting the German contribution to the EU budget. And territorially differentiated interests in domestic politics are externalized in equally differentiated territorial interests in EU politics. Bavaria does not share Saxony-Anhalt's interest in industrial regeneration, Rhineland-Palatinate is not moved by Brandenburg's concerns to find the best mechanisms for cross-border co-operation with the EU's applicant states, the CAP is irrelevant for Bremen and the other city-states, but not of course for the larger Länder, and the Saarland does not share Bavaria's more heroic aspirations to decentralize the Union.

Greater territorial diversity, and a greater willingness to give expression to it, have implications for Article 23, just as they do for domestic co-operative federalism. With the exception of the EU's constitutive politics, to which the discussion returns below, the co-operative solidaristic intention of Article 23 amounts, in practice, either to fairly meaningless lowest common denominator positions or provides a framework for the construction of shifting and transitory issue coalitions. The latter is the case in particular where EU policies impinge on areas in which the Länder still hold exclusive competence in Germany, as Rüdiger Wurzel and Jörg Monar point out in Chapters 14 and 15 in this volume. In other fields, the formal Article 23 process is just one route among many through which the Länder can make their concerns felt, including direct lobbying in Brussels, the Committee of the Regions, and the manifold organizations of cross-border and transnational regional co-operation which have sprung up, especially since the mid-1980s (Schmitt-Egner 2000). The strategic mix of 'routes' chosen by any Land naturally varies (Jeffery 1998); the common point is that Euro-political strategies of the Länder are now increasingly differentiated by territorial interest.

In these circumstances, the co-operative federalism of Article 23 is in part ill-attuned and in part irrelevant to the territorialized definition of interests that characterizes the post-unification Länder community. It is a residue of *West* German thinking about Europe, appropriate to the late 1980s, which became more or less immediately redundant and anachronistic as soon as it came into force. There is now a new misfit rooted in the domestic politics of united Germany; attendant on it are new pressures for adaptation.

Dynamic II: EU Enlargement

Article 23 and the treaty changes agreed at Maastricht were aimed at improving the goodness of fit of German federalism with the EU as it stood at the end of the Cold War. Like German federalism, the EU has since undergone a transformation. Key issues decided in principle at the beginning of the 1990s—e.g. Economic and Monetary Union, Common Foreign and Security Policy and eastern enlargement—are only now becoming a tangible reality. The goalposts of better fit of the early 1990s are clearly not the same as those of the early 2000s.

From the Länder perspective the most critical change has been the eastern enlargement process. In the early 1990s, the prospect of eastern enlargement was given unequivocal support by the Länder; enlargement was an all-European version of the German 'growing together that which belongs together'. It was in principle and in the abstract a good thing, an inherently positive by-product of the end of the Cold War (Jeffery and Collins 1998). But as the concrete details and implications of enlargement began to emerge in the later 1990s, it lost its abstract quality. For Länder in receipt of substantial EU structural funding, for Länder on the enlargement borderline facing low-cost competition, for Länder worried for labour-market or internal security reasons about migration flows from the east, enlargement increasingly became understood as a problem that threatened their interests. Support for eastern enlargement as a result became hedged with qualifications. Unequivocal support transformed into a new 'yes, but' politics on enlargement. There follow two examples, both from policy statements of the Bavarian government:

> The Bavarian European Minister, Kurt Faltlhauser, declared that Bavaria supported eastern enlargement without reservation. '*But*, precisely because our border regions are interested in harmonious integration we have to make sure that border areas do not suffer disadvantage from the enormous gaps which exist vis-a-vis the neighbour countries to the east in terms of economic strength, agricultural structures and also in the question of internal security (January 1998, emphasis mine).[4]
>
> Bavaria supports the eastern enlargement of the EU as a means of securing enduring peace in Europe. Eastern enlargement also opens up interesting new markets for the Bavarian economy in particular. *But* enlargement has to be organized in an acceptable way for the current member states through a satisfactory calculation of transitional periods. This is a precondition for EU eastern enlargement being accepted by the people (September 1999, emphasis mine).[5]

This 'yes, but' politics is an externalized expression of the new territorialism of domestic Länder politics. It is expressed largely in differentiated, Länder-specific terms rather than co-ordinated nation-wide ones. The core theme has been the protection of particular Länder interests. The VW subsidy controversy in Saxony in 1996 (Hrbek 1996) is one example of an unsubtle economic protectionism that is by no means an isolated practice in eastern Germany. The mobilization of the eastern Länder to retain existing levels of Structural Funding in the Agenda 2000 negotiations was another (Jeffery 1998). A third has been the lobbying efforts of a German-led grouping of enlargement border regions, which has aimed at winning subsidies for the western side of the border, long transition periods before the full operation of the Single Market on the eastern side, plus the retention of border controls until internal security standards to the east are raised (*Hofer 20-Punkte Katalog* 1998).

---

[4] Pressemitteilungen der Bayerischen Staatskanzlei, 29 January 1998, at http://www.bayern.de/ Politik/Pressemitteilungen, downloaded on 4 November 1999.
[5] Pressemitteilungen der Bayerischen Staatskanzlei, 28 September 1999, at http://www.bayern.de/ Politik/Pressemitteilungen, downloaded on 4 November 1999.

Most vocal among these territorial–protectionist responses to enlargement has been Bavaria. But here the agenda goes beyond protectionism. Bavaria has sought to construct an 'issue-linkage' (Jeffery and Collins 1998) between enlargement and a wider agenda of EU reform. This wider agenda is about a decentralized Union which does less and, therefore, leaves the member states—and their constituent units, like the Länder—more leeway to construct distinctive, 'tailor-made' responses to the dynamics of globalization. Enlargement is instrumentalized to support that agenda. The CAP and the Structural Funds (so the Bavarian government has argued in a series of well-publicized policy papers from 1995 onwards[6]) clearly cannot function in the same way post-enlargement without the Union becoming unfinanceable. Responsibilities in these areas, therefore, need to be renationalized (which in Germany would mean re-regionalized), with European subsidy controls also loosened to allow the member states (and their regions) to deploy their own resources flexibly to meet locally decided priorities.

Changing Values of Europe—A Changing Europeanization Dynamic?

There is a congruence in this vision for Europe with the changed territorial politics of domestic federalism. The Bavarian agenda expresses in other words the aspiration of reshaping Europe (again) to match Länder needs in a doubly changed, domestic and European environment. Though inspired and endlessly propagated by Bavaria, this is by no means an agenda restricted to the Bavarian government under Minister-President Edmund Stoiber. A growing number of Länder have come on board with statements about the need to limit the scope of the EU through better-defined competences, the need to protect national and regional identities against over-Europeanization, and to ring-fence the core roles of the German member state and within it the Länder (see, e.g., Beck 2001; Clement, 2001; Gabriel, 2001). Wolfgang Clement (SPD), North Rhine-Westphalian Minister-President until October 2002, provides a key example. His comments on the 'unreasonable limits' on 'our scope' imposed across a wide field of policies by the European Commission (Clement 2001: 2) or on the need to prioritize 'decentralized coordination over central steering, initiative and creativity over direction from above, diversity over uniformity' (Clement 1999: 9–10) have clearly echoed the Bavarian position. His suggestions on the delimitation of

---

[6] See *Memorandum der Bayerischen Staatsregierung zur Neuausrichtung der Agrarpolitik der Europäischen Union* (Munich 1995) and *Positionspapier der Bayerischen Staatsregierung für eine Reform der Struktur- und Regionalpolitik der EU* (Munich, 1996); *Anmerkungen zur Reform der EU-Strukturpolitik und zur Zukunft der Beihilfenkontrolle* (Munich, 1998).

European-level competences have probably gone even further (Clement 2001: 9–13).

These themes have, in other words, now moved far beyond their Bavarian origins. They are increasingly put forward by other key players in German politics, including the CDU/CSU (Schäuble and Bocklet 2001) and the SPD, whose programmatic statement of November 2001 on the allocation of competences in the EU reads in part like a rehash of Bavarian policy papers on enlargement from 1995–6 (SPD 2001*a*: 15–16, 2001*b*: 50)! Much of this German debate on competences gets overlooked, as commentators tend to focus instead on proposed institutional reforms which tend to follow fairly well-worn German lines on greater supranationalization, in particular of the Council of Ministers. The important point, though, is that the German position in the round would have this more supranationally organized Union do rather less, and do so within tightly circumscribed legal limits (Kreile 2001: 251).

There is a sense that this vision of a rolled-back Union gets overlooked because of its Bavarian origins. Bavarian ideas are, at times, not taken seriously enough by observers, because so many of those observers dislike Bavarian politics. A major research project in Germany has, for example, recently reported its findings on how far significant change has emerged in German European policy since 1990. The broad finding is one of continuity. In a book of 864 pages there is barely a comment on Bavaria or Edmund Stoiber (Schneider, Jopp and Schmalz 2002). But it would be misleading if preconceptions were to lead to an underestimation of the role Bavarian actors have had in disseminating new ways of thinking about the EU. The broadening commitment among German actors to express and pursue essentially narrow, territorial interests in a European frame suggests that values of European integration are changing and converging on a 'Bavarian' position. The Länder are certainly now not as instinctive and unequivocal in their commitment to European integration as they once were. The attitude to integration is now more conditional on its capacity to meet territorially defined needs and preferences. Parts of the old élite consensus on Europe are beginning to refocus on a new priority of national (and/or regional) interest.

This can be seen most vividly in Länder contributions to the constitutive politics of the EU at Amsterdam, Nice, and in the post-Nice process focused on the next IGC in 2004. Two issues stand out. First is the focus on protecting the Länder role in what they rather preposterously call *öffentliche Daseinsvorsorge* (i.e. subsidies to regional banks, regional broadcasting, and other regional services) from the restrictions of EU competition policy. This has probably been the main Länder preoccupation at the last two IGCs. Following on from the Union-shaping efforts the Länder made at Maastricht, the naked protectionism of the *öffentliche Daseinsvorsorge* issue testifies to a breathtaking narrowing—or territorialization—of their vision. This territorialization of vision is also reflected, secondly, in the competences issue. Invoking for once their enhanced Article 23-based powers to a common purpose, the Länder succeeded in persuading Chancellor Schröder to insist on a follow-on IGC after Nice which would *inter alia* focus on a clearer delineation of competences of the EU *vis-à-vis* the member states (which in German means the federal authorities *and* the Länder). The aim is to stop action by the EU that goes beyond what is formally set out in the European treaties, to close off possibilities for evolutionary 'spillover'.

This concern about competence-creep to the European level is entirely logical and understandable now that the Länder are assuming a stronger territory-specific rationale and vision. Their concern is as far as possible to retain the wherewithal to shape conditions in their territories as they deem appropriate. The transformation, though, is a remarkable one. Their refrain from the Single European Act to Maastricht was one of 'let us in'; it is now one of 'leave us alone' (Duchacek 1970: 356). And just as the Länder sought to adapt the EU to their needs in the 'let us in' phase by sensitizing the Union to domestic co-operative federalism, so they are now seeking to adapt the EU to their changing needs in this 'leave us alone' phase by pushing for an enhanced level of territorial autonomy. The underlying aim, as the Europeanization literature suggests, is to achieve better fit, but:

- The goalposts of fit have moved on as the character of both German federalism and the EU have changed.
- The pressure for adaptation is not one-way; arguably more significant are the attempts by the Länder in the early 1990s and now to change 'Europe' to suit their needs.
- And, curiously, the current phase of Länder-led Euro-adaptation pressure has the tendency not to 'Europeanize', but to 'de-Europeanize', to roll back and restrict the Union. In this sense too, Europeanization is not necessarily a one-way street.

Conclusion

A number of issues related to the wider themes of this book emerge from the above discussion. The first is to confirm the point by Dyson and Goetz in Chapter 1 in this volume that Europeanization is both dynamic and interactive in the relation between EU and member states. The pace of change in the example of the German Länder since the mid-1980s has been rapid, and the causal directions of change have been complex, with obvious 'top-down' and—even more so—'bottom-up' elements. The latter point tells us something about Germany which may not apply so much in other EU member states: Germany remains a polity with an unusually high degree of institutional pluralism. The impact of Europe 'from above' is experienced differentially in different institutional settings; and a range of different institutions, clearly extending beyond the branches of central government, have the scope to impact on Europe 'from below'. Dynamic, interactive stories equivalent to that related here about the German Länder could certainly be written about the Bundesbank, the Federal Constitutional Court, and the German private sector (Jeffery and Paterson 2001).

From all this can be read some answers to the questions of what, why, how, who, and when that drive this volume. *What* has been affected is the capacity of the Länder to pursue their interests in EU matters. And this capacity has been affected—and understood—differently in different time periods (the *when* question): prior to, and for a short period after, German unification the Länder had a vision of collective pursuit of interests, and their strategies for Europe 'from below' sought to create a collective platform for expressing their interests in European decision-making. More strongly territorial definitions of interest since unification have transformed the Länder strategy from one claiming access to expanding European competence to one seeking increasingly to restrict European competence and allow the Länder to pursue their interests differentially in a national framework. A judgement on whether their success in realizing their strategy 'from below' in the earlier period will be replicated now will have to await the conclusions of Convention on the Future of Europe and the 2004 IGC.

The *why* question can clearly be answered as one of misfit. The achievement of good fit in the early 1990s was fleeting; as domestic and European dynamics have moved apart to create new misfit, the Länder have sought to reimpose (a very different kind of) fit with their interests. *How* they have done so reflects the possibilities of an institutionally plural polity. At Maastricht and at Nice (and beyond) the Länder were able to shape the German position by imposing demands that the Federal government was forced—on pain of non-ratification of the respective treaties—to accept. The question of *who* put forward those demands has changed and has been driven by a strong normative element. At Maastricht, all the Länder subscribed to a pre-unification, West German élite consensus on the desirability of 'ever closer union'. That élite consensus has been challenged by the domestic demands of unification and the external demands in particular of eastern enlargement. New ideas on Europe emerged, in particular in Bavaria. These were initially isolated views, but have over time percolated through on a wider front to challenge and at least in part supplant the older 'Kohlian' consensus. They set out a vision of a recalibrated Union, perhaps more coherent at its centre, but also more 'national', more differentiated in its policy outputs.

Note. This chapter has been informed by research conducted for the project 'Germany and the Reshaping of Europe', funded as part of the ESRC Research Programme 'One Europe or Several?', Grant No. L213252002.

6

Public Law:
Towards a Post-National Model

GUNNAR FOLKE SCHUPPERT

The European Union as a Community Based on Law

'EUROPEANIZATION' OF THE GERMAN LEGAL SYSTEM is an inescapable consequence of the character of the EU as a legal community. The EU has evolved as an economic community, a legal community, a political community, and—last but not least—a community consisting of values. Not only has it acquired its own Charter of Fundamental Rights; also—in a fit of 'constitutional fever', *'Verfassungsfieber'* (Schuppert 2002*a*)—it is about to declare its own constitution—whatever it might look like. The EU started as a purely economic community, based on the calculation that shared interests could form the basis for a bigger and deeper community amongst states that had been engaged in bloody war (Oppermann 1991). The underlying concept of integration was clear: a process of gradual integration through a fusion of economic interests would create a dynamic and inner logic that would lead from economic integration to political integration.

Concurrently, the establishment of an economic community gave birth to a legal community, because the common market could not work without the institution of a unitary legal system (Matzner 1984), as stressed by the literature on the economics of institutions (Homann and Suchanek 2000). Thus, from the outset, the purpose of European integration was to accompany the development of a unitary European economic space by a unitary legal space. The implementation of a European economic community required enforcement by a European legal system. The European Court of Justice (ECJ) promoted the application of this insight and negotiated with the European Commission the simultaneous process of an integration of economy and law. The first requirement for the success of such a process was the recognition of the European legal system as an independent legal system.

The Recognition of the European Legal System as an Independent Legal System

The primary and secondary law of the EU forms an independent Community legal system. This legal system possesses—just like national systems—a

Proceedings of the British Academy, **119**, 109–125. © The British Academy 2003.

legitimizing foundation (Ipsen 1972) and a legal protection system (Article 220 ff. of the EC Treaty) that establishes its autonomy. The ECJ paraphrased this autonomy of the Community legal system as follows: (Case 26/62, *Van Gend and Loos* [1963] ECR 1):

> The objective of the EEC Treaty, which is to establish a common market, the functioning of which is of direct concern to interested parties in the Community, implies that this Treaty is more than an agreement which merely creates mutual obligations between the contracting states. This view is confirmed by the preamble to the Treaty which refers not only to governments but to peoples. It is also confirmed more specifically by the establishment of institutions endowed with sovereign rights, the exercise of which affects member states and also their citizens. Furthermore, it must be noted that the nationals of the states brought together in the Community are called upon to cooperate in the functioning of this Community through the intermediary of the European Parliament and the Economic and Social Committee. In addition the task assigned to the Court of Justice under Article 177, the object of which is to secure uniform interpretation of the Treaty by national courts and tribunals, confirms that the states have acknowledged that Community law has an authority which can be invoked by their nationals before those courts and tribunals. The conclusion to be drawn from this is that the Community constitutes a new legal system of international law for the benefit of which the states have limited their sovereign rights, albeit within limited fields, and the subjects of which comprise not only member states but also their nationals. Independently of the legislation of member states, Community law therefore not only imposes obligations on individuals but is also intended to confer upon them rights which become part of their legal heritage. These rights arise not only where they are expressly granted by the Treaty, but also by reason of obligations which the Treaty imposes in a clearly defined way upon individuals as well as upon the member states and upon the institutions of the Community.

If the European legal system is an autonomous Community legal system, it requires its enforcement within national legal systems.

The Enforcement of the Community Legal System within National Legal Systems

The enforcement of the Community legal system was successful in every respect (see also formation C I). It was achieved mainly through three mechanisms.

The Principle of the Primacy of Community Law

The ECJ deduced the primacy of Community law as follows (Case 6/64, *Costa* v. *ENEL* [1964] ECR 585):

> By contrast with ordinary international treaties, the EEC Treaty has created its own legal system which, on the entry into force of the Treaty, became an integral part of the legal systems of the member states and which their courts are bound to apply.

By creating a Community of unlimited duration, having its own institutions, its own personality, its own legal capacity and capacity of representation on the international plane and, more particularly, real powers stemming from a limitation of sovereignty or a transfer of powers from the states to the Community, the member states have limited their sovereign rights, albeit within limited fields, and have thus created a body of law which binds both their nationals and themselves.

The integration into the laws of each member state of provisions which derive from the Community, and more generally the terms and the spirit of the Treaty, make it impossible for the states, as a corollary, to accord precedence to a unilateral and subsequent measure over a legal system accepted by them on a basis of reciprocity. Such a measure cannot therefore be inconsistent with that legal system. The executive force of Community law cannot vary from one state to another in deference to subsequent domestic laws, without jeopardizing the attainment of the objectives of the Treaty set out in Article 5 (2) and giving rise to the discrimination prohibited by Article 7.

In the case of conflict between Community law and national law, the primacy of Community law does not lead to the invalidity of national law, but involves a primacy to execution of Community law. The disregarded national law remains valid and can be applied in national cases or cases concerning non–member states (Richter, Schuppert and Bumke 2000: 20 f.)

The Principle of Direct Effect of Community Law

In the landmark ruling of *Van Gend and Loos* (Case 26/62, 1963), the ECJ established the principle that Article 12 of the EC Treaty (now Article 25) confers rights and obligations on individuals, although the wording of the Article refers only to member states. National courts are bound to recognize and enforce these rights and obligations:

> The wording of Article 12 contains a clear and unconditional prohibition which is not a positive but a negative obligation. This obligation, moreover, is not qualified by any reservation on the part of states which would make its implementation conditional upon a positive legislative measure enacted under national law. The very nature of this prohibition makes it ideally adapted to produce direct effects in the legal relationship between member states and their subjects. The implementation of Article 12 does not require any legislative intervention on the part of the states. The fact that under this Article it is the member states who are made the subject of the negative obligation does not imply that their nationals cannot benefit from this obligation. In addition the argument based on Articles 169 and 170 of the Treaty put forward by the three governments which have submitted observations to the Court in their statements of case is misconceived. The fact that these Articles of the Treaty enable the Commission and the member states to bring before the Court a state which has not fulfilled its obligations does not mean that individuals cannot plead these obligations, should the occasion arise, before a national court, any more than the fact that the Treaty places at the disposal of the Commission ways of ensuring that obligations imposed upon those subject to the Treaty are observed, precludes

the possibility, in actions between individuals before a national court, of pleading infringements of these obligations.

The Principle of an Interpretation Agreeing with Community Law

National law that is contrary to Community law may not be applied. This leads to the obligation on the judicial institutions of the member states to make national law conform to Community law, so that discrepancies will not occur. The ECJ described the process of interpreting Community law as follows: (Case 106/89, *Marleasing SA* v. *La Comercial Alimentación SA* [1990], ECR I — 4153):

> In order to reply to that question, it should be observed that, as the Court pointed out in its judgement in Case 14/83 *Von Colson and Kamann* v. *Land Nordrhein-Westfalen* [1984] ECR 1891, paragraph 26, the member states' obligation arising from a Directive to achieve the result envisaged by the Directive and their duty under Article 5 of the Treaty to take all appropriate measures, whether general or particular, to ensure the fulfilment of that obligation, is binding on all the authorities of member states including, for matters within their jurisdiction, the Courts. It follows that, in applying national law, whether the provisions in question were adopted before or after the Directive, the national court called upon to interpret it is required to do so, as far as possible, in the light of the wording and the purpose of the Directive in order to achieve the result pursued by the latter and thereby comply with the third paragraph of Article 189 of the Treaty.

Europeanization as a Process

Europeanization as a Problem of Method and Concept

Discussions about Europe are embroiled in complex and difficult questions about its basic character. These questions include: Is the EU already a federal state? Is there a European democratic deficit? Does a European society exist? Is there a European public sphere? Does a European identity exist? Closed questions of this type should be avoided, if one does not want to be caught up in a categorical trap of 'either–or', 'state or non-state', 'existing or non-existing'. European integration and the emerging European polity are activities in process, part of an evolution from an organized economic community into a political union with common values.

The process of Europe becoming a state can be comprehended only as an evolutionary transnational process that extends beyond interstate relations. The traditional contrast between a confederation of states and a federal state or the idea of national constitutional law are not relevant in this context. This process follows its own development and has its own momentum, creating a structure of constitution, law, and organization that corresponds to the particular stage of integration.

More relevant to understanding and classifying the integration process and making it comprehensible is the concept of *scaling* (Schuppert 1994: 53 f). It seems more sensible to discard arguments of 'does it exist or not' in favour of an analysis of the 'Europeanization' of states against the background of the increasing integration of Europe. This process involves the Europeanization of national societies, politics and legal systems and takes the form of interlocking in a European multi-level system of governance rather than of contest between the EU and member states.

This notion of 'multi-level governance' permits us to distance ourselves from the question of whether the Federal Republic of Germany is sovereign. Whereas the dichotomic approach rapidly leads to a war of words on this issue (Jachtenfuchs 2002), an analysis of semi-sovereignty is more consistent with the nature of change in a transnational Europe (Biersteker and Weber 1996; Dyson 2002*a*; Krasner 1999). Change is evident on three dimensions (Jachtenfuchs 2002):

- Multi-level systems of governance increasingly shape domestic policies and politics of states. EU regulation becomes more detailed and improves in quality. Its application often requires a transformation of historically conditioned domestic regulatory systems. Supranational elements (majority decisions, delegation to independent bodies) increase.
- The number of affected policy sectors grows. Sectors that are in no way affected by international or European regulations might soon be considered an exotic species.
- The quality and significance of the affected sectors change. Above all, this appears in a long-term view. Prime symbols of collective identity, such as nationality, military, diplomacy, police, and money are included to a substantial extent not only in European but also in international regulatory systems.

Different Depths of Europeanization of National Legal Systems

One cannot assume that the depth of Europeanization is equal everywhere. The Europeanization of national legal systems has to make distinctions in terms of levels between different fields of law—environmental law, law relating to food and drugs, telecommunications law, etc. The level of Europeanization reflects the level at which competences are located (see also Schmidt 1999). Hence one can arrange the particular level of Europeanization on a scale (see Lindberg and Scheingold 1990; Schmitter 1996):

- All policy decisions by national processes
- Only the beginnings of Community decision processes
- Policy decisions in both, but with national processes predominating

- Policy decisions in both, but with Community activity predominating
- All policy decisions by joint Community processes.

A corresponding scale of different fields of law could be developed, perhaps with criminal law at one end of the scale (the national one) and law relating to food and drugs at the other end (the Community one). Though not attempting this exercise, this chapter seeks to select cases from different fields and different perspectives to get an impression of the manner and extent to which the German legal system has been 'Europeanized'.

Six Cases Illustrating the Level of Europeanization of the German Legal System

The cases that are considered in this section are not selected from every field of law to assess their particular levels of Europeanization, as this procedure would be too time-consuming and not necessarily meaningful. Instead, the chapter selects its cases in order to illustrate how the Europeanization of the German legal system actually operates, and what has been 'Europeanized'.

Europeanization of Enforcement: The Principle of Efficacy of Community Law

As a general rule, Community law has to be executed by the member states, their so-called 'execution-autonomy'. In consequence, it has to be accepted that Community law is executed in different ways, because the legal systems of member states differ. But a problem arises when a certain definition of the national law would impair the importance and efficacy of Community law. In its legal rulings, the ECJ interpreted this so–called 'commandment of effectiveness' as a limit on the autonomy of execution of the member states. In this way the ECJ clarified the position with respect to enforcement. Two examples should suffice:

- The most important example is the recovery of illegally paid state aid. Two central regulations of German procedural administrative law (§§ 48, 49a *Verwaltungsverfahrensgesetz*) were totally penetrated by Community law (Schoch 1997). These regulations provided a wide protection for the recipient, precluding a recovery of illegally paid state aid. The ECJ stated that they were in contradiction to the European interest in enforcement. Furthermore, the ECJ ruled that the relevant national law could not be executed or must be executed in a modified form (ECJ Slg. I 1997: 1591).
- The second example concerns state liability law. According to German law, there is no state liability for so-called 'legislative injustice'. In the event of an omitted, belated, or defective transposition of a Directive by

Germany, there would have been no liability, resulting in benefit for German citizens. The ECJ developed a European right for liability, which supersedes national law. It ruled that individuals are entitled to financial compensation if they are adversely affected by the failure of a member state to transpose a Directive within the prescribed period. It justified this position as follows (Case 9/90 *Francovich and Bonifaci* v. *Italy* [1991], ECR–I 5357):

33 The full effectiveness of Community rules would be impaired and the protection of the rights which they grant would be weakened if individuals were unable to obtain redress when their rights are infringed by a breach of Community law for which a member state can be held responsible.

34 The possibility of obtaining redress from the member state is particularly indispensable where, as in this case, the full effectiveness of Community rules is subject to prior action on the part of the state and where, consequently, in the absence of such action, individuals cannot enforce before the national courts the rights conferred upon them by Community law.

Europeanization of Legislation: Transposing Community Law

In a study of legislation in the 13th Bundestag (1994–8), Brandner (2002) investigated to what extent it involved the transposition of Community law. In the case of legislation during the ninth Bundestag (1980–3), eight laws had been identified as transposing Community law (Schulze-Fielitz 1998). This corresponded to 9.41 per cent (a total number of eighty-five laws were passed in this period). During the 13th period, sixty-seven laws transposed Community law. They served to incorporate Directives into national law, or they contained regulations for the execution of directly applicable Community regulations. This amounted to 20.12 per cent, twice as much as during the earlier period, and reflected an increasing 'Europeanization' of national legislation.

Europeanization of Constitutional Law

The process of Europeanization also extends into constitutional law (see Scheuing 2000). But this process is not part of the process of European constitution-making (Schwarze 2000). Nor is it about a Community constitutional law (Häberle 1995) or about 'multi-level constitutionalism' (Pernice 1999). It involves the modifications of German constitutional law caused by Community law and interaction between the two levels. These modifications and interactions are so far-reaching that one could call this a case study of eroding sovereignty: a transformation of the classic concept of sovereignty through European law (see Schwarze 2000: 140 ff). Hartmut Bauer (2000) has identified the following examples of effects on German constitutional law:

- Modification of the binding effect of the basic rights on the executive, legislature and judiciary when transposing and executing Community law. This effect is enshrined in the German constitution (*Grundgesetz*, GG) in Article 1 (3).
- Community law as a component of the constitutional order referred to in Article 2 (1) GG and therefore as a constraint on personal freedom.
- Strengthening of the constitutional provision on equality before the law in Article 3 (1) by the European prohibition on discrimination.
- Application of those basic rights that are specified in the constitution (Article 8, Article 9 (1), Article 11, Article 12 (1)) as applying to 'all Germans' to EU nationals consistent with the European prohibition on discrimination.
- Abolition of the exclusion of women from armed service (Article 12a (4), 3rd sentence) because of the European precept of equal treatment,
- Loss of the importance of national citizenship (Article 16 GG) in favour of a new Community membership (Article 17 ff. [ex-Article 8 ff.], above all Article 20 [ex-Article 8c] EC Treaty).
- European influence on the application of basic rights to foreign artificial persons (Article 19 (3)) and on the guarantee of recourse by them to the courts in case of violation of constitutional rights (Article 19 (4)).
- Change of the German democratic model of legitimacy as a consequence of increasing Europeanization.
- Erosion of German constitutional principles as there is, for example, the principle of protection of legitimate expectation because of the different preferences of European law.
- Transfer of the German constitutional provision on political parties (Article 21) to the EU level in Article 191 of the Treaty, facilitating their EU-wide activities, with effects on the notion of political party.
- Impact of EU provisions on the freedom of movement for workers (Article 139 (1) [ex-Article 48 (1)] of the Treaty) on the law governing the public service (Article 33).
- Community amendment of the German law on state liability for violation of official duty under Article 34.
- Major Community law effects on the division of legislative powers between the federation and the Länder under Articles 70–74a.

In the light of these examples, Bauer (2000: 758) draws the following conclusion:

> In combination with the preceding report, these cases seem to establish clearly that German constitutional law is not exposed across the board to European influence, but that Community effects are still wide-ranging. The contents of the constitution are at least partially influenced by the Community legal system. Modification, interaction and change of meaning through Community law have to be taken into account in almost every provision of the German constitution.

Europeanization of General and Specific Administrative Law

General Administrative Law   All academic observers agree that German administrative law is undergoing a profound process of Europeanization. Accordingly, Friedrich Schoch's (1998) identification of a 'structural depths effect of the process of Europeanization' seems justified. This structural effect makes itself felt in every element of the system of administrative law being influenced by the process. The effects cover:

- The organization of administration (Kahl 1996)
- The doctrine of the legal sources as well as the forms of action of the administration (von Danwitz 1993)
- The concept of subjective public rights (Ruffert 1998)
- The legal responsibilities of the administration (Schmidt-Aβmann 1993)
- Administrative procedure (Classen 1998)
- The protection of legitimate expectation in the field of administrative law (Kokott 1993)
- Preliminary legal protection (Schoch 1997)
- So-called 'secondary legal protection' through the law on state liability (Bröhmer 1997).

Rather than tracing the whole process of Europeanization of general administrative law, this section focuses on specific examples drawn from the case of enforcement.

Specific Administrative Law: The Case of Law Relating to Food and Drugs
Europeanization involves cases in which Community law has had profound effects in changing German administrative law. But there are also fields of administrative law that are so totally Europeanized that national law almost loses any importance. National law has lost nearly all of its importance in the field of law relating to food and drugs (Dannecker 2002). This field was standardized by the European basic regulation about food and drugs in 2001 (Abl. EG C 096: 247 ff.) It established general principles and requirements of law relating to food and drugs, provided for a European authority for food and drugs, and put in place procedures for food and drugs safety. Not only did it regulate the field of food and drug law extensively; it also developed—seen from the point of view of German law—a new concept of responsibility. This concept included every stage of production—from farm to table. It also attempted to define and balance the responsibilities of those who manufacture food and drugs, of consumers and of public authorities.

Thus EU-wide regulation of food and drugs deals with more than just the technical aspects of national law. It also imports new concepts of regulation and of supervision. In this sense it has more fundamental implications for German legal culture.

Europeanization of Legal and Administrative Culture: Public Administration and the Mobilization of the Citizen by Community Law

The European Directive that deals with restricted access to information about the environment has been transposed into the German information law on the environment. Consequent on the duties of information that are spelled out in the directive, the interested citizen can obtain widespread access to all relevant environmental data. Moreover, the data is not pre-sorted or edited (Masing 1996). The aim of this transparency is an open discussion about the environment and public participation in the process of decision-making. In particular, the target is better co-operation with environmental groups, non-governmental organizations and other parties involved. This open access to environmental data should strengthen the participation of citizens in procedures for controlling and preventing pollution. It should encourage widespread Community action to protect the environment.

The sectoral changes (Erichsen 1992) to the German legal and administrative system consequent on this EU Directive have been outlined by Schmidt– Aβmann (1993: 525):

> In the large field of administrative environmental law, the Directive not only changes the traditional role allocation between secrecy and access to files. . . . Rather it deals with a changing understanding of the function of the public, which reacts to the position of the state administration. The general public here is no longer defined as an addressee of information by the executive or—from a fundamental point of view—as the concerned public. Rather, the Directive attempts to include the public in a process of communication that is designed to enhance legitimization and control.

Through this use of information as an instrument, the relationship between administration and citizen that underlies German administrative law is being fundamentally changed. This relationship was traditionally supported and understood in terms of the doctrine of public subjective law, which states that the individual citizen can only make use of legal remedy, if he/she can show that their public subjective legal status has been violated. The principle of individual legal remedy thereby excluded so-called popular action. As Masing (1996) claims, the Directive involves a European mobilization of the citizen for the general public interest of environmental protection. So the citizen becomes a holder of competence (*status procuratoris*). Masing (1996: 43) summarizes the aims of the Directive as follows:

> The form and functioning of the law on the environment shall not be determined by the nostrums of the national administrative authority. It shall be made public with the

participation of alert citizens. The responsibility is not left just with the national apparatus of execution, but citizens themselves shall be mobilised as advocates of the environment. They, too, shall look after their environment. The citizen and the administration work together because of public data about the environment: not only the administration guards, but also the citizen. Not only the public sector deliberates and takes the initiative, but also private associations.

Europeanization of Governance: Policy-Making without Legislating?

Europeanization of the German legal system is not only illustrated by effects on, and interaction with, national law, whether statutory or constitutional, by the transfer of whole fields of law from the national level into the regime of Community law, and by a change of national legal culture and administrative culture consequent on the import of new concepts of regulation and supervision. It also means that new tendencies towards the co-operative creation of law that already exist in the national legal system are strengthened. This development will be illustrated by examples of new forms of governance at the European level.

Adrienne Héritier (2002) outlines the hypothesis that the European level is increasingly characterized by innovative forms of governance. European governance is not just associated with classic legal regulation by law and decree but also with target agreements, timetables, monitoring, and recommendations and a new vocabulary of 'naming and shaming', benchmarking and the like. Héritier sums up these new trends as follows:

> There has been an increase in the political salience of the new modes of governance (CEC White Paper), in particular, of target definitions and the publications of performance, on the one hand, and of voluntary accords with and by private actors, on the other. These new modes of governance are guided by the principles of voluntarism (non-binding targets and the use of soft law), subsidiarity (measures are decided by member states) and inclusion (the actors concerned participate in governance). The mechanisms of governance are diffusion and learning, persuasion, standardization of knowledge about policies, repetition (iterative processes of monitoring and target readjustment are employed) and time management (setting of time-tables).

Classic law is not being phased out, but is changing in function, acting more and more as threat, its role being to enforce or facilitate consensual solutions:

> These modes are thought to have specific advantages. They evade the lengthy, unwieldy, and cumbersome process of legislative decision-making. At the same time, the threat of legislation is used to increase the willingness of actors to act voluntarily. Since these new forms of governance avoid regulatory requirements, it is expected that they will meet with less political resistance from the decision-makers and the implementing actors alike. After all, the latter would have to carry the costs of regulation. At the substantive level the advantages are seen in the greater

flexibility of the policy measures and the greater adaptability of those measures to a rapidly changing social, economic, and technological environment.

In short, Héritier argues that the avoidance of norms is a governance strategy in the expanding field of EU politics. This view is confirmed by the White Paper of the European Commission on European governance, which speaks of a new form of co-regulation (European Commission 2001*a*). One can hypothesize that these developments will encourage tendencies to a co-operative creation of law and a co-operative avoidance of norms (Schuppert 2000*a*). Furthermore, they will exploit the potential of self-supervision by non-national actors (Schuppert 2001). Europeanization involves co-evolution at EU and German levels with parallel techniques of control.

This process of mutual adjustment in the development of co-operative legislation is flourishing in Germany (Schuppert 2002*b*). While it is continually exposed to criticism (Huber 2002), its momentum is visible in the increasing use of voluntary accords as governance strategies. For Héritier (2002: 12):

> Voluntary accords to achieve specific targets may also be the first to initiate European policy-making in an area previously entirely reserved to member states. They have a 'bridging or transition function' (DeClercq *et al.* 2001: 18) and constitute a stage preliminary to legislation.

The individual instruments and decision-making components of this mode of governance are summarized in Table 6.1.

Héritier (2002) gives some examples of these new modes of governance from environmental law:

- The new Sixth Environmental Action Programme, which the Commission agreed at the end of January 2001, emphasizes the need for co-operation between industry, green groups, and national authorities when tackling major environmental problems. Wherever possible,

Table 6.1.   Target development and implementation by voluntary accords.

Instruments:

- Target development plus timetables
- Definition of contributions to reaching the target
- Monitoring mechanisms
- Sanctions in case of non-compliance

Actor involvement and participatory structure:

- Targets and contributions set solely by private actors (self-regulation)
- Targets and contributions set jointly by private and public actors (co-regulation)

voluntary agreements among various stakeholders are to be used rather
than binding rules (*European Voice* 11–17 January 2001: 6).

- Under the energy efficiency programme, new voluntary agreements
between the Commission and a number of industries are to boost
energy efficiency and to support the EU climate-change strategy.
Voluntary agreements with big industrial consumers such as the chemical, steel, pulp and paper, cement, and textile industries, are seen as
making it possible to tailor mandatory energy efficiency to the needs of
the specific industry (*Agence Europe* May 2000 III: 58).

- Minimum energy efficiency standards are also to be used more
effectively by linking them to labelling schemes for certain products
(household appliances, commercial and other end-use equipment).

- Another new voluntary accord is being prepared between the automobile
and oil industries to reduce vehicle emissions. The first automobile-oil
initiative was negotiated and set up at the beginning of the 1990s.

- Under the road-safety programme, the Commission announced measures to make cars safer for pedestrians; then the automobile industry
announced that it was beginning work on a voluntary agreement. A deal
was negotiated with the Commission to ensure the manufacture of safer
vehicles with softer bumpers and low-impact metals. If this attempt at
co-regulation fails—with policy-makers setting informal targets and
leaving it to industry to meet them—industry may be threatened with
binding rules (*European Voice* 14–20 June 2001). The Belgian
Presidency was very critical of the voluntary code (a system testing the
impact of a car in collision with a pedestrian) and called for binding
rules in the form of a directive (*European Voice* 28 June–4 July 2001).

- The proposal for the End-of-Life Vehicles Directive in 1999 included
using voluntary agreements as an instrument of implementation in
member states.

Provisional Appraisal

Europeanization is a process of mutual penetration in a system of multi-level
governance (Figure 6.1).

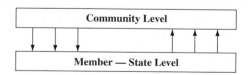

Figure 6.1. The Europeanization process.

Daniel Thürer (1991) describes the consequences:

> I believe that the European striving for unification reached a certain level. At this level, it is no longer possible to comprehend the constitutional law and the superior law on its own. Furthermore, it is not possible to understand these fields of law as stable and self-sufficient systems. Above all, this applies to Community law. It intervenes in the legal systems of the member states in a remarkably comprehensive, deep and intense way and pervades them. To varying degrees, it has resulted in a multifarious interaction of all member states and Community organs.

Accordingly, it is important not only to examine Europeanization in a hierarchical or 'top-down' manner (as we have done till now), but also to analyse how the German legal system affects the Community legal system, and what kind of marks it leaves on that system. The next section attempts such an analysis.

The Interaction between Community and German Constitutional Law: The 'Uploading' Dimension

The rest of this chapter focuses on the interaction between Community and German constitutional law. Its investigation is particularly difficult (cf. Heintzen, 1997; Schwarze 2000). The following examples illustrate the uploading of German constitutional law to the European level.

The 'Uploading' of the German Doctrine of Basic Rights: The Liselotte Hauer *Case*

The *Liselotte Hauer* Case (Case 44/79 *Liselotte Hauer* v. *Land Rheinland-Pfalz* [1979], ECR–I 3727) was about the prohibition on planting new grapevines and was based on a regulation of the European Council (No. 1162/76, 'Council Regulation on measures designed to adjust wine-growing potential to market requirements'). This case looked at interference in both the basic right of ownership and the right of freedom of occupation from restrictions both on the use of land and on being a vine-grower. The ECJ had to decide if basic rights—especially the right of ownership—that were also protected within the Community were violated. Owing to a referral from the German administrative court the ECJ examined the case in a preliminary ruling.

In so doing, the ECJ distilled basic rules from the constitutional traditions common to the member states as Community legal norms, otherwise known as general principles of law. The Court used an ascending or 'bottom-up' procedure, whose value it described as follows:

> Basic rights form an integral part of the general principles of the law, the observance of which is ensured by the Court. In safeguarding those rights, the latter is bound to draw inspiration from constitutional traditions common to the member states, so that measures which are incompatible with the basic rights recognized by the con-

stitutions of those states are unacceptable in the Community. International treaties for the protection of human rights on which the member states have collaborated or of which they are signatories, can also supply guidelines which should be followed within the framework of Community law.

The Court not only examined the arrangements for the protection of property in the constitutions of Germany, Italy, and Ireland, but also chose a procedure for the examination of basic rights in question. This procedure bears striking similarity to the procedure common to German constitutional law. It follows three steps (Richter, Schuppert and Bumke 2000) which are derived from Article 14 of the German constitution, dealing with property:

- the law that is restricting the right of ownership has to serve the common good;
- it has to stay within the scope of the proportionality rule;
- it may not violate the *Wesensgehalt*, the essence of the basic right.

The ECJ agreed with a ruling of the German Federal Constitutional Court as follows:

> Taking into account the constitutional precepts common to the member states, consistent legislative practices and Article 1 of the First Protocol to the European Convention for the Protection of Human Rights, the fact that an act of an institution of the Community imposes restrictions on the new planting of vines cannot be challenged in principle as being incompatible with due observance of the right to property. However, it is necessary that those restrictions should in fact correspond to objectives of general interest pursued by the Community and that, with regard to the aim pursued, they should not constitute a disproportionate and intolerable interference with the rights of the owner, such as to impinge upon the very substance of the right to property.

In other words, this ruling demonstrated a successful 'uploading' of the German doctrine of basic rights into the legal space of the Community.

The 'Uploading' of the German Principles of Protection of Confidence and Proportionality

The principles of protection of confidence and proportionality are pillars of German constitutional thinking. They have been incorporated into the ECJ's jurisprudence (Schwarze 1997). In so doing, they influenced other national legal systems that were not centred around these principles. Schwarze (1997: 423) describes this procedure as follows:

> The formative power of general European principles of administrative law that were developed by jurisprudence can be seen in the principle of protection of confidence. For a long time, this principle has been accepted as a general principle of law by the jurisprudence of the ECJ. It is connected closely with the principle of legal certainty

and became important in Court practice at the Community level, namely in the context of revocation and retraction of administrative acts. . . . Furthermore, it plays an important part in the legal judgement of normative acts, especially in the question of whether and to what extent the passing of a retrospective norm is permitted.

Originally, other member states of the Community did not recognise the principle of protection of confidence. For example, British law did not accept such a principle for a long time. The French legal system traditionally acts in a reserved manner towards restricting administrative authorities. Under the influence of Community law both legal systems changed; but the changes are better established in Britain than in France.

The process of interaction between European and national constitutional law can be understood as a circular flow model (Figure 6.2).

Conclusion: The 'Post-National' as a Copernican Turn

The argument of this chapter can be situated in the context of Ulrich Haltern's notion of the post-national as a Copernican turn (2003: 3–4):

> Community law places demands on and brings innovation to national legal thinking. On the one hand, it challenges traditional concepts. The Union needs conceptualisation in terms that are different from old national notions. On the other hand, Community law adds to the national legal system a European dimension that is valid for constitutional law as well as for other areas (administrative law, family law, procedural law, etc.). In this respect, fundamental changes are taking place: The importance of this cannot be overestimated (for example in the structure of competence of parliament and government, the procedural law of public administration as well as of courts and in state liability). One cannot speak about two opposing legal systems, but only about a complicated symbiosis that changes both European law and national law in its essence and substance.

This implies that the understanding of German and other national legal systems requires a broader multi-level model of comparative law (Wahl 2000). Haltern (2003) argues that two processes are simultaneously at work, in essence 'top-down' and 'bottom-up', though he prefers the notions of 'reaching-in' and 'reaching-out'. 'Reaching-in' points to the way in which Community law influences, is superimposed on and transforms German law; 'reaching-out' draws

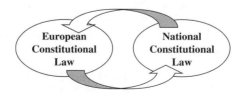

Figure 6.2.   Circular flow model of interaction between European and national constitutional law.

attention to the way in which German law opens to the outside. The German constitution opted for an international openness (e.g. Article 23 on the EU), even if not always happily (Haltern 2003: 4).

This view supports the value of a post-national theory of the German constitution. The concluding statement is best left to Haltern (2003: 4–5):

> The Copernican turn has to be welcomed, at least to a large extent. Observations about a superimposed European constitution, the conceptualisation of European integration as a bond of constitutions, the talk about co-operation, complementarity, transnationalising and supranationality are accurate. The challenges to the state in its competence, form, autonomy and authority resulted in changes of its material condition of acting. Why should one not conceptualise this into post-national notions as integrated statehood (Kaufmann 1999), a European process of de-nationalization (Hofmann 1999), a co–operative constitutional state (Häberle 1978), or relative nationalization (Pernice 2001) and regard international relations as on its way to constitutionalism?

Part III
Europeanization of German Politics

7

The Party System: Structure, Policy, and Europeanization

OSKAR NIEDERMAYER

Introduction

SINCE THE 1980S, THE GERMAN PARTY SYSTEM has changed. The relatively stable
'two-and-a-half party system' (Crotty 1985) of the 1960s and 1970s has become
a fluid five-party system (Niedermayer 2002a). This development can be linked
to three groups of causal factors: the demand and supply sides of party competition and the institutional framework. The demand side of party competition is
influenced by the cleavage structure of the society, the supply side is shaped by
the political behaviour of the party élites. Concerning the institutional framework,
to which party competition is subject, previous analyses have concentrated exclusively on the national political system, emphasizing the electoral law as well as
the rules concerning the ban on parties and their financing. As a member state of
the EU, however, Germany is embedded in a supranational political system. The
European integration process is part of the institutional framework of the national
political process, and the possible domestic responses to the supranational
institutional framework cannot, therefore, be neglected.

Although political parties are core institutions of the political systems of all
European states, up to now there has only been minor academic interest in study-
ing their domestic response to European integration. The international literature
on Europeanization of formal organizations focuses on governmental–
administrative institutions, national parliaments, the judiciary and interest associations (Hix and Goetz 2000a); comparative analyses of the impact on party systems
have only recently become a topic (Mair 2000). The first German study of the
Europeanization of the national political system (Sturm and Pehle 2001a, 2001b)
neglects the party system, and the German party literature deals almost exclusively with the responses of the national parties at the European level, i.e. the
establishment of party groups in the European Parliament and the development of
transnational party federations (Damm 1999; Dietz 1997; Jansen 1996; Jasmut
1995; Kuper 1995; Lesse 2000; Neßler 1997; Niedermayer 2002b; Pöhle 2000;
Tsatsos and Deinzer 1998; Weidenfeld and Wessels, several volumes). In this

Proceedings of the British Academy, **119**, 129–146. © The British Academy 2003.

chapter, we will try to close this research gap by answering the question of whether a Europeanization of the German party system has occurred, i.e. whether its development has been influenced by the European integration process.

Party System Properties

To analyse systematically the possible impact of the European integration process on the German party system, one has first to discuss the general characteristics of party systems. A party system is defined as a 'set of political parties operating within a nation in an organized pattern, described by a number of party-system properties' (Lane and Ersson 1994: 175). There is no consensus in the literature, however, as to which properties have to be included in the analysis (Niedermayer 1996). Following a comprehensive approach, one can develop a typology which structures the variety of system properties according to (1) the two dimensions that are usually distinguished in the analysis of political parties, i.e. the structural and the policy dimensions, and (2) the two central levels of party competition, i.e. the electoral and the parliamentary levels (see Figure 7.1).

The obvious choice to describe the structure of a party system is the number of parties. This property, here called format, has dominated the analysis of party systems for a long time. More recently, however, the property mostly used to describe the structure of party systems is their fragmentation, which takes into account not only the number, but also the relative strength of the parties, measured by their electoral success. To operationalize this property, several indices have been developed. Only two of them, however, are widely used: the fractionalization of vote shares (Rae 1967), and its linear transformation, the effective number of parties (Laakso and Taagepera 1979), which will be used here because of its greater vividness. The effective number of parties corresponds with the real number when all parties receive the same percentage of votes. The more unequal the distribution of the vote,

Level of party competition	Dimension of analysis	
	Structure	Policy
Electoral level	Format Fragmentation Asymmetry Volatility	Polarization Legitimacy
Parliamentary level	Format Fragmentation Asymmetry Volatility	Polarization Legitimacy Segmentation Coalition stability

Figure 7.1.   Party-system properties.

the smaller is the effective compared to the real number, and in party systems clearly dominated by one party, the index approaches the value 1.

Indices of fragmentation take into account all parties of a party system. For party systems that are dominated by two big parties, in particular, it is, however, appropriate to look at the relative size of these parties. When party democracy is seen as a system of changing party governments, the equality of chances to gain power is very important and the degree of inequality in this respect is indicated by the asymmetry of a party system, measured by the difference in the percentages of votes of the two biggest parties.

The previous properties show the state of a party system at a specific point in time and information about developments can be gained only by comparing two points of time. If one follows Pedersen's claim (1980: 388), however, that 'the student of party system change ought to use measuring tools that tap the phenomenon of change rather than the states of systems resulting from change', one has to look for indicators measuring the effects of electoral instability on the party system. The most frequently used indicator of this kind — which will also be used here — is the volatility of a party system, defined as 'net electoral change between two consecutive elections' (Bartolini and Mair 1990: 19) and measured by the cumulated gains in votes of the successful parties.

The structural properties of a party system are usually measured at the electoral level, i.e. the parties taking part in national parliamentary elections are counted and the size of the parties is operationalized by the proportion of votes. However, all structural properties can be measured at the parliamentary level, too, by taking into account only those parties represented in the national parliament and measuring their size by the proportion of parliamentary seats. In the following, we will refer to both levels.

At least since the work of Sartori (1966, 1976), who used the ideological distances of the relevant parties as an important criterion for his party system typology, party systems have been characterized not only by structural properties but also by a policy property: their polarization. An analysis of this property has to distinguish between its dimensionality and its strength. On the one hand, one has to ask what are the central policy dimensions characterizing the party system; on the other, one has to determine how homogeneous or heterogeneous it is on these dimensions, i.e. how far away the parties are from each other in their policy positions. In most cases, the theoretical starting point for an analysis of the dimensionality of the polarization is the cleavage theory of Lipset and Rokkan (1967). According to this theory, the political parties of Western Europe represent coalitions between political élites and social groups that have emerged from enduring and organized social conflicts. The social upheavals of the nineteenth century formed the background of the development of European party systems. They came into being as a reflection of four central conflict lines, or cleavages: the conflict between the centre and the periphery as well as the cleavage between the church and the state reflected conflicts arising from the nation-building processes, the urban–rural cleavage and the employers–workers cleavage reflected conflicts consequent on the industrial revolution. The class conflict between employers and workers was of particular importance, because this cleavage structured most party systems of Western Europe and 'laid the foundation for the traditional political distinction between "left" and "right"' (Elff 2000: 70).

It is often argued that it is an 'extreme simplification of reality' (Falter and Schumann 1992: 203) to cram parties into the left–right schema, because party systems are in almost all cases characterized by various relevant conflict lines and the party distances on these cleavages could be different (Stokes 1963). Nevertheless, most experts see this dimension as the only or at least the most important dimension (Huber and Inglehart 1995). This can be substantiated even if one takes into account a decreasing relevance of the traditional class conflict, because the left–right schema is a 'generalized political symbolic structure for the perception, interpretation and evaluation of central political conflicts' (Bauer-Kaase 2001: 235; see also Fuchs and Klingemann 1989), which can change its concrete meaning in the course of time.

The individual parties can be placed on this—or on any other—dimension by examining the party literature or party documents (i.e. electoral programmes), by using expert judgements, or by referring to the orientations of the general population (Niedermayer 1996). The strength of the party system's polarization is then operationalized by the ideological distance between the two extreme parties or by measures including all parties. More and more, the index constructed by Taylor and Herman (1971) is used, which measures the polarization on the basis of the variance formula. In the following, we will also use this measure.

An analysis of the policy dimension would remain incomplete if it did not take into account the legitimacy of a party system, especially in Germany, where the topic of 'weariness' or 'vexation' with the party system (*Parteienverdrossenheit*) has been discussed for many years. Following Easton's (1965; 1975) reflections on political support, we operationalize party system legitimacy on the basis of the citizens' positive or negative evaluation of the totality of the parties constituting the respective system. In analogy to an instrument developed for the measurement of weariness with the political élite (Niedermayer 2001), we use party scales that measure the general orientations of the respondents towards the individual parties. To structure the orientations, we have constructed a typology which distinguishes four types of general orientations towards the party system: enthusiasm (all parties without exception are evaluated positively); goodwill (on average, the evaluation of the parties is positive); scepticism (on average, the evaluation of the parties is not positive, i.e. this category includes not only those with a negative, but also those with a neutral average evaluation); and weariness (none of the parties is evaluated positively).

Both polarization and legitimacy can be measured for the electoral and the parliamentary levels by including either all parties or only those represented in the national parliament. The last two-party system properties to be analysed here, however, refer only to the parliamentary level of party competition and deal with inter-party relationships based on their governmental role. 'Throughout the course of their historical development West European party systems have been closely involved with the exercise of governing power in a parliamentary framework' and it is, therefore, 'unrealistic not to add' this dimension (Smith 1989: 351). We distinguish two system properties here: the first, segmentation, deals with the possibilities of the formation of governments, the second, coalition stability, with their duration.

Since, over time, most West European governments have been coalitions, the possibilities and limits of coalition formation are crucial for system maintenance. Owing to their ideology, policy positions, and strategy, single political parties are more or less willing to co-operate with others, especially in the form of government coalitions. At the system level, the result is a more or less segmented party system. In party systems with an extreme segmentation, all parties clearly insulate themselves against each other, whereas in party systems without segmentation, all parties are in principle willing to build coalitions with one another. Once formed, the coalitions are more or less stable over time. To operationalize coalition stability, one has to decide which event should indicate the end of the life of a cabinet. The most obvious solution is to use any change in the party composition of the cabinet as the criterion, because it 'clearly offers the optimal combination of validity and simplicity' (Lijphart 1984: 278), and measure coalition stability by calculating the average cabinet duration in months. Another approach is to look for coalition breaks and define only those coalitions as unstable that break asunder during the legislative period. This approach will be used here, because we are interested in the European policy positions of the parties as a possible reason for coalition instability.

The individual party system properties mentioned above vary more or less over time. To characterize the amount and direction of these variations within the party system as a whole, one can differentiate between four distinctive kinds of party system change (Smith 1989: 353): temporary fluctuations (the normal ebbs and flows of party fortunes); restricted change (change of only one or a few properties); general change (several changes taking place at the same time); and transformation (altering of all properties, so that a completely new system comes into existence). An analysis of the domestic response to the European integration process at the level of the party system has to ask which party system properties are influenced by European integration and what kind of party system change results from these influences.

The inclusion of Germany into the systemic context of the EU can potentially influence all party system properties. The format of the party system can be influenced by a change in the number of parties taking part in the parliamentary elections at the federal level. This can occur either by the emergence of new parties linked directly to the issue of European integration or by splits of already existing parties owing to internal conflicts about European policy positions. If these parties have electoral success, the fragmentation of the party system will be changed. However, this system property can also be influenced without the emergence of new parties. This occurs when the pro- or anti-European positions of the existing parties in general, or their positions on specific European policies, become relevant for the decision-making process of the voters and influence the election results, thereby changing the relative size of the parties. In addition, there is the possibility that changes within the national electoral arena are indirectly influenced by European integration, because successes of certain parties at the European electoral level could help them to do well at the national level. If splits of existing parties or changes in the electoral behaviour of the voters caused by European policies affect the two biggest parties, the asymmetry of a party system is influenced, too. Finally, the total amount of changes of the parties' relative size is reflected in the volatility of the party system. When the change caused by the process of European integration exceeds a certain degree, both the electoral and the parliamentary levels of party competition will be influenced, thereby changing the structural party system properties at this level, too.

The emergence of a pro- versus anti-European dimension of the national party competition would have an impact not only on the structural party system properties, but also on the policy dimension. It would influence the polarization of the party system either by modifying the ideological distances separating the parties or by supplementing or even replacing the usual left–right dimension as the central dimension of national party competition. If one modifies the cleavage theory of Lipset and Rokkan (1967) by generalizing and 'de-historicizing' (Mielke 2001) the cleavages described there, one can fit the conflict between supporters and opponents of the European integration process in this approach. It is nothing else than a centre–periphery conflict under changed social circumstances. A replacement of the usual left–right conflict by the pro- versus anti-European cleavage would lead to a completely new clustering of the parties because those 'that emerge more generally as being strongly opposed to European integration . . . are, in the main, parties of the extreme right or of the extreme left' (Mair 2000: 34; see also Ray 1999; Taggart 1998).

If citizens conceive of the European policy sphere as very important and there is a great contrast between their European orientations and those of all party élites, the result can be a decline of the party system's legitimacy. If Europe is relevant and the dissent exists not between the parties and the citizens, but among the individual parties themselves, the segmentation of the party system is influenced. In this case, the inclusion of specific parties in considerations about possible coalitions or their exclusion from this process would depend on their pro- or anti-European position or on experiences of inter-party co-operation at the European level. Last but not least, the European integration process can also influence coalition stability, if conflicts between the coalition parties about European policy positions lead to coalition breaks.

Structural Change of the Party System?

In federal parliamentary elections, the voters in Germany have always been able to choose from several parties. Up to unification, twelve parties on average took part in the elections.[1] Afterwards, the number increased considerably and reached its preliminary peak in 1998 with thirty-two. The number of parties represented in parliament, however, varied since 1953 only between three and five (Table 7.1).[2]

Changes in the number of parties taking part in national elections in the form of new parties explicitly referring to the European integration process occurred in the period 1965–72 and in 1998. In 1965, Ernst Ruban—a merchant from Bremen—founded the *Europapartei* (*Europäische Föderalistische Partei*). This party was the German section of the *Föderalistische Internationale der Europäischen Föderalistischen Parteien* (FI), an organization of the European-wide federalist movement that tried to establish a European-wide confederation of national pro-European parties to promote the European integration process. This party took part in the 1965 national elections, but only in Bremen and without any success (Table 7.2). After organizing in other parts of Germany, too, it gained 0.2 per cent in the 1969 elections. However, this was not the beginning of an improvement (Stöss 1986). The party, which was renamed *Europäische Föderalistische Partei* (EFP) in 1971, suffered from severe internal conflicts, did not succeed in 1972, and has not contested any other national election since that time.

The EFP was a decidedly pro-European party. The two new parties of the 1990s, however, the *Bund Freier Bürger—Offensive für Deutschland* (BfB), founded in 1994 by Manfred Brunner, and the *Initiative Pro D-Mark—Neue Liberale Partei* (Pro-DM), founded 1998 by Bodo Hoffmann, were heavily critical of European integration. Their catalyst was the Maastricht Treaty and the introduction of a single European currency. The basic programme of the BfB in 1995 propagated a Europe of free peoples in the form of a confederation. The EU was blamed for having taken a fatal step with Maastricht, and the Germans were

---

[1] As it is usual for analyses at the party-system level, the Christian Democratic Union (CDU) and the Christian Social Union (CSU) are counted as one party, because they do not compete territorially and have a joint parliamentary group.

[2] The high number of parties in the first legislative period is due to the fact that the 5 per cent hurdle of the German electoral law referred in 1949 to the level of the individual Länder.

Table 7.1. Development of the structure of the German party system, 1949–98.

Year	Format[a]		Fragmentation[b]		Asymmetry[c]		Volatility[d]	
	Elect.	Parl.	Elect.	Parl.	Elect.	Parl.	Elect.	Parl.
1949	13	10	4.84	4.01	1.8	2.0		
1953	12	6	3.31	2.79	16.4	18.9	22.6	41.7
1957	12	4	2.76	2.39	18.4	20.3	9.5	15.5
1961	8	3	2.83	2.51	9.1	10.4	11.5	18.5
1965	10	3	2.56	2.38	8.3	8.7	7.7	7.1
1969	11	3	2.50	2.24	3.4	3.6	6.8	8.9
1972	7	3	2.39	2.34	−0.9	−1.0	6.0	6.9
1976	15	3	2.36	2.31	6.0	5.8	4.1	7.3
1980	11	3	2.54	2.44	1.6	1.6	4.6	7.0
1983	12	4	2.55	2.51	10.6	10.2	8.4	17.9
1987	15	4	2.87	2.80	7.3	7.4	6.0	10.9
1990	23	5	3.13	2.65	10.3	12.1	7.9	17.1
1994	21	5	3.15	2.91	5.1	6.3	7.7	18.8
1998	32	5	3.31	2.90	−5.8	−7.9	8.4	15.9

Notes:
[a] Number of parties that take part in the election/are represented in the Parliament.
[b] Effective number of parties (reciprocal value of the squared and summed up vote shares/
    parliamentary seats for each party).
[c] Difference of the percentages of votes/parliamentary seats of the CDU/CSU and SPD.
[d] Net electoral change between two consecutive elections, measured by the cumulated gains in
    votes of the successful parties.

Source: Own calculations on the basis of the official electoral statistics.

Table 7.2. Federal election results of EFP, BfB, and Pro DM, 1965–98 (per cent).

	1965	1969	1972	1994	1998
EFP	0.0	0.2	0.1	–	–
BfB	–	–	–	–	0.2
Pro DM	–	–	–	–	0.9

Source: Official electoral statistics.

called upon to defend the D-Mark and the independence of the Bundesbank. The
1998 programme of the Pro-DM claimed that an early commitment to the Euro
would not bring Europe together, but destroy it.

    With respect to their policy positions, their personnel and their networks, both
parties are right-wing. The BfB got 1.1 per cent of the vote in the 1994 European
Parliament elections. In 1999, however, vehement internal conflicts about the
opening to extreme right-wing parties led to the resignation of the party founder.
In the 1998 federal election, the party gained only 0.2 per cent of the vote, and at

the end of 2000 it dissolved. The Pro-DM took part in the 1998 federal election with a massive and very expensive advertising campaign in newspapers against the Euro. It gained 2.2 per cent in East Germany, but only 0.6 per cent in the West (Table 7.2). Since then, the party has not appeared at the federal level. It no longer pursues seriously the aim of the repeal of the Euro, which is expressed in the fact that the 'DM' as part of the party's name now means *'Deutsche Mitte'*.

Changes in the format of the party system can occur not only by the emergence of new parties linked directly to the issue of European integration but also by splits of already existing parties owing to internal conflicts about European policy positions. Up to now, there have been no such splits in Germany. It is true that there are regularly different European policy positions within the parties, and in some cases this dissent increased in the 1990s (Table 7.3).[3] But this has never led to the danger of a split. Thus, the sole effect of European integration on the format of the German party system was that three marginal parties temporarily appeared on the scene.

Owing to their electoral failure, these three new parties only marginally changed the fragmentation of the party system. This party system property could have been influenced in another way, however, if the pro- or anti-European positions of the existing parties had become relevant for the decision-making process of the voters, thereby influencing the federal election results. Until the mid-1990s, this was not the case, as various analyses of voting behaviour show.[4] The

Table 7.3. Extent of internal dissent over European integration,[a] 1984–96 (means).

	1984	1988	1992	1996
FDP	1.17	1.17	1.29	1.29
PDS	–	–	1.83	1.60
REP	–	–	1.71	1.71
CDU	1.17	1.00	1.57	1.86
CSU	1.57	1.57	2.00	2.43
GRÜNE	2.57	2.57	3.00	2.57
SPD	1.67	2.00	2.29	2.86

Note:

[a] 5-point-scale: 1 = complete unity, 5 = leadership position opposed by a majority of party activists.

Source: Ray (1999: 299).

[3] More critical views are taken by parts of the Social Democrats' (SPD) left, the national–liberal part of the Liberals (FDP) and elements of the CDU right (Lees 2002). These internal differences are not comparable, however, with the severe in intra-party conflicts in some of the parties of other EU member states (see Ray 1999).

[4] On the theoretical and empirical analysis of voting behaviour in Germany see, e.g., the overviews by Falter and Schoen (1999), Gabriel and Thaidigsmann (2000), Kaase (2000), and Schultze (2000);

irrelevance of Europe for the fragmentation of the German party system implied that the development of the other two structural characteristics, asymmetry and volatility (Table 7.1), was also not influenced.

In view of the much-evoked 'European tiredness' of the Germans since the 1980s, this irrelevance of Europe is not self-evident. Indeed, the Germans could 'thoroughly count as "EU-model pupils" till the mid-1980s' (Niedermayer 1994: 66). Afterwards, however, their EU support was mostly below the EU average. In the years after the signing of the Maastricht Treaty in 1992, their scepticism was primarily related to the monetary dimension, i.e. the introduction of a single currency. From 1992 to 1997, the opponents of a single currency were more numerous than the supporters in Germany, while the European average indicated majority approval (Figure 7.2).[5] In addition, in 1997, the relevance of the EU issue for German citizens increased for a short time (Figure 7.3). Until 1997, Europe was not present among the ten most-mentioned issues by citizens, when they were asked about the most important problems. In June 1997, however, when the Amsterdam Treaty was adopted by the heads of state and government and got high media coverage, Europe ranked second among the ten most-mentioned issues for a short period. One has to add, however, that there was an extremely wide margin between this and the most important issue, unemployment, which was mentioned six times more often than Europe. After a considerable decline in the second half of 1997, the European issue gained attention again at the beginning of 1998, and in May 1998, the month of the decision to enter the third stage of the Economic and Monetary Union, it ranked second again (Figure 7.3). But there was then an even wider margin between the European and the unemployment issue.

Thus, in the run-up to the 1998 federal elections, optimal conditions were in place for an impact of Europe on the structure of the German party system. The majority of citizens opposed the pro-European course of the traditional parties on an important topic, the issue was perceived as relevant, and the BfB and the Pro-DM offered the opportunity to express EU opposition. Nevertheless, the impact of Europe on the federal election result and, therefore, on the structure of the party system kept within narrow bounds. BfB and Pro-DM together gained 1.1 per cent of the vote (Table 7.2), and the loss of votes that could be ascribed to the

---

the introductory works by Bürklin and Klein (1998) and Roth (1998); anthologies dealing with the individual elections, such as Kaase and Klingemann (1990, 1998), Klingemann and Kaase (1994, 2001); the series of publications of the working group on electoral and opinion research of the German Association of Political Science: Falter *et al.* (1989), Gabriel and Falter (1996), Gabriel and Troitzsch (1993), Plasser *et al.* (1999), Rattinger, Gabriel and Jagodzinski (1994), Schmitt (1990), Van Deth, Rattinger and Roller (2000) and Brettschneider, Van Deth and Roller (2002); and the anthology by Klein *et al.* (2000).

[5] Figure 7.2 shows the net support, measured by the difference between supporters and opponents, in percentage points. Owing to different wordings of the question, the data up to the second half of 1992 and after the first half of 1993 are not fully comparable.

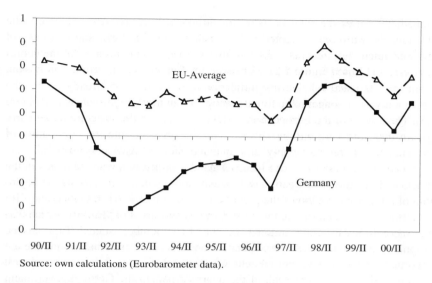

Source: own calculations (Eurobarometer data).

Figure 7.2. Attitudes to the single currency (index values).

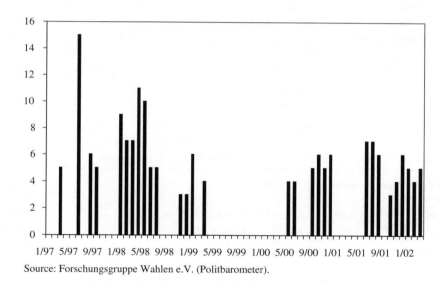

Source: Forschungsgruppe Wahlen e.V. (Politbarometer).

Figure 7.3. Relevance of the EU (percentages, two mentions possible).

pro-European policy of the Kohl government was 'below half a percentage point' (Pappi and Thurner 2000: 435).

The minor influence of Europe can be attributed to the considerable change of citizens' attitudes shortly before the election. A process of adaptation began immediately after the final decision to introduce the Euro. Already before the election, the Euro was accepted by the majority of Germans, and this has not changed since, despite a decrease in support in 1999–2000 because of the depreciation of the Euro (Figure 7.2). Moreover, the European issue immediately sank again into its usual relative insignificance for citizens, and already before the election it was no longer to be found among the ten most important issues (Figure 7.3). The impact of the European integration process on the structure of the party system therefore kept within narrow limits in 1998, despite the cumulation of influence factors on the 'supply' and 'demand' sides of party competition.

Since 1998, these influence factors have developed in a way that leads to the conclusion that the 1998 election was an exception rather than marking the beginning of a Europeanization of the party system. In spring 2001, less than one-fifth of Germans was interested in taking part in discussions about Europe, which was the second-lowest value among all the EU member states (Europäische Kommission 2001). Since 1999, either Europe has not been found among the ten important issues for German citizens or it has taken one of the lowest places. Even in early 2002, at the peak of the quarrel between the German government and the European Commission over the threat of an 'early warning' to Berlin because of the high budgetary deficit, the Germans did not perceive the issue as very relevant (Figure 7.3). In addition, since 1998 approval of the Euro has exceeded disapproval (Figure 7.2). After its introduction as legal tender, two-thirds of Germans have made their peace with the single currency (Table 7.4).

Thus, it does not seem as if in the near future Europe will play a greater role in the electoral behaviour of Germans than in the past. 'The issue of Europe simply does not influence electoral decisions' (Sturm 2002: 78). From the 'demand'

Table 7.4.   Support for the Euro after its introduction as legal tender (per cent).

I think the introduction of the Euro as the single European currency is:	
Good	69
Not good	27
No answer	4
Are you for or against the single European currency?	
For	61
Against	19
Don't care/no opinion	20
Had the introduction of the Euro been the right decision?	
Right	65
Wrong	31
No answer	3

Source: Forschungsgruppe Wahlen e.V. by order of ZDF, *Politbarometer* 1/2002; Institut für Demoskopie Allensbach by order of *Frankfurter Allgemeine Zeitung*, IfD-poll 7016; Emnid by order of n-tv, broadcasting, 1 February 2002.

side of party competition, almost nothing points to the pro- versus anti-European conflict line becoming a relevant cleavage dimension. This is mainly due to the fact that Europe is not perceived as a relevant issue by citizens.

Change of the Policy Dimension of the Party System?

From the 'supply' side of party competition, too, such a cleavage is not recognizable. All in all, in no other large member state has the élite consensus around the European project been so stable (Lees 2002). This does not mean, however, that there is no difference between the parties about their European positions (Table 7.5).

The most pro-European parties are the CDU and the FDP. For tactical reasons, the SPD assumed a sceptical position towards monetary union for a short time in the mid-1990s. Since then, however, it has taken decidedly pro-European positions again (Gloser 2001).[6] This did not prevent Chancellor Gerhard Schröder from strongly criticizing the European Commission when he claimed that Brussels did not sufficiently respect German interests. The European policy of the CSU, too, is determined by the defence of specific—Bavarian—interests and became more critical with respect to certain EU developments in the 1990s, whereas the Greens became more pro-European during this period. Of all parties represented in the Bundestag, the PDS remains the most critical. In the draft of the new basic programme, presented by its leader Gabi Zimmer, the PDS blames

Table 7.5. Position of party élite on European integration,[a] 1984–96 (means; index of polarization).

	1984	1988	1992	1996
CDU	6.86	6.86	7.00	6.86
FDP	6.71	6.71	6.71	6.71
SPD	6.29	6.29	6.14	5.71
CSU	6.50	6.29	5.43	5.43
GRÜNE	3.57	3.71	4.71	4.86
PDS	–	–	3.57	3.57
REP	–	–	1.29	1.29
PS-mean	6.39	6.35	6.17	5.88
EI-polarization	0.60	0.63	1.71	1.12
Percentage of max. EI-polarization	7	7	13	12

Note:

[a] 7-point-scale: 1 = strongly opposed to European integration, 7 = strongly in favour of European integration.

[6] In 1998, citizens perceived the SPD as the most pro-European party after the CDU (Pappi and Thurner 2000).

the European Union for being a 'powerful but unsocial and undemocratic reality' and propagates a new, socially and ecologically oriented integration concept which overcomes the democratic deficit and safeguards a lasting peace.

The strongest opponents of European integration in its current form are the three parties of the extreme right. The Republican Party (REP) flatly rejects the Maastricht Treaty, which, in their programme, is seen as a 'coup d'état' by the political élites. The German People's Union (DVU) objects to the 'dissolution' of Germany in a European Union. In the European programme of the National Democratic Party (NPD), it is argued that 'the treaties of Maastricht and Amsterdam are immoral and therefore null and void from the beginning'.

Despite these differences, the German party system is not strongly polarized on the pro- versus anti-European dimension, mainly because of the minor electoral weight of the Euro-sceptical or anti-European parties. Polarization has increased during the 1990s, but—with 12–13 per cent of the maximum value— it still remains low, and the party system as a whole is still clearly on the pro-European side, as the party system mean shows (Table 7.5).

There are several explanations for this low polarization on Europe. The parties that have shaped the Federal Republic of Germany since its foundation all take pro-European positions, reflecting the traditionally pro-European orientations of the post-war German political élite. Despite differences about specific European policies or the tempo and final shape of the European integration process, there has been a positive consent since the beginning of the 1960s. This consent was based on the expectation that the inclusion of Germany in the European integration process would enduringly advance Germany's main interests and aims. These aims included, in particular, the guarantee of peace and security in the context of the East–West conflict, economic recovery, the achievement of political and legal equality as well as the international capacity to act, the consolidation of the internal democratic order, and the re-establishment of German unity (Niedermayer 2002*b*). In the 1950s, the question of the compatibility of efforts to reunify Germany and its inclusion in the (West-)European integration process led to considerable controversies between the parties. Since the beginning of the 1960s, however, this question was answered positively with the formula of the 'Europeanization of the German question'. Thereafter, a pro-European orientation has been the norm for political and administrative behaviour (Sturm and Pehle 2001*b*).

This basis of the pro-European élite consensus shows that the Europeanization of party systems is a dynamic interaction between 'bottom-up' and 'top-down' processes. Germany's broad success in meeting its core national interests through European integration contributes much to the low salience of EU-related issues in domestic party competition. Kitschelt (1997: 147 f.) identifies a second set of reasons for the low EU polarization in Germany. First, 'opposition to European integration may be particularly vocal in countries with exceptionally large or small welfare states'.[7] Second, 'beyond these economic factors, countries' foreign-policy trajectories—whether or not they are NATO members or had a colonial empire—may affect national politicians' willingness to support European integration'. Finally, 'European integration tends to be more politicised within countries deliberating entry or having recently entered'. Taking these variables, Germany is among the states with 'the least potential for political mobilisation around European integration'.

An additional factor merits attention. The ethnocentric–authoritarian or extreme right-wing party family, whose anti-European attitude[8] is responsible for the rise of pro- versus anti-European conflicts in the party systems of many West European states, is only marginally represented in Germany. This is due to several reasons (Niedermayer 2003). The attitudinal and institutional framework for the establishment of such parties is not very different from other states. Germany faces rapid and deep-seated socio-economic change, which is differently perceived and digested by individuals according to their life situation and mental capacities and leads to the development of a conflict between libertarian and authoritarian value systems. In the second half of the 1980s, the increasing number of immigrants and asylum-seekers served as a 'catalyst-issue' for the transformation of the authoritarian side of this social cleavage into the party system. This transformation was facilitated by German federalism, which gives new parties the opportunity to acquire status at the regional level before they contest at the federal level. The result has been some electoral successes for ethnocentric–authoritarian parties at the Land level.[9] At the federal level, however, this party family remained marginal. Several factors help to explain this situation. The ethnocentric–authoritarian parties are generally discredited by historical memories of the authoritarian National Socialist dictatorship. Accordingly, they do not get any significant media support. They cannot overcome their organizational fragmentation into three parties (DVU, NPD, Republikaner). They lack a charismatic leader. They are also hampered by the ability of the bourgeois parties to partially integrate their potential clientele.

---

[7] 'Large and redistributive welfare states prompt anti-European feelings among supporters of the economic left, who fear that integration will require a levelling-down of social benefits and protection to near a European norm in order to enable domestic industries to stay competitive. Conversely, in countries with small welfare states, the economic right may see integration as an inflationary source of demands for new entitlements' (Kitschelt 1997: 148).

[8] 'European integration provides a further identifying issue for the extreme right and its electorate. As mainstream left and right parties subscribe consensually to fuller integration, the extreme right . . . serves as an oppositional voice of protest against the undermining of national sovereignty and against Euro-élites' (Hainsworth 2000: 13).

[9] Note the success of the Republikaner in the Land elections in Baden-Württemberg in 1992 (10.9 per cent of the vote) and 1996 (9.1 per cent), as well as the success of the DVU in Saxony-Anhalt in 1998 (12.9 per cent).

At the regional level of the federally structured German party system, too, the pro- versus anti-European cleavage is of minor relevance. The commitment of the Länder to European integration is not as instinctive and unequivocal as it once was, and their attitude to integration is now more conditional on its capacity to meet territorially defined needs and preferences (Jeffery, Chapter 5 in this volume). However, this change has not led to a greater relevance of the European issue for regional party competition and therefore for the structure of the party systems of the Länder. Only a few examples can be found to suggest such a relevance (Lees 2002).[10] Even in Bavaria, where the governing CSU increasingly took an anti-interventionist position towards Brussels in the 1990s (Jeffery and Collins 1998), the EU issue was not relevant in the electoral campaigns.[11]

With such a minor relevance of the pro- versus anti-European cleavage in national party competition, it is unlikely that the legitimacy of the party system is considerably influenced by European integration. Indeed, this issue did not play a role in at least two of the three time periods during the last two decades where one could speak of a decrease of the party system's legitimacy. Although citizen orientations towards the party system are characterized by relatively high and increasing scepticism, the share of those expressing 'weariness', i.e. evaluating none of the parties represented in the national parliament positively, is very small (Figure 7.4).[12] Party system 'weariness' above the average emerged in 1988, 1992–3 and 1996–7. In the first and third phases, the increasing values could clearly be attributed to an increasing discontent only with the governing parties, CDU/CSU and FDP. In 1988, this discontent had nothing to do with Europe. In 1996–7, however, the discussions about the single currency could have contributed to the increasing 'weariness', even though this issue was of minor relevance for the 1998 election (see above).

The greatest legitimacy crisis of the party system occurred in 1992/93. In this period, all traditional parties—i.e. not only the CDU/CSU and the FDP, but also the SPD—were affected by the increasing discontent, while in West Germany the Greens and in the East the post-communist PDS achieved increasing support. Three factors can be blamed for the decreasing legitimacy: growing perception of deteriorating economic development, discontent with the course of the reunifica-

---

[10] One example is the 1996 Land election in Baden-Württemberg. For tactical reasons, the SPD assumed a sceptical position towards EMU and pushed this issue into the limelight. The voters perceived this strategy as inconsistent and opportunistic (Rheinhardt 1997), and the party suffered a considerable loss of votes.

[11] For the campaigns of 1990 and 1994 see Schultze (1991) and Jung and Rieger (1995). Even in the Länder electoral campaigns of 1998 shortly before the federal election, the EU issue did not play an important role (Renz and Rieger 1999).

[12] Figure 7.4 shows the legitimacy at the parliamentary level because there are no data about the small parties. Even at this level, there are gaps. In West Germany, the PDS was not included between 1991 and 1993.

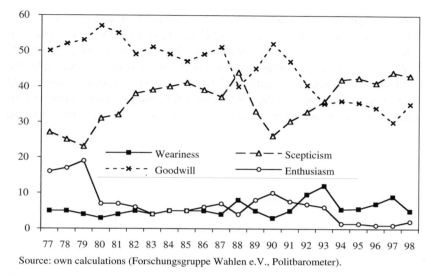

Source: own calculations (Forschungsgruppe Wahlen e.V., Politbarometer).

Figure 7.4.   Attitudes towards the party system (per cent).

tion process, and the discussion about asylum-seekers, which dominated the public agenda from autumn 1991 in West Germany. After the political compromise on this issue in summer 1993 and a considerable change in public sentiment about economic development in early summer 1994, the negative development was reversed (Niedermayer 2002*a*).

Because of the minor relevance of the European dimension for the conflict structure, there has been no impact of European integration on the segmentation and coalition stability of the German party system. The European policy positions of a party have not played an important role for their inclusion in—or exclusion from—considerations about possible coalitions. Conflicts about this issue among the governing parties have not led to the breakdown of coalitions. Breakdowns of coalitions during the legislative period occurred only twice. In 1966, the FDP withdrew its ministers from the coalition with the CDU/CSU because of economic policy conflicts (Jesse 2002). The replacement of the SPD–FDP coalition by a CDU/CSU–FDP coalition in 1982 was also caused by economic and social policy conflicts (Süß 1986).

Conclusion

This chapter has shown that one cannot speak of a Europeanization of the German party system in the sense of a considerable impact of the European integration process on its development. Up to now, the inclusion of Germany into the systemic context of the EU has not led to noticeable changes of the party system properties. At the parliamentary level of party competition, an influence cannot be detected. Also, at the electoral level, the effects have stayed within narrow limits. On the 'demand' side of party competition, this is due to the fact that the EU issue does not influence citizens' electoral decisions. On the 'supply' side, the lack of Europeanization can be explained mainly by the traditional, interest-based pro-European élite consensus, the low potential for political mobilization around European integration, and the marginal role of ethnocentric–authoritarian parties.

8

Interest Groups: Opportunity Structures and Governance Capacity

RAINER EISING

Introduction

THE INCREASING NUMBER OF POLICIES now dealt with, in one form or another, at the EU level has altered the context within which interest intermediation occurs and provided great incentives to interest organizations to promote their cases more readily to the EU institutions. The acceleration of the integration process since the Single European Act and the increasing use of qualified majority decisions in the Council led them to organize and look for coalition partners at the EU level. In part, the groups anticipated or responded to the threats and opportunities posed by EU policies and tried to shape their regulatory requirements. To some extent, their strategies paralleled the general institutional development of the EU. Moreover, some organizations simply mimicked the responses of other organizations, and some felt the need to respond to actions taken by competing groups. While the EU opens up new opportunities to interest organizations to pursue their interests, it also puts great demands on their capacities. Their strategies of interest representation must take account of a multi-level politics that binds together state institutions at different levels of government during all stages of the policy process.

International and German Context

This chapter looks at continuity and change among German interest groups and patterns of interest intermediation in the context of European integration. In other words, it analyses the Europeanization of interest intermediation. It is helpful to put both the impact of the EU and Germany into context. Here one must bear in mind that the EU is an important, but by no means the only, influence on German interest groups. The establishment of international organizations such as the World Trade Organization (WTO) can provide powerful incentives to be present in the global arena and voice concerns, be it directly or indirectly, *vis-à-vis* these international institutions. The internationalization of the economy changes the logic of membership (see Schmitter and Streeck 1981) in many business and

Proceedings of the British Academy, **119**, 147–172. © The British Academy 2003.

employer associations because they need to admit 'foreign' firms such as IBM or Toyota as members. Also, their domestic member firms extend economic activities to other states, thereby potentially reducing the importance of German associations to them.

But the impact of international competition and of widespread liberalization policies is by no means straightforward. On the one hand, both can enhance the pressures of members on associations to cut down costs, streamline activities, and develop a reasonable division of labour with other associations (see Wartenberg 2000 on the Federation of German Industry). They may also decrease the members' willingness to co-operate. On the other hand, they can lead to the emergence of associations and to the strengthening of associational systems of quality control and standardization (see Waarden 1994: 238). Technological dynamics can influence the role of associations in the product cycle and may even lead to the erosion of sector boundaries, sometimes promoting the setting up of cross-sectoral associations, as was the case in the German machinery and information technology industries. The effects of each of these factors on the definition, organization, and representation of interests must be disentangled in comparative case studies—though this is beyond the scope of this chapter. The chapter will also not consider in detail the impact of EU policy change on interests.[1] Instead, it analyses the impact of the changing institutional opportunity structure on German interest groups and patterns of interest intermediation.

Germany differs from other member states in several respects. Germany is the largest member state; it is a founding member of the European institutions; and it belongs in the group of the economically advanced member states. As the largest member state, it has a very large number of interest organizations that cover a broad spectrum of interests, whereas smaller member states have fewer interest organizations that may cover a narrower range of interests. It has also greater political clout in EU decision-making and greater formal decision-making rights (in qualified majority decisions) than smaller member states, even though this power is generally exercised in a multilateral way (Katzenstein 1997*b*: 4). As a result, German interest organizations may be more inclined to rely on their government as a representative for their interests than organizations from other member states.

However, the long duration of membership counters this influence to some extent. German interest groups have been socialized into European politics for a long time so that they have gradually integrated the EU institutions into their strategies of interest representation. As a result, they may find it easier to act within the EU multi-level system than interest groups from those member states that joined the EU only in the mid-1990s. Being economically advanced, the

---

[1] Eising and Jabko (2001) trace changes in domestic interest coalitions and definitions of interests in the French and German electricity supply industries to EU electricity liberalization.

socio-economic structure of the German interest group system differs to some extent from those of the worse-off member states (Portugal, Spain, Ireland, and Greece).

Governance Capacities and the Degree of Fit

Germany is an interesting case because the impact of the EU on the German domestic setting is fairly contested. The debate centres around the question of whether the German institutional setting fits well with that of the EU. On the one hand, Katzenstein (1997*b*: 40) asserts that 'the similarity of European and German institutions and practices (such as multilevel governance systems, subsidiarity, an activist court, and an autonomous central bank)' has created 'a milieu in which German political actors can feel at home' (also Bulmer 1997: 67). On the other hand, Risse, Green Cowles and Caporaso (2001: 8) are rather sceptical that Germany faces significantly less adaptational pressures than other member states.

Such contrasting views are also apparent when it comes to analysing interest intermediation. Green Cowles (2001: 176–8) claims that élite pluralism in the EU (on this concept, see Coen 1998) puts great pressure on German neo-corporatism, while it fits well with British pluralism because firms become directly involved in the political process instead of acting through their associative intermediaries. But Schmidt (1999: 161–2) posits that the EU's 'quasi-pluralism' resembles German neo-corporatism and puts far greater pressure on statism in France or in the UK. Despite their opposing views, all authors have in common the assumption that the degree of fit between the EU-level situation and the domestic situation explains domestic change and continuity to a great extent.

However, as a moving target, the degree of fit cannot be easily established, and its implications are less than clear and sometimes indistinguishable from those of competing explanations. This chapter illustrates these points by arguing that governance capacities shape the abilities of groups to represent their interests and their adaptation to European integration. On the one hand, organizational resources and professionalization of this function are preconditions for an effective representation of interests. On the other, the abilities to recognize the needs of state actors in decision-making processes, to mediate between the competing demands of state institutions and their members, and to contribute to the compliance with, and the implementation of, public policies by self-regulation are crucial.

The corporatist mode of interest intermediation supports the development of these abilities more than any other mode because state institutions involve interest organizations regularly in policy formation and implementation. As Germany is often said to have a (weak) neo-corporatist mode of interest intermediation (Streeck 1999), German interest organizations should not face major difficulties in representing their interests in the EU multi-level system—even when the EU mode of interest intermediation differs from that prevalent in Germany.

In the context of adaptation to the EU institutional context, the emphasis on governance capacities has four implications. First, German interest organizations face fewer difficulties in representing their interests in the EU multi-level system than those from non-corporatist states. Second, at the macro level, the power structure within the German interest group system and its established division of labour are extended to the EU context. Third, at the micro level, actors with different capacities perform differently. Well-resourced interest organizations such as large firms or large business associations represent their interests routinely both at the EU level and at the national level. Less well-equipped organizations are unable to do so or face substantial difficulties in doing so. This is because the management of access, timing, and influence in the EU multi-level system puts high demands on the resources and skills of interest organizations. Finally, at both the macro and the micro levels, embeddedness in the EU leads to manifold changes that extend and modify established practices, but reaffirm the domestic situation and accommodate EU influences without major problems.

These implications are fairly similar to those one would expect from a good degree of fit between the German and the EU modes of interest intermediation. Only in the case of a perfect fit would one expect no change at all because domestic interest groups are perfectly adapted to EU politics. In the case of a poor degree of fit, two scenarios are possible: on the one hand, interest organizations find it too difficult to respond to European integration pressures because the EU situation differs too much from the domestic situation. Hence, interest organizations are unable to extend interest representation to the EU level. On the other hand, tremendous adaptation pressures could trigger a restructuring of the landscape of interest groups, leading to the foundation of new domestic interest organizations that cover EU affairs. They might cause a reshuffling of the power structure and of the division of labour among established groups, leading to a fundamental transformation of the domestic situation.

This chapter tests these hypotheses and scenarios in the following way. The next section juxtaposes the EU and the German systems of interest intermediation. It analyses the role of interest groups in policy formulation and implementation, the modes of interest intermediation, and the composition of the interest group systems. Then, the chapter outlines the broad trends in the strategic responses of German interest groups to European integration: their membership in EU associations, their direct contacts with EU and national political institutions to represent their interests, and their co-operation with other interest organizations. Thereafter, the chapter tests the 'capacity' hypothesis. Using cluster analysis techniques, it develops a five-fold typology of interest organizations (multi-level players, EU players, traditionalists, occasional players, and niche organizations). This analysis illustrates how the domestic division of labour in the associational system is by and large transferred to the EU level. Tests of cluster membership demonstrate that large firms and German associations find it easier to act as multi-level players than French or British associations. The chapter also shows that cluster membership depends on organizational resources.

Evidence is drawn from a variety of sources. First, the analysis relies on the official databases of interest organizations that the European Commission and the German Bundestag maintain. Second, it uses a survey analysis of German interest groups registered by the German Bundestag and a sample of German trade associations and large firms. Finally, the study of organizational responses to European integration builds on case study analysis. Drawing mainly on cross-sectoral data, the chapter hopes to provide an adequate account of the overall responses of German interest groups to European integration by the late 1990s and early 2000s.

German and EU Interest Group Systems

The Composition of the Interest Group Systems

In terms of their composition, the interest group systems in Germany and the EU show important similarities, but they also differ to some extent. Both reflect highly differentiated socio-economic structures. Unlike party systems that function according to a uniform logic of party competition (see Niedermayer, Chapter 7 in this volume), neither functions according to an overarching logic of interest group competition. In the highly segmented interest group systems, the activities of many interest organizations are not related to one another. The interest group systems are more loosely coupled than the party systems, and collective action varies tremendously from loose, small, specialized, and local movements to highly organized, large, and comprehensive peak organizations at the federal level (see Reutter 2001: 75 on German associations).

The EU interest group system is more complex than the German one in that it is not only divided across functional lines, but also consists of national, subnational, EU, and international interest organizations. Divisions of interests along national lines can be at least as important as those along functional lines. In contrast, power in the German associational system often resides at the top federal level and not at the Länder level below, even though many interest associations are organized along Land lines as well as functional lines. In 2000, the European Commission listed about 902 EU interest organizations. Besides them, some 320 firms, 131 representations of national interest organizations, 135 regional and subnational bodies, 142 public affairs firms, 160 legal firms, forty-six chambers of commerce and fourteen think tanks had offices at the sites of the EU institutions (Rucht 2000: 198). The German Bundestag registered some 1,572 national interest organizations in the mid-1990s (Table 8.1).

In both political systems, business interest organizations clearly outnumber organizations for 'weak' interests that can be articulated, mobilized, and organized less easily and have generally less sanctioning power at their disposal (see

Table 8.1. The interest group systems of Germany and the EU.[a]

Type of interest	EU interest organizations No. (%)		German interest organizations No. (%)		Percentage difference (EU–German org.)
Agriculture, forestry, and fisheries	129	(14.3)	128	(8.1)	6.2
Industry	289	(32.0)	277	(17.6)	14.4
Services	313	(34.7)	750	(47.7)	−13.0
Small and medium-sized enterprises	10	(1.1)	13	(0.8)	0.3
Regions, regional development, and cities	15	(1.7)	19	(1.2)	0.5
Development aid and human rights	30	(3.3)	47	(3.0)	0.3
Consumers, social policy, and welfare organizations	37	(4.1)	168	(10.7)	−6.6
Trade unions	16	(1.8)	36	(2.3)	−0.5
Animal, nature and environmental protection	23	(2.6)	38	(2.4)	0.2
Religion	10	(1.1)	9	(0.6)	0.5
Various public interests	30	(3.3)	7	(0.5)	2.8
Various interests	–		80	(5.1)	−5.1
Total	902 (100.0)		1,572 (100.0)		–

Note: [a] The table is based on the European Commission's database that registers EU-level interest organizations dated 30 March 2000 and the database of the German Parliament that registers German interest organizations for the year 1994 as presented in Sebaldt (1997). Since then, the number of interest organizations registered in the latter database has remained fairly stable. For the purposes of this study, the categories were adapted from the Commission database and the German interest organizations were regrouped accordingly. The databases do certainly not cover all interest organizations but provide a useful overview of those groups addressing the EU or the German political institutions.

Sources: Own calculations according to European Commission (2000); Sebaldt (1997).

Willems and Winter 2001: 14). Only 16.2 per cent of the EU organizations represent weaker interests (environmental, social and welfare groups, trade unions, religious organizations, human rights groups, and so forth). In Germany, 19.5 per cent of the groups fall into the category of weak interests. To some extent, the small shares of weaker interest groups reflect greater capacities of business to organize. But they also mirror the great fragmentation of business interests that range from employer to producer interests, on the one hand, and from cross-sectoral issues to specific products and production processes, on the other. Accordingly, about 82 per cent of the EU associations organize employer, industry, or professional interests in agriculture, services, or industry. In Germany, about 74 per cent of the interest groups fall into these categories.

The interest group systems are more asymmetric with regard to business interests than with regard to weaker interests. While in Germany, interest organizations related to services outnumber industry associations by almost three times, at the EU level both types of interests are relatively evenly represented. This is related to the fact that the bulk of so-called 'third-sector' activities in Germany is in health and social services.

The Europeanization of interest intermediation has generally not taken the form of founding new EU-related groups in Germany. Only thirteen out of the 1,572 interest organizations that are registered by the German Bundestag focus only or mainly on EU or Europe-related matters. And about two-thirds of these may be qualified as EU interest organizations that are also present in Germany. Rather, EU issues are dealt with by established associations that have extended the scope of their activities to European institutions and policies (see below). Furthermore, European politics are not very contentious in Germany even though they may of course lead to conflicts of interests among and within groups. Owing to the complexity of the EU system, the lack of a European 'public', and the difficulties surrounding transnational mobilization, social movements have barely Europeanized their activities (see Imig and Tarrow 2001). Protest events within Germany that are related to European integration or European institutions are so few in numbers that Rucht (2002: 165) claims that the Europeanization of protest 'is a myth'.[2]

In sum, in both political systems manifold interests are represented with a bias in favour of economic interest organizations. At this aggregate level, the structure of the interest group systems does not exert much pressure for change in Germany, although the absence or presence of an EU group in a given issue area may create some opportunities and constraints for political action on the part of German interest groups.

Participation in Policy Formulation and Implementation

In both the EU and Germany, political institutions welcome the political participation of interest organizations. These organizations may be able to provide the expertise needed to formulate public policies, communicate the reasons for these policies to their members and the broader public, build up support for the programmes and ensure compliance, and even have the organizational capacities necessary to implement them. Accordingly, the joint rules of procedure of the German federal ministries explicitly allow for the consultation of nation-wide interest organizations, which need to register with the German Bundestag to participate in its legislative activities. Similarly, the European Commission has

---

[2] In a data set of protest events that is based on newspaper coverage from 1950 to 1994, among the total of 13,201 protests only twenty-three 'explicitly address matters of European integration' (Rucht 2002: 181). However, of the ninety-six protests in agricultural policy, thirty-eight address EU-related issues.

repeatedly stated that it welcomes an 'open and structured dialogue' with interest organizations because it 'believes this process to be fundamental to the development of its policies' (Commission of the EC 1992: 3).

However, involvement in policy implementation is more mixed. In some policy areas, perhaps most notably in labour relations, health, and social policy, German interest organizations enjoy a privileged status to implement public policies and regulate issue areas with great relevance for social integration and economic prosperity. Thus in many fields of social policy, action on the part of state agencies is subsidiary to the work of welfare organizations. Given a quite centralized and integrated associational setting, several German peak associations can provide a uniform implementation across the country and alleviate state institutions from internal negotiation pressures and administrative burdens. Hence German political institutions often come to regard self-regulation as a value in itself.

In comparison, the EU institutions are more wary of granting interest groups a public status in the implementation of EU policies, even if they do so in some policy areas such as the social dialogue and environmental policy. The European Commission (2001*b*: 17) defines such 'co-regulation' as the combination of 'binding legislative and regulatory action with actions taken by the actors most concerned'. It cautions that co-regulation must be embedded in a clear legal framework with 'enforcement and appeal mechanisms.' Co-regulation should 'only be used where it clearly adds value and serves the general interest' and where EU law need not 'apply in a uniform way in all member states'. Unlike in Germany, EU associations can generally neither alleviate the EU institutions of negotiation pressures nor guarantee uniform implementation in the Union. On the one hand, the member states, the European Parliament, and the supranational bureaucracy usually insist on their decision-making rights and would not delegate them to interest organizations. On the other, many of the umbrella associations do not cover all EU member states, they are split along national lines, and the governance capacities of their member associations vary tremendously. It is therefore of little surprise that, compared to Germany, EU institutions regard self-regulation as second best to implementation by public authorities.

Hence, the EU regime for self-regulation differs somewhat from the German regime, and European legislation or rulings of the European Court of Justice might undermine self-regulation in Germany. Nonetheless, in his comprehensive overview of this topic, Waarden (1994: 255) comes to the conclusion that European law will not 'impede associational self-regulation as much as has been the case in the US'. Regarding self-regulation as an important element of regulatory traditions in several member states, he sees these traditions as 'strongly anchored in sets of national legal and administrative institutions and hence resistant to some pressure for change' (1994: 256). As German competition law has long been in line with major aspects of EU competition law (see Lodge, Chapter 11 in this volume), repercussions of EU competition law on the role of associations ought to be quite limited. For the most part, German competition law has already ruled out those interest group practices that EU competition would prohibit.

Nevertheless, the European Commission and the European Court of Justice (see Frenz 2001: 140–55) demand transparent and formalized adjudication procedures for resolving conflicts among the partners involved and discount self-regulation as a value *per se*. This has consequences for the prospect and the shape of national self-regulation. While strengthening enforceability, redressing imbalances of power, and providing for control by affected third parties, the Commission's criteria have equally the potential to reduce the functionality of self-regulatory arrangements: They circumscribe the eligible areas of agreement, they hamper the importance of informal negotiations as their *modus operandi*, and thereby reduce the flexibility of the arrangements over time.

The Mode of Interest Intermediation

What is the precise impact of European integration on 'the' German mode of interest intermediation beyond its pressure on associational self-regulation? It is very difficult to identify clear-cut changes in this mode and attribute them to European integration. As mentioned earlier, European integration needs to be separated from other factors. But, more fundamentally, these difficulties stem from problems inherent in typological analysis. The literature on state–society relations still distinguishes among three major modes: pluralism, corporatism, and statism. Network governance is a more recent conceptualization, reflecting socio-economic dynamics and institutional changes currently occurring within western Europe (see Kohler-Koch 1999).

Difficulties in identifying modal change have a fundamental root in the link between these modes and the cases that they denote. The usage of these types is founded on the assumption that there are characteristic or at least average combinations of properties and relations that capture the main features of interest intermediation. But the elements entering these concepts need not always co-vary in the way envisaged (see Czada 1994). In such instances the countries or sectors that are allotted to one type do not have identical values on all variables but are grouped together according to their overall similarity. As a result, these modes are bound to hide important variations across countries and sectors. This also makes it difficult to establish the exact 'degree of fit' between the EU mode of interest intermediation and any national mode of interest intermediation. Furthermore, confusion may arise if, at the empirical level, authors have based their typology and sorting of cases on different periods, levels of analysis, or even single events. Finally, even if authors have the same empirical background problems result from differences at the conceptual level. For example, Schmitter (1974) characterized neo-corporatism mainly on the basis of the organizational elements of associations and of the associational system. In contrast, Lehmbruch (1974) emphasized the way in which interest organizations were involved in public policy-making and implementation.

Hence it is of little surprise that different authors have characterized the EU as well as Germany in different ways. The EU has been regarded as pluralist (Streeck and Schmitter 1991), élite pluralist (Coen 1998), quasi-pluralist (Schmidt 1999), governed in a network mode (Kohler-Koch 1999), and showing inroads to corporatism in some issue areas (Falkner 1999). Germany has been labelled a case of corporatism (Streeck 1999), organized pluralism (Sebaldt 1997), and even corporative pluralism (Maier 1977).

Thus, expectations for changes in the German mode of interest intermediation are based on concepts, units of observation, and the link between these two. How then is the impact of the EU on German modes of interest intermediation to be understood? Drawing on a case study of foreign trade policy-making, Green Cowles (2001) finds major changes in this mode and attributes them to the impact of the EU and its role in the Transatlantic Business Dialogue (TABD). The extent of change that is found rests to a large degree on conceptualizing the German mode of interest intermediation as strongly neo-corporatist and the EU mode as highly élite-pluralist. In other words, it rests on a perceived strong misfit between the EU and Germany. In particular, Green Cowles (2001: 161) finds that the direct involvement of large German firms in the TABD erodes the 'authoritative voice' of the Federation of German Industry (BDI) *vis-à-vis* the German government.

However, an inspection of the German literature indicates that the Federation of German Industry has never been a monopoly player in German foreign trade policy. The importance of large firms and even individual entrepreneurs is a long-standing feature of German state–economy relations. For Imperial Germany after 1871 it has been noted that 'great firms and concerns have usually been the link between prominent businessmen and powerful interest groups' in the 'German industrial system' (Feldman 1978: 241). In this tradition, BDI positions are often shaped by large firms (see Bührer and Grande 2000: 167). This sometimes gives rise to controversies within industry—which, in the context of the TABD, came into the open. Prior studies also emphasized the important role of sectoral associations and of large firms in German foreign economic policy (Kreile 1978: 195–205). Thus, it seems more appropriate to conclude from this case that European integration has led to an extension of practices already present in the German business system rather than to paradigmatic change. The findings accord well with the proposition that resourceful actors such as large firms are best equipped to use the options that the changes in the political opportunity structure offer to them and that their positions in the interest group system are strengthened rather than weakened.

The last finding is supported if one analyses which German business interest organizations represent their interests routinely *vis-à-vis* national and EU institu-

Table 8.2. German firms and business associations: correlations between contacts with national and EU institutions.

	Eur. Com.	EP	Council of EU	EU regul. auth.	Nat. gov.	Nat. parl.	Nat. regul. auth.
Eur. Com.	1.000						
EP	0.737	1.000					
Council of EU	0.685	0.736	1.000				
EU regul. auth.	0.457	0.345	0.301	1.000			
Nat. gov.	0.604	0.570	0.463	0.291	1.000		
Nat. parl.	0.545	0.710	0.491	0.283	0.648	1.000	
Nat. regul. auth.	0.336	0.268	0.222	0.616	0.424	0.379	1.000

Note: All correlations (Spearman's rho) are asymptotically significant at the level p = 0.000.

tions. Those organizations that are prominently placed in their contact patterns with German institutions also figure notably at the EU level (see Table 8.2). Those organizations responsible for the representation of interests *vis-à-vis* German political institutions are also the voices of their constituencies *vis-à-vis* the respective EU institutions. More generally, German interest organizations transfer domestic practices and the domestic division of labour onto the European level of governance. A one-to-one transfer of domestic activities to the European level is unrealistic given that the EU institutions do not fully replace the functions of domestic institutions. Hence the high correlations between the contact patterns with the national government and the European Commission (0.604), between contacts with the German Bundestag and the European Parliament (0.710), and between contacts with regulatory and standardization authorities at both levels (0.616) are sound evidence that European integration has not lead to a major realignment of German interest organizations.

Interest Organizations in Multi-level Governance

Strategic Responses of German Interest Groups to European Integration

Domestic interest groups have broadened their repertoire of organizational strategies to cope with the changes in the institutional opportunity structure. Much like associations in other member states, German interest organizations have employed the four strategies available to domestic interest groups. They have formed or joined EU interest organizations. They have represented their interests directly to EU institutions. They have relied on the German political institutions to promote their causes. They have coalesced with other national, transnational, or EU interest organizations. These four strategies and the changes within the organizations are outlined below.

Strategy 1   At present, German interest organizations are members in 298 of those 311 European interest groups listed in the Commission database that provide information about their members (European Commission 2002). French organizations are involved in 293 of these groups. Groups from Belgium and Italy are members in more than 280 EU umbrella groups, and groups from the Netherlands, the UK, and Spain have joined between 263 and 275 EU associations. Interest groups from the latest member states—Austria, Sweden, and Finland—as well as Denmark have joined between 231 and 244 EU associations. At the bottom of the scale are Luxembourg and Greece, which are present in fewer than 170 EU associations. This pattern accords well with the initial assumption that country size, the duration of membership, and the level of economic advancement all have an impact on the representation of domestic interests in Brussels. Five of the six founding members and the four largest member states are among those six countries whose interest groups have the largest number of memberships in EU associations. All of these six countries belong to the group of the economically advanced member states.

However, the mode of interest intermediation seems to be of little importance for the decision to join EU associations. France and Italy are considered to be statist, Germany and the Netherlands are deemed corporatist, and the UK is regarded as pluralist. Hence, membership in EU associations is almost a *sine qua non* of domestic interest organizations as they try to cope with European integration.

Therefore, about 86 per cent of German interest organizations participate in least one EU umbrella organization (see Sebaldt 1997: 193).[3] The latter have established themselves as interlocutors of the EU institutions, in particular during the agenda-setting and policy formulation stages of the policy cycle when they are clearly more involved than national associations.

Strategies 2 and 3   Owing to the heterogeneity of their members, several of the EU associations face collective action problems. The compromise pressures built into their work encourage the direct representation of interests at EU institutions if important interests are at stake. Furthermore, EU policies often have a framework character and contain several elements of flexibility (Eising 2000), such as transition rules and exemptions which lead to continued discussions and negotiations with EU institutions when Directives are transposed into national law and implemented in the member states. At that stage, the expertise of national experts rather than of EU associations is required. As a result, many German interest organizations have established direct contacts with EU institutions to pursue their goals. The following parts of this chapter analyse how German business interest

---

[3] In his survey, Martin Sebaldt addressed 1,397 of the interest organizations registered by the German Bundestag and received 602 responses which amounts to a response rate of 43.1 per cent (Sebaldt 1997: Appendix 1).

organizations have responded to European integration, because data on a large number of these organizations are available.[4]

Figure 8.1 shows the average number of contacts that German business associations and large firms maintain with EU and national political institutions to represent their interests. Substantially more contacts are targeted at the executive institutions than at the parliaments, underlining the dominance of the former over the latter. Large firms enjoy a far better access to the political institutions at each level than German business associations. In contrast to associations, German firms are also regularly involved in standard-setting and regulatory activities at both the EU and the national levels. Their contacts at the EU level outnumber even those of the EU associations.[5] In sum, these firms routinely cultivate contacts at both the national and the EU levels to represent their interests.

In comparison, most business associations are still rooted in the domestic political context. The median association maintains monthly contacts with the German federal government and its bureaucracy but approaches the supranational bureaucracy only twice a year. Contacts with the other institutions also reflect national embeddedness. The median association meets representatives of the German Bundestag, the Länder or the Bundesrat, and German regulatory and standardization authorities twice a year. It maintains no contact at all with the European Parliament, the Council of the European Union or EU regulatory and standardization authorities.

Thus, even though membership in EU associations is widespread and even though they have established direct contacts with EU institutions, the majority of German interest organizations rely still on their established domestic channels of communication to promote their case in EU affairs. The German government remains their most important political addressee. It is therefore safe to conclude that, for the majority of German business associations, activities at the EU level have a complementary function to those at the domestic level. They remain rooted in their domestic context. Unlike German firms, they are tied to domestic constituencies and operate mostly on this main working level. Hence relations at the domestic level do not necessarily loosen as a result of European integration. Disintegration is but one of several outcomes. In fact, European integration can strengthen ties at the domestic level (see Benz 1998: 583): the uncertainty of

[4] The data is based on the survey EUROLOB which I co-ordinated at the Mannheim Centre for European Social Research. Beate Kohler-Koch was the principal investigator. Based on the relevant EU and national directories, the survey addressed a population of 1998 German, British, French, and EU trade associations (excluding professional associations) as well as sixty-eight large firms in these countries. The overall response rate was 40.9 per cent (860 responses), and the response rate for German associations amounted to 44.2 per cent (321 responses).

[5] On average, EU associations maintain the following levels of contact with the EU institutions: European Commission: 4.83 (SD 1.35, N 160), European Parliament 3.79 (SD 1.62, N 154), Council of the European Union 3.05 (SD 1.58, N 150).

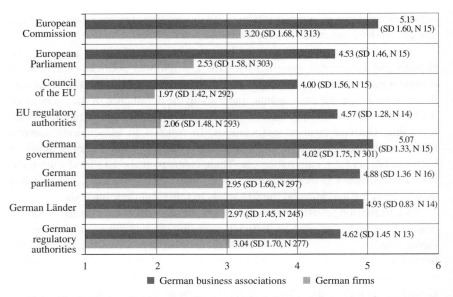

Notes: The figures provide the means, the standard deviations, and the number of cases.

1 = No contact: 2 = Annual contact: 3 = Half-yearly contact:
4 = Quarterly: 5 = Monthly contact: 6 = Weekly contact

Figure 8.1.   German firms and business associations: average number of contacts with political institutions.

public and private actors about the consequences of EU legislation can prompt or increase the exchange of information. Shared concerns about the impact of EU regulation may start up new or reinforce existing domestic alliances as national bureaucrats worry about national competitiveness and domestic regulatory practices, and trade associations are concerned that new European rules impose costs on their members.

Strategy 4   Given the interlocking of EU and national institutions in multi-level governance, national interest groups are located in a complex organizational field. As a result, they co-operate frequently with other actors in order to represent their interests in relation to EU policies. This co-operation ranges from loose 'issue alliances' to institutionalized co-operation within EU associations: 66.3 per cent (N = 207) of the German associations in the EUROLOB sample co-operate frequently with other organizations, and 31.3 per cent (N = 98) do so occasionally. The majority (56.3 per cent, N = 9) of the large German firms also co-operate habitually with other organizations while 43.8 per cent (N = 7) do so occasionally. Apparently, firms rely to a greater extent than associations on their own capacities once they have decided to remain outside of the associational loop.

Usually, the economic actors co-operate with other national, EU, or international trade associations as well as with firms. Co-operation with consultants, scientific institutes, trade unions, and environmental, social or welfare organizations is less frequent and also regarded as less useful. In general, associations and firms do not differ significantly in how they judge their co-operation with other organizations. Both regard co-operation in national trade associations as most useful, co-operation in EU trade associations as slightly less useful, and co-operation with trade unions as least useful. However, they differ clearly with regard to the role they envisage for firms in lobbying the EU. While the large firms attribute much importance to firms in EU-level interest representation, associations regard them as far less important. As a corollary, German firms find co-operation with other firms at the EU level useful, while associations attribute less utility to it.[6]

Within the associations, embeddedness in the EU has brought about organizational change (see Eising 2000). Associations have set up special EU divisions, but with the rising tide of EU regulation, EU policy is also routinely handled in line divisions that can mobilize the relevant legal, economic, or technical expertise. More important than this formal allocation of EU competencies is the impact of European integration on the internal processes of opinion formation. Here, two problems are mutually reinforcing. First, national representatives need some leeway for manoeuvre in their EU-level negotiations in order to not preclude conceivable compromises. And second, owing to the dynamic and sometimes non-transparent development of the EU policy process, position papers must often be provided in a hurry. The association's staff and the leading executives in the relevant committees must therefore often work directly with the EU institutions and associations without further consultation.

This entails a loss of control for the associational members and increases the danger that EU-level negotiations may be conducted to their disadvantage. In part, this development has been compensated for by the extension of organizational routines to EU affairs. First, associations do not usually resort to majority voting but try to seek a consensus to which each member can agree even if this may occasionally lead to least common denominator positions. These positions form a binding framework for negotiations at the EU level. Second, in controversial questions, the neutral behaviour and the role of the associations' staff as arbiters are regarded as highly important. Third, different groups in the membership are often proportionally or even equally represented in the EU 'delegation'

---

[6] Asked to rank the importance of firms in EU-level interest representation on a scale ranging from 1 (not important at all) to six (very important), German associations scored an average of 3.33 while German firms scored 4.88. Asked to assess the usefulness of their co-operation with firms on a scale from 1 (not useful at all) to 6 (very useful), German associations scored an average of 3.83 and firms scored 4.69.

to ensure that the interests of the entire membership are considered in EU-level interest representation. Fourth, in several associations both their staff and firm executives are delegated to the working groups and committees of the EU associations or the negotiations with EU institutions to ensure mutual control. Finally, heads of committees usually enjoy a high level of trust among all members and must act and speak for the overall interests of the members and not just for a specific sub-section or their firm.

Types of Interest Organizations in the EU Multi-Level System

The previous analysis described the general organizational responses of German interest organizations to the challenges posed by European integration. This section systematically tests the hypothesis that governance capacities have a decisive influence on these strategies of interest representation. Being relatively well equipped and relying mainly on insider lobbying, business associations and large firms are a good plausibility probe for the hypothesis that resourceful actors have the least difficulties in responding to changes in their institutional environment. If that should not prove to be the case, the 'capacity' hypothesis would be null and void. German business associations are placed in the context of their French, British, and European counterparts and large firms from the three member states are treated as one group.

In a first step, a cluster analysis serves to construct types of interest organizations in the EU multi-level system as the previous section has identified substantial variation among organizational strategies. In a second step, the international comparison of cluster membership demonstrates that not only large firms but also German interest organizations find it easier to represent their interests in multi-level politics than French or British interest organizations. In a third step, comparing the organizational and sectoral features of the German cluster members indicates that those organizations with great organizational capacities outperform those that are less well-equipped.

First, the cluster analysis of the contact patterns with the EU and national political institutions, lobbying activities throughout the policy-making cycle, and access to information from the political institutions leads to the identification of five clusters of interest groups.[7] There are *niche organizations, occasional*

---

[7] Cluster analysis assigns cases to clusters on the basis of distance or similarity measures. This cluster analysis has been calculated by k-means clustering which assigns the interest organizations by means of an algorithm into k clusters so that the within cluster sum of squared Euclidean distances (the 'error') is minimized. Using SPSS starting values, those interest organizations with the largest distances to each other were the starting points. Missing cases were excluded pairwise. There were ties in the data. Apart from theoretical considerations, the number of clusters has been determined on the basis of test statistics for solutions ranging from one to ten clusters that include the explained variance (ETA $= 1 - Sq_{in}(k)/SQ_{total} = 1 - Sq_{in}(k)/SQ_{in}(1)$), the proportional reduction of error (PRE $=$

players, traditionalists, EU players, and multi-level players. Table 8.3 presents the centres (means) of each cluster in detail. Because they had different scales, all variables were standardized so that they have approximately means of zero and standard deviations of one. Positive deviations from the mean that are equal to or larger than half a standard deviation have been marked in bold numbers, and negative deviations of that size are marked in bold and italics.

Table 8.3 illustrates that *multi-level players* are clearly more active and present throughout the entire policy-making cycle at both the EU and the national levels than the average interest organization and members of the other clusters. They have far more than average contacts with each national and EU institution, their activities throughout the policy-making cycle exceed those of the average association, and they find it easier than the average association to obtain relevant information from political institutions. They maintain as many contacts with national institutions as with the equivalent EU institutions.[8] It is therefore safe to conclude that interest representation in the EU multi-level system has become a matter of routine for them. Their high level of EU activities and contacts sets them apart from those associations concentrating on the national level, while their activities at the national level clearly distinguish them from the EU players. Overall, the multi-level players are the most important business interest organization in EU policy-making and implementation.

Traditionalists have a more specialized profile. They maintain only very occasional contacts at the EU level to supplement their national activities, and they have more difficulties obtaining relevant information from the EU institutions than from national institutions. Occasionally, they are active when the political agenda is set. But, mostly, they get involved when German political institutions develop their positions on EU policy and when EU Directives are transposed into national law and implemented. Their activities on the EU level concentrate on these last two stages of the policy-making cycle. At the national level, their level

---

$1 — Sq_{in}(k)/SQ_{in}(k—1))$, and the explained variance that is adjusted for by the number of clusters (F-Max$_k$ = $(Sq_{between}(k)/k—1)/(Sq_{total}/n—k))$. N denotes the number of cases, k denotes the number of clusters, Sq_{total} denotes the total sum of squared Euclidean distances, $SQ_{in}(k)$ denotes the sum of squares within the k clusters ('error sum of squares') and $Sq_{between}(k)$ denotes the sum of squares between the k clusters ('explained sum of squares') (for details, see Bacher 2001). The five-cluster solution presented explains 32 per cent of the variance and is stable. Comparing cluster membership with that obtained by a five-cluster solution based on a random starting partition indicates substantial agreement among the results. The amount of agreement for the different clusters was as follows: niche organizations 81.6 per cent, occasional players 69 per cent, traditionalists 61.2 per cent, EU players 94.2 per cent, and multi-level players 90.1 per cent (kappa = 0.717, p = 0.000). Hence, the greatest problem of this solution is in deciding whether actors are occasionally or routinely involved in national policy-making and implementation. A three-cluster solution that fares better on the F-Max statistics but not on the ETA statistics is far less stable (kappa = 0.452).

[8] The Appendix to this chapter presents the average values of the original variables and the number of cases on each variable that were included in the cluster analysis.

Rainer Eising

Table 8.3. Clusters of interest organizations in the EU multi-level system.

	Niche organizations	Tradition-alists	Occasional players	EU players	Multi-level players
EU-level agenda-setting	*-0.89*	-0.17	-0.12	0.36	**0.70**
European Commission contacts	*-0.99*	-0.28	-0.37	**1.02**	**0.84**
European Commission info	-0.03	0.01	*-1.12*	0.24	0.44
EP contacts	*-0.90*	-0.39	*-0.52*	0.97	**1.01**
EP information	0.02	-0.17	*-1.08*	0.05	**0.59**
Council of the EU contacts	*-0.74*	-0.42	-0.46	0.76	**1.00**
Council of the EU info	0.21	0.00	*-0.98*	-0.29	**0.56**
EU regulatory and standardization authorities	*-0.60*	-0.12	0.13	0.31	0.38
EU-level transposition	*-1.03*	**0.57**	-0.04	*-0.88*	**0.51**
EU-level implementation	*-0.91*	**0.57**	-0.02	*-0.97*	0.45
National-level agenda-setting	*-0.62*	0.15	-0.02	*-0.97*	**0.65**
National government contacts	*-1.09*	0.43	-0.07	*-0.65*	**0.74**
National government info	0.22	0.47	*-1.27*	*-0.61*	0.29
National parliament contacts	*-0.85*	0.24	-0.34	*-0.71*	**0.95**
National parliament info	0.35	0.32	*-1.13*	*-0.74*	0.32
National-level position formulation	*-0.98*	0.42	0.01	*-0.91*	**0.57**
National regulatory and standardization authorities	*-0.69*	0.35	0.25	*-0.79*	0.44
National-level implementation	*-0.88*	**0.60**	0.18	*-1.36*	0.33
National-level transposition	*-1.02*	**0.59**	0.20	*-1.41*	0.45
N	158	227	142	104	203

Note: Originally, contacts were measured on a 6-point scale: 1 (no contacts), 2 (yearly), 3 (half-yearly), 4 (quarterly), 5 (monthly), 6 (weekly). Activities to represent interests throughout the policy-making cycle have been measured on a 3-point scale: 1 (no activities), 2 (sometimes), 3 (often). Access to information from political institutions has been measured on a 6-point scale from 1 (very difficult) to 6 (not difficult at all).

of contacts, activities, and information does not differ much from that of the multi-level players. But in contrast to the latter, their contacts concentrate on the German government and extend rarely to the German Bundestag. Thus, these groups are traditional in that they are still firmly rooted in the German political setting and are 'policy-takers' at the EU level.

Occasional players resemble the traditionalists in that they concentrate on the national level, except that almost all of their their activities, their contacts, and the information they obtain are clearly on a lower level. They are only rarely involved in national policy-making and implementation.

EU players are very active at the EU level and entertain manifold contacts with the EU institutions. Even though they do not have fewer contacts with the EU institutions, they find it more difficult to obtain relevant information than multi-level players. During the policy cycle, they concentrate mainly on the agenda-setting and policy formulation stages rather than on the transposition and implementation of EU Directives. In addition, they are hardly involved in national political processes about EU policies. Hence, these organizations are specialized in representing interests at the EU level during the early stages of the policy-making process.

At the bottom end, *niche organizations* are hardly active at all during the policy cycle. Their contacts with both national and EU institutions are well below average, as are their activities during all the phases of the policy cycle. Nevertheless, their estimates of the access to information from national institutions are above average and those of the access to information from EU institutions are about average. Here, one has to take into account that only a minority of these organizations is in touch with political institutions and has access to information from them (see Appendix). Hence, their overall degree of information must be considered to be below that of the other clusters.[9] These actors depend almost entirely on other interest organizations in the associational division of labour when it comes to monitoring political developments and advocating their political interests. Even though they maintain fewer than average contacts with regulatory and standardization authorities, these authorities, rather than executives or parliaments, are their most frequent contact partners.

The Governance Capacities of the Cluster Members

The international comparison of cluster membership supports the first implication of the 'capacity' hypothesis. German business associations differ significantly from British and French associations.[10] While just about one-fifth of the German interest organizations falls among the *niche organizations*, this holds for about one-quarter of the British and French associations. More than half of all national associations represents their interests occasionally or routinely at the national level, without attempting to become active at the EU level. But compared to French associations, British and German groups are more likely to become routine interlocutors of their national institutions rather than only *occasional players*. Furthermore, while 82 per cent of the EU players are EU associations, only a very small minority of national associations from each country is included in this group and exits from the domestic political system. This minority is either shut out from domestic political processes, or heavily affected by EU regulation, or involved in running EU associations from domestic grounds. Finally, almost

---

[9] As an alternative to the pairwise exclusion of cases, a listwise deletion of cases would have ensured the same number of cases on all variables but would also have lowered the overall number of cases immensely.

[10] The formal test that cluster membership differs systematically across German, British, and French trade associations is highly significant ($CHI^2 = 28.171$, df $= 8$, p $= 0.000$).

three-quarters of the large firms—among whom are thirteen of the sixteen German firms—and 29 per cent of the German business associations are *multi-level players*. Only 22 per cent of the British associations and 14 per cent of the French associations fall into this category. Hence, German associations are less likely to be uninvolved in EU policy-making and implementation than French or British associations, and they are more likely to include the EU institutions routinely in their strategy of interest representation (Table 8.4). In sum, this is empirical support for the assumption that associations that have the ability to intermediate between state institutions and their members find it easier to act in the EU multi-level system than others.

The organizational characteristics of the German business associations in the clusters (see Table 8.5) confirm that organizational resources are an important determinant of cluster membership. Two organizational features stand out. First, multi-level players are far better equipped than interest organizations in the other clusters. On average, they have about two and half times to three times as many financial resources at their disposal than niche organizations, occasional players

Table 8.4.   Cluster membership of firms and of associations according to political systems.

			Associations and firms					
			EU assoc.	German assoc.	British assoc.	French assoc.	Large firms	Total
Clusters	Niche organizations	N	18	62	49	29		158
		% of associations and firms	11.1%	19.3%	24.0%	25.7%		18.9%
	Occasional players	N	17	57	33	33	2	142
		% of associations and firms	10.5%	17.8%	16.2%	29.2%	5.9%	17.0%
	Traditionalists	N	18	105	72	28	4	227
		% of associations and firms	11.1%	32.7%	35.3%	24.8%	11.8%	27.2%
	EU players	N	85	4	5	7	3	104
		% of associations and firms	52.5%	1.2%	2.5%	6.2%	8.8%	12.5%
	Multi-level players	N	24	93	45	16	25	203
		% of associations and firms	14.8%	29.0%	22.1%	14.2%	73.5%	24.3%
Total		N	162	321	204	113	34	834
		% of associations and firms	100.0%	100.0%	100.0%	100.0%	100.0%	100.0%

Table 8.5. German business associations: sectoral and organizational characteristics according to clusters.

Sectoral and organizational properties	Niche organizations	Occasional players	Tradition-alists	Multi-level players	EU players[a]	Sig.
Average degree of inter-nationalization (foreign turnover as percentage of total turnover)	19.6	24.6	24.1	27.9	28.5	0.119[b]
Average degree of concentration (turnover of largest three firms as percentage of total turnover)	25.3	30.8	30.8	33.0	33.7	0.282[b]
Average no. of employees in member firms (1,000)	71.1	173.4	134.8	280.8	50.0	0.001[b]
Average budget size (1,000 Euro)	925.0	1,084.3	1,366.0	3,309.4	750.0	0.000[b]
Average resources for interest representation (per cent)	40.3	49.1	51.5	54.8	51.7	0.007[b]
Average resources for services (per cent)	38.5	32.8	32.5	33.3	28.3	0.382[b]
Average resources for market co-ordination (per cent)	12.8	15.3	10.8	7.6	10.0	0.008[b]
Average degree of organization (per cent)	64.3	65.7	73.7	74.2	63.0	0.018[b]
Average number of members	270.1	394.9	332.1	422.3	369.5	0.206[b]
Average number of memberships in EU associations	1.7	2.0	1.8	2.6	3.4	0.057[b]
Liaison office in Brussels (percentage of cluster members)	12.1	22.0	21.1	45.1	50.0	0.000[c]
Type of association						0.694[c]
Sub-sector association	37.3	30.4	37.6	27.2	100.0	
Sector association	54.2	58.9	55.4	60.9		
Cross-sector association (percentage of cluster members)	8.5	10.7	6.9	12.0		
Type of members						0.019[c]
Firms, individuals, organizations	80.0	80.4	61.6	57.1	50.0	
Associations	6.7	8.9	14.1	18.7		
Firms and associations (percentage of cluster members)	13.3	10.7	24.2	24.2	50.0	

Notes:
[a] EU players have been omitted from the analysis of variance and the CHI^2 tests because of the small number of cases.
[b] One-way analysis of variance.
[c] CHI^2 test.

or traditionalists. Unsurprisingly, they can therefore afford to show greater presence in Brussels than the other types of interest organizations. While only 12 per cent of the niche organizations and little more than one-fifth of the occasional players and the traditionalists can afford an office in Brussels, this holds for forty-five out of 100 multi-level players. Their liaison offices serve to regularize contacts with the EU institutions and other interest organizations as well as to participate in the work of the EU associations. Their higher ratio of memberships in EU associations indicates that multi-level players are more firmly embedded in EU policy networks than members of other clusters.

Second, the functional profiles of the different types of associations vary significantly: the routine interlocutors of the political institutions, the traditionalists at the national level and the multi-level players at both levels spend more than half of their resources on the representation of interests. Hence, they are highly specialized on that function. Interest representation is less important for niche organizations who allocate most of their resources to the provision of services and to the co-ordination of markets. The former two types of interest organizations manage to organize about three-quarters of their potential members, while niche organizations and occasional players must content themselves with organizing about two-thirds. Apparently, the provision of collective goods such as the representation of interests in conjunction with the services these organizations offer provides a strong incentive to join these associations.

As a corollary, the clusters differ significantly with regard to the type of members that they organize. Four-fifths of the niche organizations and occasional players organize firms, individuals, and various organizations directly. This holds only for about 60 per cent of the traditionalists and the multi-level players. The latter two types of associations are located at the higher echelons of the associational division of labour: they organize significantly larger shares of associations or of associations and firms directly.

Sectoral features are less strongly associated with cluster membership of German business associations. Here, surprisingly, cluster membership does not differ significantly with respect to the degree of internationalization. This factor is often associated with the assumption that EU policy gains in relevance for interest organizations and triggers activities in the EU multi-level system. However, apparently, even in the internationalized sectors of the German economy the established division of labour among associations is more important in determining which association will act at the national level and which will act in the EU multi-level system. Similarly, the degree of concentration in a sector is not significantly associated with cluster membership. Problems of collective action that result from the number and relative size of the represented firms are only of secondary importance in deciding whether interests are represented at the domestic level or in the multi-level system.

Among the sectoral factors, only economic weight is significantly associated with cluster membership. The multi-level players are more important in economic terms than occasional players, traditionalists, and niche organizations that organize smaller slices of the economy. In part, this results from the fact that multi-level players are situated at the top end of the associational pyramid and aggregate interests on a great scale. But as traditionalists also organize interests at a fairly aggregate level, multi-level players seem to organize genuinely larger economic sectors than these or may be located at even higher levels of the associational pyramid.

Conclusion

Although European integration can trigger profound conflicts among domestic interest groups, it has not been very contentious in Germany in that it has hardly ever led to political protest activities. Only on rare occasions has it fostered the foundation of domestic interest groups that specialize in EU affairs. But since European law can change the framework within which interest groups and their constituencies act, established interest organizations have responded to EU politics in manifold ways to shape EU legislation and take advantage of EU political programmes.

The results confirm the implications of the 'capacity' hypothesis: in general, the changes in the institutional opportunity structure have not led to a major reshuffling of the domestic power structure or to a transformation of the weakly corporatist mode of interest intermediation in Germany. Only the traditionalists that are routinely involved in domestic political processes but not in EU politics might lose political ground at home owing to European integration. But, for the most part, European integration stimulated extensions and modifications of established practices and in general reaffirmed the power of those organizations that had already built up capacities to articulate, aggregate, organize and represent the interests of their members. Establishment in the domestic interest group system and *vis-à-vis* national political institutions, material resources that permit complex multi-level strategies, professionalism in the representation of interests, and sufficient economic weight seem to be crucial for national business interest organizations if they want to establish themselves as relevant for the representation of a specific territorial-functional interest *vis-à-vis* EU institutions.

Furthermore, the domestic mode of interest intermediation matters when it comes to representing interests in the EU multi-level system. German interest organizations find it easier than French or British organizations to represent their interests in the EU multi-level system because their routine involvement in domestic policy formulation and implementation has supported the development of substantial governance capacities. Statism in France and informal pluralism in the United Kingdom did not support such developments to the same extent. Nevertheless, one has to bear in mind that most national business interest organizations remain rooted in the domestic polity: more than 50 per cent of them represent their interests occasionally or routinely *vis-à-vis* national institutions but not *vis-à-vis* EU institutions.

German interest organizations cope with European integration by extending and modifying tried-and-tested routines. The relative smoothness of adaptation processes and the results of the international comparison do not suggest that there is a poor degree of fit between the EU mode of interest intermediation and the German mode, even though EU institutions circumscribe and formalize patterns of associational self-regulation to a greater extent than is usual in Germany. However, the findings do not necessarily support the contrary assumption that these developments are based on a good degree of fit between Germany and the EU. The evidence in this chapter supports the more basic proposition that the distribution of governance capacities among interest organizations shapes their responses to European integration.

Note. I would like to thank the participants of the two workshops that helped in preparing this book for their valuable comments. I owe special thanks to Kenneth Dyson, Klaus Goetz, and Ulf Sverdrup for their detailed and helpful critique.

Appendix: Average number of contacts with political institutions, average level of activity in the policy-making cycle, and average access to information by clusters

	Niche organizations	Occasional players	Traditionalists	EU players	Multi-level players	Total
EU-level agenda-setting	1.46 (0.58) [134]	2.03 (0.70) [131]	1.99 (0.67) [207]	2.38 (0.66) [94]	2.64 (0.53) [193]	2.12 (0.74) [759]
European Commission contacts	1.66 (1.08) [155]	2.77 (1.57) [140]	2.92 (1.37) [218]	5.25 (0.93) [102]	4.92 (0.98) [194]	3.43 (1.79) [809]
European Commission info.	4.44 (1.34) [55]	2.97 (1.19) [100]	4.49 (1.28) [174]	4.81 (1.12) [103]	5.08 (0.97) [198]	4.48 (1.35) [630]
EP contacts	1.29 (0.68) [150]	1.93 (1.25) [135]	2.16 (1.08) [215]	4.44 (1.17) [95]	4.52 (1.10) [194]	2.81 (1.69) [789]
EP info.	4.37 (1.36) [41]	2.83 (1.24) [87]	4.10 (1.26) [159]	4.40 (1.22) [100]	5.16 (0.98) [192]	4.33 (1.40) [579]
Council of the EU contacts	1.09 (0.33) [149]	1.53 (0.97) [132]	1.59 (0.96) [204]	3.41 (1.43) [95]	3.79 (1.46) [184]	2.24 (1.55) [764]
Council of the EU info.	4.17 (1.50) [36]	2.37 (1.10) [84]	3.86 (1.40) [142]	3.42 (1.37) [92]	4.69 (1.20) [182]	3.85 (1.51) [536]
EU regulatory and standardization authorities	1.42 (1.00) [153]	2.65 (1.82) [133]	2.23 (1.58) [203]	2.96 (1.67) [96]	3.08 (1.74) [181]	2.43 (1.69) [766]
EU-level transposition	1.43 (0.53) [129]	2.20 (0.70) [132]	2.68 (0.57) [218]	1.55 (0.58) [95]	2.64 (0.57) [192]	2.24 (0.78) [753]
EU-level implementation	1.49 (0.58) [125]	2.18 (0.69) [132]	2.64 (0.59) [218]	1.44 (0.56) [93]	2.55 (0.61) [185]	2.20 (0.78) [753]
National-level agenda-setting	1.83 (0.66) [132]	2.26 (0.67) [136]	2.38 (0.67) [214]	1.57 (0.66) [77]	2.75 (0.44) [194]	2.27 (0.72) [753]

Appendix: *Continued*

	Niche organizations	Occasional players	Traditionalists	EU players	Multi-level players	Total
National government contacts	1.88 (1.23) [147]	3.66 (1.56) [136]	4.55 (1.14) [221]	2.66 (1.77) [102]	5.09 (0.98) [191]	3.79 (1.76) [797]
National government info.	4.94 (0.92) [71]	2.99 (1.12) [111]	5.27 (0.86) [210]	3.86 (1.31) [49]	5.04 (1.03) [193]	4.65 (1.31) [634]
National parliament contacts	1.44 (0.89) [142]	2.29 (1.39) [128]	3.25 (1.36) [214]	1.67 (1.27) [96]	4.45 (1.18) [190]	2.86 (1.67) [770]
National parliament info.	5.04 (0.91) [57]	3.21 (1.17) [100]	5.01 (0.91) [195]	3.69 (1.24) [39]	5.01 (0.98) [185]	4.61 (1.23) [576]
National-level position formulation	1.93 (0.63) [135]	2.56 (0.55) [139]	2.82 (0.41) [219]	1.97 (0.75) [79]	2.92 (0.28) [195]	2.56 (0.64) [767]
National regulatory and standardization authorities	1.90 (1.34) [137]	3.60 (1.79) [125]	3.78 (1.59) [191]	1.71 (1.26) [96]	3.93 (1.66) [166]	3.15 (1.81) [715]
National-level transposition	1.72 (0.51) [132]	2.57 (0.51) [136]	2.84 (0.38) [219]	1.45 (0.53) [77]	2.74 (0.46) [194]	2.43 (0.69) [758]
National-level implementation	1.74 (0.58) [131)	2.50 (0.60) [134]	2.81 (0.42) [217]	1.39 (0.49) [76]	2.61 (0.57) [188]	2.37 (0.72) [746]

Note:
The figures in each cell present the mean, (the standard deviation), and [the number of cases].
Contacts have been measured on a 6-point scale: 1 (no contacts), 2 (yearly), 3 (half-yearly),
4 (quarterly), 5 (monthly), 6 (weekly). Activities to represent interests throughout the
policy-making cycle have been measured on a 3-point scale: 1 (no activities), 2 (sometimes),
3 (often). Access to information from political institutions has been measured on a 6-point scale
from 1 (very difficult) to 6 (not difficult at all).

9

The Media Agenda: The Marginalization and Domestication of Europe

KATRIN VOLTMER & CHRISTIANE EILDERS

Introduction

EUROPEAN INTEGRATION IS A COMPLEX PROCESS that involves a multitude of dimensions of interaction both across national boundaries and within the domestic political arena. What started in the late 1950s as an economic association in a limited area of co-operation has now developed into a political project that is unique in the history of international relations. However, to be successful European integration requires more than the implementation of efficient institutions and the harmonization of national and European policy-making. It also involves processes of cultural integration and the emergence of a communicative sphere that allows citizens to get involved in public discourse about European politics. Since in modern societies the mass media are the dominant arena of public debate, this chapter aims to explore the media's role in communicating Europe. Introducing the media into Europeanization studies enables us to come to grips with the complex and important cognitive aspects of integration including collective identities, symbolic politics, and public communication.

In normative democratic theory, public communication is widely recognized as an essential prerequisite of the legitimacy of political institutions, because it provides for the accountability and transparency of decision-making (Dahl 1989; Sarcinelli 1987). Democratic governance requires political decisions to be justified in public and subjected to critical debate. In this way, citizens get the chance to consider alternative viewpoints and to participate in an informed manner. While this undoubtedly holds for domestic politics, it seems that for a long time European governance has operated without and beyond public debate, and thus lacks a vital resource of legitimacy. Over decades, European integration could count on broad, albeit passive popular support leaving decision-making largely in the hands of the political élites. However, this 'permissive consensus' has been dramatically eroding since the early 1990s, coinciding with, and maybe even responding to, an intensification of integration after the Maastricht Treaty. Failed or extremely close referendums on ratification of this treaty in Denmark and France and Ireland's initial rejection of the Nice Treaty are alarming indicators

Proceedings of the British Academy, **119**, 173–197. © The British Academy 2003.

that policy-makers have been much less successful than expected in convincing citizens of the necessity and the benefits of further European integration (Niedermayer 1998).

Given the vital role of public communication in modern democracies, there are good reasons to assume that the diminishing popular support for the EU can be traced back to a lack of communication between the decision-making level, on the one hand, and the citizens who are affected by these decisions, on the other. In fact, many authors (Eder, Hellmann and Trenz 1998; Neidhardt, Koopmans and Pfetsch 2000) attribute the democratic deficit of the EU to a communication deficit. More than in the case of domestic politics, European decision-making appears as something that takes place behind closed doors, hidden from the public eye and sheltered from critical debate. Consequently, most people perceive 'Brussels' as remote from their personal lives and even in contradiction to their own interests.

The problems arising from the growing gap between public scepticism towards Europe and the transfer of an increasing range of competencies to the supranational level highlights the fact that successful integration is a multi-dimensional process that involves not only institutional changes from above, but also cultural changes from below. Almond and Verba's concept of the cultural underpinnings of democratic institutions (1963) supports the idea of the inter-action of 'top-down' and 'bottom-up' processes which, although developed to analyse national politics, can be easily applied to European politics as well. This chapter argues that the viability of democracy depends on the congruence of micro and macro variables, i.e. attitudes and values held by the public, on the one hand, and the institutional structure, on the other. The mass media can be regarded as serving a central linkage function between these two levels of European integration, implying that European integration from above must be accompanied by a Europeanization of public communication in order to overcome its lack of legitimacy and popular involvement.

This chapter investigates whether the assumption that the media contribute to the communication deficit of the EU is reflected in the empirical pattern of polit-ical coverage. In particular, it explores the extent to which German media take a Europeanized perspective on political affairs and whether or not they promote the politics of European integration. So far, only a few empirical studies have inves-tigated how Europe is represented on the national media agenda (see for an overview Semetko, de Vreese and Peter 2000; Semetko and Valkenburg 2000). An early comparative project on the elections for the European Parliament in 1979 (Blumler 1983) shows that both campaigning and media coverage were pre-dominantly national in focus. This pattern does not seem to have changed very much over the past two decades (Kevin 2001). More research is currently under way (de Beus and Mak 2001; Medrano 2002), but the area is still little explored. This chapter aims to fill this gap by providing empirical evidence for a state that is one of the key players in the European project.

The study is based on a content analysis of the editorials of German national quality newspapers covering the period between 1994 and 1998. It begins with a theoretical discussion of different approaches to the relationship between European integration and public communication, and the specific role of the media in representing political matters. It then presents empirical evidence for the media's limited capability to bring Europe into the national agenda of public debate about the future course of supranational governance. Although the data do not allow us empirically to test for the actual effects of media coverage on public opinion, we believe that the analysis of the structure of public discourse on Europe is a valuable enterprise that has been widely neglected in European studies so far. As we know from a large body of research, the media do guide citizens' opinion formation, especially when it comes to issues that evade the grasp of everyday experience (Bryant and Zillman 1994; Zaller 1992). However, even if individuals do not follow the media's particular interpretation of an issue, public deliberation is a normative *sine qua non* that endows European integration with the rationality and legitimacy required of any kind of democratic politics.

Three Models of the Europeanization of Political Communication

There are basically three different models of how and where Europeanization of public communication could occur. They involve both normative expectations of an ideal European public sphere in terms of its reach and deliberative quality and empirical observations regarding the actual possibility of implementing these ideas in the media's day-to-day coverage of European affairs. The most comprehensive approach is the notion of a *transnational European public sphere* with European media addressing a pan-European audience across all member states of the EU (Gerhards 1992, 1993; see also special issue of *Javnost/The Public* 2001). In this model, the role of the media in European integration is assumed to be comparable with their role in the emergence of nation-states and nationalism in Europe (Neidhardt, Koopmans and Pfetsch 2000). 'Nation-building' is understood as a long-term and complex process involving the unification of formerly divergent parts of a territory, the centralization of power, cultural homogenization, and the creation of popular loyalty to the central authority. The invention of the printing press by Johannes Gutenberg in the sixteenth century was a first and crucial step in this process as it fostered the standardization of language, which was important not only for the development of a common culture but also for communicating and enforcing the decisions of the centralized political authority throughout the expanse of the state territory (Schulze 1999; Thompson 1995). The emergence of a mass-circulation press during the nineteenth century further accelerated and intensified the interrelationship between the media and nation-building. Anderson argues that the nation is an 'imagined community', a social construct that does not exist *per se* and, therefore, has to be 'invented' and inter-preted—in other words, needs to be communicated to become perceived as real (1983, Chapter 3). The mass consumption of newspapers created an unpre-cedented density, frequency, and simultaneity of public communication, which enabled people to link themselves to larger, and more remote, social realities existing beyond their own immediate environment.

Given the history of the media in promoting the integration of large-scale nation-states it appears to be a logical assumption that they could serve a similar function in European integration. 'Europe' is an even more abstract political structure than the nation-state, requiring symbolic mediation in order to be 'imag-inable' for individual citizens as a political community that deserves loyalty and support. Owing to their access to political decision-makers, on the one hand, and technologies of mass distribution, on the other, the media are probably the only intermediary capable of performing this function.

However, this function may require a new infrastructure of mass communica-tion, ideally a European media system, or at least single media outlets that oper-ate on a transnational scale addressing a pan-European audience (Gerhards 1992). In view of recent technological innovations such as satellites and digital televi-sion, eliminating the limitations of the national boundaries of mass communica-tion, this does not seem to be too utopian. In addition, media corporations are more and more becoming 'global players' who operate on international markets. At the same time, a couple of factors counteract the development of a European media system or European media, one of which is political. So far European policy-makers have confined European media regulation to economic aspects, focusing on de-regulation of the media market and (to some extent) on competition and anti-concentration measures. Cultural aspects and content have been left in the competence of national regulatory policy, arguably in response to strong domes-tic interests of the governments of the member states (Hoffmann-Riem 1985). Thus, compared to other policy fields, there has been only marginal transfer of responsibilities in media regulation from the national to the European level (Dyson *et al.* 1988; Humphreys 1996; Levy 1999).

There are also economic impediments to the emergence of a pan-European media system. Since most media aim at maximizing audiences in order to be prof-itable, they are primarily interested in homogenous target markets. These can best be found within national boundaries where people speak the same language, share similar values, and follow similar daily routines of media consumption. Thus, while the management structure and the production of the dominant media corporations is highly globalized, audience markets are still national. With regard to cultural constraints, language is undoubtedly the main factor that prevents the successful operation of transnational broadcasting. It is, therefore, not accidental that the only transnational television channels that attract large audience shares are not, or only marginally, dependent on language, notably MTV (a music channel) and Eurosport. However, neither of them contributes to a European public sphere of political debate.

The experiences of television channels that provide political information to audiences across national boundaries are mixed (Hasebrink 1998). There have been several attempts, but most of them were unsuccessful because the production costs, in particular dubbing when the programme is not transmitted in English, turned out to be too high to justify the operation. Those programmes that did survive—such as Euronews or Arte—have been able to establish themselves in a niche market of European culture and politics.[1] The situation is hardly different when we look at the printed press. Language diversity seems to be even more problematic here than in broadcasting. There is no pan-European multilingual newspaper. Newspapers that have been launched as genuinely European outlets are the exception and apparently not successful. Instead, it is the *Financial Times* and *The Economist*, both London-based newspapers, that are more and more growing into the role of truly European media. Both attract a significant readership beyond their country of origin, although this is again a very small segment of the population in terms of its social composition. The two papers clearly aim at the top level of political and economic decision-makers who operate in a cosmopolitan environment and to whom English is a familiar (second) language of professional life (Schlesinger 1999).

The conclusion to be drawn from this discussion is that pan-European media, be they audiovisual or print, are unlikely to appear. Besides the particular problems of transcultural, multi-lingual publishing, media markets in general are undergoing a process of segmentation and diversification. Thus, European integration takes place in a situation where the media, even public-service broadcasting, is losing its unifying force. The few existing pan-European media hardly contribute to a European public sphere. Rather than integrating a European citizenry they may even foster the growing knowledge gap between 'information-rich' and 'information-poor' parts of the population (Bonfadelli 1994; Donohue et al. 1975).

Instead of the apparently unrealistic view of a single encompassing European public sphere, some authors propose the model of *segmented transnational public spheres*. This approach refers to those normative ideas of pluralist democracy that suggest integration through competition between divergent interests and ideas rather than a uniform arena of public debate. Accordingly, Schlesinger (1999: 270; Schlesinger and Kevin 2000) dismisses the notion of an overarching European public sphere altogether, arguing that a model of 'overlapping public spheres' is more adequate if we are to understand communication processes in the context of the complexity of multi-level governance.

---

[1] See Dill (1991), Machill (1998), and Schlesinger (1999) for a detailed account of channels like Europa TV and Euronews; see also Krüger (2000) on Arte.

Following a similar line of argument, Eder, Hellmann and Trenz (1998) point out that there exists an extensive network of communication in Europe where specific segments of the public crystallize around particular issues. Drawing on Habermas' (1989) notion of the 'structural transformation of the public sphere' in response to late-capitalism, Eder (2000) conceptualizes European public communication as undergoing another transformation. This transformation involves issue-specific transnational communication replacing, or at least supplementing, the traditional national public sphere which is based on cultural and linguistic communalities of general national audiences. Indeed, a multitude of interest groups and social movements have discovered Europe as an arena of mobilization that sometimes provides even more efficient channels of influence than the national arena (Imig and Tarrow 2001). These 'issue publics' are not necessarily confined to élites. They often include grassroot activists and even citizens who only occasionally become actively involved in an issue of personal concern, dropping out again after an adequate political decision has been achieved. Using migration policy as an example, Eder, Hellmann and Trenz (1998) demonstrates the dynamics of communication within a particular 'issue public' in the course of European-level decision-making.

While 'issue publics' are rather exclusive in the sense that the general public is not involved, they are inclusive in terms of transnational participation and exchange. In this process, the mass media are only of marginal significance, partly because—as outlined above—there is an inadequate infrastructure of mass communication on the European level, and partly because the issues that are deliberated in segmented public spheres are often too complex to be easily communicated via the mass media. Instead, the internet is increasingly becoming the first-choice medium for issue activists to address an attentive public that is willing to become involved in complex issues and, if necessary, can be mobilized for both formal and unconventional participation (Hill and Hughes 1998).

However, both models discussed so far suffer from a crucial deficit: they systematically exclude large parts of the citizenry from participating in public debate. The pan-European model in its present empirical manifestation addresses only the political and economic élites, whereas the 'issue-public' model is confined to highly specialized activists. At the present stage, universal access to European public communication for all citizens seems to be possible only by way of a third model, the *Europeanization of the national public sphere*. As we argued above, the majority of the media in Europe, both print and audiovisual, are primarily reaching out for national audiences. At the same time, European institutions of political decision-making are closely linked to the national governments of EU member states. Therefore, policy-makers address their domestic electorates, rather than a European audience, to legitimize European politics, and they do so by using the national mass media. Further, since politicians aim for re-election by their domestic electorate, it can be assumed that decisions made on the European level are packaged as being in the national rather than the European interest. In this way, Europe does enter a broader public sphere, although more often than not through the looking glass of the national perspective.

Students of political communication dispute whether or not this model is conducive to European integration (Gerhards 1993). From a critical point of view, Europeanization of the national public sphere may be more adequately conceptualized as a 'domestication' of Europe[2] promoting national egoisms, parochial thinking, and even aggressive nationalism rather than a perspective that recognizes the shared interests of European citizens across borders. On the other hand, emphasizing the impact of European politics on domestic politics is an important and legitimate aspect of communicating Europe. After all, Europe is not an end in itself, but a means designed to safeguard and promote the interests—political, economic and cultural—of the people of the member states. It can even be argued that the domestic view on Europe perfectly reflects the present state of European politics, in which the most powerful body of decision-making, the Council of Ministers, is composed of national actors negotiating national interests. By contrast, the competencies of the European Parliament, a body that represents ideological rather than national divisions, are still fairly limited. Hence, the most effective way for citizens to sanction European politics is still through participation in national elections. Information about the impact of European politics on domestic conditions of life is, therefore, a valuable—albeit restricted—contribution to enabling citizens to make informed choices.

Comparing the three models of Europeanization of political communication the notion of a pan-European public sphere appears to coming closest to the normative assumptions of a European polity based on open and critical debate. In comparison, the notion of Europeanization of national political communication—or domestication of European politics—seems to be a drawback, as it hardly reaches out for a perspective beyond the limits of national boundaries. It also fails to approximate the high level of deliberation that is possible in transnational 'issue publics', in particular when European issues become part of election campaigns that make excessive use of simplification, polemics and symbolic politics. At the same time, from the normative viewpoint of democratic theory, the Europeanization of the national public sphere carries some significant advantages. Since there are no systematic barriers for all types of national media to pick up European issues, this model is the only one that does not systematically exclude large parts of the population, be it due to social stratification or to patterns of political involvement.

Following this theoretical discussion, our empirical analysis investigates the degree to which German media are Europeanized. In particular, we operationalize the concept of Europeanization of public communication in the following way:

---

[2] We are indebted to Philip Schlesinger who drew our attention to this perspective of interpreting current patterns of public discourse on Europe.

- the extent to which the media address European issues, thus making Europe visible to a general audience

- the extent to which the media relate European issues to domestic politics, thus demonstrating the relevance of European integration to the national electorate

- the media's own position, indicating whether they generally support or oppose further European integration

- the way in which the media evaluate the day-to-day business of European politics represented by European actors.

The Role of the Media in Communicating Europe

The role of the media in modern society is often—quite naively—perceived as merely reflecting reality and serving political actors as a channel of communication to campaign for their own cause. This is a very inadequate picture of the dynamics of political communications. Along with other political actors communicating in the public realm, the media are actively involved in a process of constructing reality, thereby imposing their own 'preferred reading' on political events (Altheide and Snow 1988; Swanson 1981). More often than not, the media's notion of political reality contradicts the interests and goals of political power holders, triggering frequent conflicts over the control of the public agenda between political actors and the media. Mazzoleni (1987) describes the relationship between politicians and the press as a conflict between 'media logic', which is guided by news values and the maximization of audiences, and 'party logic', which is determined by strategies of power-seeking. In fact, public communication can be understood as different notions of reality competing with one another and seeking to dominate the public agenda. The media contribute to this debate not only by providing a forum of exchange but also by expressing their own preferences and opinions for which they try to find resonance among their audience and policy-makers alike.

Given the media's genuine role in shaping the symbolic environment, they have to be regarded as a political actor in their own right (Eilders 2000; Page 1996; Patterson and Donsbach 1996). While this applies to news coverage in general, it holds even more with regard to editorials and commentaries. Owing to the journalistic professional norm of separating facts and opinion, it is mainly in the designated opinion sections where the media explicitly take part in actual controversies. By supporting or criticizing certain political actors and policies, they frequently act as powerful opinion leaders, creating a particular 'climate of opinion' (Noelle-Neumann 1984) that may eventually cause politicians to change the course of policy-making. From the viewpoint of the audience, editorials are becoming more and more important, as they respond to people's need for orientation (Voltmer 1998; Weaver 1977). With the ever-growing amount of information that is available through different media, most notably the internet, and politics becoming increasingly complex, 'biased information' (Calvert 1985) helps individuals to make sense of the political world. Newspapers that pursue a fairly consistent editorial policy provide their audience with valuable clues as to how to structure and to interpret the daily flow of political information (Dalton, Beck and Huckfeldt 1998; Page, Shapiro and Dempsey 1987; Zaller 1992).

Editorials are, therefore, an important aspect that has been largely neglected in political communication research. Unlike news reports that require balance and objectivity, editorials are the place where the voice of the media can be heard most clearly and where the media's own political positions are most openly and legitimately expressed (Eilders 2000, 2002). However, the vast majority of media content research has been concerned with the structure of news rather than with the opinion sections of newspapers. This chapter aims to fill this research gap by focusing exclusively on the media's direct contribution to the political debate as it is expressed in editorials. It is based on the belief that for European integration the media's interpretation of political events plays a particularly crucial role. Europe is a typical example of 'non-obtrusive' issues (Lang and Lang 1984) that cannot be immediately experienced in everyday life, so that people's perception depends to a high degree on mediation and interpretation by public opinion leaders such as the media. Analysing commentaries and editorials will enable us to explore the media's genuine contribution to the symbolic construction of Europe in public communication.

The structure of our analysis of Europeanization of German newspaper editorials draws on the three basic functions of the media in modern societies.

Agenda-Setting

As agenda-setters, the media draw the attention of the audience to a particular section of political reality. By selecting a few issues out of the stream of current events and putting them into the public spotlight, the media structure public debate and provide for a thematic frame of reference for individual opinion formation (Dearing and Rogers 1996; Iyengar and Kinder 1987; Protess and McCombs 1991). Agenda-setting and selective emphasis not only meet basic requirements of individual information processing, but also serve an important role in the macro-integration of society. In his seminal article on 'Public Opinion', Luhmann (1970) argues that modern societies can no longer be integrated by consensus because the value pluralism of liberal democracy precludes any uniformity of opinions. Rather, integration can be achieved only by focused attention on particular issues. Issues that enter the public agenda can be seen as an indicator of the existence of a problem or malfunction. They trigger public debate and force decision-makers to propose possible measures for solving the problem. Thus, a simple but crucial precondition of cultural integration is Europe being a visible and frequent part of the public agenda. In his analysis of public communication on the corruption scandal of the European Commission in 1999, Trenz (2000) shows how a focus event, even a negative one, can activate public involvement in European issues and promote organizational learning to the benefit of democratic politics in the EU.

Recent research has expanded agenda-setting theory to so-called 'second-level agenda-setting' (Ghanem 1997; McCombs, Lopez-Escobar and Llamas 2000). Processes of agenda-setting not only involve the salience of particular issues, but also the salience of particular aspects of these issues, for example personality attributes of political candidates or the connection of an issue to other problems.[3] Since these attributed aspects endow an issue with meaning and significance, they are assumed to dominate individual and collective opinion-building. Our operationalization of Europeanization includes these considerations insofar as we analyse the national context of European issues on the media agenda.

Position

The media express their own position in political conflicts. Editorials allow them to do this freely without the professional restrictions that apply to regular news coverage. Historically, the media in most western European states developed political standpoints in interaction, often in close alliance, with political parties. This persistent relationship has been termed 'press–party parallelism' (Seymour-Ure 1974), indicating various levels of organizational co-operation and ideological concordance. Although in the German case the Nazi regime interrupted the free development of the media, ideological parallelism between the German press and political parties is still clearly discernable (Kepplinger 1985a; Voltmer 1997). However, since European integration does not fit into the usual left–right distinction of politics, it remains to be seen which position the media take on this issue.

Evaluation

Finally, the media evaluate actual political events and the performance of political actors. A supportive position on Europe does not necessarily coincide with a

---

[3] Conceptually, second-level agenda-setting is closely related to the framing concept, a process whereby the media choose a particular context of meaning to address an issue (Entman 1993; Nelson, Clawson and Oxley 1997).

positive evaluation of the concrete course of European integration. On the contrary, in the light of overall preferences, daily politics may fall far short of the expectations related to positions of principle. Evaluation is part of the media's role of a 'fourth estate', or 'watch-dog' who alerts the public to any problems related to the process of European integration, be it the emergence of unforeseen difficulties, misconduct of political élites, or inefficient implementation of decisions.

Our analysis of the Europeanization of the German press will be guided by these analytical concepts:

- *Agenda-setting*: To what extent do the media select European issues and actors as topics for commentary, thus providing them with additional salience besides the current news agenda? Do the media draw connections between European politics and other national policy areas, thus demonstrating Europe's significance for domestic policy-making?
- *Position*: Which preferences regarding European integration do the media put forward? Is the issue contested between the media? What is the level of conflict/consensus compared to other policy areas?
- *Evaluation*: How do the media evaluate European institutions and political actors, both European and national, that are involved in policy-making on the European level? Compared to other policy areas, is there a more positive or negative tenor of evaluation?

The results of this analysis will enable us to draw inferences about the extent to which the media might be conducive or detrimental to European integration. Although we do not imply a clear causal relationship between media coverage and public opinion, we know from the existing literature that the media do have the power to affect people's attitudes. At the same time, it has to be kept in mind that the media also reflect the environment in which they operate. Hence, media coverage may be, at least in part, a response to the public mood as well as the result of the public relations activities of the sources of information on which the media depend.

Study Design

The empirical data presented in this chapter derive from a larger project on editorial discourse in the German quality press conducted at the Wissenschaftszentrum Berlin (Eilders and Lüter 1998; Neidhardt, Eilders and Pfetsch 1998). The analysis is based on a content analysis of 8,946 editorials in *Die Welt*, *Frankfurter Allgemeine Zeitung* (*FAZ*), *Süddeutsche Zeitung* (*SZ*), *Frankfurter Rundschau* (*FR*), and *Tageszeitung* (*TAZ*) between 1994 and 1998. In Germany, editorials do not represent views of single journalists, but indicate the editorial stance of a media outlet. It has been shown that the issues and opinions brought up in editorials correspond with the general news content (Hagen 1993;

Schönbach 1977). Thus, editorials provide an efficient way of assessing the range of opinions in the media agenda on European integration. Although none of the above papers has institutional links to a particular party, political ideologies rooted in the party structure are still reflected in the press, especially in the national quality newspapers. They cover almost the entire political spectrum with the *Die Welt* located at the right and the *Tageszeitung* at the left end of the continuum. Between these poles beginning from the right and proceeding to the left, there are the *Frankfurter Allgemeine Zeitung*, the *Süddeutsche Zeitung*, and the *Frankfurter Rundschau* (Hagen 1993; Kepplinger 1985a; Schönbach 1977; Donsbach, Wolling and Blomberg 1996; Schulz 1997: 104).

Apart from the horizontal or ideological segmentation of the media system showing most clearly in the quality press, the media are also divided vertically. The quality newspapers represent the élite media, whereas the tabloids, regional and local newspapers and most television programmes are considered the popular media. Owing to their particular position in the media system as opinion leaders, however, the élite media reach a much larger segment of the citizens than their immediate audience. By determining issues and perspectives of the news, they develop a strong quantitative significance (Kepplinger 1985b). In a survey among journalists of all types of media most respondents indicated that the élite press plays an important role for their own work (Kepplinger 1985a). Inter-media agenda-setting with one media outlet influencing the agenda of the other media is well documented not only for Germany (Kepplinger 1985a; Mathes and Pfetsch 1991; Noelle-Neumann and Mathes 1987), but also for the USA (Edelstein *et al* 1989; McCombs 1992). Reese and Danielian (1989) describe it as a 'bandwagon-effect' between different media. Another series of studies found a high level of consonance even across the horizontal and vertical segmentations of the media system[4] showing that basically all media focus on the same issues.

Regarding the evaluation of political issues, however, a uniform media voice cannot be expected. The horizontal segmentation of the media market is likely to result in considerable ideological differences determined by the newspapers' position on the left–right spectrum. From a strategic point of view, the editorial policy of newspapers is not only the result of historical 'press-party parallelism' (Seymour-Ure 1974); it also serves an important economic function in the competition between newspapers. Establishing a specific ideological profile makes newspapers clearly distinguishable from their competitors, thus allowing them to position themselves on the audience market. This applies also to the tabloid press. Since most German tabloids, notably the *Bild-Zeitung*, are characterized by conservative viewpoints, their political position corresponds with the conservative spectrum of the quality press. The conclusion is that the high level of consonance

---

[4] See Bruns and Marcinkowski (1997); Kepplinger (1985b); Knoche and Lindgens (1988); Trebbe and Weiß (1997); see also the summary in Rössler 2002.

in the media system, inter-media agenda-setting, and, in particular, the opinion leadership of the quality newspapers are unlikely to produce entirely different agendas in the élite and the popular press. Instead, conflicts are more likely to be located on the horizontal, i.e. evaluative dimension between liberal and conservative newspapers.

In order to cover a substantial period of time, our sample consists of all political editorials taken from two quarters of each year with the exception of editorials that deal exclusively with international news without reference to Germany or the EU. Unlike a single-issue study on Europe, this study design allows us to compare the pattern and tone in which European and domestic issues are covered in the media. For each editorial up to three issues, three positions on these issues, as well as four actors could be coded. We employed a detailed coding scheme comprising the following elements:

- *Issues*: The initial coding list contained of 600 single-issue categories that were aggregated to forty-five larger issue areas, one of them being European integration. An all-issue study like this covering a time period of five years inevitably involves a trade-off between a broad, generalizable approach and specific in-depth analysis. Therefore, we were forced to move away from concrete event-type issue categories (restricted by time and space) and define issues on a fairly abstract level. Thus, we differentiate between issue areas like EU policy and its different sub-issues, welfare policy or legal policy, but not between specific debates or decisions related to those issue areas.

- *Positions*: In order to measure the general political positions of the newspapers on certain issue areas, we employed a parsimonious instrument that theoretically covers the entire range of political conflicts (Voltmer 1998). For each policy issue addressed in the editorials one of sixteen bipolar conflict dimensions and the particular policy preference could be coded. For the purpose of the analysis of European integration we concentrate on two conflict dimensions only. 'Co-operation versus conflict' and 'supranationalism versus sovereignty' refer to either a co-operative approach in international relations with the willingness to give up competences or to an approach where national interests are pursued in confrontation with other states and the preservation of national sovereignty is seen as the primary goal.

- *Actors*: We coded individual and collective actors at both the supranational and national levels.

- *Evaluation*: The commentators' evaluations of the actors were coded on a three-point scale ranging from positive to negative assessment.

Our analysis centres on 771 EU-related editorials that either address the issue of European policy or refer to EU actors. We found more editorials addressing EU

Table 9.1. Agenda-setting: representation of the supranational level regarding issues and actors (N = Number of editorials).

	With EU issue N = 679	Without EU issue N = 8,267
With EU actors	378	92
N = 470	4.2%	1%
Without EU actors	301	8,175
N = 8,476	3.4%	91.4%

issues than editorials referring to EU actors. 378 editorials complied with both criteria, 301 addressed only EU issues, and ninety-two referred only to EU actors (Table 9.1). The content analysis will focus on agenda-setting, the general position on Europe, and evaluation. It examines how much attention the newspapers direct toward Europe, to what degree they support European integration, and how they evaluate European actors.

Empirical Findings

Agenda-Setting

To address the role of Europe in the media agenda, we measured Europeanization by the number of references to the supranational level, on the one hand, and the presentation of interrelatedness between EU policies or EU actors with domestic policies or domestic actors, on the other. The data show a very low representation of the supranational level on the German media agenda. Most attention was directed to domestic politics, with EU issues mentioned only 884 times,[5] representing 5.6 per cent of all issue references in the sample (Table 9.2). Attention to the supranational level was accounted for mainly by the sub-issues of 'different areas of co-operation', 'problems of EU functioning', and 'EU enlargement' (Table 9.3). Even foreign policy and alliance policy (7.8 per cent and 1.9 per cent, respectively, which traditionally range low on the domestic media agenda and are less likely to affect the German electorate than European issues, received more attention than Europe. Some optimism, however, can be drawn from the slight increase of European issue references between 1994 and 1998 (1994: 5.8 per cent; 1995: 1.9 per cent; 1996: 4.1 per cent ;1997: 7.3 per cent; 1998: 9 per cent). As the level of attention to foreign policy remained the same over this period of time, the increase of EU issues cannot be explained by a growing interest in international relations in general, but points to a growing awareness of the media of

---

[5] These references were found in 679 editorials.

Table 9.2. Agenda-setting: representation of EU policies compared to foreign, alliance, and domestic policy across newspapers (per cent) (N = Number of issue references).

Policy	TAZ	FR	SZ	FAZ	WELT	Total
EU policy N = 884	4.7	5.9	7.1	6.1	3.9	5.6
Foreign policy N = 1,233	8.3	8.0	8.5	7.2	7.0	7.8
Alliance policy N = 300	1.7	1.5	2.1	2.0	2.1	1.9
Domestic policy N = 13,473	85.3	84.6	82.3	84.7	87.0	84.7

Table 9.3. Agenda-setting: representation of EU sub-issues (N = Number of issue references).

Sub-issues (N = 884)	%
Areas of co-operation	33.1
Problems in functioning	15.6
EU enlargement	10.1
EU institutions	7.6
EU agriculture	7.4
EU policy in general	5.5
European integration	4.1
Monetary policy	3.6
Other EU issues	12.4

the European level of governance. Comparing the newspapers of our sample, we found only few differences in the salience that the individual outlets assigned to EU issues, with the liberal newspaper spectrum directing slightly more attention to Europe than their conservative counterparts.[6]

The representation of EU actors was even lower than the interest expressed in EU issues. EU actors were addressed 542 times,[7] accounting for only 1.6 per cent of all actor references. More than half of them concerned the EU as a whole, less than one-fifth referred to the Commission, and less than one tenth each to the European Parliament and to the Council of Ministers (Table 9.4). Again, there were only few differences between the newspapers, with a little more attention for

---

[6] The precise numbers for EU policy are: *TAZ* 4.7 per cent, *FR* 5.9 per cent, *SZ* 7.1 per cent, *FAZ* 4.1 per cent, *WELT* 3.9 per cent; for EU actors: *TAZ* 1.6 per cent, *FR* 1.7 per cent, *SZ* 2.3 per cent, *FAZ* 1.4 per cent, *WELT* 1.3 per cent.

[7] Actors references were found in 470 editorials.

Table 9.4.   Agenda-setting: representation of EU actors
(N = Number of actor references).

EU actors (N = 542)	%
Entire EU institution	53.3
European Parliament	6.5
Council	6.6
Commission	18.8
Court of Justice	3.0
Other European institutions	11.8

EU actors in the liberal newspapers.[8] Parallel to the increase in issue attention, the share of EU actors also showed a slight increase over the years (1.2 per cent; 7 per cent, 1.6 per cent, 2.1 per cent, 2.3 per cent, respectively). Still, against the background of the increasing relevance of the European level in many policy areas, the clear focus on domestic policies and actors is somewhat surprising. Apparently, the media failed to assign significant salience to Europe and supplied only insufficient information to enable the audience to come to an 'enlightened understanding' (Dahl 1989) about the benefits and disadvantages of European integration. However, lacking a precise quantitative yardstick, it is difficult to judge how much coverage would adequately reflect the significance of European politics and promote the formation of informed opinions.

Apart from the representation of Europe on the domestic media agenda, we also investigated the degree of interrelatedness between the two levels of governance as an indicator for the Europeanization of political communication. Although there is a strong domestic focus in the German media, indicating only limited Europeanization regarding the representation of Europe, it does not follow that there is a total lack of Europeanization. In the editorials that addressed Europe, we found a high degree of interrelatedness of the European and domestic levels: 633 editorials relate Europe to domestic policies as compared to only forty-seven exclusively addressing the EU without reference to the national realm. The same holds true for the interrelatedness of actors operating on different levels: all 470 editorials addressing EU actors relate them to domestic actors. This indicates the high relevance assigned to the domestic perspective in discussing European politics. European politics is not presented as entirely self-contained and without consequences for the domestic arena. Instead, the editorials highlight the relations between the European and domestic arena and

---

[8] The precise numbers for EU actors are: *TAZ* 1.6 per cent, *FR* 1.7 per cent, *SZ* 2.3 per cent, *FAZ* 1.4 per cent, *WELT* 1.3 per cent.

point out the possible effects of European politics on domestic policies. While incorporating the domestic perspective in the presentation of European politics might be considered 'domestication' rather than Europeanization, it still has to be noted that one part of 'communicating Europe' is to reflect the growing influence of the European level on the domestic arena. Given the majority of editorials that do not relate domestic policies to the European level, however, the significance of multi-level governance is far from being adequately emphasized.

In order to explore the media's focus on particular areas of this interrelatedness, we investigated the specific contextualization of domestic policies and actors in editorials on Europe. Domestic actors addressed in EU editorials include individual or collective actors representing the established German political élite, in particular Chancellor Helmut Kohl, German ministries or the government in general (Table 9.5). The predominance of established political actors on the agenda of EU editorials shows that European integration tends to be almost exclusively presented as a matter of political élites. Citizens accounted for only less than 6 per cent of all references to domestic actors in the EU editorials. Regarding the thematic contextualization, foreign relations, monetary, economic and budgetary policy, migration, and the environment turned out to be the main areas discussed in EU editorials (Table 9.6). The distribution of domestic policy areas addressed in editorials with EU actors shows a very similar picture. The focus on foreign policy points to the strong interdependence between the EU and bilateral relations with other European countries, and the relevance of economic and financial matters reflects the history of the EU as primarily a common market. Migration issues and environmental policy represent problems that can no longer be solved within national boundaries, a fact that has moved them into the spotlight of the public discourse on European integration.

While in the vast majority of the editorials of the German national press, Europe is not addressed at all, the small share of editorials that do represent the supranational level always relate it to domestic politics and actors. The commentators deserve some credit for pointing out the consequences of European politics for the domestic arena, thereby drawing Europe closer to the better-known

Table 9.5. Agenda-setting: representation of selected domestic actors in EU editorials (N = Number of actor references).

Domestic actors (N = 1,686)	%
Chancellor	16.6
Ministries/Ministers	15.3
Government	13.3
Citizens	5.9

Table 9.6. Agenda-setting: contextualization of EU issues with selected domestic policies (per cent) (N = Number of issue references).

Domestic policies	In editorials with EU issues N = 976	In editorials with EU actors N = 734
Foreign relations	19.0	18.8
Monetary policy	8.2	6.5
Economic policy	6.6	6.5
Budgetary policy	4.8	3.4
Migration policy	4.3	3.8
Environment	4.0	4.5
Alliance policy	2.9	4.1
Tax policy	2.7	1.6
Health policy	3.4	3.8
Research policy	2.3	4.1
Media policy	1.7	3.4
Commercial law	0.3	3.8

domestic realm of politics and making it more tangible to the immediate concerns of their audience. Since national media can be expected to devote far more attention to domestic than to European issues, it is not surprising that the Europeanization of the media agenda takes place by way of 'domestifying' relevant areas of European politics rather than relating the whole range of domestic issues to Europe.

General Positions

Employing a content analytical instrument that conceptualizes political positions as general preferences for fundamental alternatives of political action, it was possible to assess the level of support for European integration in the newspapers under study. The most important alternatives regarding the EU are represented by the conflict dimension 'supranationalism versus sovereignty'. This conflict centres on the question of whether and to what extent sovereign rights should be delegated to supranational or international organizations. 'Supranationalism' points to the necessity to delegate rights from the nation-state to supranational organizations. 'Sovereignty', on the other hand, reflects the position that the state should insist on sovereign rights and endeavour to maintain the structures of the nation-state. More than two-thirds of all EU references related to this conflict. Another relevant conflict accounting for almost one-quarter of the EU references in our newspapers is 'co-operation versus conflict'. It focuses on general principles of international relations in bilateral foreign policies. Whereas 'co-operation' points to shared interests and joint action with other states, 'conflict' emphasizes the state's own national interests and puts these interests first. Together, these two conflicts represent 91.7 per cent of all policy debates regarding EU issues.

We found a stable and high level of support for both the 'supranationalism' and the 'co-operation' positions. The average position across all newspaper was 1.60, with 1 representing the 'supranationalism' and 'co-operation', 3 representing 'sovereignty' and 'conflict', and 2 representing an ambivalent position between the alternatives (Table 9.7). This corresponds with the positions on foreign policy (1.76), reflecting the newspapers' generally more liberal positions on issues regarding relations with other states. In fact, individual newspapers hardly showed any differences in the level of support for European integration. In contrast, the positions of the newspapers on most other policy areas—which, of course, relate to different kinds of policy alternatives—represent more diverse and overall more conservative opinions.[9] Thus, unlike many domestic issues, foreign and European policy did not provoke strong cleavages between liberal and conservative newspapers.[10]

While the media assign only little relevance to the EU, European integration can nevertheless be described as a highly consensual issue in media discourse. The Euro-scepticism that has been observed in opinion surveys does not correlate with the media's position on this issue. At the same time, the low representation of Europe in the media is unlikely to promote sufficient awareness in the broader audience. As Zaller (1992, 1994) has pointed out in his work on élite leadership of mass opinion, the attentive public tends to follow élite opinion. But the less informed segments of the public are generally characterized by a significantly lower level of support for élite policies. They are unfamiliar with the positions and arguments put forward by the élites and mediated by the media and lack this orientation for their own opinion formation. Following Zaller's argument, it is not surprising that the broader public shows a lower degree of support for integration than the élites, if the audience is provided with very little information on European issues.

Evaluation

Complying with the media's 'watch-dog' function, editorials can be expected to express clear opinions and predominantly critical positions. However, the high level of press support for European integration is paralleled by our findings on the general evaluative tone of EU editorials. While more than three-quarters (75.5 per cent) of our total sample were clearly evaluative, EU editorials were characterized by a more neutral and diagnostic tone (only 69.3 per cent evaluative editorials). German national newspapers tended to provide their audience with a comparably

---

[9] See the average positions for other policies in Eilders (2002).

[10] See the finding on the high level of consonance in comparison to other policies in Eilders (2002).

Table 9.7. General position: newspapers' positions on EU policy and foreign policy across newspapers (N = Number of policy preferences expressed for EU policy) ('1' = supranationalism and cooperation, '3' = sovereignty and conflict).

Policy area	*TAZ*	*FR*	*SZ*	*FAZ*	*WELT*	Total
EU policy N = 759	1.52	1.44	1.65	1.52	1.74	1.60
Foreign policy N = 889	1.86	1.95	1.69	1.72	1.69	1.76

large amount of explanations, comparisons, and prognostic statements on European matters. As in the total sample, negative evaluations outnumbered supportive statements, but the editorials on EU issues remained clearly below the average level of criticism (37.5 per cent as opposed to 44.9 per cent).

This also holds true for the evaluation of EU actors. Considering the 'watchdog' function, it is not surprising that most actors received negative evaluations. EU actors, however, were judged comparably little at all (only 49 per cent as opposed to 61 per cent of domestic actors) and assessed more positively. The average evaluation of EU actors was 2.1 (with 1 representing positive and 3 representing negative assessment). Most positively evaluated was the Court of Justice (1.6), whereas the EU as a whole received the highest share of criticism (2.3) (Table 9.8). Domestic actors in EU editorials were evaluated more critically. They averaged 2.3, with the most frequently addressed actors between 2.2 (Chancellor Kohl) and 2.4 (ministries and government) (Table 9.9). Citizens played only a minor role in the editorials, but received a fair level of support (1.6).

Table 9.8. Evaluation: evaluation of EU actors (N = Number of actor evaluations) ('1' = positive, '3' = negative).

EU actors (N = 269)	Evaluation
Entire EU institution (N = 132)	2.3
European Parliament (N = 20)	2.2
Council (N = 26)	2.2
Commission (N = 67)	2.1
Court of Justice (N = 10)	1.6
Misc. European institutions (N = 36)	1.8

Table 9.9. Evaluation: evaluations of selected domestic actors in EU editorials (N = Number of actor evaluations) ('1' = positive, '3' = negative).

Domestic actors (N = 1,087)	Evaluation
Chancellor (N = 280)	2.2
Ministries/Ministers (N = 258)	2.4
Government (N = 224)	2.4
Citizens (N = 99)	1.6

Corresponding with the stable level of support for domestic actors, the evaluation of EU actors did not show much change either (1994: 2.2; 1995: 2.9; 1996: 2.2; 1997: 2.1; 1998: 1.9).

In contrast to the strikingly high level of agreement on the supportive position toward European integration, the newspapers displayed relatively clear differences in the evaluation of EU actors. Liberal newspapers were significantly more critical than their conservative counterparts (*TAZ*: 2.3, *FR*: 2.2, *SZ*: 2.3, *FAZ*: 1.9, *WELT*: 1.7). This can—on an even higher level of criticism—also be observed regarding the evaluations of domestic actors (*TAZ*: 2.5, *FR*: 2.4, *SZ*: 2.2, *FAZ*: 2.2, *WELT*: 2.0). Since the unanimous support for integration across the newspaper spectrum is not paralleled by an equally consistent support for political actors involved in the process, there is evidence for a divided opinion on the performance of the actors and institutions involved in European policy-making. Thus, we cannot conclude that there is a generally consensual support. Editorials distinguish between the abstract idea of European integration, on the one hand, and concrete policies and the performance of actors and institutions, on the other.

Conclusion

The mass media are playing an increasingly important role in modern politics. Not only the success of single political proposals, but also the survival of governments are becoming more and more dependent on the way in which they are presented and commented by the media. Much research has been done on mass communications and elections, but so far we know only little about the role of the media in the process of European integration. This deficit of understanding is all the more serious when—with the introduction of the Euro and enlargement to new member states in the near future—European integration has entered a critical phase. Our study is based on the assumption that institutional integration has to be accompanied by a process of 'cultural integration' that involves the emergence of a Europeanized public sphere where European politics is publicly discussed and citizens get involved in a discourse on European matters. Since in modern societies it is primarily the mass media that provide for an arena of public debate, their role in representing Europe to a broader public is of crucial importance.

This chapter explored the extent to which the media in Germany have become Europeanized during the 1990s. The empirical analysis focused on the editorials of the national quality press assuming that—although they cover only a relatively small portion of the total audience share—these newspapers function as powerful opinion leaders whose agenda and interpretations are adopted by other parts of the German media system.

Our notion of Europeanization of the public sphere dismisses more advanced—partly utopian—ideas of 'truly' transnational communications. Instead, what can be expected, at least for the present, is national media bringing Europe into the domestic agenda of public discourse. This hypothesis would not only involve an adequate amount of attention to European matters, but also an awareness of the interdependence of European and domestic politics. Further, we investigated the degree to which the media support European integration and how they evaluate the actual policy-making of European and domestic actors.

The results of our empirical analysis show a divided picture. Europe makes up for only a small, though slightly increasing, part of the German media agenda. In particular, European matters are almost always addressed within the framework of the domestic political agenda, whereas the EU as a self-contained political entity is discussed only occasionally. It is difficult to evaluate the performance of the German media in the light of these findings, as it is impossible to precisely specify what a sufficient level of Europeanization would be. Even so, it seems obvious that the media agenda is far from reflecting the growing significance of the supranational level of modern governance. We can only speculate on the implications that the marginalization and domestication of Europe may have for German public opinion. Addressing European issues in the light of domestic affairs may foster the understanding of Europe's relevance as a political force that affects the individual lives of people. But it may also contribute to the persistence of a national, parochial perspective that puts the national interest first.

Besides the issue of setting Europe on the public agenda, another aspect of Europeanization refers to the affective dimension of communication. Here we distinguished between the German media's general support of European integration and their evaluation of the specific course of European politics. Comparing the general positions that the individual newspapers take on European integration, there did not appear to be a cleavage along the left–right dimension of political ideology that usually divides them. Both liberal and conservative German newspapers showed strong and surprisingly unanimous support for European integration. At the same time, we found considerable criticism of actors, in particular national politicians, involved in European politics. In contrast to the newspapers' positive positions on European integration in general, the extent of criticism revealed a left–right pattern. The liberal newspapers expressed more negative evaluations than the conservative newspapers.

The discrepancy between the positive general position on European integration and the negative evaluation of the actual performance of policy-makers can be interpreted as the German media fulfilling the role of Europe's 'loyal opposition' — a pattern that has frequently also been found with regard to domestic politics. While the media support the established institutional order and the basic values set by the political élites, they take a much more critical and adversarial stance on the actual performance of power holders. From a normative point of view, this can be seen as a positive contribution to the political process as the media are expected to take an active part in the system of checks and balances and act as a 'watch-dog' or 'fourth estate'. Critical debate is not necessarily a threat to European integration. On the contrary, it can even contribute to its legitimacy, as it responds to the legitimate concerns of the citizens and opens the opportunity to revise specific policies or procedures.

However, what is normatively expected might not necessarily work in practice. There is a growing cleavage between German political élites and the media, especially the national quality press, on the one hand, and the broader public, on the other. It seems that keeping the salience of Europe low on the public agenda and avoiding any controversial debate is no longer a guarantee for popular support. Better to understand the communication of discontent further research is needed that includes not only a broader range of media, but also the diffusion of opinions in personal networks of face-to-face communication. Since our sample is restricted to quality newspapers, we do not know with certainty what happens when local papers and tabloids pick up European items. Although the national media usually serve as influential agenda-setters within the media system, it could well be that other media emphasize different, predominantly negative aspects of European politics.

What could be possible reasons for the overall rather limited ability of the media to provide for a public sphere of debate on European matters? One explanation refers to 'media logic', that is the professional norms and operational constraints of news-making. To select topics for their agenda the media follow relatively established criteria of what makes for an interesting and professional news story. These so-called 'news values' typically include conflict, crisis, unexpectedness, personalization, and proximity to the audience. Further, news are structured along the conventions of storytelling as they tend to focus on distinct events centred around central figures who are involved in a conflict on right or wrong, winning or losing. It is obvious that European politics lacks the main ingredients that usually attract media attention. There are no outstanding personalities in the

European arena with whom audiences across national boundaries can positively identify. On the contrary, the main occasions recently when personalities became recognizable objects of media coverage were corruption scandals. In addition, the European political process is characterized by long policy-cycles with only few events that bear enough symbolic and visual power to attract public awareness. European Council summits could serve as 'focus events', but hardly overcome the problem. They are executed as routine events with group photographs designed to demonstrate harmony in the European 'family' rather than bringing up problems and issues for public discussion.

Another explanation for the low degree of Europeanization of media coverage points to the role of the sources of information that the media rely on to make up their news stories. Without a steady flow of relevant and reliable information from European policy-makers the media are unable to develop a European agenda of public discourse. However, as Neidhardt, Koopmans and Pfetsch (2000) point out, there are only weak, if any, incentives for European actors to seek publicity. This is demonstrated by the three core institutions of European politics. The Council of Ministers represents primarily national interests, its members presenting themselves to their home publics as people who defend national concerns rather than promote European interests. Since the members of the Council have developed extremely sophisticated communication strategies in the national arena, the lack of communication has to be put down to a reluctance to open the door of public debate. Secondly, the members of the Commission also avoid public communication partly because they are responsible to the national governments by which they are appointed, and partly because the Commission as any bureaucratic organization, is primarily committed to efficiency of problem-solving rather than to public accountability. Nevertheless, even in comparison to other international organizations, the Commission devotes only a small amount of resources to public relations and makes only limited efforts to professionalize the flow of information to the media and the general public. The European Parliament is special in that it is the only European institution that is directly constituted by elections and hence depends on publicity to sustain popular support. However, election campaigns for the European Parliament are highly nationalized, with the parties and candidates using the outcome as an instrument in the domestic power struggle rather than pursuing a genuinely European agenda (Niedermayer, Chapter 7 in this volume). Therefore, it comes as no surprise that the media do not cover previous elections as a European event, but as segmented national campaigns (Blumler 1983; Kevin 2001).

The conclusion to be drawn from this discussion is that blaming the media for Europe's marginalization and domestication in public communication misses the full picture. Equally responsible are the political élites who—owing to the EU's institutional set-up and domestic political constraints—avoid 'going public' on European issues. The resulting poor knowledge and understanding on the part of the citizens, and the lack of critical public discourse and transparency, may well have contributed to the current erosion of popular support for European integration.

Note. We would like to express our gratitude to Philip Schlesinger and Robert Worcester for their critical and thorough comments which were extremely helpful for improving this chapter. We are also grateful to the participants of the workshops on 'Germany and Europe' for their thoughtful comments. Of course, all shortcomings of this chapter are the responsibility of the authors.

Part IV
Europeanization of Public Policies

10

Economic Policies:
From Pace-Setter to Beleaguered Player

KENNETH DYSON

The Erosion of the Pace-Setter Role: A Changing Narrative about Germany

GERMANY'S EXPERIENCE WITH ECONOMIC AND MONETARY UNION (EMU) underlines the complex, dynamic and interactive nature of Europeanization, the extent to which it has generated unanticipated consequences, and the contingent character of 'fit' between German and EU policies. In the creation of EMU Germany was able to play the role of 'pace-setter' in a classic way, based on its capacity to 'upload' its own policy preferences and institutional practices to the EU level. This capacity rested on an essentially hegemonic position for the Bundesbank within European monetary policies, the D-Mark's role as the anchor of stability within the Exchange Rate Mechanism (ERM) after 1979, and Germany's 'model' character based on its record of superior economic performance (Dyson 1994). EMU seemed to represent the high point in Germany's capacity to exercise 'soft' power in the EU.

Germany's incentives for playing this 'pace-setter' role were complex. At the level of 'high' politics they involved enhanced geo-strategic security by minimizing the adaptational problems for other European states from a sudden and unexpected German unification in 1989–90. This took the form of a clear and irrevocable demonstration of German political will to accelerate and complete European unification (Dyson and Featherstone 1999). The economic incentive was to capitalize on the existing commercial advantages that Germany gained through a Single European Market by securing exchange-rate stability. German policy-makers anticipated growth and employment gains from increased trade with partners in EMU. In consequence, EMU seemed a classic case of 'goodness of fit', with minimal adaptational problems for Germany. Whereas German policy-makers anticipated that EMU would involve serious adaptational problems for others, it seemed likely to reinforce continuities in German economic policies rather than act as a catalyst for domestic change.

For a number of reasons 'goodness of fit' soon appeared more precarious and contingent. With a single monetary policy Germany lost the key relative advantage

Proceedings of the British Academy, **119**, 201–229. © The British Academy 2003.

of lower interest rates *vis-à-vis* other EU states. In consequence, other states benefited from a greater stimulus to both investment and budget deficit reduction via lower debt servicing charges. The result was a more substantial improvement in their economic and fiscal performance and a growing perception that Germany was a key problem within EMU, no longer a pace-setter but increasingly a laggard. In 2002 this came to a head over the European Commission's threat of a formal warning to the German government about its fiscal performance in relation to the Stability and Growth Pact. Germany no longer appeared as the model pupil in the EMU class.

Secondly, the EMU of eleven states that was created in 1998–9 (then twelve with Greece) was larger than the EMU of five–six states clustered around France and Germany that most policy professionals had expected in 1995–6. In consequence, the monetary policy of the European Central Bank (ECB) was less oriented around German interests and took greater account of potential inflationary pressures in other states. Consequently, the Schröder government of 1998–2002 found itself with a tighter monetary policy than Germany's position in the economic cycle warranted. A pro-cyclical monetary policy for Germany and a relative improvement of economic and fiscal performance by most neighbours encouraged a heavy reliance on the German exporting sector to reduce unemployment. This context provided an incentive for German policy-makers to define an interest in a weak Euro that would offer stimulus to exports.

Thirdly, and crucially, the transition to EMU was accompanied by a relative deterioration in German economic performance during the 1990s. Economic growth was below both the EU and the OECD averages, and unemployment grew and remained stubbornly high. The result was a loss of reputation and consequent credibility and presentational problems for German policy arguments. Germany appeared as a laggard in structural economic reforms. Hence there was a new emphasis on policy learning from other more successful states like Denmark, the Netherlands, and Sweden (similar 'managed' economies) or from emulating features of Anglo-American 'liberal' capitalism. Europeanization was subsumed in a wider discourse of the 'requirements' to adapt in the interests of competitiveness.

The result was a 'misfit' issue that caused political problems for the Schröder government and the Social Democratic Party (SPD) in the 2002 federal elections. They were deprived of the domestic mechanism of interest-rate adjustment, faced with the novel situation for Germany of a 'top-down' inappropriate monetary policy, and confronted with intensified competitive pressures from the internal market and the single currency. Hence the onus fell on structural reforms to labour, goods and services markets, and to the welfare state to speed adjustment and reduce unit labour costs. These pressures ran up against powerfully organized domestic interests, notably in labour-market and welfare-state policies where social partnership was strongly entrenched (see Haverland, Chapter 13 in this volume). Germany was no longer pictured as an embodiment of the virtues of consensual economic management but as an expression of the vices of a 'blocked' society in the grip of veto players and 'sub-optimal' policy-making. The dominant narrative about the German economy and its relationship to Europe had changed.

The German government faced strategic constraints in dealing with these new adaptational pressures (see Hirschman 1970). 'Exit' was not a viable option when Germany had invested so much in EMU and Germany's most fundamental national interests were bound up with it. 'Voice' was similarly a strategy of limited value, as the short period with Oskar Lafontaine as Finance Minister demonstrated in 1998–9. Criticisms of current EMU policies and practices threatened to create a crisis of confidence in the Euro and draw down negative consequences for German and EU economic policy (higher ECB interest rates). Not least, they invited severe criticisms of the Berlin government for irresponsibility and lack of consistency and credibility. After Lafontaine, ideas about developing EMU into a system of active macro-economic demand management were discredited by association.

Hence the Schröder government was limited to the strategy of 'loyalty', suppressing internal misgivings within the SPD about the lack of political manoeuvre to initiate a fiscal stimulus in 2001–2. Primacy was given to budget consolidation, though this was politically presented as done for good German and social demo- cratic reasons (notably intergenerational equity) rather than just because of the Stability and Growth Pact (Dyson 2002b). The Schröder government made a limited attempt to 'upload' the principle of social partnership into the arrangements for EMU in the form of the Macro-Economic Dialogue. But this was an exercise in exchanging information among the ECB, European Commission and employers and trade unions and fell well short of any attempt at explicit macro-economic policy co-ordination.

Otherwise, the Schröder government pursued a domestic economic reform strategy of reliance on the innovative power of consensus (Hogrefe 2002). The result was a complex combination of defensive domestic measures notably in labour markets (tightening regulation of part-time employment and extending employee participation through works councils)—designed to placate organized labour and the left of the SPD—with tax reform and pension reform measures— to appeal to employers. In particular, the pension reform and the abolition of tax on sale of cross-shareholdings in industry served to promote a stronger share- holder culture. The German model of 'managed' capitalism retrenched in the face of a stronger political assertion of shareholder rights. Companies like Daimler Chrysler and Deutsche Bank were globalizing and Europeanizing and pressuring government to enable them to make a more efficient use of their assets in a more competitive context. At the same time the co-operative management of economic change remains deeply politically entrenched and supported by a culture that places high value on solidarity. Notably it was not fundamentally challenged by Edmund Stoiber as the Chancellor candidate of the centre-right Christian

Democratic Union/Christian Social Union (CDU/CSU) in the federal elections of 2002. The discourse of a neo-liberal logic to the EU and EMU was only partially adopted and used within the German political establishment, mainly within the liberal Free Democratic Party (FDP) and parts of the CDU/CSU.

How Europeanization Affects Economic Policy: Complexity, Continuity, and Change

Europeanization of German economic policies is a complex process that evades simple, one-dimensional characterization. 'Goodness of fit' has proved contingent rather than fixed and given. In fiscal policy it has been a subject of multi-level renegotiation (see later); in structural reforms a matter of domestic contest about what is the European model to which Germany has to adjust and just what are the requirements of Europeanization. In short, there has been a strong 'bottom-up' dimension to Europeanization as it has been drawn into the domestic politics of reform.

Europeanization has been associated with complex changes in the strategic behaviour of domestic actors, playing a role as an intervening variable in economic policy reform. It changes domestic political opportunity structures, including a subtle politics of 'turf-fighting'. Domestic institutional actors seek to use European integration to alter the balance of power over economic policy and legitimate their own role and policy ideas. Thus the Finance Ministry used Europeanization to justify the need for a robust framework of fiscal rules to bind the budgetary policies of the Länder and of local authorities to the requirements of the Stability and Growth Pact, citing the preservation of German political credibility and reputation. The Bundesbank sought to compensate for loss of monetary policy by carving out an enhanced role in banking supervision and financial stability. The fact that both had only limited success in pursuing these aims is testament to the powerful constraints of managing economic policy in a semi-sovereign state characterized by a high degree of institutional pluralism in economic policy (Katzenstein 1987).

The domestic institutional structure of a semi-sovereign state, with its complex distribution and sharing of responsibilities, creates a bias to negotiated change and modesty in outcomes, to incremental rather than radical policy innovation. At the same time, Europeanization represents a more potent factor in domestic politicking about economic policy. It is associated both with an increased level of contest about economic policy management ('who manages what?') and with the introduction of a greater sense of urgency into domestic policy reform as interests seek to use it to strengthen their relative positions ('what is the appropriate pace of change?'). Europeanization is, in short, associated with heightened political conflict about the spatial and temporal dimensions of German economic policy and who has power over policy. It affects the distribution of power among federal ministries, between federation and Länder, and—as we shall see—between employers and trade unions in collective bargaining and labour markets.

In another respect, and adding to its complexity, Europeanization resonates even more deeply in the body politic, raising fundamental longer-term cultural questions about the kind of polity and of political economy that Germany aspires to be and whether that aspiration is sustainable. The central constraint on change at this deeper level is set by the domestic institutional 'fit' between the federal, corporatist and coalition government features of the German polity (the main elements of its 'negotiation' democracy) and an economy that displays strong elements of co-ordination and privileges strong producer groups and the practice of social partnership in labour-market and social policies (Dyson 2002a; Hall and Soskice 2001: 47–9; Wood 1997). Mechanisms of EU economic governance that weaken the capacity for this domestic co-ordination by undermining the power of the producer groups and social partnership have, in consequence, a high political resonance. Like three other variables—the transition to a post-Fordist economy, globalization, and German unification—Europeanization prompts questions about the credibility and sustainability of German 'managed' capitalism and of what precisely is happening to it. These questions are in turn essentially about the political dynamics of 'fit' between what is understood to be happening in economic policy at the EU level and what are understood to be the key features of the German political economy (Dyson 2002b). Can German 'managed' capitalism be accommodated to mechanisms of EU economic governance? Or will 'misfit' unleash powerful 'top-down' pressures for domestic policy transformation that make 'managed' capitalism unviable, except in the short- to medium-term? It is too soon to judge whether Germany is simply introducing greater flexibility into its 'managed' capitalism by reconfiguring its institutional arrangements or whether 'shareholder' is replacing the 'stakeholder' nature of German capitalism and Germany undergoing a painful and possibly protracted adjustment. The answer is tied up with developments in the international economy and the extent to which Anglo-American 'liberal' capitalism is able to retain its model character. The dynamics of Europeanization are inseparably bound up in this larger context.

There is a broad consensus about the direction of systemic change linked to Europeanization—it has strengthened the discourse of competitiveness and promoted market liberalization. In this respect, Europeanization reinforces ideas and practices associated with globalization and post-Fordism. But there is no consensus about the likely outcome for Germany. The outcomes of Europeanization are bound up with a domestic policy process that traditionally favours co-operation and consensus over imposed change and confrontation. This process also gives institutional support to a continuing preoccupation with issues of redistributive justice and provision of collective goods (Dyson 2002a). It also conditions the timing and tempo of policy change, encouraging slow and incremental change. But, in part because of Europeanization, the domestic policy process is being reconfigured and becoming more complex. This increased complexity and reconfiguration in turn affects the dynamics of Europeanization.

On the one hand, constraints on reform are set by a powerful constellation of successful German firms, notably in 'mid-technology' manufacturing. They have established market leadership on the basis of product quality, reliability and innovation, the cultivation of a highly skilled and committed workforce, and the containment of unit labour costs through co-option of the workforce into the management of corporate change. These firms have high sunk costs in sectoral co-ordination (e.g. in training, wage bargaining, and technology transfer) as well as in employee security and participation (especially works councils). Their continuing reputation and loyalty is an essential underpinning of German 'managed' capitalism.

On the other hand, the domestic policy process is being reconfigured as powerful corporate actors—like Daimler Chrysler and Deutsche Bank—redefine their interests in a context of globalization and Europeanization and seek to reposition themselves as global and European as well as German players. Their message has been assimilated by the Federation of German Industry (BDI), which has adopted a more assertive and confrontational pose. In order to prevent corporate 'exit' German business associations have voiced more criticism of the restrictions imposed by domestic institutional arrangements, for instance in labour-market policy, and called for priority to business-friendly taxes and lower social charges. Their advocacy of 'hire and fire' labour-market policies went further than the CDU/CSU in 2002, though by then both main parties agreed on promoting a 'low-wage' sector and reform of social benefits to encourage work.

Europeanization of economic policy involves powerful systemic changes in the direction of a discourse of competitiveness and market liberalization. But the form that these changes take, their timing and tempo, are bound up with the domestic policy process, and this process has become more complex under the combined impacts of globalization, post-Fordism, and Europeanization. Key corporate actors welcome and encourage EU-led market liberalization (e.g. in energy, transport, and telecommunications) and use the discourse of Europeanization to legitimate an increased tempo of domestic reform. Hence 'fit' and 'misfit' are not static givens. At the same time the domestic combination of constitutionally shaped 'negotiation' democracy with attributes of 'managed' capitalism lends a powerful degree of 'path dependency' to economic policy change. German economic policy has demonstrated a remarkable degree of resilience and continuity as it has adjusted to Europeanization.

A Case of 'Fit' or 'Misfit'?

The complex, multi-faceted and interactive effects of European integration on German economic policy elude attempts to shoehorn their outcome into a simple category like 'accommodation', 'transformation', 'retrenchment', and 'inertia'. Different actors are affected in different ways, depending on the kind of mechanism of EU economic governance with which they are involved, on the opportunities that they are offered or create to push through their own policy ideas, and on the strength of domestic veto players that they confront. They define whether there is a 'misfit' problem and, if confronted by such a problem, can seek to solve it by transforming EU economic governance.

'Downward' processes of Europeanization are also accompanied by, and dynamically interrelated with, 'upward' and 'horizontal' processes through which policies, practices, and discourses are transferred. They are bound up with Germany 'uploading' certain aspects of its economic model (its notions about the requirements for economic stability), but not others (in particular the co-operative arrangements of 'managed' capitalism). The result is a complex compound of 'fit' and 'misfit' between the two levels. The complexity is accentuated by the 'misfit' between EU competition and internal market rules and the territorially-specific interventionist policies of the Länder to promote inward investment (see Jeffery, Chapter 5 in this volume). In fiscal policy the federal government has been drawn into a difficult multi-level process of negotiating 'fit' between EU-level requirements enshrined in the Stability and Growth Pact (which it shaped) and the recalcitrance of Länder governments about submitting to a national stability pact with sanctions. Hence traditional assumptions about accommodation are very questionable.

'Misfit' was to a considerable extent bound up with the unanticipated consequences of European integration. German support for the principles of the Single European Market and of EMU as consistent with, and an extension of, the domestic principles of the social market economy was followed by a trail of unanticipated consequences for powerful domestic actors. These European projects created adaptational pressures for German financial markets, the Bundesbank, key sectors such as utilities, and regional policies. In each of these areas the Länder were adversely affected and their governments—via the Bundesrat—had a potential veto on change. The Stability and Growth Pact was also followed by unanticipated consequences. Germany faced increasing difficulties in meeting the fiscal rules and in making appropriate structural reforms (e.g. accelerated privatization, welfare-state reforms). Hence the story of how European integration affects German economic policy interweaves aspects of accommodation, transformation, and inertia.

Types of Policy Effect

One way of analysing the complex, multi-faceted effects of European integration on German economic policy is by distinguishing between cognitive and material effects and between direct and indirect effects. 'Cognitive effects' refer to policy ideas and preferences, 'material effects' to policy instruments and to markets. 'Direct effects' encompass the transposition and implementation of specific EU legal provisions, 'indirect effects' occur in the absence of a specific EU model and include 'spillover' into related policies at domestic level and changing domestic opportunity structures consequent on market changes induced by EU action. An example is the use of Europeanization as a discourse to legitimate certain policy changes and generate new solutions without a clear and specific EU requirement. It is also possible to identify direct and indirect institutional effects, notably on the structuring of responsibility for economic policy within the federal executive, the role of the Financial Planning Council (*Finanzplanungsrat*), the organization of the Bundesbank and of financial market supervision, and the role of labour-market institutions. These institutional effects are examined later.

The Single European Market had important direct cognitive effects on economic policy. It involved direct 'downward' effects from an EU model, as in telecommunications regulation (e.g. the requirement for an independent regulator) and in competition policy. This helped domestic reformers to shift liberalization of goods, services, and other markets to the centre of the political agenda as a European 'requirement'. By changing the terms of political argument, and using Europeanization as a legitimating discourse, they were able to overcome the power of domestic veto players over policy changes. Here Europeanization was associated with transformation of sectors. The direct cognitive effects were less obvious with EMU because the Maastricht Treaty negotiations in effect institutionalized the German model of economic stability. This took the form of 'non-monetary' financing of budget deficits, the importance attached to fiscal rules, and an independent ECB, to which responsibility for price stability was assigned. Similarly, the strict fiscal rules laid down in the Stability and Growth Pact of 1997 reflected German 'sound' finance ideas (albeit not German institutional arrangements). On both an independent ECB and fiscal rules German actors took the initiative within the EU to 'upload' German preferences (Dyson and Featherstone 1999). In these respects EMU was associated with an underlying accommodation between Germany and the EU, albeit an accommodation that was to come under strain.

Indirect cognitive effects of the single market and of EMU were most visible on the political Left in Germany. Beginning under Oskar Lafontaine's period as party chair, the SPD sought actively to promote the idea of a 'social' Europe to promote solidarity and prevent 'social dumping' by a 'race to the bottom' in standards of employment, real wages, and social benefits. This was related to the idea of an EMU for employment and growth, designed to put in place a counter-weight to a potential bias to deflation in the Euro-Zone (Lafontaine and Müller 1998). Hence the SPD pushed the notion of an Employment Pact to flank the Stability and Growth Pact—threatening to block ratification of the Amsterdam Treaty without it. Similarly, the Left took up the idea of an optimal 'policy mix' of monetary, fiscal, and wage policies at the EU level. It questioned the notion of the neutrality of money and placed renewed emphasis on the role of demand management in reducing unemployment and stimulating growth. In essence, a cognitive feedback loop to the EU level emerged, facilitated by the emergence of centre-Left governments across the major states in 1997–8. Linkage was established between EMU and a new commitment to an 'active' employment policy. But indirect cognitive effects in the form of new structures to pursue an optimal 'policy mix' at the EU level and promote neo-Keynesian ideas ran up against the entrenched institutional barriers of an EMU designed on German ordo-liberal lines.

More important were the direct and indirect material effects of the Single Market and of EMU. Europeanization unleashed a sequence of changes to the context within which German economic policy is made. Direct material effects were most strongly felt in available policy instruments (Dyson 2000a). EC competition policy created new political difficulties for Länder governments in pursuing regional subsidy policies to attract investment. The result was new tensions between them and the European Commission. Similarly the privileged status of state banks and public savings banks was challenged as incompatible with a 'level playing field' in financial market competition. German sectors—for instance, electricity and gas—also came under EU pressure to replace a reliance on voluntary codes, negotiated by firms and consumers, with formal regulatory arrangements for promoting market access. The reliance on negotiated codes as instruments for domestic reform was also tested in relation to takeover issues and corporate governance. In both areas the Schröder government established representative commissions, including employee representatives, to design new codes, and in the case of takeovers resisted the proposed EC directive. Hence Europeanization has its limits in the defence of those basic instruments of 'managed' capitalism that are seen as essential to maintaining co-operation in dealing with change. The defence of the 'self-management' elements of German capitalism was also exhibited in the Schröder government's resistance to European Commission proposals in 2002 to liberalize the European car market. These proposals threatened the ability of the big German car producers to regulate the market. The result of this accumulation of conflicts was German government complaints by 2002 that European Commission policy was biased against German industrial policy.

The direct material effects of EMU were considerable. With EMU German actors lost key policy instruments for promoting economic adjustment, notably interest-rate policy and exchange-rate policy, while fiscal policy instruments were constrained by EU rules. By default wage, labour-market, and social policies became more important, were assimilated within a discourse of competitiveness and shifted to the centre of the political agenda as objects of reform. They attracted the greatest political attention of the Schröder government and were the centre point of the work of the tripartite Alliance for Jobs (*Bündnis für Arbeit*). Their importance was reinforced by the disappearance of the disciplinary role of the Bundesbank in domestic collective bargaining and in containing unit labour costs. The consequent policy vacuum on how to secure German competitiveness was in essence filled by the new collective bargaining formula (productivity-oriented, multi-annual wage deals) agreed by employers and trade unions in July 1999 and subsequently endorsed by the Alliance for Jobs. Equally, the serious political and electoral difficulties facing the Schröder government in 2002 were bound up with the distancing of key trade unions from this wage-policy formula, under pressure from their memberships. These difficulties were further aggravated by scandal about the conduct of labour-market policy by the tripartite Federal Agency for Labour (*Bundesanstalt für Arbeit*). Labour-market reforms were central to the federal election campaign of 2002.

The indirect material effects of the Single Market and EMU were powerful in creating a context of greater competition for investment, jobs, and tax revenue. These effects were felt in financial markets where the big German commercial banks came under increased pressure from both global and European competition and in domestic retail banking. They lobbied more actively and assertively for an end to domestic restrictions on their ability to compete and for the capability to mobilize their assets for the role of global investment bankers. The commercial banks were instrumental in pushing for European Commission investigation into the privileges of state banks and public savings banks in the retail sector. They were also beneficiaries from the Schröder government's surprise decision to enable them to divest their shareholdings in German companies by abolishing capital gains tax on their sale.

Other indirect effects came from the creation of new, large Euro financial markets, notably a thriving market in Euro corporate bond issues. Their growth was tied to key features of EMU: the disappearance of exchange-rate risk and the elimination of big differences between state bonds. The effects of EMU and of the Single Market combined with those from globalized financial markets to produce potentially powerful consequences. German firms were less tied to domestic banks as sources of capital; the big commercial banks were transforming themselves away from their domestic base into international investment banking; and foreign investors in Germany took a more assertive position on issues like corporate governance and financial reporting, notably the issue of transparency. Hence EMU played a key role in opening up and transforming the debate about the way in which German investment was financed and corporate governance organized, empowering reformers who promoted a strengthening of shareholder values.

The indirect effects of EU economic governance were discernible in collective bargaining and labour-market institutions. Here there was little in the way of EU models: no mechanism for EU-wide collective bargaining, the main innovation being the provision for European works councils in companies operating cross-nationally.

But the Single Market and EMU promoted the sense that traditional forms of wage-setting and employee participation were under pressure and a greater interactivity: in effect, 'soft' co-ordination' through benchmarking, but without an EU institutional model. The result was a shared discourse of competitiveness that has been linked to new efforts to co-ordinate wage bargaining and to reconfigure the role of works councils as crucial to corporate restructuring. Other EU states were using German wage-setting as a benchmark to achieve competitive advantage through lower growth in unit labour costs. Consequently, German employers and trade unions were under increasing pressure to take account of wage developments elsewhere and set wages as a function of relative competitiveness (defined by past inflation and current productivity). German trade unions promoted the idea of co-ordinated wage policy at the EU level to prevent 'wage dumping' and a race to the bottom in employment standards. German employers increased the role of works councils in corporate restructuring, again subsuming them in a shared discourse of competitiveness and creating a greater distance between the works councils and the trade unions (Hancke and Soskice 2002). Europeanization of collective bargaining and labour-market institutions was one additional strand in a discourse about the 'need to adapt' to competitive pressures (Kallestrup 2002).

The complexity and multi-facetedness of the Europeanization of German economic policies are further accentuated by three other factors that require examination—the dynamic and changing nature of EU economic governance, the internal changes within German capitalism, and the relationship between Europeanization, globalization, and German unification.

EU Economic Governance as Changing Variable

EU economic governance is a dynamic process, involving the complex accretion of policies and practices over time. In short, the explanatory variable is itself subject to change. Both the Single European Market programme and EMU are ongoing processes, evolving in different ways and according to different time-scales. Thus financial market policies, tax harmonization, and energy regulation proved more intractable than other issues relating to the Single Market. EMU, too, has evolved as an asymmetric system of co-ordination (Dyson 2000a). Supranational integration, with a single monetary policy operated by an independent ECB (agreed at

Maastricht in 1991), is now flanked by 'hard' co-ordination of national fiscal policies (the Stability and Growth Pact of 1997) and by new evolving 'soft' forms of co-ordination of economic and employment policies. 'Hard' co-ordination of fiscal policies involves continuing national responsibility for budgetary policies, but within a framework of rules and sanctions. 'Soft' co-ordination involves an even weaker institutional framework that relies on guidelines, peer pressure, and learning through 'benchmarking' best practices.

The result is that German economic policy is embedded in a complexity of different processes of co-ordination, each with different logics. Monetary policy involves a hierarchical, 'top-down' element. Through its governing council (of which the Bundesbank is just one member) the ECB sets interest-rate policy independently of national governments. Fiscal co-ordination takes the form of a sensitive negotiation in what is a three-level game. The interests of the EU (represented by the rules of the Stability Pact) in safeguarding the Euro, of the Länder in protecting their sovereignty, and of the Federal government in its reputation and credibility have to be reconciled. For the Schröder government negotiating its way out of the threat of a formal warning on its budget deficit in 2002—just before the federal elections—was a difficult learning process about the constraints and complexities of EMU.

The complexities are further aggravated by the accumulation of different processes of 'soft' co-ordination around policies for the promotion of growth and employment: the Luxembourg (employment), Cardiff (structural reform), Cologne (macro-economic dialogue) and Lisbon processes. What they share is a belief that, in policy sectors where national responsibility is pre-eminent and institutional legacies and practices very different, policy deliberation and learning from best practice is more efficacious than either hierarchical determination by a supranational body or multi-level negotiation. 'Soft' co-ordination encompasses an increasing scope of Europeanization of economic policies, including employment policy, vocational education and training, structural economic reforms, and dialogue about 'policy mix' at the EU level. The result is that a wider range of domestic actors is being drawn more deeply into the European integration process. Thus *Länder* education ministries and the Federal Ministry of Education, Science and Research are central on issues related to the creation of a European 'knowledge' society; the Federal Ministry of Labour and Social Affairs on employment and training. They have been brought into closer contact with the Federal Finance Ministry because of its co-ordinating responsibility, notably in relation to the Lisbon process and to the national employment action plan.

This increasing emphasis on benchmarking best practice and encouragement of policy learning via 'soft' co-ordination highlights a further difficulty in using Europeanization to explain domestic economic policy change. European integration is not just about 'top-down' effects from Treaty provisions and other forms of EU legislation, most visible in the monetary and, to a lesser extent, fiscal pillars of EMU. It is more and more about developing the EU as a forum for 'horizontal' learning about how best to promote growth and employment. But it is by no means clear whether and to what extent bilateral learning is linked to mechanisms of EU governance or reflects domestic actors' attempts to use Europeanization—understood as what leading EU states are doing, but not necessarily related to the EU—as a discourse to legitimate domestic reforms.

The German government's *Annual Economic Report* of 2000 represented a watershed in stressing the importance of what could be learned from others, notably the Netherlands and Denmark (Bundesministerium der Finanzen 2000: 11). The value of the 'best practice' approach was summarized in the *Annual Economic Report* of 2001 as follows: 'This comparison (peer review) and this assessment (benchmarking) will also increase the pressure on member states to tackle the necessary reforms at home (peer pressure)' (Bundesministerium der Finanzen 2001: 22). The work of the Alliance for Jobs in boosting employment was explicitly framed in terms of the Dutch model of the Wassenaar agreement of 1982 and the Dutch practice of dialogue and negotiation (Schröder 1999: 50–1). One result was legislation in 2001 to improve the organization of labour-market policy so that it promoted a more active and efficient process of job-seeking. Though not copied directly from elsewhere, its organizing principles were based on experience in a range of states, notably Denmark, the Netherlands, Britain, and the USA. Similarly the high-profile Hartz Commission report of August 2002 on labour-market reform made considerable use of cross-national comparison to legitimate its proposals.

However, these difficulties of complexity of logics of co-ordination, extension of scope, and opacity of processes can be seen as second-order. Europeanization of economic policy can be said to have a central strategic direction. It creates pressures for convergence around economic liberalization, from financial to labour markets, and around policies consistent with economic stability. At a broad ideological level there is a 'goodness of fit' between this broad strategic direction at the EU level—market competition, sound finance, sound money—and German economic policy. It is a fit with a domestic ordo-liberalism whose image is of a 'liberal' state creating and sustaining the conditions for a competitive market economy. In essence, Europeanization has domestically empowered, and been used by, ordo-liberals. They see in the Single European Market and in EMU external disciplines capable of constraining and forcing appropriate changes on those holding veto power and blocking necessary domestic reforms. Symptomatic of this use of the European dimension has been the shift in attitudes of German ordo-liberal academic economists to EMU. In the 1990s they tended to oppose EMU because of the perceived threat to domestic economic stability from the lack of discipline of Germany's EU partners. EMU had to be designed to discipline others. With the introduction of EMU it was increasingly identified as a necessary discipline for Germany itself and as a stimulus for market-oriented

reforms to goods, services and labour markets and for structural reforms to social
policy (Dyson 2002*b*).

German Capitalism as Changing Variable

On closer examination this tidy picture of convergence around a liberal
American-style market economy soon dissolves. The German economic policy
model is not so much unitary as a dynamic, Janus-like process whose face
changes over time (Dyson 2002*a*); while the economic structure has taken on
greater complexity with the transition to a post-Fordist, service-based economy in
which part-time employment is becoming increasingly typical. The traditional
business associations and trade unions have greater difficulties in organizing a
more complex and fast-changing structure and face threats and problems of 'exit' by
members and recruitment problems. These threats and problems create incentives to
seek profile by acting assertively and place additional strains on traditional forms
of 'managed' capitalism.

The German economic policy model has always defied simple characterization because it incorporates a complex interdependency between ordo-liberalism
and 'managed' capitalism which live in complex tension and conflict with each
other. Ordo-liberalism has powerful sponsors among academic economists,
within the Bundesbank and the FDP, as well as important parts of key federal
ministries including their advisory councils, the Federation of German Industry,
and the CDU/CSU. Tensions between the ordo-liberal and 'managed' capitalism
elements make less comfortable the 'fit' between the EU and the German levels
of economic policy. This discomfort and sense of 'misfit' comes from the
difficult combination of ideological consistency between German ordo-liberals
and the liberalizing, competitive market ethos of the Single Market and EMU
and inconsistency between both and domestic 'managed' capitalism. Hence
Europeanization has been associated with a 'managed' capitalism on the
defensive.

'Managed' capitalism has deep historical roots in German economic history,
in its prowess in manufacturing exports, in a powerful domestic political constituency including strong producer groups, and in a symbiotic relationship with
a political system that is consensus-oriented. The political image associated with
'managed' capitalism is an 'enabling' state, one that moderates the relationship
between capital and labour by encouraging negotiated economic change. A liberal state of the ordo-liberal type limits itself to safeguarding basic economic
principles, essentially economic stability and a competitive market, through a
clear framework of rules (*Ordnungspolitik*). An enabling state is linked to an
evolutionary view of economic policy, one that reflects the changing needs of
economic actors and the outcomes of their interactions (Dyson 2002*a*). The institutional roots of 'managed' capitalism are within German firms in the system of

works councils and of employee participation in supervisory boards; within sectoral co-ordination of wages, training, and technology transfer; and within social
partnership in the management of labour-market and social policies (Hall and
Soskice 2001). These roots are nurtured by German legislation promoting co-
determination and social partnership. They support a preference of German firms
for high-quality products, skilled and committed labour forces and continuing
incremental innovation.

A key feature of the Schröder government was the attempt more firmly to
institutionalize the practices of 'managed' capitalism in the processes of macro-
level structural economic reforms. The embodiment of this approach at the
domestic level was the Alliance for Jobs. Similarly, the German presidency at the
Cologne European Council of June 1999 was used to initiate the Macro-
Economic Dialogue, to exchange information between the social partners, the
ECB, the European Commission, and EU governments. In effect, by 'uploading'
the practices of 'managed' capitalism to the EU level, in this case seeking an optimal policy mix of monetary, fiscal, and wage policies, the Schröder government
sought to reduce the 'misfit' with the EU and the resultant pressures on Germany.
Hence under Schröder there was a rebalancing in domestic economic policy
towards 'managed' capitalism and an attempt to project this rebalancing onto the
EU level by means of the Macro-Economic Dialogue. Though their purposes differ, the domestic Alliance for Jobs and the EU Macro-Economic Dialogue share
two features. They involve a common process of negotiated economic change
involving the social partners and a common agenda change towards seeing wage
policy and containment of unit labour costs as central to economic stability,
growth, and employment.

The Schröder government attempted to redefine the nature of the economic
problem, focusing on wages and collective bargaining and the importance of
manufacturing consensus behind structural reforms. The result was a subtle and
complex politics of redefining the accommodation between Germany and the EU
over economic policy, away from what was seen as the excessive ordo-liberalism
of Kohl and Waigel in constructing EMU. Hence, above all at the level of process,
the change of government in 1998 was significant, and change of process was
important in shaping the form, sequencing, and substance of domestic economic
reforms. It involved the careful political balancing of liberalization measures
(e.g. pension reform) with measures designed to shore up 'managed' capitalism
(e.g. extension of works councils to smaller and medium-sized firms (SMEs)).

Changing Context of EU Economic Governance: German Unification, Globalization, and Post-Fordism

But perhaps the greatest difficulty is distinguishing the independent effects of
Europeanization on domestic economic policies from the effects of other

variables. One part of the problem is distinguishing Europeanization from globalization and from the transition to post-Fordism; another—specific to
Germany—of distinguishing both from the effects of unification. German unification, globalization, and post-Fordism were important in introducing greater
complexity into German capitalism and presenting new adaptational problems,
and points of reference, for economic policy. Like Europeanization they were
used and assimilated into a domestic discourse of competitiveness that legitimated
policy reforms.

German Unification

German unification aggravated Germany's problems of accommodation with
both the single European market (especially as Bundesländer used subsidies to
compete for investment) and EMU (fiscal discipline, especially the deficit and
debt problems consequent on the financing of unification). Germany became a
more notable sinner against EU competition policies, and by 2002 was still using
German unification (and the related adjustment problems of the construction
sector) to argue a special case for failing to fulfil its convergence programme.
Moreover, though unification involved substantial institutional transfer from West
to East, 'area-wide' collective bargaining (*Flächentarifverträge*) was one of the
least successful exports. In contrast, the traditional Western collective bargaining
system was challenged by the greater flexibility of plant-level bargaining in
the East.

Unification also influenced German policies towards the EU budget and in
particular the financing of the EU Structural Funds and the CAP. These issues
became important in the context of EU enlargement to take in a large number of
relatively poor states in east central Europe. Unification decisively contributed to
German perceptions that it could no longer continue to be the paymaster for EU
enlargement and that EU budgetary and financial reforms were essential. In this
context, the German government brought forward proposals to replace the
Structural Funds and CAP by a system of financial transfers modelled on
Germany's method of funding its own federal structure.

Globalization

Even more problematic is the relationship between Europeanization and globalization. EMU, the Single Market, and globalization are bound together by their mutually reinforcing role in promoting a shared discourse of competitiveness. This
discourse has had profound effects across policy sectors. But it is by no means easy
to disentangle their respective influences. In one sense Europeanization seems more
significant: the interdependencies in trade and investment are much greater between
Germany and the EU than with the rest of the world and grew in relative impor-

tance immediately after EMU. EMU's significance was suggested by an increase in Germany's trade with the EU from 27.2 per cent in 1998 to 32.2 per cent in 2001 (Eurostat 2002). In discourse legitimating domestic reforms, however, globalization figures more prominently. This was apparent in the German government's claims in the *Annual Economic Reports* until 2000, in the debates about structural economic reforms under the Kohl government, and in the 1998 federal election campaign.

Financial Market Reforms   An analysis of the discourse surrounding the four laws for promotion of the financial markets reveals a preoccupation with globalization. Policy reforms showed that globalization had both direct effects and effects mediated by EU legislation. For reformers, the central issue was competition among global financial centres and the need to secure the competitiveness of Germany as a centre, for instance by clear rules on insider trading, technical improvements to German exchanges, and a new framework of financial supervision (modelled on London). Reform of banking supervision has its origin in work within the Group of Ten rather than in the EU, which was in effect an implementing level on this issue rather than of independent importance. As far as financial markets are concerned, the single European market and EMU can be said to mimic globalization and reinforce its effects. They had some limited cognitive effects in encouraging German banks to redefine the competitive battle as within the newly emerging 'European financial area' rather than just within Germany. But this was by no means an exclusively European identity. Deutsche Bank in particular saw itself as first and foremost a global player. On the other hand, the Single Market and EMU were important in altering the competitive conditions within which banks had to operate, notably by eliminating exchange-rate risk. In this way—through their indirect as well as direct material effects—they eased the process of domestic financial reform.

Globalization, the single European market and EMU formed reinforcing parts of a rationale for financial market reforms that could be deployed against those domestic interests, notably at the Land level, that were resistant to liberalization, especially where it involved costs to regional exchanges and regional banks. This rationale stressed the challenge of competitiveness and the vital need for Germany to raise its collective game as a financial centre within Europe and globally.

The impetus for reform was strengthened by other factors that favoured a strengthening of Frankfurt. As a Hesse Land politician, Finance Minister Hans Eichel (1999–2002) was more sympathetic to the needs of Frankfurt as an international exchange than his Bavarian predecessor, Theo Waigel. The Bundesbank was also more alert to how its own policies influenced financial markets in the wake of losing its role in monetary policy. Additionally, the big commercial banks—mostly headquartered in Frankfurt—were driven by problems of diminishing profitability in the domestic retail sector to pursue a more assertive stance. In this context interregional competition lost its earlier capacity to constrain financial market reforms and Frankfurt emerged as the undisputed leading financial centre. But the underlying catalyst was a discourse of competitiveness that did not distinguish between Europeanization and globalization.

Distinct Effects of EMU: Away from the 'Hard' D-Mark However, Europeanization and globalization also had distinct and different effects on German economic policy. At least since the 1960s German economic policy had operated in the context of a 'hard' D-Mark, manifested in the secular tendency for it to appreciate. With the end of the Bretton Woods system in 1973 and a floating D-Mark this tendency was more evident. In consequence, the development of global financial markets was associated with a powerful disciplinary effect from the 'hard' D-Mark on domestic costs. This effect supported the efforts of the Bundesbank to safeguard domestic price stability. At the same time it placed Germany's export sector under powerful competitive pressures, threatened the export of investment and jobs to lower-cost locations, and placed a premium on competing by product quality and reliability and on a highly skilled work force. The ERM involved not so much the Europeanization of German economic policy as the Europeanization of other states' economic policies based on German 'hard currency' leadership. In essence, reflecting the Bundesbank's stress on its overriding obligation to safeguard domestic stability and its power within the ERM, it was a D-Mark Zone (Dyson 1994).

But with EMU the situation changed. Both the constraint of the 'hard' D-Mark and the Bundesbank's role as the monetary policy leader in the EU were ended. As merely a part of the European System of Central Banks (ESCB), the Bundesbank was no longer the monetary policy leader but under pressure to radically restructure in the interests of greater efficiency and effectiveness. In short, EMU triggered a major reform of the Bundesbank to streamline its decision-making and strengthen its credibility within the ESCB.

More importantly, two key domestic economic disciplines had gone with EMU. Monetary policy was no longer made by the Bundesbank with the purpose of securing domestic price stability but by the ECB for the Euro-Zone as a whole. The Bundesbank was no longer able to use the threat of a non-accommodating monetary policy to discipline industry-level wage bargaining by powerful employer and trade union organizations. In practice, this did not matter in the short run because the ECB—facing what it saw as excessive inflationary pressures in other faster-growing states—set a tighter monetary policy than German needed. Hence it acted as an external discipline on wage bargaining. However, 'monetarist' co-ordination of wage bargaining could no longer be taken for granted.

More immediately important was the end of the long period of currency appreciation with the adoption of the Euro. In some respects this was a welcome relief from intensifying competitive pressures. Indeed Waigel had raised the spectre that failure to implement EMU could cost German investment and jobs as a consequence of further appreciation of the D-Mark. But a depreciating euro made urgent a process of self-discipline within collective bargaining based on constructing an agreed formula between employers and trade unions that would help secure responsibility in containing unit labour costs and in maintaining some freedom of manoeuvre for increasing employment. On this issue Schröder was active in seeking out alliances within the trade unions. In particular, IG Bergbau, Chemie and Energie (under Hubertus Schmoldt) was encouraged to play a stronger leadership role in place of IG Metall. Here we see the indirect effects of EMU.

Post-Fordism

Potentially even more significant in the long-term as a variable is a fundamental transition within the economic structure, bound up with the cluster of technological changes associated with the IT revolution, and christened 'post-Fordism'. This transition involves a shift away from mass assembly-line manufacturing and more flexible and temporary forms of organization and employment. It places new adaptational pressures on traditional forms of 'managed' capitalism.

The way in which new technologies are adopted and used has been shaped by the institutional context of German capitalism. German firms have been effective in using new technologies to improve product quality, reliability and innovation (e.g. 'smart' textiles and product innovations across the capital goods sector), and production processes. They have strengthened links with works councils to achieve greater flexibility of working and to invest in a high skilled and committed workforce. The reform of the works constitution law (*Betriebsverfassungsgesetz*) in 2001 facilitated the extension of works councils to the 'new' economy sector. Though the German employer organizations took up a critical position on this new law, in practical terms they had little difficulty with it. Hence post-Fordism was absorbed into 'managed' capitalism.

But in another respect post-Fordism challenges German policy-makers to develop labour-market policy, especially taxation and social insurance, in ways that accommodate the development of service-sector employment as a means of increasing participation rates and creating new jobs. Though there is contest about how best to develop a 'low-wage' sector, there was by 2002 a new consensus about strengthening this element of the German economy. In part, the 'benchmarking' of states like the Netherlands that had been successful in job creation and horizontal policy learning were important in legitimizing this development, especially on the political Left. Another development was the rapid growth of part-time employment during the 1990s. Here again 'benchmarking' states like Denmark and the Netherlands was important in influencing views about the appropriate degree of state regulation of part-time employment. What is important is

the choice of states for 'benchmarking' and the significance of this choice in legitimating how post-Fordism is managed. In essence, German policy-makers had a
preference for seeking to learn from other 'managed' economies rather than from
liberal market economies.

Europeanization of the Institutional Arrangements for Economic Policy

The Federal Executive

The changes in the organization of responsibility for economic policy within
the federal executive—consequent on the Schröder government in 1998—
highlight the difficulties of 'process-tracing' in what is ostensibly a case of
Europeanization. The effects of European integration were evident in institutional
adjustment to the imminence of stage three of EMU and in mimetic effects from
the organization of economic policy responsibility in Britain and France. But crucially Europeanization was also bound up with domestic politics: the economic
policy ideology of Oskar Lafontaine, the new Finance Minister, his personal
ambitions as a big player within the SPD (its party chair) and within the new
government, and the bureaucratic self-interests of the Finance Ministry. EMU's
arrival was important in opening up an opportunity both for Lafontaine and for
the Finance Ministry to pursue agendas that would have been present without
EMU.

Lafontaine wanted to demonstrate that the SPD could make a difference in
government by ending a period of deflation in Europe emanating from German
ordo-liberal policies. This required a radical neo-Keynesian reorientation of economic policy, stressing that money was not neutral and that aggregate demand
was the key to growth and employment. The priority was, accordingly, new
German initiatives to actively co-ordinate economic policies for growth and
employment at the EU level. They were essential to Lafontaine's idea of a bold
new social democratic agenda for Europe. Hence it was crucial to strengthen his
Finance Ministry's role in co-ordinating policies for Europe. This meant in particular disempowering the Federal Economics Ministry whose track record under
successive FDP ministers suggested that it would act as an ordo-liberal counter-
weight to his more Keynesian-style policies. In addition, Lafontaine wished to
secure a strong political influence within the coalition, not least to neutralize
Schröder whose image as a Chancellor close to big industry he distrusted. His
personal influence depended on having a powerful ministry behind him, with
clear responsibility for macro-economic co-ordination.

Lafontaine's impact was seen in his success in securing responsibility for
European policy co-ordination from the Economics Ministry (with consequent
staff transfers) and in bringing in the macro-economic sub-division from the

Grundsatzabteilung of the Economics Ministry. The result was a Finance Ministry with a more powerful role in both cognitive leadership of economic policy and European policy co-ordination. But Lafontaine's role as catalyst is evident when one sees that these changes outlasted him on the appointment of Eichel. They outlasted him because they conformed to the long-standing bureaucratic interest of the Finance Ministry in unifying these responsibilities within its own sphere. They also had a clear rationale in the Europeanization of economic policy consequent on EMU and the need for Germany to speak with a single clear voice on these issues.

The Finance Ministry—and especially its new European Division—took up a position on the importance of Europeanization of economic policy that represented a convergence of bureaucratic self-interests with conviction. The European Division staked out a powerful position, extolling the virtues of 'top-down' Europeanization. Its position was that: 'In future German economic and fiscal policies can no longer be conducted exclusively from the national point of view. As the EU moves ever closer together, it will have to be embedded in the general European context' (Bundesministerium der Finanzen 2002: 22). In contrast, the *Grundsatzabteilung*'s approach to Europeanization was more cautious and 'bottom-up'. It based its views on economic policy co-ordination on the principles of subsidiarity (suggesting an area of autonomy for the national level) and of market-based co-ordination. These tensions within the Finance Ministry between the necessity and the limits of co-ordination were first clearly exhibited in the *Annual Economic Report* of 2000 (Bundesministerium der Finanzen 2001: 19–20).

But overlaying these tensions was a shared commitment to the Finance Ministry taking a leading role reframing domestic debate about economic policy in a European context. The European Division sought to involve the relevant Bundesrat and Bundestag committees more closely in early-stage dialogue about the draft Broad Economic Policy Guidelines and about the German convergence programme. It also favoured reframing economic policy debate within EU and Euro-Zone rather than just German statistics, notably the work of the Council of Economic Experts (*Sachverständigenrat*). However, this objective proved difficult to realize. Members of the Bundestag showed relatively little interest (see Saalfeld, Chapter 4 in this volume); Länder representatives were more concerned about their specific territorial interests and fears about their sovereignty. From the perspective of the Finance Ministry's European Division economic policy debate within these arenas was only very imperfectly Europeanized.

The Bundesbank

The institution most directly and dramatically affected by EMU was the Bundesbank. The ERM had *de facto* represented a Europeanization of German economic policy in the sense that the Bundesbank set monetary policy for the

ERM via the D-Mark's role as 'anchor' currency (Dyson 1994). It was in essence 'the bank that rules Europe' (Marsh 1992). Its capacity to project 'soft' power to the EU level was reflected in the Federal government's political requirement to 'bind in' the Bundesbank to all decisions about the design and implementation of EMU (Dyson and Featherstone 1999). Only in that way could a German public opinion that was wedded to historical memories of rampant inflation in the 1920s and preoccupied with economic stability be reassured that the Euro would be as stable as the D-Mark.

But with stage three of EMU the Bundesbank ceded its monetary responsibility to the ECB, its president sharing in decision-making as just one member of its governing council. In consequence, two key issues arose: the functions of the Bundesbank and its structure. The Bundesbank sought out an enhanced role in financial stability to replace the loss of monetary policy, especially by centralizing banking supervision inside the Bundesbank. It based its claim on a superior competence in analysing and assessing the macro-economic effects of financial market regulation. Its directorate argued that a smaller, more centralized and streamlined Bundesbank structure was required, that the present structure of nine Länder central banks could no longer be justified, and that the Bundesbank council should be abolished. There were also problems for the Bundesbank president when presidents of the Länder central banks—who were Bundesbank council members—offered opinions about ECB monetary policy when he and not they were responsible for that policy. Hence EMU triggered a complex and difficult reform of the Bundesbank.

In January 2001 Eichel presented two interrelated legislative reform proposals that in part offered what the Bundesbank directorate sought and in part were a surprising setback to its ambitions. In his proposed amendment of the Bundesbank Act he accepted the idea of a small, centralized, and single-tier governing board (to be federally nominated) and the replacement of the Länder central banks by regional offices of the Bundesbank. This attack on the federal principle triggered the opposition of the Länder governments, notably of Bavaria. It involved abolition of the executive boards of the Länder central banks and the removal of their autonomous powers as well as an end to the remaining tasks of the Bundesbank council. But, in a separate but linked reform, Eichel also proposed that responsibilities for supervision of banking, insurance and securities markets—which had been divided—should be amalgamated in a single new Federal Authority for Financial Supervision (*Bundesanstalt für Finanzaufsicht*), modelled on the British Financial Services Authority (FSA). This proposal had the strong backing of the big commercial banks. The concerns of the Bundesbank that it was risky to separate central banking too much from banking supervision were supported by the ECB. Overall, Eichel legitimated these two proposals by the need to strengthen the European role of the Bundesbank by centralizing authority and by the need to reinforce Germany's role as a financial centre.

Faced with political difficulties in the Bundesrat, the Federal government made two concessions to secure the passage of the two bills in March 2002. The rights of the Bundesbank to share banking supervision with the new federal authority were more clearly recognized. Also, the new slightly larger (eight rather than six), single-tier governing board of the Bundesbank was to be nominated half by the Federal government and half by the Bundesrat. This meant a return to a plurality of nominating bodies, represented a concession to the Länder and was justified as better securing the Bundesbank's independence. More serious for the Bundesbank were the difficulties that it faced in securing a role as a competent authority in banking supervision at the EU level through the new Committee of European Banking Regulators.

Following EMU, the Bundesbank had to fight for a new role for itself in economic policy. It was no longer the key player in a 'bottom-up' Europeanization but a beleagured player in a more complex process of Europeanization that offered new political opportunities for other players like the Finance Ministry, the commercial banks, and the interests of Germany as a financial centre. In particular, banking supervision was Europeanized, but in the absence of a clear and explicit European model to 'download'.

Federal–State Relations

The problems of Europeanization of economic policy were most manifest in the work of the Financial Planning Council (*Finanzplanungsrat*), a body bringing together the Länder finance ministers and local authorities with the Federal Finance Ministry to co-ordinate fiscal policy in a longer-term framework. Only really from June 2001 was the European dimension strengthened in the working group that prepared its meetings.

As early as 1996 Waigel had proposed a national stability pact. The main aim was to strengthen the credibility of the Finance Ministry's proposal for an EU stability pact by being able to point out that Germany had similar domestic arrangements: what was good enough for the EU was good enough for Germany. There was a paradox here. In the creation of monetary union Germany had sought to uplift not just its policy preferences but also its institutional model and its ways of doing things. But the proposed EU Stability Pact did not involve the export of a German model or practice, only a policy preference. The Waigel proposal also reflected new and mounting political concern that Germany itself might have difficulties in meeting the fiscal convergence criteria for stage three. The Finance Ministry proposed various formulae for distributing deficits not just between different levels of government but also among different Länder, as well as sanctions for those that exceeded their targets. But Waigel's proposal failed, in part because of irreconcilable conflicts between rich and poor Länder about the nature of the formula, but largely because the Länder governments—led by Waigel's own

Bavaria—would not tolerate the use of European commitments to erode their sovereignty in such a sensitive area. Europeanization of fiscal policy ran up against the constitutional and political constraints of the German federal system.

Eichel eventually achieved a negotiated agreement with the Länder in the Budgetary Principles Law (*Haushaltsgrundsätzegesetz*) of 2001 (para. 51A). It committed them to the objective of balanced budgets, but deferred till after 2004 and without a specific agreed timetable. It also lacked sanctions. But no sooner was the new law in place than the idea of a national stability pact again surfaced. The trigger was the European Commission's threat of a formal warning to the German government that it was in danger of contravening the requirements of the Stability and Growth Pact. As part of the negotiated package in ECOFIN in February 2002 that averted this threat, the Finance Ministry committed itself to strengthen fiscal policy co-ordination with the Länder and with the local authorities. This commitment fell short of the Commission's original insistence on a national stability pact with numerical deficit ceilings and sanctions. The Finance Ministry argued that such a proposal was politically unrealistic in the context of German federalism. But it was critical to agree a deal in the Financial Planning Council that would help realize the German commitment in ECOFIN to bring its total deficit 'close to balance' by 2004.

The main advance was the agreement of the Länder to bring forward to 2002 the aim of budgets 'close to balance', to immediately reduce deficits, to commit to a target for expenditure growth, and to agree rules for distributing the total deficit between the three levels according to a formula. The need for such rules was now accepted as attractive by the Länder as a protection against the Federal government placing future extra commitments on them. This protective role of fiscal rules was used to sell the deal to otherwise reluctant Länder.

Despite this outcome—which was better than most of those involved anticipated—the Financial Planning Council remains imperfectly Europeanized, at least from the standpoint of the Federal Finance Ministry. Its European Division tends to see the Länder governments as an obstacle to an effective and credible German role in EU economic policy co-ordination. Germany's national stability pact of 2002 relied on public pressure and a domestic 'stability culture' to meet commitments rather than formal 'hard' sanctions that would bind the Länder to fiscal responsibility.

Conclusions

By 2002 Europeanization had had comprehensive 'scope' effects on German economic policies, institutional arrangements for economic policy, and the politics of economic policy. These effects had sometimes been direct and relatively easy to trace but often been indirect and more difficult to clarify, especially when mediated through changed market conditions or policy 'spillovers' (e.g. to wages policy) or institutional 'spillovers' (e.g, to federal executive co-ordination or federal–state relations). 'Depth' effects have reflected different types of mechanisms of European economic governance, from 'top-down' supranational monetary policy through 'hard' co-ordination of fiscal policy to a rapid expansion of 'soft' co-ordination across other policies. But overall the policy effects were incremental rather than radical, associated with changes in available policy instruments and how they were used. Similarly, polity effects involved a reconfiguration of institutional roles and power, with the greatest effects being felt by the Bundesbank.

As far as political effects were concerned, in the federal elections of 1998 and 2002 the domestic economic effects of European integration played a very marginal role. Europeanization figured more prominently in party economic programmes, notably of the SPD which stressed European economic co-ordination. But neither ECB monetary policy nor the Stability and Growth Pact were problematized in the election campaigns. The constraint on doing so was German public opinion which was seen to be wedded to the values of a 'stability culture' in economic policy, values that had been successfully 'uploaded' by Germany in the negotiation of EMU. By 2002 EMU was much less disruptive for élite–mass relations than many anticipated.

More politically problematic was the perceived interventionist role of the European Commission in eroding the autonomy of the Länder in regional economic policy. There was a new attempt to redefine the logic of the single market and EMU as justifying not greater supranational intervention but rather more competition among Länder for inward investment and greater freedom for them to pursue industrial policy. The perceived need for strong German industrial policies came into conflict with the Commission, with Schröder taking a lead role (not least to prevent Stoiber exploiting the political potential of this issue).

Neither the Single Market nor EMU had been linked to a crisis of institutional development of the German political economy, to a critical juncture in economic policy and a new trajectory of domestic policy development involving paradigm change. To the extent that reforms were spurred by crises, they were linked either only very indirectly or not at all to Europeanization. The scandal besetting the Federal Agency for Labour (*Bundesanstalt für Arbeit*) in 2002 led to its restructuring, greater competition in job placement, and debate about reforming unemployment benefit to encourage work. Big corporate insolvencies and scandals, like the Schneider group and Metallgesellschaft in the mid-1990s and the Kirch group in 2002, spurred reforms to corporate governance. But these reforms were essentially framed within domestic politics and left the essential features of 'managed' capitalism intact.

This point about continuity is underlined when we consider the cognitive effects. Unlike their Greek and Italian counterparts, the problem for German policy-makers has not so much been to learn about new standards of appropriate economic policy behaviour as to abide by their own traditional standards of sound finance. EMU was important in reinforcing established beliefs that were under increased domestic political pressures. Europeanization in the form of policy learning has occurred in labour-market policy, spurred by good practice elsewhere, notably in job placement, encouragement of older workers, and reform of social benefits. But it has been indirect and very selective, tailored to German practices. For the Schröder government it was also framed within a reappraisal of social democratic ideas about citizenship, a rebalancing of rights and duties, and a new image of the 'activating' state. Far more important in labour-market policy was a reaffirmation (and reform) of the traditional German apprenticeship system and a 'qualification offensive', essentially legitimated in terms of reactivating the strengths of domestic 'managed' capitalism rather than in terms of Europeanization.

Europeanization of economic policy has been conditioned by three key variables:

1. *The domestic goodness of 'fit' between 'managed' capitalism and a political system that has a strong bias to centrality and consensus.* The co-operative aspects of German capitalism are replicated in a political system in which majoritarian politics is strongly qualified. Germany has features of a 'negotiation' democracy—federalism, coalition government, and neo-corporatism (Holtmann and Voelzkow 2000). This consistency between political and capitalist structures lends a degree of robustness to German 'managed' capitalism, not least by extending it to the management of social and labour-market policies. Schröder's governing style—stressing the innovative power of consensus over majoritarian politics—sought to adapt to this reality. Governing by consensus represents the dominant policy style at political and corporate levels. It does, however, raise the question of whether the innovative power of consensus can be strangled by the veto power of key players in an economic policy system characterized by institutional differentiation and complexity.

2. *The use of Europeanization as discourse by ordo-liberal reformers.* By altering market conditions the Single Market, EMU, and globalization—and future EU enlargement—create opportunities for domestic reformers to develop and use a powerful discourse of competitiveness to legitimate change and to suggest new 'imported' solutions to problems. They seek to frame domestic policy in terms of the 'requirements' of Europe, even in the absence of an explicit European institutional model. By pressing the case for confrontation ordo-liberals serve to shift the nodal point of consensus towards greater market liberalization. Externally, the ECB—notably through Otmar Issing, its chief economist—acted as a powerful advocate of market-oriented reforms to German goods, services, and labour markets as well as to the welfare state. Internally, the BDI took up

similar policy positions, supported by the large majority of academic economists. Manufacture of a 'crisis' consciousness can be a useful method for overcoming veto politics, for instance in pension or labour-market reforms.

3. *The continuing loyalty of German firms to 'managed' capitalism, its consensus style of managing change, and its neo-corporatist features.* A key problem for the domestic legitimacy of 'managed' capitalism comes from the decline in membership of the trade unions. This decline has undermined their credibility as negotiating partners. Arguably more significant is the threat of exit by firms from business associations and from 'area-wide' collective bargaining agreements. Faced by increased competitive pressures, in part unleashed by Europeanization, firms have become much more assertive in pursuit of their business interests, pressing for more flexibility over wages, working conditions, and employment. This assertiveness was fuelled by the continuing relatively poor growth performance of the German economy from the early 1990s and again in 2001–2. Firms also threatened exit from Germany as a production base. Both economic policy and the trade unions have reacted defensively in this context of corporate threat. Sharp cuts have been made in business taxation, and greater flexibility introduced into collective bargaining and into plant-level negotiations involving the works councils. Business associations like the BDI have sought to respond by being more vocal and confrontational in approach. The result has been difficult problems in making the Alliance for Jobs work effectively.

Europeanization of economic policy has been caught up in the constraints of domestic 'negotiation' democracy, in a complex rebalancing of power between ordo-liberal reformers and 'managed' capitalism, and in a greater assertiveness by key firms and business associations. The result has not been the abandonment of 'managed' capitalism, in part because of the political constraints of a 'negotiation' democracy and the symbiotic relations with the domestic political process, and in part because German firms continue to draw strengths from it. It is associated with a steady process of incremental innovation in product quality and reliability, a highly skilled work force, and the effective implementation of corporate change. In short, 'managed' capitalism—and the political system that supports it—has shown sufficient capacity for reform to retain the loyalty and commitment of German firms. Though economic reform involves difficult and protracted negotiations, it is not paralysed by multiple veto points and 'joint decision traps', leading to a 'blocked society' (Heinze 1998; Scharpf 1992). The policy process has demonstrated sufficient flexibility to maintain a capacity for co-operative problem-solving. This was evident in the tax reform in 2000, the trade-off between trade union concessions on pension reform and gains with the renewal of the Works Constitution Law in 2001, and the Hartz Commission on labour-market policy in 2002. But the loyalty and commitment of firms cannot be taken for granted, any more than the capacity of 'managed' capitalism and the body politic to make rapid enough adjustments for this purpose.

Although there have been direct cognitive and material effects from Europeanization, they have been overshadowed by the many complex indirect effects, notably in altering the material context of collective bargaining and welfare-state reforms. In German economic policy Europeanization has been more important in 'context-altering' than 'preference-shaping'. Policy-makers have been operating in transformed contexts of incentives and constraints. The political effects have been very important. In fiscal policy politicians have had to learn just how very restricted their room for manoeuvre is to make a distinctive party political difference in the framework of the Stability and Growth Pact. This Pact—and the prospect of an early warning from the EU—was the silent guest at the federal elections of 2002, constraining what contending politicians could promise the electorate. It also raised serious questions about the room for manoeuvre available to the Länder and to local authorities in a context of external fiscal discipline. Fiscal policy was an area in which there were strong pressures for accommodation between Germany and the EU. Quite simply, political credibility—both domestically, from an electorate that valued 'sound' finance and money, and within the EU, which expected consistency and predictability—was directly at stake. There was too much to lose from conflict with the EU on this subject. Such a conflict would mobilize the ordo-liberal elements in the German model on a matter seen as fundamental to economic stability, and politicians shied away from any association with lack of credibility here. But a transforming context of incentives and constraints in relation to liberalization and competition policy brought more serious adaptation problems (e.g. over subsidy policies, the car market, takeover rules). Here there was a real sense of the need to defend 'managed' capitalism and of the electoral benefits from doing so.

The assumption of a basic goodness of 'fit' between mechanisms of European economic governance and the German 'social' market economy is deeply problematic for two key reasons. First, Germany lacks a unitary German economic policy model. It combines an ordo-liberalism that stresses firm clear rules for economic stability and market competition with a 'managed' capitalism that emphasizes negotiated change and policy evolution. They co-exist in complex and dynamic tension with each other. Astute German economic statesmanship amounts to political skill in managing this relationship. In their different ways Helmut Schmidt and Gerhard Schröder proved masters of this skill. Europeanization upset this equilibrium by creating new patterns of incentive and constraint that empowered ordo-liberal arguments about liberalization of goods, services, and labour markets. But this Europeanization as discourse of competitiveness took place within a domestic context that, during the Red–Green coalition of 1998–2002, favoured a process of co-operatively managed change consistent with rejuvenating 'managed' capitalism. In this respect the domestic politics of Europeanization remains central: the way in which domestic actors frame reforms, how domestic political opportunity structures are changed, and the role of the Chancellor in manufacturing consensus.

Goodness of 'fit' is also problematic because new mechanisms of European economic governance are associated with unanticipated consequences. Germany was a 'pace-setter' in 'uploading' its policy preferences in monetary and fiscal policies. But in both areas Germany had to cope with unanticipated consequences: a pro- rather than anti-cyclical monetary policy, and serious problems in meeting its fiscal commitments. In fiscal policy Europeanization forced Germany to confront deep-seated domestic constitutional constraints on 'top-down' rules and sanctions that exceeded those to be found in negotiating the EU Stability and Growth Pact among member states. Another instance of unanticipated consequences was the difficulties that the Bundesbank had in carving out a new role for itself on terms with which it was happy.

Above all, Europeanization of economic policy proved complex. This complexity was evident in the varying nature of the effects: cognitive and material, direct and indirect. It was also apparent in the different mechanisms of European economic governance and the directions of change that they involved. Europeanization was most easily traced in causal terms as a hierarchical, 'top-down' process of adaptation to ECB monetary policy and to aspects of the Single Market such as competition and state-aid policy. But Europeanization also involved the evolution of a horizontal process of cross-national policy learning and 'lesson-drawing', in part organized under EU auspices. For Germany under Schröder this process was shaped by an ideological disposition to favour comparison with states that were both social democratic and favoured dialogue and negotiation in economic change. Hence the tendency was to look to the Netherlands, Denmark, and Sweden rather than Britain (social democratic but without the partnership theme). In so far as Germany 'converged' it was with the economic policy process and policies of these states. Europeanization did not mean a simple unilinear trend to Anglo-American 'market' capitalism. It also supported voluntary processes of cross-national policy learning that were consistent with the inherited values and strengths of the German model. Finally, Europeanization had a 'bottom-up' dimension as domestic actors sought to use Europe to construct a discourse of domestic reform, even in the absence of a European model to 'download'. Europeanization was assimilated as discourse into the domestic contest of ideas about what had to be done in economic policy, about adaptational requirements.

11

Competition Policy:
From Centrality to Muddling Through?

MARTIN LODGE

Wettbewerbspolitik war jahrzehntelang eine Philosophie; das war kein Gewurschtel, das war ganz zentral.[1]

(Senior Official, July 2001)

COMPETITION POLICY HAS BEEN SEEN TO LIE at the heart of the German social market economy with its firm emphasis on the control of markets through a strong and non-discretionary rule-based framework. Post-1945, the German law on restrictive practices was widely defined as the 'constitution' of the social market economy. Its rule-based character, emphasizing the importance of market competition, represented a major departure from previous German competition policy, which had been mainly based on the rationale of fostering cartels (Gerber 1998: 369). Apart from being at the heart of the post-1945 political economy of Germany, it was also highly influential in shaping EU policy and subsequently other states' competition policies. DG Competition (or DG IV in old parlance) of the European Commission was long regarded as a traditional German 'stronghold'.[2] This EC 'offspring' rapidly outgrew its German 'parent' during the 1980s, when EC competition policy enjoyed institutional assertion as part of the Single Market initiative.

The notion of 'competition policy' is characterized by substantial definitional ambivalence, which reflects the dual character of the social market economy in emphasizing both 'ordo-liberal' and 'managed capitalism' styles in German economic policy-making (Dyson 2001). On the one hand, competition policy was defined by the ambition to prevent the emergence of market power, in particular with regard to the formation of cartels, the abuse of dominant market positions, and the emergence of significant market concentration. Competition policy was a

---

[1] 'For decades, competition policy was a philosophy; that was not muddling through, it was at the very centre.'

[2] See, for example, the protests by the German government concerning the replacement of Alexander Schaub as Director General of the Competition Directorate in the wake of the European Commission's policy of beginning to rotate top civil service positions in early 2002.

Proceedings of the British Academy, **119**, 231–250. © The British Academy 2003.

central part of *Ordnungspolitik*, a system, constituted by law and, more importantly, derived from a set of principles, which aimed to enforce and sustain a market-led economy in order to protect the freedom of an individual against the abuse of power by private or state actors. On the other hand, competition policy also concerned industrial policy goals, including, for example, state aids and exemptions for 'essential services', associated with the administrative principle of *Daseinsvorsorge*. This dual character of competition policy goals pointed to the ill-defined nature of the social market concept with its blurred borders between those areas where competition was advocated and those where exemptions were regarded as favourable to the wider public good.

This chapter focuses on competition law policy in the domain of 'cartel law'. The case studies nevertheless reflect on wider debates within the German political system and between Germany and the EU.[3] Europeanization in formal terms, i.e. in terms of legal regimes, occurred in at least four specific ways that set this specific domain of competition policy apart from other policy domains affected by internal market provisions. First, competition policy represented the 'first supranational policy' in the European Union (McGowan and Wilks 1995). The European Commission exercised a key executive role in competition policy with only a highly restrictive, consultative role given to member states through an advisory committee in comitology. The Commission was not only directly involved in the administration of competition policy—unlike any other EU policy domain where there was a reliance on execution by national and sub-national administrations—it was also granted monopoly power on exempting the formation of agreements under Regulation 17/62.[4]

Second, until the late 1980s, the national and the EC regimes operated largely in parallel; they had different foci, with the result of limited friction between the two systems. This state of peaceful co-existence has changed considerably since then, especially following the emergence of the EC merger regime in 1989 (Regulation 4064/89). Subsequently, the competition policy era of the 1990s was arguably characterized by growing 'system frictions' (Doern 1996: 30) between different levels of competition policy, in particular in merger policy in relation to the 'German' and 'Dutch' clauses (Articles 9 and 22 of the merger regulation).

---

[3] This chapter uses 'competition law' synonymously with 'cartel law'. It thereby ignores the existence of another 'competition law', the 'fair trading law' ('Gesetz gegen unlauteren Wettbewerb', UWG) whose purpose was to safeguard the (moral) quality of competition. It rose to prominence once again in early 2002 when the clothes retailer 'C&A' was fined (on the basis of provisions dating from 1932 and 1935) for offering a discount, despite two court orders, in the early days of the introduction of the Euro.

[4] Regulation 17/62 granted sole authority to the European Commission to apply Article 81 (3), while concurrency existed with regard to Articles 81 (1) and 82. The passing of Regulation 17/62 marked the beginning of an EC competition policy. The European Court of Justice subsequently confirmed that the doctrines of direct effect and supremacy applied to competition law.

Third, while EC competition law was a 'prototype' requirement for accession countries, such 'coercive' Europeanization did not apply to the existing member states. Hence, throughout the first decades of European integration, national competition policies were shaped by diverse philosophical, administrative and legal arrangements. Nevertheless, the years since 1980 have been characterized by the adoption of EC law-type provisions on the lines of Articles 81 and 82 across all EU member states, including the UK and Germany (Eyre and Lodge 2000). Finally, the Treaty also provided for the application of EC law by national competition authorities. Thus, Article 84 allowed member states to apply Articles 81 and 82 in parallel to national competition law. In the German context, provisions allowing the Federal Cartel Office to utilize these provisions were included following demands by the agency.[5]

Apart from these formal interactions and relationships between two sets of laws originating from the same intellectual sources, Gerber (1998) points to the peculiar 'European' character of European competition policy, which cannot simply be regarded as a diluted version of US-type anti-trust law. Gerber highlights three particular features of 'Europeanized' competition law regimes: the continuous interaction between the national and EC regimes, and between the different national competition regimes, as well as the shared foundations in a uniquely European model of competition policy.

Analysing Europeanization and German competition policy, therefore, addresses at least three concerns. First, in both the German and EU systems, competition policy represented a crucial, if not defining policy area. Second, the EU regime has traditionally been regarded as 'offspring' of the German system. Third, and related to the previous point, both systems were linked by continuous interaction. The remainder of this chapter does three things. The next section provides an overview of the German competition law regime and existing accounts of the continuing role of German competition law and its authorities in the face of internationalizing markets, changing economic thinking, and the growing importance of the EC competition regime. Then three case studies of Europeanization of competition law policy are considered. It discusses three diverse dynamics of Europeanization, namely those of 'domestic adjustment', 'informing EC legal change', and 'collision' between national exemption and the European Commission. The final section explores the actors and 'carriers' of Europeanization, while also placing this account in the wider literature on Europeanization.

---

[5] For example, EC law was used by the Federal Cartel Office to challenge the practice of two German tourist operators (TUI and NUR) which had abused exclusivity clauses in their purchase of room quotas at select Spanish hotels. In general, national competition authorities utilized European provisions only very rarely.

German Competition Law and Challenges of Europeanization

As already noted, the German competition law regime evolved interdependently with the European regime. It emerged in the context of post-Second World War economic policy in interaction between 'ordo-liberal' thinking espoused by the so-called 'Freiburg School' of legal–economic thinking and demands by the US occupying force for sustained deconcentration of German industry. The final 1957 law (*Gesetz gegen Wettbewerbsbeschränkungen*, GWB) to some extent followed these demands for a prohibition approach against cartels (for full account, see Berghahn 1986: 151–81). Earlier proposals, such as the 1949 Josten draft, had demanded the outright prohibition of cartels and of discriminatory behaviour as well as strict merger control within a judicial framework. These proposals were, however, strongly opposed by German industry interests and various sectoral federal government ministries, which claimed that reconstruction could be achieved only by 'large' and 'competitive' businesses. It was also critically received at the Federal Economics Ministry. The final approach towards competition policy reflected a mixture of prohibition and administrative approaches towards competition policy, drawing on US anti-trust law, ordo-liberal principles, and a residual inheritance from previous German regimes, exempting numerous 'sensitive' sectors and allowing derogations from the scope of the law. A merger regime, although proposed in the initial 1949 draft, was not included, but was added to the regime in 1973.

The German domain involved a small number of actors forming a relatively closed policy community, which, however, prevented neither substantial internal conflict nor agenda-setting by external actors and events. Policy development took place in the face of legal interaction with the appeal courts, with political initiatives to 'modernize' competition law and with the EU level. The Federal Economics Ministry operated not only as framer of the domestic law and as negotiator at the EU level, but also as policy-maker in other domains that affected the legal competence of the Federal Cartel Office, such as in energy policy, postal services and telecommunications. Within the ministry, the competition law sections were insulated from other, more interventionist, policy domains. The law provided for the so-called *Ministererlaubnis*, which allowed the minister to overrule the Federal Cartel Office in merger cases and in specific cartel cases on grounds of the wider national economic interest. This authority was rarely used (sixteen times in total which, up to early 2002, led to six cases of ministers overruling the cartel authority's decision). The Federal Cartel Office was established as an independent agency, subordinate to the Economics Ministry. While for some the Federal Cartel Office represented the 'guardian' of the social market economy, for others its role was that of a 'court-type federal agency', tasked with applying and interpreting competition law. Similar differences existed with regard to the (entirely abstract) question whether the Economic Ministry was legally allowed to intervene directly in a case, or whether directions could be only of a 'general' nature.

Three mechanisms, in particular, made the Federal Cartel Office 'independent' from direct political influence, in addition to the relative transparency ensured by the fact that Cartel Office decisions could be challenged through the courts (the *Oberlandesgericht* Düsseldorf and, as last instance, the *Bundesgerichtshof*). First, its organization separated policy-making from decision-making units. The latter, named *Beschlußkammern*, were constituted as court-type arrangements and were granted full decision-making authority within the organizational structure of the Federal Cartel Office. A second mode to signal independence was physical separation from the government—traditionally the Federal Cartel Office occupied premises in Berlin, but it was moved to Bonn once most of the federal government had transferred to Berlin. The third mode was the appointment of the Cartel Office's President as a technical civil servant rather than as a 'political' senior civil servant, thereby excluding the possibility of politically convenient early retirement.

The overall discourse on competition policy was further shaped by the Monopoly Commission, which was formed in 1973 to investigate and report on market concentration, but also produced special reports on economic and competition policy issues and played a consultative role in the case of ministerial merger reviews. The domain was united in a shared background in legal–economic thinking originating in the so-called Freiburg school of 'ordo-liberalism' and was reinforced by regular meetings, most prominently in the Working Group on Cartel Law (*Arbeitskreis Kartellrecht*). Key actors of the competition policy community, also involving officials from the European Commission, regularly met in such venues. At the heart of these gatherings was a commitment to the importance of competition policy, in particular, and the wider 'Freiburg school', in general, emphasizing the importance of establishing a non-discretionary legal framework in which market relationships could be technically assessed. At the same time, these meetings were crucial for the discussion of international and national competition law developments (see, for example, Bundeskartellamt 2001).

While, for many, the Federal Cartel Office represented a technocratic 'guardian' role in the German political economy, it did not evade substantial criticism, often justified on the basis of perceived Europeanization processes and (coinciding) changing economic circumstances and thinking. In the early 1970s, criticism centred on the argument that despite all the rhetoric about the important 'constitutional' role of cartel law, there was an increasing concentration across German industry. This criticism eventually led to the integration of a merger policy regime into the GWB in 1973. There was also a shift in the perception of 'competition', which moved away from 'perfect' competition towards a 'dynamic' and 'workable' understanding of competition. In due course, merger policy became a far more important element in the policy arsenal of the Federal

Cartel Office. Thus, the cartel law provisions—said to be the foundation of the social market economy—became increasingly less relevant.

By the mid-1990s, arguments pointing to the growing challenges to the authority of the Federal Cartel Office and competition law policy focused increasingly on Europeanization processes. For example, Wilks with Bartle (2002; see also Wilks and McGowan 1995*a*: 61) suggest that the Federal Cartel Office increasingly lost its pivotal role as 'guardian' and was continuously undermined by the appeal courts and the Economics Ministry, in particular with regard to merger policy in the EU context. Similarly, Sturm (1996: 218) argued that Europeanization undermined the role of the Federal Cartel Office. He suggested that the 'day-to-day fact that political decision-making is now a larger element in the shaping of merger control', meant that the Cartel Office was relegated to a subordinate position, with influence at the European level being primarily exerted by the political calculations of the Economics Ministry and the lobbying of German firms. Furthermore, the Federal Cartel Office was said to have manoeuvred itself into inward-looking isolation with an exaggerated self-belief in its mission and an over-legalistic and case-oriented approach towards competition policy (Wilks with Bartle 2002: 166).

In terms of the relationship between the European and the German competition regimes, there was also a notable increase in hostility, in particular from the German competition authority against the European Commission in the case of merger policy. The Commission was accused of over-lenient empire-building tendencies and a politicized policy approach, grounded in different understandings of 'market dominance'. From the early 1990s, this led to calls for an independent European Cartel Office on the lines of the German competition authority (Wolf 1994). For some, this reflected an attempt by the Federal Cartel Office to export its own ethos to the EC level, in the face of growing insignificance as a national institution (Wilks and McGowan 1995*b*). There was also increasing hostility between the European Commission's competition policy and German governments' political preferences (Smith 2001*a*), not only in areas such as coal subsidies, public sector banking systems, fines imposed on Volkswagen for discriminatory distribution techniques, opposition towards Commission initiatives to alter the exclusivity of car distribution schemes, aid to shipbuilding, or the amount of subsidy being spent on 'modernizing' eastern Germany (even following the initial unification problems illustrated by Anderson 1999*a*: 113–51). These tensions explained to some extent Chancellor Schröder's hostility towards the European Commission, which he accused of failing to comprehend the nature of Germany's industry base.

Dynamics of Europeanization in German Competition Policy

The examination of case studies allows for a differentiated analysis of the potential diversity of the implications of Europeanization for German competition policy. This section offers case studies of three distinct dynamics of Europeanization. They concern 'highly visible' cases, neglecting small-scale Europeanization effects at the domestic level, such as the adoption of 'whistle-blower' provisions by the Federal Cartel Office in 2000, which were derived from similar European Commission practices. The following first discusses the Europeanization of German competition law in the 1998 GWB Act as a process of 'assimilation' of the German law with EC provisions. Second, it considers the response of the German policy community to the European Commission's proposals to radically modify the procedural provisions of Regulation 17/62. In so doing it, it assesses the Europeanization of German advocacy in influencing a regime that it had fundamentally shaped in the past. Third, it examines a case of 'Europeanization collision', where European Commission initiatives based on EC competition law challenge domestic policy arrangements. The case in question is the drawn-out conflict between the European Commission, the German government, and the German book trade association concerning the fixed book-price agreement.

The selection of the cases is based on two major considerations. First, the three cases are crucial and important. In each case, Europeanization, in its various forms, affected issues of fundamental importance to the character of the German competition policy regime. Second, the cases are representative, in that they fall into three broad Europeanization 'dynamics' (as noted above) that are central to the study of Europeanization in a diversity of policy fields (Lodge 2002: 44–51). Looking at different 'dynamics' permits the analysis to highlight the potential significance (or insignificance) of different decision-rules, coalition-building requirements, and actor constellations.

The Europeanization of Domestic Competition Law

This case concerns a 'typical' example of Europeanization research: the impact of European provisions at the national level. In this case, Europeanization occurred via 'assimilation' or (very selective) 'mimicry' rather than following any demands by the European Commission. Arguably, the 'Europeanization' idea was most likely to cause substantial ideational resistance, given the German belief of having substantially shaped the EC regime and the fact that the EC regime represented a 'diluted' version of the German regime. Furthermore, any alteration to the domestic regime was likely to be opposed on the assumption that changes would dilute its consistency, legal clarity, and limits on discretionary activity.

Suggestions about 'Europeanizing' national competition law had started to be made at least since the late 1980s. The Economics Ministry finally took them up in the early 1990s as part of the broader debate concerning the competitiveness of Germany as a location for economy activity. The initiative's main proponents in the Economics Ministry were successful in placing the 'Europeanization of competition law' idea into the 1994 *Standortbericht*. It was claimed that for German business the European or even the global, rather than the domestic, market had become most relevant. Harmonization of competition law would reduce the transaction costs of business dealing with different legal systems. Following the 1994 general election and the positive reception of the Europeanization proposal, especially by the Federation of German Industry (*Bundesverband der deutschen Industrie*, BDI), the Economics Ministry established a working group to prepare detailed proposals as to what 'Europeanization' of competition law might entail. Prior to these internal considerations, there had been little discussion on the implications of 'Europeanization' for the domestic law. Following internal discussions, it was proposed that harmonization should mean the large-scale adoption of the wording of the law according to the 'reference model Europe'. The first 'corner-stones' (*Eckpunkte*) of May 1996 proposed the full adoption of Articles 81 (1), 81(3), and 82 as well as the European merger regime, in particular the criterion of control by 'decisive influence'. While these suggestions were supported by the BDI, they met strong opposition from the Federal Cartel Office, the Monopoly Commission, and the Academic Advisory Council (*Wissenschaftlicher Beirat*) to the Economics Ministry. This opposition claimed that the government was behaving negligently in putting the status and the 'toughness' of the existing domestic regime at risk, as the 'imported' EC provisions were said to offer scope for the consideration of industrial policy goals (Wissenschaftlicher Beirat 1996). It was claimed that it was perverse to adopt an inferior version of competition law, when the German law offered clearer differentiation and legal clarity. As a response to these criticisms, ministerial requests to accommodate the Federal Cartel Office rather than the BDI, and the demand that the modified law had to be perceived as a 'strengthening' of the law, a joint working group of ministry and competition authority officials was established to co-ordinate further legislative initiatives. As a consequence, the draft legislation of July 1997 suggested that the overall emphasis of the proposals had shifted towards a reform that maintained, despite adaptations in the light of EC law wording, the main substantive provisions of the existing domestic regime (BMWi 1997; BDI 1998; BT 13/10633).

In terms of formal provisions, §1 and §19 GWB represented Europeanized provisions by adopting the prohibition approach of Article 81[6] and Article 82, respectively. Previously, the practice of horizontal agreements had been outlawed. An exemption clause on the lines of Article 81 (3) was also added. Nevertheless, following the Federal Cartel Office's criticisms, the previous approach of relying on 'exempt' sectors was maintained (with some reductions in the number of exempted sectors). Also, the EC article 81 (3) provision to exempt cases which

---

[6] The German regime did not adopt the then existing provisions with regard to vertical agreements.

'promoted technical and economic progress' was not transferred in order to avoid 'public interest' considerations.[7] Thus, the 1998 Law remained less discretionary or 'flexible' than EC law under Article 81 (3), indicating the continued dominance of the 'German' provisions.

In terms of the 'import' of Article 82 concerning the abuse of dominant position, the prohibition approach replaced provisions where sanctions had been applied only if administrative findings of abuse had been ignored by the undertaking in question. At the same time, there was a continued German interpretation of market dominance, based on facing little or no competition, which was, however, joined by the EC- (and ECJ)-based criteria of market share, financial strength, market access, market entry barriers, extent of potential competition, and availability of alternatives. A further example of the influence of European, if not international (US) legal discourse (drawing on the 1912 case *United States v. Terminal Railroad Association*) was the introduction of the 'essential facilities' doctrine into the German law. While the BDI attacked the utility and potential scope of this doctrine within the German law, for officials it offered one way to make competition law applicable to so-called 'network industries'.

The third major area of harmonization concerned mergers. Here, the existing split between *ex ante* and *ex post* controls was replaced by a pure *ex ante* approach for mergers above DM 1bn (€ 0.51bn). Following lobbying by the Agriculture ministry, mergers that strengthened or established 'market dominance' were prohibited, except in cases where the merger improved the competitive position of the industry in other markets. Furthermore, the European provision of 'decisive influence' was introduced into German law, its potential impact being moderated, however, by the parallel maintenance of, and insistence on, priority being attached to the previous German approach which relied on fixed thresholds of market shares.

After the initial battle on the degree of 'Europeanization' had been decided in favour of the Federal Cartel Office's preferences, the politics of competition law reform mainly concerned purely domestic, and mostly non-competition law-related, debates. These included sectoral associations and federal government ministries that demanded 'special treatment' for their respective constituencies. Particularly prominent, and eventually successful, was the repeated lobbying in favour of measures targeted against the supposed market power of food retailers. Following threats by the CSU to veto any proposed changes should the law fail

---

[7] The relevant §7 GWB allowed for exemptions which facilitated 'development, production, distribution, acquisition, return or disposal of goods and services', and where agreements did not damage competition disproportionally. Officials used this paragraph as a 'dumping ground' for specific demands for exemptions by other departments. For example, specific demands by the Research and Technology ministry (agreements regarding R&D) and Environment (regarding exemptions for wastage recycling systems) were thereby sidetracked.

to include special provisions to please the small-scale Bavarian food supply sector, a broad prohibition of the 'not only occasional sale below acquisition cost' was included. The inclusion of 'sports' as an sector exempt from competition law followed sustained lobbying of the football industry following a *Bundesgerichtshof* judgement of December 1997 in favour of the competition authority, which had ruled that the central marketing by the German football association of television rights for the UEFA cup home matches of the German teams contravened competition rules (Lodge 2000: 97–8).

The supposed Europeanization of national competition law suggested that the main justifications and the main 'triggers' for policy development were domestic. More far-reaching 'Europeanization' in terms of wording was blocked by domestic opposition and, as a consequence, the substantive character of the law remained largely 'German', with an emphasis on fixed categories and thresholds.

Domestic Competition Policy Informing European Policy Change

Europeanization is also concerned with the interaction of domestic policies with the European level. Member states are said to favour the exporting of the domestic policy in order to reduce the adaptation costs of national policy change due to the requirement of transposing European provisions (Héritier 1997). In competition law policy, potential overlaps of legal provisions, attempts of actors to 'venue shop' and consequent system frictions caused pressure for national adaptation. Furthermore, given the decline in significance of the German competition law, which was accompanied by the growing importance of EC law, one of the most important ways of legitimizing the German law was its power to influence the evolution of EC law. This pattern followed, as noted in Chapter 1, the perception that Germany had traditionally been successful in 'uploading' its policy preferences to the EU level.

German influence on the development of the EU competition regime had been prominent, for example, in the formulation of the first merger regulation (Armstrong and Bulmer 1998: 93–115). The merger regime accommodated the Federal Cartel Office's demands for higher thresholds for the applicability of EC law than initially proposed by the European Commission. More significantly, it included the 'German claw back' clause (Article 9), which allowed national authorities to apply for the transfer of a 'European case' to the national authority where the merger mainly affected the domestic market. These arrangements were soon to cause considerable tension following early instances in which the European Commission refused to 'refer back' cases that the Federal Cartel Office argued were subsequently passed too leniently by the Commission. Decision-making among the college of Commissioners was condemned as non-transparent and politicized. In contrast, German business, which had been strongly in favour of a European merger regime, repeatedly called for an expansion of the EC regime by lowering the thresholds of applicability. A further example of the EU regime becoming similar to the German law was the change towards a threshold-based approach concerning vertical agreements in 2000. However, the 'match' between the two systems was incomplete, leading to 'gaps', where certain areas were exempted in the European regime while being prohibited under German law, or where the 'non-mentioning' of certain sectors in the EC law seemed to contradict a German prohibition. This was likely to lead to an informal accommodation of the German practice, despite an absence of domestic law change.

The proposals regarding Regulation 17/62, first issued in 1999, had potentially large-scale consequences for domestic competition policy and pointed to a decreasing influence of the formal German approach on EC law developments. The suggested amendment to Regulation 17/62 was potentially the most significant change in European competition law 'for over 40 years' (Ehlermann 2000: 537; see also Apeldoorn 2001; European Commission 1999). The context was provided by claims that the procedures under Regulation 17/62 had led to a Commission overload, diverting its resources away from serious breaches of competition principles, and to legal uncertainty given the existing practice to issue 'comfort letters'. DG Competition published, in July 1999, a White Paper that outlined proposals for amending its procedures under which Articles 81 and 82 were to be applied. It suggested making competition policy more similar to internal market policies by decentralizing its authority under Article 81 (3) to national competition authorities and courts and by moving away from the *ex ante* notification procedure to an *ex post* control regime that would rely heavily on the self-assessment among businesses. These proposals were to allow the European Commission to focus on so-called 'hard-core' cartels. Overall, these proposals to some extent reflected not only a move towards themes drawn from the US anti-trust system, but also a system of cartel law governance where the Commission acted as standard-setter, with national authorities and courts representing decentralized executive agencies operating under EC law and Commission guidance.

The Commission proposals met with a hostile reception from the German competition policy community (see Fikentscher 2001; Möschel 2000; Wissenschaftlicher Beirat 2000; Monopol-Kommission 2001). Particular criticism was targeted at the proposed move from a notification and exemption regime to an *ex post* regime. It was claimed that such proposals put the coherence of EC competition policy at risk, given the inevitable inconsistency of national interpretation of EC law, and that the proposals represented an disproportionate response to the Commission's problems in administering Article 81 and 82 cases. However, despite intensive lobbying at the EU level, Germany was unable to organize a blocking majority among other member states to veto the Commission's initiative.[8] In order

---

[8] Arguably, this was due to the fact that in the other member states where the notification procedure had just been introduced, the immediate effect had been a massive increase in workload because of

to provide a 'constructive' counter-offer to the Commission's proposal, a joint working group of ministry and competition authority staff was established. The outcome was the realization that the system of *ex ante* notification was not as effective in practice as suggested by the opponents of the Commission's proposals. In response, both organizations adopted a less hostile and more pragmatic approach towards the Commission's proposals, nevertheless warning of the potential legal uncertainty to business implicit in the shift to an *ex post* control- and 'economics effects'-based approach towards cartels. It was proposed that an internet-based register for horizontal agreements should be established to provide for some public information and enhance the potential for preventive action to be taken. However, while the Commission initially accepted a weak version of the German proposal, other member states were hostile to the 're-introduction' of notification provisions and the proposal did not survive Council working group deliberations.

Following discussions on the basis of Commission 'non-papers', and in an effort to respond to member states' concerns about the potential for increased incoherence of national application of EC competition law, the Commission produced its draft regulation of September 2000. This draft proposed that in all areas where there was a 'cross-national' effect, EC law should apply and the Commission was to be granted the right to intervene in particular cases. The national authorities were to supply continuous information on their application of Articles 81 and 82 (Wesseling 2001). The relevant provision (Article 3 of the draft regulation) was later watered down in applying only to Article 81. But, nevertheless, it was regarded as a marginalization of national competition law, by banning national authorities from applying national law to cases with any form of 'cross-border effect'. It was, accordingly, seen as a reduction in the status and authority of the Federal Cartel Office to that of a cartel-law executive agency of the European Commission (Bechtold 2000: 2428–9). The issue of applicability of national competition law meant that discussions in the Council working group went beyond the expected agreement date of spring 2002 (reflecting the unwillingness of subsequent Council Presidencies to force the issue). In the meantime, the German Monopoly Commission, in a special report, called for judicial action to be taken against the Commission should the draft regulation be passed (Monopolkommision 2001). Such suggestions, as well as further angry attacks by German academics, were dismissed by the Economics Ministry, which claimed that the Commission proposals were mainly concerned with alterations in policy instruments rather than with changing competition policy philosophies. However, the ministry stressed that the Commission's proposals were too radical and that a more gradual, 'bottom-up' approach would offer a more appropriate method to achieve desirable policy harmonization. The Federal Cartel Office resisted the

---

the number of (often irrelevant) notifications. This contrasted with the embedded nature of German practices where only a limited and relevant number of cases was notified.

Commission proposals more strongly, suggesting that the national law was far superior to EC law. Therefore, it proposed that Article 81 was to be used as a 'minimum standard', with national competition law being allowed to offer stricter formulations. Although the Economics Ministry tolerated this domestic opposition and even sympathized with parts of the Cartel Office's reasoning, it regarded the office's suggestions as politically not feasible and too negative towards the Commission's proposals.

The shift of the EC law towards a more US-type approach, which was supported by international bodies such as the OECD, also implied a potentially significant impact on national procedural autonomy and subsequent changes in national competition regimes, not least because of the constant oversight by the European Commission. However, this potential trend towards criminal sanctions-type national procedures being adopted across national competition regimes was less likely to occur through a 'top-down' process than as a result of horizontal diffusion.

In conclusion, the case of the proposed amendments to Regulation 17/62 illustrates the decreasing influence of the German approach on informing competition law development at the European level. Faced with a set of European Commission proposals, a lack of potential coalition partners among fellow member states, and growing dominance of the US-influenced 'economic' approach to competition policy, the German competition policy domain was unable to 'inform' or, in this case, veto, EU policy. Its position was further weakened by its inability to suggest strong alternatives to the overload perceived to be inherent in the existing notification procedure of the EC regime. Apart from the EC regime's shift beyond traditional German assumptions, there were also potentially significant feedback effects on the national regime.

On Collision Course: European Competition Policy and National Policy Preferences

This section concerns the Europeanization of competition policy in the form of a new opportunity structure for new actors to challenge existing national provisions. The following example considers a conflict between German policy preferences for state subsidies and exempt treatment and the preferences of the European Commission and other member states in an area where supposedly 'cultural' values were said to require protection from economic values in the name of cultural diversity. The fixed book-price agreement that applied across Germany, Austria, and Switzerland led to a direct conflict between a national 'exempt' sector and the EC competition regime. It also led to a shift in governance mechanisms at the domestic level, away from associational agreements involving the national book association (*Börsenverein*) towards legislation.

These agreements, dating from 1887, to prevent differential pricing across the

German-speaking territories, included a fixed-price agreement for cross-border economic activities between Germany, Austria, and Switzerland administered by the respective national book associations. In preparation for Austria's accession to the EU, an application for exemption was made to the European Commission in 1993. In August 1994, the Commission issued a 'comfort letter' allowing trans-border fixed-book pricing with a time-limited exemption until the end of June 1996. In June 1996, the Austrian discount bookseller Librodisk (later Libro) lodged a complaint with the European Commission against the trans-border price agreement. This complaint marked the beginning of increasingly adversarial relations between the German government, German booksellers, publishers, and authors, on the one hand, and DG Competition, on the other, especially after January 1998, when the European Commission launched formal proceedings against the German price-fixing agreement.

The initial DG Competition initiative to investigate the German–Austrian agreement received substantial hostility among member states and even within the Commission. The Commission President, Jacques Santer, supported the German government against Competition Commissioner Karel van Miert. Van Miert argued that the trans-national aspects of the agreement violated EC competition law. In July 1997, the Culture Council called on the Commission to tolerate 'cultural' policies that seemed to counter internal market principles, while the German book association produced three studies that suggested that the German–Austrian agreement was not incompatible with EC law in legal and economic terms. Despite these interventions, campaigns by authors, suggestions by the book association that DG Competition was attacking the 'core' of German 'culture', and European Parliament resolutions, DG Competition issued a complaint to Austria and Germany in mid-January 1998, demanding the abolition of the existing book-price agreement, as there was no evidence for the supposed utility of this particular mechanism to support the book industry. The German book association responded with the claim that the Commission was putting up to 25,000 jobs, 2,000 bookshops, and 800 publishing houses at risk. As a compromise, it offered to partially lift the fixed-price regime on particular book products with a 'lower' cultural value. However, the Commission rejected these proposals. The Commission was also backed, in June 1999, by the advisory committee of member states, where a large majority supported van Miert's stance against the German–Austrian agreement. However, van Miert's attempt in mid-July 1999 to outlaw the German agreement failed. In the light of the resignation of the Commission earlier that year and a subsequent unwillingness among Commissioners to tackle politically controversial issues, van Miert did not succeed in obtaining the necessary support from his fellow Commissioners. Further negotiations between the European Commission and the German federal government and the book association received new urgency when Libro threatened, in early January 2000, to take the European Commission to court for non-action, if a decision had not been reached by mid-February. By then, the German book association had consented to the European Commission's proposals. Two national systems of book price control emerged, thus removing competition issues from the scope of EC competition law, while cross-border trade was to be price-controlled only where the sole purpose of the book import and re-import was the subversion of the national fixed-price regime. This compromise solution, which came into force on 1 July 2000, also required some alterations to the cartel law (GWB) in order to clarify the purely national character of the price-fixing agreement.

However, within days this agreement was challenged by cross-national discount selling by Libro, which offered 20 per cent online discounts for selective titles to be purchased in Austria. In its German shops, it installed computer terminals so that customers could order these cheaper offers. In response, the publishing houses and distributors refused to provide Libro with any further stock, arguing that its selling techniques represented a purposive attack on the fixed book-price agreement. Following legal confusion, owing to two successful court injunctions against the publishers and a judgement by the Berlin state court that Libro's behaviour was a purposive subversion of the fixed-price agreement, Libro (later joined by the Belgian firm 'Proxis') complained to the European Commission. By late July, it cancelled its online discounts in agreement with the publishers. The European Commission claimed that online sales were not part of the 'protected' areas of the remained fixed book-price agreement.[9] DG Competition renewed its proceedings against the German fixed book-price agreement and with the support of the Federal Cartel Office launched raids on publishers, distributors, and the book association, suspecting illegal agreements.[10]

Following accusations by the book association that the European Commission was involved in a 'crusade' against German publishers and German government promises to provide publishers with a legal basis for their agreement, a further compromise between the various parties emerged in early 2002. Until national legislation was put into force in the course of 2002, the German publishing industry agreed to the (limited) circumstances in which it would take action against the discounted sale of German books by a non-domestic provider. The Commission ended its investigations, while the Federal government agreed on draft legislation in late March 2002.

---

[9] The re-import of books for the purpose of a sale to an individual customer was not regarded as a purposive subversion of the fixed book-price agreement. A purposive subversion would occur only in cases of large-scale export and re-import of books.

[10] The affected businesses were the Aufbau Verlag, Bertelsmann (Random House), the distributors KNO and K&V, the *Börsenverein*, and Libro itself. The latter was investigated because of its sudden change in sales strategy.

To a certain extent, therefore, the collision between the EC competition regime and an exempt national sector ended with a shift of German policy according to the preference of DG Competition. However, despite the heated exchanges, the policy shift did not lead to an assertion of competition policy principles in the book domain; rather, national regimes replaced the previous transnational fixed-pricing regime. Arguably, however, the lifting of the transnational barriers invited 'externalities' and 'contagion effects' as initially initiated by Libro. Thus, Europeanization, although not directly able to enforce adjustment of national provisions, may still reduce the viability of national policy solutions by lifting market barriers.

Europeanization and German Competition Policy: From Centrality to Muddling Through?

The case studies have shown the diverse dynamics and impacts that Europeanization has on a specific aspect of competition policy. Two patterns are particularly noteworthy. On the one hand, there was substantial national resilience. Given the non-'coercive' sources for national change, the Europeanization of competition law was, in the case of Germany, mainly a domestic affair. Even the 'collision' case of the fixed book-price agreement did not challenge the existence of a national 'exempt' domain as long as it did not affect cross-border trade. On the other hand, the debate and discourse on national competition law policy was inherently international and 'European', with expert networks operating across different levels of government. This section concludes with a discussion of the nature of 'Europeanization' triggers and then assesses the claims made in the literature against observations stemming from the case studies. It concludes with a discussion of the role of national competition policy in the Europeanized German political economy.

At the national level, three distinct triggers for Europeanization can be distinguished. First, business interests have traditionally been at the forefront of demanding a more lenient domestic competition regime. The context of the Single European Market with increased trans-border activities and mergers led to the call for 'one-stop shops', i.e., a European merger regime applying from low thresholds. The functional explanation for such claims was that increased transactions incurred increased transaction costs in having to deal with diverse national regimes. More interest-driven accounts would suggest that business was mainly attracted by the more discretionary European provisions, given that the European Commission was taking the EU rather than the national market into consideration. Both approaches explain to some extent the initiative to 'Europeanize' the domestic competition law. They also account for the demands by business to establish a EU-wide competition regime that would reduce the administrative burden of notification procedures and legal uncertainty produced by 'comfort letters', and eliminate different competition approaches by national authorities. At the same time, Europeanization engendered not only an advocacy of increased 'harmonization' among business interests. As the example of the book association suggested, the Europeanization of policy domains also threatened privileged institutional positions and governance agreements, thereby triggering defensive reactions.

The 'second' trigger was the Federal Cartel Office itself, which acted both as a proponent as well as an opponent of 'Europeanization' of domestic policy, while being in any event 'Europeanized' in its activities, for example because of its constant communication with DG Competition on the allocation of merger cases. This interaction also allowed for diffusion effects, as in the adoption of the domestic 'whistleblower' provision.[11] In general, the Federal Cartel Office advocated Europeanization where it expanded its arsenal of instruments, as in the case of utilising EC law. It was also interested in the Europeanization of national competition authorities in order to establish a 'network' of agencies as a means to prevent increasing centralization by DG Competition. It was opposed to 'Europeanization' where this was seen as infringing on its own authority and turf.

The third 'trigger' was the Federal Economics Ministry. It introduced the proposal for Europeanizing domestic competition law policy. Furthermore, it was centrally involved in assessing and debating the evolution of national and EC competition law, in terms of both underlying principles and case-specific issues. Its nodal position between academic, political, and business demands meant that it faced a constant balancing act across these three constituencies. In addition, within the ministry, competition law faced permanent tension between more 'sector-friendly' and more competition-focused divisions and sections.

While the role of the 'triggers' was characterized by ambivalence, competition policy itself was difficult to separate between a national and an EC competition law regime. This fusion of legal domains was partly due to the permanent interaction of officials as part of the merger regime and the application of cartel law, and partly to the shared background in the 'Freiburg' school and the joint origins of the competition law frameworks. It is doubtful whether Europeanization led to the marginalization of the Federal Cartel Office, as suggested by earlier studies. In the area of the 'national claw-back' clause of the merger regulation, there had been, over time, a gradual learning and embedding of procedures between the national and the EC authorities. In the early years, the Federal Economics Ministry had served as a 'bottleneck' between the Cartel Office, requesting the case to be delegated to the national competition authority, and European Commission. In consequence, it had been exposed to substantial industry lobbying, and decision-making occurred at the highest levels. Later years saw a

---

[11] Although an informal practice had been operated previously.

routinization of procedures, an increased willingness by the European Commission to delegate cases 'downwards', and a reduction of lobbying attempts. Furthermore, there was little evidence to suggest an increased hostility of the appeal courts to the Federal Cartel Office in terms of economic analysis. The most difficult period in the relationship between appeal court and Federal Cartel Office occurred in the immediate period after the Federal Cartel Office's move to Bonn (and the subsequent shift from the Berlin to the Düsseldorf court). The Düsseldorf court demanded substantially higher procedural requirements from the Federal Cartel Office, rebuking the latter for its insufficient investigations against the alleged abuse of a dominant market position in a case concerning the discriminatory sale of petrol of established operators to 'independent' petrol stations.

Nevertheless, the ideational 'match' between national and EC law was giving way to growing ideational 'mismatch', most visibly expressed in the European Commission's proposals regarding the reform of Regulation 17/62. These proposals fundamentally challenged one of the sustaining myths of German competition law—namely that, despite its decreasing significance in the face of the growing importance of EC competition law, the German law's character as the ultimate source of EC law allowed it to have an disproportional influence on the 'offspring's' development. Alterations to the EC competition law approach represented not just challenges to the philosophy underlying the German competition law. They also exposed the German inability to veto such change in the absence of potential coalition partners in the Council and the inability to generate an alternative to a *status quo* that was widely regarded as untenable. The success of the European Commission in becoming the overarching standard-setting and review body for all cartel cases with a cross-national impact (virtually any economic activity apart from hairdressers and the like) was regarded as a fundamental threat to the institutional viability of the Federal Cartel Office.

In the longer term, there was also a European Commission-led change of 'competition law' thinking, partly in support, partly in opposition to, the German competition policy community. Based on a mix of incentives, ranging from changing ideas, overload, institutional self-interest, and rhetoric about the superiority of the economic performance of the USA, the European Commission was seen to move away from the more legalistic thinking inherent in the German approach. Increasingly, it adopted a more 'Chicago-School' based view of competition policy that allowed for more flexibility and 'economic effects-based' application of competition law.

The epigraph to this chapter noted the centrality of principle in German competition policy. Similarly, Gerber (1998) suggested that German competition law and the overarching ordo-liberal economic policy domain represented a mutually re-enforcing relationship. Europeanization processes arguably challenged both this system and its ordo-liberal environment. The case of the Europeanization of the domestic competition law represented a 'triumph' for the Federal Cartel Office. It was able to reverse a policy commitment towards its own favoured position, although it still suggested that the 1998 Competition Law had been abused by special interests. Its ability to utilize academic and public opinion against business and (initial) ministry opinion were clear signs that it was hardly marginalized in the domestic politics of competition law reform. The Federal Cartel Office was less successful in the EU arena, unable to persuade other national governments of its opposition to the European Commission's proposals amending Regulation 17/62.

Nevertheless, the status of the Federal Cartel Office as the representative of the significance of the competition law in the wider German political economy remained precarious. It showed both signs of continued centrality and even assertion, while also facing a loss of centrality in the face of growing transnational business activity and challenges to its methodological approach (see also Gerber 1998: 337). Its continuing centrality was expressed in its capacity to regularly mobilize public opinion as 'guardian' of the social market economy and its ability to sustain its organizational authority despite its move from Berlin to Bonn.

However, the competition law policy domain was challenged not only by European Commission activity in the fields of cartel and merger policy, but also by the domain's coupling with other increasingly Europeanized policy domains that led to an extension and fragmentation of competition law. In telecommunications, this coupling led to the emergence of a sectoral regulator. In railways, the Federal Office for the Railways (*Eisenbahn Bundesamt*) was provided with increasing investigative powers. Meanwhile, in electricity, the Cartel Office was faced with overload, criticism about its capacity, and continuous calls for the creation of a sectoral regulator (see Bulmer *et al.*, Chapter 12 in this volume). The liberalization envisaged in EC provisions encouraged regulatory reform and the subsequent emergence of new, often European, entrants, who litigated to enforce more favourable terms of access. The consequence was a challenge to the Cartel Office's capacity to assess technological change, for example, in its decision to prohibit the sale of a number of Deutsche Telekom's regional cable networks to 'Liberty'.

There was also an increasing change in the political preferences concerning ordo-liberalism. Partly, this was reflected in the decline of the standing of the Federal Economics Ministry in the overall ranking of federal ministries and especially *vis-à-vis* the Finance Ministry. Partly, it was reflected in the decline of competition policy *vis-à-vis* other (industrial) policy domains within the Federal Economics Ministry, with many critics suggesting that the ministry's appropriate function was that of a Ministry for Industry (Hood, Lodge and Clifford 2002: 11). Apart from these domestic shifts in political preference, the growing federal and Länder hostility towards EU competition policy responded to the increasing attention by DG Competition on German state aids and other subsidy programmes.

More importantly, there was a growing political perception that Europeanization and globalization had placed Germany in an environment of locational competition that required a policy emphasis on promoting (and sustaining) domestic employment and national champions able to compete on global markets. Thus, both within the Federal Economics Ministry and in the wider political system, ordo-liberal arguments were increasingly regarded as outdated and irrelevant. The result was a marginalization of 'competition' in official government discourse, making the application of competition policy goals *ad hoc* rather than central to policy formulation.

Therefore, during the early years of the twenty-first century, the Europeanization of German competition policy presents an increasing and continuous challenge to established competition law policy. The coherence of economic policy principles and competition law has been under increasing pressure from arguments stressing the importance of 'competitiveness' and the internationalization of business and markets, as well as the nature of technological innovation. In this respect, domestic competition policy has moved from centrality to 'muddling through', with, ironically, Europeanization of national policy by European Commission activity arguably being more ordo-liberal than national policy.

12

Electricity and Telecommunications: Fit for the European Union?

SIMON BULMER, DAVID DOLOWITZ,
PETER HUMPHREYS & STEPHEN PADGETT

Europeanization and Policy Transfer

CONVENTIONAL INTERPRETATIONS SUGGEST THAT GERMANY has experienced a gradual and smooth adaptation to European integration (see Chapter 1 in this volume). A broad congruence has been noted between European integration and Germany's constitutional order, norms and conventions, its patterns of meso-level governance, and its policy goals (Bulmer 1997). Similarly, the multi-tiered nature of the EU has fitted well with Germany's character as a 'semi-sovereign' state (Katzenstein 1997a: 33). But how fit is sectoral governance in Germany for the imperatives of the contemporary global economy and, specifically, for the rules of the EU's internal market? What has been the impact of Europeanization on Germany? This chapter explores these questions using evidence from the utilities sectors of telecommunications and electricity. Our research is based *inter alia* on semi-structured interviews with officials in the German and European policy processes, designed to chart the dynamics of interaction between the two institutional systems.

In the absence of a generally accepted 'theory' of Europeanization, our understanding of the concept builds on work by Börzel and Risse (2000); Bulmer and Lequesne (2002); Green Cowles, Caporaso and Risse (2001); Knill (2001); and Ladrech (1994). It is based on a definition developed by Radaelli (2000a):

> A set of processes through which the EU political, social and economic dynamics interact with the logic of domestic discourse, identities, political structures and public policies.

This definition is broadly consistent with that of Dyson and Goetz (Chapter 1 in this volume). That is to say, our principal concern is with the impact of the EU on the policies, institutions, and norms of sectoral governance at the domestic level. Our definition of 'Europeanization' identifies it as an interactive process. Accordingly, we recognize that member states—here, Germany—may attempt to shape EU legislation in line with their own institutional arrangements and

Proceedings of the British Academy, **119**, 251–269. © The British Academy 2003.

policy preferences, thereby reducing any misfit and alleviating subsequent adaptational pressures (Green Cowles, Caporaso and Risse 2001). Thus, we also examine the extent to which Germany has been able to exercise 'soft' power in the EU by exporting ideas and policy prescriptions to the supranational level.

The main focus of the chapter is, however, on the domestic institutional environment through which Europeanization occurs and associated adaptational pressures are mediated. We deploy an institutionalist framework, arguing that the policy outcomes of Europeanization are institutionally mediated, i.e. they are a function of the interaction of the institutional system of the EU with that of Germany. In identifying the institutional variables, the research draws on an established literature about the institutional mediation of the adaptational pressures generated by EU policy (Börzel 1999, Green Cowles, Caporaso and Risse 2001; Harmsen 1999; Haverland 2000; Knill 2001).

Our understanding of the processes at work is as displayed in Figure 12.1. It recognizes the shifting global and technological context of national and EU regulatory regimes, but focuses analytically on what is occurring within the 'oval'. Our assumption is that the evolving European regulatory system places some form of adaptive pressure on existing German public policy and actor behaviour in the two utilities sectors. This pressure is in part coercive in nature. Compliance with EU legislation is inevitable, given that the two sectors are regulated through the law. A second source of adaptive pressure, however, is interaction amongst member governments arising out of, for example, policy co-ordination, benchmarking, or the exchange of best practice (Wallace 2000: 32–3). Fitness for the EU is therefore not simply a matter of complying with 'hard' EU legislation, but also with 'softer' models of good policy practice and the pressures of competitive emulation on the part of corporate interests.

Following the actor-centred institutionalist approach, as elaborated by Fritz Scharpf (1997), we explain the changes taking place in German utilities regulation in terms of the way in which the interests and preferences of policy and corporate actors are mediated and shaped by the domestic institutional arena. The specific institutional variables that we explore are the veto points, opportunity structures, and policy norms operative in the domestic environment. Domestic institutions are, however, not fixed and static, but are subject to the impact of European policy.

Europe may impact on the domestic environment in two ways. First, it impacts on the way actors calculate their interests. These calculations are not just a response to changing rules; socialization effects during Europeanization may also lead to change in the normative yardstick against which domestic actors define their interests and policy preferences. Social learning through interaction or discourse is central to constructivist perspectives on Europeanization (Radaelli 2000*a*, 25; Schmidt 2001; Soysal 1993: 179). Secondly, they alter the distribution of resources amongst actors, for instance through strengthening reform elements

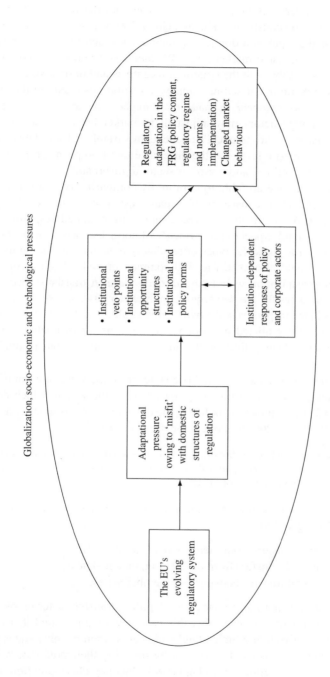

Figure 12.1. Europeanization and adaptation of regulatory regimes.

against their opponents (Börzel 1999: 577–80) and/or offering new opportunities to exit from domestic constraints (Hix and Goetz 2000). This occurs both in terms of how they make input into domestic policy debates and in terms of corporate behaviour in the regulated market place. We therefore see regulatory policy and corporate actors as subject to the structural incentives and normative cues arising in the domestic institutional setting. Domestic institutions make up the arena in which policy actors compete to make their impact on the regulatory regime. Separately, corporate actors may adjust their market behaviour to reflect the changing regulatory environment. The dependent variable is formulated in terms of outcomes at domestic level, i.e. the difference that Europeanization has made to the policies, institutions, and norms of sectoral governance.

A key issue that we are able to explore by comparing two utilities sectors is whether there is a consistent 'German' response to the challenges of Europeanization. Alternatively, is there a more differentiated response? In the former case, we would expect to find evidence of normative bias in the institutional environment towards particular types of regulatory outcomes, including the extent of change. We would also expect to find common procedural norms of conflict resolution. Europeanization would pass through German translator mechanisms, with similar outcomes for the two sectors. In the latter case, we would expect distinct contrasts in the responses in the two German utilities sectors. Causes would be attributable to a differentiated institutional structure or, alternatively, to different market conditions (thereby limiting the analytical purchase of our institutionalist account).

Europeanization is conceived in this chapter from the vantage point of policy transfer, which provides a distinctive perspective on the way in which developments at the EU level impact on policy at the domestic level (Bulmer and Padgett 2001; Radaelli 2000*a*, 2000*b*). Policy transfer is defined as:

> A process by which ideas, policy, administrative arrangements or institutions in one political setting influence policy development in another political setting, mediated by the institutional system of the EU.

EU policy transfer can be seen in terms of multi-directional influences as follows (Bulmer and Padgett 2001):

- upward transfer (from member states to the EU);
- downward transfer (from the EU to member states);
- horizontal transfer between EU member states.

Europeanization normally conceives of policy transfer in terms of 'downloading'. We maintain, however, that this is overly simplistic and that analysis must also be sensitive to the 'uploading' that occurs when member states seek to pre-empt domestic adjustment processes by inserting their preferences into an emergent EU policy regime. This chapter will thus pay close attention to interaction between 'uploading' and 'downloading'. Identifying Europeanization exclusively with downward transfer also tends to presume that the pattern of EU policy is hierarchical, implying the use of instruments of command and control. Pluralist patterns of integration entail horizontal transfer between member states (Metcalfe 1996), with the EU acting as a facilitator of best practice rather than imposing a model on member states. This pattern of transfer is particularly prevalent in the post-Maastricht era. It will be seen to be a feature of the co-ordination of national regulatory regimes.

The Europeanization of Sectoral Governance I: Telecommunications

Between 1988 and 1999, a series of EU Directives incrementally opened up European telecommunications markets to full liberalization. The European Commission's apparently 'coercive' use of a series of Article 90 (now 86) Directives, allowing it to by-pass the Council and European Parliament (in contrast to the electricity sector), is deceptive. After early controversy, the Commission took care to proceed only with the support of member state governments (Interview, EC, 12 July 2000). Moreover, harmonization directives, negotiated intergovernmentally, provided the new regulatory framework. This process allowed scope for 'uploading', and Germany's support for EU reform—along with that of France—was pivotal; it played an important role in determining its incremental pace and timing (Schneider and Vedel 1999).

German support for EU reform was constrained by the country's incremental domestic policy style and particularly by the need to steer telecommunications reform through a highly pluralist domestic institutional regime that allowed veto actors considerable purchase. During the 1980s, despite the Federal government's 'strong will to reform', the policy process was characterized by the state's 'limited capacity to act' and reform was at first limited (Grande and Schneider 1991: 42; Humphreys 1992). In the early 1990s, Germany helped set the moderate pace of further EU reform, assuming a position in significant respects in the vanguard of liberalization only at the end of the decade (Table 12.1).

Interests

Because of the need to achieve a broad political consensus, German telecommunications reform could occur only as fast as conservative forces underwent a 'learning process' about the new realities in the sector. Thus, liberalization of the telecommunications equipment market by the end of the 1980s was helped by Siemens' re-orientation from 1987 onwards of its former protectionist position, in recognition that the Single European Market and 'globalization' offered it exciting business opportunities (Humphreys 1992: 123; Humphreys and Simpson

Table 12.1.   The key directives and their transposition into German law.

Liberalization Directives (Commission)	Harmonization Directives (European Parliament and Council)
1988 'Terminals' Directive 88/301/EEC, liberalising the market for terminal equipment, is transposed by the 1989 Postal Constitution Act (Postreform I) 1990 'Services Directive' 90/388/EEC, liberalising services but not voice telephony, is transposed by the 1989 Postal Constitution Act (Postreform I) 1996 'Full Competition' Directive 96/19/EC, providing for the early liberalization of alternative networks from July 1996 and setting a 1 January 1998 deadline for the full liberalization of voice telephony and telecoms infrastructure (transposition deadline: October 1997), is transposed by the July 1996 TKG (Postreform III)	1990 ONP Framework Directive 90/38/EEC, amended by Directive 97/51/EC (October 1997), is substantially transposed by the July 1996 Telecommunications Law (TKG, Postreform III) and regulations on consumer protection (December 1997), universal service (January 1997), and network access (October 1996) Voice Telephony Directive 95/62/EEC (transposition deadline: 31 December 1996) is substantially transposed by the TKG and regulations on consumer protection, network access and tariffs (October 1996) New Voice Telephony Directive 98/10/EC is substantially transposed by the TKG and regulations on consumer protection, universal service, network access and tariffs (October 1996) Licensing Directive 97/13/EC of April 1997 (deadline: 31 December 1997) is transposed by the TKG Interconnection Directive 97/33/EC of June 1997 (deadline: 31 December 1997) is substantially transposed by the TKG and regulations on universal service, network access, data protection (July 1996) and tariffs

Source: 3rd and 5th Implementation Reports.

1996: 114). During the early 1990s, key actors—including politicians in all main parties, German manufacturing industry, and DBP Telekom managers themselves—came to embrace the need for further reform, notably first the corporatization, then the privatization of DBP Telekom. These reforms helped to meet the huge infrastructural costs of unification and to respond to the risks and opportunities of international competition in the sector (Schmidt 1996).

However, the domestic reform process was still significantly slowed down in Germany's consensual political system. It faced the resistance of DBP Telekom's highly unionized workforce, the federal government's need to accommodate the concerns of the Länder that had always had a significant say in telecommunications policy, and the need for agreement with the opposition SPD because privatization—if not its close relation, liberalization—constitutionally required a two-thirds parliamentary majority (Schmidt 1996). Thus, the domestic process of liberalization required three major laws between 1989 and 1996.

Germany's Position in the 'Uploading Process'

Germany's pivotal place in the EU system made its support crucial (along with France's) for progressing liberalization. Thus, Lüthje (1997: 165) observes that Germany's 1989 reform of telecommunications services actually created the 'political weight' that allowed the EC to proceed further with liberalization. Broadly, Germany was in a northern 'coalition for reform' alongside the UK, the Netherlands, Sweden, and Finland,[1] but it was constrained by domestic politics regarding the pace of change. Reflecting the concern of Deutsche Telekom (and other domestic actors) about a too rapid liberalization, the German government supported the agreed 1 January 1998 EU deadline for full liberalization (Council 1993, 1994), while other 'northern' pro-liberalization states had favoured an earlier deadline (Bartle 1999: 170–1, 2002: 16). Consequently, the 'national champion' DTAG benefited from a 'window' during which returns from its core monopoly could be maximised prior to competition (Waesche 2001).

Adaptation Pressures

The adaptation pressures were considerably reduced by the incremental pace of reform that allowed for the emergence over time—as domestic pressures (unification) and external pressures (international competition) mounted—of a broad enough political consensus for full-scale reform (Bartle 1999; Schmidt 1996). Germany was able to move from being a half-hearted reformer in the 1980s, reflected in the limited degree of liberalization (terminals, services but excluding voice telephony, mobile telephony) introduced by Postreform I in 1989 (Humphreys 1992). There followed a laborious domestic political process in the early 1990s which—involving a compromise package that included delayed full liberalization—led to the corporatization and then partial privatization of DBP Telekom by Postreform II during 1994–6[2] (Bartle 1999: 170; Schmidt 1996). Finally, Germany endorsed the prompt and in key aspects early transposition of the EC's full telecommunications liberalization package by Postreform III, the 1996 Telecommunications Law (TKG) (see Table 1). Germany's adaptation was eased by the fact that the EU regulatory package allowed for a degree of 'domestification' of

---

[1] Our numerous interviews invariably pointed to such an alignment of liberalizers facing a southern alliance of liberalization laggards.
[2] DBP Telekom was legally privatized in 1994 and a 39 per cent share floated on the stock exchange in 1996. In 2002 57 per cent of its shares are in free float, the FRG holds 31 per cent and the KfW a further 12 per cent.

regulation, notably by placing regulation in the hands of national regulatory authorities (NRAs).

Institutional Opportunity Structures and Constraints

Despite the domestic politics constraint, incrementalism meant that 'downloading' proved to be largely unproblematical. Germany enacted the measures needed to transpose the most important harmonization Directives in all cases before the deadlines. In three notable cases—licensing, interconnection, and new voice telephony—Germany had legislated even before their enactment by the European Parliament and Council (see Table 1; also CEC 1998). The 1996 Telecommunications Law established a fairly liberal licensing regime and clear rules regarding access to the incumbent's network (Werle 1999: 114–18). It provided, for instance, the basis for the regulator to mandate carrier pre-selection from the start and also comparatively early unbundling of the local loop (Interview, RegTP, 27 March 2001).

Europe provided manifold 'opportunity structures' for German domestic reform. In general, as Schneider (2001: 77) explains, 'supranational pressures from the EU supported and amplified the process of structural reform in Germany [and France]'. Europeanization gave leverage to German policymakers who were able to carry through liberalization measures against domestic opposition by presenting them as *faits accomplis* from Brussels (Bartle 1999, 2002). Thus, the German government played a two-level game with regard to the EU's 1998 deadline for full liberalization. On the one hand, at the EU level, the government could point to domestic pressures preventing it from signing up to an earlier deadline than 1998. On the other hand, in 1993–4,the German government signed up to a 1998 deadline for voice telephony liberalization (Council 1993) and infrastructural liberalization (Council 1994), thereby constraining resistant domestic actors to accept the 1998 deadline (Bartle 1999: 171). The Commission's direct application of competition law played a role, too. In March 1995,the EU Competition Commissioner notified the German and French governments that approval of the Atlas international alliance between DTAG and France Télécom, the focal point for their international strategies, would be conditional on their liberalization of existing alternative infrastructures for all services except telephony (Schmidt 1997: 17; also Bartle 1999: 172; Schneider and Vedel 1999: 88). According to Susanne Schmidt, the German Post Minister had actually encouraged this measure at a 1993 Council meeting, but domestic support had been lacking.

Policy learning and socialization effects occurred through a number of EU institutional mechanisms (Humphreys 2002). For instance, the 1992 'Telecommunications Services Review' paved the way for a broad EU-wide consensus about the need for full liberalization of voice telephony (Interview, EC, 12 July

2000)[3]; Humphreys and Simpson 1996: 112). At the level of detailed regulation, EC comitology and implementation reports promoted the exchange of best practice. For instance, the German regulators followed the UK's Oftel in introducing flat-rate internet call origination (FRIACO) and a flat-rate wholesale interconnection tariff for unmetered internet access (Interview, RegTP, 27 March 2001).

Policy Change

Generally, the European Commission's implementation reports have suggested that Germany has been a comparatively good performer. The third implementation report, looking principally at the national transposition of the EU Directives, lacked any criticism of Germany (CEC 1998; Werle 1999: 125). The EC's sixth implementation report (CEC 2000a), looking at the effective application of the principles contained in the Directives, did note a number of remaining concerns about regulatory practice over cost-accounting, licence fees, and the powers of the NRA with regard to interconnection issues. On the other hand, the report confirmed the rapid expansion of German telecommunications services and infrastructure market and the competitive pressure created by new entrants. It pointed to a consequent reduction of prices in nearly all market segments and a sharp reduction of long-distance and international prices, a market in which the DTAG's aggregate share of call minutes was now less than 60 per cent. Germany was second only to the UK in the number of local operators authorized to offer public voice telephony, and 100 per cent of the population now had a choice of operators for local calls. However, at the end of 1999, the incumbent DTAG's share of the local call market still stood at about 95 per cent (CEC 2000a, Annex 1: 2, 15).

This was hardly surprising. The domestic politics compromise that had smoothed the way for reform—and perceptions of DTAG as a 'national champion'—had resulted in DBP Telekom/DTAG's retention of ownership of its key assets and its exploitation of a position of market dominance for a crucial period of 'reprieve' (i.e. until 1998). Moreover, under pressure from the Commission, DTAG started selling off its cable television network, an important potential national telecommunications 'alternative infrastructure', only in 2000. In February 2002, this process was further delayed by a Federal Cartel Office ruling blocking the sale of the last six of DTAG's regional cable companies to the US corporation Liberty Media Inc. The Post Ministry mandated the implementation of local loop unbundling in May 1997 (well ahead of the EC Regulation in

---

[3] The interviewee indicated that France Télécom (and Telefonica) came around first and Deutsche Telekom followed suit; 'once the monopolies had change their minds, then the member states had to follow. . . . That was the turning point, the 1992 review.'

December 2000 doing the same) to force through competition in the 'last mile'. But it was delayed by court appeals and 'hard' negotiation between the RegTP, new entrants, and DTAG over pricing, which was set relatively high, so that at first it was slow to take off (Waesche 2001: 186–201; Interview, Bundeskartellamt, 27 March 2001). Thus, until the turn of the century, local calls in Germany—and internet access, which DTAG had hitherto supplied on a metered basis—remained costly in international comparison, as DTAG made the most of the last bastion of its former monopoly. However, the evidence suggests that regulation has become increasingly effective. By 2001, Germany—with nearly half a million unbundled local lines, far ahead of any other member state, and a wholesale flat-rate interconnection tariff (FRIACO) introduced since 2000 (Roy 2002)—was at last assuming a vanguard position in the liberalization stakes. Thus, clearly, over time far-reaching policy change has occurred.

Institutional Change

'Domestification' is clearly illustrated by the manner of operationalization of the idea of a sector-specific independent regulatory authority, a recommendation of the 1987 Green Paper and a measure required by the liberalization Directives from 1988 onwards. Not until the establishment in 1998 of the Regulatory Authority for Telecommunications and Posts (RegTP), specified by the 1996 Postreform III, was the problem of guaranteeing independent regulation formally resolved. Ever since Postreform I in 1989 had first introduced the separation of regulation and operation, the Bundespost Ministry had been suspected by some of having been too close to the incumbent (Humphreys 1992). In order to underpin its *de facto* political independence despite its not being granted the full independent status of the Bundesbank or the Federal Audit Office, the RegTP was modelled on the *Bundeskartellamt* (Interview, Economics Ministry, 28 March 2001). It had independent decision-making chambers covering the various functional areas of the RegTP's operation (network access and interconnection; universal service; licensing; allocation of scarce frequencies, etc). Characteristically, its mode of regulation is legalistic. Unlike the *Bundeskartellamt*, however, the NRA's decisions take immediate effect and are not suspended while the administrative courts consider complaints. This is a very important innovation for the purpose of controlling the incumbent operator, which could not therefore hope to delay liberalization through constant appeals to the courts (Interview, RegTP, 27 March 2001).

Nonetheless, on occasion DTAG has managed to claim temporary legal protection (*einstweiligen Rechtschutz*—interview, VATM, 29 March 2001). Coen (2001: 23) suggests that the tendency for business-regulator exchanges to be played out in the courts has created cost barriers to new entrants. Moreover, the twin facts that DTAG remains part-owned by the German government and that the

RegTP is accountable to the Economics Ministry (BMWi).[4] which could overturn its decisions on grounds of national economic interest, led Coen (2001: 9) to view the RegTP as an 'institutionally constrained quasi-independent regulator'. New entrants felt that the RegTP was still too weak (Bartle 1999: 174; CEC 2000a) and politically pressured (Interview, VATM, 29 March 2001; Coen 2001). Against this, the RegTP has been judged by the EC's implementation reports (e.g. CEC 2000a) to be a comparatively effective and independent regulatory agency.

'Domestification' was also reflected in the residual influence granted to the Länder in the new regulatory structure. In the old order, they had had a significant voice in telecommunications policy through their representation on the Bundespost's 'corporatist' Administrative Council (*Verwaltungsrat*). Their main concern over liberalization was the future scope of universal service provision, particularly regarding the more rural Länder.[5] Thus, in June 1996, the Bundesrat rejected the liberalization reform bill (Postreform III), and arbitration produced a compromise that both widened the definition of universal service and guaranteed representation for the Länder on an Advisory Council for the RegTP[6] (Bartle 1999: 173). Finally, the RegTP marked a degree of continuity with the past in that its large staff were simply transferred from the Posts and Telecommunications Ministry and the Federal Office for Posts and Telecommunications, the agency responsible for technical regulation and standards (Werle 1999: 114). This was politically highly expedient—in terms of the domestic politics compromise—because it saved numerous civil service jobs.

Normative Change

The degree of normative change should not be underestimated. Telecommunications liberalization clearly ran counter to a historically deeply entrenched sectoral governance structure based on public monopoly. The concept of sector-specific pro-competitive regulation by an independent regulatory agency, the key provision of the EU 1998 regulatory package, was 'essentially unknown in the Federal Republic until telecommunications liberalization' (Interview, Economics Ministry, 28 March 2001). This concept not only challenged the forty-year tradition of reliance on competition law, with which it could at least be technically reconciled; it also ran counter to the embedded neo-corporatist German ethos of self-regulation. On balance, therefore, it might be concluded that—despite the litigation and possible political pressure—the RegTP has performed relatively well, even setting the pace in local loop unbundling.

---

[4] DTAG's government shares are held by the Finance Ministry, not by the Economics Ministry.

[5] Half of its twenty-four members came from the two sides of industry, five more were federal politicians, and five were *Land* politicians. The *Verwaltungsrat* had to approve the Bundepost's budget and had an important say in infrastructural matters and the setting of tariffs (Humphreys 1992: 110).

[6] The Advisory Council is composed of nine Bundestag and nine Bundesrat members.

The Europeanization of Sectoral Governance II: Electricity

The European liberalization of the electricity sector was a protracted and difficult process spanning eight years from the European Commission's Green Paper of 1988 to the adoption of Directive 96/92/EC (EP and Council 1996). During the early part of this process, Germany was a 'liberalization laggard', mobilizing the Franco-German axis to retard the European policy process (Padgett 1992). European liberalization was thereby slowed down to match the tempo of domestic reform, with the additional advantage of allowing to German utilities breathing space to adapt in anticipation of EU legislation. Once the legislation had been adopted, however, it required 'Big Bang' reform delivered in a relatively short time-scale, challenging domestic interests and exerting pressure on a policy process geared to incrementalism.

Interests

Domestic interests were divided along quite complex lines. The pro-liberalization lobby initially centred on industries that were electricity-intensive and acutely concerned with relatively high German power prices. These concerns found a ready ear in a liberal-oriented Federal Economics Ministry that was heavily pre-occupied with competitiveness issues, as well as the Federal Cartel Office, the Deregulation Commission and the Monopolies Commission, where liberalization was an institutional vocation. In the electricity sector itself, the effects of the external economic environment and technological change were somewhat less pronounced than in telecommunications. In the absence of these market-opening forces, territorial market protection remained the dominant objective well into the 1990s.

Large German power producers, however, have progressively re-oriented themselves towards European market opening as an opportunity for expansion as 'European super-utilities'. As they have done so, territorial market protection has given way to a 'game of movement', with a sharp increase in cross-national merger and acquisition activity. At the same time, the embrace of market liberalization by the utilities has been moderated by the potential export threat from cheap French nuclear electricity to German utilities already awash with excess capacity (*Economist* 13 November 1999).

Opposition centred on the municipal power undertakings and authorities which faced the loss of around DM 6bn in revenues deriving from exclusive distribution contracts that had served to cross-subsidize other municipal services. These financial considerations drew the Federal Finance and Interior Ministry into an opposition that was further augmented by the Länder, jealously guarding their regulatory competences against the potential threat of a federal authority (Eising 1999: 24–7). This left both government and the sector divided on liberalization issues. As we shall see below, the German reform was driven in large part by the imperative of reconciling this complex configuration of competing interests within a highly pluralist institutional environment. The result was a self-referential policy process that was largely impermeable to the influence of externally inspired policy innovation.

Germany's Position in the 'Uploading Process'

Germany's position reflected divided domestic constituencies within a pluralist institutional setting. Domestic divisions were reflected in Germany's schizophrenic position in the Council and its working groups.

> It seemed to us [in the working group] that . . . official policy was directed not towards the rest of us but towards the Ministry of the Interior and the Ministry of the Environment . . . they brought their internal political fights to the Union. The [Energy] Minister was very liberal at meetings. . . . And then he was taken back to the Ministry and given a lesson . . . because he had said too much. (Interview, 22 November 2000)

A similar ambivalence characterized Germany's position in the bilateral and trilateral negotiations that ultimately brokered agreement on Directive 96/92/EC. From 1994, Germany lined up as a liberalization ally of the UK, and there was fairly intensive bilateral activity on this axis. The strongest bilateral axis, however, was with France, the most entrenched of the anti-liberalization states, based on a mutual agreement that neither would support a proposal to which the other was opposed (Schmidt 1998: 13). UK officials repeatedly found that agreements they had reached with Germany would unravel following Franco-German bilaterals (Interview 30 November 2000). The most important amendments to the directive were the products of Franco-German deals.

Amendments had the effect of opening up a number of options permitting national discretion in the implementation of the Directive. Discretion applied, in particular, to provisions governing access to transmission networks, a key principle of competition in network-bound sectors. Alongside the initially proposed regulated access regime were two alternative options: a provision for access by negotiation between commercial parties, introduced by Germany, and the single-buyer option put forward by France. Moreover, whilst member states had an obligation to ensure transparent and non-discriminatory terms of access to transmission networks, they were given wide discretion over how to discharge that responsibility.[7] There was no obligation to install a free-standing, sector-specific regulatory authority. Another casualty of the adoption process was the

---

[7] This was in sharp contrast to the Interconnection Directive in telecommunications, in which the responsibilities of the national regulatory authorities were defined in detail (Directive 97/33/EC, OJ L199, 26/07/97 p. 0032–0052).

requirement for a legal separation between generation and transmission. The final Directive required merely that transmission system operations should be 'independent at least in management terms' from the other activities of vertically integrated utilities. For the advocates of liberalization, the latitude of national discretion risked compromising the objective of an open and competitive European market (Interview 30 November 2000).

Adaptation Pressures

In one sense, the structural adaptation pressures imposed on Germany by the Directive were relatively low. The sector consisted of over 500 regional and municipal undertakings, clustered around nine dominant utilities on regional monopoly lines. These monopolistic arrangements were exempted from federal competition law in return for the utilities accepting co-responsibility for a range of policy objectives. (Padgett 1990: 183–4). Liberalization could be accomplished simply by revoking the exemption from competition law, thus 'animating' the competitive potential of a pluralist sector (Interview 14 February 2001). Compliance with EU legislation, however, posed three main adaptation problems: the danger of exposing German utilities already carrying excess generating capacity to the French export threat; the potential loss of municipal revenues derived from exclusive distribution concessions; and the constitutional problem of reconciling a federal regulatory authority with the regulatory competence of the Länder. As we shall see below, German actors took steps to reduce these adaptation problems by exploiting the latitude for discretion in the implementation of the Directive.

Institutional Opportunity Structures

In the Introduction to this chapter it was postulated that the domestic institutional context will exert a decisive influence in shaping the downloading of EU legislation. In the German case, a highly pluralist institutional environment replete with veto points allows domestic interests free reign to intervene in transposition legislation to minimize the adaptation pressures upon them and to implement EU legislation in accordance with domestic norms. Electricity reform provides a graphic illustration of these tendencies (Eberlein 2000).

The German reform was initiated in 1994, some two years before the adoption of the Directive, but was not brought to a conclusion until 1998. The initial Federal Economics Ministry draft law was vetoed in the cabinet by an alliance of the ministers of Finance and the Interior (concerned with the threat to municipal revenues), Environment (with a priority on promoting renewable energy sources), and Urban Planning (fearing the emergence of cross-regional price differentials) (Eising 1999). Thus deadlocked, the reform process was revivified only by the adoption of Directive 96/92/EC. The subsequent draft failed to win Bundestag assent, thwarted by the defection of government Christian Democrats articulating the concerns of the municipalities. In an attempt at appeasement, the draft was amended once again to allow the municipalities to protect their revenue by opting for 'single-buyer' status under a provision of the Directive that Germany had previously opposed in the Council. Successful in the Bundestag, but threatened now by veto in an upper house (Bundesrat), controlled by the opposition, the draft was amended yet again, deleting regulatory provisions that impinged on the competencies of the Länder in a device to circumvent the constitutional requirement of Bundesrat assent. Following an unsuccessful opposition challenge to this stratagem in the Federal Constitutional Court, the Electricity Act was finally passed in March 1998 (Oxera, 15 April 1998).

As argued earlier, the adaptation pressures generated by European policy may serve to redistribute resources among domestic actors, strengthening reform elements against their opponents. On the evidence of the above, it may be concluded that EU adaptation pressures catalyzed a change in the distribution of institutional resources by bolstering the pro-liberalization coalition against its opponents. In particular, it has been argued that Europe strengthened the autonomy of the Federal Economics Ministry, the main sponsor of German legislation (Eising 1999: 30). European reform was thus instrumental in breaking the deadlock surrounding domestic liberalization intitiatives. On the other hand, the succession of amendments to proposals that occurred after the adoption of Directive 96/92/EU shows that EU effects on the distribution of institutional resources were not so decisive as to free the Economics Ministry from the need to make concessions to veto players.

Policy Change

In cross-national perspective, the German response to Directive 96/92/EC appears somewhat paradoxical (Padgett 2003: 235–40). Germany was one of only four states to have opted for an immediate 100 per cent market opening. Other member states exploited the latitude in the Directive over the time-scale for market opening. In relation to the institutional design of sectoral governance, on the other hand, Germany stands out from a general pattern of cross-national assimilation, making more use than other member states of the zones of discretion contained in the Directive. First, having itself pressed for the inclusion of the option in the Directive, Germany was one of only two member states to have opted for a negotiated rather than a regulated form of transmission network access, with a temporary provision for municipalities to opt for 'single-buyer' status. Second, although it imposed a legal requirement on network owners to grant access rights, it stopped short of prescribing a regime of access rules. Instead, the framework for negotiated access was left to voluntary agreement between sectoral associations (the *Verbändevereinbarung*). Thus, while all electricity producers and consumers are legally eligible to participate in the liberalized market, the structure of sectoral governance does little to promote genuine competition (*Economist* 13 November 1999). To be sure, liberalization triggered a frantic wave of merger and acquisition activity and a ruthless price war that has seen consumer prices reduced by around 40 per cent. The result, however, has been a concentration of market power among the big utilities, with new players struggling for market entry (*Power in Europe*, 13 September 1999).

The domestic policy process appears to have been relatively impervious to external influence, proceeding almost exclusively 'from a consideration of the German situation' (Interview 26 January 2001). Thus, the choice of a negotiated access regime was 'the obvious choice, reached largely without even discussing the alternatives; it was just clear from the existing situation' (Interview 16 February 2001). Little systematic attempt appears to have been made by the Federal Economics Ministry to monitor developments in other member states. Policy learning was restricted largely to matters relating to the technical operation of a competitive electricity sector. Utility officials spent some time in Scandinavia, examining transmission system operation and the Nordic power pool. There is some evidence that lessons learned here were incorporated in certain technical aspects of the *Verbändevereinbarung*. In interviews, however, utility officials expressed the view that transfer potential was limited by cross-national differences in the structure of the sector (Interview 16 February 2001). Overall, neither the EU policy process nor horizontal learning from other member states appears to have had a significant effect on policy (Interview 14 February 2001).

Institutional Change

Germany is the only member state to have rejected the model of a sector-specific regulator, opting instead for self-regulation via the industry agreement (*Verbändevereinbarung*). The Federal Cartel Office deals with market abuse under competition law, with disputes resolved by the courts, and the Federal Economics Ministry playing an ill-defined 'mediation' role (Interview, 26 January 2001). It has been argued that the system privileges the large incumbents that occupied a dominant position in the negotiation of the industry agreement (Coen 2001: 35), and that new market entrants are further deterred by the commercial uncertainties endemic to *ex ante* judicial regulation (*Power in Europe*, 321, 4 April 2000; 330, 4 August 2000). New market entrants lack confidence in both the *Verbändevereinbarung* and the *Bundeskartellamt*, and have launched pro-competition initiatives calling for clearer rules of network access and a sector-specific regulatory body (Coen 2001: 37; *Power in Europe*, 338, 24 November 2000).

Resistance to independent regulation, however, was reiterated at the Stockholm European Council of 2001, where Germany blocked a draft Directive requiring member states to implement regulated network access regimes under an independent regulatory authority (*Power in Europe*, 348, 9 April 2001). Even the generally pro-liberalization Economics Ministry and *Bundeskartellamt* remain obdurate on the issue. 'Our position is quite clear . . . under certain circumstances we may not exclude it . . . But that is a question we will decide upon as a member state, not be forced to by the Commission' (Interview 26 January 2001).

Normative Change

Evaluations of congruence or 'fit' between EU legislation and domestic policy norms are clouded in the German context by the split between 'ordo-liberalism' and 'managed capitalism' which runs through national political economy (Dyson 2001, *Handelsblatt* 5 June 1986; Padgett 1990; *Wirtschaftswoche* 14 August 1987). While the EU electricity legislation was in accord with the former, it was sharply incongruent with the neo-corporatist ethos of managed capitalism. Cultural misfit is seen most clearly in relation to the regulatory implications of the directive. Regulation by external rules runs counter to a deeply entrenched neo-corporatist ethos of self-regulation:

> Germany stands for the principle of self-regulation . . . it was like that under monopoly conditions; much was regulated between the different *Verbände* . . . we just transferred the idea to a liberal market. (Interview 26 January 2001)

> There is a strong tradition of self-regulation and allowing market forces to operate. A regulated access system would very clearly be seen as a step backwards—a less 'liberal' system than one with negotiated access. (Interview 16 February 2001)

Subjecting privately owned transmission network assets to external regulation, it is argued, would have been 'alien to German constitutional law' (Interview 26 January 2001). Sector-specific regulation, moreover, runs counter to 'a forty-year-long tradition of competition law' (Interview 14 February 2001). There is little evidence, then, of the socialization effects of interactions in the EU policy process making a significant impact on the norms and values of sectoral governance in Germany.

Conclusion

The research presented above indicates that Germany's structural position within the EU gives it a degree of 'soft power' over the European legislative process that is matched by few other EU members. Its status as a 'swing state', especially when acting in concert with France, provides it with considerable influence in the development of European governance regimes. Acting in this way to minimize 'misfit' with domestic policy norms helps Germany reduce subsequent adaptation pressures. This is particularly important in the context of a highly pluralist institutional regime with numerous veto actors capable of blocking implementation. Most German interventions in the EU legislative process surrounding the agreement of telecommunications and electricity directives can be explained in terms of compromises reached with domestic interests exercising potential veto powers over possible transposition measures.

Comparison between the two sectors also highlights the importance to Germany of the tempo of EU reform. The slower tempo of EU legislation in telecommunications meant that adaptation pressures were lower here than in electricity. Incremental legislation over a decade permitted Germany to liberalize the sector at its own pace in line with a domestic policy style of incrementalism. Always in the liberalizer camp, but seriously constrained over the pace of change, Germany evolved from being a half-hearted reformer in the late 1980s to a policy leader in key respects by the end of the 1990s. In contrast, after the passage of two fairly uncontroversial Directives in 1990, electricity liberalization took the form of a single 'Big Bang' package (albeit one that took six years to agree). So, unlike telecommunications, which saw a series of Directives using the implementation of one Directive to guide the next, domestic actors in the electricity sector had less time to respond to change. This mismatch between the EU regime and the domestic policy process left Germany as a policy laggard.

Another reason why adaptation was less problematical in telecommunications than in electricity relates to market conditions. With demand for telecommunications services growing exponentially, competition was less of a threat than in electricity where market growth was only modest. Indeed, in light of the speed at which technological change was occurring, most actors in the telecommunication market perceived the need to introduce greater competition. In electricity, on the other hand, key German veto players saw the existing regime as providing adequate competition, especially in light of the high cost of German electricity, which made German incumbents vulnerable to competition from French nuclear power exports. Additionally, unlike in telecommunications where their concerns could be accommodated, the municipalities and Länder were strongly opposed to change. Thus, while a pluralist institutional environment meant plentiful veto opportunities in both sectors, there were fewer potential losers in telecommunications.

Differences in the tempo of EU reform and in the resultant adaptation pressures explain differences in the German response between the two sectors. In telecommunications, Germany has been significantly more activist in 'downloading' EU legislation, and ahead of minimum EU requirements. In electricity, it has made considerable use of the zone of discretion (which it helped establish) in the directive to 'domesticate' European legislation. Moreover, the slow tempo of domestic reform permitted the large power producers to progressively re-orientate themselves towards a competitive market.

It is noteworthy that domestic institutions have proved especially resistant to European norms in electricity but not so in telecommunications. In electricity, Germany has resisted the European trend towards sector-specific regulatory authorities. In telecommunications, a compromise was available in the 'conversion' of the Posts and Telecommunications Ministry into the RegTP. In electricity, no such compromise was available, and Germany remains the only member state without a sector-specific regulator. Because of this, Germany is not permitted to participate in the European Council of Energy Regulators, which may potentially isolate them in relation to future European energy matters.

While we have identified a number of differences between the two sectors in the response to EU reform, it is also possible to identify some overarching features indicative of a characteristically German response to the challenges of Europeanization. Both sectors display the power of the domestic actors operating in a highly pluralist and incremental policy process. In telecommunications the incremental development of the EU governing regime fits Germany's natural style, ensuring that, while there was significant normative change, indigenous forces could shape and adapt to the emerging liberalization regime. In electricity, Germany's ability to act, in concert with France, at the European level allowed its domestic policy style to shape the Europeanization of its electricity sector. During the course of negotiations leading to the final Directive in 1996, Germany was able to shape the reform package to minimize the reform its domestic electricity market would have to undergo. More importantly, by being able to set the tempo of European-level reform, Germany was able to 'bring along' the key players who could have acted as veto points at the national level in both sectors. There is little doubt that sectoral governance regimes have been influenced by Germany's participation in the process of EU reform, although the experience in electricity shows a degree of insularity to externally inspired innovation. It is equally clear that the EU regimes have themselves been influenced by Germany's participation in the uploading of policies and ideas into the Union's legislative process.

Note. This chapter forms part of the ESRC project 'The European Union as a Medium of Policy Transfer; Case Studies in Utilities Regulation' under the Future Governance programme.

13

Social Policy: Transforming Pensions, Challenging Health Care?

MARKUS HAVERLAND

Introduction

IN THE CASE OF SOCIAL POLICY, research into Europeanization runs into problems. In contrast to areas like monetary policy or utilities regulations, there is, as yet, no explicit European model or paradigm. There are European Directives in the social policy area requiring a certain 'institutional model' (Knill and Lehmkuhl 2002: 252) to be implemented. However, these Directives merely regulate specific—mostly labour-related—aspects of social policy, such as gender equality in pay or health and safety at work. But they do not deal comprehensively with broader issues of income security, redistribution, and poverty alleviation. In particular, the European Union (EU) lacks the competencies and budgets necessary for large-scale inter- and intragenerational redistribution. This is not to say that European integration cannot have a profound impact on national social policy. Yet, if these pressures exist, they are rather indirect. Consequently, there might be several functionally equivalent ways to make national policies compatible with them. In the absence of a blueprint of a European social model, it is hard to tell to what extent German social policy has converged towards Europe. Hence this chapter does not associate Europeanization with a substantively defined end-state. In line with the definition proposed in Chapter 1 in this volume, 'Europeanization' will be defined as the degree to which direct and indirect effects of European integration have been causally important for continuity and change in German social policy.

Research on the politics of social policy falls into two categories: comparative welfare state research and European social policy research. These strands of research arrive at different judgements about the relative importance of the EU. Comparative welfare state researchers usually employ large-N comparisons. Concentrating on aggregate social expenditure as a dependent variable and socio-economic features, national institutions, and strength of political and corporatist actors as independent variables, they tend to neglect adaptation pressure generated as spillovers from EU market and monetary integration. It is precisely these

Proceedings of the British Academy, **119**, 271–288. © The British Academy 2003.

indirect effects, however, that produce the largest pressures on national welfare states (Leibfried and Pierson 2000). Case-oriented comparative welfare state research also tends to ignore the potential EU impact. It usually starts by identifying globally or domestically generated adaptation pressures as background variables and then analyses the way in which national political and societal actors react to them within the context of nationally distinctive institutional settings. Even accounts of recent social policy development pay almost no attention to EU effects (see Alber 1998; Jochem 2001; Kania and Blanke 2000). At the most, authors comparing welfare states concede a weak impact on national social policies (Schmidt 1998).

Research on European social policy has claimed that the EU has an important impact on national social policy. Leibfried and Pierson (2000: 268) argue, for instance, that 'the process of European integration has eroded both the sovereignty and autonomy of member states in the realm of social policy. National welfare states remain the primary institutions of social policy, but they do so in the context of an increasingly constraining multi-tiered polity.' Many case studies have corroborated the importance of EU regulation, in particular in health and safety at work (Eichener 1995) and gender equality (Caporaso and Jupille 2001; Ostner and Lewis 1995; van der Vleuten 2001). However, this strand of research usually employs a vertical, 'top-down' view (see Chapter 1). It identifies potential EU sources of adaptation pressure and follows their (assumed) causal effects down to the nation-state. If one generalizes from these findings to social policy in general, one is likely to suffer from selection bias. Cases are selected in which EU pressures are clearly identifiable, based on a criterion that is likely to be related to the dependent variable, the degree of Europeanization (Geddes 1990; see King, Keohane and Verba 1994).

Having worked in both traditions, I aim at clarifying the relative importance of EU factors *vis-à-vis* other—domestic and global—factors in shaping German social policy development (Haverland 2000, 2001).

For the sake of brevity, the chapter does not cover social policy as a whole, but concentrates on two sectors: old-age pensions and health care. These sectors have been chosen for three reasons. First, they are representative for social policy more generally, as they reflect the two basic rationales for provision, namely income transfer (in the case of pensions) and service (in the case of health care). Second, the policy arrangements as developed until the mid-1970s, the starting point of my empirical analysis, nicely reflect the constitutive elements of the German welfare model, that is generosity, status maintenance, male-breadwinner orientation, work-based compulsory social insurance, and corporatism. For this reason, a focus on pensions and health care permits general conclusions about the strength of the German model after twenty-five years. Moreover, as Germany has been the empirical reference point for the Continental model of the welfare state, this case study can generate wider implications for the Europeanization of this type of member state (Chapter 1). Thirdly, in substantive terms, these two sectors are by far the largest within the area of social policy, almost universal in terms of contributors and beneficiaries and huge in financial terms. The size of the annual budget of the statutory pensions insurance, for instance, equals the size of the budget of the Federal government.

The chapter begins by establishing the specific properties of German social policy from a cross-national perspective. This will be done for the mid-1970s, hence prior to any major potential direct or indirect EU effect. Next, the chapter reviews the potential European, global, and domestic pressures on old-age pension arrangements and health care. Hence, it contextualizes social policy development to isolate EU integration as a variable from other factors such as demographic change ('greying' of the society), individualization, technological change, German unification, and economic and financial globalization, which may point in similar directions. The major part of the discussion reviews the development of German pension and health care policy over the last decades, and analyses the extent to which these developments can be attributed to EU integration.

German Social Policy in Comparative Perspective

'Social policy' in the narrowest sense aims at protecting against the risks of unemployment, disability, sickness, old age, and poverty. A broader conception includes the goal of gender equality and of a fair distribution of income. Social policy usually assumes the form of publicly provided—subsidized or regulated—income transfers and service delivery. Comparative welfare state research has demonstrated that advanced democracies vary significantly in the generosity of social policies; the extent to which they aim at poverty alleviation, redistribution, and status maintenance; and their relative emphasis on states, markets and families. It is common to distinguish between three different types of welfare state (Esping-Andersen 1990; Titmuss 1974). The liberal or residualist welfare regime, exemplified by the USA and the UK, is the least generous. It aims at poverty alleviation, benefits are often means-tested, and the role of the market in welfare services is emphasized. The social democratic or institutionalist welfare state, dominant in Scandinavia, is generous in financial terms. Gender equality and an equal distribution of income are important aims. Benefits are tax-financed, and there is a strong emphasis on the state as provider of services.

The Christian-democratic or 'industrial-achiever' welfare regime is typical for continental Europe. Germany is usually identified as the empirical reference of this regime type (see Goodin *et al.* 1999; Pierson 1996). The continental welfare state is as generous as the social-democratic welfare state, but it aims at maintenance of status and living standard rather than redistribution. The benefit formulae reflect the male-breadwinner model, which is also reflected in the importance of the family (and voluntary intermediary associations) for the provision of social services. Benefits are typically financed by wage-based contributions (pay-roll taxes) to compulsory social insurance. The social partners jointly administer the insurance funds, which points to the corporatist nature of the arrangement.

Central to German old-age income security is the statutory retirement insurance (*Gesetzliche Rentenversicherung*, GRV), which provides retirement, disability, and survivor benefits on a pay-as-you-go basis (Nullmeier and Rüb 1993). The insurance is compulsory for persons in dependent employment above a (very low) income threshold. Civil servants fall outside the scheme; their pensions are tax-financed. The GRV currently provides more than 80 per cent of the household income of persons aged sixty-five years or older (Börsch-Supan 2000). Contributions and benefits are earnings-related, reflecting the goal of maintaining status and living standard. To maintain this standard, long-term uninterrupted employment of forty to forty-five years is assumed. Along with gender differences in the statutory retirement age and in the system of survivor benefits, this reflects the male-breadwinner model.

The pension insurance institutions are public-law bodies (*Körperschaften des öffentlichen Rechts*) and organized according to status groups. There are separate bodies for blue- and white-collar workers, farmers, craftsmen, and other categories. Representatives from trade unions and from employer organizations manage the institutions. The system is financed by pay-roll taxes (*Sozialbeiträge*). Employers and employees contribute equally (the principle of *Beitragsparität*). However, the insurance principle is weakened at the expense of the solidarity principle by the fact that the GRV also provides benefits that are not matched by previous contributions. State subsidies compensate for this. The subsidy has always been significant. In 2001, it amounted to some 50 billion Euro, covering one-quarter of pension expenditures and absorbing one-quarter of the German federal budget (Bundesministerium für Arbeit und Sozialordnung 2002: 420).

The health care system displays similar features. The statutory health insurance (*Gesetzliche Krankenversicherung*, GKV) is compulsory for those employees (including civil servants) above the same income threshold that applies in the case of the GRV. However, above an income ceiling of roughly one-and-a-half times the average wage, employees can opt for a private health insurance scheme. The GKV currently covers some 90 per cent of the population (Bundesministerium für Arbeit und Sozialordnung 2002: 128). The insurance provides earnings-related benefits in cash (sick pay) and benefits in kind. Benefits in kind are comprehensive. The aim is to provide all diagnosis and all therapy that is necessary to improve the health of the patient or to prevent it from getting worse (*Bedarfsprinzip*). The need for medical care is generally determined by office-based medical experts who work on a self-employed professional basis

(Kötter 1999). Contributions are earnings-related. By providing benefits in kind irrespective of the amount of contributions, the insurance principle is weakened to the benefit of the solidarity principle. As in the case of the GRV, the GKV is financed by pay-roll taxes, with equal shares from employers and employees. Government does not contribute to the scheme.

As in pensions, the health insurance institutions are based on occupational or status group, have public-law status, and are managed by employer and employee representatives. Public-law status is also provided to the doctors, the key providers of health care. They are united in the associations of doctors (*Ärtzekammern*). As Giaimo and Manow (1999: 976) aptly remark, the public-law status privileges the insurance institutions and the association of doctors in legal terms and provides them with 'a (near) monopoly in social welfare provision but, at the same time, constrains their freedom of action by requiring that they fulfil certain public functions' (see also Katzenstein 1987). The role of the state is restricted to framework regulation, setting the general procedures and goals of health policy. The insurance institutions and the association of doctors have a great leeway in negotiating collective contracts that stipulate the conditions, fees, and prices of health care provision. This principle of 'self-administration' (*Selbstverwaltung*) reflects the corporatist character of the German health care system (Giaimo and Manow 1999; Jochem 2001; Kötter 1999, Dyson, Chapter 10 in this volume).

European, Global, and Domestic Pressures on German Social Policy

Social policy is an unlikely case for European integration for a number of reasons. Providing and expanding a solidaristic system of social benefits has been an important source of legitimation for the nation-state and produces party political allegiance. In addition, the great heterogeneity of national welfare regimes (see above) makes European harmonization difficult. Also, the importance of social policy for the nation-state has recently been reinforced as 'the welfare state remains one for the key realms of policy competence where national governments still appear to reign supreme' (Leibfried and Pierson 2000: 270). For these reasons, member states have been extremely reluctant to delegate social policy competencies to the EU level.

Gender equality and health and safety at work have been two important issues, however, where integration has taken place and has changed the national status quo. European gender equality policy is a relevant source of direct adaptation pressure as it potentially threatens the German male-breadwinner model in pensions. The policy is laid down in Article 141 (Consolidated Version of the Treaty establishing the European Community, CTEC, ex-Article 119) and a number of Directives, among others the Directive stipulating equal treatment for men and women in statutory social security schemes (79/7/EEC). European gender policy has gained strength from the Commission's enterpreneurship and from legal activism by the Court of Justice (ECJ) (Falkner 2000; Ostner and Lewis 1995; van der Vleuten 2001). Another potential source of direct adaptation pressure has emerged from the mid-1990s, as the ECJ increasingly applies provisions of European competition and Single Market policy, in particular the free movement of goods and services, to the area of social security. This especially challenges the corporatist character of the health care system (Kötter 1998; Lamping 2001).

European integration can also have indirect effects on German social policy. The completion of the Single European Market programme has enhanced intra-EU competition. Contributions to health and pension insurance significantly contribute to labour costs, making up roughly one-third of the gross wage, because contributions are work-related and have to cover generous benefits. In an era of increased European competition amplified by the Single Market programme, social insurance contributions—especially of the employers—may have to be cut to safeguard the competitive position of Germany. This potentially threatens the generosity of the scheme and the principle of parity of contributions that reflects its corporatist character, because employers' contributions can be reduced by either replacing them by state subsidies—financed by taxes or increasing budget deficits—or by private contributions (e.g. co-payments by the employees) or by cutting benefits.

The adaptation pressure is aggravated since reducing or at least curbing social contributions of employers at the expense of the public budget may be difficult to reconcile with the proper functioning of EMU (Dyson, Chapter 10 in this volume). During the Swedish Presidency in the first half of 2001, the European Council decided that the Broad Economic Policy Guidelines (Article 99 CTEC), the central instrument of the European co-ordination of national economic policies, should address the budgetary challenges posed by demographic ageing. Accordingly, member state strategies to cope with this challenge were to be examined in the context of the multilateral surveillance procedure. Strains caused by demographic changes will also be included in peer group review of the member states' stability and convergence programmes, submitted in the context of the Stability and Growth Pact (Article 104 CTEC). Moreover, pension and health care policies will be subjected to the 'open method of co-ordination', a comparatively 'soft' method of co-ordination based on benchmarking, target-setting, and peer review. But arguably it lacks the degree of peer pressure exerted under the Stability and Growth Pact, and also lacks—at least as far as pensions and health care are concerned—a firm base in the Treaty (see Anderson 2002; Dyson, Chapter 10 in this volume; European Council 2001*a*, 2001*b*).

Still, it is important to bear in mind that national social policies are not affected only by EU pressures. The male-breadwinner model is challenged from above by EU gender policy, but also from below by a combination of individualization, changing gender relations, shifts in work–family organization, and rising female labour-market participation (Esping-Andersen 1999; European Commission 1997). The enforcement of Single Market freedoms and EU competition law may undermine the corporatist management of health care, but corporatism is also challenged by the process of individualization. Individualization increases the pressure for more choice and diversity in income security and health care and has enhanced intra-organizational conflicts. All of this does not go well with the collective bargaining logic that underpins corporatist arrangements.

The generosity and wage-based character of German social policy arrangements is affected by global—and not only European—competition and financial market integration (Anderson, Chapter 2 in this volume). Moreover, financing generous pensions and health care arrangements out of labour income has become more difficult owing to the decrease in real wage growth over the last decades, which has been related to the shift from the industrial to the service economy (Iversen and Wren 1998; see also Pierson 2001). Other strains are high levels of unemployment and inactivity (Scharpf 2000). In addition, demographic ageing reduces the number of contributors to social security schemes and increases the number of their beneficiaries. As far as health care is concerned, demographic ageing in combination with changing consumer preferences, in particular higher expectations about quality and privacy, increases the demands on health care, while technological and scientific progress increase the potential supply (Freeman and Moran 2000: 39). Meeting the rising costs with higher social contributions (or taxes) may encounter electoral resistance. It may also result in a reduction of labour supply on the regular labour market. The rise of the 'shadow' economy may result in a vicious circle that may make the social policy arrangements financially unsustainable (Konrad and Wagner 2000: 17). In short, German social policy arrangements would almost certainly be challenged without European integration and probably even without economic and financial globalization (Pierson 2001).

Old-Age Pensions

During the first three post-war decades, European governments of all colours gradually but continuously increased the replacement rates and coverage of their public pension arrangements and reduced the statutory retirement age. Germany established a generous scheme in 1957, which was subsequently further expanded. The generosity peaked with a reform in 1972. Therefore, Germany entered the era after the golden age with one of the most generous public pension systems in the world. From the mid-1970s on, however, the social-liberal SPD–FDP government, which held office until 1982, and the succeeding Christian-liberal CDU/CSU–FDP government engaged in cost-containment reforms. These reforms unfolded against the background of a global economic recession, triggered by the oil crisis of 1973, which resulted in a high level of unemployment and, in turn, threatened the financial sustainability of pensions. From the late 1970s, the government came to learn that the crisis had not been temporal and that Keynesian economic policy—which would justify generous benefits under certain conditions—was difficult to sustain in an era of large international trade and capital flows. In line with a new supply side oriented economic orthodoxy, the focus was on sound public finances and the reduction of taxes and contributions to social insurance (Scharpf and Schmidt 2000). In addition, the destructive effect of demographic ageing on the long-term financial sustainability of the German pension arrangements, which had occasionally surfaced in the pension debate from the 1950s onwards, became more widely recognized (Jochem 2001; Nullmeier and Rüb 1993: 113–38). This combination of factors, rather than any direct or indirect effects of European integration, pushed cost-containment reforms onto the political agenda in the 1970s and 1980s.

Until a more significant reform in 1989, a series of incremental reforms were adopted, employing 'technical' measures to reduce benefits, such as postponing annual adjustments or changing their basis of calculation (Alber 1998; Nullmeier and Rüb 1993). Governments confined themselves to these relatively invisible measures because a more blunt attempt in 1976 to reduce benefits met with huge public resistance and was perceived by policy-makers as a débâcle (Nullmeier and Rüb 1993: 117–23). During the 1980s, however, both the Christian-liberal government and the opposition Social Democrats increasingly recognized that technical measures were insufficient to cope with the rising load of problems. Accordingly, their preferences converged and a more significant pension reform was adopted in 1989; it, too, remained, however, within the basic parameters of the existing system. This reform abandoned the principle of gross-wage adjustment that had already been weakened by *ad hoc* measures. Benefits were now adjusted to the development of net wages, which implies lower benefits when taxes and social contributions rise. The reform also increased the reference age for retirement for all categories, including women, to sixty-five and diminished the early retirement incentives built into the reform of 1972. Employers and employees had used these incentives extensively to soften the consequences of economic adjustments (Nullmeier and Rüb 1993).

The federal Ministry of Labour estimated that, without the reform in 1989, the contribution rate would have to increase from 18.7 per cent (in 1989) to 36.3 per cent in 2030, while as an effect of this reform the rate would merely increase to 26.9 per cent (Schmähl 1993: 47). These cost-containment reforms reduced the generosity of the public pension system, but they did not significantly threaten the aim of maintaining the living standard after retirement, as the reform largely reversed expansionary effects of the 1972 reform that had not yet fully materialized (Alber 1998). But the 1989 reform also contained expansionary elements. It increased the earning credits (periods of non-contribution credited as contribution equivalent) for raising children. This has to be seen as part of a long-term strategy to encourage higher birth rates with a view to sustaining the pension system against a background of demographic ageing.

Whether these earning credits weaken or strengthen the male-breadwinner model is disputed in the literature (Nullmeier and Rüb 1993). There were two other reforms, however, that certainly weakened the model, though they did not necessarily improve the situation of women. A 1985 reform removed gender inequality in the survivor benefit system, and, as mentioned above, the reform in 1989 equalized the statutory retirement age. As the male-breadwinner model did not fit well with EU gender policy, one may hypothesize that the changes made in Germany were causally related to the EU. This is not the case, however.

The 1985 reform was the consequence of a 1975 decision of the German Constitutional Court regarding equal treatment, which forced the government to change a number of social security provisions, in particular the survivor benefit system. Only because the German government had to adapt anyway did it support the 1978 EC Directive on equal treatment in statutory social security. It wanted other member states to be subjected to the same norm (van der Vleuten 2001: 192). This Directive, therefore, provides a fine example of 'bottom-up' Europeanization. The equalization of retirement ages was also unrelated to EU pressures. The German government had consistently joined forces with those who opposed the Commission's attempts to make equal retirement ages in statutory pensions part of the *acquis*. As a result, the Directive on equal treatment in statutory social security does not demand equal retirement ages (van der Vleuten 2001: 192). Germany equalized the statutory retirement ages to improve the financial sustainability of the scheme. It increased the statutory retirement age of women (by five years) rather than decreasing the retirement age of men.

Although the 1989 reform implied significant savings in the long term, reform of pensions remained on the agenda, because one hour (sic!) after the reform had been legislated for, the fall of the Berlin Wall made the assumptions on which it had been based partly redundant. This became clear when the government decided to rely on the GRV to cope with the social consequences of economic adjustment by providing benefits unmatched by contributions (Czada 1998; Deutsches Institut für Wirtschaftsforschung 1997).

In political terms, the period from the early 1990s until the pension reform in 2001 was fundamentally different from the preceding one. All reforms of the late 1970s and 1980s had been characterized by consensual policy-making involving the two major parties in parliament—the CDU/CSU and the SPD; the employer organizations and trade unions as social partners; and the association of pension insurers (VDR), which itself is made up of representatives from the social partners. Thereafter, consensus-seeking within closed networks was replaced by a more conflict-oriented policy approach. Pension policy became subject to party competition, in particular in the 1998 federal election. The traditional pension policy network was opened up, and solutions have been sought and found outside the main parameters of the existing pension regime.

In the mid-1990s, the CDU/CSU–FDP government unilaterally adopted a number of incremental cost-containment measures, which were partly stalled or reversed by the SPD–Green government when it entered into power in 1998. The new government also aimed at curbing contributions, but it did so by broadening the financial base of the GRV. This broadening has been achieved by increasing the value-added tax and by devoting the revenue from the new ecological tax to this purpose (Bundesministerium für Arbeit und Sozialordnung 2002). These new financial resources are generated from relatively immobile tax bases, which makes the reform consistent with the economic globalization argument. As the new resources are used to finance the state subsidies to the GRV, they help to avoid budget deficits, which is consistent with arguments about financial global- ization and the restrictive effects of EMU.

The reforms of the SPD–Green government had still been rather incremental, though the increase in tax financing weakened the contribution-based character of the GRV. In 2001, however, the government enacted the most radical pension reform since 1957. It was the first significant reform that was not supported by the major opposition party in parliament, in this case the CDU/CSU. The reform had two main elements: retrenchment of public pensions and financial support for private pensions. The new GRV benefit formulae implied that the standard pen- sion would be gradually reduced from 70 to 64 per cent of the average net wage. Moreover, a partial transition to the funding system was decided. Private savings were not made compulsory, but generously supported by tax allowances if certain financial instruments such as private pension insurance or occupational pension funds were chosen. This pension reform marked a remarkable deviation from the traditional German social policy model. Though GRV retrenchment and the partial shift to private pensions are interrelated, each element will be discussed separately for analytic purposes.

With the decrease in benefits, the government gave up the principle that the GRV alone is capable of income and status maintenance after retirement. Given that many employees, in particular women, never achieve a working history of forty to forty-five years, the new benefit formulae will make more of the retired dependent on means-tested social assistance. Moreover, the practice that capital and labour contribute equally to the financing of social policies, reflecting the principles of social partnership and corporatism, was weakened. There were no compulsory employer contributions to the emerging private pillar, though collec- tively agreed occupational pension plans took precedence over private provisions. This element strengthened German corporatism. In particular, it provided the trade unions with a voice in private pensions. As Schludi (2001) points out, this ele- ment was the government's concession to the trade unions to secure their support.

This example demonstrates that global pressures are mediated by domestic factors, in this case sectoral institutions.

Economic globalization and domestic concerns have shaped the decision to retrench public pensions as part of the solution to the ongoing problem of demographic ageing and inactivity amplified by German unification. The pressure generated by economic globalization is reflected in the overall objective of the reform, namely to curb the employers' contributions rather than the employees' contributions. However, net wage adjustment of pension benefits, introduced by the reform of 1989, implied that measures that decrease labour taxes and social contributions to safeguard the competitive position of German industry are in part ineffective as they increase pension benefits (Lamping and Rüb 2001: 15).

At the same time, retrenchment was also informed by domestic reasons, namely the need to prevent companies from evading contributions by shifting activities into the 'shadow' economy (see Jochem 2001: 209). It is difficult, however, to identify the influence of EU factors on the retrenchment of public pensions. This is due not least to the fact that the German government and the major opposition party have had an incentive to avoid the association of unpopular reforms with the EU. They have an interest in further European integration, e.g., eastern enlargement, and are, therefore, careful not to blame Brussels. Hence, whereas globalization as a pressure to change the German welfare state system figures prominently in official government documents, Single European Market imperatives are not invoked in the public debate (see for instance Bundesministerium für Wirtschaft 1997; also Dyson, Chapter 10 in this volume). In striking contrast to the pension reform in Italy, for instance, EMU was not used as a 'vincolo esterno' or 'external tie' (Dyson and Featherstone 1996). It remains to be seen whether the purported decline in German élite consensus about the benefits of EU integration (Chapter 17 in this volume) will result in scapegoating the EU or at least in an increased emphasis on EU pressures in future pension reform discussions.

The second element of the reform, the path-breaking establishment of a heavily subsidized private-funded pillar, is more obviously related to European integration, in particular to the integration of capital markets, which is in part spurred by EMU and by EU Directives designed to remove barriers to capital flows. In an ever more integrated capital market, funded pensions become increasingly advantageous over unfunded pensions. Note that in Germany, in contrast to most other countries, the vast majority of supplementary occupational pension schemes are unfunded. They assume the form of 'book reserves', implying that pension savings are invested back into the firm, hence in an existing and often mature firm. As capital can move ever more freely, such investments are increasingly inefficient (*Financial Times* 21 May 1999). Also, the move towards more funding was informed by the government's preference to stimulate pension funds so as to strengthen the German position in the ever more integrated global and European capital market. The government estimated that the 2001 reform would increase the volume of the private pension market by some 35–50 billion Euro annually (*Süddeutsche Zeitung* 2 February 2001).

While the partial shift to funded pensions is consistent with the claim that increased capital market integration matters, the decision to generously subsidize this shift is inconsistent with the pressures generated by EMU. It was estimated that the government subsidies would amount to 11 billion Euro by the time the new scheme was fully operational in 2008 (Lamping and Rüb 2001: 9). This places a considerable burden on the public budget and may contribute to rising debts; it is likely to be punished by the global capital market and may endanger the fiscal commitments under the Stability and Growth Pact. The initial government proposal had not included generous subsidies. Rather, it proposed to make savings compulsory, which would have saved public money and would have been consistent with EMU imperatives. However, the government sought a broader consensus for the overall reform in order to share the blame with other actors. It, therefore, dropped the compulsory character and introduced subsidies and tax allowances. This aspect of the reform also confirms the view that external adaptation pressure is mediated by national negotiation capacity — or incapacity — for reform.

The 2001 pension reform marks a transformation of German pension policy. Moreover, it is likely that further reforms will follow and that these will be more directly related to European integration, in particular monetary integration. The new pension system enjoys even stronger state subsidies than the old one. The requirements of the Stability and Growth Pacts and recent EU-level developments, such as extending the scope of the Broad Economic Policy Guidelines and the 'open method of co-ordination', suggest that these subsidies will be viewed as an increasingly painful burden on the public budget.

Though it is unlikely that EU pressures translated directly into national policy reform, there is evidence that the EU contributed to a change in the domestic political opportunity structure in favour of those who concentrate on financial sustainability rather than those privileging adequacy or generosity. In the course of the 1990s, the German Ministry of Labour, the main defender of the traditional GRV, had already lost its dominant position in the pension policy networks to the Chancellor's Office and the Ministries of Economics and Finance (Lamping and Rüb 2001: 21). In recent years, the positions of the Ministries of Economics and Finance have been strengthened by increased EU economic policy co-ordination and its extension to public pension issues. The ministries are powerfully entrenched in the emerging EU co-ordination machinery, such as the Economic Policy Committee and the organizational framework responsible for the national stability and growth plans. It is doubtful that the Social Policy Committee established in 1999, which includes the national Ministries of Social Affairs and joins the Economic Policy Committee in implementing the 'open method of co-ordination', can redress the balance, given its weaker institutional base (De La Porte and Pochet 2002).

Health Care

Since the mid-1970s, cost-containment concerns have dominated not only the pension agenda, but also the health care debate. Health care has been exposed to the same global and domestic adaptation pressures as pensions. However, this sector is confronted with additional cost-inducing pressures: rising expectations about quality and privacy increase the demand for health care, while technological and scientific progress increases potential supply.

Various incremental reforms of the GKV were enacted in the late 1970s and 1980s, followed by a more radical reform in 1992, and again by a number of subsequent incremental reforms. The first cost-containment reform, adopted in 1977, introduced the principle of 'stability of contribution' (*Beitragssatzstabilität*), which became the guiding idea of almost all later reforms. The principle states that sickness funds' expenditure is tied to the development of their revenues, which in turn depend on the development of wages and employment (Freeman and Moran 2000: 38). By introducing this principle, the government used the opportunity to manipulate the framework of the collective bargaining system in health care without intervening directly in it (Giaimo and Manow 1999: 981). This principle does not mean, however, that benefits are rationed in cases of financial strains. The *Bedarfsprinzip* supersedes the principle of contribution stability, if both are in conflict with each other (Kötter 1999). The explicit focus on contribution stability fits well with 'supply-side' economic orthodoxy and with increased international economic integration.

To achieve contribution stability, the 1977 reform made pensioners into contributors to the GKV. Another strategy was to introduce or increase prescription fees, and co-payments for stays in hospitals, rehabilitation, and transportation costs. This strategy was repeatedly employed, irrespective of the government in office between 1977 and 1997. The overall magnitude of fees and co-payments remained relatively low, however. The 1997 reform, in which the level of co-payment peaked, included a ceiling for co-payments of 2 per cent of the gross wage, reduced to 1 per cent for the chronically ill (Alber 1998: 29; Freeman and Moran 2000: 39, 41). Making pensioners into contributors to the GKV and introducing fees and co-payment reduced the relative importance of pay-roll taxes in financing health care and is, therefore, consistent with the economic globalization argument. More importantly, the government introduced fees and co-payments to reduce the demand for health care, which, in turn, reduces costs and, by implication, contributions, which is also in line with the economic globalization argument (Kania and Blanke 2000: 580).

Another strategy to achieve contribution stability has been the regulation of the provision of health care. Yet, health care provider interests are very powerful. The government is dependent on them for smooth corporatist self-regulation, and providers control two veto points in the decision-making process. Physicians and the pharmaceutical industry can rely on the liberal party, the FDP, as a defender of their interests, and the FDP was a member of all governing coalitions between 1969 and 1998. The hospitals, many of them owned by the Länder or local authorities, found their ally in the Länder governments. These governments are represented in the Bundesrat, the upper chamber of the legislature, which has a veto on all legislative proposals that touch on issues relevant to them (Mayntz 1991; Rosewitz and Webber 1990). For these reasons, regulating provision is notoriously difficult and mostly unsuccessful.

The reform adopted in 1992 was the major example of a government's success in significantly regulating the provision of health care (for an overview, see Döhler 1995; Giaimo and Manow 1999). This reform introduced fixed budgets for drug prescriptions by office-based physicians, for physician fees, for user charges from hospitals, and for administrative costs of sickness funds. Moreover, physicians and the pharmaceutical industry became financially liable for overspend of the drugs budget. Also, the financing method for the operational costs of hospitals was changed from retrospective cost coverage to modes of prospective coverage and case payment, supported by an increase in the planning competencies of sickness funds.

The most innovative element of the reform of 1992 was the introduction of competition between sickness funds to achieve cost containment through greater efficiency. Competition was introduced by allowing the insured to choose their insurance fund. This decision was informed by the view that budgeting can be viable only for the short term. Such strong state involvement ran counter to the ideology of the CDU/CSU–FDP government, while it was difficult to get the powerful self-governing actors to adhere to the principle of stable contributions (Giaimo and Manow 1999). Although the introduction of competition was informed by cost-containment concerns, it had the side effect of levelling the stratification and the symbolic status maintenance implied by the old system of organizing sickness funds along occupational lines.

The 1992 'victory against pressure groups' may be explained by a combination of factors. There was a sudden increase in problem pressure owing to higher costs caused by German unification. The SPD majority in the Bundesrat at the time created an opportunity to outmanoeuvre the FDP. The fragmentation of provider interests, which was itself partly a result of earlier health reforms, also facilitated reform (Döhler 1995). Not least, there was the skilful management of the decision-making process by the Minister of Health, Horst Seehofer, who carefully engineered a supportive political coalition and kept the interest groups at a distance (Döhler 1995; Freeman and Moran 2000; Hassenteufel 1999).

However, despite this relatively radical reform, GKV contributions stabilized only for a few years. Against the background of a continuing debate about the damaging effects of high non-wage labour costs in an era of global (not European) economic internationalization, the CDU/CSU–FDP government adopted additional cost-containment measures in both 1996 and 1997. It reduced the scope of benefits and the replacement ratio of sick pay, and significantly increased co-payments, in particular in the case of rehabilitation. Also, the insured were allowed to choose between benefits in cash or kind, and to take on own risks in exchange for lower premiums. The latter measures were aimed at increasing the transparency of costs and the responsibilities of the insured. This was expected to depress health care consumption (Kania and Blanke 2000: 580).

As in pensions, the SPD–Green government that took office in 1998 almost immediately repealed most of the latest reforms of the old government, but also aimed at a significant health care reform. The new government wanted to strengthen office-based general practitioners as gatekeepers of the health system; to increase the role of insurance funds in managing health care; to restrict the range of pharmaceuticals for which the insurance funds have to pay (the so-called 'positive list'); and to operate an exclusively case-based mode of hospital financing (Bundesministerium für Arbeit und Sozialordnung 2002; Kania and Blanke 2000: 584–7). These proposals were heavily opposed by the vested provider interests and became subject to intense party-political competition. Unlike in pensions, the SPD–Green government did not succeed in adopting a significant health care reform in the legislative period 1998–2002.

The story of twenty-five years of health care reform can be plausibly told without any reference to the EU. The EU has merely been important to the extent that the Single Market programme amplified the global competition pressures that informed the principle of contribution stability. The health care system has not changed as radically as the pension sector. The guiding principles have remained untouched. There are neither significant increases in inequality nor an erosion of solidarity in access to, or the financing of, health care, and there is still a broad range of universally provided statutory benefits (Alber 1998: 9; Giaimo and Manow 1999; Kötter 1999).

Although corporatist self-regulation has been weakened by more state control and by more competition, it is still at the core of the health system. That corporatism is still operating can be explained by its ideological embeddedness in the worldviews of both major parties, the CDU/CSU and the SPD. It corresponds to the subsidiarity principle of Catholic social doctrine and to the social democratic concept of co-determination. Corporatism also serves the organizational self-interest of social partners who have a strong voice in health care. In addition, corporatist self-regulation allows the government to share the blame for unpopular cost-cutting measures with the social partners (Giaimo and Manow 1999).

As in pensions, the impact of the EU may increase in the near future, but, unlike in pensions, direct pressures rather than indirect pressure will probably matter most. As the state does not contribute to the GKV, the health care sector is less susceptible to EMU imperatives. Moreover, the 'open method of co-ordination' is only slowly entering this area and is still institutionally weak. The

Single Market freedoms and the European competition regime, however, potentially restrict the range of options available to the German government to reform its system. The provider-oriented strategy: that is fixing budgets, quality standards, efficiency, and price controls are based on the assumption that patients cannot exit the system, an assumption which is legally backed by the territorial principle of German social law. This principle has been undermined by ECJ decisions that have established that health care is not exempt from EU law (Kötter 1999: 12). More specifically, the ECJ has ruled that national legislation that stipulates that insured persons can obtain reimbursement for treatment abroad only after prior authorization of the competent social security institution constitutes an unjustified barrier to the free movement of goods (*Decker* C-120/1995) and the freedom to provide services (*Kohll* C-158/1996). Provider-oriented cost control will be rendered ineffective, however, if patients have the right to exit the system. The ECJ rulings imply that 'if they [member states] cannot substantiate that rules restricting the free market of goods or services are necessary to protect the financial balance of their health insurance systems or public health, they will have to find other instruments to guarantee efficiency and quality than restricting access to health care delivered in other member states' (Kötter 1999: 16). The application of these Single European Market freedoms to health care is a consequence of judicial activism of the ECJ and was not anticipated by the member states. In fact, the German government, like others, has repeatedly argued that the market freedoms are not applicable to the area of social security (Kötter 2002: 2).

In the longer run, Single Market provisions—in combination with EU competition law—may even hollow out the corporatist core of the German health care system. Competition law may jeopardize the monopolistic organization of the supply side, the association of doctors, and the oligopolist behaviour of the demand side, the insurance funds (Lamping 2001). The corporatist core may, thus, be weakened at the expense of both the state taking more direct responsibility for all solidaristic and redistributive elements of the health care system to which EU competition law does not apply, and the emergence of a European health care market governed by EU competition law. In this case, direct EU effects would lead towards a transformation of the health care systems.

The ECJ has been very careful not to impinge radically on national social security. Moreover, as a seminal case regarding occupational pensions (*Barber* C-262/88) shows, member states are in certain circumstances willing and able to restrict the domestic effects of Court decisions by changing the legislation on which the Court decision is based (Garret, Keleman and Schulz 1998). There are, however, at least a few examples in which Court decisions have already shaped the domestic agenda of reform. The German government and the sickness funds associations have discussed, for instance, the possibility of delegating the fixing of maximum prices for prescribed drugs—now negotiated between the insurance funds associations and the providers' associations—to the Federal Health

Ministry. This would avoid the risk that the ECJ might judge the current practice as an illegal price cartel (Lamping 2001).

Conclusion

The cases of pensions and health care point to the differential impact of the EU. The male-breadwinner orientation of the pension system did not fit well with the EU gender equality policy. Yet, the weakening of the model by reforming the system of survivor benefits and by equalizing the statutory retirement age has not been causally related to EU policy. Indirect EU effects have, however, amplified global and domestic pressures to transform the German pension system as far as its financial dimension is concerned. They have made the status quo more difficult to maintain and the alternative, a multi-pillar system, more attractive. Yet, it is difficult to estimate the significance of the EU effect on the generosity of provision; in particular the decision to curb the employers' contributions to the GRV and to give up the GRV objective of maintaining living standards after retirement cannot easily be related to the effects of enhanced competition owing to the Single Market programme. Global and domestic factors were probably more important. Significantly, domestic reformers did not used EU factors to try to increase the credibility of retrenchment.

However, the decision in favour of a partial shift to funded pensions has been more obviously informed by increased European integration, in particular the integration of capital markets. At the same time, the heavy subsidy that accompanied this shift runs against the EMU imperative of budgetary austerity. Moreover, the weakening of the corporatist character of the pension system, by giving up the principle of contribution parity as far as private pensions are concerned, has been partly offset by granting trade unions a say in the running of private pension schemes. Both the heavy subsidies and the trade unions' say in private pensions show how domestic political processes and institutions mediate national adaptation to external pressures. Pension reform will most probably remain on the political agenda, and there are number of good reasons to believe that the impact of European integration will increase.

Most reforms in health care were geared towards cost containment and contribution stability. The focus on contribution stability reflects concerns about Germany's competitive position in the global economy. That the role of work-based financing has been slightly reduced by co-payments and by the inclusion of pensioners as contributors is consistent with these concerns. European integration has indirectly contributed to these reforms to the extent that the Single Market programme has increased European competition; but EU pressures have not been used to support the credibility of reforms. Despite two decades of cost-containment measures, health care is still relatively generous, based on solidarity and universal access. Its corporatist core has been partially weakened by a combination of 'more state' and 'more market'. More state involvement has taken the form of a tighter regulation of the health sector and a closer monitoring and adjustment of corporatist self-governance. The introduction of competition among sickness funds is the main example of the introduction of market mechanisms in health care. None of these reform strategies has been directly influenced by EU pressures. Direct EU pressures may become more important in the future, however, as the free movement of goods and services and the EU competition regime interfere with the government's strategy to achieve cost containment by regulating the supply of health services. More generally, these pressures challenge the corporatist core of German health arrangements. European integration would, in this case, not only reaffirm domestic developments already under way, but would significantly increase their speed.

14

Environmental Policy:
A Leader State under Pressure?

RÜDIGER K. W. WURZEL

Introduction

BROADLY SPEAKING, THREE PHASES OF THE 'EUROPEANIZATION' of the German environmental policy system can be identified. First, during the 1970s, German environmental policy was only moderately affected by the EU. As will be explained below, the origins of contemporary German environmental policy can be traced to 1969, while the EU's environmental policy was launched in 1972 (Bungarten 1978; Weale *et al.* 2000). Germany was therefore in a strong position to influence the fledgling EU environmental policy. It strongly supported many of the EU's early pollution control measures (such as directives on car emissions, noise, and detergents) and acted as a provider of ideas, as can be seen from the 'uploading' of the precautionary principle (*Vorsorgeprinzip*) to the EU level. However, during the 1970s, Germany sometimes also dragged its feet. Mainly for competitive reasons, it opposed significant reductions in sulphur dioxide emissions from large combustion plants and in toxic discharges into the Rhine from its chemical industry (*Die Zeit* 9 May 1974; Grant, Paterson and Whitson 1988; Moltke 1984; Wurzel 2002: 193, 230). Moreover, it opposed the implementation of the 'polluter pays principle' (PPP) on the international level out of fear that this could lead to compensation claims. For many observers Germany exhibited an 'ambivalent attitude' (*Zwiespältige Haltung*) in EU and international environmental politics (*Frankfurter Allgemeine Zeitung* 8 November 1974; *Frankfurter Rundschau* 12 August 1975).

During the 1970s, the impact of the Europeanization process on German environmental policy was largely taken for granted, although some early EU policy measures (such as the directives on bathing water (76/160/EEC) and shellfish waters (79/869/EEC)) had no basis in domestic environmental law. The federal government, which strongly supported deeper European integration, disregarded repeated complaints by the Länder which disputed the EU's environmental and water policy competences, in particular, as the latter fell within their competences on the domestic level (Bohne 1992; Stoiber 1987; Weinstock 1984).

Proceedings of the British Academy, **119**, 289–308. © The British Academy 2003.

Until the 1987 Single European Act (SEA), the EU lacked explicit environmental Treaty provisions. As a consequence, much of the early EU environmental policy consisted of harmonized national environmental laws, which constituted a trade barrier within the Single European Market (SEM). The direct link between EU environmental policy and the Single European Market was strengthened by a legally non-binding information and standstill agreement in 1973. It obliged member states to both inform the Commission about draft national environmental laws with a potential impact on the Single European Market and put them on hold in order to allow for the adoption of EU measures as an alternative (Bungarten 1978; Rehbinder and Stewart 1985; Wurzel 1993; 2002: 75–7). The initial effect of the standstill agreement was that '[s]trongly environmentalist member states were more or less able to set the pace and direction for Community action by unilaterally proposing strong national environmental legislation' (Rehbinder and Stewart 1985: 17). The full impact of early EU environmental policy measures on the domestic environmental policy system became clear only in the 1980s when the Commission insisted on their correct implementation.

The second phase, in the 1980s, was characterized by Germany adopting an environmental policy leader role on the EU and international levels (Héritier, Knill and Minger 1996; Pehle 1997; Weale 1992*a*; Weidner 1999; Wurzel 2002). Its new role was very much a reaction to scientific findings that suggested that air pollution was the main cause of dying forests *(Waldsterben)* (Boehmer-Christiansen and Skea 1991; Weale 1992*a*). In 1983, the German government issued a threat to 'go it alone' *(Alleingangsdrohung)* if the EU refused to adopt the best available technology (BAT, *Stand der Technik)*—which, at the time, was the three-way catalytic converter in order to reduce car emission pollution (Arp 1995; Boehmer-Christiansen and Weidner 1995; Holzinger 1994; Wurzel 2002). This was an unusual step for a strongly pro-integrationist member state which, for historic reasons, normally 'punched below its weight' (Paterson 1996: 170) and strongly relied on joint initiatives. It illustrates the high political salience of the environment at the domestic level where the Green Party entered the Bundestag for the first time in 1983. The long drawn-out car emission saga, which led to the EU-wide introduction of the three-way catalytic converter only in the early 1990s, seemed to confirm the widely held view in Germany that EU environmental policy acted mainly as a brake on domestic environmental policy. Observers who pointed out that at least occasionally the EU also took on an innovating role for German environmental policy were largely ignored (Hartkopf and Bohne 1983: 169–70; Kromarek 1986, 1989; Krämer 1989; Moltke 1984; SRU 1978: 514).

During the third phase, in the 1990s, Germany came under 'top-down' pressure from the EU to reform its environmental policy system. This adaptational pressure came from the Commission abandoning its preference for detailed 'command and control' regulations, which stipulated EU-wide emission limits that were derived from the BAT principle, in favour of more flexible environmental quality objectives (EQOs), framework directives, procedural measures, and 'soft' policy instruments. Most German environmental policy-makers perceived the Commission's 'new approach' (see, for example, CEC 1996) as incompatible with existing domestic structures and the preferred national regulatory style which relied heavily on detailed BAT-derived emission limits (Friedrich, Tappe and Wurzel 2000; Héritier, Knill and Minger 1996; Knill 2001; Knill and Lenschow 1998; Kraack, Pehle and Zimmermann-Steinhart 2001; Pehle 1998; Sturm and Pehle 2001:187–210; Weale et al. 2000; Wurzel 2002). In short, 'misfit' was generating new adaptational pressures. The German government responded by trying to alter some of the Commission's proposals based on its new approach during the adoption or implementation phase.

The Causes of the Europeanization of Domestic Environmental Policy

Three variables are commonly used to explain the Europeanization of domestic environmental policies. First, functional 'spillover' pressures; second, regulatory competition; and, third, policy transfer and lesson-drawing. Neo-functionalists have long argued that market harmonization (or 'negative integration') will create 'spillover' pressures that trigger regulatory activities in other policy sectors (see Weale 1996). The Commission, which holds the formal monopoly to initiate common legislation, is often seen as the most important policy entrepreneur because it occupies a central node within the EU decision-making process. It can exploit 'spillover' pressures to foster European integration and to extend its competences (Arp 1995; Héritier, Knill and Minger 1996). However, because the Commission is a relatively small bureaucracy with limited in-house technical expertise, it often makes use of (draft) national legislation as a base for its environmental policy proposals.

The Europeanization of member state environmental policies can also be the result of regulatory competition between member states. The states try to export their national standards and problem-solving philosophies to the EU level in order to avoid adaptation costs on the domestic level (Héritier 1996; Héritier, Knill and Minger 1996; Knill 2001; Sbragia 1996; Vogel 1995). However, the EU policy-making process grants veto actors (such as member governments and the European Parliament) various access points (Haverland forthcoming; Weale 1996; Wurzel 2002). In consequence, EU environmental policy as a whole (Héritier, Knill and Minger 1996; Knill 2001), and often also individual policy measures, exhibit a patchwork character (Weale 1996). Even member states that initiated a particular proposal by, for example, passing on to the Commission draft national legislation under the standstill agreement, will usually have to undertake some domestic adaptation measures.

Policy transfer and lesson-drawing may also lead to changes in member state environmental policies (Jordan *et al.* 2001; Kern, Jörgens and Jänicke 2000). The EU is said to offer a 'massive transfer platform' (Radaelli 2001: 26). The emergence of epistemic communities (i.e. transnational networks of policy experts) is of particular importance within the environmental policy field which is characterized by a large technical core and dependent on the emergence of new policy ideas for problem-solving (Weale 1992*a*). The sixth Environmental Action Programme (CEC 2000*b*), as well as its *White Paper on European Governance* (CEC 2001*a*), strongly advocate networking activities which can lead to benchmarking of best practices and the exchange of new policy ideas. Andersen and Liefferink (1997: 19) have pointed out that 'environmental policy has probably become one of the most internationalised policy fields with a universal tool-kit and policy concepts and strategies ranging from sustainable development to life cycle analysis'. The international politics of the environment can have an impact on policy ideas and discourses, while acting as an intervening variable on both the EU and German environmental policy systems, which in turn can exert influence on the global level. The climate change convention might not have been adopted at the 1992 United Nations Earth Summit in Rio without the determined efforts of the EU and the German government. The United States, which was reluctant to agree to domestic actions to cut climate change gases, insisted on the use of tradeable permits as a means of complying with the 1997 Kyoto protocol. The EU and Germany in particular initially resisted tradeable permits. However, the Commission later used the Kyoto protocol to propose an EU directive on tradeable permits in 2001 (CEC 2001*b*). In order to be able to influence EU developments, the German government set up a working group on tradeable permits (*Arbeitsgemeinschaft Emissionshandel*) in 2000.

'Spillover' pressures, regulatory competition, and policy transfer help to explain why the Europeanization of member state environmental policy has occurred and who the driving forces are. However, they offer little guidance about *what* exactly is being Europeanized and *how* this process takes place. In order to operationalize the concept of Europeanization this chapter differentiates for analytical reasons between (1) the institutional structures; (2) policy content; and (3) the environmental regulatory style, including core action guiding principles. Paul Sabatier (1999) has convincingly argued that public policy should be studied over a time period that spans at least one decade. A longitudinal perspective is particularly important for environmental policy because the full implications of both environmental pollution and pollution control measures often become apparent only after a considerable time (Wurzel 2002: 51).

The Europeanization of Institutional Structures

Germany is often characterized as a 'semi-sovereign state' (Katzenstein 1987) because the power of state officials is both severely circumscribed and widely diffused; unification has not changed this (Katzenstein 1997a, 1997b). As a federal state, Germany has been called 'a state without a centre' (Smith 1992). Large-scale reforms are difficult to achieve for any German government, especially if they involve changes to deeply embedded institutional structures. Major reform efforts in the environmental policy field were, nevertheless, attempted by a newly elected centre-left (SPD–FDP) coalition government which came to power in 1969 (Bechmann 1984; Genscher 1980; Hartkopf and Bohne 1983; Müller 1986; Wey 1982). The centre-left government set up environmental administrative capacities, adopted an ambitious domestic environmental programme, experimented with novel procedural approaches (such as integrated pollution control), and introduced new policy instruments (such as the 1976 waste water levy). However, the reform euphoria came to an abrupt end when the 1973 oil crisis pushed German environmental policy into a 'defensive phase' (Müller 1986). German environmental policy subsequently conformed again to more traditional patterns of domestic policy-making even before it was discovered that some of the early reform measures suffered from an implementation deficit (Mayntz 1980).

The core institutional environmental policy structures were created on the federal level during the early 1970s. They have remained remarkably stable despite the fact that a Federal Environmental Ministry (BMU) was set up in 1986 (Pehle 1998). The BMU took over the environmental competences from the Federal Interior Ministry (BMI), which had been the lead department for environmental policy since 1969. In 1974, the Federal Environmental Agency (UBA) was established as an agency which provides the ministry with scientific expertise. The German debate about the need for a reform of the domestic structures in order to deal successfully with pollution has focused primarily on the federal ministry in charge of environmental policy (Müller 1986; Pehle 1998). It centred mainly on three issues. The first issue was whether a new ministry could be more effective in conducting environmental policy than a classic ministry (such as the BMI) which commands more extensive staff and power resources.

The second issue was how best to achieve interdepartmental co-operation in order to integrate environmental requirements into other policy sectors (such as transport and agriculture). In the early 1970s, the government introduced new procedures to improve cross-departmental co-operation (Interviews in 2001; Hartkopf and Bohne 1983: 144–50; SRU 2002). However, these procedural changes brought about disappointing results and were largely abandoned until the EU adopted, in the late 1990s, the so-called 'Cardiff strategy'. This strategy aimed at implementing the integration of environmental requirements into all common policy sectors. The BMU's internal organization still largely reflects the traditional media-centred (for example, air, water, and soil) approach to environmental policy-making. Overall the BMU has remained a relatively isolated ministry, with weak interdepartmental links (Müller 2002; Pehle 1998). However, shortly before the Cardiff strategy was adopted on the EU level, the UBA underwent a major internal reorganization, which resulted in the establishment of cross-sectoral units such as 'environment and transport'. The Cardiff strategy led to a revival of earlier indigenous reform efforts and strengthened the arguments of domestic reformers who had put forward similar ideas. However, it has also triggered considerable adaptational pressures because ministerial independence (*Ressortprinzip*) is a core guiding principle that is deeply embedded within the German government structure.

The final major (and related) issue within the domestic institutional reform debate focused on the question of whether governmental structures which are geared towards the implementation of the BAT principle for different environmental media can take sufficient account of cross-cutting strategies that are aimed at reducing pollution in the round. Again the EU has revived a reform debate which stalled on the domestic level in the early 1970s (Müller 2002; SRU 2002). The EU's environmental policy integration strategy is largely based on procedural measures which have caused considerable adaptational pressures within the German environmental policy system because they have led to a 'misfit' with existing domestic structures (Lenschow 2002).

Within the Federal government, the BMU is 'one of the most Europeanized ministries', with EU dossiers amounting up to about '90 per cent' for some units (Interview in 1992). However, according to a survey by Pehle (1998: 262), 49 per cent of BMU officials think that the EU's influence on domestic environmental policy is a negative one.

Germany's EU policies are co-ordinated largely by officials in Bonn/Berlin. The Permanent Representation acts mainly as the interface between Brussels and Bonn/Berlin, although it takes on a more prominent role when Germany holds the EU Presidency. The number of BMU officials in the Permanent Representation has increased from one in the late 1980s to three since the late 1990s. This is a reflection of the EU's growing importance in the environmental policy field. A small EU co-ordination unit was set up within the BMU during the 1980s. However, its ability to co-ordinate Germany's input into the Environmental Council is limited because much EU business—apart from co-ordination of the Presidency—is left to technical units which act relatively independently (Demmke 1998, 1999; Demmke and Unfried 2001; Wurzel 1996). For a long time, the BMI/BMU perceived EU environmental policy 'mainly as interior environmental policy [*Umweltinnenpolitik*] rather than foreign environmental policy [*Umweltaußenpolitik*]' (Interview, BMU official, 1992; Genscher 1980). The loose co-ordination of German EU policy reflects this normative belief, although it is also the result of existing institutional structures.

In 2000, a reform of Germany's EU policy co-ordination procedures took place. It was partly triggered by the political damage caused by the German government's last-minute intervention during the negotiations of the End-of-Life Vehicles (ELV) directive (Bulmer, Jeffery and Paterson 2000; Kraack, Pehle and Zimmerman-Steinhart 2001; Müller 2002; Wurzel 2000, 2001). During Germany's 1999 EU Presidency, Chancellor Gerhard Schröder (SPD) instructed the Environmental Minister, Jürgen Trittin (Greens), who personally favoured the proposal, to keep the ELV dossier off the Environmental Council's agenda for fear that Germany might be outvoted. Germany had already agreed in principle to the ELV Directive in 1998. However, frantic lobbying by the German automobile industry had alerted the Chancellor to the cost implications of the proposed Directive. He subsequently overruled Trittin and persuaded the British and Spanish Prime Ministers to help Germany form a blocking minority (Wurzel 2000, 2001). This constituted a rare abuse of the EU Presidency, which is supposed to act as an honest broker, and damaged Germany's reputation as a pro-integrationist environmental leader state.

In 2000, a three-stage procedure was introduced aimed at ensuring better co-ordination of Germany's input into EU negotiations (Interviews 2001). First, the heads (or their deputies) of the European units in the ministries (*Europabeauftragte*) discuss EU issues approximately once a week. Second, the heads (or their deputies) of the European divisions (*Europaabteilungsleiter*) meet approximately every two weeks. Third, the State Secretaries of the key ministries dealing with the EU (*Europastaatssekretäre*) meet about once a month in order to resolve the remaining co-ordination problems and agree on medium-term strategic aims. However, according to one official, 'medium term means anything within the next few *weeks'* (Interview 2001, emphasis added). Repeated calls for a European Ministry by Chancellor Schröder and the opposition's chancellor candidate, Edmund Stoiber (CSU), during the 2002 federal election campaign suggest that leading German politicians favour a more radical reform of Germany's EU co-ordination machinery (*Frankfurter Allgemeine Zeitung* 8 March 2002; *Süddeutsche Zeitung* 11–12 May 2002). This stands in contrast to much of the academic literature which argues that the 'German pattern of *ex post* co-ordination . . . is ultimately superior to a proactive or *ex ante* co-ordination' (Derlien 2000: 56).

The co-ordination of a unified national position is made difficult by the fact that German EU delegations sometimes reach the size of football teams, depending on the allocation of domestic competences (Pehle 1997; Wurzel 2002: 61). There have been occasions when German delegates spoke with different voices. One spectacular example took place during the inaugural meeting of the Auto-Oil II Programme in 1997. The Commission wanted to continue its controversial Auto-Oil I Programme, which aimed to arrive at cost-effective car emission limits and fuel standards derived from (urban) air quality objectives. However, since the 1980s, the BMU and BMI had consistently lobbied for the adoption of stringent emission limits derived from the BAT principle. The German delegation was headed by a BMU official who strongly condemned the Commission's new approach and walked out of the inaugural meeting while threatening a boycott. However, after his exit, an official from the Federal Economics Ministry actually praised the Commission's proposal, clearly undermining the official German negotiating position (Wurzel 2002: 160).

The Federal System

The federal system also constrains the German government's ability to come up with a unified national position on the EU level. This is particularly the case in the environmental field where the allocation of domestic competences for different environmental media has remained split between the Länder and the federal government. In the 1970s, the Länder successfully defended their competences for water management and nature protection by blocking a constitutional amendment which would have granted the federal government powers similar to those which it had acquired for air pollution, waste management and noise pollution control (Bohne 1992; Möbs 1991). This explains why Germany abandoned early domestic efforts to adopt a cross-media approach and finds it difficult to comply with the EU's environmental policy integration strategy, with subsequent 'misfit' problems. The Länder have often accused the Federal government of seeking to extend its powers by agreeing to environmental legislation on the EU level that falls within Länder competences on the domestic level. This has frequently led to a lack of co-operation by the Länder during the implementation phase.

Implementation of EU legislation is generally more complex and time-consuming in federal states than in unitary states. However, the ECJ has not accepted difficulties with internal domestic structures as a legitimate excuse for the incorrect implementation of EU legislation. For many years, the federal government could put political pressure on the Länder only by, for example, pointing out that Germany's reputation as a 'good European' and environmental leader state was at stake. However, the Amsterdam Treaty allows the Commission to fine member states that fail to implement ECJ decisions. The Federal government announced immediately that it would pass on to the Länder any fines that were due to their failures (Interview 2000).

During the 1970s and 1980s, the Länder often relied on passive resistance during the implementation phase in order to prevent a loss of their competences and/or simply to save money. For example, under the EU bathing water directive the Länder initially identified only very few bathing waters and simply claimed that the quality of the water was good although monitoring had been carried out only insufficiently. The number of German bathing waters shot up from 118 to 1,714 between the 1987 and 1988 bathing seasons after the Commission had initiated legal action (Wurzel 2002: 208–9). The Länder strategy ran into difficulties when, in the late 1980s, the Commission tried to improve the poor implementation of EU environmental legislation by taking an increasing number of member governments to the ECJ. This triggered considerable adaptational pressures on the Länder level. The unsubstantiated allegation by Jürgen Salzwedel (1989: 49) that the Commission tried to set up an 'occupational regime' (*Besatzungsregime*) by attempting to change the well-embedded domestic administrative structures and procedures for water management has to be seen within this context.

In the 1990s, the Länder adopted a more pro-active approach to the Europeanization process. They used their veto position during the ratification of the Maastricht Treaty, which had to be agreed on by both the Bundestag and the Bundesrat, in order to demand greater involvement in the EU policy formulation phase. The federal government subsequently agreed to a constitutional amendment that obliged it to keep the Länder better informed. Moreover, the Länder have been granted the right to represent Germany in the Council on issues that fall within their exclusive competence on the domestic level (Bundesrat 2001*a*, 2001*b*; Demmke and Unfried 2001; Maurer and Wessels 2001). However, in the Environmental Council, the Länder have made use of their new powers only very sparingly. Since the 1980s, the Länder increased considerably their EU representation by setting up their own offices in Brussels where they occasionally compete with the federal government for access to the Commission. The Länder are also represented in the Committee of Regions. Since the 1990s, the Länder have become more competent on European matters (*europafähig*) and have developed a proactive approach towards European integration. In 2001, the Länder had 308 representatives for eighty Council and 127 Commission working groups (Bundesrat 2001*a*: 13). The Bundesrat's experiment of putting one Land representative in charge of several environmental Directives that are related to similar themes was judged successful and has been extended to other policy sectors (Demmke and Unfried 2001: 41).

The 'Uploading' and 'Downloading' of Environmental Standards

Germany has been characterized as a 'high regulatory state' (Héritier, Knill and Minger 1996) that has adopted a dense body of environmental legislation (Demmke 1998: 99; Kloepfer 1998; Müller-Brandeck-Bocquet 1996). This fits the claim that German policy-making is characterized by a high degree of juridification (Dyson 1982, 1992; Weale 1992*b*; Weale, O'Riordan and Kramme 1991). Germany initially made wide use of the EU's 1973 standstill agreement in order to set the agenda (Héritier, Knill and Minger 1996; Rehbinder and Stewart 1985: 17; SRU 1978: 512–14; Wurzel 2002: 75–8). However, occasionally the German government decided not to inform the Commission about draft national environmental legislation because it was concerned that this could lead to a watering down of national standards (SRU 1978; Wurzel 2002: 102).

The bulk of early EU environmental legislation dealt with harmonization measures (such as car emission regulations and dangerous chemicals) which were aimed at the prevention of new barriers to trade (Rehbinder and Stewart 1985). As a densely populated and highly industrialized country at the centre of Europe, Germany had a strong ecological and economic interest in pushing for the EU-wide harmonization of national environmental laws (Grant, Paterson and Whitson 1988: 245–65; Weale 1992*b*; Weale *et al.* 2000; Wurzel 2002). Domestic public environmental awareness was high and most German environmental interest groups demanded that the EU should prevent ecological dumping by harmonizing national environmental standards on the highest level while German industry was keen on achieving a level playing field with its competitors. Thus the German government had strong incentives to export its relatively stringent domestic environmental standards to the EU level.

Broadly speaking, the Europeanization of German environmental standards can be grouped into three major categories. First, relatively progressive German standards were 'uploaded' to the EU level. Examples include Directives which regulated the sulphur content of liquid fuels (75/176/EEC), the lead content in petrol (78/611/EEC), the large combustion Directive (88/609/EEC), and many car emission Directives (Hartkopf and Bohne 1983: 169). However, the EU often adopted German proposals only after a considerable time-lag. Moreover, they became subject to modifications that took account of the core demands of veto actors (Demmke and Unfried 2001; Weale 1996; Wurzel 2002). Often this led to vague requirements (which were wide open to different interpretations) and complex compromises (which stipulated exemptions, derogations and phased-in deadlines). However, the final EU legislation also usually stipulated new requirements that went beyond the original German demands because the environmentally minded European Parliament or other environmental leader states tried to tighten the standards even further during the adoption process. Hence even 'uploaded' standards often trigger adaptational pressures, especially when they are resisted by domestic veto actors (Haverland 1998).

Second, EU standards were 'downloaded' to the domestic level. Examples include standards for bathing waters, shellfish waters, and conservation measures for wild birds. Compared to 'uploaded' standards, the implementation of 'downloaded' standards has triggered greater adaptational pressures on the domestic level (Knill 2001; Moltke 1984). 'Downloaded' standards that required significant institutional and/or procedural changes on the domestic level have generally caused the most serious implementation problems.

Third, an intermediate category consists of EU measures that the BMU and BMI were prevented from adopting on the domestic level owing to the resistance of national veto actors (such as the Chancellor, the Federal Economics Ministry, and the Länder). Examples include EU environmental laws on dangerous chemicals, nature protection laws and the ELV directive (Hartkopf and Bohne 1983: 169; Moltke 1984; SRU 2002; Wurzel 2000). However, the BMU's domestic opponents also tried to exploit the EU decision-making arena for their own purpose. This can be seen from the following quote from a Federal Economics Ministry official (Wurzel 2002: 11): 'Brussels is often our last hope when it comes to toning down some of the extreme measures put forward by the BMU.'

Over time, EU environmental laws expanded in terms of both numbers and issues covered. By 2000, the EU had adopted almost 700 items of environmental legislation (Haigh 2001). However, the EU's legislative activism has slowed down since the Danish 'no' to the Maastricht Treaty in 1992. British lobbying against a steady outpour of detailed environmental legislation, the increased maturity of EU environmental policy, and economic recession constitute important additional explanatory variables. Over time, EU legislation changed also in terms of content, which points to a change in the underlying regulatory philosophy or environmental regulatory style.

The EU's procedural measures, for example on environmental impact assessment (85/366/EEC), freedom of access to environmental information (90/313/EEC), and integrated pollution prevention and control (96/61/EC) have triggered considerable domestic adaptational pressures in Germany where they have been implemented often only belatedly and incorrectly (Börzel 2002; Breuer 2000; Héritier, Knill and Minger 1996; Kraack, Pehle and Zimmermann-Steinhart 2001; Knill 2001; Knill and Lenschow 2000; Pehle 1997, 1998). The adaptational pressures relate mainly to institutional 'fit' or 'misfit' (i.e. the institutional structures) and, as will be explained below, to the relationship between government and societal actors (i.e. the preferred regulatory style). In Germany the EU's recent preference for procedural environmental policy measures is perceived as alien and has variously been attributed to 'Anglo-American' (Kloepfer 1998: 614), 'Anglo-Scandinavian' (Baacke 2000) or 'British' (Héritier, Knill and Minger 1996; Pehle 1998: 235) influence. Many of the EU's procedural measures adopt a cross-cutting integrated pollution control approach, while German environmental law is still largely geared towards the implementation of the BAT principle for different environmental media. A national environmental code (*Umweltgesetzbuch*), which would have pulled together the specialized media-centred environmental laws, could have made easier the implementation of procedural EU environmental policy measures (but see Knill 2001). However, the Federal government had to shelve well-developed plans due to the resistance of the Länder.

In anticipation of the implementation difficulties on the domestic level, the German government has tried to alter some of the EU's procedural measures. In the case of the integrated pollution prevention and control (IPPC) Directive, Germany used its 1999 EU Presidency in order to present, at a very late stage in the EU decision-making process, a compromise proposal that included the BAT principle. But Germany failed to gain sufficient support for its proposal and was instead accused of abusing the office of the Presidency (Wurzel 1996: 285). It subsequently withdrew its proposal, although the BAT principle later found its way into the IPPC Directive.

On other occasions, Germany has tried to divert the adaptational pressures resulting from procedural measures during the implementation phase. This was the case with the environmental impact assessment (EIA) Directive, which was initially implemented in such a manner that it lost most of its cross-cutting approach. Ironically, Germany had been one of the pioneers in Europe when it adopted national EIA legislation in 1975 (Hartkopf and Bohne 1983: 98–9; Kloepfer 1998: 237–8; SRU 2002). However, its effect was severely curtailed by more specialized media-centred environmental laws which prescribed the BAT principle.

Policy Instruments

Traditional 'command-and-control' regulation (*Ordnungsrecht*) is the most widely used environmental policy instrument in Germany. Until recently, it was also the most important policy tool on the EU level. EU and German preferences therefore mutually reinforced each other. However, voluntary agreements (VAs) have also been widely used in German environmental policy (Pehle, forthcoming; UBA, 1999). In the EU, Germany has adopted one of the highest numbers of environmental VAs (Jordan *et al.* 2001). As will be explained below, this fits the claim that the German policy style exhibits moderately corporatist features (Dyson 1982, 1992). German VAs are often adopted 'in the shadow of the law', although they are legally non-binding policy tools. The use of VAs can be traced to the beginnings of German environmental policy and has much to do with industry trying to pre-empt government legislation. However, their importance increased significantly when a centre-right (CDU/CSU/FDP) coalition government adopted a coalition agreement in 1994 that stated a general preference for VAs over regulation (Pehle, forthcoming; UBA 1999). Germany's first ever SPD–Green coalition government, which came to power in 1998, was initially highly sceptical about VAs, although Chancellor Schröder considered them a useful policy tool. The SPD–Green coalition accepted several environmental VAs, including a major voluntary commitment by industry to cut climate change gases.

The EU has adopted only very few VAs despite the Commission's recent emphasis on non-regulatory policy tools (Jordan *et al.* 2001; Knill and Lenschow 2000; Mol, Lauber and Liefferink 2000). In some cases German VAs have actually been overwritten by EU legislation, as with the ELV Directive. The EU's reluctance to adopt VAs stems from the lack of legitimacy and transparency from which this tool suffers, especially on the supranational level. However, the Commission has tried hard to overcome the fact that there is no Treaty base for VAs, which remain outside the normal EU decision-making procedures and are therefore viewed with suspicion by the European Parliament. German VAs have not acted as a model for the EU despite the fact that Germany has a lot of experience with this policy tool. Most EU policy actors consider the majority German VAs as lacking in transparency, monitoring commitments, and explicit sanctions.

In 1978, Germany acted as a pioneer when it adopted the world's first national eco-label scheme. This voluntary informational device is used both to raise environmental awareness and to change consumer and producer behaviour. This 'soft' policy instrument quickly achieved a considerable market uptake in Germany and influenced the EU's eco-label scheme that was adopted in 1992. However, German environmental policy-makers initially viewed with great suspicion EU voluntary informational devices such as the eco-audit and management system (EMAS). German companies nevertheless made up almost two-thirds of all EMAS applications in the EU (Knill and Lenschow 2000; Kraack, Pehle and Zimmermann-Steinhart 2001).

Overall, the EU has constrained rather than facilitated the development of eco-taxes in Germany. In 1999, the first stage of an ecological tax reform was introduced by the Red–Green coalition government (Reiche and Krebs 1999). Its implementation had to be postponed by three months in order to incorporate amendments that took into account objections raised by the Commission about generous exemptions for high-energy industrial users and subsidies for renewable energy sources (Interviews 2001). The previous centre-right government supported the adoption of an EU-wide carbon dioxide/energy tax which was blocked first by Britain on sovereignty grounds and then by Spain which was concerned that its industrial development might be stifled. However, it refrained from adopting unilaterally an eco-tax owing to fears about its impact on German industry's competitiveness (Wurzel 1996; Zito 2000).

The Commission's proposal for an EU-wide emission trading system to cut climate change gases was the main driving force behind the German government's decision to set up a national emission trading working group in 2000. But Germany's large chemical industry, in particular, remains opposed to tradeable permits and instead favours VAs as tried-and-tested instruments—although the banking sector, which would be involved in running such a scheme, strongly supports tradeable permits. BMU officials, who had made three unsuccessful attempts to set up small-scale pilot schemes during the 1990s, used the Commission's proposal to overcome considerable industry resistance. They argued that Germany would be unable to influence the EU scheme without some prior experience with this novel policy tool which has already been tested in other member states such as Britain, Denmark, and the Netherlands (Interview 2001).

Environmental Regulatory Style and Action Guiding Principles

German governments are said to prefer a moderately active stance that relies on consensus and consultation when trying to solve public policy problems (Dyson 1982, 1992; Katzenstein 1987). This fits well the German preference for regulation (*Ordnungsrecht*) and for VAs 'in the shadow of the law'. The traditional German policy style featured corporatist elements because government consultation extended mainly to employers and unions while environmental groups remained largely excluded from the policy formulation phase (Kitschelt 1986; Paterson 1989; Rose-Ackermann 1995). Environmental groups often had to rely on court action during the post-decision phase which was made easier by the high degree of juridifcation of German politics and the strong 'state ruled by law' (*Rechtsstaat*) tradition that was revived after the lawlessness of the Nazi regime (Dyson 1982; Weale 1992*b*). The dominance of officials with legal training within the BMI and, to a lesser degree, the BMU further encouraged the wide use of detailed technical regulations derived from general legal principles (such as the precautionary and BAT principles). Germany therefore became a high regulatory state with a dense body of detailed environmental rules.

Kitschelt's claim that the German environmental policy-making process is characterized by 'closed opportunity structures' (1986) holds true more for certain sub-sectors (such as nuclear power) than others (such as eco-labels). It also ignores the fact that BMI officials actively encouraged the setting up of environmental groups during the early 1970s (Hartkopf and Bohne 1983). Moreover, it cannot explain why (unlike their British counterparts) German environmental groups have been slow in making use of the EU's opportunity structures to influence environmental policy. It is only since the 1990s that many of the large German environmental groups have started more actively to lobby the EU, which they for long perceived mainly as a free-trade area and brake on domestic environmental policy.

The EU's Directive on environmental information has given domestic environmental groups greater access to information. It was initially opposed by a centre-right German government that failed to sign the so-called 'Aarhus Convention' on access to environmental information and public participation. However, Germany finally signed the Aarhus Convention when the Red–Green government—which welcomed the existence of the EU's environmental information Directive—came to power. This shows that certain EU measures which pose a problem for one particular coalition government may be seen as a model by another (Baacke 2000). It also shows that 'a given policy sector or a particular case may display various styles as well as shifts in the dominant style over time' (Dyson 1982: 21; see also Beyme 1985). However, as a rule these shifts take place incrementally, as they are curtailed by institutional constraints and deeply embedded cultural norms about the role of state actors in the domestic policy-making process and Germany's place in Europe.

Many of the EU's procedural measures have caused concern among German environmental policy actors who instead have shown a preference for relatively detailed substantive standards. The core features of the traditional domestic environmental regulatory style (together with the institutional constraints) explain why the EU's recent procedural measures (such as EIA and EMAS) have led to a misfit on the domestic level and triggered considerable adaptational pressures (Börzel 2002; Demmke 1998; Knill 2001; Knill and Lenschow 2000). As Woolcock, Hodges and Schreiber (1991: 5) have pointed out: 'every regulatory regime or set of standards represents a form of national social contract that reflects a particular consensus or balance between competing interests. . . . [I]ndividual governments are generally reluctant to see them eroded by EC proposals.' This is even more the case when EU policy measures clash with deeply embedded national policy styles which can be seen as distinctive processes of policy-making (or standard operating procedures) that are used to arrive at core action guiding principles for particular policies (Weale *et al.* 2000: 150).

The social market economy (*soziale Marktwirtschaft*) doctrine became a dominant macro-political action guiding norm for German policy-makers after the economic miracle (*Wirtschaftswunder*) of the 1950s (Dyson 1982, 1992). It allows state actors to set the framework conditions for private actors within the market place. In the late 1980s, there was considerable cross-party support for developing the social market economy into a 'social and ecological market economy' (*soziale und ökologische Marktwirtschaft*) (Jänicke 1993; Schröder 1989; Töpfer 1989; Weale 1992*b*; Weale *et al.* 2000). Proponents of ecological modernization, who rejected the conventional (neo-liberal) view that there is a trade-off between environmental policy and economic prosperity by claiming that stringent environmental standards can be beneficial for both the environment and the economy, gained considerable political influence in Germany in the 1980s. Their arguments seemed to be confirmed by a significant rise in the number of jobs related to environmental protection and the boom in Germany's environmental technology exports (UBA 1997). The closest that the EU came to embracing the ecological modernization doctrine was the Commission's 1994 White Paper on *Growth, Competitiveness, Employment* (CEC 1994). However, one year later the *Report of the Group of Independent Experts on Legislative and Administrative Simplification* turned back the clock on the EU level by again embracing the conventional wisdom of a trade-off between stringent environmental regulations and economic growth (CEC 1995). The chair of this expert group was a Federal Economics Ministry official, illustrating that there was also considerable opposition to the ecological modernization doctrine amongst domestic actors in Germany (Interview 1999).

In the 1990s, proponents of ecological modernization found themselves on the defensive in Germany where they were faced with declining public environmental awareness (CEC 1999), the economic impact of unification and a fierce debate about *Standort Deutschland*—i.e. Germany's capacity to attract and retain investment (BMWi 1993; Harding and Paterson 2000). Within the *Standort Deutschland* debate, questions were raised about the future of the 'model Germany' *(Modell Deutschland)* which has widely been seen as an alternative to Anglo-Saxon capitalism (Harding and Paterson 2000; Hodges and Woolcock 1993). In Germany, the EU's recent emphasis on self-regulation, procedural measures, and 'soft' policy instruments has been connected to a much more fundamental policy discourse about the future of the German model. Many BMU and UBA officials rejected the Commission's new approach to environmental governance as alien to the German environmental regulatory style and a danger to the guiding principles that governed domestic pollution control strategies. They raised fears that the EU's new approach could lead to a rolling back of hard-won achievements in the environmental policy field.

Weale *et al.* (2000: 385) have identified EU environment policy as an area in which the German and British governments have been engaged in serious disputes about the best approach to pollution control that form part of 'a more general conflict between Rhineland capitalism and Anglo-Saxon capitalism'. In the 1970s, many EU environmental policy measures stipulated EQOs. But in the 1980s, the Commission's Directorate-General for the Environment (DG Environment) relied more heavily on EU-wide emission limits derived from the BAT principle. This was partly due to German pressure and partly out of necessity as there was simply insufficient data for a science-based EQO-centred approach (Wurzel 2002: 69–70). However, in the 1990s, the Commission moved away from a BAT-derived emission limits approach and returned to its earlier preference for EQOs. It subsequently tried to supplement (and in some cases substitute) detailed substantive 'command and control' regulation with more flexible framework Directives, procedural measures, and 'soft' policy instruments while emphasizing cost-effectiveness considerations (CEC 1996, 2000, 2001*a*; Friedrich, Tappe and Wurzel 2000; Knill and Lenschow 2000; Kraack, Pehle and Zimmermann-Steinhart 2001; Héritier, Knill and Minger 1996)

In 1988, Germany used its EU Presidency to organize a ministerial seminar in Frankfurt on water policy, the policy sector where Anglo-German differences were most pronounced (Wurzel 1996: 283). This led to the accommodation of core elements of both British and German action guiding norms. However, many EU laws stipulate vague compromises. Thus the BATNEEC principle has usually been interpreted by German policy-makers as the 'Best Available *Technology* Not Entailing Excessive Costs', which is close to the German BAT principle. In the UK, it has usually been defined as the 'Best Available *Techniques* Not Entailing Excessive Costs', which is closer to the preferred British regulatory style and its emphasis on short-term costs (Wurzel 2002).

It can be argued that the Europeanization of domestic environmental policies led member governments to define more clearly, and in some cases codify, their national environmental regulatory styles and action guiding principles. In this way they would be better able to defend on the EU level what are perceived as long-established national practices and principles. However, important differences of opinion have remained among German policy actors about the best approach to environmental policy. Occasionally they resurfaced during EU negotiations, as was illustrated by the above-mentioned differences between the BMU and the Federal Economics Ministry about the merits of the Commission's Auto-Oil programme.

Another example relates to the debate about sustainable development, which largely replaced the discourse about environmental modernization on the EU level in the 1990s. The EU's sustainable development strategy, which itself is a reflection of developments on the UN level, gives equal weight to environmental, economic, and social requirements. The Federal Economics Ministry has interpreted the sustainable development strategy as an obligation on environmental policy-makers (on the EU and domestic levels) to take more seriously the economic and social consequences of their decisions. For the BMU this interpretation constitutes a (potential) threat to ambitious environmental policy measures (Interviews 2001). However, the BMU also considers the sustainable development strategy as 'a foot in the door of the Lisbon strategy', which initially excluded the environment (Interview 2002). After considerable lobbying by the BMU, which at the time of the Lisbon summit in 2000 was 'preoccupied with phasing out nuclear power' (Interview 2001), this omission was rectified at the 2001 Gothenburg summit with the help of the Swedish Presidency (SRU 2002). The BMU (and its domestic and EU allies) may have been able to prevent a further downgrading of environmental policy within the wider political discourse about the EU's future. However, compared to the 1980s, German environmental policy-makers (and their allies on the domestic and EU levels) have lost influence with respect to the 'uploading' of ideas and policy principles to the EU level.

For some practitioners, the neglect of the 'politics of staffing' within DG Environment of the European Commission, in particular, has contributed to Germany's decline in influence over the EU's ideational agenda. Considering the salience of environmental issues on the domestic level, it is surprising that only one German national ever held (between 1982 and 1985) the post of Environmental Commissioner and none has ever been promoted to the post of director-general or deputy director-general within DG Environment. Moreover, the German government has not provided BMU or UBA officials with sufficient incentives (such as fast-track promotion after a successful stint in Brussels, as introduced by the British government in the 1990s) for accepting temporary postings as national experts on secondment with the Commission. However, the 'mainstreaming of DG Environment' (Weale *et al.* 2000: 89) and the alleged under-representation of German nationals within DG Environment have been discussed at a senior level by German government officials (Interview 2001). On the other hand, the traditional German approach to environmental policy has lost some of its appeal on the EU and international levels owing to other factors.

In the 1980s, BAT-derived emission reduction targets were an attractive policy concept for the EU (as well as on the international level) for three main reasons. First, they were relatively easy to determine and monitor (Gündling 1991); second, they dealt mainly with pressing environmental and health issues at a time when relatively few environmental policy measures had been adopted; third, they ensured a level playing field. By the 1990s, EU environmental policy matured and covered a much wider range of issues. Moreover, international competition increased at a time when environmental awareness declined. Cost-effectiveness considerations therefore became more important, while the resistance against ambitious EU-wide standards rose (Holzinger and Knoepfel 2000). The BAT principle became branded as encouraging 'end-of-pipe' technology, and new policy ideas such as the 'critical loads' concept entered the wider policy discourse. The 'critical loads' concept, which aims to reduce environmental pollution to a threshold level at which environmental damage no longer occurs, takes more explicit account of cost-effectiveness considerations than EU-wide emission limits for all member states, regardless of their pollution levels. Canada and Sweden pioneered this concept within the international negotiations to reduce acidification by stipulating variable threshold levels (rather than uniform reduction targets) which depend on the existing degree of pollution. It was initially viewed with suspicion by German policy-makers, but has found its way into international environmental treaties and the EU's acidification strategy (Wurzel 2002). This is not to argue that BAT-derived regulation and the precautionary principle no longer play a role on the EU level. However, both EU and domestic environmental policy content are now based on a more complex mix of competing concepts.

Conclusion

The Europeanization process had a highly variegated impact on the German environmental policy system. Its direct material impact on the policy content differs from its cognitive effects on the ideational level. In the 1970s and 1980s, the Europeanization process was largely taken for granted, while the EU was primarily perceived as a brake on German environmental policy. In the 1980s, Germany was relatively successful in exporting to the EU level some of its environmental standards (e.g., on car emissions), regulatory principles (e.g., the precautionary principle), and policy instruments (e.g., traditional regulation).

However, the EU's impact on domestic environmental policy increased in the 1980s when the Commission started to take more seriously the correct implementation of EU environmental laws. Germany was subsequently the subject of several adverse ECJ rulings that resulted in considerable adaptational pressures, especially on the Länder level. There was a gradual realization in Germany that the Europeanization process also brought about the 'downloading' of a significant number of standards to the domestic level, while 'uploaded' standards often contained additional requirements. Since the early 1990s, there has been a partial misfit between German and EU preferences on a range of environmental issues. The EU's recent procedural measures have created considerable adaptational pressures on the domestic level because they constitute a challenge to deeply embedded institutional structures and procedures as well as the dominant environmental regulatory style.

The impact of the EU on domestic structures is most evident with regard to the federal system. Up to the late 1980s, the Länder relied primarily on a strategy of passive resistance by frequently failing to implement fully EU environmental legislation, which on the domestic level fell within their competence. Since the 1990s, the Länder have tried to increase their formal responsibilities and involvement in EU issues, while insisting on domestic constitutional changes in order to be able better to participate in the EU policy-making process (see Jeffery, Chapter 5 in this volume).

The national regulatory style has arguably been least affected by the EU. However, there are signs that this may be about to change. Environmental groups have gained greater access to information owing to EU legislation and are taking the EU more seriously as an important decision-making arena. The EU's emphasis on procedural measures and self-regulation poses a challenge to the more formalistic German environmental policy style which relies heavily on general legal principles and detailed substantive regulation as well as VAs. The BMU and UBA have raised concerns that some of the EU's procedural measures could lead to a weakening of hard-won environmental policy achievements.

However, the partial misfit between national and EU preferences should not be exaggerated. First, important domestic policy actors (such as the Federal Economics Ministry) also favour a less interventionist approach to environmental policy that relies more strongly on self-regulation. In this way the Europeanization process is strengthening certain aspects of the social market economy (neo-liberalism) *vis-à-vis* others (ecological modernization) (see Dyson, Chapter 10 in this volume). It has created new political opportunity structures for domestic actors to use, empowering some actors over others. Second, some of the EU's recent procedural measures (such as EIA and environmental policy integration) had already been demanded by environmental policy actors on the domestic level in the early 1970s. Moreover, Germany still exerts considerable influence within the EU decision-making process on a wide range of issues (such as car emission regulation and climate change) on which it has taken the lead, despite the fact that its overall environmental record has again become a mixed one. This is not to deny that the Europeanization process has been an important factor. However, overall it has been an incremental and reasonably subtle process that has allowed the gradual adaptation of the German environmental policy system to new demands.

Note. This chapter has benefited from discussions with participants at the workshop and conference on 'Germany and Europe: A "Europeanized" Germany' in London at the British Academy in November 2001 and May 2002. The author would like to thank the discussant, Christoph Knill, and editors, Kenneth Dyson and Klaus Goetz, for their highly valuable comments on earlier drafts. The author is grateful to all interviewees for giving up their precious time and providing valuable information. The research has benefited from grants from the Anglo-German Foundation (1043 and 1258) and the ESRC (L216252013), the main findings of which are published elsewhere.

15

Justice and Home Affairs: Europeanization as a Government-Controlled Process

JÖRG MONAR

Introduction

THE RAPID DEVELOPMENT OF EU JUSTICE and home affairs (JHA) from loose inter-governmental co-operation to a partially communitarized policy-making area and the fundamental Treaty objective of establishing an 'area of freedom, security and justice' have been among the most remarkable and surprising phenomena of the European integration process since 1990. Germany played a key role in trigger-ing this development. It was one of the founding members of the Schengen group in 1985. It can also be argued that without the strong German insistence in the 1990–1 Intergovernmental Conference (IGC) on bringing justice and home affairs into the Treaty on European Union (TEU)—which took the form of the 'third pillar'—the extraordinary growth of EU justice and home affairs through-out the 1990s would hardly have been possible. Germany has also been at the forefront of a range of other significant elements of progress in EU justice and home affairs. They include the establishment of Europol (completed with the entry into force of the Europol Convention in 1998) and the communitarization of substantial parts of the 'old' third pillar (achieved with the entry into force of the Amsterdam Treaty in 1999). With Germany having been among the principal driving forces of EU justice and home affairs, it seems worthwhile to ask whether this leading role in Europeanizing this sector at the European level has been accompanied by a similarly extensive Europeanization of justice and home affairs at the German level. In line with the agenda set out in Chapter 1 in this volume, the present chapter will look at both the 'uploading' and the 'downloading' dimensions of Europeanization in justice and home affairs. It will thus take into account both the impact of the growth of EU policy-making and structures in this area on Germany and the impact of domestic German preferences and factors on the development of EU justice and home affairs.

Proceedings of the British Academy, **119**, 309–323. © The British Academy 2003.

Driving Factors and Actors of Europeanization in Justice and Home Affairs

At a general level, the factors that led Germany to support increased European co-operation and even integration in justice and home affairs were largely identical to those of its other EU partners. They included the need for common compensatory measures for the abolition of internal border controls on goods and persons in the context of the European internal market, a mounting immigration pressure with its effects on the asylum system since the end of the 1980s, and new or increased threats of international crime in the 1990s, some of which—such as the emergence of Russian organized crime—were closely linked to the collapse of the Communist systems. Yet, these general factors cannot explain why successive German governments developed such a particular interest in bringing justice and home affairs on the European agenda that they often ended up being one of the protagonists or even the main driving force at EU level. There were three more specific reasons that made Germany play a much more active role through most of the 1990s.

The first of these was—and to a large extent still is—exposure. Because of its geography, Germany found itself at the beginning of the 1990s in the position of a 'frontline' state to central and eastern Europe whose revolutionary transformation—besides many benefits and opportunities—also generated some actual—and perhaps even more perceived—risks to internal security in the broadest sense. The new permeability of borders to Germany's eastern neighbours led to substantial numbers of illegal border crossings and illegal immigrants, a phenomenon that was largely new, in that the Iron Curtain had previously spared Germany this problem. Substantial numbers of asylum seekers also took the new open routes through central and eastern Europe, with Germany in most cases being their first and intended final destination. This was already seen as enough of a problem, but on top of that came the rapid increase of organized crime in several of the central and eastern European countries and Russia. It operated across borders and was seen as a serious risk by German authorities (Schelter 1999: 16–17). In 1996, when the enlargement process to the central and eastern European countries was already well under way, German Minister of the Interior Manfred Kanther called the border lands east of Germany a 'crime zone'.[1] Public scares fuelled by the media, such as those about the smuggling of nuclear materials by Russian criminals at the beginning of the 1990s, added to the perception of particular vulnerability as a frontline state.

At the end of the 1990s, illegal immigration and the smuggling and trafficking of people had developed into a firm part of this threat perception. The German Federal Border Guard (*Bundesgrenzschutz*) regularly emphasized the exposure of

---

[1] Quoted in Bort (2000: 95).

German eastern and southern borders to illegal immigration via all three of the main European immigration routes: the Eastern (through the EU candidates), the Southeastern European (through the Balkans) and the Maghreb (through France and Italy) routes (Grenzschutzdirektion 2000: 23–39). The perception of serious external threats to German internal security was again reflected in the first 'Periodical Report on Crime and Crime Control' of July 2001. It pointed to the penetration of Germany by Italian, Turkish, and Kosovo Albanian modern 'mafia'-type organized crime groups (Federal Ministry of the Interior and Federal Ministry of Justice 2001: 20). All of these problems have been seen as part of the wider transformation and challenges of Europe and extending beyond German borders and national possibilities of control. Hence, seeking European solutions and solidarity with other EU partners in the form of common policy responses to common challenges has continued to appear as an obvious choice for successive German governments.

An important second reason for Germany's role as a protagonist was the interest of the German government, at least during the first half of the 1990s, in reducing internal pressure by an attempt at Europeanizing the asylum problem. As already mentioned, the German government played a crucial role in 1990–1 both in bringing justice and home affairs on the agenda of the Inter-governmental Conference leading to the Maastricht Treaty and in making the introduction of the third pillar possible. This proactive role was to a large extent motivated by the enormous increase of asylum applications in Germany during this period and its disproportionate share in the total number of applications in the EC-12, which reached 78.76 per cent in 1992 (Reermann 1997: 122). In this situation, the German government was, on the one hand, hoping that a move towards a common European asylum policy would lead to a more even distribution of asylum applications among the member states and/or the introduction of a burden-sharing mechanism. On the other hand, Europeanizing the issue also offered the prospect of defusing to some extent the increasingly bitter debate about a restrictive revision of the relatively liberal German legislation on political asylum. Against the background of domestic outbursts of racism and xenophobia, this issue not only caused major polarization in the political landscape and public opinion, but also generated serious controversies in the ruling Christian-Liberal coalition. The new European dimension of the asylum issue was repeatedly used as an argument by politicians favouring a restrictive revision of the German legislation, which eventually took place in 1993. They pointed to the need to arrive at a common European approach that would enable Germany to bring its asylum legislation into line with the more restrictive approach taken by most of its European partners. Although the attempted Europeanization led only to very limited immediate progress towards common EU asylum policy-making, it at least partially fulfilled its role in the internal German political debate.

A third, although less prominent, reason was that from the mid-1980s onwards the Kohl government regarded co-operation and eventually integration in justice and home affairs as one of the building blocks of political union. Chancellor Helmut Kohl himself repeatedly declared that the European construction could and should play a role in providing European citizens with a higher degree of internal security and should contribute to a better management of the problems in the asylum and immigration spheres. He stressed that citizens were expecting this and that it could help to increase the legitimacy and improve the public image of the Union. In the European Council, Kohl defended the idea of establishing Europol as a sort of European FBI with the argument that it could make a contribution to a better visibility of the EU as taking care of citizens' interests (Funk 2000: 302–3). Making the development of justice and home affairs part of the debate about the deepening of the European construction can be regarded as a deliberate and—in the most neutral sense of the word— ideological choice, which was occasionally also presented as such to the German public.

Looking at these main driving factors and reasons for Germany's protagonist role in justice and home affairs, it comes as no surprise that the main agent of Europeanization has been the government itself. It has tried to instrumentalize the European level both in the search for more effective common European responses to transnational challenges to its internal security and, for domestic political reasons, as a means for diffusing internal political pressures over the asylum issue. Yet it has also pursued Europeanization of justice and home affairs as an objective in its own right, presenting it as an essential part of the European political project.

To say that the government has acted as the primary agent of Europeanization does not mean, however, that it has acted in isolation. The strong insistence of the German government on effective compensatory measures for the abolition of internal border controls in both the Schengen context and the third pillar of the 1990s responded to concerns and urgent calls for such measures by law-enforcement agencies at both the federal level—the *Bundesgrenzschutz* and the *Bundeskriminalamt*—and the Länder level—the *Länderpolizeien*.[2] Their arguments about potentially increasing internal security risks were taken more than seriously by the Federal Ministry of Interior (*Bundesministerium des Innern*).

The change of government in 1998 made little difference in this respect, as the new SPD Minister of the Interior—Otto Schily—was at least as interested in not appearing 'soft' on European internal security issues as his predecessor. Given the clear threat perception developed by the agencies, it would have been difficult

---

[2] On the internal German debate about compensatory measures at the European level in the Schengen context see Fijnaut (1993: 41–2).

for any federal minister to take a different line. The emerging European issues were increasingly closely followed by Länder governments, especially Bavaria, which were concerned about increased internal security risks. Any compromising by the Federal government would have been eagerly seized upon by the opposition. This can help explain Germany's reputation as an advocate of tough restrictive and controlling measures at the European level and its insistence on a strict application of the Schengen *acquis* by the future central and east European EU member states.

By contrast, neither the Länder governments nor economic and social interest groups have emerged as major driving forces in the process of Europeanization of justice and home affairs. The former followed the process with more suspicion than enthusiasm (see below). The latter realized only after the entry into force of the Treaty of Amsterdam and the decisions of the Tampere European Council in 1999 that decisions at the European level could well make a major difference at the German level, too. Only a few of the groups defending the rights of asylum seekers and immigrants started to lobby the German government on European issues in the mid-1990s. Nor have the media been effective agents of Europeanization in this area. Reporting on the European dimension of national justice and home affairs issues in newspapers and television was extremely rare at the time of the old third pillar and is still fairly sporadic and fragmentary today. The complexity and lack of transparency of decision-making on justice and home affairs in Brussels and the mostly indirect and delayed impact on the national setting have not encouraged the media to spread the news to German citizens that justice and home affairs has become a major EU policy-making area, with considerable long-term implications for German internal policies in this area.

Obstacles to Europeanization

In one sense, the federal organization of the German state has made it easier for Germany to become one of the leading protagonists of the development of EU justice and home affairs. German representatives at the various levels of decision-making in the EU Council have been used to a system of division of competences in internal security matters in the domestic context. Hence, they have often found it easier than many of their other EU counterparts to accept the emergence of a new level of decision-making and the transfer of decision-making powers to this level and to operate effectively between the different levels. German law-enforcement authorities have also been used for a long time to the sort of functional co-operation between territorial and central agencies that is required at the European level in the context of the Council bodies, Europol, Eurojust and other structures. Although its powers are much more limited, Europol, for instance, fits quite well the central federal agency model on which the German Federal Crime Office (*Bundeskriminalamt*) is based. This can partially explain why Germany has become the by far most important and comprehensive supplier of data to Europol, through the Federal Crime Office, whereas other member states—not used to a similar federal agency model—have been much less forthcoming and effective in this respect.

Yet in another sense, the federal structure has proved to some extent to be an obstacle in the process of Europeanization. The Länder governments have extensive powers in police matters, a say in legislation in the areas of civil and criminal law, asylum and immigration, and important administrative competences. Hence—although supporting the development of EU justice and home affairs in principle—they have tended to regard the growth of the new European dimension as a potential source of erosion of their own role and authority. In addition, there have been concerns that the Länder—as the main executive agents of national policies—could be left facing the administrative, social, and even financial bill of decisions taken in Brussels in the sphere of justice and home affairs. In consequence, the Länder have made the most of their rights of participation under Article 23 of the Basic Law and the relevant implementing legislation. They have insisted on extensive information and consultation before the federal government adopts a position in the Council and co-ordinated their positions in the *Innen- und Justizministerkonferenz* (the interior and justice ministerial conference of the Länder). They have also sent Länder ministers to the Justice and Home Affairs Council meetings, and delegated Länder ministry officials to the German Permanent Representation in Brussels to follow the decision-making process continuously.

There have been a number of occasions when the Länder have prevented the federal government from adopting a position that they perceived to be contrary to their interests. The most dramatic was the final night of negotiations on the Treaty of Amsterdam in June 1997, when a threat by the German Länder to block the Treaty in the Bundesrat forced Chancellor Kohl—to the consternation of Italy and a number of other member states—to backtrack on his previous support for majority voting on asylum and immigration issues. The result was a reconfirmation of the unanimity principle and, therefore, to a *de facto* veto possibility of Germany against measures that the Länder might find detrimental to their interests. This principle is to last at least until 2004, when the Council will have to decide by unanimity on whether to pass to majority voting from then on.[3] The case demonstrates the very considerable impact that the German Länder can have on the development of justice and home affairs at the European level, and highlights the fact that they are willing to make full use of their internal powers in this respect.

The German federal system also adds an element of complexity to the implementation of EU justice and home affairs decisions. In 2001, for instance, the

---

[3] Article 67 TEC.

Federal Office for the Recognition of Foreign Refugees (*Bundesamt für die Anerkennung ausländischer Flüchtlinge*) had to delay the implementation of the Council Decision establishing the European Refugee Fund[4] because the necessary co-decision procedure with the Länder had not yet been defined and legally codified.

The Europeanization of justice and home affairs has met some opposition within the ministries, the law-enforcement agencies and the judiciary. At the time EU justice and home affairs co-operation developed a new dynamism in the first half of the 1990s, the Federal Interior Ministry was one of the most inward-looking of the whole ministerial bureaucracy in Bonn. Whereas most other ministries had been involved in intense co-operation with their EU counterparts for many years, the comparative neglect of justice and home affairs in the integration process until then had prevented the Interior Ministry from developing a similar culture of co-operation. A telling detail is the fact that in preparation for entry into force of the Maastricht Treaty—which introduced third pillar co-operation—the Ministry felt obliged to introduce extensive language training for officials likely to be engaged in the new co-operation structures. The situation in the Federal Ministry of Justice was slightly better, because of decades of involvement in Council of Europe negotiations, but even there the rapid growth of EU justice and home affairs brought a change of culture that was not universally appreciated by officials.

The extraordinary pace of developments at EU level raised concerns not only in the ministries, but also in the police forces, the Federal Border Guard, and the judiciary. They centred on an insufficient consideration of the likely implications of certain measures taken in Brussels for internal German legislation, law enforcement, judicial procedures, and aspects of internal security. In the early years of Europol, there were also widespread concerns among German police forces about adequate data protection when sharing sensitive data with their European counterparts. Senior officials tried to restrain rather than encourage ministers when it came to new initiatives in the Council, and the ambitious agenda set by the Tampere European Council in October 1999 has been received with more misgivings than enthusiasm within the ministries.

In this context, one should also not underestimate the impact of the generally rather conservative-minded legal establishment. The opposition of the German delegation to the full abolition of the principle of double criminality in the negotiations on the introduction of the European Arrest Warrant—one of the measures of the anti-terrorism action plan adopted in response to the 11 September attacks—was due to the orthodox position taken on this issue by senior German lawyers. The same can be said about German opposition to higher minimum penalties in the negotiations on the Framework Decision on combating terrorism,

---

[4] *Official Journal of the European Communities* 2000 No. L 252.

which was finally adopted in December 2001. It is fair to add, however, that this sort of difficulty in engaging in full-scale Europeanization of justice and home affairs on the part of administrative and legal establishments is a widespread phenomenon in other member states, motivated by legal conservatism and the unwillingness to consider deviations from established national rules and practices.

The 'Downloading' Dimension of Europeanization

Despite the reluctance of ministries, law-enforcement agencies, and the judiciary fully to support the process of Europeanization of their domains, they have not escaped its effects. Because of the enormous widening of the European agenda, the emergence of a considerable number of new EU Council committees and working groups, and more and more EC and EU legislative initiatives which need to be dealt with,[5] hundreds of officials are now involved in the European process on a regular basis. This involvement has increased their understanding of the different situations in other member states, and of the requirements, potential, and limits of co-operation and harmonization. Both the Ministry of the Interior and the Ministry of Justice have become 'normal' Europeanized ministries in the sense that they have all established special European units for the evaluation and the horizontal co-ordination of cross-sectoral European questions. This is particularly true for the Ministry of the Interior, which has set up European units in each of its major divisions, with two out of eight units of the division dealing with aliens' and asylum issues having a distinctly European set of tasks.[6] Special European units have also been set up in the Länder ministries, and both the Bundesrat and the *Innen- und Justizministerkonferenz* of the Länder have developed effective scrutiny and deliberation procedures for EU justice and home affairs. For the law-enforcement agencies, co-operation with other EU partners and involvement in the new European structures have also become a matter of routine, although there are still complaints about lengthy procedures and lack of efficiency of cross-border co-operation.[7]

The impact of Europeanization on German national legislation is more limited. This is partly to be explained by the fact that most of the decisions taken at EU level until 1999 were of a non-binding character and left wide margins of discretion to national implementation. Since 1999, an increasing number of binding EC and EU legislation has been adopted, but these, too, tend to provide a margin of discretion, and most of them are still in the process of being implemented. Yet, there are some cases in which Europeanization has clearly had an impact. One of

---

[5] In 2001, the Council adopted no less than ninety-nine texts, most of which were legally binding.
[6] Referat A 6 *'Europäische Harmonisierung'* and Referat A7 *'Zwischenstaatliche Innenthemen der Ständigen Vertretung Bundesrepublik Deutschland bei der EU'*.
[7] For the case of the Federal Border Guard see Rippert (2001: 104–7).

the most notable examples is the new German nationality law, which entered into force on 1 January 2001. The new nationality law retains for the first time an element of *ius soli*. It breaks with the traditional German emphasis on the *ius sanguinis* by providing that children of foreigners born in Germany may acquire German nationality if one of their parents has been a legal resident for at least eight years or has been in the possession of an unlimited residence permit for at least three years. This change was brought about by a recognized need to facilitate the acquisition of German nationality by the children of long-term residents. It was also prompted by an effort to bring German nationality law closer to the EU mainstream and notably to the French nationality law. This was seen as an important step towards a common EU approach to immigration.

However, the EU dimension played only a marginal role in the intense political debate on the new German Law on Immigration (*Zuwanderungsgesetz*), which finally passed the Bundesrat with difficulty on 22 March 2002.[8] In this important new law, the EU level has to be taken into account only where—because of an existing EC/EU *acquis*—this is legally inevitable, such as in the case of the rules on granting temporary protection and on the recognition of readmission decisions. Very little effort has been made in the Immigration Law to facilitate a compromise at EU level on difficult issues such as family reunification, where Germany has been among the least flexible EU member states.

Another example of the impact of EU justice and home affairs integration can be found in the current reform efforts of the German government in the area of criminal procedure. One of the cornerstones of these reform efforts is the improvement of victim protection. In April 2001, the Federal Ministry of Justice published an explanatory memorandum on the intended reforms in which it explicitly referred to the EU Framework Decision on the standing of victims in criminal proceedings[9] as one of the reasons for the necessary changes to existing German legislation (Bundesministerium der Justiz 2001: 1–2). Characteristically, however, this was given as the last of a series of reasons.

During the debate on the Law on Civil Procedure Reform (*Zivilprozessreformgesetz*), which entered into force on 1 January 2002, the Federal government also mentioned the new tasks for courts of first instance resulting from the harmonization efforts at EU level as one of the reasons for the structural reorganization of key areas of civil procedure.[10] An SPD paper made it clear that the elimination of the value-based restrictions on access to appellate remedies in civil proceedings through the reform act was partially inspired by

---

[8] Gesetz zur Steuerung und Begrenzung der Zuwanderung und zur Regelung des Aufenthalts und der Integration von Unionsbürgern und Ausländern (Zuwanderungsgesetz), Bundesrats-Drucksache No. 157 of 1 March 2002.

[9] *Official Journal of the European Communities* 2001 No. L 82.

[10] Deutscher Bundestag, 14. Legislaturperiode, Drucksache 14/4722.

the absence of such restrictions in other EU states. But here, again, the European dimension was cited only at the end of the respective section (SPD-Fraktion, Arbeitgruppe Rechtspolitik 2001).

Apart from the penetration of public administration and—to a much more limited extent—legislation by EU justice and home affairs, there is little evidence in Germany of a significant Europeanization of these areas. Party programmes, media reports and the political debate about key issues of justice and home affairs contain few, if any, references to the European dimension which—since the Treaty of Amsterdam—has been elevated to a major treaty objective under the ringing title of an 'area of freedom, justice and security'. Whenever major justice and home affairs issues come up, the political debate about them tends to be an almost purely national one, with the European dimension being notably absent. A striking example was the major debate over the move towards a new positive approach towards immigration, which started with the 'green card' issue in 2000. The development of a common asylum system and common action on a range of immigration aspects are firmly on the EU agenda since the Tampere European Council. But the European level was almost completely absent in this domestic debate, and the proposed new German law on immigration was developed in 'splendid isolation' from other EU partners, who were presented with a *fait accompli*. In the 320-page report submitted in 2001 by the independent Commission on Immigration, chaired by Professor Rita Süssmuth, which consti-tutes the most substantial evaluation of the immigration situation commissioned by any German government so far, the EU dimension was mentioned for the first time—and rather briefly—on page 176 (Bundesministerium des Innern 2001). It seems that the impact of the rapidly growing EU justice and home affairs agenda on the national setting has so far remained limited. It has applied to cases where either this has been absolutely inevitable because of existing or newly adopted EU decisions, or where the EU dimension could be invoked as a convenient additional—albeit never primary—reason for changes at the national level.

What are the reasons for this overall rather limited Europeanization of justice and home affairs? One is clearly that EU justice and home affairs is still a rather new area of EU policy-making, which has acquired a significant legislative dimension only over the last few years. The media, economic, and social interest groups and other societal actors may just be in the process of realizing that in this area something quite significant is happening at the European level. The primary responsibility for raising public awareness should be with the federal govern-ment, the political parties, and the Länder governments, but none of them has made any major effort to bring the European dimension into the public domain. Successive German governments have limited themselves to bringing domestic problems onto the EU agenda whenever politically desirable and feasible, with-out really attempting to invoke the EU dimension of justice and home affairs in the domestic context—with the temporary exception of asylum policy at the beginning of the 1990s. Political parties have been happy to continue treating justice and home affairs as primarily national issues, being fully aware that asylum, immigration, and internal security have a strong vote-winning potential in national elections. In this respect, little is to be gained from making these evaporate into the blue European sky.

All this has not helped in accelerating changes in the rather conservative attitude of the practitioners of justice and home affairs, i.e., ministry officials, judges, prosecutors, lawyers, police officers, and border guards. While accepting the need for some action at European level, most of them continue to think that 'the politicians' are moving far too fast with the construction of the 'area of freedom, security and justice'. Additional efforts and a considerable amount of time will be needed to change mentalities amongst those who are the primary agents of implementing of EU justice and home affairs. A useful step in this direction are some of the proposals on the new draft law on the reform of the education of lawyers (*Gesetz zur Reform der Juristenausbildung*), currently under deliberation in both chambers of the German parliament. It places a greater emphasis on mandatory education and training of lawyers in European legal issues, potentially including even a mandatory minimum study time at another EU university.[11] A better knowledge of the legal systems of other EU member states and of the growing EU justice and home affairs *acquis* could certainly help with the Europeanization of the next generation of judges, prosecutors and practising lawyers.

The 'Uploading' Dimension of Europeanization

The previous sections have already provided some evidence of a certain imbalance between the 'uploading' and 'downloading' dimensions of the Europeanization of justice and home affairs in the German case. The full extent of this imbalance becomes clear if one looks at some of the many cases in which Germany has tried—quite often with some success—to bring domestic preferences in justice and home affairs onto the European agenda.

By the second half of the 1980s, Germany played a key role in the development of the wide range of 'compensatory measures' adopted in the context of the Schengen system to reduce potential internal security risks resulting from the abolition of internal border controls. As a 'frontline' state, successive German governments regarded tight external border controls as an absolute priority, and the quite extensive and sophisticated Schengen *acquis* on external border controls—now part of the EC/EU *acquis*—has been to a very considerable extent influenced by German standards and priorities.

---

[11] See the explanatory statement of the draft law introduced by the SPD/Bündnis 90/Die Grünen parliamentary groups on 26 September 2001 (Deutscher Bundestag, 14. Wahlperiode, Drucksache 14/7176), pp. 12 and 14.

German preferences and priorities have also been brought in a quite significant way into the justice and home affairs dimension of the EU enlargement process. These stem from concerns about increased internal security risks that might result from ineffective external border controls, organizational and capability problems, and corruption in the future central and east European member states. They prompted Germany to work successfully for the incorporation of the entire Schengen *acquis* into the EU—which makes it part of the *acquis* that the candidate countries have to adopt. It has also insisted on a very strict application of Schengen rules by the future member states and their tight monitoring in this respect before accession. Germany was one of the driving forces behind the setting up in 1998 of the Council's 'Collective Evaluation Group' on the justice and home affairs situation in the applicant states. Its confidential reports have since then highlighted—often in a much more critical way than the Commission's 'Progress Reports'—a range of problems in many of the applicant states. They have included such sensitive areas as border control, the fight against organized crime and illegal immigration, corruption, and shortcomings in data processing and modern search equipment. Germany is also clearly at the forefront of those Schengen states that have insisted that this *acquis* be non-negotiable[12] and that Schengen external border controls towards the new member states should be unlikely to be lifted on accession.

The internal security implications of enlargement are also the primary reason for the German government's backing for the idea of introducing a common European border guard. According to Otto Schily, such a common border guard would not leave responsibility for the new external EU borders, 'in whose security we are also interested' to the new member states.[13] Unsurprisingly, German experts—particularly from the *Bundesgrenzschutz*—played a leading role in drawing up the 'Feasibility Study to Set up a European Border Police', which was presented to the special Ministerial Conference organized in Rome on 30 May 2002[14] and which reflected to a considerable extent German experiences and preoccupations.

All this constitutes a clear case of EU structures and opportunities for action being used to satisfy specific domestic political interests, which Germany—as a state bordering on applicants for membership—has in protecting against illegal immigration and cross-border crime.

[12] Giving evidence on 5 July 2000 before Sub-Committee F of the European Union Committee of the House of Lords, Dr Gerald Lehnguth, *Ministerialdirektor* at the German Ministry of the Interior, declared that it was the German position that 'there can be no dropping of security standards and that the newcomers must keep to the standards laid down by the old members' and that 'no exceptions can be made for any particular country' (House of Lords Select Committee on the European Union: Enlargement and EU External Frontier Controls, Session 1999–2000, 17th Report, October 2000, Minutes of evidence, para. 270–271).

[13] Bettina Vestring, 'Schily für europäische Grenzpolizei', *Berliner Zeitung* 16 March 2001.

[14] Council document No. 9834/02, 11 June 2002.

As already mentioned, it was to a considerable extent the enormous increase in the number of asylum applications that in 1990–1 that made the German government emerge as the protagonist of the introduction of justice and home affairs into the Treaty on European Union. It advocated a communitarization of asylum policy even at that early stage (Mazzuchelli 1997: 147–8). Against the background of an increasingly bitter internal debate about the asylum problem, the German government had a clear domestic interest in common European restrictive measures. The Dublin Convention of 1997,[15] which is intended to prevent multiple asylum applications by allowing only one member state to examine an application, is the most prominent example. While EU action in this area fell short of initial expectations, the German government played a major role in keeping the asylum issue high on the Union's agenda throughout most of the 1990s. It was key to securing the communitarization of substantial elements of asylum policy through the Treaty of Amsterdam in 1997.

The strong German interest in a burden-sharing between EU member states in asylum and refugee policy is directly linked to the asylum issue and to the fact that—especially in the second half of the 1990s—Germany had to cope with a disproportionate share of the refugee flows resulting from the wars in former Yugoslavia. This has been a constant priority of the Federal government since the early years of the Third Pillar. The central motive was, again, that of reducing pressure on the domestic system through a system of national quotas or financial compensation. Germany failed in its attempts to secure agreement on a comprehensive burden-sharing mechanism. But its insistence—backed by other member states facing high numbers in this area, such as Austria and Italy—played a key role in the adoption in 1999 of the Joint Action on practical support in relation to the reception and voluntary repatriation of refugees, displaced persons, and asylum seekers.[16] It allowed, for the first time, EC funding of refugee policy measures in areas such as the improvement of reception infrastructures, legal assistance and counselling services, and basic standards of living conditions. German influence was also apparent in the Council decision of 2000 on the establishment of a European Refugee Fund,[17] which earmarked 216 million Euro for refugee support measures until 2004.

The leading role played by Germany in the establishment and development of Europol is another example of the 'uploading' dimension of the Europeanization of justice and home affairs. At the beginning of the 1990s, the creation of a European police office was seen by Chancellor Helmut Kohl as the basis for development of a sort of European FBI. It was regarded as a necessary response to new threats of cross-border crime, most of which were related to the massive

---

[15] *Official Journal of the European Communities* 1997 C No. 254.
[16] 1999/290/JHA.
[17] *Official Journal of the European Communities* 2000 No. L 252.

rise of organized crime in Russia and some central and east European countries after the transition. The existing forms of bilateral and multilateral police co-operation between the EU member states were no longer considered sufficient for meeting Germany's needs in its exposed position. The strong German support of, and influence on, Europol—its first and so far only director, Jürgen Storbeck, is a German national and Germany still supplies close to 50 per cent of the data received by Europol—have to some extent also to be seen as an attempted 'system export'. In its position—though not yet powers—*vis-à-vis* national police forces, Europol comes fairly close to the central agency model represented by the German *Bundeskriminalamt*. Germany has also looked more favourably than most of the other member states on the idea of granting operational powers to Europol which is clearly a case of trying to 'export' a national preference and model.

These are only a few major examples from a much longer list of cases of Germany 'uploading' its domestic preferences and models to EU justice and home affairs. Germany has played a key role in creating this new arena of European policy-making that the 'area of freedom, security and justice' has become, and has clearly been using it in several respects to serve specific domestic policy interests.

Conclusion

The general conclusion to be drawn from this brief analysis of Europeanization of justice and home affairs in Germany is that these areas have been much less Europeanized at the national level than Germany's previously leading role at EU level might lead one to expect. Germany has been quite active—and in some cases, such as Schengen and Europol, also at least partially successful—in trying to 'upload' domestic preferences and models to the European level. But Europeanization has remained very much a government-led and controlled process with hardly any impact on public opinion and society. The 'downloading' has been largely limited to selective legislative changes as a result of the growing EC/EU *acquis* and to the enhanced involvement of public administration and law-enforcement agencies in European co-operation procedures and structures. There are several reasons for this imbalance between the 'uploading' and 'downloading' dimensions of Europeanization in justice and home affairs. With the exception of a few issues, the political establishment has shown a fairly limited interest in the Europeanization of internal security issues that are still considered as valuable national vote winners. Another factor is the recent development and the lack of transparency of EU justice and home affairs. Finally, this sector is characterized by the conservatism of 'practitioners' in ministries, courts, and law-enforcement agencies.

Although the importance of the Europeanization of parts of the German state should not be underestimated, the absence of a wider Europeanization of state and society makes German participation in the further development of EU justice and home affairs unduly dependent on changes in government policy and priorities. The Schröder government has made little effort to bring the European dimension into current national debates about justice and home affairs issues, such as the major national debate on immigration in 2000 and 2001. In addition, many Länder governments have voiced more concerns than enthusiasm over developments at the European level. In consequence, Germany has over the last few years played a less active role in the development of EU justice and home affairs than previously under the old third pillar. It seems that, if the federal government does not play the Europeanization card, nobody else can or is willing to do so. If one divides member states in the Council into 'floggers' and 'hangers,'[18] Germany is currently—with a few exceptions such as the idea of a common European border guard—clearly more among the 'hangers' of progress in EU justice and home affairs. This has been shown again in the negotiations on the European arrest warrant and the framework decision on combating terrorism following the events of 11 September 2001. This could well deprive it of some of the opportunities to actively shape the further construction of the 'area of freedom, security and justice'. It would not be a small price to pay for a Europeanization of justice and home affairs, which has remained too much at the surface of state and society.

---

[18] A characterization which the author owes to a senior official of the Council of the European Union.

16

Foreign and Security Policy:
On the Cusp Between Transformation
and Accommodation

ALISTER MISKIMMON & WILLIAM E. PATERSON

Introduction

COMPARATIVISTS ARE CONGENITALLY SUSPICIOUS of arguments that appear to rely on a claimed singularity for a particular state or sector. Singularities do occur, however, and the situation of the Federal Republic in foreign and security policy prior to 1989–90 was undoubtedly singular. In terms of traditional power resources, it was by the 1980s clearly one of Europe's leading states. This was, however, often less important than the constraints associated with its semi-sovereign status and its associated vulnerabilities, most especially West Berlin. Its semi-sovereign status and the proximity to a shaming past had led successive governments to adopt a policy of exaggerated or reflexive multilateralism and to define its external goals in terms of shared European, rather than specifically national, interests. This European vocation was flanked by a constitutionally anchored commitment to overcoming German division and a predominant NATO/Atlanticist orientation in security policy.

The restoration of full sovereignty in October 1990 might have been expected to end Germany's singularity. But the consistent success of the external policy of the old Federal Republic, which had culminated in a new unified state 'encircled by friends', encouraged the maintenance of the semi-sovereign multilateral *mentalité* of the political class, and restored sovereignty was associated initially with deeper multilateralism. (Paterson 1996).

If the policy choices of the immediate post-unity years had persisted, we would be dealing in the foreign and security policy areas with a relatively uncomplicated narrative of Europeanization in which the new Germany would have been singular, primarily in its zeal and shaping capacity (Goetz 1996; Bulmer, Jeffery and Paterson 2000). Yet, over a longer time perspective, the picture is more complicated, more dichotomous. The discourse and to some extent the practice of Europeanization persists and it remains the reflexive mode of the Foreign Ministry (*Auswärtiges Amt*). In contrast to the Foreign and Commonwealth

Proceedings of the British Academy, **119**, 325–345. © The British Academy 2003.

Office and the Quai D'Orsay, the German Foreign Ministry does not have a history of several hundred years of defending national sovereignty. It was re-established in 1951 within an already existing multilateral context. Therefore, adaptation within German foreign and security policy has taken place under different conditions from France and the UK. Alongside this and slowly gathering strength, there is a discourse of normalization culminating in Chancellor Schröder's October 2001 Bundestag speeches (Hyde-Price and Jeffery 2001). This chapter focuses on the Common Foreign and Security Policy (CFSP), the policy area most likely to demonstrate Europeanization in German foreign and security policy.

Europeanization as a Conceptual Framework of Analysis

This chapter assesses the extent to which the EU has exerted adaptational pressures on German foreign and security policy-making. While there has been an erosion of separate notions of foreign policy as argued by much constructivist thought, harmonization of foreign and security policy within the EU is very incomplete, despite the moves towards the interwovenness of national policies since the 1970s. In order to answer this question a study of international relations will not be sufficient to analyse the complexities of Germany's security policy. This study examines domestic and EU policy-making structures and practices that impact on Germany's attitudes towards CFSP in order to assess the extent to which German policy-makers have gone through a process of rethinking policies and institutions.

The Europeanization literature deals with the effect of the integration process on the national level (Börzel and Risse 2000; Bulmer and Burch 2001; Green Cowles, Caporaso and Risse 2001; Hix and Goetz 2000; Knill 2001; Kohler-Koch and Knodt 2000; Ladrech 1994; Radaelli 2000; Torreblanca 2001). How can the concept of Europeanization be applied to the study of German institutional adaptation in light of the growing role of the EU as an international force? De la Serre (1988) concluded that member states benefited from collective foreign policy endeavours without the need for major national adaptation. Alternatively, Smith (1997; 2000) argues that there has been considerable adaptation. In turn, can Europeanization successfully encapsulate the impact of how Germany has influenced CFSP policy through its involvement in the EU?

The extent to which a member state can influence the policy-making process will impact on the Europeanization of domestic institutions and policy-making. Bomberg and Peterson (2000: 1) state:

> European integration shapes domestic policies, politics and polities, but member states also 'project themselves' by seeking to shape the trajectory of European integration in ways that suit national interests.

Crucially, Germany does not passively comply with EU legislation, but seeks to place its imprint on the course of European integration (Bulmer 1997). This has been very evident in EU foreign policy where Germany has often been at the fore-front of calls for deeper integration of national policies, fulfilling its well-practised role as 'model pupil' (*Musterknabe*) of the EU integration project. As Bulmer, Jeffery and Paterson (2000) posit, Germany's diplomacy in Europe has been driven by its strategy and national interest in seeking to shape its surround-ing milieu. The projection of German ideas and interests within the EU has not, however, extended to the ability to decisively shape policy direction in EPC (European Political Co-Operation)/CFSP. This is in stark contrast to Germany's ability to shape the negotiations on EMU using the Bundesbank in an advanced form of institutional export (Dyson and Featherstone 1999).

Europeanization is, therefore, a challenge to intergovernmentalism and bounded national sovereignty (Favell 1998: 1). However, member states may contribute to the process of Europeanization through an institutional and/or ideational 'export' of their domestic norms and practices. European policies are essentially an amalgam of policy proposals presented by a wide array of actors. Here the German imprint has been most clearly visible in the ideational export in matters concerning CFSP. Pedersen's 'co-operative hegemony' thesis (1998) is an excellent portrayal of the Franco-German efforts to co-ordinate policy proposals bilaterally, before exporting their ideas to the EU level. Germany, predominantly in tandem with France, has sought to suggest the way forward for CFSP, for example, Eurocorps or common European defence.

Wessels' 'fusion thesis' posits the impact of the EU on national polities (Wessels and Rometsch 1996; see also Hanf and Soetendorp 1998). This identi-fies the deep impact that the EU has on national policies and which should be clearly noticeable in the case of Germany and the CFSP. A state's capacity to co-ordinate its aims and policies within the European Union, 'vary[s] considerably, depending on the mix of ideological ambition, institutional capacity and political constraints' (Wright 1996: 149). An examination of German policy-makers on a cross-ministerial comparison will, therefore, pinpoint the ideological conditions, institutional capacity and political constraints affecting Germany's CFSP policy.

Ladrech's initial formulation of the concept of Europeanization states that it is an

> Incremental process re-orienting the direction and shape of politics to the degree that EC political and economic dynamics become part of the organizational logic of national politics and policy-making. (Ladrech 1994: 69)

In the case of Germany and the impact of the EC/EU on foreign and security policy, it is difficult to assess the extent to which there has been a reorientation of Germany's policy-making. From the very beginning, West Germany based its for-eign policy around an intensely multilateral rationale, in an attempt to reintegrate itself both into the international environment and into its interwoven institutional landscape. Aspects of domestic discourse and identities are significant here in tracing the impact of the EU on Germany's foreign and security policy—and vice versa. Within Germany, policy discourse reinforces Germany's CFSP preferences; it does not challenge policy élites. The singularity of this sectorized policy was clear, for instance, at Maastricht, when public opinion was firmly behind policy areas in which Germany did not go far enough and opposed policy sectors, such as EMU, where Kohl sought to push forward.

There remain considerable obstacles to the comprehensive Europeanization of German foreign and security policy (Schmidt 1999). Most significantly, talk of a communitarization of foreign and security policy is considered anathema within German policy élites. While moves to further strengthen co-operation among the fifteen member states in foreign and security policy would be welcomed by Germany, any moves towards weakening the intergovernmental basis of such co-operation, especially in terms of military deployment, would be opposed by German policy élites.[1]

The process of Europeanization does not always prescribe concrete templates for domestic adaptation to European developments. A large degree of flexibility is in evidence. Olsen states that:

> European level developments do not dictate specific forms of institutional adaptation but leave considerable discretion to domestic actors and institutions. There are significant impacts, yet the actual ability of the European level to penetrate domestic institutions is not perfect, universal, or constant. Adaptation reflects variations in European pressure as well as domestic motivations and abilities to act. European signals are interpreted and modified through domestic traditions, institutions, identities and resources in ways that limit the degree of convergence and homogenization. (Olsen 2002: 23)

Nowhere is this more the case than in foreign and security policy. The singular strategic cultures of the EU member states define the realms of the possible in terms of the ability and scope to adapt to EU-level institutional change (Cornish and Edwards 2001; Longhurst 2000). The domestic 'traditions, institutions and identities' referred to by Olsen are framing conditions for the degree of institutional and policy adaptation at the German level.

---

[1] Interviews conducted in Berlin and London, 2001. The SPD launched a series of bilateral meetings with Social Democratic sister parties across Europe. Central to the conclusions of the SPD were that the parliamentary aspect of the CFSP process should be strengthened, the institutional relationships within CFSP should be clarified, there should be a phased plan for a communitarized European foreign policy, crisis management and conflict prevention should be strengthened, a common defence and arms export policy and the integration of a common European deployment co-operation policy within CFSP should be developed; SPD Bundestagsfraktion, *Die Zukunft der GASP: Sozialdemokratische Perspektiven für die 'Gemeinsame Außen- und Sicherheitspolitik' der Europäischen Union*, Berlin, December 2000.

Europeanization in the field of foreign and security policy has been associated with a number of dynamics and beliefs. It implies the move by EU member states towards regarding the EU as a key actor for foreign and security policy-making, with the implied pooling of collective resources that this entails. Europeanization has also been driven by the desire to achieve EU solutions to European problems. This has resulted in the realization of the need to co-ordinate better militarily and the willingness to consider some supranational organization to achieve foreign and security policy goals. A good example is the development of the EU's conflict prevention policy (European Parliament 2001; Lalumiere 2000; Secretary General/High Representative 2000; Swedish Presidency 2001).

While the dynamics driving Europeanization in foreign and security policy as outlined above infer commitments to co-operate, they have not, until the post-1998 developments, inferred heavy costs. However, the development of CFSP/CESDP (Common European Security and Defence Policy) has necessitated the willingness among the member states to consider some degree of policy adaptation/learning, as they seek to act as a more credible and effective international actor. Looking at the degree of policy adaptation and policy learning within EU member states can pinpoint the extent to which they have committed themselves to making the EU a truly effective international force to be reckoned with.

Applying Europeanization to Foreign and Security Policy

Applying Europeanization to German foreign and security policy comes up against a number of puzzles. On the formal side of the EU's CFSP/CESDP, co-operation and co-ordination exist, rather than 'integration' in the purest sense of the word. There are a number of reasons. Firstly, the 'pillar' structure of the Treaty on European Union means that the European Court of Justice does not have jurisdiction over the second pillar, CFSP/CESDP (Winn and Lord 2001). Therefore, compliance in this policy area is not enforceable. Treaties, not legislation, govern CFSP/CESDP.[2] However, Smith (2001) argues that one can regard CFSP as a legal regime owing to the fact that the member states often act as though they are subject to legal guidelines. Secondly, foreign and security policy

---

[2] For example, the Preamble to the Single European Act stated, 'Aware of the responsibility incumbent upon Europe to aim at speaking ever increasingly with one voice and to act with consistency and solidarity in order more effectively to protect its common interests and independence, in particular to display the principles of democracy and compliance with the law and with human rights to which they are attached, so that together they make their own contribution to the preservation of international peace and security in accordance with the undertaking entered into by them with the framework of the United States Charter.', The Single European Act, Preamble, 17 February 1986. Although this section of the text seeks to bring co-operation within foreign policy among the member states, the framing of this aim is loose and offers flexibility. While the Treaty on European Union increased the degree of co-operation among the EU member states (Articles J1–J13), a large degree of flexibility remains.

remains one of the most jealously guarded areas of government policy and national sovereignty. Finally, it is clear that each member state has contrasting, and sometimes conflicting, foreign policy traditions that impact on policy preferences, policy style and *Weltanschauung*. There does not yet exist an accepted 'logic' of foreign and security policy. Taking into account national positions when analysing CFSP remains key to the understanding of how CFSP/CESDP has developed.

In the aftermath of the Second World War, West Germany sought to reintegrate itself into the international system through a policy of multilateralism. The establishment of the Western European Union (WEU) and attempts to create the European Defence Community (EDC) were early manifestations (Haftendorn 2001: 31–8). The clear paradox of the German situation in the post-unification period is that, on regaining full-sovereignty, Kohl consistently sought to deepen European integration. This has been part of an overall strategy of balancing *Selbstbehauptung* (self-assertion) with *Selbstbeschränkung* (self-limitation) (Haftendorn 2001).

The structural aspects of external semi-sovereignty disappeared with German unity. Semi-sovereignty persisted externally as a *mentalité* in the Franco–German relationship and informally in the semi-sovereign institutions, with the crucial exception of the Bundesbank. Indeed, through institutional export, German institutions were sometimes projected onto the European level. In other areas, the thrust was in the other direction of continued Europeanization. CFSP and security policy more widely are located at the executive level and are not constrained by domestic institutions of semi-sovereignty. Change is, therefore, along the axis of Europeanization.

A final issue concerning Europeanization and foreign and security policy is that the EU and its member states do not exist in a vacuum. They are actors in a highly integrated and sophisticated international environment. It is, in consequence, difficult in some cases to attribute national foreign and security policy adaptation solely to EU dynamics—often these pressures for change have originated from NATO, for example. Many of the adaptational pressures that have impacted on Germany stem from Germany's concern to balance its commitments to the EU with those to the Organisation for Security and Co-operation in Europe (OSCE), the United Nations and NATO (NATO 1999*a*, 1999*b*). Indeed, the major leaps forward in CFSP since 1998 have taken place parallel to developments in NATO. Both of these processes have sought to be mutually reinforcing rather than competing exercises.

These developments have come about as a result of equipping NATO to meet the new challenges of the post-Cold War environment. However, there has also been a discernible 'Europeanization' of NATO. The major debates within NATO and the EU during the 1990s have centred on how NATO's European states might increase their influence without weakening the cohesion of the alliance (Albright

1998; Miskimmon 2001; North Atlantic Council Summit 1999; North Atlantic Council 1999; Robertson 1999). The desire on the part of European NATO members to have a greater say has led in part to the EU developing autonomous military capabilities. The Washington Summit in 1999 with the agreement on the so-called 'Berlin Plus' decision was a key moment in codifying the relationship between NATO and the EU in light of these new capabilities. This chapter addresses the areas where the EU has impacted in a discernible way on Germany's foreign and security policy. In this way, we isolate the 'EU effect' on foreign and security policy-making within Germany.

The Dimension of 'Downloading': German Foreign and Security Policy as a Case of Policy Adaptation

As already stated, Europeanization seeks to assess the extent to which the EU has impacted on national policies. Smith (2000) posits four key areas of national adaptation to CFSP, as a means to systematically assess policy change. By applying Smith's four expressions of domestic adaptation to EU foreign policy, it is possible to determine the extent to which Germany's security policy has developed over the course of the 1990s and to pinpoint some additional aspects of Europeanization. Smith argues that élite socialization, bureaucratic reorganization, constitutional change, and the increase in public support for European political co-operation will be the most visible indicators of domestic policy and institutional adaptation (see Figure 16.1).

Élite socialization is one of the defining characteristics of the CFSP process. Sjursen (1998: 17) asserts that 'The internalisation of a European dimension of foreign policy is most advanced and explicit in Germany where it forms part of the overall strategy of reflexive multilateralism'. Hill and Wallace (1996: 6) have noted the 'transformationalist effects' that the interaction between policy-makers on the EU level has had on traditional foreign policy-making practices. Glarbo (1999) persuasively argues that diplomats do not become blindly socialized through interaction with diplomats from other states, but rather are constantly weighing up national and European foreign policies. The process of internalization of international norms and procedures can best take place under conditions of structural or procedural asymmetry (Schimmelfennig 2000). The socialization and internalization of EU foreign and security policy within Germany can be viewed as stemming from the asymmetry of EU member states' security capabilities, leading German policy-makers to favour involvement in EPC/CFSP. Germany has gained significantly through its involvement in CFSP, which emerged from a process of socialization within EC frameworks, leading to greater co-operation in this field. It is important to note that socialization is not a result of greater co-operation, but rather, 'is a process, not an outcome. Socialisation does not, by definition, have to be successful. If it is, it

	German European Council and WEU Presidencies
Elite socialization	New government had little time to adjust to pressures of foreign and security policy dilemmas in the Balkans — came to accept intervention on the basis of German 'responsibility' — conceptual shift.
Bureaucratic organization	The introduction of the PSC, EUMC, EUMS has altered the form of security policy co-ordination and development. PSC has taken away role of EUKOR from Berlin — now co-ordination undertaken by Brussels Ambassador. (Interviews in Berlin, 2001) *Bundeswehrreform.* Establishment of the Human rights and humanitarian assistance section in the *Auswärtiges Amt* under Gerd Poppe (Fischer's decision) — No equivalent in London or Paris.
Constitutional change/legislative adaptation	Constitutional change in the broadest sense due to the impact of the Cologne, Helsinki, and Feira Declarations and with the impact of the Treaty of Nice on the German political system (should it be ratified). This has also been in the context of the Federal Constitutional Court's decisions to sanction the deployment of the Bundeswehr throughout the course of the 1990s. Establishment of a Bundestag European Committee for European Affairs as a result of the domestic German debate during the IGC 1990/1991 (Art.45, BL).
Adaptation of public opinion	Signs that the German public is moving towards grudging acceptance of Bundeswehr involvement in EU 'Petersberg Task' missions — but still only if it is clear that all diplomatic avenues have been explored. Importance of a Conflict Prevention (CP)-type foreign policy. With the development of the ERRF in the future, Germany's pressing for a CP-oriented CESDP approach may become all the more important in light of continued German reluctance to develop a military interventionist security policy. Minimalist versus maximalist approaches to CESDP/ERRF. General support for the creation of a European Army, but not a leading role within such a venture (Rattinger 1994).

Figure 16.1.   Adaptation of German foreign and security policy under CFSP/CESDP.

results in the actor's internalisation of beliefs and practices' (Schimmelfennig 2000: 112).

In terms of bureaucratic reorganization, the introduction of the Political Security Committee (COPS), the EU Military Committee (EUMC), and the EU Military Staff (EUMS) has affected the role of the Foreign Ministry in the co-ordination of CFSP policy (Interviews, Foreign Ministry, Berlin 2001). The potential of COPS to be a powerful forum for formulating CFSP/CESDP policy by bringing together political and military experts will be an important factor in the development of the EU's capabilities. The introduction of the EUMS and the EUMC may also raise the profile of the Defence Ministry (for wider trends in German European policy-making see Bulmer, Maurer and Paterson 2001).

Constitutional change took place in Germany throughout the course of the 1990s. Germany's international commitments have increasingly come into opposition with constitutional brakes from the pre-unification period. Most significantly, the Federal Constitutional Court's decision of 12 July 1994 to allow the use of the Bundeswehr in 'out-of-area' missions has extensively increased the range of operations and commitments in which Germany may become involved. The constitutional change that has taken place concerning security and defence policy is an example of wider international developments impacting on Germany's role within CFSP. This has had 'knock-on' effects for Germany as the EU attempts to work out the operational scope of any future European Rapid Reaction Force (ERRF) missions. Constitutional shifts have also taken place in a less specific sense. The constant process of refining the EU treaties has impacted on the German polity. One manifestation of this was the decision to establish a Committee for European Affairs in the Bundestag in order better to scrutinize the snowballing raft of EU legislation (Article 45, Basic Law of the Federal Republic of Germany; see Saalfeld, Chapter 4 in this volume).

There are signs that German public opinion is becoming more at ease with the thought of Germany participating more fully in CFSP, even to the extent of a reluctant acceptance of the need to sanction the use of the Bundeswehr in future Petersberg Tasks (Bundesverteidigungsministerium 2001). This comes with the reservation that the German public and also policy élites are insistent on the need to exhaust all diplomatic avenues before military intervention is sanctioned. Germany favours a conflict prevention approach to the development of CFSP, which is mirrored in its minimalist views on CESDP/ERRF/Petersberg Tasks. Clearly, there is a major paradox here. German public and élite opinion has been consistently in favour of developing CFSP. Germany supports the idea, but has misgivings about the implementation and the implications of such a policy relating to the need for a potentially much wider deployment of the German armed forces. While public opinion is firmly behind Germany's stance on CFSP, it does not act as a dynamic driving force behind the project. No sectoral interest or domestic institution exists to press the government to make progress in CFSP. As a consequence, public opinion may act as a blessing and a curse for the Foreign Ministry, as it seeks to generate momentum for German CFSP policy.

Policy adaptation in the German political system takes place under considerable institutional constraints. Katzenstein (1987) has stated that 'Divergent interests are brought together through a policy process that resists central reform initiatives and defies sustained attempts to steer policy developments', resulting in a sectorized policy-making structure (see also Bulmer and Paterson 1996). This is further constrained by the 'preference for defining responsibilities clearly and devolving them widely' (Johnson 1983). The lack of co-ordination of German policy-making within the EU and the need to incorporate a myriad of actors in negotiations make an important imprint on Germany's European policy (Bulmer and Paterson 1987). Co-ordination among ministries produces difficulties owing to the jealously guarded ministerial autonomy enjoyed by German ministers. The consequence is what Collins (1998: 63) has termed 'small empires' within the policy-making system. Hill and Stavrides (1983: 189) have noted the 'permissive inactivity' of national parliaments in the sphere of EPC. This no longer applies to the same degree as European foreign and security policy takes on a more conspicuous presence in international relations and consequently becomes of more interest to national parliamentary scrutiny.[3]

Germany's power in Europe during the Kohl period is better seen in pushing for long-term strategic goals rather than the nitty-gritty bargaining over individual policy areas (Bulmer 1997). This has not hampered Germany's influence on the integration process, but has discredited realist claims that Germany seeks to wield power over its partners in the pursuit of German national interests (Mearsheimer 1990). With the Schröder government, Germany has appeared more pragmatic in its approach to EU policy areas, perhaps the defining change in its approach to EU policy-making. These institutional constraints have resulted in the 'stickiness' of national policies in the face of adaptation of EU legislation (Haverland 2000) and are also visible in German approaches to CFSP policy.

These pressures developed in conjunction with a domestic reassessment of the role of the Bundeswehr on the international stage, impacting also on its perception within Germany. The streamlining of the armed forces that Defence Minister Rudolf Scharping set in train, the most wide-ranging reform of the Bundeswehr ever put in place, also affects the position of the armed forces in German society. The closing down of many barracks within Germany and the shake-up of forces to meet the demands of a greater German involvement in international operations will inevitably mean that the image of the Bundeswehr soldiers as 'citizens in uniform' in the future will no longer hold as much symbolic potency. The von Weizsäcker report on the reform of the Bundeswehr raised many questions about the role and future of the Bundeswehr in German society and as part of Germany's multilateral commitments (von Weizsäcker-Kommission 2002).

---

[3] In the case of Germany, the Bundestag has *de jure* constitutional powers in decisions concerning deploying the Bundeswehr. The Netherlands is the only other EU country where the national parliament has such powers. The influence of such a constitutional power was seen during the difficulties the Federal government had in the debates over the deployment of the Bundeswehr in Macedonia. Whilst the government secured a majority for the deployment, there were notable dissenting voices among the SPD backbenchers.

The high costs of unification have led to the growing importance and influence of the Finance Ministry under Hans Eichel, reflected in the redistribution of competencies between the Economics and Finance Ministries that took place after the Red–Green coalition entered government in September 1998 (Bulmer, Maurer and Paterson 2001). This has also been seen in the recent measures to combat terrorism within and without Germany. The proposals to raise taxes on tobacco and insurance from 1 January 2002 to meet the high costs of implementing an anti-terrorism programme were made by Hans Eichel. It was made very clear to the Defence Ministry that these funds would not be diverted into its coffers to aid the reforms of the federal armed forces currently being undertaken (*FAZ* 19 September 2001). This is seen by the Ministry of Defence and Germany's partners as an essential step to making the Bundeswehr more operational and raising Germany's credibility in multilateral endeavours.

The dynamic for the development of a EU military capability to conduct military operations in cases where NATO declined to participate was provided by the British Prime Minister Tony Blair and subsequently in tandem with France. (Austrian Presidency 1998; Franco-British Summit 1998) Hence, analyses of developments within CFSP and the subsequent framing of CESDP tend to focus on the leading role played by France and the UK, with Germany, in many ways owing to its traditional reservedness in military affairs, not receiving sufficient attention. However, thanks to Germany's joint presidencies of the EU/WEU and the G8 during the first half of 1999, Germany had an important part in recent developments in CFSP. It played a key role in the negotiations that led to the Cologne Declaration in June 1999 and the successful conclusion of a diplomatic solution to the Kosovo crisis based on the Stability Pact for the South East Balkans. This role is vital to understanding both forces within the EU and the international system moving towards greater EU military capabilities and for appreciating the domestic developments taking place within Germany (Miskimmon 2001).

The Dimension of 'Uploading': Germany's Contribution within the Process of Europeanization of Foreign and Security Policy

As already stated, Europeanization is not a simple 'downloading' process. If it can be posited that Germany's foreign and security policy has been affected as a direct result of its involvement in the EPC/CFSP/CESDP, then it surely follows that, as a constituent member of this process, there must conversely be signs of German influence or participation (see Figure 16.2). Whereas 'milieu-shaping' within the CFSP process is certainly an overstatement of German influence, Germany has made its mark in recognizable ways. In a process where Germany has not been able to determine the pace of integration, it has sought to influence the process of Europeanization within EU foreign and security policy by persuading its main

Aim	Method	Target audience/Milieu	Outcome/ Manifestation
Ideational export	Persuasion Franco-German co-operation	EU15	Influence within a policy area in which Germany has been traditionally weak
Example-setting	*Musterknabe* role	EU15	Capabilities Commitment Conference, pledged most troops for ERRF
Strengthening co-operation	Multiple bilateralism — bilaterals within a multilateral framework around issues — not long-term co-operation	Bilateral relations — minilateralisms	Franco-German Corps/Eurocorps
Discursive influence	Provoking grand debates on long-term visions of Europe	EU15+	EU-wide debates over the future of Europe sparked by Fischer's Humboldt Speech
Exaggerated multilateralism — mitigating Germany's foreign and security policy weaknesses	Institution-building	EU15+	Stability Pact ERRF PSC, EUMC, EUMS

Figure 16.2.   How Germany contributes to the Europeanization process in CFSP.

partners, France and the UK, of the rationale of deepening co-operation in this policy area. This is perhaps the defining method or mechanism of Germany's role in Europeanizing foreign and security policy.

The main actors involved in making German CFSP policy have the following tools or strategies at their disposal, as outlined in Figure 16.2. The main actors are the Chancellor and his Chancellery, the Foreign Office, to a lesser extent the Defence Ministry, and also the Bundestag. The Bundestag has the dual function of an arena where government decisions are ratified, and, as CFSP becomes more politicized, the Bundestag may assume a greater role to play. However, the Bundestag as a veto player within CFSP is not imaginable. Potential veto players come from within the EU's member states on the basis of perceived national interest or foreign policy strategy. This is a major inherent weakness in institutional export within the CFSP process. The overall aim of Germany's CFSP strategy is to create a German–EU institutional fit in order to lessen the cost of adaptation to the German system. In this way, Germany has exercised what Nye (1990) refers to as 'soft power', in which it has sought to influence the ideas and preferences of its EU partners by suggesting the way forward for EU foreign and security policy co-operation.

Germany has been successful in keeping the idea of a common European defence policy on the agenda, as outlined in Article 17 (1) of the Treaty of Nice. German governments during the 1990s consistently argued for a common European defence as one of the key issues concerning the finality of European integration. This has been generally viewed with suspicion in some quarters in the UK as an attempt to weaken the Atlantic Alliance. However, since the St Malo Declaration in December 1998, the UK has begun to view this more pragmatically, while maintaining a cautious approach. Germany has also been supportive of attempts to strengthen the EU's conflict prevention capabilities, a goal that has particular resonance within Nordic EU member states. Indeed, while the Nice summit produced some unsatisfactory results and witnessed a cooling in the Franco-German relationship, the key advances within the treaty may well have been within the area of CESDP. Duke (2000: 175) suggests that Nice's immediate aftermath showed up the new importance that CFSP/CESDP had taken on: 'the stakes are higher since more progress has been made along the road to the CESDP goal and more political capital has been invested in the security aspects of the EU than ever before'.

Schmalz (2002) has defined Germany's input into the CFSP/CESDP process on the basis of three role conceptions, which correspond to historical stages in the development of Europe's foreign and security policy presence. First, the Federal Republic's input into EPC is defined as one of 'opinion leadership' (*Meinungsführerschaft*), as it sought to sketch out a role for the EC in conjunction with France. Secondly, the developments since the end of the Cold War have seen Germany's role develop into one of an 'impulse giver' (*Impulsgeber*), generating a dynamic for greater integration with the quest for political union. Finally, events since 1998, and in particular during the Germany European Council Presidency of early 1999, have witnessed a more self-confident Germany willing to take on a '(co)-leadership' role ((*Mit*)-*Führungsrolle*). The paradox inherent in the current quest to play a (*Mit*)-*Führungsrolle* is that Germany does not yet have the military capabilities to play such a role.

The EU Convention initiated by the Laeken summit presents the EU member states with a considerable opportunity to streamline and improve the workings and effectiveness of CFSP/CESDP (Laeken Declaration 2001). Indeed, Germany has been a major supporter of this process. Policy élites within Germany have raised a number of proposals in the sphere of foreign and security policy. First, German élites view the merging of Javier Solana and Chris Patten's jobs as a prerequisite to representing the EU more effectively (Everts 2002; Friedrich Ebert

Stiftung 2002; Pflüger 2001; Scharioth 2002). Linked to this, the practice of rotating the Presidency of the European Council has proved disruptive in external relations. Merging Solana's role with that of Chris Patten in the form of a permanent chair of the Council and perhaps even a specialized Council on foreign affairs would replace the troika and, thus, prove more effective, especially in international negotiations. Secondly, a move towards the more widespread use of Qualified Majority Voting (QMV) within CFSP would result, according to the head of policy planning at the Foreign Ministry, in a change in mentality among the EU member states towards a more proactive role (Scharioth 2002). Thirdly, there should be a greater emphasis on conflict prevention and post-conflict management to reduce the need for military intervention in Europe. Fourthly, the connection between defence and national sovereignty needs to be addressed through greater European arms co-operation, with the aim of forging complete interoperability between EU and NATO forces. Fifthly, according to the Foreign Ministry, there is a real need to involve candidate countries in CFSP/CESDP in building co-operation and understanding. This may be achieved by establishing a European security and defence college to train the policy élites of an enlarged EU. Finally, the question of democratic accountability can no longer be avoided in light of the EU's growing capabilities in CFSP/CESDP.

Muddled Discourses: Limitations on the Europeanization of German CFSP Policy

CFSP/CESDP is primarily the product of intergovernmental negotiation. Hence, EU foreign and security policy is not involved in, and deeply constrained by, domestic struggles. Political support for CFSP/CESDP is broad, but shallow. In consequence, this a policy area whose dynamic and focus are easily blown off course, as witnessed in the post-11 September international environment. Currently, there is an emphasis on capabilities rather than process. Consequently, there has been the emergence of a *directoire*, or leading coalition, within the CFSP/CESDP process—France, Germany and the UK—which has caused considerable hostility from other member states (Everts 2002; Miskimmon 2002).

The limitations impacting on the Europeanization of German CFSP policy are recognizable in the mixed policy discourses emanating from the Foreign Ministry, the Chancellor's Office, and the Defence Ministry. Rather than aspiring to the EU foreign policy ideal of speaking with one voice, the federal ministries in Bonn and Berlin are more polyphonic than monophonic. The Foreign Ministry maintains a consistently Europeanized discourse in CFSP matters. The *Kanzleramt* has since 1998 developed a more normalizing foreign and security policy discourse that reached new heights in Schröder's Bundestag speeches of October 2001 and in his statements on Iraq in 2002 (Hyde-Price and Jeffery 2001). The Defence Ministry maintains a broadly Atlanticist discourse, although some Europeanization is creeping in, in part down to the inclusion of EU defence ministers in discussions about the development of CESDP. However, the Bundeswehr maintains its focus of being integrated into NATO command structures, and is wary of plans to strengthen the European pillar if it will have a detrimental effect on NATO partnership. At the European Council meeting in Gothenburg, it was Germany that considered France and the UK were in danger of weakening the Atlantic Alliance, with tabled proposals to further strengthen CESDP (Interview, Defence Ministry, Berlin, 2001).

This has a major impact on German policy-making. While each of the ministries involved will state their public support for the CFSP, there are competing rationales in place. Co-ordination among the ministries is also limited in scope concerning German CFSP policy. The problems of co-ordination are exacerbated by the system of coalition government in Germany in which the junior coalition partner receives the Foreign Ministry portfolio. Joschka Fischer, of the Bündnis '90–Greens, was also directly responsible to his party which expected him to represent Green interests, something that in the pressures of government was very difficult for him to achieve.

CFSP as a policy sector has significant singularities, which distinguish it from other policy areas where Europeanization has made an impact. The Foreign Ministry, while being the sponsoring ministry of CFSP policy, needs to co-ordinate with the other key ministries of Defence, Finance, and the Chancellery. Despite this, the mixed discourse emanating from these ministries can uncover the latent tensions and puzzles within CFSP policy within Germany. Along with the costs of unification and the sensitivities of the German polity about the use of military force, the problems of co-ordination within the German system and the lack of a dynamic sectoral interest to drive the process forward have impinged on the process of Europeanizing German foreign and security policy, and hampered Germany's impact on the process at the EU level.

As the most pro-European ministry, the Foreign Ministry is instinctively orientated towards working within the highly institutionalized Franco-German relationship (de Maiziere 1991; Pederson 1998). There is a reflexive co-ordination with France on major foreign and security policy issues within the EU, which is facilitated by regularized meetings between the two governments. The CFSP process was reliant on Franco-German proposals until the decision of the UK to take up a greater role in events after December 1998. The Defence Ministry, by contrast, while predisposed to the Franco-German tandem, is instinctively Atlanticist. Different policy accents are, therefore, recognizable on foreign and security policy issues between these ministries.

Military effectiveness and capabilities are the key goals for CESDP. Without this and the EU's ability to share more of the burden for regional stability with the USA, transatlantic relations will inevitably come under strain. The EU has long suffered from what Hill (1993, 1998) dubbed the 'capabilities–expectations gap'. However, this may now be an unfair label in light of the major steps forward that the EU has undertaken in recent years. While it is true that the EU has yet to become a fully credible military actor, the EU does have the potential to develop into a truly encompassing foreign and security policy actor. It is this very aim that the EU draws on to derive much of its legitimacy in international affairs.

The 'Capabilities Commitment' Conference of 20 November 2000 was an initial step to meet the expectations for reaching the 'headline goal' and the 'headline goal force catalogues' (Military Capabilities Commitment Statement). The goal of creating a force of between 50,000–60,000 troops to be deployable within sixty days and for at least one year to conduct the types of missions envisaged within the so-called Petersberg Tasks (Article 17 TEU) represents a major commitment on behalf of the EU member states. The deployment of the ERRF is on a purely voluntary basis. The creation of COPS, EUMC, and EUMS will add to the ability of the EU to react effectively to regional instability and play a more proactive role in hindering any such instability in the future (Council Decision 2001*a*, 2001*b*, 2001*c*).

The demands of the 'headline goal' have placed the spotlight on the defence expenditures of EU member states. For the 'big three' of France, Germany, and the UK in CFSP/CESDP this spotlight is all the brighter. Defence expenditure within the EU has steadily fallen since the end of the Cold War. At the same time, the USA has exerted pressure on politicians in France, Germany, and the UK to take up a greater share of the crisis management burden. The increasing demands placed on budgets to meet the burdens of social security provision in Western Europe have meant that defence has often been seen as an area for 'penny-pinching' in order to reach public expenditure targets. This has been most evident within Germany, where the effects of unification still present the Federal government with huge challenges. Europe has still not managed to benefit from the kind of economies of scale all too evident within the US defence industry, and a solution to these problems does not appear to be in sight, especially in light of the difficulties in the A-400M project[4] (Schmidt 2000, 2001).

The adaptation of the Bundeswehr under pressures stemming from the Europeanization of national foreign and security policy has exhibited a number of characteristics. First, the process of adaptation has been relatively reluctant. The reforms of the Bundeswehr that are currently being tentatively carried out have been considered largely internal German matters. The initial pressure to reform the Bundeswehr has come from the international environment and the incremental pressure of involvement in international peace-keeping missions. But the German political establishment has sought to reform the Bundeswehr along the

---

[4] Rudolf Scharping, the German Defence Minister until August 2002, had considerable trouble in finding the necessary funds to meet Germany's commitment to buy seventy-three A400Ms. In comparison, the UK has a relatively modest commitment to buy twenty-five.

lines of what they consider best for Germany, rather than accepting much outside advice on what is to be done (Sarotte 2002; Interviews in Berlin 2001). In the words of former Defence Minister Scharping: 'Die Bundeswehr ist zu einer Armee im Einsatz geworden—*im Dienste deutscher Friedenspolitik*' (Scharping 2002, emphasis in the original).

Secondly, and following on from the first point, the Bundeswehr exhibits considerable misfit in terms of any Europeanization of defence and armed forces policy. All the blueprints for the future of the Bundeswehr view conscription as being vital for the long-term success of the German armed forces. This is a deeply held cultural belief among many of the German military and political élites, which will ensure its existence for the foreseeable future, despite the attempts of Germany's major allies to have Germany phase out conscription.

Nevertheless, the Defence Ministry does not have the same influence as the Foreign Ministry and Chancellery in CFSP/CESDP, despite the inclusion of matters pertaining to defence and the higher profile being given to joint European defence procurement ventures. The lessons learned by policy-makers in Bonn and Berlin over the past decade have shown up the need for Germany to play a more active military role in order to have a greater influence on the EU level (Miskimmon 2001).

The increased role of the Defence Ministry has the potential for creating several tensions in German policy-making. First, the Defence Ministry and the Bundeswehr have been predominantly Atlanticist in outlook owing to the highly integrated structure of the German armed forces within NATO. The transfer of loyalties to fledgling European structures will be a gradual process. This can perhaps be overstated as a braking mechanism for developments within the armed forces towards creating a credible CESDP/ERRF. Secondly, if budgetary restrictions remain in place, then the Bundeswehr may feel that it is not in a position financially to carry out its responsibilities. This may lead to friction in political–military relations within Germany. Finally, the greater involvement of Defence Ministers on the EU level may create greater incentives within the German policy-making system for competition between ministries, especially in light of the fact that the Foreign Ministry considers itself to be the 'sponsoring ministry' of CFSP/CESDP.

Germany's Stance on Iraq

The foreign and security policy environment has changed dramatically since the attacks on New York and Washington on 11 September 2001, affecting not only America's position in the world, but also having a major impact on America's major allies. Germany has not been exempt from this. Chris Hill has documented the response of EU member states in terms of renationalizing and regrouping: renationalizing in the sense of looking for solutions from national capitals rather than within the CFSP/CESDP framework, and regrouping in terms of a clear break from the past traditional assumptions of multilateral co-operation in Europe (Hill 2002). Evidence of both these dynamics can be found in Germany's foreign and security policy, most noticeably in relation to the US determination to seek 'regime change' within Iraq.

Two ideas have been central to Germany's stance on Iraq that are in many ways consistent with the 'Europeanization/normalization' dynamic which this chapter has sought to define. Firstly, there is the notion of Schröder and his 'normalizing' discourse. This comes through most clearly in his refusal for German participation in military action against Iraq without a UN mandate. Secondly, however, this is not a claim for leadership, but a signal from the *Kanzleramt* that Germany is more *selbstbewußt* (self-confident) in this apparent retreat from multilateralism.

Polyphony within Germany's foreign and security policy establishment has also been evident over the Iraq issue. In this case, the Foreign Ministry under Joschka Fischer has sought to distance itself from Schröder's normalizing discourse. This has been further encouraged by the Greens' strong performance in the September 2002 German Federal Elections. Fischer has been keen to disassociate himself and the *Auswärtiges Amt* from Schröder's new definition of a 'deutsche Weg' (Hooper 2002; Naumann 2002). The *Auswärtiges Amt* has consistently pursued a complementary agenda, and now that its head has emerged strengthened from the 2002 elections, it has sought to prevent any attempt by Schröder to wrestle European foreign and security policy to the *Kanzleramt* (*Financial Times Deutschland* 2002). The *Auswärtiges Amt*, as the CFSP 'sponsoring ministry', continues to follow the institutional logic moving towards greater co-operation in CFSP/CESDP. In addition, the *Auswärtiges Amt* remains less subject to public opinion than the *Kanzleramt*, as has been shown in Schröder's instrumentalizing of the Iraq issue to claw back the popular support in the federal election of 2002 (Krägenow 2002).

Renationalizing and regrouping have, thus, been evident in German foreign and security policy. There are essentially two Schröders on display here: Schröder's ready support for the USA in the aftermath of the 11 September attacks, particularly in his support for the intervention in Afghanistan, and Schröder's *alter ego* who has sought to delineate a more independent German voice on Iraq. Schröder has become more comfortable with defining a singular German foreign and security policy on Iraq, and no longer views the traditional multilateral groupings of the Cold War and the immediate post-Cold War period as reflexive tenets of German policy. Schröder is now faced with what Hellmann (2002) has described as a *Gratwanderung*—a tight rope walk between pursuing a 'deutscher Weg' and the necessity to restate Germany's multilateral vocation under new international conditions, attempting to balance the 'Europeanization/ normalization' pressures on German foreign and security policy.

Conclusion

The substantial changes brought about by unification in 1989–90 continue to have ramifications for German domestic and foreign policy. In many ways this has caused the process of European integration to decelerate, but there has been sufficient instability affecting the EU's global role to necessitate the development of a closer and more effective foreign and security policy. As this chapter has attempted to show, Germany has been both an agent for Europeanization, but also an object of policy adaptation, with the EU and its member states acting as a policy paradigm.

There are positive and negative factors affecting the Europeanization of Germany's foreign and security policy, which also highlight the singularity of CFSP in German policy. The facilitating circumstances have been enough to maintain Germany's support for the CFSP process. However, these have been checked by a number of conditions limiting the impact of CFSP on German policy. Perhaps the most important positive factor has been firm support from public and élite opinions for CFSP as a process. This marks out CFSP as a singular policy sector within Germany, as there are no opposing sectoral interests. Secondly, the Foreign Ministry, as the sponsoring ministry of the project, is very much behind the development of CFSP. Finally, Foreign Minister Fischer has been more active in advancing the course of CFSP in the Schröder government than his predecessor in the Kohl government, Klaus Kinkel. Fischer took advantage of the fall-out from the break-up of Yugoslavia to persuade his main European foreign policy allies, France, the UK, and Italy, of the merits of expanding the co-operative links in foreign and security within the EU. His success in convincing and persuading his EU colleagues of the value of deepening CFSP/CESDP was evident during the German Presidencies of the European Council, WEU, and the G8 in 1999. Fischer's difficulty has been that he is flanked by a Chancellor who has been increasingly seen as a normalizer. In addition, the 'vote of confidence' that Schröder called in November 2001 to justify his policy of supporting the USA in the war on terrorism resulted in the subjugation of the Greens' position on foreign and security policy matters, leaving the Chancellor more room for manoeuvre (Bannas 2001). Since the 2002 federal elections, Fischer has attempted to reassert his position in foreign and security policy, bolstered by his party's good showing at the polls.

The fact that CFSP is associated with the Foreign Ministry is an inherent advantage within the German policy-making system—from the perspective of organization and continuity—in that it always plays the role of a central ministry. In addition, thanks largely to the fact that the junior coalition partner in the government usually holds the Foreign Ministry, it is allowed a degree of policy space in which to work.

However, there are a number of limiting conditions affecting the Foreign

Ministry's role in CFSP policy-making. Its influence fluctuates according to two main factors. First, the influence of the Foreign Ministry is largely reliant on the personality of its head. Hans-Dietrich Genscher was a successful foreign minister because of his extended incumbency and the wide experience that he was able to accrue. However, not every foreign minister has the luxury of such a long time in office to place his imprint on German policy. The second limiting condition is the Chancellor and his involvement in foreign policy. While the 'departmental' principle (*Ressortsprinzip*) asserts that the Foreign Minister has the responsibility to conduct foreign policy with relative autonomy within the cabinet, responsibility for strategic direction rests with the Chancellor. This can affect the overall strategy and direction of policy. Finally, the Defence Ministry was for a long time more concerned with a different project from CFSP, i.e. NATO. However, more recently there have been signs of a growing acceptance by the Defence Ministry of the need for Europeanization. While potentially complicating the CFSP policy-making process within Germany, this aids the CFSP's chances of success by strengthening the institutional involvement and interests in the project.

What, then, have been the limitations on CFSP that have militated against the full Europeanization of German policy? Germany finds itself on the cusp between accommodation and transformation of its foreign and security policy. There are internal and external factors acting as a brake in this process. Internally, the Foreign Ministry dominates this policy sector. The Defence Ministry's role is growing, but co-ordination is patchy, as each ministry seeks to assert its policy territory. While the Chancellor's Office maintains a co-ordinating role over all policy sectors, it does not play a dominant role in German CFSP policy. The mixed policy discourse emanating from Bonn and Berlin is evidence of ministerial singularities. A second internal factor is that, despite its multilateral vocation, there is a policy of resisting extensive communitarization of European foreign and security policy within the Foreign Ministry. This sets obvious boundaries on the realms of the possible in German CFSP policy. As mentioned earlier, public opinion is behind Germany's CFSP policy, but no organized sectoral interest puts pressure on the government to pursue CFSP policy more actively. As a consequence, it is difficult to inject any degree of dynamism into the project.

Central to the external factors hindering the Europeanization of German policy is the absence of an external agent or compliance mechanism that could force through greater co-operation among the EU-15. As the terrorist attacks on the US in 2001 showed, in times of crisis the knee-jerk reaction has been to turn to intergovernmental co-operation and co-ordination from national capitals rather than to work through the Brussels bureaucracy (Black 2001; Dempsey 2001). The trilateral meeting between Chirac, Schröder, and Blair before the European Council meeting in Ghent in October 2001 was a clear case of multiple bilateralism, and a sign that the UK, France, and Germany are the key players in foreign and security policy within the EU (Paterson 2001). To complicate matters, uncertainty remains about the division of labour between Javier Solana working for the Council and Chris Patten working for the Commission. The result is problems of co-ordination, an issue that will be addressed within the Convention. However, some analysts have posited the beginnings of a European strategic culture, which will, if developed, go a considerable way towards further Europeanization of foreign and security policy (Cornish and Edwards 2001). The second external factor acting as a brake is the nature of EU treaty reform. The constant process of renegotiation, however consensual, is a hindrance to progress.

The Europeanization of German foreign and security policy has been accompanied by a normalization dynamic — a 'push/pull' dynamic as Germany seeks to adapt to new circumstances, post-unification and post-Cold War. Germany will continue to be a leading actor within CFSP/CESDP, but the limitations of CFSP policy-making within Germany will continue to impinge on its ability to shape the CFSP policy sector.

Note. The authors would like to thank the following for their helpful comments on initial drafts of the text: Elizabeth Bomberg, Tanja Börzel, Gunther Hellmann, Chris Hill, and Lord Wallace of Saltaire.

Part V
Europeanization Compared

17

Europeanization Compared: The Shrinking Core and the Decline of 'Soft' Power

KENNETH DYSON & KLAUS H. GOETZ

Introduction

THE CONTRIBUTIONS TO THIS VOLUME HAVE EXPLORED the implications of living with Europe in terms of Germany's power to project its institutional forms and policies; the balance between enabling and constraining implications of European integration; and domestic contestation about European integration. Our main findings call for a revision of the 'conventional wisdom' regarding Germany's Europeanization experience.

First, while Germany continues to engage intensively in all aspects of the integration process, its power to 'upload' — 'hard' and 'soft', 'deliberate' or 'unintentional', 'institutional' or 'ideational' — appears in decline. Germany's capacity to 'shape its regional milieu' (Bulmer, Jeffery and Paterson 2000) is challenged both by changes in the integration process and the ever more apparent weaknesses of the 'German model'. The traditional regional core milieu is shrinking in size and importance in an enlarging Europe, and Germany's milieu-shaping power is being challenged. As a result, the 'systemic empowerment' through a 'virtuous cycle . . . in which indirect institutional power is influential for the configuration of European institutions and the style of their interactions, and subsequently "pays back" through systemic empowerment' (Bulmer, Jeffery and Paterson 2000: 135) is becoming increasingly questionable. The rise of new power constellations within the enlarged EU robs Germany of much of its previous gatekeeper-role; and Eastern enlargement, which was initially seen by many as a further boost to Germany's centrality, is increasingly showing up the limitations of both Germany's financial resources and ideational attraction. It is, in fact, highly debatable whether the Central and Eastern accession states still 'seek access to the secrets of Germany's success as they embark on their *Drang nach Westen*' (Jeffery and Paterson 2001: 208). It would overstate our empirical findings to suggest that the virtuous cycle has been replaced by a vicious cycle, in which growing limitations to 'uploading' spell systemic disempowerment. But the virtuous cycle appears perilously close to being broken.

Proceedings of the British Academy, **119**, 349–376. © The British Academy 2003.

Second, and as a consequence, the coincidence of enabling and constraining effects is being progressively replaced by a discourse that notes unwelcome constrictions associated with EU membership. The emphasis here has been not on the limitations to Germany's actions in the international arena, but rather on the foreclosing of domestic policy options. Too much can be made of the more censorious and confrontational tone adopted by leading figures in the Schröder government, notably the Chancellor himself, *vis-à-vis* the European Commission, and of more frequent references to the German 'national interest'. They might owe more to changing perceptions of the costs and benefits of integration amongst the new generation of German political leaders than to a marked increase in policy 'misfits'. Rather, our findings suggest a more basic constraint, with potentially more serious consequences. Thus, the chapters in this volume dealing with the Bundestag, the party system, and the media agenda, in particular, demonstrate that key political institutions and processes in the Federal Republic have not co-evolved with the integration process, but lead an, at times, uncomfortable coexistence. Such co-existence need not necessarily be problematic; but if domestic institutions and processes, notably those involved in political communication, representation, and legitimation, do not appear capable of, or interested in, co-evolution, then a systematic gap opens up between their ostensive responsibilities and their real capabilities.

With respect to the impact of Europe on elections and party systems, Peter Mair (2000: 46) has pointed to the paradox that in much of Europe, including Germany 'national elections continue to be dominated by conflicts over policy alternatives, the scope for the exercise of which is severely constrained by the European dimension. By contrast, European elections tend to be dominated by debates over Europe itself, despite the fact that the room for institutional manoeuvre concerning Europe is severely constrained by national governments . . . contests in each arena involve questions that can often be resolved only outside the arena itself.' It is this mixture of effective constraint combined with the absence of co-evolution that lies at the heart of the problematic consequences of integration for domestic democratic politics. As Niedermayer (Chapter 7 in this volume) and Saalfeld (Chapter 4 in this volume) make clear, it is not purposeful resistance that explains the limited impact of Europe on electoral behaviour, the party system, and parliament. Rather, domestic opportunity structures would appear to provide few incentives to parties, elected national politicians and the Bundestag as an institution to seek a deeper engagement with Europe (see also Lees 2002).

Third, domestic contestation over both the everyday EU policy and the constitutional politics of integration seems set to increase. There are, as yet, no indications that these domestic conflicts will reach an intensity comparable to that of the 1950s, when, as noted in Chapter 1 in this volume, Adenauer's policy of Western integration was fiercely criticized by the opposition and challenged within his own party and government. However, both the 'permissive' mass consensus and, perhaps more importantly, élite consensus, are being tested to their limits. In the case of the former, there is already a domestic West–East divide in terms of the level of support for integration. This divide is likely to widen in the wake of enlargement. The visible costs of enlargement will be most immediately felt in the five Eastern Länder, where support is already consistently lower than in the West. More worryingly, basic differences have opened up between the SPD–Green government and the CDU/CSU over the issue of the long-term prospects of Turkey's accession to the EU. While Chancellor Schröder has successfully pushed for a clear timetable for the start of accession negotiations, any prospect of full Turkish membership has been categorically ruled out by the leaders of both the CDU and the CSU. This debate will not be easily contained, and it has the potential for partisan polarization over the future of the EU.

The following will, first, summarize the empirical findings of the contributions on the polity, politics, and policy dimensions of Europeanization, with an emphasis on the variegated patterns of Europeanization that can be detected. On that basis, we will return to the question of how our received understanding of Germany's Europeanization experience might need to be revised. Both sections primarily address the contribution of Europeanization research to our understanding of the German political system. We then turn to the implications of our findings for comparative Europeanization studies. How exceptional is the German case? And are there wider implications of our project for students of comparative Europeanization? Finally, we conclude with a set of arguments about the likely future trajectory of the Europeanization of the German political system.

Asymmetry and Temporal Differentiation: Variegated Patterns of Europeanization

Chapter 1 set out a number of questions to guide the empirical inquiry into patterns of Europeanization: what is being Europeanized, why, how, by whom, and when? Not all of these five guiding questions have been addressed in all of the contributions and with equal attention. Accordingly, our empirical conclusions are more robust in respect of some of these questions than others. In terms of substantive effects, what is striking is the—at best—loose linkage between policy, polity and politics effects. Spillover effects from policy to polity and, in particular, to politics have been much less pronounced than we expected at the outset. Changes in policy have not translated into correspondent change in institutional development; key structures and procedures of democratic representation and legitimation, in particular, remain very firmly centred on the nation-state. It is also clear that the time, timing, and tempo of Europeanization processes have differed and that these differences matter in terms of substantive adaptation. As new forms and methods of intergovernmental co-operation supplement the traditional Community method of integration, the substantive profile of Europeanization changes. In particular, there are indications that in those policy areas where the open method of co-ordination has been particularly important—EMU (Dyson, Chapter 10 in this volume) and Justice and Home Affairs (JHA) (Monar, Chapter 15 in this volume)—Europeanization has been associated with a pronounced trend towards the creation of executive-centred policy networks that more or less exclude parliamentary and societal actors. Europeanization patterns across the policy, polity, and politics dimensions are, in short, asymmetrical and dynamic over time.

The disparity between policy, polity, and politics effects is, in itself, not very surprising, for there is a broad consensus in the literature that the most discernible effects of Europeanization can be seen in public policies. However, given that the creation, consolidation and maturation of the political system of the Federal Republic were so firmly placed in the context of progressive integration, the limited direct effects on basic features of the political process—like cleavage formation, electoral behaviour and party system development, and the functioning of institutions such as the Bundestag—are noteworthy. Few institutions have been affected so centrally as the Bundesbank. Rather, in many instances, European integration has not been a mobilizing and polarizing issue, and the effects on institutional opportunity structures have been either too limited or too diffuse to create strong incentives or pressures to Europeanize. 'Co-existence' rather than 'co-evolution' constitutes the typical Europeanization pattern in these cases.

Effects on the Polity: Ambiguous Institutional Incentives to Europeanize

Europeanization of the German polity has occurred in complex, dynamic, and interactive ways. Institutions such as the federal executive, the Bundestag, and the Bundesbank have undergone internal restructuring, albeit to varying degrees. The distribution of power both within and amongst institutions has changed, for instance between ministries within the federal executive; between the federal executive and the Bundestag; and between the federation and the Länder. There has been evidence of a new activism as German actors, notably the Länder, seek to 'upload' German domestic models and preferences to the EU level in order to counteract the weakening of their autonomy. Above all, reflecting a high degree of institutional pluralism, the German polity has experienced Europeanization in a differential way. Central to understanding the effects of European integration have been the institutional incentives to Europeanize.

At the level of the polity, the institutions most bound up in Europeanization have included the federal executive, the Länder, and the Bundesbank. The federal executive is most directly and intensively engaged because of its day-to-day involvement in the work of the Council of Ministers, with its associated deadlines. But even here evidence of significant structural change is limited and more apparent at administrative levels than the level of executive politics. Many ministries have divisions and sections (*Referate*) specializing in European policy, a total of nine of the former and ninety-nine of the latter by 2001 (Sturm and Pehle 2001: 45). The effects were, however, differentiated. Defence lacked any European policy unit, and Transport, Family, Environment and Health ministries had three or fewer sections. In contrast, the Finance Ministry had twenty-eight sections specializing in Europe, and the Foreign Ministry eighteen. The main co-ordinating structures for European policy—the Committee of State Secretaries for European Questions and the 'Tuesday' Committee of division heads—date back, respectively, to 1963 and 1971, and have altered little in functioning. Although their work is more formalized than is typical of interministerial committees, they reflect a German administrative tradition of horizontal co-ordination rather than the emergence of a strong central co-ordinating mechanism on the British and French models.

Before 2002, no serious attempt had been made to enhance the status of European co-ordinating units, though there was a debate about whether a European minister—perhaps in the Federal Chancellor's Office and with responsibility for chairing these committees—was required. Also, until the second Schröder government in 2002—when a European division was established in the Chancellor's Office—it maintained a relatively low complement of relevant administrative expertise, with only two sections focusing on European policy. Co-ordination is characterized by a division of labour between the Foreign Ministry (which chairs the Committee of State Secretaries) and the Finance Ministry (which chairs the 'Tuesday' Committee), with the Chancellor's Office seeking to play a role especially in preparing the Chancellor for the meetings of the European Council. Overall, the primacy of the principle of departmental autonomy—aided and abetted by the effects of coalition politics—has closed off opportunities to emulate more centralized systems of European policy co-ordination in other member states, although it has been suggested that this might help rather than hinder the effective promotion of German interests at EU level (Derlien 2000). Undoubtedly, however, it encourages a 'diplomacy of improvisation, which contrasts especially strongly with the more choreographed diplomacy of its British and French counterparts' (Maurer and Wessels 2001: 123).

Europeanization has more clearly manifested itself in the way in which political and administrative actors in the federal executive have exploited the associated opportunities to augment their own power and profile. This process was seen with the new Red–Green government in 1998. Oskar Lafontaine, as Finance Minister, created a new European division by bringing in key European policy officials from the Economics Ministry and gained the main co-ordinating responsibility for European policy alongside the Foreign Ministry. A key part of the rationale was provided by the need for Germany to match the administrative capacity of the French Finance Ministry and of the British Treasury with the establishment of the final stage of EMU on 1 January 1999. EMU was, accordingly, associated with empowerment of the Finance Ministry and disempowerment of the Economics Ministry, a phenomenon that was generally discernible across the EMU (Dyson 2000*b*). Despite this 'logic of EMU' argument, macroeconomic policy was returned to the new expanded superministry of Economics and Labour in 2002. This provided a platform for Wolfgang Clement, the new minister, to carve out a role in EMU on macro-economic co-ordination questions.

Otherwise, outside the realm of seeking out the opportunities offered by Europeanization to enhance domestic power and profile, the political level of the federal executive showed limited and intermittent evidence of the effects of European integration. This relatively low level of involvement from executive politics reflects the weakness of institutional incentives when European issues have low electoral saliency and when the links between European engagement and making a visible difference to what the electorate perceives to be the pressing problems are tenuous and uncertain (Goetz, Chapter 3 in this volume).

The relevance of institutional incentives is also clear in the case of the Bundestag (Saalfeld, Chapter 4 in this volume). In one respect, the Bundestag has an institutional interest in strengthening its role in the European integration process. It has seen an erosion of its legislative competence to the EU, an enormous growth in EU-related legislation, and a European integration process that has empowered the federal executive at the expense of its own powers. These are important and real constraints associated with Europeanization. Yet, members of the Bundestag have not on the whole actively exploited opportunities to Europeanize their work. The Bundestag has been slow to develop a structural specialization on European policy, with the Committee for EU Affairs dating only from 1994. The ratification of the Maastricht Treaty in 1993, notably the associated new Article 23 of the Basic Law (which gave the new committee constitutional status), and the Amsterdam Treaty strengthened the information rights of the Bundestag. But these developments were linked more to active political lobbying by the German Länder than to independent initiatives by the Bundestag and produced only limited behavioural change. The Committee on EU Affairs has improved the potential for control over what German politicians are doing in the EU and for more searching debates on EU matters. But it has proved difficult to realize this potential because of the lack of incentives for individual MdBs. Members of the Bundestag tend to see the democratic legitimation function for the EU as a matter for the European Parliament rather than for themselves (Katz 1999). They also have little incentive to specialize in Europe when it has low electoral salience, when there is a high opportunity cost in doing so, and when the connection between this engagement and policy outcomes is tenuous and uncertain.

The institutional incentives to Europeanize have been greater in the case of the Länder and of the Bundesrat (Jeffery, Chapter 5 in this volume). As with the

Bundestag, the Bundesrat has lost legislative competences to the EU and has had an incentive to defend its power and status by acquiring new rights. The Federal government has had a particular incentive to listen. because the Bundesrat could threaten to veto treaty change. Thus, at Maastricht, the German government pressed the case for a new EU Committee of the Regions to cement the role of the Länder at the EU level. Similarly, at Amsterdam, Kohl reversed the German position to argue for the retention of unanimity in Council voting on justice and home affairs matters, again to pacify the Länder. In order to safeguard ratification of the Single European Act and of the Maastricht Treaty, the federal government was willing to tolerate new rights of both information and participation for the Länder in EU policy. Particularly notable was the right to represent Germany in Council meetings dealing with matters falling into the Länder sphere of competence. Because European integration has had wide-ranging effects on the distribution of competences, it has introduced increased sensitivities into federal–Länder relations. Above all, it has spurred the Länder, led by Bavaria, to seek to redefine and clarify the proper constitutional balance of powers between Brussels, Berlin, and themselves, with the objective of securing more freedom of manoeuvre notably in internal market and competition policy. The result has been an increasingly proactive role by the Länder in seeking to shape the debate about the future EU.

But perhaps the most startling example of Europeanization was provided by the Bundesbank (Dyson, Chapter 10 in this volume, 2002b). Under the old ERM, the Bundesbank effectively dictated the terms of monetary policy to other ERM members because of the D-Mark's role as the anchor currency. This was a case of the Bundesbank 'exporting' its own monetary policy through the ERM rather than of the ERM 'Europeanizing' the Bundesbank. Consistent with the institutional incentives created by the Bundesbank Law of 1957, it took account only of domestic monetary stability. This changed after the Maastricht Treaty committed Germany to realize EMU by 1999 at the latest and following the ERM crises of 1992–3 that threatened this timetable. In particular, the logistics of working as part of the European Monetary Institute (EMI) from January 1994 in preparing the final stage three placed the Bundesbank firmly in a framework of Europeanization. Institutional incentives pointed to it playing the role of loyal and constructive player in this treaty-driven process, not least to shape the specific features of EMU on its own terms and to underwrite its own long-term interest.

The transfer of monetary policy to the new European Central Bank (ECB) in January 1999 was the final catalyst in prompting a domestic debate about reform to both the structure and the functions of the Bundesbank. This reform engaged the interests of the Länder in maintaining an influence on the future Bundesbank and of the big banks and financial institutions that wanted a new integrated financial services authority to combine regulation of banking with insurance and the stock markets. Both found themselves ranged against the Bundesbank, which preferred a streamlined single-tier Bundesbank board in place of the old two-tier structure to ensure more coherent policy and also sought to strengthen its own position in banking supervision. The outcome of the reform in 2002 was a smaller single-tier board, but with scope for the Länder to share in appointments, and a new integrated financial services authority in which the Bundesbank was given guarantees of a role in banking supervision. Crucially, as now an operating part of the European System of Central Banks (ESCB), institutional incentives pointed to a thorough Europeanization of the Bundesbank.

In many ways more problematic have been the effects of European integration on the Federal Constitutional Court (Schuppert, Chapter 6 in this volume). The Court was reluctant to recognize the primacy of the European Court of Justice (ECJ) in matters of European law, especially where they touch on basic rights. In the process—notably after its ruling of 12 October 1993 on the constitutionality of the Maastricht Treaty—it has been drawn into considerable controversy. It was seen to be challenging the right of the ECJ, under Article 234 of the Treaty of Rome, to interpret the treaty in favour of stressing its own role in ensuring an interpretation that was consistent with the German Basic Law. This view of a judicial activism of the Court on matters of European law went back to the so-called 'Solange I decision' of May 1974, which saw EU and national law as 'independent of each other' and standing 'side-by-side'. This reluctance seemed to have been qualified in the 'Solange II decision' of October 1986, when the Court argued that as long as the ECJ provided an effective protection for basic rights its own jurisprudence on matters of European law was not necessary. But the element of conditionality was revealed in the Maastricht ruling where the Court claimed the right to rule whether EU institutions were acting in conformity with their powers. It was reiterated in the 1995 decision on the Banana Directive, which asserted the primacy of the basic right to property as guaranteed in the Basic Law over EU law. At the heart of the Federal Constitutional Court's jurisprudence in EU law was a strong institutional incentive to define its role as ensuring the conformity of EU law with the Basic Law and doing so in a manner consistent with the doctrine of judicial activism that it had practised. By 2000, however, there were signs of change, in part consequent on new appointments to the Court (and the departure of Paul Kirchhof, regular *rapporteur* on European cases since 1987). But perhaps more significant, and spurred on by public criticisms, the Court identified an institutional incentive to avoid a fundamental clash with the ECJ and other Community institutions at some future point. The banana market decision of June 2000 indicated a new self-restraint and willingness to accept the overriding constitutional role of the ECJ in interpreting Community law.

What emerges from this review of effects on the German polity is the decisive role of institutional incentives to Europeanize and how these incentives have differed. These incentives have been in part shaped by the political context of institutions, and hence it is appropriate to look next at the effects of Europeanization on German politics. The Federal Constitutional Court shows the difficulties of sustaining a practice of co-existence and a difficult process of alternation between co-evolution and contestation. The Bundestag illustrates how a measure of co-evolution has complemented rather than overturned a preference for co-existence. The Bundesbank has trodden a track from co-existence, through a measure of contestation over the design and timing of EMU, to co-evolution. By contrast, the federal executive combines firmly rooted co-evolution at administrative levels with co-existence and occasional contestation at political levels. The major source of contestation has come from the bigger and more prosperous Länder, which have had the clearer institutional incentive to redefine the rules of the European game and have sought to draw the Federal government along with them.

Effects on Politics: Manoeuvring within Cultural Constraints

The effects of integration on German politics have been less obvious. Their limited nature in relation to the widening range of public policies affected by the EU reflects the strict, historically conditioned, cultural constraints at élite and mass levels. The limited effects on German politics, in turn, have shaped and constrained the Europeanization of the polity. Processes of opinion formation, identity construction, and élite–mass interactions have not been notably affected, whether one looks at the party system, interest groups, or the media. The prime reasons are to be found in a strong pro-European élite consensus, which defines macro-political strategies at home as well as within the EU and constrains polarization about European integration, and in a permissive public consensus. Élite and public consensus might seem precarious in relation to issues like the loss of the D-Mark and the German budget contribution, but have, nevertheless, proved resilient.

Although there have been changes in the party system since the early 1980s, notably from a relatively stable 'two-and-a-half' party system to a more fluid five party system, these changes have no clear relationship to Europeanization (Niedermayer, Chapter 7 in this volume). European integration has not influenced such party system properties as polarization, fragmentation, or coalition stability. Parties advocating a national populism, especially on the extreme right, failed to establish a sizeable electoral base, with the European issue remaining marginal to electoral behaviour and, therefore, lacking a mobilizing potential. Even the issue of losing the D-Mark, to which so much symbolism was attached, did not prove a polarizing issue and a successful launch pad for new parties. Issues like the loss of the D-Mark and Germany's large net EU budgetary contribution were latent issues of contestation, but they remained framed within a continuing élite consensus about the overriding German national interest in the integration process and within a permissive public consensus. The result was a lack of centrality for

European issues. By 1998–9, the German public had made its peace with the Euro.

For the same reasons, the media were not polarized into pro- and anti-European camps, tended to avoid sensationalized European reporting, and preferred to domesticate European news in terms of national political figures and their activities (Voltmer and Eilders, Chapter 9 in this volume). There was no agonizing debate about Europe between or within the parties or within the federal government to draw the attention of the media. In short, the media lacked exciting 'newsworthy' stories about Europe. They also showed little willingness to set the agenda on Europe. Negative reporting was in the context of the more general assessment of the policy performance of the Chancellor and ministers rather than of an attempt to lead on an anti-European agenda.

More complex were the effects of European integration on the major interest groups, especially the business associations (Eising, Chapter 8 in this volume). At one level, the market liberalization ethos of the internal market and EMU challenged German traditions of self-regulation and encouraged firms to see less incentive in membership of these associations and more advantage in lobbying EU institutions directly (Bührer and Grande 2000). The EU threatened the cultural basis of German industrial capitalism, noticeably self-regulation, which formed the backbone of the highly organized interest group system. But, at another level, German business associations were effective players at the EU level compared to their counterparts in Britain and France. This effectiveness reflected above all their organizational capabilities as well-resourced, highly professional multi-level players. They had an institutional incentive to transfer their domestic strengths upwards to the EU level and play an influential role within EU policy networks, not least in order to retain membership loyalty. This loyalty was the very basis of their organizational capability. The open question was whether further EU market liberalization would weaken their future organizational capability to sustain this multi-level influence.

Effects on German Public Policies: Managing Veto Players

By far the clearest and strongest effects of Europeanization were demonstrated in public policies. These effects were most evident in regulatory policies, especially those associated with the Single Market and competition policies, and in policies designed to secure economic stability. The EU approximated a form of 'regulatory' and 'stabilization' state (see Dyson 2000*b*; Majone 1996), specializing in the performance of these functions and legitimating itself in an essentially technocratic manner as promoting economic efficiency and 'sound' money and finance. As these values were broadly congruent both with German macro-political strategy for European integration and with domestic 'ordo-liberalism', they enjoyed a broad-based support in principle. Indeed, the German federal government—led by the Federal Economics Ministry—had strongly promoted the internal market and a strict competition policy regime. It had also backed the Bundesbank in ensuring the 'uploading' of German ideas about 'sound' money (an independent ECB) and 'sound' finance (clear fiscal rules) to the EU.

But, in practice, policy adaptation has proved more problematic since the 1990s. In regulatory and competition policies, these problems have reflected the complex interaction between the changing nature and direction of policy development at the EU level—putting in question earlier German success in 'uploading' its institutional models, policy preferences, and 'ways of doing things'—and entrenched sectoral-level policy structures, discourses and veto players. In stabilization policy, the problem has been that fiscal rules have implications for the capacity of the German state to provide policies whose function is distribution and redistribution, for instance generous social policies.

In environmental policy, Germany was long able to play a strikingly successful leadership role as the Community expanded its competence, for instance in the larger combustion directive, car emission standards, eco-labelling and climate change (Wurzel, Chapter 14 in this volume). But EU-level policy developments since the 1990s have challenged Germany's rather formalistic style, which relies heavily on detailed substantive regulation, by a 'softer', less interventionist, self-regulatory approach. This approach involved new requirements on Germany to introduce the principle of shared responsibility, to pay more attention to cost-effectiveness of regulation, and to strengthen its procedural measures (notably environmental impact assessment (EIA) and right of access to environmental information). Also, Germany had institutional difficulties in implementing the EU 'integrated pollution prevention and control' approach embracing air, water, and soil. The Länder had a veto position consequent on their key competence in water management and were resistant to the EU's approach and any idea of a national environmental law. On occasion, the Chancellor and the Federal Economics Ministry acted as veto players, preventing the Federal Environment Ministry from agreeing to the End-of-Life Vehicles Directive in 2000 and frustrating EU legislation on dangerous chemicals and nature protection. Hence, the co-existence and co-evolution of the 1970s and 1980s gave way to a complex of co-evolution and contestation from the 1990s.

Competition policy had a similar trajectory of development (Lodge, Chapter 11 in this volume). Here, again, Germany had been a policy leader, promoting the idea of a strong rule-based approach to mergers. This idea was institutionalized in, and promoted by, the Federal Cartel Office, which took a tough, case-oriented approach in line with traditional German ordo-liberalism. By the 1990s, the Cartel Office was fighting a defensive rearguard action in the face of what it saw as the politicization of merger policy by the European Commission and by the Federal Economics Ministry and the Chancellor's Office. Seen from the EU level, Germany presented a divided picture. The Chancellor's Office and Länder governments appeared as veto players in relation to the Commission's attempt to apply competition policy as a level playing field within the internal market. In so doing, they tapped into a well of broad political support. On the other hand, the Federal Cartel Office seemed a bastion of old-fashioned competition policy beliefs that acted as a veto player in mobilizing German domestic opposition to a more economics-based approach to merger control.

Two developments were important. First, in developing competition policy within the framework of the internal market, the European Commission shifted to a more evolutionary, economics-based approach to merger, which the Cartel Office saw as the abandonment of a rules-based approach in favour of a discretionary approach that offered scope for the consideration of industrial policy goals. Notably the Cartel Office failed to export to the EU level the model of an independent European Cartel Office. It was also unable to prevent the amendment to Regulation 17/62 that shifted competition policy decisively from the formal German *ex ante* notification procedure to a US-style of *ex post* control.

Second, within this EU-level context, the Federal Economics Ministry and the Chancellor—sensitive to the worries of German firms, especially in the case of Schröder—were concerned to ensure a strong German corporate presence in a larger and growing European market. The result was what the Cartel Office saw as a politicization of merger policy and its subordination to industrial policy. An example was the Economics Ministry's approval of the giant Eon–Ruhrgas merger in 2002, on the basis that it raised no problem of competition in the European energy market. In doing so, it overruled the Cartel Office. The European Commission chose not to intervene. The federal government was also increasingly sensitive to what it saw as excessive interference by the Commission in pursuing its competition policy. Examples included: an end to the privileges of public-sector savings banks; faster phasing out of huge coal subsidies; fines imposed on Volkswagen for discriminatory distribution arrangements; an attack on the exclusivity of car distribution schemes; and aid to shipbuilding and steel in east Germany. The accumulation of these cases of tension and conflict led Schröder to a general assault on the Commission for not taking Germany's industrial interests sufficiently into account in its policies.

Sectoral regulation in areas that were earlier exempted from the German competition law regime illustrates how German EU policy positions have been influenced by the specific problems of achieving negotiated compromise in pluralist institutional environments in which potential veto players shape the nature and tempo of reform. It also reflects Germany's relative success in influencing the terms of EU liberalization in different sectors against a background not just of domestic veto players, but also of contrasting market conditions. Thus, liberalization of road haulage came as one of the earlier internal market reforms, reflecting the strength of competitive pressures. Here Germany had to adapt quickly. In telecommunications, too, competitive market conditions pushed the agenda of liberalization, especially driven by telecommunications users who wanted lower costs. But Germany was successful in gearing the pace of EU liberalization to domestic difficulties of adjustment (Bulmer *et al.*, Chapter 12 in this volume). The key here was the shift of strategic direction by Siemens and Deutsche Telekom, both of which had been veto players, but recognized that liberalization and an end to their monopoly position were a necessary price to be paid for their European and global ambitions. Telecommunications was characterized by co-evolution, with Germany shifting to a greater policy leader role by the late 1990s and adopting a more rules-based approach. A striking outcome was the establishment of a new regulatory authority for telecommunications to replace the Federal Posts and Telecommunications Ministry.

Electricity was different, partly because market pressures were less intense and partly because veto players like the Länder and local authorities had much more to lose, notably revenues. Here, Germany worked closely with France to control the pace of adjustment and was distinctive in an EU context for preferring negotiated sectoral adjustment over an independent regulatory authority. Until the electricity liberalization directive of 1996, Germany was characterized by co-existence, and thereafter caught up in a dynamic of contestation about a stronger rules-based approach versus a negotiated self-regulation that would allow co-evolution. Hence, there were pronounced differences in the Europeanization of sectoral regulation.

The most spectacular instance of Europeanization was economic policy (Dyson, Chapter 10 in this volume). EMU's effects were both wide-ranging and complex, reflecting its three main pillars. First, monetary union represented the transfer of authority to a new supranational authority, the ECB, and the relegation of the once powerful Bundesbank—the 'bank that rules Europe'—in both power and status to a member of the ESCB. This transfer did not promise radical policy shifts in the sense that in essentials the ECB had been modelled on the Bundesbank to ensure a continuity of 'sound' money policies. It was independent and obligated to ensure price stability. But there were, nevertheless, effects. Germany found itself with an ECB monetary policy that was set with the interests of the Euro-Zone as a whole in mind, but was less appropriate for its own economic circumstances of low growth and stubbornly high unemployment. Between 1998 and 2002, the problem was to some extent alleviated by a weak Euro, which boosted German exports and hence helped employment and incomes in the manufacturing sectors. However, in the absence of a domestically geared monetary policy, the onus fell on wages policy and on labour-market policies to speed economic adjustment. Between 1999 and 2001, there was success in negotiating and implementing two-year, productivity-based wage agreements. By 2002, however, pent-up wage frustrations surfaced in a tougher wage round. More seriously, political resistance to labour-market reforms remained high, with powerful veto players within the trade unions, the SPD, the

CDU, and the Federal Ministry for Labour and Social Affairs. It took the scandal at the Federal Labour Office in early 2002 and the subsequent Hartz Commission report to enable the Chancellor's Office to create an atmosphere of crisis that could give momentum to labour-market reforms. It was by no means clear that these reforms would be sufficient to generate major reductions of unemployment in the context of EMU. Yet, the German government was not prepared to call for reforms to the structure or mandate of the ECB that might have made it more politically accountable or its mandate more inclusive of other goals, including growth and employment.

In the second pillar of fiscal policy, by contrast, the EU—led by German proposals—had established a system of 'hard' policy co-ordination in the form of the Stability and Growth Pact. Under it terms, member states were required to submit and gain approval for national stability programmes that spelt out how they intended to achieve 'close to budgetary balance' over the economic cycle. In 2001, the European Council specified a deadline of 2004 for meeting this objective. The Pact also required that states avoid a budget deficit greater than 3 per cent of GDP. If they broke this requirement, they would be the subject of recommendations for action and, ultimately, of heavy sanctions. The overall purpose of the Pact was to prevent 'free-riding' by states that—once deprived of the direct exchange-rate constraint—might be tempted to pursue expansionary budgets and offload the costs to other states in the form of higher ECB interest rates. It was also to provide a fiscal flank of 'sound' finance to support the ECB.

Embarrassingly, in February 2002, Germany was threatened with a letter of warning from the European Commission that it risked breaching the 3 per cent limit. This was averted by a negotiated agreement in ECOFIN, with Schröder heavily involved because of the high political stakes in an election year. A key result was agreement that the Federal government would once again try to negotiate a national stability pact with the Länder and the local authorities, which would bind them to budgetary targets consistent with achieving an overall 'close to balance' by 2004 and thereby meeting Germany's commitments. However, there remained a striking difference between the rules and sanctions of the Stability and Growth Pact and the 'soft' fiscal policy co-ordination that characterized German federalism. The Länder vetoed the idea of a national stability pact with sanctions. By October 2002—just after the election—it was clear that Germany would breach the 3 per cent limit. The result was another major bout of budget consolidation. A key effect of the Stability and Growth Pact was to reinforce—rather than to create—the domestic political rationale for continuing budgetary consolidation. Schröder and Eichel were careful to distance themselves from fundamental criticism of the Pact, but with the election behind them began to talk of the need for a more flexible interpretation of its provisions.

Perhaps most importantly, the Pact reinforced the domestic political status and power of the Finance Ministry. It became an increasingly Europeanized ministry (led by its European division) and with an interest in spreading Europeanization to the Länder (through the Financial Planning Council), the Council of Economic Experts, and the Bundestag and Bundesrat. From its perspective, these bodies were only imperfectly Europeanized and could, potentially, act as veto players on EMU-related matters. Its influence reached out to constrain the scope for the Defence Ministry to engage in the emerging European security and defence policy and press the case for its reliance on restructuring to release necessary resources. It was also felt in terms of pushing the agenda for social policy reforms, notably to pensions and health. In these ways, EMU had important indirect effects on German public policies.

In the third pillar of economic policy, especially in policies to promote growth and employment, the EU proceeded by 'soft' co-ordination. This involved a reliance on guidelines, peer review, benchmarking best practice, and policy learning. These processes informed the Macro-Economic Policy Guidelines (Maastricht Treaty), the national employment action plans (Luxembourg process since 1997), the structural reform reports (Cardiff process since 1998), the Macro-Economic Dialogue (Cologne process since 1999), and the Lisbon process (since 2000) for improving the longer-term growth, productivity, and employment performance of the EU. This approach has been strongly promoted by the German federal government as consistent with the principle of subsidiarity in economic policy. Thus, in 1997, Kohl rejected the idea of the Community being given formal responsibility in employment policy. In its 1999 EU Presidency, the Schröder government proposed the Macro-Economic Dialogue as a way of involving the social partners in EMU in a dialogue and information exchange about optimal policy responses of wages to monetary and fiscal policies.

The overall result of this widening range of EU initiatives was to broaden the circle of German policy actors involved in the process of Europeanization, particularly to include the Federal Ministry of Labour and Social Affairs, the Federal Ministry for Education and Research, and the Länder education ministries. In co-ordinating the German input to the Lisbon process, the Finance Ministry was inhibited from being able to make commitments and act as a policy leader by the difficulty of reconciling the plurality of different institutional interests. In labour-market and education policies, there was a new interest in benchmarking best practice elsewhere, for instance in the UK, a need that was reinforced when in 2001 the OECD's Pisa study showed Germany to be falling well behind in international educational league tables of pupil attainment. But this practice was *ad hoc*, pragmatic horizontal Europeanization with no real connection to EU processes. What was interesting, however, was the tendency to take similar examples: Denmark, the Netherlands, Sweden, and the UK. German policy was less introverted and framed in terms of a German model. With that model in question, or even discredited, domestic policy space was being opened up from within to a wider range of experiences.

EMU meant that fewer policy sectors and actors could continue to co-exist with Community policy, treating it as marginally significant. Its effects were invading labour-market policies, education policies, and social policies, especially though the reframing of policies as discourse shifted to how Germany could improve policy performance by benchmarking best practice and drawing appropriate lessons. Here, direct and indirect cognitive effects were apparent, strengthening the agenda for promoting vocational education and more precise standard-setting and monitoring in education, attention to retaining older people and promoting the role of women in the labour market, and more competition in health and pension policy provision.

The overall pattern of Europeanization that emerges is then characterized by intensive and intensifying Europeanization effects in most fields of public policy. Effects are evident not just where the EU has been a long-standing legislator, but in fields as diverse as social policy (Haverland, Chapter 13 in this volume), justice and home affairs (Monar, Chapter 15 in this volume) and foreign and security policy (Miskimmon and Paterson, Chapter 16 in this volume). In contrast, direct effects on core state institutions seem often marginal rather than central. More strikingly, the evidence about political effects is much more ambiguous. At the risk of oversimplification, one may contrast Europeanized public policies with a semi-Europeanized polity and a largely non-Europeanized politics. This conclusion might be used to suggest that traditional institutions of democratic politics have failed to keep pace with Europeanization, that there is a dangerous and growing gap between policies and politics. Alternatively, it might be cited as evidence for the resilience of national democratic institutions.

A different explanation might be offered for this broad macro-pattern of Europeanization of the German political system. As the Introduction to this chapter noted, the Europeanization literature suggests two basic explanations for the 'differential impact of Europe' (though, as we stressed, these explanations are not mutually exclusive): 'fit'/'misfit', and the impact of integration on domestic opportunity structures. The 'fit'/'misfit' explanation suggests that the greatest resistance to Europeanization will occur where the 'misfit' is most pronounced. One might posit such a 'misfit' between the EU and traditional national arrangements of representation, in line with the 'democratic deficit' debate. On the one hand, EU decision-making structures and processes are not easy for national parliaments and parties to 'penetrate', in contrast to national executives. In other words, there is weak 'political' 'uploading'. On the other hand, national elections, representative institutions, and the patterns of political communication are closely tied to the principle of territorial representation. A pronounced 'misfit' between EU governance and the traditional patterns of domestic democratic legitimation seems accordingly evident.

'Misfit' can, however, only be part of an explanation and does not appear generalizable. Comparative studies show that in some other European member states the electorate, parties, the party system, and legislatures show rather different patterns of adaptation to European integration from Germany. Thus, in many member states there is evidence of a pro- versus anti-integrationist cleavage; of a European effect on party choice; and, although the evidence must not be overplayed (Mair 2000), of clear party system effects. Several parliaments, perhaps most notably in the Nordic states, have taken bigger steps to guarantee a more powerful say in EU affairs than the Bundestag. Although such comparative remarks do not contradict the basic point about the obstacles facing the 'Europeanization of nation-based democracy', they suggest that the German case of non-adaptation cannot be explained simply by high degrees of 'misfit' alone.

It would appear that the opportunity structures for actors in the representative institutions of the German political system differ significantly from those in other parts of the political system. For political actors, there would appear to be a disjunction between what one might call 'intra-institutional' incentives and electoral incentives (see also Lees 2002). Any intra-institutional incentive for MPs to carve out a niche for themselves in the legislature by specializing in EU affairs is largely dissociated from, and cancelled out by, the incentive structure for MPs in the electoral arena. Similarly, executive politicians find themselves inevitably drawn into decision-making at the EU level, but their performance there has no demonstrable effect in terms of electoral performance at the national level. They play at two levels, but they do not play a two-level game, where gains at the EU level can be translated into advantages in the domestic political arena (Goetz, Chapter 3 in this volume). The point here is not so much that it does not pay to be a Euro-sceptic or a Europhile in the German political system. As far as elections and parties are concerned, a 'two-level' game does not appear to exist or, if so, only a very weak version of it.

There is no ready answer to account for this non-contestation of European integration in the German political system. It certainly contrasts quite sharply with the situation in some other European states, where integration policy is strongly controversial, giving rise to a—conflictually—Europeanized politics. The mainstream answer would be sought in arguments about congruence (partly based on Germany's 'uploading' capacity) and 'enabling constraints'. However, as will be argued in the next section, these basic conditions of Europeanization are subject to increasing challenges, with the result that we can also expect a growing contestation of integration policy in future.

Beyond Congruence and 'Enabling Constraints': Towards a More Contested Relationship

The chapters on the Europeanization of institutions and public policies provide sufficient evidence to call into question whether 'congruence' and 'enabling constraints' will continue to be dominant influences on patterns of Europeanization in Germany. Briefly, there are growing indications of 'incongruence', and that the tensions between constraints and enabling effects are becoming more pronounced, as the character of the EU and the character of Germany are changing.

A key theme to emerge from this study has been the mounting paradox between a more politically self-confident Germany, represented by Schröder's pursuit of a discourse of 'normalization', and a Germany whose resources of 'soft' power are diminishing. Of course, the normalization discourse itself can be read as evidence that, in the eyes of German policy-makers, the external 'enabling' constraints have been largely realized. Put differently, one of the decisive motives behind integration as pursued by Adenauer and his successors—to re-establish Germany as a power in Europe—has been achieved, and further integration is unlikely to lead to significant gains in this respect. The paradox is that, just when Germany is seeking to project itself more effectively at the European and international levels, in the seemingly secure knowledge of a place 'at the top table', its credibility to do so is diminishing. Generational change points to a more relaxed view about how Germany exercises power, one not freed from the legacy of the past, but one that is less personally burdened by it. At the same time, relative economic decline has gathered pace: the 'fading' economic miracle of the 1980s (Giersch, Paque and Schmieding 1992) has been followed by its disappearance. Contrary to some earlier political expectations, German unification has not led to a new economic miracle. It has created an extra economic and fiscal burden that has accelerated relative economic decline. In consequence, Germany's role as 'paymaster' of Europe has been abrogated. This means that the solution to European problems no longer leads immediately to Berlin; decisive political leverage at the European level has been lost. No less importantly, German is losing another decisive resource of 'soft' power: the reputation and credibility that comes with superior policy performance. This leads on to further paradoxes. Just as the EU embraces 'benchmarking' as a key policy instrument, Germany no longer appears as an appropriate model of best practice for others to emulate and from which to draw appropriate policy lessons. In addition, just as Eastern enlargement starts to become a political and institutional reality, Germany ceases to be as convincing a model for these new members as it was for earlier waves of entrants.

This paradox between increasing self-confidence and declining 'soft' power suggests a major underlying change in the way in which Germany interacts with Europe and in how Germany experiences Europeanization. 'Uploading' domestic institutions, policies, and 'ways of doing things' to the EU level will be more difficult. The result is greater potential for a more conflictual relationship in which the options of resistance and inertia are likely to play a greater role than in the past and the traditional image of a Germany that simply accommodates Europe will be more difficult to sustain.

This potential for a more contested relationship is decisively increased by the diminishing grip of the traditional 'North-West' core on the EU. Large-scale expansion of membership, combined with a greater diversity of interests within the EU, means that it will become more difficult for Germany to set and control the EU agenda. New, much poorer member states will have an interest in externalizing at least some of the costs of rapid economic adjustment, especially in the context of exchange-rate stability under ERM2, by pushing the case for increased EU fiscal transfers and seeking out allies for this purpose. There is the potential for conflict with Germany and for Germany to find itself on the defensive. EU enlargement implies that the 'periphery' is growing at the expense of the traditional 'centre'. Germany also faces the prospect of tension between domestic industrial policy objectives, which involve claims for greater autonomy especially of Länder governments from EU internal market and competition policies, and German support for the objective of ensuring that there is a rigorous implementation of these policies in the new member states. This poses a credibility problem for German EU policy.

These twin developments are occurring in the context of a long-term trend towards an expansion in the scope and depth of EU policies so that their effects are experienced more directly and intrusively by domestic institutions, political actors and the public. An arm's-length relationship of co-existence with the EU in which generalized support for integration does not translate into very tangible effects is becoming unsustainable. In short, the German pattern of Europeanization is shifting from co-existence and co-evolution to co-evolution and contestation.

Is Germany Still Exceptional?

What can be learned by situating Germany in the comparative Europeanization literature? At first sight, the potential of such an approach might appear limited. After all, there has been a strong tendency to discuss the German Europeanization experience in terms that stress the exceptionalism of the German case. As far as 'uploading' is concerned, the literature on European integration has long emphasized the apparent German willingness to prioritize integration over the national interest and not just to accept, but also to seek limitations on sovereign powers. Analysts have sought to capture this with concepts and notions such as the 'penetrated polity' (Hanrieder 1967), 'semi-Gulliver' (Bulmer and Paterson 1989), 'shaping the regional milieu' (Bulmer, Jeffery and Paterson 2000, building on Wolfers 1962), 'tamed power' (Katzenstein 1997b) or even *Machtvergessenheit* (Schwartz 1985). It was even suggested that integration may be part of the 'genetic code' of the German political system (Goetz 1996), a variant of the long-established argument about integration as part of the *raison d'être* of the Federal Republic. At least prior to unification, the Federal Republic was said to be willing to punch below its weight, to be less assertive than other member states in defending its interests and more willing to bear a disproportionate share of the financial costs of integration. This orientation, it was argued, was further accentuated by a system of co-ordinating EU-related policies that limited the German state's capacity to influence day-to-day EU decision-making. In short, where Germany sought to exercise influence, it was—in terms of its domestic institutional arrangements—not especially well equipped to do so.

As regards patterns of domestic effects, German exceptionality has been a less prominent theme, although the congruence argument, with its stress on macro-institutional factors, points to the particular adaptability of the German system. More recently, the comparative literature has focused on meso-level and micro-level institutional and actor-centred variables to account for the 'differential impact' of Europe. In line with such an explanatory approach, the diversity of national experiences of Europeanization has been emphasized.

However, a brief comparative contexualization of the German case suggests that it is, in fact, closer to that of other member states than much of the German-centred Europeanization debate suggests. Both in terms of its predominant pattern of participation in European integration (the 'uploading' dimension) and the predominant pattern of domestic effects (the 'downloading' dimension of Europeanization), Germany does, in fact, share a great deal with other members of the North-Western founding core of the European Communities. The basic tenets of integration are shared: including length of membership in the EU and its predecessors; full engagement across all the three pillars of integration; and membership of EMU. Moreover, the founder members are bound together by a dense network of intra-regional ties, a point that applies to Germany, the Benelux countries and France.

If, as this study suggests, Europeanization in the sense of co-evolution is a much more restricted phenomenon than received wisdom on Germany tends to argue, the commonalities in the Europeanization experiences of the North-Western founding members also come to the fore. Thus, while European integration has not, of course, remained politically uncontested in the North-Western world, it did not emerge as a strong social cleavage and, until recently, it does not appear to have had major party system effects. Élite consensus and permissive mass consensus on European integration were no less strong in the Benelux countries than in Germany, and while support may have been more brittle and conditional in France, it remained sufficiently stable for France to act as one of the motors of integration. Moreover, in terms of effects on state organization, while it may have been differential, there is no evidence of pronounced transformative or fragmentary effects that would have challenged the cohesion of the ensemble of core state institutions. Of course, as was argued above, it is primarily sector-specific opportunity structures that determine detailed Europeanization trajectories. But commonalities in the integration experience constitute important context variables or parameters that shape the repertoire of possible domestic responses.

Comparative contextualization of the German case also reveals, first, that in important respects the North-Western core experience has not been fully replicated in Southern, Nordic and the emerging Central and Eastern European worlds of Europeanization. The traditional North-Western world, with Germany at its heart, is becoming increasingly less typical both in terms of patterns of member participation in the Union and in terms of domestic Europeanization effects. This is a point worth making, given that the bulk of the Europeanization literature draws on the founder states and tends to generalize from their experience. Second, however, and following on from the arguments developed in the preceding sections, there are some signals that the German Europeanization experience may, in future, come to resemble more closely Europeanization patterns so far principally associated with the European periphery. Both points require brief elaboration.

Even a cursory review of the integration and Europeanization patterns in Southern, Northern, and Eastern Europe shows up important differences from the core experience. In the Nordic world, Denmark acceded to EC in the early 1970s and both Sweden and Finland joined the EU only during the enlargement round of the mid-1990s. One should also include Norway in this world, not only because European integration has also far-reaching effects on non-members, but also because, as far as domestic effects are concerned, there are very strong similarities to other members of the Nordic family. With the partial exception of Finland, the Nordic pattern of Europeanization can be described in terms of conditional participation and engagement. Finland is the Nordic exception, in that it both participates fully in all three pillars and belongs to the EMU area. By contrast, Denmark has secured a number of significant opt-outs. Thus, under Article 69 of the revised and renumbered Treaty of Rome, Denmark wishes to be inside the free-movement area, but formally under an intergovernmental regime. It also gained significant exemptions under the Maastricht Treaty. Importantly, neither Denmark (opt out) nor Sweden (derogation) had joined the single currency by 2002. Even more than in the North-Western world, there is a strong tradition of intra-regional co-operation among the Nordic states.

The pattern of effect is gradual, pre-accession Europeanization, followed by acceleration since accession. In terms of state organization, there is little evidence of strong fragmentary effects, but particular emphasis has been placed on the role of parliaments, leading to a certain 'reparlamentarization' of public policy-making. However, European integration has had high political salience and has left its marks on the Nordic party systems. Nick Sitter (2001) has compared the impact of Euro-scepticism on the party systems of Norway, Sweden and Denmark. Operating with Bartolini and Mair's definition of political cleavages, he argues that, while classifying opposition to European integration as a cleavage may stretch the concept too far, the translation of European issues into the domestic party systems of the Nordic states has been associated with a strong government–opposition dynamic. With the exception of Finland, integration has been strongly contested in the EU's Nordic periphery, with direct effects on electoral competition and party systems.

As regards the overall pattern of membership, the Mediterranean world resembles the North-Western core. Membership occurred later, but there are no formal opt outs, and Spain, Portugal, and Greece all participate in EMU. But it is doubtful whether this formal description of participation patterns fully captures their role in Europe. Thus, it is arguable that Spain is only gradually growing into a major role when it comes to shaping the trajectory of European integration in terms of 'uploading' policies, while Portugal and Greece still exhibit a more passive pattern of membership, with limited proactive engagement outside areas of immediate concern to them. The Mediterranean world is proactive where its specific interests are affected, but does not consistently seek to 'upload' its preferences across the range of EU regulatory and constitutive policies. A notable lack of institutionalized intra-regional co-operation further reduces their overall influence.

The differences from the North-Western core are even more noticeable when we look at integration effects. Europeanization has been gradual and appears to have remained partial. The overall societal and institutional effect has been summed up by Featherstone and Kazamias (2001), who identify 'dynamism, asymmetry and fragmentation' as the key attributes of the southern experience of Europeanization. Thus, 'Europeanization creates and reinforces domestic cleavages based on competing notions of reform, economic interest and identity. The impact is felt in social, cultural, economic and political terms as change and continuity are juxtaposed as domestic faultlines across the domestic system" (Featherstone and Kazamias 2001: 13).

Finally, as far as Europeanization in Eastern Europe is concerned, the main outlines of current and likely future participatory patterns are now emerging reasonably clearly. The process of negotiation for accession has been structured by the adoption, implementation, and enforcement of the *acquis communautaire*, organized around the negotiation of individual chapters. This has turned out to be a much more drawn-out process than many had envisaged in the late 1980s and early 1990s. It has proceeded through various stages marked by the conclusion of Europe agreements, the development of a pre-accession strategy, and the opening of accession negotiations with Hungary, Poland, the Czech Republic, Estonia, and Slovenia at the end of March 1998. Co-operation among the CEE applicants during the negotiation process has been weak, a reflection of a broader pattern of weakly institutionalized intra-regional linkages. What appears to be emerging is EU membership of a different quality, characterized by transitional arrangements, derogations, and aspects of bilateralization. Importantly, most of the new CEE members are also likely to remain outside EMU for the foreseeable future.

If we turn to Europeanization effects, they have not just been differential—as different parts of the state have been affected in different forms and to different degrees by European integration—but there is evidence of fragmentation. Thus, the requirements of managing accession negotiations and of ensuring legal harmonization have led to the creation of Europeanized 'enclaves' in the executive systems of the CEE applicants. These 'islands of excellence' consist of small teams of politicians and officials operating under the authority of the head of government. They tend to operate outside many of the constraints of mainstream executive administration—be they political or budgetary. But they are also in permanent danger of becoming dissociated from the main body of the executive machinery (Goetz 2000*a*; for a recent case study of the 'administrative and institutional duality between domestic and EU affairs' in Hungary see Ágh 2002). Similar consequences become apparent when one examines the administrative arrangements that have been set up for the management of pre-accession EU funds, including PHARE, IPSA (Instrument for Structural Policies for Pre-Accession) and SAPARD (Special Pre-Accession Programme for Agriculture and Rural Development) (van Stolk 2002). Institutional fragmentation is mirrored in increasingly evident cleavage and party system effects. These are especially pronounced in the case of Poland, where European integration is emerging as a major salient issue in party competition.

What follows from this brief comparative contextualization for our understanding of the German case? First, specific features notwithstanding, the historical German Europeanization experience appears to show close parallels to that of the other North-Western founding states, both in terms of patterns of participation and in terms of patterns of effects. This is not to deny that there are elements of singularity—notably, European integration as part of the *raison d'être* of the Federal Republic. But what appears striking is the impression of commonality rather than difference. The North-Western experience has been based on common founder member status, the emphasis on unanimity in EU decision-making, coupled with the predominance of the Community method, and the existence of strong intra-regional links.

Second, the Europeanization experience of this core does not provide a template for later members. Through various enlargements—South, North, and now East—and through changes in the way in which the EU works, the traditional core experience has become progressively less 'typical'. Put differently, the 'peripheral' variants of Europeanization are increasingly becoming the norm; the traditional 'core' variant becomes the exception, with potential far-reaching repercussions for the shrinking core.

Third, there are indications that the Europeanization pattern at the centre itself may be showing increasing signs of 'peripheralization', especially as far as social cleavages and party system effects are concerned. What appears of most immediate relevance here is the growing evidence of anti-integrationist sentiments among significant parts of both the electorates and the political élites not just in the Nordic world and CEE, but also in France, Italy, Belgium and, most recently, the Netherlands. In fact, considered in this context, Germany does, indeed, appear exceptional—but is it likely to stay so? It would be wrong to attach too much long-term significance to recent controversies between the German government and the European Commission; Germany has no Jörg Haider, no Umberto Bossi (and no Ian Duncan Smith). But it is clear that the generational shift in the German political leadership marked by the end of the Kohl era has not only led to a change of tone in domestic discussions of European integration. It has also been accompanied by a greater willingness of political élites to respond to—or, as critics might have it, pander to—real or perceived uneasiness amongst the electorate about the deepening and widening of integration. At the same time, as this volume has shown, there is a growing willingness to 'blame' the EU and to criticize openly the EU institutions.

Germany as a Test Case?

If comparative contexualization helps to avoid the pitfalls of unwarranted singularization, are there any broader implications of our study for the future of Europeanization studies? As we noted in Chapter 1, there is a danger of a growing gap between increasingly ambitious conceptualizations of Europeanization and concomitant research desiderata and what empirical investigations are likely to be able to achieve. We would claim that the definition of Europeanization that we have advanced at the outset has helped to yield tangible insights and may, thus, provide a basis for advancing the comparative debate. First, our contributions have borne out the extent to which Europeanization is an interactive and dynamic process. The study of Europeanization cannot be divorced from the study of integration, although the two are analytically distinct. In fact, for students of Europeanization there is much to be learned from the latter and also from the considerable amount of Europeanization research *avant la lettre*. Given the scarcity of current research in this field with a strong historical dimension— short time horizons predominate—'reanalysis' of this earlier work is an important part of gaining a fuller understanding of the temporal patterns of Europeanization.

Second, the contributions underline that 'misfit' is not a necessary precondition of Europeanization, and should not, therefore, be made part of the definition. To be sure, misfit—or, perhaps, the perception of misfit at EU or domestic levels—may create adaptational pressures and, thus, trigger Europeanization. But this should not be treated as the norm. Misfit as part of an explanatory account is most relevant where European policy relies on standardizing EU legislation that conflicts with domestic legislation. Even under those restrictive conditions, associated with the classical Community method, misfit is best understood as a trig-

ger or catalyst of change, but does not explain patterns of Europeanization themselves. Moreover, a 'top-down' perspective needs to be complemented by attention to 'bottom-up' dynamics, or, put more concretely, the tactical and strategic
use domestic actors may make of 'Europe' as leverage for achieving change at the
domestic level. In short, especially in a member state such as Germany, which has
traditionally been a vigorous 'uploader' in the integration process, 'misfits' do not
just appear 'from above', but may be purposefully engineered 'from below'. Of
equal importance is the fact that more horizontal forms of integration—as
through the open method of co-ordination or benchmarking—are associated with
a greater degree of voluntarism, discretion and negotiability in domestic
responses, not least since the powers of the European Court of Justice are drasti-
cally curtailed in these domains. Here, the explanatory power of misfit is further
reduced.

Third, our definition of Europeanization was substantively indeterminate, in
the sense that unlike some recent contributions, such as Buller and Gamble
(2002), we leave open the question of whether Europeanization entails a transformation of public policies, political institutions, and processes. As many of the
contributions to this volume bear out, Europeanization may take many forms and
to equate Europeanization with transformation is to 'define away' much of the
subtlety of the European effect.

Turning from conceptual to empirical questions, the preceding chapters bear
out the unevenness of our empirical knowledge of Europeanization patterns, not
just in terms of their historical evolution, but also in terms of the disparities in the
depth and detail of what we know about different policy sectors, different institutions, and different processes of political communication, representation and
legitimation. Much of the received wisdom on the Europeanization of Germany
is derived from the analysis of a fairly narrow range of exemplary cases, and even
here appeals to intuition and common sense must often make up for a lack of
systematically collected information.

If this holds for Germany, a founder member, the largest state of the EU, and
often seen as the touchstone of Europeanization, it applies with similar, if not
greater force, to other countries, notably those outside the North-Western core. In
terms of the key empirical questions that guided the present inquiry, comparative
research is still very much at the beginning. For example, it is clear that more
attention needs to be given to a longer time perspective, which helps to trace
changes in the nature of the integration process and of the European institutions
over time and their implications for patterns of Europeanization; that there is a
great deal of work to be done on the political dimension of Europeanization—
parties, party systems, representation, identities, and the role of media; that we
are still at the beginning of understanding the implications of the plurality of integration within the framework of the EU, let alone its interaction with other forms
of regional integration; and that the 'unbundling' of integration must be

accompanied by efforts to investigate the linkage between integration and other drivers of change, such as democratization, liberalization, and privatization in the case of the Eastern European accession countries.

Living with Europe

The main findings of this volume do not just pose a challenge to analysts of European integration and Europeanization. They imply an even greater challenge to those actively engaged in shaping the political course of Germany and of the European project. Our analysis of the three themes introduced in Chapter 1— power, constraint, and contestation—will make uncomfortable reading for those committed to the 'widening and deepening' of integration. Germany's resources of 'soft power' to shape the EU's policies and constitutive politics are dwindling; domestic restrictive constraints are becoming more apparent; and domestic arguments about the balance between the costs and benefits of integration, which were notable by their absence since the late 1950s, are resurfacing, giving rise to growing contestation. It may well be argued that—in comparison to such states as France, Italy, the UK or Denmark—contestation is sporadic rather than consistent and is of low intensity. This is true, but for reasons that should worry proponents of further integration.

Contestation does not, as yet, feature prominently in the politics of electoral competition, media reporting, representation, and legitimation, precisely because, after more than half a century of European integration, the politics of the Federal Republic remain fundamentally inward-looking. Party competition and the party system, the Bundestag, and political communication do not provide effective fora for engaging with European issues. The sanguine view is that this is because citizens are more or less content with, or at least resigned to, the overall direction of European integration and there is, therefore, no demand for public debate. Where 'permissive consensus' reigns, there is no need for a continuous engagement with the public. However, our study suggests a less optimistic explanation. Institutional opportunity structures work against the Europeanization of key institutions and processes of democratic politics, resulting in growing tensions between Europeanized public policies and non-Europeanized politics.

The tensions, if not disjuncture, associated with the integration project within the German political system, considered together with arguments about the decline of Germany's 'soft' power, rooted in both domestic and EU-level developments, have profound implications for both German policy-makers and the integration project. Briefly, Germany's commitment to 'deepening and widening' is subject to growing domestic constraints and qualifications, while 'soft' power declines. Both developments combine to restrict the capacity of German policy-makers to set the pace and direction of integration. For the EU, this implies that it is less and less able to rely on Germany as an engine for 'widening and deepening'.

If, perhaps, past analyses have been in danger of overstating Germany's 'soft' power in Europe and the solidity of its domestic foundations, it would be equally misguided to subscribe to a gloom-and-doom scenario of inevitable restrictions and limitations and to underplay opportunities for action at both domestic and European levels. The above analysis points to a dual agenda of domestic reform: one that enables Germany to regain its benchmark status in key policy domains—most centrally in economic policy—and one that addresses the apparent unresponsiveness of domestic politics to pressures of Europeanization. The former is, of course, very widely debated in both politics and academe, and the details of the reform agenda—as well as the obstacles to its realization—need not be repeated here. There is much less public debate, if any, over how the domestic structures and processes of democratic politics may evolve in a way that allows for a positive engagement with Europe instead of increasingly problematic co-existence.

Our account has emphasized the importance of institutional opportunity structures in explaining divergent patterns of Europeanization. Accordingly, it is here that the potential for a democratic engagement with integration must be explored. As has also been noted, the standard repertoire of Europeanization responses—centred on the creation of dedicated 'linkage structures' (Goetz 2000a) such as specialized EU affairs committees—is ill-suited to advance a Europeanized politics. Moreover, in those states where signs of effects from European integration on electoral behaviour and party systems can be clearly detected, this is invariably tied to the presence of a strong Euro-sceptic undercurrent. This suggests that the Europeanization of politics may be achieved only at the price of growing contestation of Europe. It is not least for that reason that German politicians have repeatedly shied away from fostering the salience of European issues in the domestic context. However, if, as we argue, the domestic constraints of integration are becoming increasingly less enabling, the incentives for contestation also increase.

Is Germany, therefore, destined to develop an organized Eurosceptic movement, as many other EU member states already possess? Past experience would suggest otherwise, for even the clearly unpopular abolition of the D-Mark was insufficient to spark the creation of organized Euro-scepticism with solid institutional foundations (Niedermeyer, Chapter 7 in this volume). However, it follows from our argument above that the past does not provide a reliable guide to the future. As Lees (2002: 263) shows: 'there is a latent potential within the German polity for the mobilisation of what remains a significant level of popular unease about aspects of the ongoing process of European integration.' But our analysis suggests that the 'systemic disincentives' that Lees sees at work in preventing the mobilization of this potential will be less pronounced in the future than in the past. Thus, instead of placing their trust in the continued restrictive effects of the institutional framework, political decision-makers might be better advised to encourage the public discussion of alternatives scenarios of European integration within the parameters of a fundamental commitment to advancing the Union. Put differently, the best way to ensure against the rise of organized Euro-scepticism is to promote the debate about the choices facing Europe.

If, domestically, Eastern enlargement has largely failed to engender such a debate, then the prospect of Turkish membership of the EU might provide such an opportunity. While the Red–Green coalition welcomes this project in principle, the CDU/CSU declared their fundamental opposition to such a move, advocating a 'privileged partnership' instead. Because the question of Turkish membership affects the very fundamentals of the nature of the EU, it can be controversially debated without the debate being structured in terms of pro- versus anti-integration. Both proponents and opponents can legitimately claim to argue from a perspective of a basic and deep commitment to the integrationist project. There are signs that the CDU/CSU are beginning to pursue just such a strategy.

Even the distant prospect of Turkish membership puts further pressure on the shrinking core and its longer-term role in Europe. Attempts by leading politicians from both France and Germany to revitalize their joint agenda and pace-setter role in Europe—led by Fischer in Germany and Chirac in France—are evidence that policy-makers are keenly aware of many of the pressures on traditional patterns of integration and Europeanization that this volume has examined. As Wolfgang Wessels (2001: 114) has argued: 'Major disappointment about an inefficient, overstretched and blocked EU of 21 or even 28 member states is bound to give rise to repeated projects of a "core Europe", or even a *directoire*.' The revitalization of the Franco-German 'motor'—notably within the European Convention—and the salience of ideas of 'flexible' integration within the Franco-German relationship from 1995 suggested the search for defensive mechanisms to counteract the threat to the power of the traditional core. The prospect that the 'shrinking' core may turn out to be a 'harder core' cannot be discounted.

Abstracts

KENNETH DYSON & KLAUS H. GOETZ

1 Living with Europe: Power, Constraint, and Contestation

This introductory chapter critically examines the concept of Europeanization and uses it to explore the changing relationship between Germany and the EU. It argues in favour of understanding 'Europeanization' as a complex, interactive 'top-down' and 'bottom-up' process in which domestic polities, politics, and public policies are shaped by European integration and in which domestic actors use European integration to shape the domestic arena. Europeanization may produce either continuity or change and potentially variable and contingent outcomes. Previous work has stressed the capacity of Germany to shape European integration through the use of 'soft' power; the coincidence of enabling and restrictive effects arising from progressive integration; and harmonious co-existence and co-evolution between the German political system and the EU level. However, a focus on Europeanization provides grounds for re-examining the conventional wisdom about the domestic conditioning and effects of integration. It highlights how momentous changes in the European integration process are combining with domestic changes, summarized as the transition from the 'Bonn Republic' to the 'Berlin Republic', to situate Germany as part of a shrinking core and as marked by declining 'soft' power.

JEFFREY J. ANDERSON

2 Europeanization in Context: Concept and Theory

This chapter explores challenges associated with the use of Europeanization as an explanatory variable in accounting for domestic institutional and policy developments. It covers a range of issues, including the conceptual and empirical relationship between Europeanization and globalization. This is an important and in many ways analytically prior task, for no other reason than that one cannot hope to assess accurately the extent of Europeanization and its implications if one cannot distinguish it from other large-scale processes at work in contemporary Europe. Domestic systems are subject to a vast range of causal forces both endogenous and exogenous, and selecting one out—in this case, Europeanization—for close, careful examination presupposes an ability to differentiate it conceptually and empirically. The chapter also presents a set of

Proceedings of the British Academy, **119**, 377–386. © The British Academy 2003.

arguments supporting the basic methodological approach adopted by the contributors to this volume, which shuns a macro or aggregate perspective in favour of one premised on the wisdom and logic of parsing: specifically, taking articulated components of the domestic system—typically policies and/or institutions—and devising rigorous searches for the presence or absence of Europeanization.

KLAUS H. GOETZ

3 The Federal Executive: Bureaucratic Fusion versus Governmental Bifurcation

The federal ministerial executive is a dual institution, which combines the attributes of a government and an administration. European integration has affected these two qualities of the executive in different ways. On the administrative side, progressive integration has been associated with growing fusion, through which the ministerial administration becomes part of a closely interconnected multi-level system. By contrast, the governmental dimension of the executive is characterized by growing bifurcation. Government takes place at two levels—the European and the domestic —but institutional linkage between the two levels is limited and key features of German government—party government, coalition government, and parliamentary government—show few signs of Europeanization. The contrasting pattern of effects can be explained with reference to the differing opportunity structures within which officials and executive politicians operate. For officials, progressive integration provides opportunities for 'bottom-up' Europeanization, in that powers and responsibilities at the EU level can be used for bureau-shaping in the domestic context. Executive politicians, too, have to operate at both levels, but European opportunities and constraints translate only loosely into power gains and losses at the domestic level. The chief reason for this lies in the continued non-Europeanization of key actors and processes of domestic politics and democratic decision-making. The main proposition of this chapter may suggest an association between European integration and the bureaucratization of public policy-making. However, the effects on the politics–administration nexus are more ambivalent, since politics and administration cannot be neatly separated.

THOMAS SAALFELD

4 The Bundestag: Institutional Incrementalism and Behavioural Reticence

The German Bundestag has been slow in its institutional adaptation to the emerging governance structures at the European level and Members of the Bundestag (MdBs) have made only hesitant use of their institutional means to hold the federal government to account for its actions at the European level. The explanation for these findings does not focus on the general institutional constraints emanating from the complex mix of inter-governmental and supranational decision-making in the EU or the general propensity of the Bundestag to emphasize committee expertise instead of communication and debate. Rather, the explanation is based on an expected-utility model that focuses on the electoral benefits that MdBs derive from legislative oversight of the national government in the EU policy process. These benefits are largely a function of the electoral salience of European integration and EU policies. In addition, the incentives of MdBs are negatively affected by high levels of uncertainty (a) about the link between a policy and its expected outcomes and (b) about the efficacy of legislative oversight. Finally, their decision to engage in oversight activities depends on the cost of the activity. Low electoral salience and high uncertainty about outcomes and responsibilities can explain why elected representatives have generally chosen not to utilize the institutional capabilities available to them to hold the federal government accountable for its policies at the EU level.

CHARLIE JEFFERY

5 The German Länder: From Milieu-Shaping to Territorial Politics

This chapter looks at Europeanization through the lens of how the German Länder have responded to challenges posed by European integration since 1985. It does this by understanding 'Europeanization' as a two-way process in which the EU imposes adaptational pressures on the Länder but is also subject to adaptational pressures from the Länder. It also uses the timescale of fifteen years to explore the dynamics of Europeanization. It finds that the Länder have persistently sought to minimize any perceived 'misfit' between the EU decision-making process and their domestic role as constituent units of the German federation. The nature of the misfit, and ideas on its resolution, have, however, changed over time as both the EU and Germany have adapted to the post-Cold War era. An initial concern for winning collective rights of access to a deepening EU is now being supplanted by a concern to protect individual Länder autonomy within the framework of the German member state from what is increasingly perceived as an unnecessarily interventionist EU.

GUNNAR FOLKE SCHUPPERT

6 Public Law: Towards a Post-National Model

The enactment and enforcement of law is regarded as one of the most important attributes of sovereign statehood. Traditionally, 'sovereignty' has been understood as meaning the special quality of a state expressed in its ability to shape its own legal system and to enforce it within the territorial limits of its jurisdiction. Hence the question of the extent to which member states of the European Union are still masters of their legal systems turns out to be a crucial test of their sovereignty. This chapter argues that the legal system of Germany is a Europeanized legal system, in terms both of a European modification of national laws and of a Europeanization of legal culture and modes of governance. This argument takes the form of testing the degree of Europeanization in six different cases, including the field of constitutional law. The conclusion is that the legal system of Germany is a Europeanized legal system and that the German legal profession is quite aware of this development. However, the relationship between the EU and the member states is not to be regarded as an exclusive 'top-down' process. Looking at two examples drawn from public law, the chapter shows that the political and legal European multi-level system can be understood as an ongoing process of interaction between the EU and the national legal systems.

OSKAR NIEDERMAYER

7   The Party System: Structure, Policy, and Europeanization

Since the 1980s, the German party system has changed. The relative stable 'two-and-a-half party' system of the 1960s and 1970s has become a fluid five-party system. This development can generally be attributed to changes on the demand and supply sides of party competition and to the changing institutional framework. The European integration process is part of this institutional framework and the chapter deals with the question of whether it has influenced the development of the party system at the national level. To systematically analyse the possible impact, eight party-system properties are distinguished—format, fragmentation, asymmetry, volatility, polarization, legitimacy, segmentation, and coalition stability. The analysis shows that one cannot speak of a Europeanization of the German party system in the sense of a considerable impact of the European integration process on its development. Up to now, the inclusion of Germany in the systemic context of the EU has not led to noticeable changes of party-system properties. On the demand side of party competition, this is due to the fact that the EU issue does not influence the citizens' electoral decisions. On the supply side, the lack of Europeanization can be explained mainly by the traditional, interest-based pro-European élite consensus, the low potential for political mobilization around European integration, and the marginal role of ethnocentrist–authoritarian parties.

RAINER EISING

8 Interest Groups: Opportunity Structures and Governance Capacity

This chapter analyses the Europeanization of German interest groups and patterns of interest intermediation. It puts the impact of the EU in the context of other factors influencing interest group organization and behaviour and situates Germany among other member states. While several analysts regard the degree of fit between the EU and the German mode of interest intermediation as a decisive influence on the responses of these groups to European integration, this chapter argues that it is mainly organizational capacities that explain interest group strategies in the EU multi-level system. The argument is tested in the following steps. First, the chapter provides an overview of the EU and the German systems of interest groups, of the prevalent modes of interest intermediation, and of associational self-regulation at both levels. Based on survey data of German, British, French, and EU business associations, as well as large firms, the general strategies of German interest groups in the EU are outlined. Next, a cluster analysis serves to distinguish fives types of interest groups according to their access to political institutions, their access to information from these institutions, and their political activities during the policy cycle: niche organizations, occasional (national) players, (national) traditionalists, EU players, and multi-level players. The composition of the clusters and the organizational characteristics of the cluster members are used as evidence to establish more precisely the adaptation of German, British, and French groups to the EU. They are used to test the proposition that organizational capacities matter greatly when it comes to representing interests in the EU multi-level system.

KATRIN VOLTMER & CHRISTIANE EILDERS

9 The Media Agenda: The Marginalization and Domestication of Europe

This chapter argues that for the EU to be successful cultural integration through public communication and deliberation of European matters is an important precondition. Three models of Europeanization of political communication are discussed: the emergence of a 'pan-European public sphere', 'segmented trans-national public spheres', and the 'Europeanization of the national public sphere'. We argue that only the latter is able to provide for the opportunity of all citizens to become involved in a public debate on European issues. Our study aims to investigate the extent to which German media have become Europeanized. The empirical analysis examines the discourse on Europe in the editorials of national quality papers. The findings show that the media under study devote only a very small portion of their attention to European issues, thus marginalizing Europe to an extent that is not warranted by the significance of the European level of governance. If the media do focus on European issues they predominantly address them in terms of national politics, which we interpret as a 'domestication' of Europe in public discourse. At the same time, the media unanimously support the idea of European integration. We conclude that this pattern of communicating Europe reflects the élite consensus on European matters in Germany and may have contributed to the alienation of the general public from European politics.

KENNETH DYSON

10   Economic Policies: From Pace-Setter to Beleaguered Player

This chapter traces how rapidly evolving mechanisms of EU governance have affected German economic policy since the Treaty of Maastricht was agreed in 1991. Its central theme is the transition of Germany from 'pace-setter' in the constitutive politics of designing EMU to 'beleaguered player' in the regulative politics of its implementation, from Germany as policy model to Germany as the main problem. Europeanization has both reinforced traditional policy beliefs in 'sound' finance and acted as a catalyst for domestic policy reforms by strengthening the domestic discourse of competitiveness. It has also led to significant pressures for institutional reconfiguration, notably within the federal executive, federal–state relations, and the Bundesbank. The chapter questions the traditional assumption of a goodness of 'fit' between German and EU economic policies, in part because of unintended effects from EMU and in part because, despite emphasis on a consensus about the 'social market' economy, Germany lacks a unitary economic policy model. 'Ordo-liberal' and 'managed' economy elements co-exist in tension and react very differently to Europeanization. The nature of the domestic governing style, with its stress on consensus and the complementing of majoritarian by 'negotiation' democracy, creates an important institutional bias to 'managed' capitalism. But the reinforcing effects of the European Single Market, EMU, and globalization raise questions about the loyalty of key German firms to 'managed' capitalism and whether at some point its defences might be overwhelmed by a process of market liberalization that escapes its confines. In that case the polity and political effects of Europeanization will prove much greater than is currently seen.

MARTIN LODGE

11   Competition Policy: From Centrality to Muddling Through?

Competition policy has been said to lie at the heart of the German social market economy and to have been a key influence on the EC competition regime. This chapter assesses the impact of Europeanization on the competition law policy domain in the light of earlier claims that suggest a marginalization of the Federal Cartel Office. The question is pursued through three case studies that involve three different Europeanization dynamics—those of domestic assimilation of EU policy provisions, of informing policy change at the EU level, and of 'collision' between national and Commission policy preferences. The cases cover three distinct policy issues—the Europeanization of domestic competition law, attempts to shape changes to the EC regime's Regulation 17/62 and efforts of the DG Competition to prohibit the fixed-book price agreement between Austria and Germany. While those cases leading to domestic policy change suggest a considerable degree of national 'resilience', the example of 'informing EC policy change' points to the declining influence of the German approach *vis-à-vis* other national competition law experiences, Commission preferences, and changing competition policy 'ideas'. Moreover, while earlier claims suggesting a marginalization of the Federal Cartel Office require some qualification, wider changes in the German political economy have challenged the previous predominance of competition policy in German economic policy.

SIMON BULMER, DAVID DOLOWITZ, PETER HUMPHREYS
& STEPHEN PADGETT

12   Electricity and Telecommunications: Fit for the European Union?

This chapter examines the processes and outcomes of Europeanization in the German utilities' sectors. Employing an institutionalist perspective, it focuses on interaction between the institutional system of the EU and that of Germany. Adaptation pressures, it is argued, are reduced by Germany's ability to exert 'soft' power to ensure that EU policy is congruent with domestic governance. The tempo of EU reform is particularly significant. Incremental legislation in telecommunications permitted Germany to liberalize at its own pace in line with domestic policy style. In electricity, by contrast, the 1996 Directive created more acute adaptation pressures. Thus, in telecommunications Germany was activist in 'downloading' EU legislation in line with EU requirements. In electricity, it made considerable use of the zone of discretion in the Directive to minimize the impact on domestic governance. In examining the way in which Germany responds to adaptation pressures, particular attention is given to opportunity structures, veto points, and institutional norms in the domestic policy process. The experience of the electricity reform suggests that adaptation pressures are exacerbated by a highly pluralist institutional regime with numerous veto actors capable of blocking implementation. Moreover, German reluctance to embrace independent, sector-specific regulation suggests the resistance of domestic regulatory norms to the effects of Europeanization.

MARKUS HAVERLAND

13   Social Policy: Transforming Pensions, Challenging Health Care?

This chapter analyses the Europeanization of German social policy, focusing on the sectors of old-age pensions and health care. It argues that indirect EU effects rather than direct pressures have mattered. These indirect effects have amplified global and domestic pressures on German social policy arrangements. Their impact has been differential, as they have been mediated by properties of the policy sector and by political institutions. European integration has contributed to the transformation in pension generosity and finances by making the status quo— generous public pensions—more difficult to sustain and by making the alternative—a partial transition to private funded pensions—more attractive. The EU was not causally important with regard to reforms weakening the male-breadwinner orientation of the pensions system, although the previous system did not fit well with EU gender equality policies. European integration has contributed to the incremental changes in health care only indirectly and marginally. Since 1975, the traditional German social model has lost coherence, but has not yet been replaced by a new model. EU pressures have been too weak to foster a fully fledged transformation of social policy and too diffuse to lead to convergence towards a European social model. There are good reasons to believe, however, that European integration will matter more in social policy in the next decade.

RÜDIGER K.W. WURZEL

14   Environmental Policy: A Leader State under Pressure?

For much of the 1980s, Germany acted as an 'environmental leader' state, successfully exporting to the EU level some of its standards, instruments, and regulatory approaches. In consequence, the Europeanization process was largely taken for granted by most domestic environmental policy actors. Overall, the Europeanization of the German environmental policy system has been an incremental and relatively subtle process that began in the 1970s, although its full implications did not become apparent until the 1980s. In the 1990s, Germany lost much of its 'environmental leader' status and came under pressure from the EU to reform its environmental policy system. At the beginning of the twenty-first century, Germany remains an 'environmental leader' state that pushes for stringent EU environment policy measures on air pollution control issues in particular. However, it has taken on a defensive position with regard to the EU's recent procedural measures, which have caused considerable domestic adaptational pressures. The recalibration of Germany's EU and environmental policy co-ordination procedures can be interpreted as an attempt to regain the initiative on the

EU level and to avoid these adaptational pressures. Overall, the Europeanization process has had a highly variegated effect on German environmental policy. Deeply engrained institutional structures and regulatory styles have been affected to a lesser extent than the substantive policy content.

JÖRG MONAR

15 Justice and Home Affairs: Europeanization as a Government-Controlled Process

Although in the 1990s Germany played a leading role in transforming justice and home affairs into a major policy-making field for the EU, these areas have been much less Europeanized at the national level than Germany's key role at the European level would suggest. Germany has been quite active—and in some cases, such as Schengen and Europol—also relatively successful in trying to 'upload' domestic preferences and models to the European level. But Europeanization has remained very much a government-led process with hardly any impact on public opinion and society. The 'downloading' has been largely limited to selective legislative changes as a result of the growing EC/EU *acquis*, and to the increased involvement of administrative and law-enforcement agencies in the European co-operation procedures and structures. One of main reasons for this imbalance between the 'uploading' and 'downloading' dimensions of Europeanization is the limited interest of the political establishment in the Europeanization of internal security issues that are still considered as valuable national 'vote winners'. Another reason is the only recent development and lack of transparency of EU justice and home affairs. In addition, the conservatism of practitioners in ministries, courts, and law-enforcement agencies plays a role. The importance of the Europeanization of parts of the German state should not be underestimated. At the same time, the absence of a wider Europeanization of state and society makes German participation in the further development of EU justice and home affairs unduly dependent on changes in government policy and priorities.

ALISTER MISKIMMON & WILLIAM E. PATERSON

16 Foreign and Security Policy: On the Cusp Between Transformation and Accommodation

Foreign and security policy-making within Germany represents a singular policy area. From its inception it emerged into an already existing multilateral framework under the conditions of semi-sovereignty. In addition, this policy area is dominated within Germany by a comparatively small number of policy élites, with little or no sectoral interests outside that of central government to push for increased co-operation. Nonetheless, central to this chapter is the question of why there has not thus far been a far-reaching Europeanization of policy, despite Germany's apparent deep commitment to European integration and EU foreign and security policy co-ordination. German foreign and security policy finds itself on the cusp between accommodation and transformation and has not progressed further as a result of internal and external factors that continue to define German security policy as a distinctive case.

KENNETH DYSON & KLAUS H. GOETZ

17 Europeanization Compared: The Shrinking Core and the Decline of 'Soft' Power

This concluding chapter summarizes the empirical findings of the volume's contributions on the polity, politics, and policy dimensions of Europeanization, with an emphasis on the implications of living with Europe in terms of Germany's power to project its institutional forms and policies; the balance between the enabling and constraining implications of European integration; and domestic contestation about European integration. First, while Germany continues to engage intensively in all aspects of the integration process, its power to 'upload' appears in decline. Germany's capacity to 'shape its regional milieu' is challenged by the ever-more apparent weaknesses of the 'German model', but also by changes in the integration process, which mean that the agenda-setting power and leverage of the traditional North-Western core of the EU are shrinking. Second, and as a consequence, the coincidence of enabling and constraining effects is being progressively replaced by a discourse that notes unwelcome constrictions associated with EU membership. Third, domestic contestation over both everyday EU policy and the constitutional politics of integration seems set to increase. The overall pattern of Europeanization is characterized by the contrast between progressively Europeanized public policies, a semi-Europeanized polity, and a largely non-Europeanized politics. This finding points to a dual agenda of domestic reform: one that enables Germany to regain its benchmark status in key policy domains—most centrally in economic policy—and one that addresses the apparent unresponsiveness of domestic politics to pressures of Europeanization.

Bibliography

Aberbach, J. D., Putnam, R. D. and Rockman, B. A. (1981), *Bureaucrats and Politicians in Western Democracies* (Cambridge, Mass.).

Ágh, A. (2002), 'The Accession Management and Europeanization in Hungary', *Budapest Papers on Europeanization*, 7, Hungarian Centre for Democracy Studies Foundation.

Alber, J. (1998), 'Recent Developments in Continental European Welfare States: Do Austria, Germany and The Netherlands Prove to be Birds of a Feather?', paper presented at the ISA Congress, RC 19, Session 7: Patterns of Reform in Western Welfare States (Montreal).

Albright, M. (1998), 'The Right Balance Will Secure NATO's Future', *Financial Times*, 7 December.

Almond, G. A. and Verba, S. (1963), *The Civic Culture. Political Attitudes and Democracy in Five Nations* (Princeton).

Altheide, D. L. and Snow, R. P. (1988), 'Toward a Theory of Mediation', in J. A. Anderson (ed.), *Communication Yearbook 11* (Newbury Park), 194–223.

Andersen, M. S. and Liefferink, D. (1997) (eds), *European Environmental Policy: The Pioneers* (Manchester).

Andersen, S. S. and Burns, T. R. (1996), 'The European Union and the Erosion of Parliamentary Democracy: A Study of Post-Parliamentary Governance', in S. S. Andersen and K. A. Eliassen (eds), *The European Union: How Democratic Is It?* (London), 227–51.

Anderson, B. (1983), *Imagined Communities: Reflections on the Origins and Spread of Nationalism* (London).

Anderson, J. J. (1995), 'The State of the (European) Union: From the Single Market to Maastricht, From Singular Events to General Theories', *World Politics*, 47, 441–65.

Anderson, J. J. (1997), 'Hard Interests, Soft Power, and Germany's Changing Role in Europe', in P. Katzenstein (ed.), *Tamed Power: Germany in Europe* (Ithaca), 80–107.

Anderson, J. J. (1999a), *German Unification and the Union of Europe* (Cambridge).

Anderson, J. J. (1999b), 'Germany: Between Unification and Union', in J. J. Anderson (ed.), *Regional Integration and Democracy: Expanding on the European Experience* (Lanham), 171–92.

Anderson, J. J. (2002), 'Europeanization and the Transformation of the Democratic Polity', *Journal of Common Market Studies,* 40, 793–822.

Anderson, K. M. (2002), 'The Europeanisation of Pension Arrangements: Convergence or Divergence?', in C. De La Porte and P. Pochet (eds), *Building Social Europe through the Open Method of Co-ordination* (Brussels), 251–84.

Anonymous (2002), 'Globalization's Last Hurrah? A. T. Kearney/Foreign Policy Magazine Globalization Index', *Foreign Policy*, 128, 38–51.

Apeldoorn, J. F. (2001), 'Are the Proposed Changes Compatible with Article 81 (3)EC?, *European Competition Law Review*, 22, 400–3.

Proceedings of the British Academy, **119**, 387–425. © The British Academy 2003.

Armstrong, K. and Bulmer, S. (1998), *The Governance of the Single European Market* (Manchester).

Arp, H. (1995), *Multiple Actors and Arenas: European Community Regulation in a Policy Centric System: A Case Study on Car Emission Policy*, Ph.D. dissertation, European University Institute (Florence).

Austrian Presidency (1998), Informal Summit Press Conference, October, Downing Street web site, http://www.number-10.gov.uk.

Baacke, R. (2000), 'Fortentwicklung des Umweltrechtes—Europa als Modell oder Problem?', speech given by the State Secretary of the Environment Ministry at the Humboldt University of Berlin, 31 May.

Baake, P. and Perschau, O. (1996), 'The Law and Politics of Competition in Germany', in G. Majone (ed.), *Regulating Europe* (London).

Bacher, J. (2001), 'Teststatistiken zur Bestimmung der Clusterzahl für QUICK CLUSTER', *ZA-Information*, 48, 71–97.

Bannas, G. (2001), 'The Subjugation of the Greens', *Frankfurter Allgemeine Zeitung*, English Edition, 14 November 2001, http://www.faz.de/.

Baring, A. (1996) (ed.), *Germany's New Position in Europe: Problems and Perspectives* (Oxford).

Bartle, I. (1999), *European Union Policy-Making and Globalization: A Comparative Study of the Liberalisation of Telecommunications and Electricity*, Ph.D. thesis, Liverpool.

Bartle, I. (2002), 'Competing Perspectives on European Union Telecommunications Policy', *Convergence: The Journal of Research into New Media Technologies*, 8(2), Special Issue on Telecommunications in Europe, 10–27.

Bartolini, S. and Mair, P. (1990), *Identity, Competition, and Electoral Availability. The Stabilization of European Electorates 1885–1985* (Cambridge).

Bauer, H. (2000), 'Europäisierung des Verfassungsrechts', *Juristische Blätter*, 750–63.

Bauer-Kaase, P. (2001), 'Politische Ideologie im Wandel?—Eine Längsschnittanalyse der Inhalte der politischen Richtungsbegriffe "links" und "rechts"', in H.-D. Klingemann and M. Kaase (eds), *Wahlen und Wähler: Analysen aus Anlaß der Bundestagswahl 1998* (Opladen), 207–43.

BDI (1998), Bundesverband der deutschen Industrie, *Stellungnahme* (Köln), 10 February.

Bechmann, A. (1984), *Leben Wollen: Anleitungen für eine neue Umweltpolitik* (Cologne).

Bechtold, R. (2000), 'Modernisierung des EG Wettbewerbsrechts: Der Verordnungs-Entwurf der Kommission zur Umsetzung des Weißbuchs', *BetriebsBerater*, 55, 2425–31.

Beck, K. (2001), 'Eröffnung der Konferenz', in Bundesrat (ed.), *Zukunft der Europäischen Union* (Berlin), 24–9.

Bennett, R. J. (1997), 'The Impact of European Economic Integration on Business Associations: The UK Case', *West European Politics*, 20, 61–90.

Benz, A. (1998), 'Politikverflechtung ohne Politikverflechtungsfalle—Koordination und Strukturdynamik im europäischen Mehrebenensystem', *Politische Vierteljahresschrift*, 39, 558–89.

Benz, A. (1999), 'From Unitary to Asymmetric Federalism in Germany: Taking Stock after 50 Years', *Publius*, 29, 55–78.

Berger, S. and Dore, R. (1996) (eds), *National Diversity and Global Capitalism* (Ithaca).

Berghahn, V. (1986), *The Americanisation of West German Industry* (Leamington Spa).

Bergman, T. (2000*a*), 'The European Union as the Next Step of Delegation and Accountability', *European Journal of Political Research*, 37, 415–29.

Bergman, T. (2000*b*), 'Introduction: Delegation and Accountability in European Integration', *Journal of Legislative Studies*, 6, 1–14.

Beyme, K. von (1985), 'Policy-Making in the Federal Republic of Germany: A Systematic Introduction', in K. von Beyme, and M. Schmidt, M. (eds), *Policy and Politics in the Federal Republic of Germany* (New York), 1–25.

Beyme, K. von (1997), *Der Gesetzgeber: Der Bundestag als Entscheidungszentrum* (Opladen).

Bianco, W. T. (1994), *Trust: Representatives and Constituents* (Ann Arbor).

Biersteker, T. (1999), 'Locating the Emerging European Polity: Beyond States or State?', in J. Anderson (ed.), *Regional Integration and Democracy: Expanding on the European Experience* (Boulder, Colo.), 21–44.

Biersteker, T. and Weber, C. (1996) (eds), *State Sovereignty as a Social Construct* (Cambridge).

Black, I. (2001) 'Calling the Shots in Europe', *The Guardian*, 26 October, http://www.guardian.co.uk/elsewhere/journalist/story/0,7792,581438,00.html.

Blumler, J. G. (with A. D. Fox) (1983) (eds), *Communicating to Voters: Television in the First European Parliamentary Elections* (London).

BMWi (1993), *Report by the Federal Government on Securing Germany's Economic Future* (Bonn).

BMWi (1997) *Referentenentwurf eines Gesetzes zur Reform des Gesetzes gegen Wettbewerbsbeschränkungen* (Bonn), July.

Boehmer-Christiansen, S. and Skea, J. (1991), *Acid Politics: Environmental Politics— Environmental and Energy Policies in Britain and Germany* (London).

Boehmer-Christiansen, S. and Weidner, H. (1995), *The Politics of Reducing Vehicle Emissions in Britain and Germany* (London).

Bohne, E. (1992), 'Das Umweltrecht—Ein "irreguläre aliquid corpus et monstro simile"', in H.-J. Koch (ed.), *Auf dem Weg zum Umweltgesetzbuch* (Baden-Baden), 181–233.

Bomberg, E. and Peterson, J. (2000), 'Policy Transfer and Europeanization: Passing the Heineken Test?', Paper for the Political Studies Association UK 50th Annual Conference (London), 10–13 April, http://www.psa.ac.uk.

Bonfadelli, H. (1994), *Die Wissenskluft-Perspektive. Massenmedien und gesellschaftliche Information* (Konstanz).

Börsch-Supan, A. (2000), 'A Model Under Siege: A Case Study of the German Retirement Insurance System', *The Economic Journal*, 110, F24–F45.

Bort, E. (2000), 'The Frontiers of *Mitteleuropa*: Problems and Opportunities at the Eastern Frontier of the European Union', in M. den Boer (ed.), *Schengen Still Going Strong* (Maastricht), 85–104.

Börzel, T. (1999), 'Towards Convergence in Europe? Institutional Adaptation to Europeanization in Germany and Spain', *Journal of Common Market Studies*, 39, 573–96.

Börzel, T. (2000), 'Europäisierung und innerstaatlicher Wandel: Zentralisierung und Entparlamentarisierung', *Politische Vierteljahresschrift*, 41, 225–50.

Börzel, T. (2002), 'Pace-Setting, Foot-Dragging, and Fence-Sitting: Member State Responses to Europeanization', *Journal of Common Market Studies,* 40, 192–214.

Börzel, T. (forthcoming), 'How the European Union Interacts with its Member States', in S. Bulmer and C. Lequesne (eds), *Member States and the European Union* (Oxford).

Börzel, T. and Risse, T. (2000), 'When Europe Hits Home: Europeanization and Domestic Change', *European Integration Online Papers*, 4, http://www.eiop.or.at/texte/2000-015a.htm.

Börzel, T. and Risse, T. (2003), 'Conceptualizing the Domestic Impact of Europe', in K. Featherstone and C. Radaelli (eds), *The Politics of Europeanization* (Oxford).

Brandner, T. (2002), 'Gesetzesänderung—Eine rechtstatsächliche und verfassungsrechtliche Untersuchung anhand der Gesetzgebung des 13. Deutschen Bundestages', unpublished Habilitationsschrift (Berlin).

Brettschneider, F., Van Deth, J. and Roller, E. (2002) (eds), *Das Ende der politisierten Sozialstruktur?* (Opladen).

Breuer, R. (2000), 'Europäisierung des Wasserrechts', *Natur und Recht*, 22(10), 541–9.

Bröhmer, J. (1997), 'Die Weiterentwicklung des ursprünglichen Staatshaftungsrechts—EuGH', *Juristische Schulung (JUS)*, 117–24.

Brück, A. (1988), 'Europäische Integration und Entmachtung des Deutschen Bundestages: Ein Unterausschuβ ist nicht genug', *Zeitschrift für Parlamentsfragen*, 19.

Bruns, T. and Marcinkowski, F. (1997), *Politische Information im Fernsehen: Eine Längsschnittstudie* (Opladen).

Bryant, J. and Zillman, D. (1994) (eds), *Media Effects: Advances in Theory and Research* (Hillsdale).

BT13/10633 (1998), *Beschluβempfehlung und Bericht des Ausschusses für Wirtschaft (9. Ausschuβ) zu dem Gesetzesentwurf der Bundesregierung BT 13/9720* (Bonn).

Buchanan, J. and Tullock, G. (1962), *The Calculus of Consent: Logical Foundations of Constitutional Democracy* (Ann Arbor).

Budge, I., Klingemann, H.-D., Volkens, A., Bara, J. and Tanenbaum, E. (2001) (eds), *Mapping Policy Preferences: Estimates for Parties, Electors, and Governments 1945–1998* (Oxford).

Bührer, W. and Grande, E. (2000) (eds), *Unternehmerverbände und Staat in Deutschland* (Baden-Baden).

Buller, J. and Gamble, A. (2002), 'Conceptualising Europeanization', *Public Policy and Administration*, 17, 4–24.

Bulmer, S. (1986), *The Domestic Structure of European Policy-Making in West Germany* (New York).

Bulmer, S. (1991), 'Analysing European Political Co-operation: The Case for Two-Tier Analysis', in M. Holland (ed.), *The Future of European Political Co-operation* (London), 70–94.

Bulmer, S. (1997), 'Shaping the Rules? The Constitutive Politics of the European Union and German Power', in P. Katzenstein (ed.), *Tamed Power: Germany in Europe* (Ithaca), 49–79.

Bulmer, S. and Burch, M. (2000*a*), 'Coming to Terms with Europe: Europeanisation, Whitehall and the Challenge of Devolution', Queens University Belfast, http://www.qub.ac.uk/ies/onlinepapers/poe9.pdf.

Bulmer, S. and Burch, M. (2000*b*), 'Die "Europäisierung" von Regierungsinstitutionen: Deutschland und das Vereinigte Königreich im Vergleich', in M. Knodt and B. Kohler-Koch (eds), *Deutschland zwischen Europäisierung und Selbstbehauptung* (Frankfurt a.M.), 265–92.

Bulmer, S. and Burch, M. (2001), 'The "Europeanization" of Central Government: The UK and Germany in Historical Institutionalist Perspective', in G. Schneider and M. Aspinwall (eds), *The Rules of Integration: The Institutionalist Approach to European Studies* (Manchester), 73–96.

Bulmer, S. and Burch, M. (2002), 'British Devolution and European Policy-Making: A Step Change Towards Multi-Level Governance', *Politique Européenne*, xx, 114–35.

Bulmer, S., Jeffery, C. and Paterson, W. (2000), *Germany's European Diplomacy: Shaping the Regional Milieu* (Manchester).

Bulmer, S. and Lequesne, C. (2002), 'New Perspectives on EU–Member State Relationships', *Questions de Recherche/Research in Question*, CERI/Sciences Po, 4, January, http://www.ceri-sciences-po.org/publica/qdr.htm.

Bulmer, S. and Padgett, S. (2001), 'Policy Transfer in the European Union: An Institutionalist Perspective', paper presented at the European Community Studies Association Biennial Conference, Madison, 31 May–2 June.

Bulmer, S. and Paterson, W. E. (1987), 'European Policy-Making in the Federal Republic: Internal and External Limits to Leadership', in W. Wessels and E. Regelsberger (eds), *The Federal Republic of Germany and the European Community: The Presidency and Beyond* (Bonn).

Bulmer, S. and Paterson, W. E. (1989), 'West Germany's Role in Europe: "Man-Mountain" or "Semi-Gulliver"?', *Journal of Common Market Studies*, 28(2), 95–118.

Bulmer, S. and Paterson, W. E. (1996), 'Germany in the European Union: Gentle Giant or Emergent Leader?', *International Affairs*, 72, 9–32.

Bulmer, S., Maurer, A. and Paterson, W. E. (2001), 'The European Policy-Making Machinery in the Bonn Republic: Hindrance or Handmaiden?', *German Politics*, 10, 177–206.

Bulmer, S. *et al.* (2001), 'European Policy-Making under Devolution: The UK's New Multi-Level Governance?', Report for the Economic and Social Research Council, University of Manchester.

Bundeskartellamt (2001), *Das Untersagungskriterium in der Fusionskontrolle— Marktbeherrschende Stellung versus Substantial Lessening of Competition?*, discussion paper for the meeting of the Arbeitskreis Kartellrecht, 8–9 October.

Bundesministerium der Finanzen (2000), *Arbeitsplätze schaffen—Zukunftsfähigkeit gewinnen: Jahreswirtschaftsbericht 2000 der Bundesregierung* (Berlin).

Bundesministerium der Finanzen (2001), *Continuing on the Course of Reform— Strengthening the Dynamic of Growth: Annual Economic Report 2001* (Berlin).

Bundesministerium der Finanzen (2002), *Vor einem neuen Aufschwung—Verlässliche Wirtschafts- und Finanzpolitik fortsetzen: Jahreswirtschaftsbericht 2002* (Berlin).

Bundesministerium der Justiz (2001), *Eckpunkte einer Reform des Strafrechts* (Berlin).

Bundesministerium des Innern (2001), *Zuwanderung gestalten—Integration fördern. Bericht der Unabhängigen Kommission Zuwanderung* (Berlin).

Bundesministerium für Arbeit und Sozialordnung (2002), *Sozialbericht 2001* (Berlin).

Bundesministerium für Wirtschaft (1997), *Reformen für Beschäftigung. Jahreswirtschaftsbericht der Bundesregierung '97* (Bonn).

Bundesrat (2001a), *Überprüfung der Mitwirkungsrechte der Länder in EU-Angelegenheiten—Vorlage für die Europaministerkonferenz* (Unterarbeitsgruppe Überprüfung der Mitwirkungsrechte der Länder in EU-Angelegenheiten (Stuttgart/Berlin).

Bundesrat (2001*b*), *Protokoll zur 30. Europaministerkonferenz der Länder am 10./11. Oktober 2001 in Goslar. Top 5 Mitwirkungsrecht der Länder in EU-Angelegenheiten; Verbesserungsvorschläge. Berichterstatter: Baden-Württemberg* (Bundesrat) (Berlin).

Bundesverteidigungsministerium (2001) *Meinungsbild zur Sicherheitspolitischen Lage* (SPL) 2001, http://www.bundeswehr.de/.

Bungarten, H. (1978), *Umweltpolitik in Westeuropa* (Bonn).

Bürklin, W. P. and Klein, M. (1998), *Wahlen und Wählerverhalten. Eine Einführung* (Opladen).

Calvert, R. L. (1985), 'The Value of Biased Information: A Rational Choice Model of Political Advice', *Journal of Politics*, 74, 530–55.

Caporaso, J. and Jupille, J. (2001), 'The Europeanization of Gender Equality Policy and Domestic Structural Change', in M. Green Cowles, J. Caporaso and T. Risse (eds), *Transforming Europe: Europeanization and Domestic Change* (Ithaca), 21–43.

CDU/CSU (2002), *Leistung und Sicherheit. Regierungsprogramm 2002–2006*, http://www.cdu.de/regierungsprogramm/, accessed 5 July.

CEC (1987), *Green Paper on the Development of the Common Market for Telecommunication Services and Equipment*, COM (87), 290 (Brussels), 30 June.

CEC (1994), *Growth, Competitiveness, Employment: The Challenges and Ways Forward into the 21st Century* (Commission of the European Communities) (Luxembourg).

CEC (1995), *Report of the Group of Independent Experts on Legislative and Administrative Simplification*, COM(95) 288 (Commission of the European Communities) (Brussels).

CEC (1996), *Proposal for a European Parliament and Council Directive Relating to Measures to be Taken Against Air Pollution from Vehicles and Amending Council Directives 70/156/EEC and 70/220/EEC, COM(96) 248 final of 18 June, 96/0163 (COD), 96/0164 (COD)* (Commission of the European Communities) (Brussels).

CEC (1998), *Commission of the European Communities, Communication from the Commission to the Council, the European Parliament, the Economic and Social Committee and the Committee of the Regions; Third Report on the Implementation of the Telecommunications Regulatory Package*, COM (1998) 80 final (Brussels).

CEC (1999), *Les Européennes et L'Environment en 1999* (Commission of the European Communities) (Luxembourg).

CEC (2000*a*), *Commission of the European Communities, Communication from the Commission to the Council, the European Parliament, the Economic and Social Committee and the Committee of the Regions; Sixth Report on the Implementation of the Telecommunications Regulatory Package*, COM (2000) 814 (Brussels).

CEC (2000*b*), *Environment 2010: Our Future, Our Choice. The Sixth Environmental Action Programme of the European Union 2001–2010*. COM(2001)31 (Commission of the European Communities) (Brussels).

CEC (2001*a*), *European Governance. A White Paper*, COM(2001) 428 final (Commission of the European Communities) (Brussels).

CEC (2001*b*), *Proposal for a Framework Directive for Greenhouse Gas Emissions Trading Within the European Community*, COM(2991)581 (Commission of the European Communities) (Brussels).

CEC Commission of the European Communities (1999), *1999 Minutes of the First Meeting of the Florence Working Group*, 8 December.

Cerny, P. (1995), 'Globalization and the Changing Logic of Collective Action', *International Organization*, 49, 595–625.

Classen, C. D. (1998), 'Das nationale Verwaltungsverfahren im Kräftefeld des Europäischen Gemeinschaftsrechts', *Die Verwaltung*, 1307–34.

Clement, W. (1999), 'Perspektiven nordrhein-westfälischer Europapolitik', *ZEI* Discussion Paper, C48.

Clement, W. (2001), 'Europa gestalten—nicht verwalten. Die Kompetenzordnung der Europäischen Union nach Nizza', *Forum De Constitutionis Europae*, FCE 3/01.

Coen, D. (1998), 'The European Business Interest and the Nation State: Large-Firm Lobbying in the European Union and Member States', *Journal of Public Policy*, 18, 75–100.

Coen, D (2001), 'Business–Regulator Interaction in German and UK Telecommunications and Energy Sectors: A Multi-Level and Multi-Institutional Study', paper presented at the Annual Conference of the European Community Studies Association, 31 May–3 June (Madison).

Cole, A. (2001), *Franco-German Relations* (Harlow).

Collins, S. D. (1998), 'Managing the Agenda? German Policy-Making with Regard to Eastern Enlargement of the European Union', Ph.D. thesis, Institute for German Studies, University of Birmingham.

Commission of the European Communities (1992), *An Open and Structured Dialogue between the Commission and Special Interest Groups* (Brussels: SEC (92) 2272 final).

Cornish, P. and Edwards, G. (2001), 'Beyond the EU/NATO Dichotomy: The Beginnings of a European Strategic Culture', *International Affairs*, 77, 587–603.

Council (1993), *Council Resolution of the 22 July 1993 on the Review of the Situation in the Telecommunications Sector and the Need for Further Development in that Market*, 93/C213/o1, 6 August (Luxembourg).

Council (1994), *Council Resolution of 22 December 1994 on the Principles and Timetable for the Liberalization of Telecommunications Infrastructures*, 94/C379/03, 31 December (Luxembourg).

Council Decision (2001*a*) 22 January 2001 Setting up the Political and Security Committee (2001/78/CFSP), *Official Journal of the European Communities*, L27/1–L27/3.

Council Decision (2001*b*) 22 January 2001 Setting up the Military Committee of the European Union (2001/79/CFSP), *Official Journal of the European Communities*, L27/4–L27/6.

Council Decision (2001*c*) 22 January 2001 on the Establishment of the Military Staff of the European Union (2001/80/CFSP), *Official Journal of the European Communities*, L27/7–L27/11.

Crotty, W. (1985), *Comparative Political Parties* (Washington).

Cygan, A. J. (2001), *National Parliaments in an Integrated Europe: An Anglo-German Perspective* (The Hague).

Czada, R. (1994), 'Konjunkturen des Korporatismus: Zur Geschichte eines Paradigmenwechsels in der Verbändeforschung', in W. Streeck (ed.), *Staat und Verbände* (*Politische Vierteljahresschrift*, Special Issue, 25) (Opladen), 37–64.

Czada, R. (1998), 'Vereinigungskrise und Standortdebatte: Der Beitrag der Wiedervereingung zur Krise des westdeutschen Modells', *Leviathan,* 26, 24–59.

Dahl, R. A. (1989), *Democracy and Its Critics* (New Haven).

Dalton, R. J., Beck, P. A. and Huckfeldt, R. (1998), 'Partisan Cues and the Media: Information Flows in the 1992 Presidential Election', *American Political Science Review*, 92, 111–26.

Damm, S. M. (1999), 'Die europäischen politischen Parteien: Hoffnungsträger europäischer Öffentlichkeit zwischen nationalen Parteien und europäischen Fraktionsfamilien', *Zeitschrift für Parlamentsfragen*, 30, 395–423.

Dannecker, G. (2002), 'Stufenverantwortung—wer haftet wofür? Verantwortlichkeit in der Lebensmittelkette (From Farm to Fork)—nach der Basisverordnung für Lebensmittelrecht', *Zeitschrift für das gesamte Lebensmittelrecht (ZLR)*, 19–35.

De Beus, J. and Mak, J. (2001), 'The Missing European Public: A Note on the Ethics and Politics of Contemporary European Integration since Nice', *Acta Politica*, 2001/4, 339–57.

DeClercq, M. *et al.* (2001), 'National Patterns in the Use of Voluntary Approaches in Environmental Policy', International Workshop on the Use of Voluntary Approaches.

De La Porte, C. and Pochet, P. (2002), 'Public Pension Reform: European Actors, Discourses and Outcomes', in C. De La Porte and P. Pochet (eds), *Building Social Europe through the Open Method of Co-ordination* (Brussels), 223–50.

de Maizière U. (1991), 'Die praktischen Folgen des Elysée-Vertrags im militärischen Bereich', in W. Loth and R. Picht (eds), *De Gaulle, Deutschland und Europa* (Opladen), 203–14.

Dearing, J. W. and Rogers, E. M. (1996), *Agenda-Setting* (London).

Demmke, C. (1998), 'Nationale Verwaltung und europäische Umweltpolitik' , in C. Demmke (ed.), *Europäische Umweltpolitik und nationale Verwaltungen: Rolle und Aufgaben nationaler Verwaltungen im Entscheidungsprozeß* (Maastricht), 85–127.

Demmke, C. (1999), 'Bremser oder Vorreiter—Deutsche Umweltverwaltung und europäische Umweltpolitik', *Die Verwaltung*, 32(1), 43–71.

Demmke, C. and Unfried, M. (2001), *European Environmental Policy: The Administrative Challenge for the Member States* (Maastricht).

Dempsey, J. (2001), 'Power to the Capitals', *Financial Times*, Comment & Analysis, 15 October.

Derlien, H.-U. (2000), 'Germany', in H. Kassim, B. G. Peters and V. Wright (eds), *The National Co-ordination of EU Policy: The Domestic Level* (Oxford), 54–78.

Derlien, H.-D. and Murswieck, A. (1999), 'Der Politikzyklus zwischen Bonn und Brüssel: Multifunktionalität der Akteure, Iterativität der Prozesse, Informalität der Verfahren', in H.-D. Derlien and A. Murswieck (eds), *Der Politikzyklus zwischen Bonn und Brüssel* (Opladen), 7–19.

Deutscher Bundestag: EU-Ausschuß (1998), *Der Ausschuß für die Angelegenheiten der Europäischen Union des Deutschen Bundestages* (Bonn).

Deutsches Institut für Wirtschaftsforschung (1997), 'Vereinigungsfolgen belasten Sozialversicherung', *Wochenbericht*, 40, 725–9.

Dietz, T. (1997), *Die grenzüberschreitende Interaktion grüner Parteien in Europa* (Opladen).

Dill, R.W. (1991), 'Europa-TV—zu Tode geliebt', in W. Gellner (ed.) *Europäisches Fernsehen— American Blend?* (Berlin).

Doern, B. G. (1996), 'Comparative Competition Policy: Boundaries and Levels of Political Analysis', in B. G Doern and S. Wilks (eds), *Comparative Competition Policy* (Oxford).

Döhler, M. (1995), 'The State as Architect of Political Order: Policy Dynamics in German Health Care', *Governance*, 8, 380–404.

Donohue, G. A. *et al.* (1975), 'Mass Media and the Knowledge Gap: Hypotheses Reconsidered', *Communication Research*, 2, 3–23.

Donsbach, W.,Wolling, J. and Blomberg, C. (1996), 'Repräsentation politischer Positionen im Mediensystem aus der Sicht deutscher und amerikanischer Journalisten', in W. Hömberg and H. Pürer (eds), *Medien-Transformation: Zehn Jahre dualer Rundfunk in Deutschland* (Konstanz), 343–56.

Döring, H. (1995), 'Time as a Scarce Resource: Government Control of the Agenda', in H. Döring (ed.), *Parliaments and Majority Rule in Western Europe* (New York), 223–47.

Duchacek, I. (1970), *Comparative Federalism* (New York).

Duchesne, S. and Frognier, A.-P. (1995), 'Is There a European Identity?', in O. Niedermayer and R. Sinnot (eds), *Public Opinion and Internationalized Governance* (Oxford), 193–226.

Duke, S. (2000), 'From Feira to Nice—More bonnes paroles?', *Eipascope*, 2000/3, 14–18.

Dunleavy, P. (1991), *Democracy, Bureaucracy and Public Choice* (London).

Dyson, K. (1980), *The State Tradition in Western Europe* (Oxford).

Dyson, K. (1982), 'West Germany: The Search for a Rationalist Consensus', in J. Richardson, (ed.), *Policy Styles in Western Europe* (London), 17–46.

Dyson, K. (1992) (ed.), *The Politics of German Regulation* (Aldershot).

Dyson, K. (1994), *Elusive Union: The Process of Economic and Monetary Union in Europe* (London/New York).

Dyson, K. (1998), 'Chancellor Kohl as Strategic Leader: The Case of Economic and Monetary Union', *German Politics*, 7: 37–63.

Dyson, K. (2000a), *The Politics of the Euro-Zone: Stability or Breakdown?* (Oxford).

Dyson, K. (2000b), 'EMU as Europeanization: Convergence, Diversity and Contingency', *Journal of Common Market Studies*, 38, 645–66.

Dyson, K. (2001), 'The German Model Revisited: From Schmidt to Schröder', *German Politics*, 10, 135–54.

Dyson, K. (2002a), 'Introduction: EMU as Integration, Europeanization and Convergence', in K. Dyson (ed.), *European States and the Euro: Europeanization, Variation and Convergence* (Oxford), 1–27.

Dyson, K. (2000b), 'The German Model Revisited: From Schmidt to Schröder', in S. Padgett and T. Poguntke (eds), *Continuity and Change in German Politics: Beyond the Politics of Centrality? A Festschrift for Gordon Smith* (London), 135–54.

Dyson, K. (2002c), 'Germany and the Euro: Redefining EMU, Handling Paradox and Managing Uncertainty and Contingency', in K.Dyson (ed.), *European States and the Euro: Europeanization, Variation and Convergence* (Oxford), 173–211.

Dyson, K. and Featherstone, K. (1996), 'Italy and EMU as a "vincolo esterno": Empowering the Technocrats, Transforming the State', *South European Society and Politics*, 1, 272–99.

Dyson, K. and Featherstone, K. (1999), *The Road to Maastricht: Negotiating Economic and Monetary Union* (Oxford).

Dyson, K., Humphreys, P. *et al.* (1988), *Broadcasting and New Media Policies in Western Europe: A Comparative Study of Technological Change and Public Policy* (London/New York).

Easton, D. (1975), 'A Re-Assessment of the Concept of Political Support', *British Journal of Political Science*, 5, 435–57.

Eberlein, B. (2000), 'Institutional Change and Continuity in German Infrastructure Management: The Case of Electricity Reform', *German Politics*, 9, 81–104.

Eckstein, H. (1975), 'Case Study and Theory in Political Science', in F. Greenstein and N. Polsby (eds), *Handbook of Political Science, 7* (Reading, Mass.), 79–138.

Economist, The (1999), 'Germany's Electrical Storm', *The Economist*, 13 November, 97.

Economist, The (2002), 'The Tortoise is Thinking of Moving: Europe's Constitutional Convention Gets Down to Business but its Wily Chairman Won't Force the Pace', *The Economist*, 20 July, 25–6.

Edelstein, A.S., Ito, Y. and Kepplinger, H. M. *et al.* (1989), *Communication and Culture : A Comparative Approach* (New York/London).

Eder, K. (2000), 'Zur Transformation nationalstaatlicher Öffentlichkeit in Europa. Von der Sprachgemeinschaft zur issuespezifischen Kommunikationsgemeinschaft', *Berliner Journal für Soziologie*, 2, 167–84.

Eder, K., Hellmann, K.-U. and Trenz, H.-J. (1998), 'Regieren in Europa jenseits öffentlicher Legitimation? Eine Untersuchung zur Rolle von politischer Öffentlichkeit in Europa', in B. Kohler-Koch (ed.), *Regieren in entgrenzten Räumen* (Opladen), 321–44.

Egeberg, M. and Sætren, H. (1999), 'Identities in Complex Organisations: A Study of Ministerial Bureaucrats', in M. Egeberg and P. Lægreid (eds), *Organizing Political Institutions* (Oslo), 96–108.

Ehlermann, C. D. (2000), 'The Modernization of EC Anti-Trust Policy: A Legal and Cultural Revolution', *Common Market Law Review*, 37, 537–90.

Eichener, V. (1995), 'European Health and Safety Regulation: No "Race to the Bottom"', in B. Unger and F. van Waarden (eds), *Convergence or Diversity? Internationalization and Economic Policy Response* (Aldershot), 229–51.

Eilders, C. (2000), 'Media as Political Actors? Issue Focussing and Selective Emphasis in the German Quality Press', *German Politics*, 9, 181–206.

Eilders, C. (2002), 'Conflict and Consonance in Media Opinion: Political Positions of Five German Quality Newspapers', *European Journal of Communication*, 17, 25–63.

Eilders, C. and Lüter, A. (1998), *Ein inhaltsanalytisches Kategoriensystem zur Erfassung von Themen und Meinungen in Pressekommentaren*, WZB-Discussion Paper, FSIII-98-107.

Eising, R. (1999), 'Reshuffling Power. The Liberalization of the EU Electricity Markets and its Impact on the German Governance Regime', in B. Kohler-Koch and R. Eising (eds), *The Transformation of Governance in the European Union* (London).

Eising, R. (2000), *Liberalisierung und Europäisierung. Die regulative Reform der Elektrizitätsversorgung in Großbritannien, der Europäischen Gemeinschaft und der Bundesrepublik Deutschland* (Opladen).

Eising, R. and Jabko, N. (2001), 'Moving Targets. National Interests in EU Electricity Liberalization', *Comparative Political Studies*, 34, 742–67.

Elff, M (2000), 'Neue Mitte oder alte Lager? Welche Rolle spielen sozioökonomische Konfliktlinien für das Wahlergebnis von 1998?', in J. W. Van Deth, H. Rattinger and E. Roller (eds), *Die Republik auf dem Weg zur Normalität?* (Opladen), 67–92.

Entman, R. M. (1993), 'Framing: Toward Clarification of a Fractured Paradigm', *Journal of Communication*, 43, 51–8.

EP and Council (1996), *Directive 96/92/EC Concerning Common Rules for the Internal Market in Electricity*, OJL 027, 30 January 1997.

Erichsen, H.-U. (1992), 'Das Recht auf freien Zugang zu Informationen über die Umwelt', *Neue Zeitschrift für Verwaltungsrecht* (*NVwZ*), 409–19.

Esping-Andersen, G. (1990), *The Three Worlds of Welfare Capitalism* (Oxford).

Esping-Andersen, G. (1999), 'Politics without Class: Postindustrial Cleavages in Europe and America', in H. Kitschelt, P. Lange, G. Marks and J. Stephens (eds), *Continuity and Change in Contemporary Capitalism* (Cambridge), 293–316.

Europäische Kommission (2001) (ed.), *Eurobarometer, Bericht Nr. 55* (Brussels).

European Commission (1997), *Modernising and Improving Social Protection in the European Union*, European Commission COM (97) 102 (Brussels).

European Commission (1999), *White Paper on Modernisation of the Rules Implementing Articles 85 and 86 of the EC Treaty*, Commission Programme No. 99/027, 28 April.

European Commission (2001*a*), *Eurobarometer 54*, http://europa.eu.int/comm/dg10/epo.

European Commission (2001*b*), *European Governance. A White Paper*, COM(2001) 428 final (Brussels).

European Commission, General Secretariat (2000), *Directory of Non-profit Making Interest Groups*, http://europa.eu.int/comm/secretariat_general/sgc/lobbies/en/dom40 dat.htm, March 30 (Brussels).

European Council (2000), *Military Capabilities Commitment Statement*, http://ue.eu.int/ pesc/military/en/CCC.htm.

European Council (2001*a*), *Gothenburg European Council (15–16 June 2001): Presidency Conclusions* (Gothenburg).

European Council (2001*b*), *Stockholm European Council (23–24 March 2001): Presidency Conclusions* (Stockholm).

European Parliament (1999), 'Protocol on the Role of National Parliaments in the European Union. Treaty of Amsterdam Amending the Treaty on European Union, the Treaties Establishing the European Communities and Certain Related Acts: Protocols Annexed to the Treaty on European Union and the Treaties Establishing the European Community, the European Coal and Steel Community and the European Atomic Energy Community', 113–14, http://www.europarl.eu.int/topics/treaty/pdf/amst-en.pdf.

European Parliament (2001) 'Instruments of Conflict Prevention and Civilian Crisis Management, Available to the European Union', Directorate General for Research-Directorate A STOA—Scientific and Technological Options Assessment Briefing Note N° 1/2001 PE nr. 296.707, March.

Eurostat (2002), *Eurostat Yearbook 2002* (Luxembourg).

Everts, S. (2002), *Shaping a Credible EU Foreign Policy* (London).

Eyre, S. and Lodge, M. (2000), 'National Tunes and a European Melody? Competition Law Reform in the UK and Germany', *Journal of European Public Policy*, 7, 63–79.

Falkner, G. (1999), 'European Social Policy: Toward Multi-Level and Multi-Actor Governance', in B. Kohler-Koch and R. Eising (1999) (eds), *The Transformation of Governance in the European Union* (London), 83–97.

Falkner, G. (2000), 'The Treaty of the European Union and its Revision. Sea Change or

Empty Shell for European Social Policies?', in S. Kuhnle (ed.), *Survival of the European Welfare State* (London/New York), 185–201.

Falter, J. W., Rattinger, H. and Troitzsch, K. G. (1989) (eds), *Wahlen und politische Einstellungen in der Bundesrepublik Deutschland: Neuere Entwicklungen der Forschung* (Frankfurt a.M.).

Falter, J. W. and Schoen, H. (1999), 'Wahlen und Wählerverhalten', in T. Ellwein and E. Holtmann (eds), *50 Jahre Bundesrepublik Deutschland (Sonderheft 30 der PVS)* (Opladen), 454–70.

Falter, J. W. and Schumann, S. (1992), 'Politische Konflikte, Wählerverhalten und die Struktur des Parteienwettbewerbs', in O. W. Gabriel (ed.), *Die EG-Staaten im Vergleich* (Opladen), 192–219.

Favell, A. (1998). 'Europeanisation of Immigration Politics', http://www.eiop.or.at/eiop/texte/1998–010a.htm.

FDP (2002), *Bürgerprogramm 2002*, http://www.fdp-bundesverband.de/buergerprog. phtml, accessed 5 July 2002.

Fearon, J. (1991), 'Counterfactuals and Hypothesis-Testing in Political Science', *World Politics*, 43, 169–95.

Featherstone, K. (2003), 'Introduction: In the Name of Europe', in K. Featherstone and C. Radaelli (eds), *The Politics of Europeanization* (Oxford), 3–24.

Featherstone, K. and Kazamias, G. (2001) (eds), *Europeanization and the Southern Periphery* (London).

Featherstone, K. and Radaelli, C. (2003a) (eds), *The Politics of Europeanization* (Oxford).

Featherstone, K. and Radaelli, C. (2003b), 'A Conversant Research Agenda', in K. Featherstone and C. Radaelli (eds), *The Politics of Europeanization* (Oxford), 331–41.

Federal Ministry of the Interior and Federal Ministry of Justice (2001), *First Periodical Report on Crime and Crime Control in Germany* (Berlin).

Feldman, G. (1978), 'The Large Firm in the German Industrial System: The M.A.N., 1900–1925', in D. Stegmann, B. J. Wendt and P. C. Witt (eds), *Industrielle Gesellschaft und politisches System. Beiträge zur politischen Sozialgeschichte. Festschrift für Fritz Fischer zum siebzigsten Geburtstag* (Bonn), 241–57.

Fijnaut, C. (1993), 'The Schengen Treaties and European Police Cooperation', *European Journal of Crime, Criminal Law and Criminal Justice*, 1.

Fikentscher, W. (2001), 'Das Unrecht einer Wettbewerbsbeschränkung: Kritik am Weissbuch und VO-Entwurf zu Art. 81, 92 EG-Vertrag', *Wirtschaft und Wettbewerb*, 51, 446–58.

Financial Times Deutschland (2002), 'Schröder pocht gegenüber der EU auf Eigeninteressen', 21 March 2002, http://www.ftd.de/pw/de/1014398922161. html?nv=se.

Fischer, J. (2000), 'From Confederacy to Federation—Thoughts on the Finality of European Integration', speech at the Humboldt University in Berlin (translation of advance text), 12 May (Berlin, Auswärtiges Amt) http://www.auswaertiges-amt.de/6_archiv/2/r/r000512b.htm, accessed 22 September.

Fischer, J. (2001), Speech delivered on the occasion of the presentation of the German–British Award 2000 (London, 24 January) (unpublished).

Fligstein, N. and Merand, F. (2001), 'Globalization or Europeanization? Evidence on the European Economy Since 1980', paper presented at the conference 'Shareholder Value-Capitalism and Globalization' (Hamburg).

Franco-British Summit, Joint Declaration on European Defence, St Malo, 4 December.

Frankfurter Allgemeine Zeitung (2001), 'Cabinet Approves Emergency Laws', 19 September, http://www.faz.de/.

Freeman, R. and Moran, M. (2000), 'Reforming Health Care in Europe', *West European Politics,* 23, 35–58.

French National Academy (2001). 'Rencontre parlementaire franco-allemande sur l'avenir de l'Europe enlargé: Actes du colloque', Paris, 10 December.

Frenz, W. (2001), *Selbstverpflichtungen der Wirtschaft* (Tübingen).

Frieden, J. (1991), 'Invested Interests: The Politics of National Economic Policies in a World of Global Finance', *International Organization,* 45, 425–51.

Friedrich, A., Tappe, M. and Wurzel, R. (2000), 'A New Approach to EU Environmental Policy-Making? The Auto-Oil I Programme', *Journal of European Public Policy,* 7(4), 593–612.

Friedrich Ebert Stiftung (2002), 'Making EU Foreign Policy More Effective', International Policy Analysis Unit: Working Group on European Integration, Working Paper, 12, May (Bonn).

Froelich, S. (2001), *'Auf den Kanzler kommt es an': Helmut Kohl und die deutsche Außenpolitik* (Paderborn).

Fuchs, D. and Klingemann, H.-D. (1989), 'The Left–Right Schema', in M. K. Jennings and J. W. Van Deth (eds), *Continuities in Political Action* (Berlin), 203–34.

Funk, A. (2000), 'Das deutsche System der inneren Sicherheit im Prozeß der Europäisierung', in H.-J. Lange (ed.), *Staat, Demokratie und innere Sicherheit in Deutschland* (Opladen), 291–309.

Gabriel, O. W. and Falter, J. W. (1996) (eds), *Wahlen und politische Einstellungen in westlichen Demokratien* (Frankfurt a.M.).

Gabriel, O. W. and Thaidigsmann, I. (2000), 'Stand und Probleme der Wahlforschung in Deutschland', *Politische Bildung,* 33, 6–19.

Gabriel, O. W. and Troitzsch, K. G. (1993) (eds), *Wahlen in Zeiten des Umbruchs* (Frankfurt a.M.).

Gabriel, S. (2001), 'Thesen von Ministerpräsidentt Gabriel für die politische und verfassungsrechtliche Struktur einer künftigen erweiterten Europäischen Union', Niedersächsische Staatskanzlei (Hannover).

Gaddum, E. (1994), *Die deutsche Europapolitik in den 80er Jahren: Interessen, Konflikte und Entscheidungen der Regierung Kohl* (Paderborn).

Garret, G., Keleman, R. D. and Schulz, H. (1998), 'The European Court of Justice, National Governments, and Legal Integration in the European Union', *International Organization,* 51, 149–76.

Geddes, B. (1990), 'How the Cases You Choose Affect the Answers You Get: Selection Bias in Comparative Politics', *Political Analysis,* 2, 131–52.

Genscher, H.-D. (1980), 'Umweltpolitik und Verfassung', in J. Jekewitz, M. Melzer and W. Zeh (eds), *Politik als gelebte Verfassung: aktuelle Probleme des modernen Verfassungsstaates* (Opladen), 113–28.

Gerber, D. A. (1998), *Law and Competition in Twentieth Century Europe: Protecting Prometheus* (Oxford).

Gerhards, J. (1992), 'Europäische Öffentlichkeit durch Massenmedien?', in B. Schäfers (ed.), *Lebensverhältnisse und soziale Konflike im neuen Europa* (Frankfurt/New York).

Gerhards, J. (1993), 'Westeuropäische Integration und die Schwierigkeiten der Entstehung einer europäischen Öffentlichkeit', *Zeitschrift für Soziologie*, 22, 96–110.

Ghanem, S. (1997), 'Filling in the Tapestry: The Second Level of Agenda-Setting', in M. McCombs, D. L. Shaw and D. H. Weaver (eds), *Communication and Democracy: Exploring the Intellectual Frontiers of Agenda-Setting Theory* (Hillsdale), 3–14.

Giaimo, S. and Manow, P. (1999), 'Adapting the Welfare State. The Case of Health Care Reform in Britain, Germany and the United States', *Comparative Political Studies*, 32, 967–1000.

Giersch, H., Paque, K.-H. and Schmieding, H. (1992), *The Fading Miracle: Four Decades of Market Economy in Germany* (Cambridge).

Glarbo, K. (1999), 'Reconstructing the CFSP of the EU', *Journal of European Public Policy*, 6, 634–51.

Gloser, G. (2001), 'Die europäische Integration voranbringen: Zum europapolitischen Leitantrag der SPD', *Integration*, 24, 303–7.

Goetz, K. H. (1995), 'National Governance and European Integration: Intergovernmental Relations in Germany', *Journal of Common Market Studies*, 33, 91–116.

Goetz, K. H. (1996), 'Integration Policy in a Europeanized State: Germany and the Intergovernmental Conference', *Journal of European Public Policy*, 3, 23–44.

Goetz, K. H. (1997), 'Acquiring Political Craft: Training Grounds for Top Officials in the German Core Executive', *Public Administration*, 75, 753–75.

Goetz, K. H. (1999), 'Senior Officials in the German Federal Administration: Institutional Change and Positional Differentiation', in E. C. Page and V. Wright (eds), *Bureaucratic Elites in Western European States: A Comparative Analysis of Top Officials in Eleven Countries* (Oxford), 147–77.

Goetz, K. H. (2000*a*), 'European Integration and National Executives: A Cause in Search of an Effect?', *West European Politics*, 23, 211–31.

Goetz, K. H. (2000*b*), 'The Development and Current Features of the German Civil Service System', in H. A. G. M. Bekke and F. M. van der Meer (eds), *Civil Service Systems in Western Europe* (Cheltenham), 61–91.

Goetz, K. H. (2001), 'Understanding Post-Communist Public Administration: Modernization, Europeanization or Latinization?', *Journal of European Public Policy*, 8, 1032–51.

Goetz, K. H. (2003*a*), 'Executives in Comparative Context', in J. Hayward and A. Menon (eds), *Governing Europe* (Oxford), 74–91.

Goetz, K. H. (2003*b*), 'Government at the Centre', in S. Padgett, W. E. Paterson and G. Smith (eds), *Developments in German Politics 3* (Basingstoke).

Göhler, G. (1994), 'Politische Institutionen und ihr Kontext', in G. Göhler (ed.), *Die Eigenart der Institutionen: Zum Profil politischer Institutionentheorie* (Baden-Baden).

Goodin, R. E., Headey, B., Muffels, R. and Dirven, H.-J. (1999), *The Real Worlds of Welfare Capitalism* (Cambridge).

Gourevitch, P. (1986), *Politics in Hard Times* (Ithaca).

Grande, E. (1994), *Vom Nationalstaat zur europäischen Politikverflechtung. Expansion und Transformation moderner Staatlichkeit—untersucht am Beispiel der Forschungs- und Technologiepolitik*, Habilitationsschrift, University of Konstanz.

Grande, E. and Schneider, V. (1991) 'Reformstrategien und staatliche Handlungskapazitäten: Eine vergleichende Analyse institutionellen Wandels in der

Telekommunikation in Westeuropa', MPIFG Discussion Paper, 3, Max-Planck-Institut für Gesellschaftsforschung (Cologne).

Grant, W., Paterson, W. and Whitson, C. (1988), *Government and the Chemical Industry* (Oxford).

Green Cowles, M. (2001), 'The Transatlantic Business Dialogue and Domestic Business–Government Relations', in M. Green Cowles, J. A. Caporaso, and T. Risse (eds), *Transforming Europe: Europeanization and Domestic Change* (Ithaca), 159–79.

Green Cowles, M., Caporaso, J. and Risse, T. (2001) (eds), *Transforming Europe: Europeanization and Domestic Change* (Ithaca).

Green Cowles, M. and Risse, T (2001), 'Transforming Europe: Conclusions', in M. Green Cowles, J. Caporaso and T. Risse (eds), *Transforming Europe: Europeanization and Domestic Change* (Ithaca), 217–37.

Grenzschutzdirektion (2000), *Lagebericht Unerlaubte Einreise und Schleusungskriminalität 1999* (Koblenz).

Gündling, L. (1991), 'Protection of the Environment by International Law: Air Pollution', in W. Lang, H. Neuhold and K. Zemanek (eds), *Environmental Protection and International Law* (London), 91–100.

Häberle, P. (1995), 'Gemeineuropäisches Verfassungsrecht', in R. Bieler and P. Widmer (eds), *Der europäische Verfassungsraum* (Zurich), 361–97.

Habermas, J. (1989), *The Structural Transformation of the Public Sphere: An Inquiry into a Category of Bourgeois Society* (Cambridge).

Haftendorn, H. (2001), *Deutsche Außenpolitik zwischen Selbstbeschränkung und Selbstbehauptung* (Stuttgart).

Hagen, L. (1993), 'Opportune Witnesses: An Analysis of Balance in the Selection of Sources and Arguments in the Leading German Newspapers' Coverage of the Census Issue', *European Journal of Communication*, 8, 317–43.

Haigh, N. (2001) (ed.), *Manual of Environmental Policy: The EC and Britain* (Harlow).

Hainsworth, P. (2000), 'Introduction: The Extreme Right', in P. Hainsworth (ed.), *The Politics of the Extreme Right: From the Margins to the Mainstream* (London/New York), 1–17.

Hall, P. and Soskice, D. (2001*a*), 'An Introduction to Varieties of Capitalism', in P. Hall and D. Soskice (eds), *Varieties of Capitalism: The Institutional Foundations of Comparative Advantage* (Oxford), 1–68.

Hall, P. and Soskice, D. (2001*b*) (eds), *Varieties of Capitalism: The Institutional Foundations of Comparative Advantage* (Oxford).

Haltern, U. (forthcoming), 'Internationales Verfassungsrecht? Anmerkungen zu einer kopernikanischen Wende', *Archiv des öffentlichen Rechts (AöR)*.

Hancke, R. and Soskice, D. (2002), 'The Europeanization of Labour Market Institutions', paper presented at the Conference on 'Germany and Europe' held at the British Academy, May.

Hanf, K. and Soetendorp, B. (1998) (eds), *Adapting to European Integration: Small States and the European Union* (Harlow).

Hanrieder, W. (1967), *West German Foreign Policy 1949–63: International Pressure and Domestic Response* (Stanford).

Hänsch, K. (1986), 'Europäische Integration und parlamentarische Demokratie', *Europa-Archiv*, 7.

Harding, R. and Paterson, W. (2000) (eds), *The Future of the German Economy: An End to the Economic Miracle?* (Manchester).

Harmsen, R. (1999), 'The Europeanization of National Administrations; A Comparative Study of France and the Netherlands', *Governance*, 12, 81–113.

Harnisch, S. and Maull, H. W. (2001) *Germany as a Civilian Power? The Foreign Policy of the Berlin Republic* (Manchester).

Hartkopf, G. and Bohne, E. (1983), *Umweltpolitik 1. Grundlagen, Analysen und Perspektiven* (Opladen).

Hasebrink, U. (1998), 'Fernsehen und Hörfunk in Europa: Angebote und Nutzung', in Hans-Bredow-Institut (ed.), *Internationales Handbuch für Hörfunk und Fernsehen* (Baden-Baden).

Hassenteufel, P. (1999), 'How do Health Insurance Systems Change? France and Germany in the 1990s', Conference Paper WS /38, presented at the European Forum, EUI (Florence), 26–27 February.

Haverland, M. (1998), *National Autonomy, European Integration and the Politics of Packaging Waste* (Thela Thesis, Utrecht).

Haverland, M. (2000), 'National Adaptation to European Integration: The Importance of Institutional Veto Points', *Journal of Public Policy*, 20, 83–103.

Haverland, M. (2001), 'Another Dutch Miracle? Explaining Dutch and German Pension Trajectories', *Journal of European Social Policy*, 11, 308–23.

Haverland, M. (2003), 'The Impact of the European Union on Environmental Policies', in K. Featherstone and C. Radaelli (eds), *The Politics of Europeanization* (Oxford).

Heintzen, M. (1997), 'Gemeineuropäisches Verfassungsrecht in der Europäischen Union', *Europarecht (EuR)*, 1–16.

Heinze, R. (1998), *Die blockierte Gesellschaft. Sozioökonomischer Wandel und die Krise des Modells Deutschland* (Wiesbaden).

Hellmann, G. (2002), 'Der "deutsche Weg": eine außenpolitische Gratwanderung', *Internationale Politik*, 18.

Hellwig, R. (1993) (ed.), *Der Deutsche Bundestag und Europa* (Munich).

Helms, L. (2001), 'The Changing Chancellorship: Resources and Constraints Revisited', *German Politics*, 10, 155–68.

Héritier, A. (1996), 'The Accommodation of Diversity in European Policy-Making and its Outcomes: Regulatory Policy as a Patchwork', *Journal of European Public Policy*, 3, 149–67.

Héritier, A. (1997), 'Policy-Making by Subterfuge: Interest Accommodation, Innovation and Substitute Democratic Legitimation in Europe—Perspectives from Distinctive Policy Areas', *Journal of European Public Policy*, 4, 149–67.

Héritier, A. (2002), 'New Modes of Governance in Europe: Policy-Making without Legislating?', in A. Héritier (ed.), *Common Goods: Reinventing European and International Governance* (Lanham).

Héritier, A., Knill, C. and Mingers, C. (1996), *Ringing in the Changes in Europe: Regulatory Competition and the Transformation of the State. Britain, France and Germany* (Berlin).

Heritier, A. *et al.* (2001), *Differential Europe: The European Union Impact on National Policymaking* (Lanham).

Hesse, J. J. and Goetz, K. H. (1992), 'Early Administrative Adjustment to the European Communities: The Case of the Federal Republic', *Yearbook of European Administrative History*, 4, 181–205.

Hill, C. (1993), 'The Capabilities–Expectations Gap or Conceptualising Europe's International Role', *Journal of Common Market Studies*, 31, 305–28.

Hill, C. J. (1998), 'Closing the Capabilities–Expectations Gap? A Common Foreign Policy for Europe?', in J. Peterson and H. Sjursen (eds), *A Common Foreign Policy for Europe* (London), 18–38.

Hill, C. J. (2002), 'European Foreign Policy since September 11: Renationalising or Regrouping?', EWC Guest Lecture, Liverpool University, 24 October .

Hill, C. J. and Stavridis, S. (1983) (eds), *National Foreign Policies and European Political Co-operation* (Hemel Hempstead).

Hill, C. J. and Wallace, W. (1996), 'Introduction', in C. Hill (ed.), *The Actors in Europe's Foreign Policy* (Basingstoke).

Hill, K.A. and Hughes, J. E. (1998), *Cyberpolitics: Citizen Activism in the Age of the Internet* (New York).

Hirschman, A. (1970), *Exit, Voice and Loyalty* (Cambridge).

Hix, S. and Goetz, K. (2000*a*), 'Introduction: European Integration and National Political Systems', *West European Politics*, 23, 1–26.

Hix, S. and Goetz, K. (2000*b*), *Europeanised Politics? European Integration and National Political Systems* (London).

Hodges, M. and Woolcock, S. (1993), 'Atlantic Capitalism Versus Rhine Capitalism in the European Community', *West European Politics*, 16, 29–44.

Hodson, D. and Maher, I. (2001), '"Soft" Economic Policy Co-ordination', *Journal of Common Market Studies*, 39.

Hofer 20-Punkte Katalog zur EU-Erweiterung (1998), Entschliessung der 2. Konferenz der EU-Grenzregionen am 24.–25. Juli 1998 in Hof, Munich, Bayerische Staatskanzlei.

Hofmann, H. (1999), 'Von der Staatssoziologie zu einer Soziologie der Verfassung', *Juristenzeitung (JZ)*, 1065–74.

Hoffmann-Riem, W. (1985), 'Kulturelle Identität und Vielfalt im Fernsehen ohne Grenzen? Zur Diskussion um die Sicherung der Vielfalt im internationalisierten Rundfunk', *Media Perspektiven*, 3/1985, 181–90.

Hogrefe, J. (2002), *Gerhard Schröder: Ein Porträt* (Berlin).

Hollingsworth, J. R. and Boyer, R. (1997) (eds), *Contemporary Capitalism: The Embeddedness of Institutions* (New York).

Hölscheidt, S. (2000), 'Mitwirkungsrechte des Deutschen Bundestages in Angelegenheiten der EU', *Aus Politik und Zeitgeschichte*, B28, 31–8.

Hölscheidt, S. (2001), 'Die neuen Bundesländer und der Parlamentarismus in der Europäischen Union', *Zeitschrift für Parlamentsfragen*, 32: 325–39.

Holtmann, E. (2001) (ed.), *Zwischen Wettbewerbs- und Verhandlungsdemokratie: Analysen zum Regierungssystem der Bundesrepublik Deutschland* (Wiesbaden).

Holzinger, K. (1994), *Politik des kleinsten gemeinsamen Nenners? Umweltpolitische Entscheidungsprozesse in der EG am Beispiel der Einführung des Katalysators* (Berlin).

Holzinger, K. and Knoepfel, P. (2000) (eds), *Environmental Policy in a European Union of Variable Geometry? The Challenge of the Next Enlargement* (Basel/Geneva/ Munich).

Homann, K. and Suchanek, A. (2000), *Ökonomik. Eine Einführung* (Tübingen).

Hood, C., Lodge, M. and Clifford, C. (2002), *Civil Service Policy-Making Competencies in the German BMWi and the British DTI* (London).

Hooper. J. (2002), 'Fischer Rejects Chancellor's "German Way"', *Guardian*, 15 October, http://www.guardian.co.uk/.

Hrbek, R. (1996), 'Eine politische Bewertung der VW-Beihilfen-Kontoverse', *Wirtschaftsdienst*, 10.

Huber, J. and Inglehart, R. (1995), 'Expert Interpretations of Party Space and Party Locations in 42 Societies', *Party Politics,* 1, 73–111.

Huber, P. M. (2002), 'Konsensvereinbarungen und Grundgesetz', in Bundesministerium für Umwelt, Naturschutz und Reaktorsicherheit (ed.), *11. Deutsches Atomrechtssymposium* (Baden-Baden), 329–45.

Humphreys, P. (1992), 'The Politics of Regulatory Reform in German Telecommunications', in K. Dyson (ed.), *The Politics of German Regulation* (Aldershot), 105–35.

Humphreys, P. (1996), *Mass Media and Media Policy in Western Europe* (Manchester).

Humphreys, P. (2002), 'Europeanisation, Globalisation and Policy Transfer in the European Union: The Case of Telecommunications', *Convergence: The Journal of Research into New Media Technologies*, 8(2), Special Issue on Telecommunications in Europe, 53–79.

Humphreys, P. and Simpson, S. (1996), 'European Telecommunications and Globalization', in P. Gummett (ed.), *Globalization and Public Policy* (Cheltenham), 105–24.

Hyde-Price, A. and Jeffery, C. (2001), 'Germany in the European Union: Constructing Normality', *Journal of Common Market Studies*, 39, 689–717.

Imig, D. and Tarrow, S. (2001), *Contentious Europeans. Protest and Politics in an Emerging Polity* (Lanham).

Interview (12 July 2000), Official, European Commission (Brussels).

Interview (22 November 2000), Former Official, Ministry for Industry (Stockholm).

Interview (30 November 2000), Official, DTI (London).

Interview (26 January 2001), Officials, Unterabteilung IIIB (Energie) Bundesministerium für Wirtschaft und Industrie, BMWi (Berlin).

Interview (4 February 2001), Official, Bundeskartellamt (Bonn).

Interviews (16 February 2001), Official Deutsche Verbundgesellschaft; Official E.on Netz (Frankfurt a.M).

Interview (27 March 2001), Official, Bundeskartellamt (Bonn).

Interview (27 March 2001), Official, RegTP (Bonn).

Interview (29 March 2001), Official, VATM (Cologne).

Ipsen, H.-P. (1972), *Europäisches Gemeinschaftsrecht* (Tübingen).

Ismayr, W. (2001), *Der Deutsche Bundestag im politischen System der Bundesrepublik Deutschland*, 2nd edn (Opladen).

Iversen, T. and Wren, A. (1998), 'Equality, Employment, and Budgetary Restraints: The Trilemma of the Service Economy', *World Politics,* 50, 507–46.

Iyengar, S. and Kinder, D. R. (1987), *News that Matters: Television and American Opinion* (Chicago/London).

Jachtenfuchs, M. (2002), 'Versuch über das Gemeinwohl in der postnationalen Konstellation', in G. F. Schuppert and F. Neidhardt (eds), 'Das Gemeinwohl: Auf der Suche nach Substanz', *WZB-Jahrbuch*.

Jänicke, M. (1993), 'Über ökologische und politische Modernisierungen', *Zeitschrift für Umweltpolitik und Umweltrecht*, 16, 159–75.

Jansen, T. (1996), *Die Entstehung einer Europäischen Partei: Vorgeschichte, Gründung und Entwicklung der EVP* (Bonn).

Jasmut, G. (1995), *Die politischen Parteien und die europäische Integration: Der Beitrag der Parteien zur demokratischen Willensbildung in europäischen Angelegenheiten* (Frankfurt a.M.).

Javnost/The Public (2001), Special Issue on 'The Emergence of the European Public Sphere?', 8(1).

Jeffery, C. (1993), 'The Länder Strike Back: Structures and Procedures of European Integration Policy-Making in the German Federal System', Leicester University Discussion Papers in Federal Studies, FS93/2.

Jeffery, C. (1998), 'Les Länder allemands et l'Europe: intérêts, stratégies et influence dans les politiques communautaires', in E. Negrier and B. Jouve (eds), *Qui gouvernent les Régions d'Europe?* (Paris), 55–84.

Jeffery, C. (1999), 'Vom kooperativen Föderalismus zu einer Sinatra-Doktrin der Länder', in R.C. Meier-Walser and G. Hirscher (eds), *Krise und Reform der Föderalismus* (Munich), 50–63.

Jeffery, C. (2002*a*), 'German Federalism from Cooperation to Competition', in M. Umbach (ed.), *German Federalism Past, Present and Future* (Basingstoke), 172–88.

Jeffery, C. (2002*b*), 'Auf den Spuren einer neuen deutschen Europapolitik', *Integration*, 25, 244–8.

Jeffery, C. and Collins, S. (1998), 'The German Länder and EU Enlargement: Between Apple Pie and Issue-Linkage', *German Politics*, 7, 86–101.

Jeffery, C. and Paterson, W. E. (2001), 'Germany's Power in Europe', in H. Wallace (ed.), *Interlocking Dimensions of European Integration* (Basingstoke), 179–214.

Jesse, E. (2002), 'Die Parteien in der SBZ/DDR 1945–1989/1990', in O. W. Gabriel, O. Niedermayer and R. Stöss (eds), *Parteiendemokratie in Deutschland* (Wiesbaden).

Jochem, S. (2001), 'Reformpolitik im deutschen Sozialversicherungsstaat', in M. G. Schmidt (ed.), *Wohlfahrtsstaatliche Politik. Institutionen, politischer Prozeß und Leistungsprofil* (Opladen), 193–226.

Johne, R. (2000), *Die deutschen Landtage im Entscheidungsprozeß der Europäischen Union—parlamentarische Mitwirkung im europäischen Mehrebenensystem* (Baden-Baden).

Johnson, N. (1983), *State and Government in the Federal Republic of Germany: the Executive at Work*, 2nd edition (Oxford).

Jordan, A., Wurzel, R., Zito, A. and Brückner, L. (2001), 'The Innovation and Diffusion of "New" Environmental Policy Instruments (NEPIs) in the European Union and its Member States', paper delivered at the Conference on 'The Human Dimensions of Global Environmental Change and the Nation State' organized by the German Political Science Association and the Potsdam Climate Change Institute (Berlin), 8–9 December, http://www.uea.ac.uk/env/all/resgroup/cserge/cframe/Temp-pages/ FutGov ernance/Home.htm.

Jung, G. and Rieger, G. (1995), 'Die bayerische Landtagswahl vom 25. September 1994: Noch einmal gelang der CSU ein machiavellisches Lehrstück', *Zeitschrift für Parlamentsfragen*, 26, 232–49.

Kaase, M. (2000), 'Entwicklung und Stand der Empirischen Wahlforschung in Deutschland', in M. Klein, W. Jagodzinski, E. Mochmann and D. Ohr (eds), *50 Jahre Empirische Wahlforschung in Deutschland* (Opladen), 17–40.

Kaase, M. and Klingemann, H.-D. (1990) (eds), *Wahlen und Wähler: Analysen aus Anlaß der Bundestagswahl 1987* (Opladen).

Kaase, M. and Klingemann, H.-D. (1998) (eds), *Wahlen und Wähler: Analysen aus Anlaß der Bundestagswahl 1994* (Opladen).

Kahl, W. (1996), 'Europäisches und nationales Verwaltungsorganisationsrecht—Von der Konfrontation zur Kooperation', *Die Verwaltung*, 341–84.

Kallestrup, M. (2002), 'Europeanization as a Discourse: Domestic Policy Legitimation Through the Articulation of a "Need for Adaptation"', *Public Policy and Administration*, 17, 110–24.

Kania, H. and Blanke, B. (2000), 'Von der "Korporatisierung" zum "Wettbewerb": Gesundheitspolitische Kurswechsel in den Neunziger Jahren', in R. Czada and H. Wollmann (eds), *Von der Bonner zur Berliner Republik: 10 Jahre Deutsche Einheit. Leviathan, Sonderheft 19/1999* (Opladen), 567–91.

Kassim, B., Peters, G. and Wright, V. (2001) (eds), *The National Co-ordination of EU Policy: The Domestic Level* (Oxford), 235–64.

Katz, R. S. (1999), 'Representation, the Locus of Democratic Legitimation, and the Role of the National Parliaments in the European Union', in R. S. Katz and B. Wessels (eds), *The European Parliament, the National Parliaments, and European Integration* (Oxford), 21–44.

Katz, R. S. and Wessels, B. (1999) (eds), *The European Parliament, the National Parliaments, and European Integration* (Oxford).

Katzenstein, P. (1987), *Policy and Politics in West Germany. The Growth of a Semisovereign State* (Philadelphia).

Katzenstein, P. (1997*a*) (ed.), *Tamed Power: Germany in Europe* (Ithaca).

Katzenstein, P. (1997*b*), 'United Germany in a Unifying Europe', in P. Katzenstein (ed.), *Tamed Power: Germany in Europe* (Ithaca), 1–48.

Katzenstein, P. (1997*c*), *Mitteleuropa: Between Europe and Germany* (Providence).

Kaufmann, M. (1999), 'Integrierte Staatlichkeit als Staatsstrukturprinzip', *Juristenzeitung (JZ)*, 814–22.

Kepplinger, H.-M. (1985*a*), *Die aktuelle Berichterstattung des Hörfunks. Eine Inhaltsanalyse der Abendnachrichten und politischen Magazine* (Freiburg/Munich).

Kepplinger, H.-M. (1985*b*), 'Systemtheoretische Aspekte politischer Kommunikation', *Publizistik*, 30, 247–64.

Kern, K., Jörgens, H. and Jänicke, M. (2000), 'Die Diffusion umweltpolitischer Innovationen. Ein Beitrag zur Globalisierung von Umweltpolitik', *Zeitschrift für Umweltpolitik*, 23, 507–46.

Kevin, D. (2001), 'Coverage of the European Parliament Elections of 1999: National Public Spheres and European Debates', *Javnost/The Public*, 8, 21–38.

King, G., Keohane, R. O. and Verba, S. (1994), *Designing Social Inquiry: Scientific Inference in Qualitative Research* (Princeton).

Kitschelt, H. (1986), 'Political Opportunity Structures and Political Protest: Anti-Nuclear Movements in Four Democracies', *British Journal of Political Science*, 16, 57–85.

Kitschelt, H. (1997), 'European Party Systems: Continuity and Change', in M. Rhodes. P. Heywood and V. Wright (eds), *Developments in West European Politics* (Basingstoke), 131–50.

Kitschelt, H. and Streeck, W. (2003) (eds), *Germany: Beyond the Stable State*, Special Issue of *West European Politics*.

Klein, M., Jagodzinski, W., Mochmann, E. and Ohr, D. (2000) (eds), *50 Jahre Empirische Wahlforschung in Deutschland* (Opladen).

Klingemann, H.-D. and Kaase, M. (1994) (eds), *Wahlen und Wähler. Analysen aus Anlaß der Bundestagswahl 1990* (Opladen).

Klingemann, H.-D. and Kaase, M. (2001) (eds), *Wahlen und Wähler. Analysen aus Anlaß der Bundestagswahl 1998* (Opladen).

Kloepfer, M. (1998), *Umweltrecht, 2. Auflage* (Munich).

Knill, C. (2001), *The Europeanisation of National Administrations. Patterns of Institutional Change and Persistence* (Cambridge).

Knill, C. and Lehmkuhl, D. (1999), 'How Europe Matters: Different Mechanisms of Europeanization', *European Integration Online Papers*, 3, http://www.eiop.or.at/texte/1997–007a.htm.

Knill, C. and Lehmkuhl, D. (2002), 'The National Impact of European Union Regulatory Policy: Three Europeanization Mechanisms', *European Journal of Political Research*, 41, 255–80.

Knill, C. and Lenschow, A. (1998), 'Coping with Europe: The Impact of British and German Administrations on the Implementation of EU Environmental Policy', *Journal of European Public Policy*, 5, 595–614.

Knill, C. and Lenschow, A. (2000) (eds), *Implementing EU Environmental Policy* (Manchester).

Knoche, M. and Lindgens, M. (1988), 'Selektion, Konsonanz und Wirkungspotential der deutschen Tagespresse. Politikvermittlung am Beispiel der Agentur- und Presseberichterstattung über die Grünen zur Bundestagswahl 1987', *Media Perspektiven*, 8/1988, 90–510.

Kohler-Koch, B. (1992), 'Interessen und Integration: Die Rolle organisierter Interessen im westeuropäischen Integrationsprozeß', in M. Kreile (ed.), *Die Integration Europas (Politische Vierteljahresschrift*, Special Issue 23/1992) (Opladen), 81–119.

Kohler-Koch, B. (1999), 'The Evolution and Transformation of Network Governance in the European Union', in B. Kohler-Koch and R. Eising (eds), *The Transformation of Governance in the European Union* (London), 14–35.

Kohler-Koch, B. and Eising, R. (1999) (eds), *The Transformation of Governance in the European Union* (London).

Kohler-Koch, B. and Knodt, M. (2000*a*) (eds), *Deutschland zwischen Europäisierung und Selbstbehauptung* (Frankfurt a.M.).

Kohler-Koch, B. and Knodt, M. (2000*b*), 'Europäisierung: Plädoyer für eine Horizonterweiterung', in M. Knodt and B. Kohler-Koch (eds*), Deutschland zwischen Europäisierung und Selbstbehauptung* (Frankfurt a.M.), 11–31.

Kokott, J. (1993), 'Nationales Subventionsrecht im Schatten der EG—Das Beispiel der Rückforderung von Subventionen', *Deutsches Verwaltungsblatt (DVBl.)*, 1235–40.

Kommission der Europäischen Gemeinschaften (2001), *Europäisches Regieren, Weißbuch* (Luxembourg).

Konrad, K. A. and Wagner, G. (2000), 'Reform of the Public Pension System in Germany', Deutsches Institut für Wirtschaftsforschung, Discussion Paper (Berlin).

Korte, K.-R. (2000), 'Solutions for the Decision Dilemma: Political Styles of Germany's Chancellors', *German Politics*, 9, 1–22.

Korte, K.-R. and Mauer, A. (2002), 'Innenpolitische Grundlagen der deutschen Europapolitik: Konturen der Kontinuität und des Wandels', in H. Schneider, M. Jopp and U. Schmalz (eds), *Eine neue deutsche Europapolitik: Rahmenbedingungen, Problemfelder, Optionen* (Bonn), 195–230.

Kötter, U. (1998), 'Die Urteile des Gerichtshofs der Europäischen Gemeinschaften in den Rechtssachen Decker und Kohll: Der Vorhang zu und alle Fragen offen?', *Vierteljahresschrift für Sozialrecht*, 26, 233–52.

Kötter, U. (1999), 'Health Care Systems between National Regulation and European Market — Recent Developments of the Belgian, the Dutch and the German Social Health Insurance System', European University Institute, Conference Paper, WS/41 (Florence).

Kötter, U. (2002), 'Die Bedeutung der Entscheidung Geraerts-Smit/Peerbooms für das Gesundheitssystem der Niederlande', unpublished manuscript (Cologne).

Kraack, M., Pehle, H. and Zimmermann-Steinhart, P. (2001), *Umweltintegration in der Europäischen Union* (Baden-Baden).

Krägenow, T. (2002), 'Schröder betont eigenen deutschen Weg', *Financial Times Deutschland*, 6 August, http://www.ftd.de/sp/ak/1028330276837.html?nv=rs.

Krämer, L. (1988), 'Keine Absichtserklärungen, sondern durchsetzbares Recht — Die Kontrolle der Anwendung von EWG-Umweltrichtlinien', in L. Gündling and B. Weber (eds), *Dicke Luft in Europa. Aufgaben und Probleme der europäischen Umweltpolitik* (Heidelberg), 227–34.

Krasner, S. D. (1999), *Sovereignty: Organized Hypocrisy* (Princeton).

Krehbiel, K. (1991), *Information and Legislative Organization* (Ann Arbor).

Kreile, M. (1978), 'West Germany: The Dynamics of Expansion', in P. J. Katzenstein (ed.), *Between Power and Plenty: Foreign Economic Policies of Advanced Industrial States* (Madison), 191–224.

Kreile, M. (2001), 'Zur nationalen Gebundenheit europapolitischer Visionen: Das Schröder-Papier und die Jospin-Rede', *Integration*, 24, 250–7.

Kromarek, P. (1986), *Vergleichende Untersuchung über die Umsetzung der EG-Richtlinien Abfall und Wasser* (Bonn/Berlin).

Kromarek, P. (1989), *Umweltpolitische Handlungsspielräume der Länder im Zusammenhang mit der Vollendung des Europäischen Binnenmarktes 1992* (Bonn).

Krüger, U. M. (2000), 'Qualitätsanspruch bei 3SAT und Arte. Struktur und Inhalte der öffentlich-rechtlichen Kulturprogramme', *Media Perspektiven*, 2/2000, 71–84.

Kuper, E. (1995), *Transnationale Parteienbünde zwischen Partei- und Weltpolitik* (Frankfurt a.M.).

Laakso, M. and Taagepera, R. (1979), '"Effective" Number of Parties: A Measure with Application to West Europe', *Comparative Political Studies,* 12, 3–27.

Ladrech, R. (1994), 'Europeanization of Domestic Politics and Institutions: The Case of France', *Journal of Common Market Studies*, 32, 69–88.

Laeken Delaration on the Future of the European Union (2001), http://european-conven tion.eu.int/pdf/LKNEN.pdf.

Lafontaine, O. and Müller, C. (1998), *Keine Angst vor der Globalisierung* (Bonn).

Lalumière, C. (2000) *Report on the Establishment of a Common European Security and Defence Policy after Cologne and Helsinki* (2000/2005(INI)) Committee on Foreign Affairs, Human Rights, Common Security and Defence Policy.

Lamping, W. (2001), 'What Does European Integration Have to do with the German Health Care System? Sorting out the Issues', paper presented at the ECPR Joint Sessions of Workshops, Grenoble, April, 6–11.

Lamping, W. and Rüb, F. W. (2001), 'From the Conservative Welfare State to "Something Uncertain Else": The New German Pension Politics', Centre for Social and Public Policy, University of Hannover, Discussion Paper, 12 (Hannover).

Lane, J.-E. and Ersson, S. (1994), *Politics and Society in Western Europe* (London).

Lang, G. E. and Lang, K. (1984), *Politics and Television. Re-Viewed* (Beverly Hills).

Lees, C. (2002) '"Dark Matter": Institutional Constraints and the Failure of Party-Based Euroscepticism in Germany', *Political Studies*, 50, 244–67.

Lehmbruch, G. (1977), 'Liberal Corporatism and Party Government', *Comparative Political Studies*, 10, 91–126.

Leibfried, S. and Pierson, P. (2000), 'Social Policy', in H. Wallace and W. Wallace (eds), *Policy-Making in the European Union* (Oxford), 267–92.

Lenschow, A. (2002) (ed.), *Environmental Policy Integration. Greening Sectoral Policies in Europe* (London).

Leonardy, U. (2002), 'Parteien im Föderalismus der Bundesrepublik Deutschland. Scharniere zwischen Staat und Politik', *Zeitschrift für Parlamentsfragen*, 33, 180–95.

Lesse, U. (2000), 'A Fully-Fledged Political Party? Die Sozialdemokratische Partei Europas', unpublished paper.

Levi-Faur, D. (1999), 'The Governance of Competition: The Interplay of Technology, Economics and Politics in European Union Electricity and Telecom Regimes', *Journal of Public Policy*, 19, 175–207.

Levy, D. A. (1999), *Europe's Digital Revolution. Broadcasting Regulation, the EU and the Nation State* (London/New York).

Lijphart, A. (1984), 'Measures of Cabinet Durability: A Conceptual and Empirical Evaluation', *Comparative Political Studies*, 17, 265–79.

Lindberg, L. N. and Scheingold, S. A. (1970), *Europe's Would-Be Polity: Patterns of Change in the European Community* (Englewood Cliffs).

Lipset, S. M. and Rokkan, S. (1967), 'Cleavage Structures, Party Systems, and Voter Alignments: An Introduction', in S. M. Lipset and S. Rokkan (eds), *Party Systems and Voter Alignments: Cross-National Perspectives* (New York), 1–64.

Lodge, M. (2000), 'Isomorphism of National Policies? The Europeanization of German Competition and Procurement Law', *West European Politics*, 23, 89–107.

Lodge, M. (2002), 'Varieties of Europeanisation and the National Regulatory State', *Public Policy and Administration*, 17, 43–67.

Longhurst, K. (2000), 'Strategic Culture: The Key to Understanding German Security Policy?, Ph.D. thesis, Institute for German Studies, University of Birmingham.

Luhmann, N. (1970), 'Öffentliche Meinung', *Politische Vierteljahresschrift*, 11, 2–28.

Lüthje, B. (1997), 'Bundesrepublik Deutschland: Von der "Fernmeldeeinheitstechnik" zum universallen Netzwettbewerb', in J. Esser (ed.), *Europäische Telekommunikation im Zeitalter der Deregulierung: Infrastruktur im Umbruch* (Münster), 147–81.

Machill, M. (1998), 'Euronews: The First European News Channel as a Case Study for Media Industry Development in Europe and for Spectra of Transnational Journalism Research', *Media, Culture and Society*, 20, 427–50.

Maier, C. (1977), 'Berichterstatter zur Abschlußsitzung: Methodologische Ansätze und Ereignisse', in H. Mommsen, D. Petzina and B. Weisbrod (eds), *Industrielles System und politische Entwicklung in der Weimarer Republik, Band 2* (Düsseldorf), 950–7.

Mair, P. (2000), 'The Limited Impact of Europe on National Party Systems', *West European Politics*, 23, 27–51.

Majone, G. (1996), *Regulating Europe* (Routledge).

Manin, B., Przeworski, A. and Stokes, S. C. (1999), 'Introduction', in A. Przeworski, S. C. Stokes and B. Manin (eds), *Democracy, Accountability and Representation* (Cambridge), 1–26.

Manow, P. (1996), 'Informalisierung und Parteipolitisierung—Zum Wandel exekutiver Entscheidungsprozesse in der Bundesrepublik', *Zeitschrift für Parlamentsfragen*, 27, 96–107.

Marks, G. and Hooghe, L. (2001), *Multi-Level Governance and European Integration* (Lanham).

Marsh, D. (1992), *The Bundesbank: The Bank that Rules Europe* (London).

Marsh, D., Smith, M. J. and Richards, D. (2000), 'Bureaucrats, Politicians and Reform in Whitehall: Analysing the Bureau-Shaping Model', *British Journal of Political Science*, 30, 461–82.

Masing, J. (1996), *Die Mobilisierung des Bürgers für die Durchsetzung des Rechts* (Berlin).

Mathes, R. and Pfetsch, B. (1991), 'The Role of the Alternative Press in the Agenda Building Process: Spill-Over Effects and Media Opinion Leadership', *European Journal of Communication*, 6, 33–62.

Matzner, E. (1984), *Der Wohlfahrtsstaat von morgen* (Opladen).

Maull, H. (1992), 'Zivilmacht Bundesrepublik Deutschland. Vierzehn Thesen für eine neue deutsche Außenpolitik', *Europa Archiv*, 47, 269–78.

Maurer, A. and Wessels, W. (2000), 'Die Ständige Vertretung Deutschlands bei der EU: Scharnier im administrativen Mehrebenensystem', in M. Knodt and B. Kohler-Koch (eds), *Deutschland zwischen Europäisierung und Selbstbehauptung* (Frankfurt a.M.), 293–324.

Maurer, A. and Wessels, W. (2001), 'The German Case: A Key Moderator in a Competitive Multi-Level Environment', in H. Kassim, A. Menon, B. G. Peters and V. Wright (eds), *The National Co-ordination of EU Policy: The European Level* (Oxford), 101–28.

Mayntz, R. (1980) (ed.), *Implementation politischer Programme: empirische Forschungsberichte* (Königstein).

Mayntz, R. (1991), 'Politische Steuerbarkeit und Reformblockaden: Überlegungen am Beispiel des Gesundheitswesens', in *Die Zukunft der Sozialen Sicherung in Deutschland* (Baden-Baden), 21–45.

Mayntz, R. and Scharpf, F. W. (1975), *Policy-Making in the German Federal Bureaucracy* (Amsterdam).

Mazzoleni, G. (1987), 'Media Logic and Party Logic in Campaign Coverage: The Italian General Election of 1983', *European Journal of Communication*, 2, 81–103.

Mazzuchelli, C. (1997), *France and Germany at Maastricht: Politics and Negotiations to Create the European Union* (New York).

McCombs, M. E. (1992), 'Explorers and Surveyors: Expanding Strategies for Agenda-Setting Research', *Journalism Quarterly*, 69, 813–24.

McCombs, M., Lopez-Escobar, E. and Llamas, J. P. (2000), 'Setting the Agenda of Attributes in the 1996 Spanish General Election', *Journal of Communication*, 50, 77–92.

McGowan, L. and Wilks, S. (1995), 'The First Supranational Policy in the EU: Competition Policy', *European Journal of Political Research*, 28, 141–69.

Mearsheimer, J. (1990), 'Back to the Future: Instability in Europe after the Cold War', *International Security*, 15, 5–56.

Medrano, J. D. (2001), 'Die Qualitätspresse und Europäische Integration', *Forschungsjournal Neue Soziale Bewegungen*, 14, 30–41.

Mehl, P. (1987), *Die Europa-Kommission des Deutschen Bundestages: Eine neue Einrichtung interparlamentarischer Zusammenarbeit* (Kehl am Rhein).

Mény, Y., Muller, P. and Quermonne, J.-L. (1996) (eds), *Adjusting to Europe: The Impact of the European Union on National Institutions and Policies* (London).

Metcalfe, L. (1996), 'The European Commission as a Network Organization', *Publius*, 26, 43–62.

Mielke, G. (2001), 'Gesellschaftliche Konflikte und ihre Repräsentation im deutschen Parteiensystem: Anmerkungen zum Cleavage-Modell von Lipset und Rokkan', in U. Eith and G. Mielke (eds), *Gesellschaftliche Konflikte und Parteiensysteme* (Opladen), 77–95.

Milner, H. and Keohane, R. (1996), 'Internationalization and Domestic Politics: An Introduction', in H. Milner and R. Keohane (eds), *Internationalization and Domestic Politics* (New York), 3–24.

Milward, A. (1992), *The European Rescue of the Nation-State* (Berkeley).

Miskimmon, A. J. (2001), 'Recasting the Security Bargains: Germany, European Security Policy and the Transatlantic Relationship', in D. Webber (ed.), *New Europe, New Germany, Old Foreign Policy? German Foreign Policy since Unification* (London), 83–106.

Miskimmon, A. J. (2002), 'Europeanising Foreign and Securities Policies—National Adaptation and the Common European Security and Defence Policy—The Case of France, Germany and the United Kingdom', paper presented to the Graduate Student Conference, 'Europe and the World: United Europe Comes into its Own', BMW Centre for German and European Studies, Georgetown University, Washington, DC, 22 and 23 March.

Möbs, H. (1991), 'Gewässerschutzrecht in Deutschland und der Europäischen Gemeinschaft—Divergierende Zielsetzungen?', in P. Beherens and H.-J. Koch (eds), *Umweltschutz in der Europäischen Gemeinschaft* (Baden-Baden), 112–26.

Mol, A. P. J., Lauber, V. and Liefferink, D. (2000), *The Voluntary Approach to Environmental Policy* (Oxford).

Möller, F. and Limpert, M. (1993), 'Informations- und Mitwirkungsrechte des Bundestages in Angelegenheiten der Europäischen Union', *Zeitschrift für Parlamentsfragen*, 24.

Moltke, K. von (1984), 'Die EG-Umweltpolitik—Notwendige Ergänzung nationaler und internationaler Massnahmen', in R. Hrbek and W. Wessels (eds), *EG-Mitgliedschaft: ein vitales Interesse der Bundesrepublik Deutschland* (Bonn), 299–321.

Moltke, K. von (1986), 'Environment and Resources Policy—the Federal Republic and the European Community', in P. Lützeler (ed.), *Western Europe in Transition. West Germany's Role in the European Community* (Baden-Baden), 61–76.

Monopolkommission (2001), *Folgeprobleme der europäischen Kartellverfahrensreform, Sondergutachten* (Bonn).

Möschel, W. (2000), 'Systemwechsel im Europäischen Wettbewerbsrecht?', *Juristenzeitung*, 55, 61–7.

Müller, E. (1986), *Innenpolitik der Umweltpolitik. Sozial-liberale Umweltpolitik—(Ohn)Macht durch Organisation?* (Opladen).

Müller, E. (2002), 'Environmental Policy Integration as a Political Principle: The German Case and the Implications of European Policy', in A. Lenschow (ed.), *Environmental Policy Integration* (London), 57–77.

Müller-Brandeck-Bocquet, G. (1996), *Die instititionelle Dimension der Umweltpolitik. Eine vergleichende Untersuchung zu Frankreich, Deutschland und der Europäischen Union* (Baden-Baden).

NATO (1999*a*), Nato's Defence Capabilities Initiative 25 April, Press Release NAC-S(99)69, http://www.nato.int/docu/pr/1999/p99s069e.htm.

NATO (1999*b*), The Alliance's Strategic Concept, Press Release NAC-S(99)65, http://www.nato.int/docu/pr/1999/p99–065e.htm.

Naumann, K. (2002), 'Schröders deutscher Irrweg', *Die Welt*, 13 October, http://www.welt.de/daten/2002/08/13/0813fo350287.htx.

Neidhardt, F., Eilders, C. and Pfetsch, B. (1998), *Die Stimme der Medien im politischen Prozeß: Themen und Meinungen in Pressekommentaren.* WZB Discussion Paper, FSIII 98–106.

Neidhardt, F., Koopmans, R. and Pfetsch, B. (2000), 'Konstitutionsbedingungen politischer Öffentlichkeit', in H.-D. Klingemann and F. Neidhardt (eds), *Zur Zukunft der Demokratie: Herausforderungen im Zeitalter der Globalisierung* (Berlin), 263–93.

Nelson, T. E., Clawson, R. A. and Oxley, Z. M. (1997), 'Media Framing of a Civil Liberties Conflict and its Effect on Tolerance', *American Political Science Review*, 91, 567–98.

Neßler, V. (1997), *Europäische Willensbildung: die Fraktionen im Europaparlament zwischen nationalen Interessen, Parteipolitik und europäischer Integration* (Schwalbach).

Niclauß, K. (2001), 'The Federal Government: Variations of Chancellor Dominance', in L. Helms (ed.), *Institutions and Institutional Change in the Federal Republic of Germany* (Basingstoke), 65–83.

Niedermayer, O. (1994), 'Maastricht und die Entwicklung der öffentlichen Meinung zu Europa', in G.-J. Glaeßner and K. Sühl (eds), *Auf dem Weg nach Europa* (Opladen), 57–73.

Niedermayer, O. (1995*a*), 'Trust and Sense of Community', in O. Niedermayer and R. Sinnott (eds), *Public Opinion and Internationalized Governance* (Oxford), 227–45.

Niedermayer, O. (1995*b*), 'Trends and Contrasts', in O. Niedermayer and R. Sinnott (eds), *Public Opinion and Internationalized Governance* (Oxford), 53–72.

Niedermayer, O. (1996), 'Zur systematischen Analyse der Entwicklung von Parteiensystemen', in O. W. Gabriel and J. W. Falter (eds), *Wahlen und politische Einstellungen in westlichen Demokratien* (Frankfurt a.M.), 19–49.

Niedermayer, O. (2001), *Bürger und Politik* (Wiesbaden).

Niedermayer, O. (2002*a*), 'Nach der Vereinigung: Der Trend zum fluiden Fünfparteiensystem', in O. W. Gabriel, O. Niedermayer and R. Stöss (eds), *Parteiendemokratie in Deutschland* (Wiesbaden), 107–27.

Niedermayer, O. (2002*b*), 'Die europäischen Parteienbünde', in O. W. Gabriel, O. Niedermayer and R. Stöss (eds), *Parteiendemokratie in Deutschland* (Wiesbaden), 428–46.

Niedermayer, O. (2003), 'Parteiensystem', in E. Jesse and R. Sturm (eds), *Demokratien des 21. Jahrhunderts im Vergleich* (Opladen, forthcoming).

Niedermayer, O. and Sinnott, R. (1995), 'Democratic Legitimacy and the European Parliament', in O. Niedermayer and R. Sinnott (eds), *Public Opinion and Internationalized Governance* (Oxford), 277–308.

Noelle-Neumann, E. (1984), *The Spiral of Silence. Public Opinion—Our Social Skin* (Chicago).

Noelle-Neumann, E. and Mathes, R. (1987), 'The "Event as Event" and the "Event as News"', *European Journal of Communication*, 2, 391–414.

Norris, P. (1997), 'Representation and Democratic Deficit', *European Journal of Political Research*, 32, 273–82.

North Atlantic Council (1999), *The Alliance's Strategic Concept*, Washington Summit Communiqué, NATO Press Release, NAC-S(99) 65, 24 April.

North Atlantic Council Summit (2000), Final Communiqué, Brussels, 14–15 December, http://www.nato.int/.

Nullmeier, F. and Rüb, F. W. (1993), *Die Transformation der Sozialpolitik. Vom Sozialstaat zum Sicherungsstaat* (Frankfurt/New York).

Nye, J. S. (1990), *Bound to Lead. The Changing Nature of American Power* (New York).

Ohmae, K. (1990), *The Borderless World* (New York).

Olson, J. P. (2002), 'The Many Faces of Europeanization', *Journal of Common Market Studies*, 40, 921–52.

Oppermann, T. (1991), *Europarecht* (Munich).

Ostner, I. and Lewis, J. (1995), 'Gender and the Evolution of European Social Policy', in S. Leibfried and P. Pierson (eds), *European Social Policy: Between Fragmentation and Integration* (Washington, DC), 159–93.

Oxera (1998), ' The European Union Electricity Directive and the German Electricity Act', *Oxera Utility View*, 15 April.

Padgett, S. (1990), 'Policy Style and Issue Environment: The Electricity Supply Sector in West Germany', *Journal of Public Policy*, 10, 165–93.

Padgett, S. (1992), 'The Single European Energy Market: The Politics of Realization', *Journal of Common Market Studies*, 30, 53–75

Padgett, S. (1994) (ed.), *Adenauer to Kohl: The Development of the German Chancellorship* (London).

Padgett, S. (2003), 'Between Synthesis and Emulation: EU Policy Transfer in the Power Sector', *Journal of European Public Policy*, 10, 227–46.

Padgett, S. and Poguntke, T. (2002) (eds), *Continuity and Change in German Politics: Beyond the Politics of Centrality?* (London).

Page, B. I. (1996), 'The Mass Media as Political Actors', *Political Science & Politics*, 29, 20–24.

Page, B. I., Shapiro, R.Y. and Dempsey, G. R. (1987), 'What Moves Public Opinion?', *American Political Science Review*, 81, 23–43.

Pappi, F. U. and Shikano, S. (2000), 'Sachpolitik und Kompetenz als Beurteilungskriterien von großen und kleinen Wettbewerbern in deutschen Bundestagswahlkämpfen', in H. D. Klingemann and M. Kaase (eds), *Wahlen and Wähler: Analysen aus Anlaß der Bundestagswahl 1998* (Wiesbaden), 309–50.

Pappi, F. U. and Thurner, P. W. (2000), 'Die deutschen Wähler und der Euro: Auswirkungen auf die Bundestagswahl 1998?', *Politische Vierteljahresschrift*, 41, 435–66.

Paterson, W. E. (1989), 'Environmental Politics', in G. Smith *et al.* (eds), *Developments in West German Politics* (Basingstoke), 267–88.

Paterson, W. E. (1994), 'The Chancellor and Foreign Policy', in S. Padgett (ed.), *Adenauer to Kohl: The Development of the German Chancellorship* (London), 127–56.

Paterson, W. E. (1996), 'Beyond Semi-Sovereignty: The New Germany in the New Europe', *German Politics,* 5, 167–84.

Paterson, W. E. (1998), 'Helmut Kohl, the "Vision Thing" and Escaping the Semi-Sovereignty Trap', *German Politics*, 7, 17–36.

Paterson, W. E. (2001), 'Britain and the Berlin Republic: Between Ambivalence and Emulation', *German Politics*, 10, 201–24.

Paterson, W. E. and Smith, G. (1982) (eds), *The West German Model: Perspectives on a Stable State* (London).

Patterson, T. E. and Donsbach, W. (1996), 'News Decisions: Journalists as Partisan Actors', *Political Communication*, 13, 455–68.

Pedersen, M. N. (1980), 'On Measuring Party System Change. A Methodological Critique and a Suggestion', *Comparative Political Studies*, 12, 387–403.

Pedersen, T. (1998), *Germany, France and the Integration of Europe* (London).

Pehle, H. (1997), 'Domestic Obstacles to an Environmental Forerunner', in M. S. Andersen and D. Liefferink (eds), *European Environmental Policy: The Pioneers* (Manchester), 161–209.

Pehle, H. (1998), *Das Bundesministerium für Umwelt, Naturschutz and Reaktorsicherheit: Ausgegrenzt statt integriert?* (Wiesbaden).

Pehle, H. (forthcoming), 'Umweltschutz', in E. Jesse and R. Sturm (eds), *Demokratien des 21. Jahrhunderts im Vergleich* (Opladen).

Pernice, I. (1999), 'Multilevel Constitutionalism and the Treaty of Amsterdam: European Constitution-Making Revisited?', *Common Market Law Review*, 36, 703–50.

Pernice, I. (2001), 'Europäisches und nationales Verfassungsrecht', *Veröffentlichungen der Vereinigung der Deutschen Staatsrechtslehrer (VVDStRL)*, 60.

Perspektiven für die 'Gemeinsame Außen- und Sicherheitspolitik' der Europäischen Union (2000), (Berlin), December.

Peters, B. G., Rhodes, R. A. W. and Wright, V. (2000), 'Staffing the Summit—The Administration of the Core Executive: Convergent Trends and National Specificities', in B. G. Peters, R. A. W. Rhodes and V. Wright (eds), *Administering the Summit: Administration of the Core Executive in Developed Countries* (Basingstoke), 3–22.

Pflüger, F. (2001), 'Das Chaos der EU-Außenpolitik', *Die Welt*, 26 April.

Pierson, P. (1996), 'The New Politics of the Welfare State', *World Politics*, 48, 141–79.

Pierson, P. (2001), 'Post-Industrial Pressures on the Mature Welfare States', in P. Pierson (ed.), *The New Politics of the Welfare State* (Oxford), 80–104.

Plasser, F., Gabriel, O. W., Falter, J. W. and Ulram, P. A. (1999) (eds), *Wahlen und politische Einstellungen in Deutschland und Österreich* (Frankfurt a.M.).

Pöhle, K. (1984), 'Die Europa-Kommission des Deutschen Bundestages: Ein politisches und geschäftsordnungsmäßiges Novum', *Zeitschrift für Parlamentsfragen*, 15, 352–9.

Pöhle, K. (2000), 'Europäische Parteien—für wen und für was eigentlich?', *Zeitschrift für Parlamentsfragen*, 31, 599–619.

Power in Europe (1999), 'More of the German Way', *Power in Europe*, 308, 13 September 1999, 4.

Power in Europe (2000), 'Germany: New Entrants Hobbling to Market', *Power in Europe*, 321, 4 April 2000, 6.

Power in Europe (2000a), 'Editorial', *Power in Europe*, 330, 4 August 2000, 2.

Power in Europe (2000b), 'Commission to Demand German Energy Regulator', *Power in Europe*, 338, 24 November 2000, 5.

Protess, D. L. and McCombs, M. (1991) (eds), *Agenda Setting: Readings on Media, Public Opinion, and Policy Making* (Hillsdale).

Radaelli, C. (2000a), 'Policy Transfer in the European Union: Institutional Isomorphism as a Source of Legitimacy', *Governance*, 13, 25–43.

Radaelli, C. (2000b), 'Whither Europeanization? Concept Stretching and Substantive Change', *European Integration Online Papers*, 4(8), http://eiop.or.at/eiop/texte/2000–008a.htm.

Radaelli, C. (2001), 'Conceptualising Europeanization: Theory, Methods and the Challenge of Empirical Research', paper presented to the Europeanization Residential Easter School, University of York, 24–25 March.

Rae, D. (1967), *The Political Consequences of Electoral Laws* (New Haven).

Ranney, A. (1962), *The Concept of Responsible Party Government* (Urbana).

Rattinger, H. (1994), 'Public Attitudes to European Integration in Germany after Maastricht: Inventory and Typology', *Journal of Common Market Studies*, 32, 525–40.

Rattinger, H., Gabriel, O. W. and Jagodzinski, W. (1994) (eds), *Wahlen und politische Einstellungen im vereinigten Deutschland* (Frankfurt a.M.).

Rau, J. (2001), Address delivered at the European Parliament on 4 April 2001, Minutes of the European Parliament, 4 April 2001, 106–10.

Raunio, T. and Hix, S. (2000), 'Backbenchers Learn to Fight Back: European Integration and Parliamentary Government', *West European Politics*, 23, 142–68.

Raunio, T. and Wiberg, M. (2000), 'Building Elite Consensus: Parliamentary Accountability in Finland', *Journal of Legislative Studies*, 6, 59–80.

Ray, L. (1999), 'Measuring Party Orientations Toward European Integration: Results from an Expert Survey', *European Journal of Political Research*, 36, 283–306.

Reermann, O. (1997), 'Readmission Agreements', in K. Hailbronner *et al.* (eds), *Immigration Admissions* (Providence), 121–45.

Reese, S. D. and Danielian, L. H. (1989), 'Intermedia Influence and the Drug Issue: Converging on Cocaine', in P. Shoemaker (ed.), *Communication Campaigns about Drugs: Government, Media, and the Public* (Hillsdale), 29–45.

Rehbinder, E. (1992), 'Rethinking Environmental Policy', in G. Smith, W. Paterson, P. Merkl and S. Padgett (eds), *Developments in German Politics* (London), 227–43.

Rehbinder, E. and Stewart, R. (1985), *Integration Through Law. Europe and the American Federal Experience* (Berlin).

Reiche, D. T. and Krebs, C. (1999), *Der Einstieg in die ökologische Steuerreform: Aufstieg, Restriktionen und Durchsetzung eines umweltpolitischen Themas* (Frankfurt).

Renz, T. and Rieger, G. (1999), 'Die bayerische Landtagswahl vom 13. September 1998: Laptop, Lederhose und eine Opposition ohne Optionen', *Zeitschrift für Parlamentsfragen*, 30, 78–97.

Ress, G. (1994), 'The Constitution and the Maastricht Treaty: Between Co-operation and Conflict', *German Politics*, 3, 49.

Reutter, W. (2001), 'Deutschland', in W. Reutter and P. Rütters (eds), *Verbände und Verbandssysteme in Westeuropa* (Opladen), 75–102.

Rheinhardt, N. (1997), 'A Turning Point in the German EMU Debate: The Baden-Württemberg Regional Election of March 1996', *German Politics*, 6, 77–99.

Richardson, J. J. (1993), 'Government and Groups in Britain: Changing Styles', in C. S. Thomas (ed.), *First World Interest Groups: A Comparative Perspective* (Westport), 53–66.

Richter, I., Schuppert, G. F. and Bumke, C. (2000), *Casebook Verwaltungsrecht*, 3. Auflage (Munich).

Rippert, L. (2001), 'Erfahrungen des Bundesgrenzschutzes mit der internationalen Gremienarbeit, der multi- und bilateralen Zusammenarbeit und künftige Erwartungen an diese Formen der Zusammenarbeit', in Grenzschutzdirektion (ed.), *Intensivierung der praktischen Zusammenarbeit bei der Verhinderung der unerlaubten Einreise und Bekämpfung der Schleusungskriminalität* (Koblenz), 101–15.

Risse, T. (2001), 'A European Identity? Europeanization and the Evolution of Nation-State Identities', in M. Green Cowles, J. Caporaso and T. Risse (eds), *Transforming Europe: Europeanization and Domestic Change* (Ithaca), 198–216.

Risse, T., Green Cowles, M. and Caporaso, J. (2001), 'Europeanization and Domestic Change: Introduction', in M. Green Cowles, J. Caporaso and T. Risse (eds), *Transforming Europe: Europeanization and Domestic Change* (Ithaca), 1–20.

Rittberger, V. (2001), 'The Debate about the New German Foreign Policy after Unification', in V. Rittberger (ed.), *German Foreign Policy since Unification: Theories and Case Studies* (Manchester), 11–33.

Robertson, G. (1999), Speech to the Annual Assembly of the NATO Parliamentary Assembly, Amsterdam, 15 November, reprinted in M. Rutten, *From St. Malo to Nice: European Defence Core Documents, Chaillot Paper*, 47, 60–5 (2001).

Rogowski, R. (1989), *Commerce and Coalitions* (Princeton).

Rometsch, D. (1996), 'The Federal Republic of Germany', in D. Rometsch and W. Wessels (eds), *The European Union and Member States: Towards Institutional Fusion?* (Manchester), 61–104.

Rometsch, D. and Wessels, W. (1996) (eds), *The European Union and Member States: Towards Institutional Fusion?* (Manchester).

Rose-Ackermann, S. (1995), *Controlling Environmental Policy: The Limits of Public Law in Germany and the United States* (New Haven).

Rosewitz, B. and Webber, D. (1990), *Reformversuche und Reformblockaden im deutschen Gesundheitswesen* (Franfurt a.M./New York).

Rössler, P. (2002), 'Von der Agenturwirklichkeit zur Pressewirklichkeit. Vielfalt und Fokussierung auf der Mikroebene: Berichterstattung von Tageszeitungen und deren Abhängigkeit von Nachrichtenlieferanten', in A. Baum and S. J. Schmidt (eds), *Fakten und Fiktionen: Über den Umgang mit Medienwirklichkeiten* (Konstanz).

Roth, D. (1998), *Empirische Wahlforschung* (Opladen).

Roy, S. (2002), 'Telecommunications Policy in the European Union', *Convergence: The Journal of Research into New Media Technologies*, 8(2), Special Issue on Telecommunications in Europe, 100–13.

Rucht, D. (2000), 'Zur Europäisierung politischer Mobilisierung', *Berliner Journal für Soziologie* 2, 185–202.

Rucht, D. (2002), 'The EU as a Target of Political Mobilization: Is there a Europeanization of Conflict?', in R. Balme, D. Chabanet and V. Wright (eds), *L'action collective en Europe* (Paris), 163–94.

Ruffert, M. (1998), 'Dogmatik und Praxis des subjektiv-öffentlichen Rechts unter dem Einfluß des Gemeinschaftsrechts', *Deutsches Verwaltungsblatt (DVBl)*, 69–75.

Saalfeld, T. (1995), 'The German Houses of Parliament and European Integration', *Journal of Legislative Studies*, 1, 12–34.

Saalfeld, T. (1998), 'The German Bundestag: Influence and Accountability in a Complex Environment', in P. Norton (ed.), *Parliaments and Governments in Western Europe* (London), 44–71.

Saalfeld, T. (1999), 'Coalition Politics and Management in the Kohl Era, 1982–1998', *German Politics*, 8, 141–73.

Sabatier, P. (1999), 'The Need For Better Theories', in P. Sabatier (ed.), *Theories of the Policy Process* (Boulder, Colo.), 3–18.

Salzwedel, J. (1989), 'Probleme der Umsetzung europäischen Gemeinschaftsrechts in das Umwelt- und Technikrecht der Mitgliedsstaaten', *Umwelt- und Planungsrecht*, 9, 41–9.

Sandholtz, W. (1996), 'Membership Matters: Limits of the Functional Approach to European Institutions', *Journal of Common Market Studies*, 34, 403–30.

Sandholtz, W. and Zysman, J. (1989), '1992: Recasting the European Bargain', *World Politics*, 42, 95–128.

Sarcinelli, U. (1987), *Symbolische Politik. Zur Bedeutung symbolischen Handelns in der Wahlkampfkommunikation der Bundesrepublik Deutschland* (Opladen).

Sarotte, M. E. (2001), *German Military Reform and European Security*, Adelphi Paper, 340, IISS (Oxford).

Sartori, G. (1966), 'European Political Parties: The Case of Polarized Pluralism', in J. LaPalombara and M. Weiner (eds), *Political Parties and Political Development* (Princeton), 137–76.

Sartori, G. (1976), *Parties and Party Systems: A Framework for Analysis* (Cambridge).

Sartori, G. (1987), *The Theory of Democracy Revisited. Part One: The Contemporary Debate* (Chatham, NJ).

Sbragia, A. (1996), 'Environmental Policy', in H. Wallace and W. Wallace (eds), *Policy-Making in the European Union*, 3rd edn (Oxford), 235–55.

Scharioth, K. (2002), 'GASP und ESVP vor internationalen Herausforderungen: Möglichkeiten—Grenzen—künftige Verfaßtheit', Mittagsgespräch, Institut für Europäische Politik (Berlin), 4 July.

Scharpf, F. (1992), 'Europäisches Demokratiedefizit und deutscher Föderalismus', *Staatswissenschaft und Staatspraxis*, 3, 293–306.

Scharpf, F. W. (1999), *Governing Europe: Effective and Democratic?* (Oxford).

Scharpf, F. (1997), *Games Real Actors Play: Actor-Centred Institutionalism in Policy Research* (Boulder, Col.).

Scharpf, F. W. (2000), 'The Viability of Advanced Welfare States in the International Economy: Vulnerabilities and Options', *Journal of European Public Policy*, 7, 190–228.

Scharpf, F. W. and Schmidt, V. (2000) (eds), *Welfare and Work in the Open Economy, 1: From Vulnerabilities to Competitiveness* (Oxford).

Scharping, R. (2002), 'Rede des Bundesministers der Verteidigung', Rudolf Scharping, anläßlich der 39. Kommadeurtagung der Bundeswehr am 8. April 2002 in Hannover.

Schäuble, W. and Bocklet, R. (2001), *Vorschläge von CDU und CSU für einen Europäischen Verfassungsvertrag* (manuscript).

Schelter, K. (1999), 'Innere Sicherheit in einem Europa ohne Grenzen: Illusion oder realistisches Ziel einer entschlossenen Politik?', in R. C. Meier-Walser et al. (eds), *Organisierte Kriminalität* (Munich).

Scheuing, D. H. (2000), 'Die Europäisierung des Grundgesetzes für die Bundesrepublik Deutschland', in Bauer et al. (eds.), *Ius Publicum im Umbruch* (Stuttgart), 47–69.

Schimmelfennig, F. (2000), 'International Socialization in the New Europe: Rational Action in an Institutional Environment', *European Journal of International Relations*, 6, 109–39.

Schindler, P. (1999), *Datenhandbuch zur Geschichte des Deutschen Bundestages 1949 bis 1999* (Baden-Baden).

Schlesinger, P. (1999), 'Changing Spaces of Political Communication: The Case of the European Union', *Political Communication*, 16, 263–79.

Schlesinger, P. and Kevin, D. (2000), 'Can the European Union Become a Sphere of Publics?', in E.O. Eriksen and J. E. Fossum (eds), *Democracy in the European Union. Integration Through Deliberation?* (London/New York), 206–29.

Schludi, M. (2001), 'The Politics of Pensions in Social Insurance Countries', Max Planck Institute for the Studies of Societies Discussion Paper, 01–11 (Cologne).

Schmähl, W. (1993), 'The "1992 Reform" of Public Pensions in Germany: Main Elements and Some Effects', *Journal of European Social Policy*, 3, 39–51.

Schmalz, U. (2002), 'Die europäisierte Macht: Deutschland in der europäischen Außen- und Sicherheitspolitik', in H. Schneider, M. Jopp and U. Schmalz (eds), *Eine neue deutsche Europapolitik? Rahmenbedingungen—Problemfelder—Optionen*, (Bonn).

Schmidt, B. (2000), *From Co-operation to Integration: Defence and Aerospace Industries in Europe, Chaillot Paper*, 40, Institute for Security Studies, Western European Union (Paris), July.

Schmidt, B. (2001) (ed.), *Between Co-operation and Competition: The Transatlantic Defence Market, Chaillot Paper*, 44, Institute for Security Studies, Western European Union (Paris), January.

Schmidt, M. G. (1998), *Sozialpolitik in Deutschland. Historische Entwicklung und internationaler Vergleich,* 2nd edn (Opladen).

Schmidt, M. G. (1999), 'Die Europäisierung der öffentlichen Aufgaben', *Politische Vierteljahresschrift (PVS) Sonderheft 30/99*, 385–94.

Schmidt, S. (1996), 'Privatizing the Federal Posts and Telecommunications Services', in A. Benz and K. Goetz (eds), *A New German Public Sector? Reform, Adaptation and Stability* (Aldershot), 45–70.

Schmidt, S. (1997), 'Behind the Council Agenda: the Commission's Impact on Decisions', MPIfG Discussion Paper 97/4, Max-Planck-Institut für Gesellschaftsforschung (Cologne).

Schmidt, S. (1998), 'Commission Activism: Subsuming Telecommunications and Electricity under European Competition Law', *Journal of European Public Policy*, 5, 169–84.

Schmidt, V. (1999), 'National Patterns of Governance under Siege: The Impact of European Integration', in B. Kohler-Koch and R. Eising (eds), *The Transformation of Governance in the European Union* (London), 155–72.

Schmidt, V. (2001), 'Europeanization and the Mechanics of Economic Policy Adjustment', *European Integration Online Papers*, 5(6), http://eiop.or.at/eiop/texte/2001–006a.htm.

Schmidt, V. (2002), *The Futures of European Capitalism* (Oxford).

Schmidt-Aßmann, E. (1993), 'Zur Europäisierung des Allgemeinen Verwaltungsrechts', in P. Badura and R. Scholz (eds), *Wege und Verfahren des Verfassungslebens* (Munich).

Schmitt, K. (1990) (ed.), *Wahlen, Parteieliten, politische Einstellungen. Neuere Forschungsergebnisse* (Frankfurt a.M.).

Schmitt-Egner, P. (2000), *Handbuch der Europäischen Regionalorganisationen* (Baden-Baden).

Schmitter, P.C. (1974), 'Still the Century of Corporatism?', *The Review of Politics*, 36, 85–131.

Schmitter, P. C. (1996), 'Imagining the Future of the Euro-Polity With the Help of New Concepts', in G. Marks *et al.* (eds), *Governance in the European Union* (London), 121–50.

Schmitter, P. C. (1999), 'Reflections on the Impact of the European Union on "Domestic" Democracy in its Member States', in M. Egeberg and P. Laegreid (eds), *Organizing Political Institutions: Essays for Johan P. Olsen* (Oslo), 289–98.

Schmitter, P. C. and Streeck, W. (1981), 'The Organization of Business Interests. A Resarch Design to Study the Associative Action of Business in the Advanced Industrial Societies of Western Europe,' WZB Discussion Paper, IIM/LMP 81/13 (Berlin).

Schneider, H., Jopp, M. and Schmalz, U. (2002) (eds), *Eine neue deutsche Europapolitik?* (Bonn).

Schneider, V. (2001), 'Institutional Reform in Telecommunications: The European Union in Transnational Policy Diffusion', in M. Green Cowles, J. Caporaso and T. Risse (eds), *Transforming Europe: Europeanization and Domestic Change* (Ithaca), 60–78.

Schneider, V. and Vedel, T. (1999), 'From High to Low Politics in Franco-German Relations: The Case of Telecommunications', in D. Webber (ed.), *The Franco-German Relationship in the European Union* (London), 75–92.

Schoch, F. (1997), 'Die Europäisierung des verwaltungsgerichtlichen vorläufigen Rechtsschutzes', *Deutsches Verwaltungsblatt (DVBl)*, 289–97.

Schoch, F. (1998), 'Die Europäisierung des Allgemeinen Verwaltungsrechts und der Verwaltungsrechtswissenschaft', *Die Wissenschaft vom Verwaltungsrecht, Beiheft 2*, 135–54.

Schönbach, K. (1977), *Trennung von Nachricht und Meinung. Empirische Untersuchung eines journalistischen Qualitätskriteriums* (Freiburg).

Schröder, G. (1989), 'Alternativen in der Umweltschutzpolitik', in H. Donner, G. Magoulas, J. Simon and R. Wolf (eds), *Umweltschutz zwischen Staat und Markt* (Baden-Baden), 43–58.

Schröder, G. (1999), 'Das Bündnis als Fokus unserer Politik der neuen Mitte', in H.-J. Arlt and S. Nehls (eds), *Bündnis für Arbeit: Konstruktion, Kritik, Karriere* (Opladen), 49–56.

Schröder, G. (2001), 'Closely Involving Citizens and Parliaments.' Europa: The Future of the European Union—Debate, http://www.europa.eu.int/futurum/documents/ contrib/ contjuin2001_en.htm, accessed 14 June,

Schultze, R.-O. (1991), 'Die bayerische Landtagswahl vom 14. Oktober 1990: Bayerische Besonderheiten und bundesrepublikanische Normalität', *Zeitschrift für Parlamentsfragen*, 22, 38–58.

Schultze, R.-O. (2000), 'Wählerverhalten bei Bundestagswahlen: Bekannte Muster mit neuen Akzenten', *Politische Bildung, 33*, 34–56.

Schulz, W. (1997), *Politische Kommunikation: Theoretische Ansätze und Ergebnisse empirischer Forschung zur Rolle der Massenmedien in der Politik* (Opladen).

Schulze, H. (1999), *Staat und Nation in der europäischen Geschichte* (Munich).

Schulze-Fielitz, H. (1988), *Theorie und Praxis parlamentarischer Gesetzgebung—besonders des 9. Deutschen Bundestages (1980–1983)* (Berlin).

Schuppert, G. F. (1994), 'Zur Staatswerdung Europas. Überlegungen zu Bedingungsfaktoren und Perspektiven der europäischen Verfassungsentwicklung', *Staatswissenschaften und Staatspraxis*, 5, 35–76.

Schuppert, G. F. (2000a), *Verwaltungswissenschaft. Verwaltung, Verwaltungsrecht, Verwaltungslehre* (Baden-Baden).

Schuppert, G. F. (2000b), 'Anforderungen an eine Europäische Verfassung', in H.-D. Klingemannn and F. Neidhardt (eds), *Zur Zukunft der Demokratie. Herausforderungen im Zeitalter der Globalisierung, WZB-Jahrbuch 2000* (Berlin).

Schuppert, G. F. (2001), 'Das Konzept der regulierten Selbstregulierung als Bestandteil einer als Regelungswissenschaft verstandenen Rechtswissenschaft', *Die Verwaltung, Beiheft 4*, 201–52.

Schuppert, G. F. (2002a), 'Europa im Verfassungsfieber. Bemerkungen zu Sinn und Unsinn der europäischen Verfassungsdebatte', in W. Lamping and I. Katenhusen (eds), *Demokratie in Europa* (Opladen).

Schuppert, G. F. (2002b), *Gute Gesetzgebung. Bausteine einer kritischen Gesetzgebungslehre. Gutachten im Auftrag des Bundesministeriums der Justiz* (Berlin), August.

Schwartz, H.-P. (1985), *Die gezähmten Deutschen. Von der Machtbesessenheit zur Machtvergessenheit* (Stuttgart).

Schwarze, J. (1997), 'Der Beitrag des Europäischen Gerichtshofs zur Europäisierung des Verwaltungsrechts', *Europarecht (EuR)*, 419–32.

Schwarze, J. (2000), 'Auf dem Wege zu einer europäischen Verfassung— Wechselwirkungen zwischen europäischem und nationalem Verfassungsrecht', in J. Schwarze and P.-C. Müller-Graf (eds), *Europäische Verfassungsentwicklung, Europarecht, Beiheft 1/2000*, 7–30.

Sebaldt, M. (1997), *Organisierter Pluralismus. Kräftefeld, Selbstverständnis und politische Arbeit deutscher Interessengruppen* (Opladen).

Secretary General/High Representative (2000), *Conflict Prevention*, Report by the Secretary General/High Representative and the Commission Council of the European Union, 14088/00 LIMITE CAB 14, Brussels, 30 November, http://register.consil ium.eu.int/pdf/en/00/st14/14088en0.pdf.

Secretary General/High Representative and the Commission (2000), Report Presented to the Nice European Council, 'Improving the Coherence and Effectiveness of the European Union Action in the Field of Conflict Prevention', 8 December.

Semetko, H.A., De Vreese, C. H. and Peter, J. (2000), 'Europeanised Politics— Europeanised Media? European Integration and Political Communication', *West European Politics*, 23, 121–41.

Semetko, H. A. and Valkenburg, P. M. (2000), 'Framing European Politics: A Content Analysis of Press and Television News', *Journal of Communication*, 50: 93–109.

Serre, F. de la (1988), 'The Scope of National Adaptation to EPC', in R. Pijpers *et al.* (eds), *European Political Cooperation in the 1980s: A Common Foreign Policy for Western Europe?* (Dordrecht), 194–210.

Seymour-Ure, C. (1974), *The Political Impact of Mass Media* (London/Beverly Hills).

Simonian, H. (1985), *The Privileged Partnership: Franco-German Relationships in the European Community 1969–1984* (Oxford).

Single European Act (1986), Preamble, 17 February.

Sitter, N. (2001), 'The Politics of Opposition and European Integration in Scandinavia: Is Euro-Scepticism a Government Opposition Dynamic?', *West European Politics*, 23, 211–31.

Sjursen, H. (1998), 'CFSP and EU Enlargement', in B. Tonra and F. T. Christiansen (eds), *CFSP and Beyond: Theorising European Foreign Policy,* Proceedings of the Conference, Centre for European Studies in Aberstwyth, 16–18 May.

Smith, G. (1989), 'A System Perspective on Party System Change', *Journal of Theoretical Politics*, 1, 349–64.

Smith, G. (1992), 'The Nature of the Unified State', in G. Smith, W. E. Paterson, P. H. Merkl and S. Padgett (eds), *Developments in German Politics* (London), 37–51.

Smith, M. E. (1997), 'Rules, Transgovernmentalism and the Expansion of European Political Co-operation', in W. Sandholz and A. S. Sweet (eds), *Supranational Governance: The Institutionalization of the European Union* (Oxford), 304–33.

Smith, M. E. (2000), 'Conforming to Europe: The Domestic Impact of EU Foreign Policy Co-operation', *Journal of European Public Policy*, 7, 613–31.

Smith, M. E. (2001*a*), 'Diplomacy by Decree: The Legalization of EU Foreign Policy', *Journal of Common Market Studies*, 39, 79–104.

Smith, M. E. (2001*b*), 'Europe and the German Model: Growing Tension and Symbiosis?', *German Politics*, 10, 119–40.

Soysal, Y. (1993), 'Immigration and the Emerging European Polity', in S. Anderson and K. Eliassen (eds), *Making Policy in Europe: The Europeification of National Policy Making* (London), 171–86.

SPD (2001*a*), 'Keynote Proposal: Responsibility for Europe', Draft, National Conference of the Social Democratic Party of Germany, http://www.spd.de/english/politics/party congress/europe.html.

SPD (2001*b*), *Zwischenbericht: Wegmarken für ein neues Grundsatzprogramm* (Nurnberg).

SPD (2002), *Regierungsprogramm 2002–2006*, http://www.spd-parteitag.de/servlet/PB/menu/-1/index.html. accessed 5 July.

SPD-Fraktion, Arbeitgruppe Rechtspolitik (2001), *Eckpunkte des Gesetzentwurfs der Koalition zur Justizreform* (Berlin).

SRU (1978), *Umweltgutachten 1978,* Bundestags-Drucksache 8/1938 (Bonn).

SRU (2002), *Umweltgutachten 2002. Für eine neue Vorreiterrolle*, Der Rat von Sachverständigen für Umweltfragen (Berlin).

Steffani, W. (1995), 'Das Demokratie-Dilemma der Europäischen Union: Die Rolle der Parlamente nach dem Urteil des Bundesverfassungsgerichts vom 12. Oktober 1993', in W. Steffani and U. Thaysen (eds), *Demokratie in Europa: Zur Rolle der Parlamente. Sonderband der Zeitschrift für Parlamentsfragen zum 25jährigen Bestehen* (Opladen).

Stoiber, E. (1987), 'Auswirkungen der Entwicklung Europas zur Rechtsgemeinschaft auf die Länder der Bundesrepublik Deutschland', *Europa-Archiv*, 19, 543–52.

Stokes, D. E. (1963), 'Spatial Models of Party Competition', *American Political Science Review,* 57, 368–77.

Stöss, R. (1986), 'Die Europäische Föderalistische Partei (EFP)/Europa Partei (EP)', in R. Stöss (ed.), *Parteien-Handbuch. Sonderausgabe, Band 3* (Opladen), 1296–1310.

Streeck, W. (1999), *Korporatismus in Deutschland* (Frankfurt a.M.).

Streeck, W. and Schmitter, P. C. (1991), 'From National Corporatism to Transnational Pluralism: Organized Interests in the Single European Market', *Politics and Society*, 19, 133–64.

Strøm, K. and Müller, W. C. (1999), 'Political Parties and Hard Choices', in W. C. Müller and K. Strøm (eds), *Policy, Office, or Votes: How Political Parties in Western Europe Make Hard Decisions* (Cambridge), 1–35.

Sturm, R. (1996), 'The German Cartel Office in a Hostile Environment', in B.G. Doern and S. Wilks (eds), *Comparative Competition Policy* (Oxford).

Sturm, R. (2002), 'Europa -kein Wahlkampfthema?', *Der Bürger im Staat*, 52, 74–8.

Sturm, R. and Pehle, H. (2001*a*), *Das neue deutsche Regierungssystem: Die Europäisierung von Institutionen, Entscheidungsprozessen und Politikfeldern in der Bundesrepublik Deutschland* (Opladen).

Sturm, R. and Pehle, H. (2001*b*), 'Europäisiertes Regieren: Erklärungsmuster der Auswirkungen der europäischen Integration auf das politische System Deutschlands', *Gegenwartskunde*, 50, 161–71.

Süddeutsche Zeitung (2001), 'Schröder für radikale Reform der EU', *Süddeutsche Zeitung*, 29 April, http://www.sueddeutsche.de, accessed 30 April.

Süß, W. (1986), 'Wahl und Führungswechsel: Politik zwischen Legitimation und Elitekonsens. Zum Bonner Machtwechsel 1982/83', in H.-D. Klingemann and M. Kaase (eds), *Wahlen und politischer Prozeß* (Opladen), 39–83.

Swanson, D. L. (1981), 'A Constructivist Approach', in D. D. Nimmo and K. R. Sanders (eds), *Handbook of Political Communication* (Beverly Hills), 169–91.

Swedish Presidency (2001), *Results of the Swedish Presidency* (final version), http://www.eu2001.se/.

Taggart, P. (1998), 'A Touchstone of Dissent: Euroscepticism in Contemporary Western European Party Systems', *European Journal of Political Research*, 33, 363–88.

Taylor, M. and Herman, V. M. (1971), 'Party Systems and Government Stability', *American Political Science Review*, 65, 28–37.

Thompson, J. B. (1995), *The Media and Modernity. A Social Theory of the Media* (Cambridge).

Thürer, D. (1991), 'Der Verfassungsstaat als Glied einer europäischen Gemeinschaft', *Veröffentlichungen der Vereinigung der Deutschen Staatsrechtslehrer (VVDStRL)*, 50, 97–139.

Titmuss, R. (1974), *Social Policy* (London).

Töller, A. E. (1995), *Europapolitik im Bundestag: Eine empirische Untersuchung zur europapolitischen Willensbildung im EG-Ausschuß des 12. Deutschen Bundestages* (Frankfurt a.M.).

Töpfer, K. (1989), 'Ecological Modernisation of the Industrialised State: A Federal Perspective', in T. Ellwein, *et al.* (eds), *Yearbook on Government and Public Administration* (Baden-Baden), 489–520.

Torreblanca, J. I. (2001), 'Ideas, Preferences and Institutions: Explaining the Europeanization of Spanish Foreign Policy', ARENA Working Papers, WP10/26, http://www.arena.uio.no/publications/wp01_26.htm.

Treaty of Nice (2000).

Treaty on European Union (Articles J1–J13).

Trebbe, J. and Weiß, H.-J. (1997), 'Lokale Thematisierungsleistungen: Der Beitrag privater Rundfunkprogramme zur publizistischen Vielfalt in lokalen Kommunikationsräumen', in G. Bentele and M. Haller (eds), *Aktuelle Entstehung von Öffentlichkeit* (Konstanz), 445–65.

Trenz, H.-J. (2000), 'Korruption und politischer Skandal in der EU: Auf dem Weg zu einer europäischen politischen Öffentlichkeit?', in M. Bach (ed.), *Transnationale Integrationsprozesse in Europa* (Opladen), 332–59.

Tsatsos, D. T. and Deinzer, G. (1998) (eds), *Europäische Politische Parteien: Dokumentation einer Hoffnung* (Baden-Baden).

UBA (1997), *Umweltschutz und Beschäftigung. Brückenschlag für eine lebenswerte Zukunft*, Umweltbundesamt (Berlin).

UBA (1999), *Selbstverpflichtungen und normsetzende Umweltverträge als Instrumente des Umweltschutzes*, Umweltbundesamt (Berlin).

van der Vleuten, A. (2001), *Dure Vrouwen, Dwarse Staten* (Nijmegen).

Van Deth, J. W., Rattinger, H. and Roller, E. (2000) (eds), *Die Republik auf dem Weg zur Normalität?* (Opladen).

Van Stolk, C. (2002), 'The EU and the CEECs: Towards More Limited Concepts of Administrative Capacity Building', paper presented at the EGPA Annual Conference, Workshop 1 (Potsdam), 4–7 September.

Vogel, D. (1995), *Trading Up: Consumer and Environmental Regulation in a Global Economy* (Cambridge).

Voltmer, K. (1997), 'Medien und Parteien im Wahlkampf. Die ideologischen Präferenzen der meinungsführenden Tageszeitungen im Bundestagswahlkampf 1990', *Rundfunk und Fernsehen*, 45, 173–93.

Voltmer, K. (1998), *Medienqualität und Demokratie. Eine empirische Analyse publizistischer Informations- und Orientierungsleistungen in der Wahlkampfkommunikation* (Baden-Baden).

von Danwitz, T. (1993), 'Normkonkretisierende Verwaltungsvorschriften und Gemeinschaftsrecht', *Verwaltungs-Archiv*, 73–96.

Von Weizsäcker-Kommission (2000), 'Abschlußbericht der Kommission "Gemeinsame Sicherheit und Bundeswehr der Zukunft"', Bericht der Kommission an die Bundesregierung, http://www.bundeswehr.de/pic/pdf/reform/refbrosch_mai2000Gem einsameSicherheit.pdf.

Waarden, van F. (1994), 'Is European Law a Threat to Associational Governance?', in V. Eichener and H. Voelzkow (eds), *Europäische Integration und verbandliche Interessenvermittlung* (Marburg), 217–62.

Waesche, N.M. (2001), *Global Opportunity and National Political Economy: The Development of Internet Ventures in Germany*, Ph.D. thesis, London School of Economics and Political Science.

Wahl, R. (2000), 'Die zweite Phase des öffentlichen Rechts in Deutschland: Die Europäisierung des öffentlichen Rechts', *Der Staat*, 39.

Wallace, H. (2000), 'The Institutional Setting: Five Variations on a Theme', in H. Wallace and W. Wallace (eds), *Policy-Making in the European Union*, 4th edn (Oxford), 3–37.

Wallace, H. (2001a), 'Introduction: Rethinking European Integration', in H. Wallace (ed.), *Interlocking Dimensions of European Integration* (Basingstoke), 1–22.

Wallace, H. (2001b), 'The Changing Politics of the European Union: An Overview', *Journal of Common Market Studies*, 39, 581–94.

Wartenberg, von L. (2000), 'Industrieller Wandel in Deutschland, Globalisierung und Europäisierung—Herausforderungen für den BDI', in W. Bührer and E. Grande (eds), *Unternehmerverbände und Staat in Deutschland* (Baden-Baden), 157–63.

Weale, A. (1992a), *The New Politics of Pollution* (Manchester).

Weale, A. (1992b), 'Vorsprung durch Technik? The Politics of German Environmental Regulation', in K. Dyson (ed.), *The Politics of German Regulation* (Aldershot), 159–83.

Weale, A. (1996), 'Environmental Rules and Rule-Making in the European Union', *Journal of European Public Policy,* 3, 594–611.

Weale, A., O'Riordan, T. and Kramme, L. (1991), *Controlling Pollution in the Round: Change and Choice in Environmental Regulation in Britain and West Germany* (London).

Weale, A., Pridham, G., Cini, M., Konstadakopulos, D., Porter, M. and Flynn, B. (2000), *Environmental Governance in Europe: An Ever Closer Ecological Union?* (Oxford).

Weaver, D. H. (1977), 'Political Issues and Voter Need for Orientation', in D. L. Shaw and M. E. McCombs (eds), *The Emergence of American Political Issues. The Agenda-Setting Function of the Press* (St Paul, Minn.).

Webber, D. (1999) (ed.), *The Franco-German Relationship in the European Union* (London).

Webber, D. (2001) (ed.), *New Europe, New Germany, Old Foreign Policy? German Foreign Policy since Unification* (London).

Weber-Panariello, P. A. (1995), *Nationale Parlamente in der Europäischen Union: Eine rechtsvergleichende Studie zur Beteiligung nationaler Parlamente an der innerstaatlichen Willensbildung in Angelegenheiten der Europäischen Union im Vereinigten Königreich, Frankreich und der Bundesrepublik Deutschland* (Baden-Baden).

Weidenfeld, W. and Wessels, W. (several vols) (eds), *Jahrbuch der Europäischen Integration* (Bonn).

Weidner, H. (1999), 'Umweltpolitik: Entwicklungslinien, Kapazitäten und Effekt', in M. Kaase and G. Schmidt (eds), *Eine lernende Demokratie: 50 Jahre Bundesrepublik Deutschland* (Berlin), 425–60.

Weinstock, U. (1984), 'Nur eine europäische Umwelt? Europäische Umwelt im Spannungsverhältnis von ökologischer Vielfalt und ökonomischer Einheit', in E. Grabitz (ed.), *Abgestufte Integration: Eine Alternative zum herkömmlichen Integrationskonzept?*, Schriftenreihe Europaforschung (Hamburg), 301–34.

Werle, R. (1999), 'Liberalisation of Telecommunications in Germany', in K. A. Eliassen and M. Sjovaag (eds), *European Telecommunications Liberalisation* (London), 110–27.

Wesseling, R. (2001), 'The Draft Regulation Modernising the Competition Rules: The Commission is Married to One Ideal', *European Law Review,* 26, 357–78.

Wessels, W. (1999), 'Strukturen und Verfahren Bonner EU-Politik—eine administrativ-politische Mehrebenenfusion', in H.-U. Derlien and A. Murswieck (eds), *Der Politikzyklus zwischen Bonn und Brüssel* (Opladen), 21–37

Wessels, W. (2000), *Die Öffnung des Staates: Modelle und Wirklichkeit grenzüberschreitender Verwaltungspraxis 1960–1995* (Opladen).

Wessels, W. (2001), 'Germany in Europe: Return of the Nightmare or Towards an Engaged Germany in a New Europe?', *German Politics,* 10, 107–16.

Wessels, W. and Rometsch, D. (1996) (eds), *The European Union and Member States: Towards Institutional Fusion* (Manchester).

Wey, K.-G. (1982), *Kurze Geschichte des Umweltschutzes in Deutschland seit 1900* (Opladen).

Wiener, A. (1998), *European Citizenship Practice: Building Institutions of a Non-State* (Boulder, Col.).

Wilks, S. and McGowan, L. (1995a), 'Discretion in the European Merger Control: The German Regime in Context', *Journal of European Public Policy,* 2, 41–68.

Wilks, S. and McGowan, L. (1995*b*), 'The Debate over a European Cartel Office', *Journal of Common Market Studies*, 32, 259–73.

Wilks, S. with Bartle, I. (2002), 'The Unanticipated Consequences of Creating Independent Competition Regimes', *West European Politics*, 25, 148–72.

Willems, U. and Winter, von T. (2001) (eds), *Politische Repräsentation schwacher Interessen* (Opladen).

Winn, N. and Lord, C. (2001), *EU Foreign Policy Beyond the Nation-State* (Basingstoke).

Wissenschaftlicher Beirat beim BMWi (1996), *Stellungnahme*, reprinted in *Wirtschaft und Wettbewerb*, 46, 689–97.

Wissenschaftlicher Beirat beim BMWi (2000), *Reform der europäischen Kartellpolitik* (Dresden), 1 July.

Wolf, D. (1994), 'Maastricht Zwei. Eine europäische Behörde für den Wettbewerb', *Frankfurter Allgemeine Zeitung*, 5 November.

Wolfers, A. (1962), *Discord and Collaboration* (Baltimore).

Wood, S. (1997), 'Capitalist Constitutions: Supply-Side Reforms in Britain and West Germany 1960–1990', Ph.D. dissertation, Department of Government, Harvard University.

Woolcock, S., Hodges, M. and Schreiber, K (1991), *Britain, Germany and 1992: The Limits of Deregulation* (London).

Wright, V. (1996), 'The National Co-ordination of European Policy-Making: Negotiating the Quagmire', in J. Richardson (ed.), *European Union: Power and Policy-Making* (London), 148–69.

Wright, V. and Hayward, J. (2000) 'Governing from the Centre: Policy Co-Ordination in Six European Core Executives', in R. A. W. Rhodes (ed.), *Transforming British Government, Vol. 2: Changing Roles and Relationships* (Basingstoke), 27–46.

Wurzel, R. K. W. (1993), 'Environmental Policy', in J. Lodge (ed.), *The European Community and the Challenge of the Future*, 2nd edn (London), 178–99.

Wurzel, R. K. W. (1996), 'The Role of the EU Presidency in the Environmental Field: Does It Make a Difference Which Member State Runs the Presidency?', *Journal of European Public Policy*, 3, 272–91.

Wurzel, R. K. W. (2000), 'Flying into Unexpected Turbulence: The German EU Presidency in the Environmental Field', *German Politics*, 9, 23–43.

Wurzel, R. K. W. (2001), 'The EU Presidency and the Integration Principle: An Anglo-German Comparison', *European Environmental Law Review*, 1, 7–15.

Wurzel, R. K. W. (2002), *Environmental Policy-Making in Britain, Germany and the European Union* (Manchester).

Zaller, J. R. (1992), *The Nature and Origin of Mass Opinion* (Cambridge).

Zaller, J. R. (1994), 'Elite Leadership of Mass Opinion', in L. W. Bennett and D. L. Paletz (eds), *Taken by Storm. The Media, Public Opinion, and U.S. Foreign Policy in the Gulf War* (Chicago and London).

Zito, A. (2000), *Creating Environmental Policy in the European Union* (London).

Weber, S. and J. Claparède (1976), 'The Debate over a European Canal Officer Corps', *Common Market Studies*, 32, 59–79.

Weiler, S. and J. Bielfeldt (1998), 'The Constitutional Consequences of German Unification', *German Politics*, 7, 195–72.

Willems, J. and T. Moen, eds. (2001), ed., *Politische Beteiligung zwischen Ost- und Westdeutschland* (Opladen).

Wind, N. and H.-P. (2001), 'Europa Politik und die Medien', Sonderheft der *Mitteilungen des Instituts BMWA* Wien Staatswissenschaftliche Vereinigung (Wiesbaden), 16, 180–97.

Wissenschaftlicher Rat beim BMWi, 'Neue Rahmenbedingungen Arbeitsmarkt' (Düsseldorf, July 2001).

Wolf, D. (1981), 'Staat, die Krise, Die europäische Bürokratie und die Wirtschaft', *Internationale Korrespondenz Europa 5* (Wiesbaden).

Wollmann, J. (1997), *Politische und Gesellschaften* (Baumgarten).

Wood, S. (1997), 'Economic Coordinations, Social Pacts and Reform in Britain and West Germany', in J. Katz, ed., *International Transitions of Governance* (Ithaca, Cornell).

Woolcock, S., Hodges, M. and Schreiber, K. (1991), *Britain, Germany and 1992: The Limits of Deregulation* (London).

Wright, Vincent, Hans and Caird, Jürgen 'Administrations Making Policies and the Determinants of Regulation', *eds.*, *European Union: power and policy-making* (London, 1996).

Wright, V. and Hayward, J. (1998), 'Governing the ... of ...: the Co-ordination of European Policy Transforming', in Kassim, P., Guéton and Wright, European British Governance, vol 3 (Clarendon, Press and Administration) (Washington, 1998).

Wright, R. K. W. (1993), *Transnational Labour in Industrial Relations: The Response of German Unions* (Oxford, 1993) in the end (Cornell, 1993).

Russell, W. E. (1993), 'The Role of the EU Presidency in the International Field: Does it Make a Difference to High Intensity State-Type the Presidency?', *European Politics and Policy*, 772–91.

Wessels, W. W. (2000), 'Nice and ... Prospects and Ambition: The Geneva ... Producing in the *European Common Affairs*', *Journal of Politics*, 3, 1–9.

Wurzel, R. K. W. (1996), 'The ... and the Environment ... in Germany: ... the Presidency', *European Integration Online Papers* vol 4 (No 1) 1–9, 35.

Wurm, B. K. W. (1993), 'Interest Groups and Policy-Making in German Central and Südosteuropa', *Central Europe*, no. 4.

Zahn, J. K. (1999), 'The Politics and History of European Unification'.

Zysman, F. F. (1994), 'Global Configuration of Institutions', in J. W. Hasu and D. S. Landes, eds. (eds), *The Anglo Public*, *Culture and 25 years Institutions of the End* (London, Harcourt).

Zürn, (2000), *European Governance and the Power of Ideas* (Oxford, Basil).

Index